Rocky's Rail

1743
1743

Rocky's Rail

A Spokane Division Trainman, 1960–2004

by John E. Langlot and
Mac McCulloch

Yakt Publishing ➻ 2020

ISBN 978-1-7351741-0-5
Library of Congress Control Number: 2020911804

YAKT PUBLISHING
620 Woodland Hts.
Holly Springs, MS 38635

Manufactured in the U.S.A.
Text design by Ariane C. Smith, Capital A Publications, LLC

PP. ii–iii The Mansfield Local descends Douglas Creek Canyon during July 1983 with forty-four loads of grain. Air brakes are set and both units are in dynamic braking to hold the train on the 2.0 percent grade. This location is near where Douglas Creek enters Moses Coulee, and is about two miles railroad west of the long-forgotten station of McCue. Palisades is about four miles ahead. The rear of the train is passing through the only tunnel of the branch. PHOTO BY BLAIR KOOISTRA.

1 2 3 4 5 6 7 8 9 10

Table of Contents

Illustrations

Maps and Diagrams

Preface

THIS BOOK GREW OUT OF THE GREAT Northern Railway Historical Society convention at Wenatchee in July of 2008. Mac McCulloch, a former clerk at Wenatchee, met John Langlot at the convention and enjoyed John's tales of working as a brakeman on the W–O in the early 1960s.

Mac and John had lunch with the late Max Ulver one day. Max complained bitterly that this was the second convention in Wenatchee and that for the second time the convention planners had not included any tour of, or information about, the Wenatchee–Oroville branch line. Max planted the seed for a book about the W–O that expanded to became this volume about John Langlot's career.

John hired on with the Great Northern as a brakeman at Hillyard in 1960 and retired from the BNSF at Spokane in 2005. John participated in, observed, and often simply endured, the most tumultuous 45 years since the introduction of rail transportation in America.

The authors enjoyed much help in this project. This work would not have been possible without that help. Long before we thought of writing this book, Jim Mattson, former Great Northern Cascade Division Station Inspector and switchman at Seattle, rescued hundreds of pounds of Authority for Expenditure files, Station Maps, and Employee Timetables from destruction. Many of those Employee Timetables are now protected in Seattle's Museum of History and Industry (MOHAI).

Two other former employees of the Great Northern provided invaluable assistance. Dave Sprau was a train dispatcher for most of his career. Portions of the book relating to dispatching incorporate so much of Dave's input that it would be fair to say he wrote them. Guy Baxter assisted John in describing switching assignments at Hillyard and Spokane and the operation of the Spokane terminal in the 1960s.

All of the following individuals reviewed our draft chapters and helped us avoid unnecessary use of jargon and assuming facts not offered. In addition, each of them provided focused assistance. Bob Kelly made the full contents of the joint NP-GN archives available to us. Mike Bartenstein of Wenatchee drew the first drafts of maps and profiles for the book, which were redrawn for publication by Dave Cooley. Dave Sprau was very helpful about historical, operating and dispatching items.

The late Bob Downing constantly encouraged us to do the book, stating several times that the subject matter was historically important and not well documented. Earl Currie, a former Officer of the Burlington Northern, also encouraged us to complete the book and reviewed all of the text.

We thank railroad employees Gene [Spanky] Sponcler, John Kerwin, Jim Weaver, Marvin Hallgreen, Jack Campbell, and Bob Shollenburger for retelling their stories to John Langlot and for reviewing our drafts for accuracy and clarity. Loren Gunther, track inspector, snow dozer operator, and work train boss helped on the Kettle Falls lines. We thank Mark McNaghten and Paul Fishburne for their help with union related negotiations with the BN. We thank Rick Avery for his help about the Lamona Rail Grinder collision and particularly thank Michael Olin for allowing us to tell his experience of the runaway train that derailed at Sprague.

The authors hope you enjoy this review of one man's career; a career which in many aspects is representative of thousands of working railroaders during the period of John's employment in the railroad industry.

Introduction

➻ WHEN WE BEGAN THIS PROJECT, IT WAS TO be a book about the Wenatchee–Oroville branch of the Great Northern Railway. We were concerned that we would not have much to say. As it turned out we ended up with two books, the previously published *The Rusty Dusty: Great Northern's Wenatchee–Oroville Branch* and this one.

This book recounts John Langlot's career and experiences during the tumultuous period of railroad history between 1960 and 2005. John hired out on the Great Northern at Hillyard in July of 1960, was forced to the W–O in 1961, and worked the line in the early 1960s. The first chapter is about John's life as a boy in Hillyard. The next eight chapters describe John's work on the lines of the Great Northern Railway's Spokane Division as it was from July 12, 1903, to February 1, 1956, and from July 1, 1967, to March 2, 1970, arranged on a geographic basis.

Two chapters describe the planning and implementation of the Burlington Northern merger, which was finally accomplished March 2, 1970. The balance of the book recounts John's career after 1970. To allow the reader a broader view, some of these chapters include a section that summarizes what was going on at the corporate level. Very fortunately, John has an excellent memory and is a great storyteller. This book is founded on his wealth of stories.

With the Burlington Northern merger, the territory available for John to work expanded to include the former Spokane, Portland and Seattle main line between Spokane and Pasco, and the former Norther Pacific main line between Spokane and Pasco, the main line between Spokane and Paradise, Montana, plus the Palouse & Lewiston and Central Washington branches. We discuss these lines in the context of John's work on them and issues related to them that impacted John's working life.

Co-author Mac McCulloch grew up in Wenatchee and worked as a clerk in Wenatchee and Seattle in the late 1960s and early 1970s. Mac was there at the end of the Great Northern era and the beginning of Burlington Northern.

This book is unique in three ways. First, it is set in Eastern Washington, a region relatively unremarked in the railroad literature. Second, it covers the time period from 1960 to 2005, a period of technological change as sweeping as the period from 1825 to 1870 when everything was new and the technology was in constant flux. Third, it provides a first-person view of the craft of trainman, a work life experience seldom discussed in the literature about the railroad industry.

On January 25, 2016, two days before my birthday, I lost a close friend and my braking partner Gene "Spanky" Sponcler. Many of my experiences recounted in this book occurred when I was working with Gene. The time spent forced on the W–O local, working the Kettle Falls Turn, plus three years on the Coeur d'Alene local were with Gene. The time we spent at our model railroad club after we both retired were moments to cherish and remember. I never met one person who didn't like Gene. Gene always had a smile on his face and his quick wit always bought laughter even during the last six years of his life while he was fighting cancer. Every time I pick up a copy of this book it will remind me of Gene and the good times we spent together.

1. A Child of Hillyard

I, JOHN ERNEST LANGLOT, WAS BORN ON January 27, 1940, and was raised in Hillyard, Washington. My father, John Henry Langlot, hired out as a brakeman on the Great Northern Railway at Hillyard on September 4, 1929, mere days before the stock market crash of 1929. Thirty-one years later I also hired out with the GN.

My parents attended Lewis and Clark High School near downtown Spokane, where they met, and stayed together from that time on, graduating in 1928. My father worked in a local sawmill until he went to work for the Great Northern in 1929. My mother worked as a waitress at the Desert Oasis Restaurant in the Desert Hotel in downtown Spokane during the Great Depression. My mother and father planned to get married, and had a joint savings account, but the bank failed when the Depression hit and they received only five cents on the dollar from the bank after a long delay. This loss prevented my parents from getting married until 1938.

My father was called for a freight trip to Wenatchee in the fall of 1929. The conductor was off the conductors' extra board. The extra board is a list of railroad employees, by craft, who do not have a bid in job. Extra board employees are called on a rotating basis as needed to fill temporary vacancies or to crew an extra train.

They were gone for about thirty-six hours. When they returned to Hillyard, my father was furloughed and the extra board conductor was cut back to brakeman. About one month later, he was also furloughed. Business was so bad, the Great Northern was running one freight train a day each way through Spokane which left 70% of the trainmen furloughed.

My father did not work for the railroad from the time he was furloughed through all of 1931, well over two years. During 1932, he worked only during holidays and now and then during the summer months. By 1934, business picked up enough that my father was able to work most of the year. Four men had been hired as brakemen behind my father in 1929. The five men hired in 1929 were sufficient to cover the available work until August 15, 1936, when the Great Northern hired ten brakemen at Hillyard.

Hillyard was a one industry town and the Great Northern was it. The community was devastated by the unemployment created by the Great Depression. The high number of railroad men furloughed caused hardships on those who were employed in town.

I remember the town well from my almost daily trips through the community as a kid. After World War II, there was one bank downtown: the Hillyard Bank, on the railroad side of Market Street, the north/south street nearest the railroad. About two thirds of the business buildings in Hillyard were brick or concrete; the rest were wood construction. Maderan Brothers Studebaker was the only auto dealership in Hillyard.

Our one department store handled furniture, refrigerators, and all sorts of other appliances. There was a new concrete Safeway store on Market Street, plus the Diamond Cash Market on Diamond Avenue two blocks west of Market. Both stores included a meat department with sawdust on the floor, and all the meat was hand cut right there. As I walked through Hillyard it seemed that every three or four blocks I would find a little "mom and pop" grocery store. One hardware store, Keyhole Hardware, sold all sorts of nuts, bolts, screws, brackets, and tools.

Hillyard also supported a bakery, the Westminster Bakery, a couple of restaurants, and about five bars. There was a Chinese restaurant and a Chinese laundry. No one working at the laundry spoke English. There were two drug stores, located only three doors apart. The more popular was Hands Drug Store. Hands featured an old-fashioned soda fountain that was popular with us kids. There was one movie theater, the Rialto. We could go to the Saturday matinee and see Roy Rogers or Tom Mix for only a dime.

It was common to see a horse team and wagon at the feed store. I recall the iceman coming down our street with his horse drawn ice wagon selling ice to everybody who used an ice box. He did a brisk business since refrigerators were rare. The iceman bought his ice at the Great Northern ice house.

Most kitchens included a wood stove. Milk was delivered to the door in glass quart bottles with paper stoppers. Most everyone had a garden in the summer months, and a lot of the neighbors kept chickens and sold eggs. Once in a while, my mother would give me a glass pint jar and a dime with instructions to go over to old man Gulars, who had a cow and some pigs, to buy a pint of whipping cream.

In 1941, my parents bought their first and only home. It was on the west side of town, right next to conductor Al Richardson, whose conductor's date was May 4, 1909. Al's brakeman date must have been in the 1890s. Al enjoyed enough seniority to work during the Depression. During those hard times, he bought land for the taxes owed, which made Al a very wealthy man after the Depression ended. Al worked chain gang to Troy, Montana and would take me with him when he took something down to his assigned caboose at Hillyard. In those days of assigned cabooses, they were a crew's home away from home.

When my father went down to the railroad yard office, he would often take me with him. We walked six or seven blocks east and about two blocks south to get to the yard office. On most of these walks to Hillyard I stood on the depot platform to watch the steam engines in the yard.

I clearly remember standing on the platform when an R-2 class 2-8-8-2 cut off its train east of the yard office and moved toward the roundhouse. I stood there as this monster crept by, with little puffs of steam. I was in total awe as this the huge R-2 crept almost silently by. I could not believe that something that big could move so quietly down the track. I was used to the big steam engines as they pulled a westbound tonnage train out of the yard bellowing smoke and booming loud cracks of exhaust steam. The quiet really impressed me as this big engine drifted by me. I always looked forward to going with my father or Al down to the depot or to the yard office so I could watch the engines moving around in the yard.

Entertainment was limited because most families were having a tough time making ends meet even in the late 1940s. Home entertainment was listening to the radio. The trainmen families would get together a couple times a month at different homes for a potluck dinner, and we kids would play while the adults played cards. I ended up braking for some of these fathers, including Bus Downing, Jim Stevenson, and Hi and Dick Stall, who were brakemen when I was a kid. The whole town of Hillyard was a big railroad family. We were all Hillyardites and proud of it. This attitude is definitely missing today.

About half of the kids I played with were sons of fathers who worked for the railroad. In the summer months we played 'kick the can.' Someone would bring an old can and someone would be 'it.' Everybody would go hide, and the person who was 'it' had to go look for the others. If he spotted you, it was a race to kick the can. If you beat him to the can, you were home free; if he beat you, then you would be 'it' for the next game. Toys were in short supply since this was after World War II when all manufacturers were busy making war supplies. The first time we ever saw toys made of plastic was after the war.

My younger years were spent playing sandlot baseball with my neighborhood friends in any open dirt and cheatgrass field close to home. The only park with grass close to home was Jim Hill Park on the north end of Hillyard, about two blocks north of the Hillyard swimming pool and across the street from the Great Northern Ice House on Market Street.

We rode our bicycles everywhere. The first thing you learned when you started to ride a bike was not to drift across the trolley tracks, or you would end upside down when your front wheel dropped into the flangeway inside of the rail. You always wanted to cut straight across the tracks at about a right angle. We rode our bikes to the swimming pool in the summer, and down to the railroad yard to watch the switch engines switching

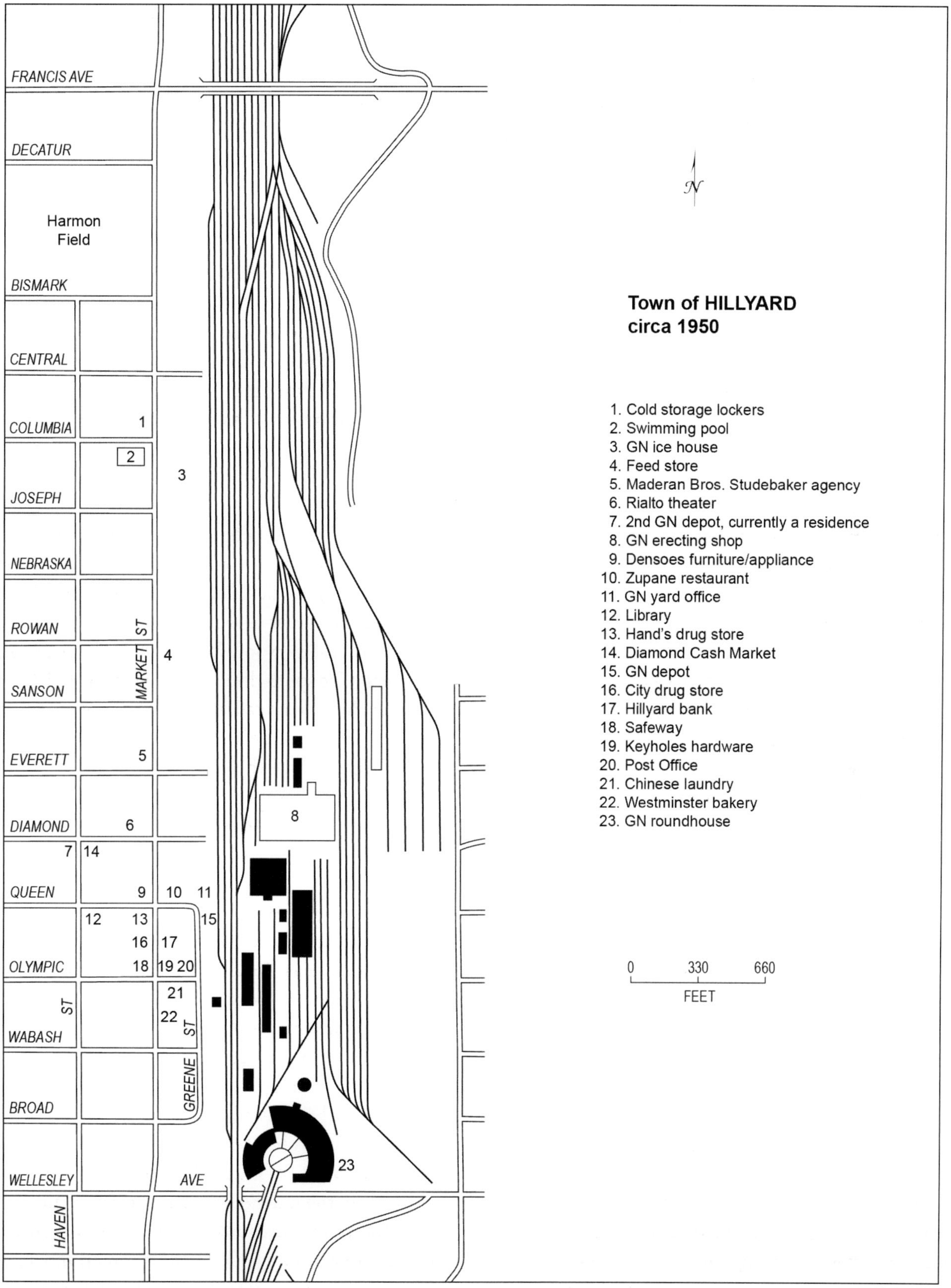
FRANCIS AVE
DECATUR
Harmon Field
BISMARK
CENTRAL
COLUMBIA
JOSEPH
NEBRASKA
ROWAN
SANSON
EVERETT
DIAMOND
QUEEN
OLYMPIC
WABASH
BROAD
WELLESLEY
AVE
MARKET ST
ST
GREENE ST
HAVEN
N
Town of HILLYARD
circa 1950
1. Cold storage lockers
2. Swimming pool
3. GN ice house
4. Feed store
5. Maderan Bros. Studebaker agency
6. Rialto theater
7. 2nd GN depot, currently a residence
8. GN erecting shop
9. Densoes furniture/appliance
10. Zupane restaurant
11. GN yard office
12. Library
13. Hand's drug store
14. Diamond Cash Market
15. GN depot
16. City drug store
17. Hillyard bank
18. Safeway
19. Keyholes hardware
20. Post Office
21. Chinese laundry
22. Westminster bakery
23. GN roundhouse
0
330
660
FEET

in the yard. On Fridays, we would ride our bikes down to the north end of Hillyard yard and watch the burning of the old worn out reefers on the burn track. Western Fruit Express stripped all metal, the ice hatches, and the doors off the old reefers and set them afire to burn to the ground, leaving only the steel frames supported by the trucks. We would watch them burn until it got close to 1:00 PM, when the swimming pool opened up for the afternoon swim.

I attended Marcus Whitman grade school, four blocks from home, from kindergarten through the eighth grade. There was a Boy Scout troop at Whitman, Troop 44, that most of my friends and I joined. I stayed in scouting until I was eighteen years old. I feel that the

ABOVE Hillyard Depot served in the 1960s as an Agency office, housing the agent and the cashier who collected money due the railroad on outbound prepaid and inbound collect freight bills. It was also a flag stop for trains 27 and 28. COLLECTION OF JOHN E. LANGLOT.

LEFT Hillyard Yard Tower was the operational heart of Hillyard. It housed the General Yardmaster and Yardmaster. The bottom story housed crew callers, billing clerks, manifest clerks, and the train order operator, who also controlled the interlocking plant at the east and west ends of Hillyard. GNRHS ARCHIVE.

things I learned in scouting stayed with me all of my life, and I made sure that my son Gordon experienced the scouting program: I got Gordon into the Cub Scouts at age eight, and I also joined as an adult leader. We both moved into the Boy Scout program when he turned eleven. Gordon and I stayed active in scouts until he turned eighteen. I have used the scout laws as a guide in my everyday life. They were also my father's rules of life, and they have been passed down to my son and to my grandson, who is now a Boy Scout. My father taught me to stand up for what was right even if you stood alone.

Of the six high schools then in the Spokane area, John R. Rogers, where I went, had the reputation of being the toughest. Michael Downing (Bus's son) and I played sandlot baseball, rode our bikes, and went to the Hillyard swimming pool together until Bus became the General Chairman for the Order of Railway Conductors & Brakemen and they moved to St. Paul, Minnesota. Bus had the same values as my father did, and was fired after he included the brakeman in a pay raise after the union president told him he could care less about the brakemen. They returned about 1959 and Bus marked up as a conductor in the Wenatchee freight pool as he had retained his seniority. Mike and I rented an apartment together. Mike had a job as a GN clerk and transferred to fireman about the time I hired out as a brakeman. Mike got married and later moved to Lewiston, Idaho, working on the Camas Prairie railroad as a fireman and engineer. I lost my longtime friend Mike when he was killed in a motorcycle accident in 1977.

I graduated from Rogers High School in 1958. I took industrial shop classes, hated English, but liked science. I love history because of one teacher, Mr. Stover, who really knew how to teach. The way he lectured made you feel like you were there, even though some of the material was ancient history. At home, I received many history lessons at the dinner table as my father read everything he could get his hands on about world history, especially all of its wars. My father had a better memory than I do and could tell me on just what page in several history books I could find the information I needed.

I got a *Spokesman-Review* morning newspaper route when I was twelve and continued to carry papers until I was sixteen. Once a year the *Spokesman-Review* and the *Spokane Dally Chronicle*, which were owned by the same company, ran a contest; if you signed up enough new subscriptions you got to go to the picnic at Spokane's Natatorium Amusement Park. We could have all the hot dogs, pop, and pie a kid could possibly eat. All the rides were free. We always rode the Looff Carousel, which had been installed in the park in 1909. My father and I, my son, and my grandson all rode this Spokane treasure. The carousel was later relocated to Riverfront Park in downtown Spokane, and is still in use today inside a building especially designed specifically for it.

One day, we boys were in the penny arcade. One boy who was a bully and always beating us up was hitting us on our arms, bragging about how strong he was. We were standing next to one of those old cast-iron machines meant to test your strength. I knew all about that machine, but the bully didn't. You could drop a penny in the slot and pull the two handles together; the more you moved them together, the more of an electrical shock you would receive. I suggested to the bully he should try the machine to see how strong he really was! The bully said that he was not going to waste a penny as knew he was very strong and didn't need to use the machine to find out. I piped up and said that I would put in the penny. Of course, he agreed. I was just about to drop the penny in the slot when the lightbulb came on! I said, "Why don't you hold the handles together, and when I drop in the penny, see if you can hold them together." Of course, he agreed. I dropped in the penny and he dropped like a rock and couldn't let go of the handles. He instantly turned a pale shade of gray hanging there on his knees. He was moaning and gurgling and shaking all over, and I thought for sure that I had killed him. As we ran out of the arcade, the manager ran back to unplug the machine.

We hid out in a different part of the park for a while; I was sure I was going to get arrested for murder. We later saw the bully sitting on a park bench, and I figured he was going to beat me up, but we were all surprised when he just sat there. He still looked a little gray. I figured he would beat me up the first time he had a chance, but he never bothered any of us again.

Every Saturday, three or four of us paper boys would ride the bus downtown to the *Spokesman-Review* building to pay our bill for the newspapers we had sold that week. After we paid our bills, we would run around town, visit the department stores, and stop by the train model shop. We would occasionally go under the Monroe Street Bridge deck and walk across over the river on the bridge arches to spook the pigeons. There was nothing but air under these arches, and if we slipped, we would have fallen about 125 feet into the swiftly flowing Spokane River.

Somehow my father found out about our walking on the bridge arches, and did I ever get chewed out! After about fifteen minutes of a good tongue-lashing, my father ran out of wind and it got really quiet for what seemed like forever. I broke the silence and said, "You know, there are a lot of names written under the bridge, and in one spot you can still read really faint the name 'Langlot,' and I didn't put it there." Neither of us said any more. Finally, dad just turned around and walked away. The subject never came up again.

I bought my first car, a 1949 Ford convertible, when I was sixteen, with the money I earned on my paper route. I worked in a grocery store as a box boy until I turned seventeen. That summer, the summer of 1957, I got a job in an auto body shop as a painter's helper. That fall I told the boss I couldn't work Monday through Friday anymore. He, in a gruff voice, asked why. I said that school was about to start and this was my senior year in high school. He stood there for a minute and said, "If I had

This photo of the Extra 454D West departing Hillyard in 1960 illustrates the typical main-line motive power consist of the time, four 1500 HP F 7 units totaling 6,000 HP. During the 1940s and 1950s, engines made up of multiple F units replaced steam in through freight service on the GN, as on most American railroads. PHOTO BY GARY GARBER.

known that, I wouldn't have hired you in the first place." He finally said, "If you want to come down to the shop on Saturday and clean up and do some work that I need done, I will keep you on until you graduate from high school and go back to full time." I worked at the body shop after I graduated from high school, and when I started college at Eastern Washington in Cheney that fall, I worked at the body shop part time. I started to take a good look at the men I worked with at the body shop and realized that this was a very unhealthy occupation.

Like many sons of railroaders, I followed in my father's footsteps, hiring out with the GN as a trainman in July of 1960. Being raised in a railroad family I knew about never knowing when you would have to go to work, as I had watched my father have to go to work with little to no notice. I realized that I could be gone for weeks at a time, as I had observed my father do hundreds of times. Working on the road was hard on the guys, and it was hard on their families as well.

Our training program consisted of seven student trips, one each to Wenatchee, to Troy, Montana, plus the Coeur d'Alene, Moscow, Newport, West Local, and the Kettle Falls Turn. All of my group of three were furloughed immediately after completing our student trips. I worked my first paid trip as a brakeman on August 6, 1960, on the Republic Local at Kettle Falls which established my seniority date. After one week, I was furloughed again. I was forced to Kettle Falls now and then that summer and I continued to attend classes at Eastern. When I was furloughed and couldn't work as a brakeman, I worked at the body shop painting hot rod cars and speed boats. I was forced to Wenatchee to work the Wenatchee–Oroville branch (W–O) in 1961 and never went back to Eastern or to the body shop. I worked the W–O line more or less continually through the spring of 1967 because I did not have enough seniority to avoid it.

I was always asking questions about the history of the track we were running on. I remember asking engineer Paul Hume why the tail on the wye at Oroville was so long. Most wye tail tracks were five to fifteen car lengths. The tail of the wye at Oroville ran out about a quarter of a mile and disappeared around a rocky hillside as it curved to the right. Paul said this was the remnant of the line to Molson. Paul said that at one time this wye was a junction of different subdivisions. Years later, working the Republic local, I asked engineer Norman Wilson where to line from Molson used to cut in at Curlew. Norman showed me exactly where the Molson line branched off at Curlew. Years later, one spring, the river washed out the area where the Molson line took off. The high water also took out the road, so when the water receded and the county rebuilt the road it ended up right where the line to Molson branched off the Republic line.

I asked about line changes on the main line to Wenatchee where you could see they moved the track but not the telephone pole line nor the old grade beside the pole line. I asked when that line change was done. I asked about industry tracks that were no longer there but obviously had been in the past. Oh, many times I had to ask several people to get my answer. I was surprised by the number of employees who didn't have a clue and could care less.

As I mentioned before, my name is John Ernest Langlot, but everyone on the railroad called me Jack, just like they did my dad, for reasons I never discovered. I told them, "No, my name is John." They would say, "OK, Jack." After about a year of this I figured that as long as they did not call me late for dinner, I could live with being called Jack. Pretty good, I worked for one company for 45 years and no one knew my real name.

The rest of this book will explain how Hillyard based crews operated the Great Northern Railway in its final decade, describe classic railroad operating practices, discuss what has changed, what has been lost, and what has been gained over the years. I will also tell some of my more memorable experiences working on the railroad.

2. Trainman

➳ Crew Duties

Safety is of first importance in the discharge of duty for all railroad employees, and obedience to the operating and safety rules is required to create a reasonably safe operating environment. The conductor and the engineer are equally responsible for the safety of the train, and for compliance with the rules by the other members of the crew.

The conductor is responsible to see that all the switching is done and done right, and is also responsible for several accounting functions. Since the conductor is responsible for assuring that the work is done correctly, and performing the business functions, the conductor has been the boss of the train for over 180 years.

The engineer is responsible for the safe movement of the train between stations. While switching, he moves the engine as directed by the brakeman giving the signs, by hand or lantern signals in days past, or today by two-way radio, instructing the engineer to come forward, go back, or stop. Engineers go forward and back, stop, and start as directed by sign. They often do not know what the trainmen are doing back there.

Some engineers would dispute the issue of who is the 'boss' of the train. When the company asked why the work was not done, why cars were not spotted in the correct locations, why loads were not picked up, or why a car was on the ground, it was always the conductor who would be asked "why," not the engineer. The engineer's classic answer, if they were ever asked, was "I just work by sign," meaning they just did what the trainmen told them to do by sign.

In addition to the conductor, a train crew always included a head brakeman and a rear brakeman, also called the flagman. If a job involved heavy switching, the company would include a third brakeman on the crew.

The head brakeman guided the engine. It was his job to take the engine from one track to another, and he was responsible for making the first joint, that is, coupling to the first car in a track. If the swing brakeman was standing at the first joint, the head brakeman would stay at the switch. One of the most important duties of the head brakeman was to keep both the swing brakeman and engineer in his line of sight so that he could relay hand or lantern signs given by the swing brakeman to the engineer.

If the crew had only two brakemen, the rear brakeman worked the list, that is, managed the switching at each station under the supervision of the conductor. In this role he was also called the swing man. He decided how the work was to be done, with the conductor's approval. The conductor gave a list of the train to his swing man, explained which cars went where, and helped the swing man mark up his list of the train for the set outs at each station. Working the list taught a brakeman how to plan his work.

When the work load required a third brakeman, he worked the rear brakeman position and was the 'long arm' of the swing brakeman when switching. He usually worked behind the swing man, that is, the rear brakeman worked farthest from the engine while the crew was switching. He was on the leading end of the cars when they were shoved into a track to 'spot' an industry, that is, put a car at a place where the customer can load or unload it. The swing brakeman worked between the other two brakemen.

If the train stopped unexpectedly on the road, the rear brakeman would flag the rear of his train to avoid having his train hit by a following train. When used as a verb, the word 'flag' refers to the act of a brakeman walking back, and sometimes ahead, to stop an oncoming train. His flagging kit included a red flag by day, plus a white light at night, to wave at the engineer of the oncoming train as a signal to stop. A brakeman would also have several fusees (approximately 10-inch-long fiberboard tubes filled with slow burning pyrotechnic material used for signaling and flagging that burned red for 10 minutes), and several torpedoes. Most people know fusees as highway flares. Torpedoes were small mounds of explosive material wrapped in waxed paper and set atop a lead strip that was long enough to wrap around the head of a rail. When run over by an engine, torpedoes made a loud bang.

Most of the time, the abilities of the brakemen were about equal. As long as the work got done, the conductor would let the brakemen use their seniority to choose which job they wanted to work. Seniority on the particular job was generally controlling, not absolute seniority by hire date. This usually resulted in the newest guy on the job working as head brakeman, with the more experienced men working as swing and third brakeman. Once the new guy learned the job, the head and rear brakemen would often agree to trade off each week. On the Great Northern, the conductor could change his brakemen's arrangements if he desired.

In the days before radio communication between the engine and the caboose, we counted telephone poles to determine when our train was past any restriction. Railroads put their telephone and telegraph lines on poles along the right of way for easy access. Great Northern set its poles 40 poles to the mile, or one hundred and thirty-two feet apart.

This distance between poles was equal to three 40-foot car lengths, including the drawbar length of two feet on each end, or 44 feet per car. Since most cars were 40 feet long in those days, we could figure three car lengths between each pair of poles. Trainmen knew how many cars were in our train, so simple math would tell you how many pole lengths to count to know when our train was clear of a speed restriction. Crews used the same logic when heading into a siding to clear an opposing train, or when leaving a siding. In either case, the rear brakeman was required to line the switch behind the train. When leaving a siding, the engineer needed to give the rear brakeman time to get onto the caboose.

Telegraph poles could be used to figure our speed if the speedometer was not working properly or not working at all. The method was to time the distance over ten pole lengths, or one quarter of a mile, then multiply that time by four to get the time for a mile, then check the time on the speed table chart printed in the back of the time table to determine our speed.

In my early days on local jobs, the station agent dealt with the customers and created the switch lists that told the conductor what to do on a day by day basis. At each agency station, the agent would leave a list of the work to be done at his station in the waybill box attached to the outside wall of the depot by the front door. The agent's list showed each track at his station(s), the cars on those tracks in standing order, and whether they were empty or loaded. His list also showed where cars on hand were to go; with us to some other station, or to hold at this particular station. The list showed where to spot any empties on hand, and included instructions to pull cars loaded or unloaded by the customer. The agent's list also showed where to spot the cars in our train for that station.

The conductor delivered waybills for cars terminating and picked up waybills for cars originating at each agency station. He also picked up the agent's switch lists and conferred with his rear brakeman about how the lists affected their plans. In addition to the waybills and switch lists, the conductor delivered and picked up company mail. In those days, company mail was transported on local trains to and from all stations. The station agent gathered up the inbound waybills for loads terminating at his station(s) that conductor left in the bill box for the agent and "took them into account" as part of the revenue collection process.

Early in my career, local trains included a 'way freight car' used to transport less than carload business (LCL). The term 'less than carload' refers to a shipment that occupies less than all of a rail car. An LCL freight rate applies to any quantity by weight. This is in contrast to a carload, a shipment that occupies substantially all of a rail car. The freight rate on a carload quantity is always much less per pound than the LCL rate.

The way freight car was always immediately ahead of the caboose. Way freight would be unloaded at the appropriate station along the line. For the most part, one man could handle unloading the boxes of merchandise onto a baggage cart, but on occasion it would take both brakemen and the conductor to get some of the heavy merchandise onto the baggage cart. Each LCL shipment travelled with a waybill, and the conductor also delivered the LCL waybills to the station agent.

The conductor wrote up all the cars that a train took from each station on the wheel report showing from what station cars were taken, as well as the time and date. When his train picked up cars, he added the cars on the wheel report. When his train set out cars, he showed on the wheel report the date, time, and location by station number, where the crew left the cars. One copy of the wheel report went to the Car Accounting office at St. Paul where it served as the foundation of the car accounting and car tracing systems.

The conductor also kept a delay report that showed the running time between each pair of stations the train stopped at, how much time was spent at each station, and what work the crew did there. Typical delay report items read as, "45 min switching," "20 min unloading way freight," and "10 min air."

Recording these details kept the conductor busy with his number 2 pencils. The conductor did most of his bookwork in the caboose while the train was moving. To get the idea of what this was like, try writing a letter at a table while somebody is continually shaking or bumping it! After a while, conductors got kind of a sixth sense as to when the slack in the train was going to run in or run out, and soon learned to lift the pencil just in time to keep from running an unwanted pencil line far up or down the paperwork. If this did happen to occur, the conductor usually started over because an errant pencil line ruined the form.

When I was promoted to conductor in March of 1968, the conductor's work was still done in the same way that it had been for decades. I figured the tonnage and length of our set outs with paper and pencil, subtracting the totals from the train's total tonnage and length. The same applied to pickups. I figured tonnage and length and added those figures to the train's total tonnage and length. When pocket calculators became available, they made the figuring part of a conductor's book work so much easier.

With the continuing improvements in computer capabilities and programming, the computer now tells the conductor car counts, length, and tonnage of each pick up and set out. Very little figuring is now required of conductors, except for the few traditional style locals that directly serve customers.

Seniority, Bidding, and Preferred Jobs

Some jobs were generally preferred to others. Passenger work appealed to those who wanted a predictable schedule, and were generally held by guys with a lot of seniority. In general, the men who worked passenger were up in years, whose children were raised, and who were close to retirement. Some were not in perfect health and could not handle the strenuous work in through freight or local freight service any longer. Passenger jobs paid a little bit less than freight jobs on a monthly basis, but were as close to perfectly predictable in terms of start time and duration as was possible on the railroad.

The freight 'pool,' or 'chain gang' service jobs at Hillyard also tended to go to senior people. These were relatively easy, for the most part 'get on and ride' jobs, and they paid well for the time involved. 'Chain gang' refers to a first in/first out call system at Hillyard and the turn back point. I believe that the term 'chain gang' came from the fact that the crews worked in a continuous cycle, each crew being a link in the chain. When you tied up at Hillyard, the time of your next call was reasonably predictable.

The local jobs based at Hillyard and Spokane appealed to those who liked a regular start time. An advantage to most of these jobs was that you could regularly sleep in your own bed. The disadvantage was that being brakemen on some of these locals was real work.

Local jobs with home terminals at Sandpoint, Kettle Falls, and Wenatchee were called 'outside jobs' by anyone who lived in Spokane, which included the vast majority of Spokane Division trainmen and enginemen.

The Sandpoint job was considered a good outside job since it was only an hour or so drive for most of the guys. Some of the men liked to work the jobs at Sandpoint. If they lived in the Spokane Valley or Post Falls, Idaho, it was quicker to drive to Sandpoint than to Hillyard.

Jobs at Kettle Falls all started in the daylight, and Kettle Falls was only 92 miles from Spokane. They were reasonably attractive outside jobs.

Outside jobs were well down anybody's preference list. If a man got called to fill a temporary vacancy on an outside job, he needed to figure out how to protect the job. The term 'protect the job' refers to a crewman's agreement to accept a call and report for duty at the place and time specified. Driving home at night from Wenatchee was out of the question due to distance; you were going to stay in a hotel, at best. At least the company paid for your drive to and from the job if the person you were relieving was off sick or on vacation. If they just laid off, that is, a man had removed himself from the normal rotation for no apparent reason, then you did not get paid for driving out and back home to protect the job. After the late 1960s, trainmen received $1.50 per day room allowance for hotel expenses; before that, the carrier did not pay for your lodging. That was at your own expense. Also, after the late 1960s, trainmen received a $1.50 meal allowance after four hours of work and another $1.50 after twelve hours of work. Before trainmen received motel and meal allowances, all we could do was to claim our 'away from home' expenses on our federal income tax.

Wenatchee was the edge of the world to Hillyard men due to the three and one-half hour drive from Spokane. In the 1960s, the I-90 freeway was not complete, so travel time by highway was longer than it is today. Until I-90 was substantially complete, the preferred route from Spokane to Wenatchee was US 2 to Davenport, then Washington 28 to Odessa, Ephrata, Quincy, and East Wenatchee, then US 2 across the Columbia River and into Wenatchee. It was a long, lonely road, especially at night. Today I-90 is a bit longer, but much faster.

All the jobs in Wenatchee were night jobs and they did not pay particularly well, except for the Alcoa Local. Summer in Wenatchee was hot, and the Wenatchee to Oroville (W–O) line was very dusty. I have heard the W–O locals referred to as 'Devil's Island,' 'the dust bowl,' 'the rusty dusty,' 'prison,' and 'the journey to the end of the earth,' along with some other descriptive phrases not fit for a family publication such as this. The W–O and Alcoa locals were my least favored jobs on the entire division due to their remote location and the dirty and dusty conditions in the Alcoa aluminum smelter.

Retired dispatcher Dave Sprau tells of Donald V. Shane, for many years a Northern Pacific and Burlington Northern train dispatcher at Tacoma, Washington, who carried this attitude to the extreme: "Don began his railroad career as a brakeman on the Spokane Division about 1945. When I asked if he ever worked the W–O line, he responded, 'Hell no!' The possibility of getting sent up there was one of the things that encouraged me to quit the Great Northern. We used to think of getting sent up there the same as a jail sentence. 'Ten Days on the W–O!' That's a direct quote of what he said to me fifty years ago, and I can still hear the emphasis in his voice!"[1]

During the fruit season on the W–O, most days on the 'long locals' between Wenatchee and Oroville were 15 hours, 55 minutes on duty. Six full 16-hour days adds up to 96 hours a week. We trainmen usually would sleep in the caboose at Oroville and go our separate ways at Wenatchee. This meant that all of our waking hours, plus the time in the caboose at Oroville, was spent together. Tempers did flare once in a while, but for the most part we all got along rather well, considering the conditions. The engine crew paid for their rooms at the cheap hotel which cost them about $1.50 per day. One engineer rented an apartment at Oroville in someone's basement; at least it was cool in the hot summer. That was better than the hotel, which was very hot in the summer and very cold in the winter.

When you are on the bottom of the seniority roster, you work all that you can because you know full well that when business slows down, you will be in the first group of brakemen to be furloughed. I personally put up with this for seven years. I worked a few more days each year, but would still get furloughed at some time after the first of the year. Fall was the busiest time of the year since the fruit and the wheat moved strongly in the fall and winter, much less in the spring, and little if any in the summer. During the winter, when the weather was bad, I could work because some trains were not making the final terminal within their crews' hours of service, so the company would call a 'dog catch' crew, a crew sent out to relieve the 'dead' crew. The dog catch crew finished the trip the original crew began. Sometime from February or March through the end of May it would become furlough time, and it would stay that way until the summer vacations started in June, when I could work filling temporary vacancies. I consider myself lucky; I was single at the time. I was working with brakemen just above me in seniority that had put up with this for 10 years or more, and they were able to work only three or four weeks more than I did each year.

In conversation among the ranks, the terms 'old,' 'older,' 'young,' and 'youngest' were always used in terms of seniority, not chronological age. Seniority was everything.

When I was on the bottom of the seniority roster, my strategy was to bid on any job that was close to home, knowing that if one of the outside jobs, like in Wenatchee, would go no bid, I could be forced onto it. The term 'bid' means to advise the crew office, in writing, that you want a job. If you were the bidder with the most seniority, you would be awarded the job. When a man was awarded a job, he was said to have 'bid in the job,' and he had to cover, or protect, the job as soon as he could do so. After a man starts to work his bid in job, he reports to the next start of the job without being called.

If that job in Wenatchee went no bid, the oldest furloughed man would be forced to that job. If no one was furloughed, then the youngest man on the extra board would be forced onto the no bid job. If that man was older than I was, and I just bid in a 'not quite so bad job,' he was required to protect the job that he was forced to. He could not bump me. because by not bidding on the 'not quite so bad' job, he was said to have 'passed that job up.'

Now, if you passed up a job and bid successfully on another job at a later date, and then got bumped off, meaning displaced from the job you had bid in by a senior man, you could not bump the man off the job that you passed up. You were said to have 'passed it up to him.' The only way you could bump a junior man off a job you passed up to him was if you were not able to go back to your former assignment. This could happen if someone older than you bid in and was working that job, or if the carrier pulled your previous job off. Then, and only then, could you bump the junior man off the job you had passed up. For example, if you were working the brakeman's extra board and you got cut off the board, then you could bump the junior man off that local that you previously passed up.

To avoid having to work the W–O jobs, some trainmen would just not mark up, that is, they would not OK themselves to go to work, or they would lay off sick. The term 'lay off' means that a crewman has removed himself from the normal rotation of the crew board by telling the crew clerk to 'lay me off.' They would stall around and wait to see if the company was going to increase the brakeman's extra board at Hillyard so they would not have to work those outside jobs.

If the company increased the brakeman's extra board at Hillyard with men who were younger than you in seniority, then you could give up the outside job you were working, come home, and mark up on the brakeman's extra board at Hillyard. To 'mark up' is to advise the crew caller that a crewman wishes to return to the normal rotation of the extra board. If the man was moving onto the extra board, the crew caller would place his name at the bottom of the board, and it would usually take 16–24 hours before the man would be called to work. The company would also put your now vacant outside job up for bid. When a job was vacant for any reason, including being up for bid, the company would call the first out brakeman on the extra board to work that job for ten calendar days while the job was up for bid.

I remember one time when the other brakeman on the W–O Local, 'Dried Apple Bill' (so called here because he once got bloated on dried apples and water at Oroville, a story we told in our other book, *The Rusty Dusty*) and I came home on our day off to mark up on the brakeman's extra board after the company increased the board with men younger than us in seniority. He rode in with me from Wenatchee in my car. At the Hillyard yard office, even before I stopped the car, he jumped out and ran into the yard office to mark up on the extra board ahead of me! I thought that was a low-down trick since I hauled him out of Wenatchee. Well, the next morning he got called to work my old job on the W–O, where he was stuck for another 10 days. I neither know nor care how he got back to Wenatchee. All I know is he did me a favor. But for Bill beating me onto the board, I would have been called to protect my old W–O job for the ten days my old job was up for bid.

When I enjoyed relatively little seniority, I consistently bid on the Pateros Turn when the company put it up for bid early in November. I knew that I would be forced to some job in Wenatchee sometime in the month of November. The Pateros Turn was only a five day a week job, Monday afternoon, 4:30 PM, through Saturday morning. The Pateros Turn gave me from Saturday afternoon until Monday afternoon to myself. I would drive to Spokane on Saturday and take an afternoon nap; hopefully I had a date for Saturday night. Sunday morning, I would get up early, go snow skiing all day, and crash into bed Sunday night. Monday morning, I would get up, drive back to Wenatchee, and work the Pateros Turn all night. It's amazing how much we abused ourselves in our youth!

The details of the bumping and bidding process were spelled out in the contract of the schedule work rules between the Great Northern and the Order of Railroad Conductors & Brakemen (ORC&B). When I started to work on the railroad, Great Northern trainmen at Hillyard was an open shop. The open shop at Hillyard meant that trainmen could belong to the ORC&B, or the Brotherhood of Railroad Trainmen (B of RT), but they did not have to belong to any union. The engineers and firemen were a 'closed shop;' a man must belong to the union or he could not work for the railroad in engine service. I personally did not like the closed shop. I felt that the union tended to get a little lazy under closed shop conditions.

As rail employment fell after World War II, the operating unions lost membership and became weaker financially. Union leaders recognized this, and on December 10, 1968, the ORC&B merged with the Switchmen's Union of North America (SUNA), the Brotherhood of Railroad Trainmen (B of RT), and the Brotherhood of Locomotive Firemen and Enginemen (BLFE, the firemen's union), to become the United Transportation Union (UTU). The Brotherhood of Locomotive Engineers, BLE, remained independent for many years but ultimately became an appendage of the Teamsters Union.

I was, and still am, a strong union supporter. I can tell you right up front that working for a railroad without a union contract, and without union representation, would be disastrous. When there was a derailment, the first people the railroad would try to blame it on was the train and engine crew. If that did not work, then the maintenance-of-way department was in the hot seat over track conditions. If that did not work, then the mechanical department was on the spot with a rolling stock failure. Without a competent union representative at the investigation, you could lose your job. The railroad long ago made up its mind that someone, or some department, will take the blame for any derailments.

When a man was set up as a conductor, he went through the extra board, being forced onto outside jobs and being constantly bumped, all over again. Again, my strategy was to bid on any conductor job close to home, in order to keep from being forced to an outside job farther away from home.

I preferred work trains when I could hold one. My second choice was a good home terminal local. As I got older, the locals became few and far between. I worked the Mead Turn that switched Kaiser Aluminum reduction plant when I could hold it, but this job was given to the switchmen when the yard limit board was moved to a point east of Mead. Yard limits are the farthest reaches of a yard, within which trains and engines may move without time table or schedule authority. Yard limits are marked by signs commonly called 'yard limit boards.'

Seniority existed on the division level. This meant that if someone, with, say, 10 years' seniority on the Spokane Division wanted to move to Seattle, which was on the Cascade Division, he would start on the bottom of the Cascade Division seniority roster. Once a man established seniority anywhere, the division level seniority system was a strong incentive not to move. The incentive to stay put increased as your seniority increased.

➻ How Does This Job Pay?

What a job paid obviously affected how attractive it was. Figuring out what a job paid involved a bit of calculation because of the 'dual basis of pay' by which earnings were calculated for each trip.

The national standard 'basic day' of 100 miles for trainmen in freight service dates to World War I, when the federal government took over management of the railroads. Since almost no trip was exactly 100 miles, there was an adjustment in the per trip rate to account for the excess miles. The adjustment was to divide 100 miles by eight hours, which came out to 12.5 miles per hour. The pay for the 'excess miles,' those over 100 miles, would be at the same rate that applied to the first 100 miles.

Overtime started after eight hours based on the 100-mile day. If a job covered excess miles, the excess miles were converted to hours at 12.5 miles per hour to determine the time on duty when overtime began. Overtime was paid at time and a half, or 18.75 miles per hour.

Let's look at two actual examples on the Great Northern in the 1960s, the chain gang pool between Hillyard and Troy, Montana, and the chain gang between Hillyard and Wenatchee. The rate for the basic day is arbitrarily assumed to be $50.00.

The distance between Hillyard and Troy was 135 miles. The employee earns 135 miles at $.50 for base earnings of $67.50. Overtime starts after 10 hours, 48 minutes. If the trip is completed in 10:48 hours or less, the pay is $67.50. If the trip takes longer, say 14 hours, overtime starts after 10:48 hours. In this case, the employee works 3 hours 12 minutes (3.2 hours) overtime at 12.5 miles per hour times 1.5 the overtime rate, or 60 miles overtime, at $.50 per mile. The employee is paid the base earnings of $67.50 plus $30.00 in overtime, or $97.50 for that trip.

The distance between Hillyard and Wenatchee was 179 miles. The employee earns 179 miles at $.50 for base earnings of $89.50. Overtime starts after 14 hours, 20 minutes. If the trip is completed in 14:20 hours or less, the pay is $89.50. If a crew works 14 hours in the Troy pool, they earn $97.50 due to the overtime, but in the Wenatchee pool they earn only the $89.50 base pay. If they both have a good day and work less than 10:48, neither incurs overtime, but the Wenatchee crew makes more money due to the higher mileage. If the Wenatchee trip takes longer, say, 15 hours, overtime starts after 14:20 hours. In this case, the employee works 40 minutes (.66 hours) overtime at 12.5 miles per hour times 1.5 the overtime rate, or 12.375 miles, at $.50 per mile. The employee is paid the base earnings of $89.50 plus $6.19 in overtime, or $95.69 for that trip.

'Arbitraries' also affected pay. Arbitraries were provisions of the brakeman's and conductor's agreements intended to "keep the company honest." These provisions flowed from the dual time and mileage basis of pay, and the craft unions' issue of trainmen's work versus switchmen's work. Arbitraries included Initial Terminal Switching (ITS), Initial Terminal Delay (ITD), Final Terminal Delay (FTD), and Final Terminal Switching (FTS). The rules for claiming arbitraries were complex and interesting only to those whose costs and earnings were affected by them.

When it was established by the federal government during World War I, the 100-mile basic day was reasonable. Travelling more than 100 miles in eight hours was an achievement. By the 1980s, however, average freight train speed had increased to the range of 20 to 25 mph and the companies thought they were overpaying based on the 100-mile day.

The companies wanted to change the basic day to 160 miles, without changing the rate of pay for the basic day. This would reduce the rate per mile and change overtime calculations. After extended negotiations, on October 30, 1985, the basic day for freight trainmen increased from 100 miles to 106 miles and increased again in steps to 130 miles over the next four years. Lengthening the basic day was intended to reduce the company's labor costs and trainmen's earnings.

To illustrate the impact of this change, we will change the basic day to 130 miles, holding everything else constant, including the initial pay rate of $50.00 per 100 miles. Going to Pasco, the employee earned the basic day of 149 miles. When the basic day was 100 miles, total miles paid was 149 at $.50 for basic earnings of $74.50. Overtime did not start until 11:56, so a trip of 11:55 made no overtime, and the total pay was $74.50 for the trip. Since the crew was now limited to 12 hours per day by the Hours of Service law, there was no opportunity for overtime.

Now change the basic day to 130 miles. The employee still earns the basic day of 149 miles. Total paid miles are 149 at $.3846 for basic earnings of $57.30. There is joy in Fort Worth.

With the 130-mile basic day, your basic day miles ran out at the rate of 16.25 miles per hour, which enabled you to go on overtime sooner. Overtime now began after nine hours and twelve minutes. If the trip took longer, say 11:55 hours, overtime started after 9:12, and was paid at the time and a half rate. The employee earned the basic 149 miles, plus 2 hours and 43 minutes, or 2.72 hours, at 16.25 miles per hour times 1.5 the overtime rate for 66.3 overtime miles, paid at $.3846 per mile. The basic earnings of $57.30, plus $25.50 of overtime earnings, totals $82.80 for that trip. There is joy in the heart of the working man.

After management tore out the Spokane, Portland & Seattle line between Spokane and Pasco, most crews between Yardley and Pasco were working the full twelve hours or going dead on their hours of service before they reached Pasco or Yardley. These dead crews were relieved by a new crew on line, which added to the original crew's total hours on duty, which meant more overtime. Even if they did not reach their hours of service work time limit, 95% of the train crews between Pasco and Yardley went on overtime before they got off duty.

If the company could get the trains over the road, the change in the basic day was to the company's advantage. If trains could not get over the road before the new overtime threshold, the company could end up paying more on a per trip basis than was previously the case. After the bean counters figured this out, the company no longer pushed to increase the basic day beyond 130 miles.

To simplify pay calculations for everyone, just after I retired, the Burlington Northern Santa Fe and the union agreed to a flat rate per trip. The company averaged the whole pool's pay per trip, and came up with a good solid average. This saved the company money in wages and benefits by cutting the number of employees in the timekeeper's office down to the bare minimum.

As required, the union submitted the proposed contract to the trainmen and enginemen for a ratification vote. I was heavily questioned by the younger trainmen about how 'old number one' was going to vote on this proposed new contract. I asked the group of them how they would like me to vote. They all responded with puzzled looks on their faces. I told them that there was nothing that the union could do to me or for me since I would be retired by the time this proposed contract was either ratified or not. I asked them, "How do you want me to vote? I will fill out the ballot right now in front of all of you and you can mail it." Again, they asked why I would do this. I told them that they were the ones who were going to have to live with this contract, not me, so how do you want me to vote? They all just looked at me and never did tell me how to vote.

Time Table and Train Order Operation

When I started with the Great Northern in 1960, the Time Table and Train Order system was the only traffic control method in use on the lines that I worked. The Time Table and Train Order system was based on schedules of regular trains published in the Employee Time Table and on train orders. Time Table and Train Order operation is now a lost art, replaced by Centralized Traffic Control and Track Warrants. The Time Table and Train Order system was defined and specified by the Consolidated Code of Operating Rules, Edition of 1959.

We must define several terms that had very specific meanings. Trains operated either as regular trains or as extra trains. Regular trains were those whose schedules were shown in the Time Table. Extra trains were trains that did not have a schedule shown in the Time Table. Extra trains were authorized by train order.

The Time Table was a document, printed for each division, in which the schedules of regular trains were published. The Time Table showed Train Number, Class, Direction, and scheduled departure times from each station for each regular train. As a matter of practice, a first class train was usually a passenger or mail train, while a second class train was usually a through freight train. Third class trains were usually local freight trains. By the book of rules, class, train number, the superior direction was whatever the Time Table said they were.

By rule first class trains were superior to all trains of lower classes, and to all extra trains. Second class trains were superior to opposing third class trains and extras, and third class trains were superior to opposing extras. By the Time Table, as between trains of the same class, westward trains were superior to eastward trains. The inferior train was required by rule to take the siding at meeting points unless otherwise directed by train order.

For many years Great Northern Time Tables showed two or three eastward second class schedules on main line subdivisions between Wenatchee and Bainville, Montana, a distance of almost 1,000 miles. During the 1960s, these schedules were numbered in the 490 series, such as 490, 492, and 494. Westward freight trains operated as extra trains. Eastward freight trains operated as either second class or extra trains. The practical effect was to make any train operating on these schedules superior to westward extras, reversing the usual directional superiority.

An engine was defined by rules as a unit propelled by any form of energy, or a combination of such units operated from a single control, used in train or yard service. The word 'power' was a commonly used slang term for an engine. The word 'locomotive' did not appear in the rule book and was not used in railroad operations.

The train dispatcher authorized movement of trains on the main track. If all of the regular trains ran on time, and if no extra trains were operated, two conditions seldom met in practice, the dispatcher could simply let the trains operate by the Time Table.

The rules required that a 'clearance' form be issued to the crew of each regular train at its initial station on each Time Table subdivision. In the case of regular trains, a clearance authorized the crew receiving it to operate their engine on the Time Table schedule designated on the clearance. The clearance form address showed the train number for a regular train, or engine number and direction for an extra train. It was made up by the operator and transmitted to the dispatcher. If the operator had orders for a train, the operator showed them by number on the clearance form. When the list of orders was correct, the dispatcher transmitted "OK," and the time. The operator added the "OK," the time, and the initials of the dispatcher on the clearance to make it complete. The clearance was the check between the dispatcher, the telegraph operator, and the crew as to what schedule an engine was to operate on and what train orders the crew was to receive. Conductors and engineers were required to confirm that they had all the orders shown on the clearance.

In the case of extra trains, a clearance was a check between the dispatcher and the operator as to the orders the crew was to receive at its initial station. An extra train always received a train order instructing the train's engine to run extra, in the applicable direction, from the initial station to the destination. As a matter of practice, 'slow and cautionary orders,' that is, slow orders and orders protecting track work and workers or hazardous situations such as falling rock, were provided to all trains at their initial stations. Conductors and engineers were required to confirm that they had all the orders shown on the clearance.

The clearance form was also used at intermediate stations. Here a clearance allowed the crew of a train to pass a train order signal indicating that the crew needed to pick up orders. As a matter of practice, train orders at intermediate stations were very likely to affect train movement. Here too, the clearance forms were made up by the operator and transmitted to the dispatcher. If the clearance form was correct, then the dispatcher would "OK" the clearance and provide the time of the OK. The operator placed the OK, the time, and the dispatcher's initials on the clearance to complete it. Obviously, the train order(s) were transmitted before the clearance.

The rules provided that if an operator held orders for a train but could not contact the dispatcher to OK the clearance, then the operator could issue a clearance bearing the notation 'wire failure' to a train. When communication was restored, the operator was required to advise the dispatcher of the time and order numbers given each train cleared during the time the wires were down. I know that wire failures occurred as late as the 1970s.

The dispatcher managed the movement of trains in his territory by issuing train orders through human operators located at stations along the line. A train order was a formatted message issued by the dispatcher which affected the movement of trains, or conveyed information about adverse track conditions. The dispatcher could and did issue train orders that annulled (cancelled), modified, or superseded the schedule of a regular train. The dispatcher routinely authorized the operation of extra trains. Extra trains were directed to meet or pass other extra trains by train order. The crewmen moved their train, or not, based on the combination of Time Table and train order authority that they held.

The dispatcher could establish 'sections' of any regular train. A section was defined as "One of two or more trains running on the same schedule displaying signals or for which signals are displayed." Each section enjoyed the rights accorded the schedule by rule and Time Table. The signals were green signal lights displayed on each side of the front of the engine on all sections except the last. Any section displaying green signal lights was required to sound the whistle signal 'long-short-short' to train and engine crews of yard engines, inferior trains, and trains of the same class at meeting points to call attention to signal lights indicating a following section. Crews receiving the whistle signal were to respond with the whistle signal 'short-short' to acknowledge the 'following section' signals.

In theory, there could be any number of sections. In practice, third sections were rare and I do not recall ever seeing a fourth section. The dispatcher could create additional sections without informing inferior trains by train order. Inferior trains were routinely informed of the existence of a following section only by the first, and each following section except the last, displaying green signals.

Every time a crew met a regular train, we always looked to see if they were 'carrying the green.' If their class lights displayed the color green, that was a signal that there was a following section of this train. If a crew met a regular train displaying green signals, the regular train was not the last section of that schedule. They were carrying the green to protect a following section of that regular train. If a crew did not have any train orders that gave them waiting time on, or a meet with, the following section(s) at another station, then they were required to wait right there until the second, or third, section passed them.

Regular trains displayed no signal lights; that is, the class lights were turned off and dark. This practice included all regular trains regardless of class. The display of no signals meant that there was no following section of this regular train.

Extra trains displayed two illuminated white classification lights on the lead engine. For many years these signals consisted of two flags by day and two lights of the same color at night. After December, 1959, the flags were discontinued and the two lights served as classification signals, both day and night. By the time I started in 1960, the classification signals were by light only and were referred to as 'class lights. '

People sometimes get 'classification signals' and 'markers' mixed up. Class lights are displayed on the locomotive, or at the front of a train; markers are displayed on the caboose, or at the rear of a train.

The display of markers on the rear of trains indicated that the train was complete, that is, it was all there physically. Seeing the markers meant that the whole train was past your location and it was safe to proceed. Crews were required to stay in the clear until the rear end of an opposing train passed, with red markers on the rear car or caboose, to make sure that the entire train was past. Markers were an important tool when a train was required to be handled in more than one piece from some point to another.

Let's say that our train met another train but there were no markers on the rear of the other train. This meant that not all of that train passed our location. Maybe the train suffered engine trouble and was forced to double the hill. That is, they left part of their train behind while taking the head end of the train to a location at or beyond the top of the hill. Then the locomotive would return for the rear part of their train. Or, perhaps the train suffered a 'hot box' or some other contingency, and the crew was forced to cut the engine, or the engine and some cars, off and run to some other location. The markers stayed on the rear car as a matter of course. We could not proceed until all of the train was by us as indicted by the markers. This rule protected both us and the other train, by ensuring that we, and any other trains, did not get between the head and rear ends of the other train. We always checked trains with a roll-by inspection and we always checked the rear end of a passing train to make sure the red markers were displayed to assure ourselves that the entire train was past our location.

The Time Table and Train Order system of railroad traffic control was created when the only communication between the dispatcher and the trains in his territory was via the train order operators at open stations. In unusual circumstances, the crew on the train could go to the company phone at a station where there was no operator to communicate with the dispatcher. During the 1960s, the conductor of snow plow extras often had to call the dispatcher from a line side phone. Radio communication was limited to operators at Wenatchee, Ephrata, Quincy, Harrington, Hillyard, Newport, Sandpoint, Bonners Ferry, and Troy.

The Great Northern operated several symbol trains that handled designated types of traffic from and to designated terminals. These were trains that the traffic department touted to customers. Their performance was monitored by senior management. They generally operated every day and had a schedule for traffic purposes, which the company tried to adhere to, but it was not mandatory as a Time Table schedule was.

Spring switch indicators at the west end of Stryker, Montana. The Great Northern placed spring switches at the ends of most sidings used to meet trains. A two-light indicator assured train and engine crewmen that the spring switch mechanism had returned the switch points to full contact with the running rail of the main track. PHOTO BY WILLIAM MCGINLEY.

Spring switch mechanism at Stryker, Montana. By rule, spring switches were lined for the main track, but because of the spring mechanism of the switch, a train could exit the siding without stopping to open the switch and then stopping again to reline the switch, thus saving at least fifteen minutes of delay for the average freight train exiting the siding. PHOTO BY WILLIAM MCGINLEY.

The symbol trains through Hillyard were numbers 97 and 83 westward and 82 and 88 eastward. The symbol trains were not identified or carried by those symbols in the Time Table so, while they operated on a daily basis, they were not 'regular trains' by operating rule definition. This created two types of nomenclature: the informal one based on the symbol, 'No. 83's train,' for example, but to the dispatcher and operating crews, 'No. 83's train' was operated as an extra, for example, 'Extra 2020 West.' This dual nomenclature was second nature to the people who dealt with it every day, but needs to be explained for present-day readers.

Between Wenatchee and Troy, the main track was equipped with an automatic block signal (ABS) system, a series of consecutive blocks of main track governed by block signals actuated by a train or engine, or by certain conditions affecting the use of a block. The automatic block signal (ABS) system was invented about 1900 and installed here during the 1920s.

The Great Northern equipped most of its main line

sidings with spring switches. A spring switch is a switch with a spring mechanism that restores the switch points to their original positions after having been trailed through. (To trail through is to make a trailing point movement of a locomotive or train over a spring switch that is lined for the opposite direction). Spring switches automatically lined themselves back to the main line after a train pulled out of the siding. That eliminated the need to pull the rear of the train very slowly over the switch, and often stop, so that the rear brakeman could line the switch back for the main track, lock the switch, and then run to the caboose to get on. Spring switches saved ten to fifteen minutes every time a train left a siding.

The spring mechanism introduced the risk that the spring might not fully return the switch points to their normal positions. Such a 'gapped switch' would almost certainly cause a derailment to the next facing point movement through the switch. To prevent that catastrophic result, spring switches were equipped with an indicator that crews leaving the switch after trailing through it were required to observe, indicating that the switch had fully resumed its normal position. As a backup, contacts attached to the switch points joined with other fixed contacts. These contacts were part of the block signal system, and would set the signals at both ends of the block that contained the switch to red.

➻ An Illustration of Time Table and Train Order Operation

To illustrate how Time Table and Train Order operation worked from the perspective of train and engine crews, we will take a round trip on the Bull Local from Hillyard to Troy, Montana, during late 1966. The Bull Local was a straightaway local manned by chain gang crews. The Bull Local did local work, that is, set out and picked up blocks of cars, and pulled and spotted cars, at several stations between Hillyard and Troy, Montana. It continued to Whitefish after a crew change at Troy. For illustrative purposes, both days of this trip are on the Bull Local. In reality, if the eastward trip was on the Bull Local, the other would not be, as the westward Bull Local was routinely called for 5:00 AM at Whitefish. We will concentrate on the traffic control aspects of the Bull Local. We will discuss the traffic that the Bull Local handled in Chapter 6.

The eastward leg of our trip began when I was called off the brakemen's extra board at Hillyard as head brakeman for the Bull Local at 5:00 AM. The conductor got our orders from the operator at the Yard Office. Before he left the operator's window, he checked the Train Register for the arrival and departure of all superior regular trains due within the previous 12 hours.

By rule, when a regular train became more than 12 hours late, it lost its schedule authority and could continue only as an extra train. For example, the westward Empire Builder, No. 31, when 12 or more hours late, had to be operated as an extra, say, 355C west. The order that authorized engine 355C to "run extra Troy to Spokane" was also likely to give it 'right over' all or specific trains and require the now superior extra to wait at Troy until 9:30 AM, Yakt until 9:45 AM, and so on, listing wait times all the way to Hillyard. Extra 355C could not leave the named stations earlier than the 'quasi-schedule' established for it by the wait times given in the order. All trains that would encounter extra 355C were provided with a copy of the order. Inferior trains were obligated by the rules to clear the superior extra based on the wait times in the order. Using a train order of this kind, the dispatcher could grant the passenger extra as much, or even more, superiority as it enjoyed as a regular train.

Our conductor wrote the arrival and/or departure times of superior trains on the back of the clearance that came with our train orders. This morning our conductor checked the register for No. 31, the westward Empire Builder, and No. 32, the eastward Empire Builder. Today both No. 31 and No. 32 have arrived and left. The conductor gave a set of orders to the rear brakeman who passed them to the head brakeman, who gave them to the engineer. All crewmen were required to read the orders for their train and call any operation not in accordance with the rules and the train orders to the attention of the conductor or engineer for the safety of everyone.

After getting our engine on the train and making our air test, we could leave Hillyard, but we first had to contact the control operator to get the signal to enter the double track at the east end of the yard. Once the caboose was on the main, we advised the operator that we had departed. He would advise the dispatcher of our departure and the time.

We usually ran with the current of traffic on the

An operator hoops up orders to an eastward train at Summit, Montana, during the summer of 1964. This operation demanded a degree of courage to stand close enough to a moving train that the crewmen could snag the orders. In this photo, the train is moving about 10–15 MPH due to the grade it is still climbing—but consider doing this in the dark of the night in a blizzard with a train approaching at 60 MPH. PHOTO BY MIKE POWER.

A trainman picks up train orders from a moving caboose, shown here at Ephrata. This was totally routine in the day, but it was later eliminated by Centralized Traffic Control. PHOTO BY GUS CHRIST, COLLECTION OF WILSON CREEK MUSEUM.

double track between Hillyard and Dean, about nine miles. There was an operator on duty at Dean 24 hours a day, seven days a week, to copy train orders from the dispatcher and hoop them up to passing trains. At the end of the double track at Dean we encountered an interlocked signal controlled by the operator. If the controlled signal at the end of the double track at Dean was red, we were required to stop before any part of our train or engine passed it. If we had a green signal, we could proceed toward the depot, checking the order board (train order signal) at the depot. If the order board was green, that meant there were no train orders for us to pick up. If the order board was yellow, it meant the operator had orders for us to pick up. These orders could be about anything affecting our movement but were most likely to be about meeting opposing trains between Dean and Newport, the next station where we could get orders.

The controlled signal at the end of double track was part of the block signal system. The train order board was independent of the block signal system.

Today the controlled signal is green and the order board is yellow, so the fireman leans out the cab window of our lead F 7 and picks up our orders out of the hoop. The rear brakeman picked up the orders while standing on the bottom step of the caboose as we went by.

Our new orders establish a flat meet at Camden, the second station east of Dean, with Extra 2502 West, which is 'No. 83's train.' No. 83 was the second hottest westward freight train on the Great Northern. A 'flat meet' means we can't leave until Extra 2502 West has arrived

Extra 1741 West at Camden, Washington, is likely 79's train. PHOTO BY DALE JONES.

at the meeting point and cleared the main line at the east switch, and Extra 2502 West can't leave the meeting point until we have arrived and cleared the west switch. Since the orders are silent about who should take the siding, since both trains are extras, and since we are inferior by direction, we will take the siding as required by the rules.

As we were pulling into the siding, No. 83's train, Extra 2502 West, called us on the radio and asked how soon we were going to be in the clear as they had a yellow block signal at the approach signal about a mile east of the east end of the siding. The block at the east switch was then red, meaning stop. Our conductor told them that we were almost in the clear, and that he would let them know as soon as we were clear of the main line. This would be a good meet, that is, a meet involving minimal delay to both trains.

Our conductor soon informed the extra west that we were in the clear of the main track and the rear brakeman had lined the switch back for the main. The extra west came around the curve and stated that they had a clear (green) block at the east switch. As they picked up speed, they mentioned that they did not have time to make the double track at Dean for No. 28, the first class eastward Western Star, so they planned to take the siding at Milan, seven miles west of Camden. The extra west was required by rule to be clear of the main track at Milan five minutes before No. 28's schedule arrival time at Milan.

When No. 83's extra cleared the east switch, we started to pull out of the siding at Camden. We were headed for Newport, a bit over fourteen miles east of Camden, to get in the siding to get in the clear for No. 28. We needed to clear the main track at Newport before No. 28 was due out of Scotia at 7:22 AM. The rule required us to clear first class trains running in the same direction that we were at the time shown at the next station to the rear. We were a little heavy, so our speed from Camden to Scotia was less than track speed due to the ascending grade from Camden to Scotia. At Scotia, the grade became virtually flat and we could get up to track speed.

We headed into the siding at Newport with the rear brakeman lining the switch behind us back for the main track. We pulled down toward the east end of the siding and stopped at the depot where we had a yellow train order board. We had cars to set out for the Newport Local that worked between Newport and Sandpoint. The head brakeman went into the depot where he gave the agent a list showing what we had for a Newport set out. He got the orders for our engineer and the switch list for our pickup from the Newport Local's work from the day before off the industry track, located parallel with the siding, from the agent.

The agent was required by the rules to continue to display the yellow order board as a signal to our rear end crew to pick up orders, but he generally did not have orders for No. 28 which had to arrive and depart before we could occupy the main track. When No. 28's crew saw the yellow order board, they expected orders and had to receive a clearance. The solution was for the agent to issue the conductor and the engineer of No. 28 a clearance showing "NO ORDERS."

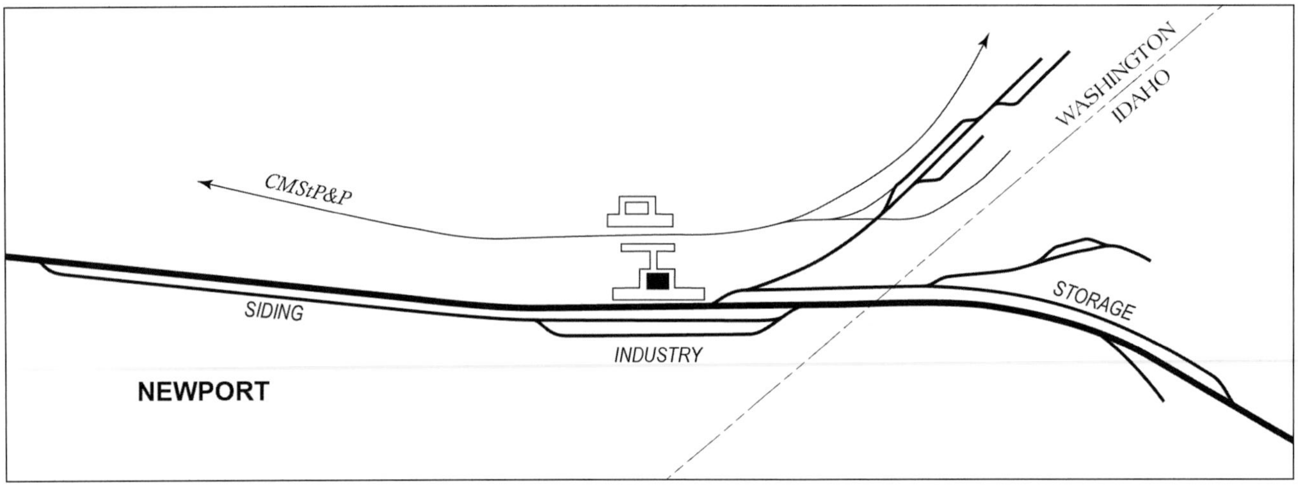

Our new orders established a flat meet with Extra 400 West, No. 97's train, at Laclede, the first station east of Priest River. We would take the siding since both trains were extras, and we were inferior by direction. Later, a new Consolidated Code rulebook, effective July 1, 1967, removed the obligation on the train inferior by direction to take the siding at meeting points. The dispatcher was then required to specify which train would take the siding at all meets.

No. 97 was the premier westward freight train on the Great Northern. Dispatchers and other freight crews did not mess with No. 97. The agent at Newport said the dispatcher figured that 97 would be in the siding at Colburn, the first siding east of Sandpoint, for No. 28. No. 28 arrived at 7:30 AM, made their scheduled station stop, and left on time at 7:35 AM.

After No. 28 departed, we made our pickup off the industry track and set out our cars in their place. We headed out of the siding for our next work at Priest River. The Newport Local told us to hurry up and leave and they would line the main track switch back for us when they came over to get the cars we set out for them in the industry track.

The train order board at Priest River was clear. The next place we might receive more train orders was Sandpoint. We stopped at Priest River, set out cars for the Newport Local, put the engine back on the train after making our set out, and headed for Laclede as soon as the air released.

As we arrived at the west switch at Laclede, the Extra 400 West called us and said they had a yellow approach block to Laclede. We told them that we were heading into the siding right now. We were about halfway into the siding when the headlight on the extra west came around the curve at the east end of Laclede. This was a good meet for both of us. When the Extra 400 West cleared the east switch, we began to pull onto the main track.

We were now at the time of day when we started to worry about eastward second class train No. 490. I should explain that Nos. 490, 492, and 494 were 'dummy' or 'straw man' schedules spaced about eight hours apart, for the dispatcher to use to operate any available train, such as symbol trains 82, 88, or anything else that otherwise might have had to run as an extra. Any of those trains could, and did, operate on whichever of those three Time Table schedules the dispatcher found convenient. When we went to work this morning, among our orders was an order stating that No. 490 was annulled today. There was evidently not enough business to run a No. 490 today. The annulment order let us work without having to clear up for No. 490.

Extra trains were allowed by the rules to run ahead of second class trains without having to clear the main track to let the second class train pass. While there was no rule requiring us to get out of the way of Nos. 490, 492, or 494, practical railroading called for the Bull Local to clear up for them to keep them moving. As a result, they got past us as we were stopped doing station work at some station, or by dispatcher's orders.

If No. 490 passed us, the crew that passed us would be in line to leave Troy ahead of us the next day. We would lose a position in the calling rotation at Troy, which often resulted in an undesirable, long layover at our away-from-home terminal. When one freight train passes another on line, the crew that was passed has been 'run around.' The next scheduled eastward second class train out of Hillyard was No. 492, which was due at Laclede 5:40 PM. We were far enough along that we did not have to worry about 492 today.

Our next stop was Sandpoint. Our train included cars for Sandpoint, and we always did some switching and spotting of cars at Sandpoint. We headed into the siding to begin at least an hour of switching. If we were to receive fresh train orders, the clerk brought them to us when he came to weigh the cars.

Switching done, and with the time rolling toward noon as we made our air test, we needed to figure out where we were going to meet No. 27, the westward first class Western Star. Today we figured we could make Colburn, the first station east of Sandpoint, some eight and one third miles ahead. We left Sandpoint the moment the air test was done and arrived at Colburn twenty minutes before No. 27 was due. We hurried into the siding and were in the clear of the main track five minutes before No. 27 was due to leave Colburn, as required by the rules. Number 27 was due at 12:23 PM, but this time came and went. No. 27 came around the curve at 1:05 PM, forty-two minutes late. As soon as No. 27 cleared the east switch, we started to pull out of the siding headed for Bonners Ferry.

The delay we incurred in this meet illustrates one of the problems with Time Table and Train Order operation: its inflexibility. Because Number 27 became superior at 12:18, we were stuck for 40 minutes waiting for a superior train that was not there. The dispatcher could have helped us but did not. In his defense, the dispatcher did not know exactly when we would leave Sandpoint, so any orders he issued to help us could further delay No. 27, which was the U.S. Mail train. He was also concerned about other trains in his territory; he had other things to worry about than helping us against a not very late No. 27.

We ran though Elmira and down the grade through Naples, where we had a clear train order board. We called the Bonners Ferry depot on the radio and told the agent that we were going to eat after we finished our work. The agent called us back and told us that the dispatcher wanted us to head in to the siding in case we could not get out of town early enough, because he had a westward train coming at Eureka, 82 miles east of Troy, that should arrive at Troy in about two hours and 30 minutes. We had a yellow train order board, so we knew we would receive orders before we left. We pulled into the siding, cut the power and our Bonners cars off the train, continued east of the east switch, and stopped on the main at the depot. The agent gave us his switch list and confirmed that the dispatcher planned to issue train orders to us before we left Bonners Ferry.

These orders would probably have to do with the extra west. It was getting to be the time of day when No. 79's train, running as an extra, usually appeared. No. 79 originated at Laurel, Montana, made up of traffic delivered by the Chicago, Burlington & Quincy (the Burlington). An important component of that traffic was alumina ore from the Gulf Coast moving to aluminum smelters at Mead, just east of Hillyard, and at Malaga, just east of Wenatchee. No. 79's train was unusually heavy because it had the ore, and because it often carried many carloads of wheat from the Great Falls area. No. 79's train was more important than the Bull Local, so we would probably have to go in the hole for him.

Switching done, we went to eat at a local restaurant and in due time were ready to leave Bonners Ferry. Our new orders set up a flat meet at Leonia, 17.82 miles east of Bonners Ferry, with Extra 724 West, No. 79's train. The order directed them to take the siding. If the orders had not put them in the siding, since we were both extras and our train was inferior by direction, we would have had to head in instead. We pulled our train slowly out of the siding at Bonners Ferry with the conductor using the radio in the depot to slow us down so that he and the rear brakeman could get on the caboose as it passed the depot.

From the east end of Crossport, a siding 4.5 miles east of Bonners Ferry, track speed is limited to 30 miles per hour for the 20.3 miles to Yakt. This part of the line is located in Kootenai Canyon which was carved by the Kootenai River.

We arrived at Leonia, but the extra west was not there. We stopped on the main track short of the east end of Leonia siding, and I walked ahead and lined the switch for the siding. This was a courtesy on my part, since the train orders made the extra west the inferior train, and they were responsible for handling their own switches, but my doing it for them expedited the move and helped both crews get over the road. About fifteen minutes later, the extra west called and said they had a yellow approach block. Our engineer told the extra west that we had them lined into the siding at Leonia. Soon the extra west came around the curve and headed into the siding. When they cleared the switch, I lined it for the main line and we were off to Troy.

This was a less than ideal meet. Since we arrived first, if we had been the train that took siding, we would have used our delay time in the process of getting into the siding. If we headed in, the extra west would have suffered little or no delay, and we would not have had to wait for him to slowly pull a mile of train into the siding. The extra west was probably delayed after the dispatcher issued his meet orders to both trains, and then it was too late to change the siding instructions. Here, the dispatcher's effort to help us went awry and delayed both trains. This delay was attributable to the inflexibility of Time Table Train Order operation.

The agent at Troy controlled the switches and signals at both ends of the siding as directed by the dispatcher. The yellow approach signal to Troy indicated that we would probably head into the siding. The agent told us to stop opposite the depot and the Whitefish crew would take over from there. We tied up at 4:00 PM, eleven hours total time on duty.

We were called for 2:00 AM for an extra west, the westward Bull Local. When we reported for duty, the operator told us that our train was at Kootenai Falls for No. 32, the first class Empire Builder, which was scheduled to arrive at Troy at 2:15 AM. Our conductor checked the train register and wrote down No. 31, the westward Empire Builder, and First 492, an eastward second class train. Now that we were moving west, we had to clear eastward second class trains. We were waiting for No. 32 so that everyone on the crew saw No. 32 arrive and depart Troy. This, and the conductor's register check on earlier regular trains we hadn't seen, was all that was required for compliance with rules requiring we not leave our initial station until knowing that all superior trains that were due had arrived or left.

About 2:45 AM, our train, Extra 466D West, came down the main since there was nothing in the yard to pick up for the west and no train to meet at Troy. We changed crews and left Troy at 3:02 AM, headed for Bonners Ferry, our first work. We held a train order stating that Second 492 would wait at Leonia until 3:45 AM and at Yakt until 4:00 AM for us. This order helped us and restricted them since they were past due at Troy by Time Table. Under that circumstance we could not advance beyond Troy without the order restricting Second 492.

We arrived at Leonia at 3:35 AM, ten minutes before Second 492's wait time, and headed in. Our engineer just set the brakes to stop at the west end of Leonia when we saw Second 492 coming up the canyon weaving around the curves along the river. I got off the engine and crossed over to the river side to look Second 492 over as they rolled by. This was a very good meet.

When their engine, the 2510, came by, we saw that they were displaying green signals on their class lights. Second 492's engineer whistled one long and two short blasts to call our attention to his green class lights, which were a signal that there was another section of No. 492. Our engineer whistled two short blasts in answer to Second 492's whistle signal. We had no orders about other sections of No. 492, so we had to stay where we were until all following sections of 492 got by us.

I got back on the engine after Second 492 cleared. Our engineer said that Third 492 was close behind the second section. About twenty minutes later we saw the headlight of Third 492. I got off the engine again and crossed over to the river side to give Third 492 a roll by inspection. Third 492, engine 444A, displayed no signals which indicated that they were the last section of 492. As soon as they were by, we started out of the siding and through the spring switch. We left Leonia at 4:30 AM.

We arrived at Bonners Ferry at 5:05 AM looking at a green order board. We stopped on the main track and picked up the car of wheat we had left on the house track the day before, made our air test, and left Bonners Ferry at 5:30 AM. We had a heavy train so the best we could do coming up the hill from Bonners Ferry through Naples with a clear (green) train order board to Elmira was 20 miles per hour. We had 20 cars of bauxite for Kaiser Aluminum at Mead, about five miles east of Hillyard. This alumina ore came from the Gulf Coast on the Burlington and moved on No. 79's train from Laurel, Montana. The day before yesterday, No. 79's train into Whitefish was so small that it was terminated there. Whitefish Yard put the alumina on the Bull Local for Hillyard.

The Bull Local arrived at Sandpoint at 6:35 AM and picked up one flatcar of telephone poles behind the wheat so we had a one car buffer between the engine and the open load of poles. We were ready to leave Sandpoint at 7:00 AM. We pulled west to the Sandpoint depot which displayed a yellow order board; the orders we picked up there established a flat meet at Newport with the eastward Bull Local. They were to take the siding since they were inferior by direction.

We figured to be at Laclede for No. 490 and we knew we would have to remain there for No. 28, the Western Star. We arrived at Laclede at 7:15 AM and headed in to the siding for No. 490 since they were superior to us by class and stopped at the west end to wait. No. 490 appeared at 7:35 AM running at track speed. They were on short time to clear the main at Sandpoint for No. 28. We sat tight for No. 28 which was due at 7:54 AM. Number 28 blew by Laclede at 8:00 AM, six minutes late. As soon as No. 28 cleared, we started to pull, leaving at 8:05 AM.

At Newport, we picked up 10 cars from the storage track, which was on the north side of the main at the east end of Newport. We then pulled to the west end of Newport, holding the main. As we approached the west switch, the eastward Bull Local was just stopping at the switch to line themselves into the siding. We told them to pull right in and we would line the main track switch behind them. Our engineer started to pull at about the time my feet hit the ground. I walked ahead, lined the switch, took a step to the west, and got on the engine as it came by me with the throttle wide open. We left Newport at 9:05 AM.

We arrived at Mead at 10:05 AM, set the 20 cars of alumina ore over onto the storage track, put our train back together, made a quick set up and release air test, and headed for Hillyard at 10:40 AM.

Leaving Mead, we called the yardmaster at Hillyard for a track to head into and he asked, "are you ahead of No. 83's train, or behind them?" We told him that we were ahead of 83's train, and that they were right behind us. His response was, "Oh great, I wanted them first." The yardmaster told us to head in to West Yard One, tie on the train's hand brakes, and take the power to the house, that is, to the diesel shop. We headed into West Yard One. The rear end crew tied about ten hand brakes on the rear of the train and I took the power to the house. No. 83 came up West Yard Four as we were taking the engine to the house. The engineer, fireman, and I walked into the yard office at 11:30 AM. The conductor registered our train on the train register, delivered his consist and waybills to the manifest clerk, completed our time slip, and we tied up, that is, went off duty, at 11:45 AM after nine hours 45 minutes total time on duty to cover the 134.57 miles from Troy to Hillyard.

ENDNOTES

1 Dave Sprau, email May 31, 2012.

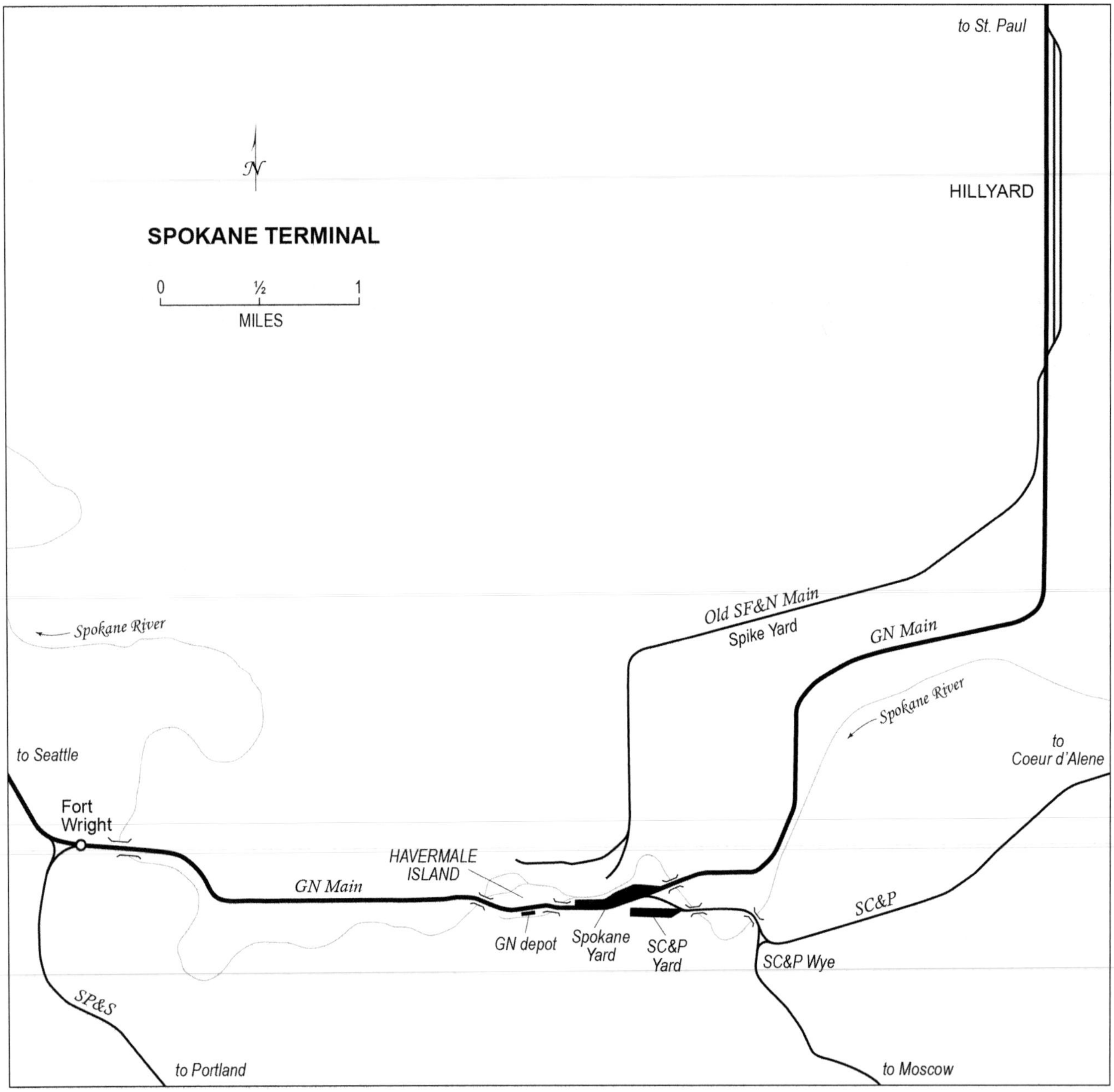

SPOKANE TERMINAL
N
0
½
1
MILES
to St. Paul
HILLYARD
Old SF&N Main
Spike Yard
GN Main
Spokane River
to Seattle
Fort Wright
Spokane River
to Coeur d'Alene
HAVERMALE ISLAND
GN Main
SC&P
GN depot
Spokane Yard
SC&P Yard
SC&P Wye
SP&S
to Portland
to Moscow

3. Hillyard Yard

➻ Introduction

This and the following chapter will describe the Spokane Terminal, all the trackage within the yard limits of Spokane during the 1960s, the final decade of the Great Northern. The east yard limit was one half mile east of the east switch at Hillyard and the west yard limit was approximately MP 1481, or about 1.5 miles west of Bridge No. 274, the long high bridge over the Spokane River near Fort Wright.

This chapter will discuss Hillyard and the three short turn locals on the main line between Hillyard and Newport. We will describe the sub yards, train blocking, various yard jobs, and three runaway engines. The next chapter will present Spokane Yard, the Spokane, Coeur d'Alene & Palouse (SC&P) Yard, the Moscow Local, and the Coeur d'Alene Local.

There were two Great Northern freight yards with yardmasters assigned: Hillyard and Spokane Yard. Hillyard, 4.7 miles east of the passenger depot on Havermale Island in downtown Spokane, was the largest and most important freight yard on the division. Hillyard switched all main line trains in both directions. Cars to and from the Spokane Terminal were placed in or removed from through trains at Hillyard. Hillyard originated and terminated several drag freights, low priority freight trains generally with just enough power to get to the next terminal, every day. Hillyard played a key role in the operation of the west end of the Great Northern.

Spokane Yard and the nearby SC&P Yard were industry support yards, each with a twist on that theme. Spokane Yard also provided the engines and crews that switched the passenger trains at the depot on Havermale Island. The SC&P Yard originated two local jobs that served the former SC&P routes which radiated from Spokane.

In 1960, the main line of the Kalispell Division extended from Conkelley, Montana, just east of Whitefish, to Fort Wright. The Cascade Division extended from Fort Wright to Seattle. Hillyard based freight crews worked from Troy, Montana to Olds Junction and the W–O line. The Great Northern restored the Spokane Division on January 1, 1967. The main line of the reconstituted Spokane Division extended from Conkelley, Montana, to Olds Junction.

Spokane passenger crews worked east to Whitefish, Montana and west to Seattle. Trainmen also covered eight baggage jobs, that is, brakemen worked as baggage men in the baggage car, four from Spokane to Seattle and four from Spokane to Havre, Montana.

The division supported many local jobs, some on the main line and others on its several branch lines. Local trains served customers on a retail level and fed traffic to the main line trains. In Great Northern practice, any local name that ended with the word 'turn' indicated a local that left its home terminal, worked to a turnaround location, and returned to its home terminal in one work day. Such jobs were also called a 'turnaround local.' The Mead Turn, Chewelah Turn, Kettle Falls Turn, Priest River Turn, all on duty at Hillyard, and the Pateros Turn out of Wenatchee were turnaround locals. The Alcoa Local and the Coeur d'Alene Local were turnaround locals that for some reason did not include the word 'turn' in their names.

Blocks and Blocking

When I started railroading, the basic unit of sale was the single car shipment. The railroads' unit of production was and is the train, not the carload. This discrepancy between unit of sale and unit of production required a network of yards to sort cars for multiple destinations, to assemble cars into trains, and to adjust train sizes at the foot of grades.

In the early days, origin yards simply gathered up all the cars headed in a particular direction. When the yard accumulated enough cars to make a train, the cars were sent to the next yard in random order where the train was switched to dig out the cars for that yard. In addition, cars might be added, and then the whole bunch moved to the next yard down the line in another train. Random order worked, but it meant each yard switched the entire train to dig out its cars, which was not a very efficient system.

Destination blocking, meaning that the origin yard builds its trains as a series of blocks with each block having a separate destination, was a major innovation. Intermediate yards also block their traffic so that yards that handle the train farther down the line can remove blocks of cars, add blocks of cars, and get the train back on the road with minimal delay.

As time went on, the railroads got smarter about blocking. They recognized that switching work could be moved between yards, to a degree. Train briefs[1] were developed and issued to communicate to all concerned what trains were to be operated, what traffic they were to carry, and where and how they would be blocked. A train brief describes the frequency, purpose, and schedule of freight trains, particularly symbol trains, including traffic to be carried, blocking, and work to be performed at various stations along the route.

During the 1960s, the 'long east' main line block at Hillyard contained cars to the hump yard at Gavin Yard in Minot, North Dakota. The block was formally called 'Gavin and beyond.' Most long east traffic was interchanged at Minneapolis for further movement eastward. All other traffic for the east was 'shorts,' meaning the car was going to a destination short of Gavin Yard. Cars for the Chicago Burlington & Quincy at Laurel was one 'shorts' block; Whitefish, Shelby, Great Falls, and Havre were others.

A hump yard is a yard in which cars are classified by shoving cuts of cars over a small hill known as 'the hump.' Cars are cut off at the top of the hump and roll by gravity into one of many classification tracks. The profile of the classification tracks is lower in the center of the tracks than at the ends, so these tracks are often referred to as 'the bowl' tracks. Humping rates of four cars per minute are common. Hump yards always involve a large capital investment and require high traffic volumes over the hump to be economical.

A flat yard is a yard with a more or less flat profile, that is, having no hump. In a flat yard, cars are pulled out of and kicked or shoved into the various tracks to classify them. In some yards, the grade is truly flat or slightly descending from the lead. In this case, cars can be kicked, or let roll free into a track, without concern that a car will roll out of the track toward the engine. In other yards, the grade is ascending from the lead to the yard tracks and cars must be shoved to a coupling and hand brakes set so that cars will not roll back onto the lead. Flat yards are by far more common than hump yards.

East of Hillyard trains No. 82 and 88 carried Gavin and beyond traffic that Gavin sorted into blocks for points east. Gavin made several blocks for Union Yard in Minneapolis that were forwarded on the same train. One block was destined to Minneapolis customers, four blocks for the CB&Q, and a block for each of the other Chicago lines including the CNW, the Milwaukee, and the Rock Island. Gavin was allowed three hours to do this work for No. 82, and four hours for No. 88. Both trains carried only Gavin and beyond traffic leaving Hillyard, except that No. 88 could also carry a block of perishables for Whitefish.

Westward traffic split at Hillyard and moved, in blocks, to Wenatchee, Everett, and Seattle via the GN main line. Traffic to California, Wishram, Vancouver, Washington, and Portland, Oregon moved, in block, via the Spokane Portland & Seattle. Gavin and Hillyard were operational mirror images of each other in that Hillyard separated west traffic and consolidated east traffic, while Gavin separated eastward and consolidated westward.

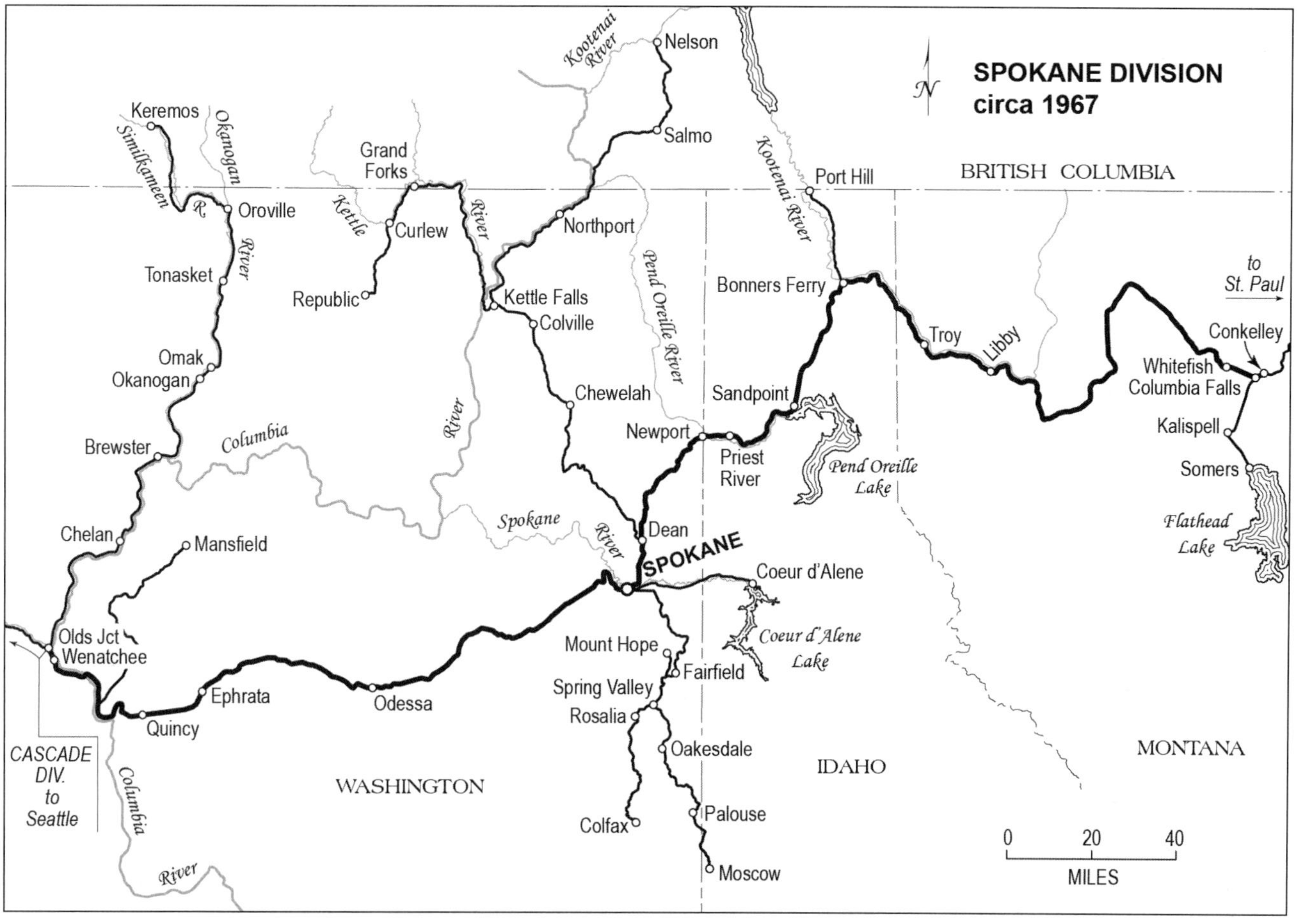

➸ Hillyard Yard

Hillyard was the heart of the division. It originated and terminated several local trains and was an important grain inspection point. Hillyard was the location of the WFE shops where refrigerator car cleaning, repair and pre-trip inspections were performed, and was the site of the largest diesel engine shop west of Havre, Montana.

Train and engine crewmen were hired at Hillyard and lived in the area. The extra boards at Hillyard were the sources of supply for crewmen for all of the division locals. As of 1960, main line freight crews worked in 'pool' or 'chain gang' service east to Troy, Montana and west to Wenatchee, Washington.

The yard lay on a north/south axis. Geographic north was Time Table east, while geographic south was railroad west. The main track extended along the geographic west edge of the yard with the yard and mechanical facilities to the geographic east of the main track. The yard included several sub yards, each used for one or more specific purposes.

Hillyard extended 2.1 miles from Wellesley Avenue to the main track switch at the east end and, while it was a 'flat yard' as opposed to a 'hump yard,' it was not really flat. From the passenger depot on Havermale Island eastward to the Wellesley Avenue overpass, the main track climbed an ascending grade of as much as 1%. The grade broke to flat at Wellesley Avenue and remained flat for about half a mile. This flat spot included the area of the diesel shops, the passenger depot, and the yard office. A few hundred feet east of the yard office, the main and yard tracks started downhill to the east and continued downgrade to the east at about .6% for the remaining length of the yard.

Because of the grade through the yard, the west end

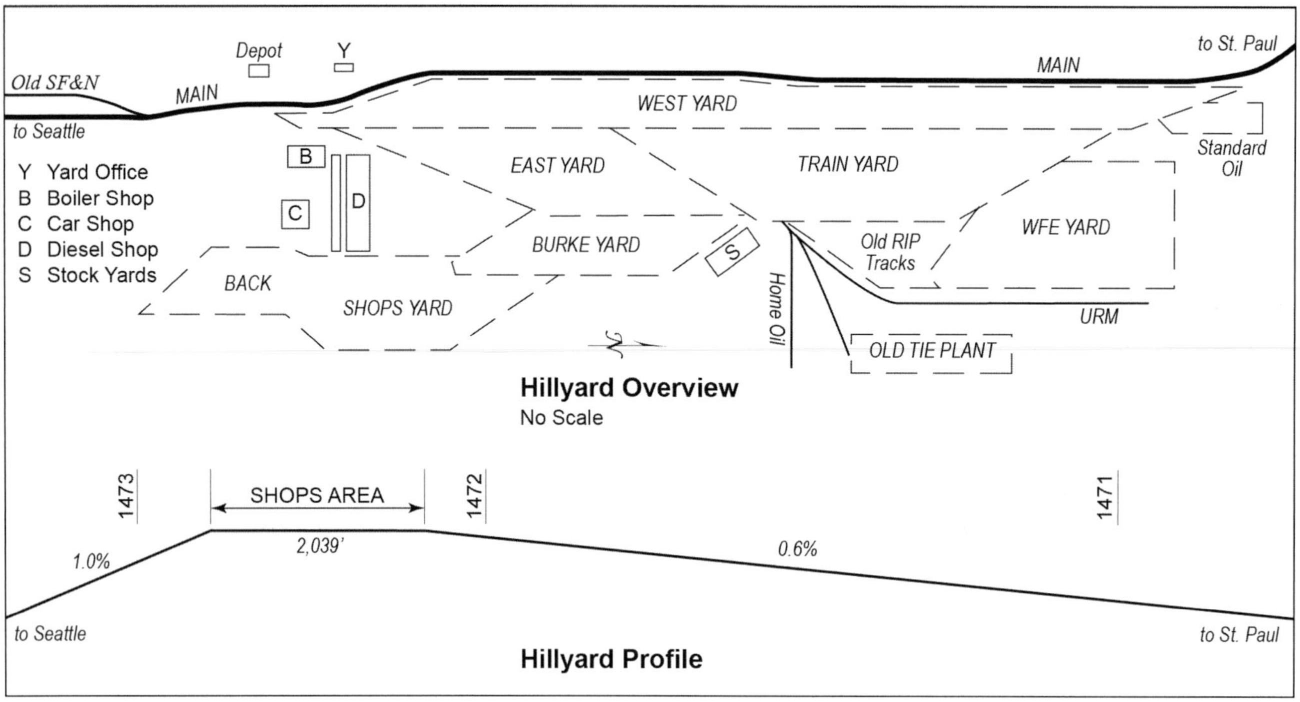

was called the 'top end' while the east end was called the 'bottom end.' This nomenclature applied to all of the sub yards. Because of the grade in the West Yard and the Train Yard tracks, it was necessary to set seven or eight solid brakes on the east end of a cut of cars in any of these tracks to prevent the cut from rolling out of its track. (The term 'cut of cars' means a group of cars physically separate from an engine or other cars.) The several cars with hand brakes set was referred to as a 'heel.' When switching from the top end, cars were kicked into the cars on the yard tracks.

Hillyard handled both perishable traffic and dead freight. Dead freight was all traffic other than perishable. Perishable traffic, perishable freight, or perishables refers to freight that must be transported quickly and with protection against extremes of heat and/or cold. All tree fruits—cherries, apricots, peaches, pears, and apples from the Wenatchee District—were perishables. Fresh fish from Puget Sound ports was also perishable.

Items that are extremely subject to decay, like fresh fish from Puget Sound ports and cherries moving at the beginning of the season to meet pent-up demand, moved in express service in baggage cars on passenger trains. During the 1960s, cherries also moved east from Wenatchee on the rear of No. 28 in steel express refrigerator cars Great Northern 2200 to 2249. These were ice bunker cars, 52-foot outside length, 42-foot inside length, having 2457 cubic feet capacity, built by Pacific Car and Foundry in 1952.[2] In season, a Wenatchee switch engine added as many as five express cars of cherries to the rear of No. 28, behind the rider car occupied by the rear brakeman. Cherries picked on Monday left Wenatchee at 2:20 AM Tuesday and arrived in Chicago at 7:00 AM Thursday.[3]

The vast bulk of perishable traffic originated at Wenatchee, but some also came off the SP&S. Because perishables required expedited transport, and needed to be re-iced in transit, they moved in block to the east. Perishables from Wenatchee arrived in block, but melding the flow of perishables from other origins complicated switching at Hillyard.

➻ General Yardmaster

The yardmasters at Hillyard and at Spokane Yard, as well as all train and engine crews working in both yards, were under the jurisdiction of the General Yardmaster. A favorite trick of the General Yardmasters was to overload the power of outbound trains. The General Yardmaster would instruct the yardmaster to add an additional 600 to 1,000 tons to a Drag West. This resulted in the train stalling at Highland or Lyons on the climb to the top of the Columbia Plateau, forcing the crew to double the hill.

The term 'double the hill' means to take a train up a hill in two pieces. It is done by taking one cut of cars to the top of a grade, setting the cut out on a siding or spur track, then returning to the bottom of the hill, bringing the second cut to the top of the hill, securing it, cutting away from it, picking up the first cut, and coupling it to the second cut to restore the original order of the train. If our train stalled at Highland or Lyons we would double to Fairchild, incurring a delay of an hour to hour and a half and blocking the main track for that entire time.

➻ Two Yardmasters at Hillyard

Two yardmasters ran Hillyard Yard. The main yard office, at the west, or top, end of the yard directly across from the diesel shop, was referred to as the Hillyard Tower. When an arriving crew called for a 'head in,' they called the tower. The yardmaster in the tower would answer and give them a head in, meaning telling them on what track to put the train, and where to put the power. When arriving from Wenatchee, the yardmaster would also tell us which lead to use to get to our track. The Hillyard Tower yardmaster handled the West Yard, the transfers, the spike jobs, and the 'Black Line,' a customer that unloaded asphalt. The Black Line was located about a quarter of a mile west of Wellesley Street on the geographic east side of the main track.

The Lower Yard Office was located at the east end of the Burke Yard, directly across from the Train Yard switching lead. The Lower Yard yardmaster and a clerk to check tracks in the Train Yard worked from this office. They handled the Train Yard, the grain in the Old Tie Plant tracks, the WFE yard and shop, the Back Shops, and the industries on the geographic east side of the yard including Home Oil, URM, Safeway and Standard Oil. The two yardmasters shared the work in the East Yard.

After the shops closed for the day, the WFE shop foreman left a list showing the switching required in a box at the west end of the WFE yard for the WFE switch job. The Back Shop foreman left a list for the shop job switch engine, indicating what cars were ready to be removed from the Back Shops and what bad order cars to bring in and where to spot them. When the shop job switch engine pulled the repaired cars out of the Back Shops, the Lower Yard Yardmaster would give the crew a track number to put the cars into. The car checker, a clerk, wrote the car numbers down on a switch list as the switch engine shoved the cars into the track. He gave the list to the Yardmaster who marked it up for switching later in the shift, after conferring with the car distributor about the disposition of the empty cars from the Back Shop. Cars from the WFE shop were handled in the same way.

➻ West Yard and Train Yard

The West Yard was adjacent to the main track. West Yard tracks were the longest at Hillyard, ranging from 138 cars on West 1, to 150 cars on West 6, based on nominal 40-foot cars figured at about 45 feet over the pulling faces of the couplers. Between West 1 and West 2 there was an open space about 20 feet wide, where the icing platform had once been.

The West Yard functioned as both an arrival and departure yard. With only six long tracks it was necessary to work both hard and smart so that inbound trains could be accepted without delay and outbound trains could depart in one piece, as opposed to being made up on two tracks and doubled over by the road crew. (To double over means to pick up one cut of cars, setting it over to a second cut on another track, and coupling them together.) Doubling over is a routine way to make up a departing train or to consolidate a block of cars.

Most westward trains headed into the west yard. All long westward trains were built on, and run out of, west yard tracks 1 through 4. Eastward train No. 82 was built in West 6. Train No. 88 was built in West 6 or West 5 with No. 78 on the other track.

GREAT NORTHERN
GREAT NORTHERN
G.N.
13465
TRAILER

Hillyard handled two groups of main line trains. The first group was the symbol trains that maintained their identity on both sides of the yard, even though they underwent substantial switching at Hillyard. The through symbol trains were No. 82 and No. 88 eastward and No. 97 and No. 83 westward.

The second group of main line trains was those trains that originated or terminated at Hillyard. These were the Drags West via the GN and the SP&S, No. 78 for Laurel, the Bull Local to and from Whitefish, and the West Local to and from Wenatchee. When traffic was heavy, No. 490 with overflow east cars on hand from the previous day, and second and third sections of today's No. 88's train would be run. These trains were generally made up on West 5 or West 6, and occasionally on Train Yard 1 depending on what tracks were clear and how many sections of No. 88's train would be run that night.

Arriving symbol trains were usually blocked, except for cars on the head end that the train picked up on line. Switching of inbound trains could get complex if the trains made several pickups, even if they were well blocked leaving their origin terminal.

No. 82 arrived with only Gavin and beyond traffic, but in two blocks: nonperishable and perishable. No. 82 typically went into west yard track 6 and was filled on the rear end with previously blocked Gavin and beyond cars received from the SP&S, from Hillyard based locals, and from Spokane. Cars to go on trains No. 82 and No. 88 were gathered and blocked on convenient tracks in the train yard throughout the day. The train brief allowed two hours for the switching and a complete inspection of the train. No. 82 was soon on its way east.

Long eastward trains, including No. 88, usually headed in Two Lead to Train Yard 1 through Train

This 1960 publicity photo shows a practice that would soon be prohibited: signaling from the top of a box car. The view is across the yard, probably taken from the Francis Avenue overpass. The WFE yard is to the left in the distance. GREAT NORTHERN RAILWAY, COLLECTION OF GNRHS ARCHIVE.

Yard 7. This left the rear of the train hanging up the lead. No. 88 picked up all the eastward potatoes from Quincy in season. The Quincy pickup was not blocked; this work was done at Hillyard. No. 88 usually arrived with perishables from Quincy on the head end, then cars for Hillyard, then Gavin and beyond traffic with Gavin perishables from Wenatchee on the rear.

Please follow along as we take you through the switching of train No. 88. Use the following legend to identify the blocks. Note that the switching is based entirely on destination blocks.

➻ *Capital letters indicate destination block, small letters indicate origin of the block.*

B	*Balmer Yard (Seattle)*
E	*Everett*
G	*Gavin*
H	*Hillyard*
q	*Quincy*
W	*Wenatchee*
WF	*Whitefish*

➻ *Other characters*

P	*Perishable*
CAB	*Caboose*
ENG	*Engine*
>	*Direction of travel*

The inbound train should arrive with three blocks, Gavin cars on the rear, then Hillyard cars, and then a block of perishable potatoes picked up at Quincy. The spuds were 'shot gunned,' meaning that they were not blocked by destination.

CAB GPw G H Pq ENG>

Before No. 88 arrived, yard crews built up to two blocks of cars on two separate tracks. Hillyard pre-blocked its Gavin fill with Whitefish perishables, if any, on the east end of a convenient train yard track. In the usual case, when the inbound train did not include spuds for Whitefish, the Gavin fill and Whitefish perishables could be set to the east end of West Yard 5 or 6 to be the head end of the train before the inbound train arrived. If there were spuds for Whitefish, it was best to leave the Gavin fill and Whitefish perishables in the train yard for ease of adding the spuds from Quincy to the east end of the Whitefish block. If the yard had any Gavin perishables on hand, they were pre-blocked on the east end of a convenient, preferably clear, train yard track. These blocks are represented as follows:

Gh WFPh

GPh

After the engines cut off and went to the roundhouse, the Quincy pickup was switched out from the east end to block the spuds to Gavin, Hillyard, and Whitefish. Gavin spuds from the Quincy pickup were switched to the Gavin perishable cars on hand to create a new block of Gavin and beyond perishables. Hillyard spuds went against the Hillyard cars from the train, and Whitefish spuds went against the Whitefish perishables.

The Gavin and beyond nonperishable fill and the Whitefish perishable block from the train yard was set over to the east end of track West 5 or West 6. This was the head of train, Whitefish perishables on the east end, to be against the power for easy set out at Whitefish.

Gh WFPh WFPq

Immediately upon arrival, a west end switch engine set both inbound Gavin blocks over to the departure track against the Gavin fill from Hillyard and any Whitefish perishables to build the bulk of the outbound train.

CAB GPw G

Cars in the Hillyard block, that is, cars for Hillyard locals, Spokane, dead freight for main line points short of Gavin, dead freight for Laurel–CB&Q, perishables for main line points short of Gavin, and perishables for Laurel–CB&Q stay in on the arrival track in the train yard. If this block happened to contain any fruit cars for Whitefish, then they would be dug out from the east end for the Whitefish perishable block of the train. The inbound block was later switched by destination, with Spokane and local cars set over to the east yard for further handling, while cars moving east stayed in the train yard to be put into eastward trains.

After setting the inbound Gavin blocks over, the west end switch engine cut the caboose off the rear of the train in anticipation of its final move. Switching the Quincy pickup from the east end created a new block of perishables. If Hillyard had perishables for Gavin, the spuds from Quincy went to that track; if not, spuds went to an otherwise clear track in the train yard. The west end switch engine went into the track holding the new Gavin perishable block with the caboose, and doubled the caboose and perishable blocks, CAB GPh GPq, to West 5 or 6 to set the rear of No. 88.

The engine came from the roundhouse and coupled to the east end of the train. The full train was blocked as shown below:

CAB GPh GPq GPw G Gh WFPh WFPq ENG>

This description assumes that Wenatchee correctly blocked the train and that some of the work was done from the west end and some from the east, which was the usual plan. About all that the yardmaster could be sure of was that No. 88 would require switching the Quincy pickup and that No. 88's inbound train would have a block of cars for Hillyard.

Hillyard often ran two or three sections of No. 88's train to handle the Gavin traffic. Overflow Gavin blocks moved on the later sections, which were not as time constrained as the first. When the traffic was available and if there was capacity on a second or third section of No. 88's train, the following sections handled cars for Havre, Great Falls, and Laurel–CB&Q. Overflow Laurel and Great Falls traffic moved on the head end of a section of No. 88 for set out at Shelby, Montana for pick up there by the next train No. 78.

When business volume was normal, Hillyard made a daily train No. 78 of Laurel, Great Falls, and Shelby traffic, along with hot cars for Whitefish. Train No. 78 left the main line at Shelby and handled dead freight and perishables for Laurel–CB&Q. From Laurel, traffic moved on the CB&Q to places like Kansas City, Denver, Houston, and off-line points south and east of the CB&Q. It also handled cars for all destinations short of Laurel on the line between Shelby and Laurel, and for the Helena line. Great Falls was the most important intermediate point between Shelby and Laurel. During and after Montana's grain harvest, No. 78 handled many empty grain cars for loading between Shelby and Laurel.

When the apples and potatoes were running heavy, train No. 88 could get too long and too heavy east of Wenatchee. When that happened, Wenatchee would reduce the inbound No. 88 so that after filling the train with fruit, No. 88 could get up Trinidad Hill and have the capacity to pick up the potatoes at Quincy. If Wenatchee removed all the Hillyard cars, then all Hillyard needed to do with No. 88 was block the potatoes and the train could be on its way with relatively little switching. Wenatchee would run the reduction from No. 88, plus dead freight from Wenatchee, plus perishable shorts as train No. 78, usually behind train No. 88. In this case, Hillyard would remove its cars from No. 78, add Laurel and Great Falls traffic from the yard along with hot cars for Whitefish, and No. 78 was on its way.

The yardmasters usually made up extras east in West Yard 5 or 6 to take advantage of the long tracks. The Bull Local and Kettle Falls turn were made up in the train yard because of their relatively short 50 to 70 car lengths. These trains were assembled from whatever cars were in the yard, from all sources, and were blocked by destination.

Hillyard gathered west traffic for Seattle, Everett, and Vancouver, British Columbia as well as Portland, Oregon, and Vancouver, Washington from locals terminating there and from Spokane. These cars were switched into west yard tracks, one track for each destination.

Westward trains No. 97 and No. 83 were received into the west yard on tracks 1 through 4. Both trains came in with a block of cars for Hillyard on the head end.

Sometimes, the bottom, or east end, switch engine would make some double overs to help switch No. 83. Switching the train from both ends shortened the switching time and expedited putting the outbound train together. In addition to the obvious benefit of getting this hot train out of town quickly for schedule keeping purposes, by clearing the high value long tracks in the west yard, Hillyard was able to dispatch many long trains with very few long tracks.

No. 83 was scheduled to arrive and depart first each day. It arrived with a block of Hillyard cars from Gavin and a block of west coast cars off the CB&Q, picked up on the head end at Shelby, Montana. The cars Gavin called 'Hillyard' were actually cars for Hillyard, Spokane, Portland, and Vancouver, Washington. What the CB&Q called 'west coast' was actually Portland, Vancouver, Seattle, Everett, and Hillyard cars. Both of these blocks required extensive switching. These blocks were followed by an Everett block and a Seattle block, both from Gavin.

The Hillyard block from Gavin was switched into four destination blocks, Hillyard, Spokane, Vancouver and Portland. The block from the CB&Q was switched the same way, except that this block also included loads for Everett and Seattle which went with hot cars for Everett and Seattle previously lined up in the yard. Cars for Everett and Seattle from the yard and the cars for Everett and Seattle from the CB&Q block were added to the head end of No. 83, with the Everett cars against the other Everett cars, and the Seattle cars in next. By holding on to the first block of Seattle cars when setting out at Everett Junction, the head and rear blocks of Seattle cars would fall together after the set out. Hillyard could add Wenatchee cars as the first block of the train as space and tonnage limits allowed.

When No. 97 arrived, its cars for Hillyard were pulled off the head end and No. 97 was turned loose in the half hour scheduled for this work. Again the 'Hillyard' block contained cars for Hillyard, Spokane, Portland and Vancouver, which were immediately switched into the appropriate tracks.

The Vancouver cars from the yard, from No. 83 and No. 97 were doubled to the west end of the Portland cars from the yard, from No. 83, and No. 97, to make up SP&S train 275, 'The Bypasser,' so called because it bypassed the Pasco hump yard. By the 1960s, most interchange between the NP and the SP&S took place at Pasco, where that traffic was naturally switched at the hump yard there.

Symbol train No. 79 came off the CB&Q at Laurel, through Shelby, Montana, and terminated at Hillyard. This train was short but heavy with loads of alumina ore, coke, and pitch binder for the Kaiser Aluminum reduction plant at Mead and Alcoa at Malaga. We referred to No. 79 as the 'weight lifter' because the train's tonnage was usually between 7,000 and 8,500 tons. Loads for Wenatchee, Seattle, and Portland moved west on GN and SP&S Drags West.

Great Northern and SP&S Drags West were made up on whatever west yard track 1 through 4 happened to be available. The drags were low priority trains that handled the dead freight such as wheat and wood chips. They also took empty cars west for loading, particularly empty boxcars for Alcoa and the W–O line, and cleaned and inspected empty reefer cars for Wenatchee and the W–O from the WFE yard.

➻ Train Yard

The Train Yard, located geographically east of and immediately adjacent to the West Yard, included 15 tracks. Track 15 was the runaround track and it was generally left open. The caboose track was off track 15 and opened on both ends. Because of the grade, the train yard was much easier to switch from the west end than from the east end. Two Lead was located on the west end of the yard and was the lead for tracks 1 through 8. Three Lead was also on the west end of the yard and was the lead for tracks 8 through 15. There was no One Lead, but the running lead extended from the main track at the west end of the yard all the way into the WFE yard.

Train yard tracks 1 through 7 were used to accumulate and block eastward cars and to accumulate cars for Spokane proper and for selected local trains. To build a long eastward train, blocks of cars were doubled out of either end of the train yard and shoved into West 6 or West 5.

Train yard track 8 was accessible from either Two Lead or Three Lead. Track 8 was the slough track used to pass 'wrong way' cars from one side of the train yard to the other. Train yard tracks 9 through 12 were used to accumulate and block westward cars and to accumulate cars for Spokane proper and for selected local trains. Tracks 13 and 14 were holding tracks for wheat previously inspected at Hillyard. Track 14 was used to hold wheat that was to go west on the GN. Track 13 was for wheat to go west on the SP&S.

The inspected wheat was held until ordered, by individual car number, to a specific export elevator, or to Fisher Flour Mill in Seattle. Customers could divert grain at Hillyard. Exporters constantly traded grain with each other, with the result that cars lined up on tracks 13 and 14 were routinely diverted to go the other way. While some of the diversions could be handled when cars were ordered to the coast for unloading, it was necessary to switch out both tracks about every other day to maintain their 'purity.'

The east end of the west yard and the train yard was switched by 'bottom end jobs.' All of the bottom end jobs employed four switchmen, a foreman, a pin puller, and two field men. The second field man was required to release and apply hand brakes before and after doing anything with a track, and to make sure that no cars kicked into a track rolled back out. If a car or cut of cars rolled out during switching, the most likely result was a sideswipe accident which could very easily also become a derailment.

➻ East Yard, Burke Yard, Back Shops, and Diesel Shop

The East Yard was located railroad west of, and immediately adjacent to, the train yard. The east yard was between the east end of the diesel shop and the west end of the train yard. Tracks in the east yard were short, only 20 to 35 cars long.

The West Local and the Chewelah Turn were made up in the east yard to avoid tying up long tracks in the west yard and the train yard to build these much shorter trains. Cuts of cars for the spike yard switch engines and cars for the transfer jobs to Spokane, including cars for the OW (Union Pacific) interchange track, were accumulated and classified in the east yard.

The scale track was located between east yard track 1 and the running lead. Cars that received heavy repairs were required to be reweighed after they were repaired to determine their light weight. Reweigh cars pulled from of the Back Shops by the east yard switch engine during the late afternoon or on midnight shift were switched into the scale track to be weighed the next morning when the weigh master was on duty. Some cars out of the WFE yard also needed to be reweighed. They too went to the scale track. After being weighed, the cars were stenciled with their new light weight, capacity, and load limit on both sides before they were put back in service.

Tracks 10, 11, and 12 in the east yard were the washout tracks where boxcars were washed out with water during daylight hours. Wheat, other grain, and anything else spilled on the floor of boxcars was washed out. Switchmen often found rodents feeding on the rotting grain in the trenches beside tracks 10, 11 and 12.

The Mead Turn regularly brought in 15 to 25 empty 40-foot boxcars each day from Kaiser Aluminum which went to the washout tracks to flush the alumina ore residue out of the cars before they could be used for wheat loading. Some days the Mead Turn brought in 30 to 40 empty alumina ore cars from Kaiser.

Gondolas and flatcars also went to the washout tracks. The gondolas were flooded with water, washing the debris to one end of the car where the debris was shoveled out of the car. Flatcars came into the yard from the consignees with wood dunnage still nailed to the flatcar's deck. This material was removed before the flatcar could be spotted to a shipper for a new load.

The afternoon bottom end job pulled the washout tracks, took the cars to the east end, and switched them out based on the destinations assigned by the car distributor. Those destinations were driven by demand as expressed in car orders and by the physical condition of the inside of the car. Cars for lumber, for example, could be rougher than cars for grain. Some of the clean boxcars went on a transfer to Spokane Yard and then the SC&P Yard to go on the Moscow local for grain loading. Others were switched into the West Local at Hillyard to be spotted for grain loading between Espanola and Wenatchee. Others moved to eastern Montana for grain loading. The afternoon bottom end job often switched out 125 cars per shift.

➻ Burke Yard

The Burke Yard laid parallel with and geographic east of the east yard. Tracks in the Burke Yard were also short, 16 to 31 cars. The Burke Yard was used to store maintenance-of-way equipment such as Snow Dozers, the Jordan Spreader, and flatcars loaded with prefabricated track panels used to repair track in case of derailments. All sorts of track materials were held in the Burke Yard.

Heavily damaged cars that would be moved to the back shops for repair were held in the Burke Yard. Cars that would be parted out and cut up for scrap were also held in the Burke Yard.

The stock yards, where cattle and hogs were unloaded and rested, was located immediately east of the east lead of the Burke Yard. Federal law required that livestock be unloaded and rested every 28 hours unless the shipper signed a release, in which case the time limit was

36 hours. Hillyard was located where stock coming from eastern Montana needed to be rested. Livestock typically arrived on the head end of westward trains. Livestock always departed on the head end of westward symbol trains.

In the mid-1960s, Safeway Foods moved from a warehouse east of Division and just north of Sprague, served by the Northern Pacific, to a new warehouse and cold storage facility east of the Burke Yard. The track ran off the Burke Yard lead, turned and ran geographic east towards Dogtown for about three hundred feet. Dogtown was the unofficial name of the low-density residential area that lay geographic east of the yard. The new Safeway warehouse was accessible by road from Dogtown for the trucks to come in and out of the new warehouse. Many Dogtown residents worked for the railroad in lower paid track and equipment maintenance crafts.

Back Shops

The Back Shops were located west of the Burke Yard and geographic east of the end of the diesel shop. The term 'back shops' usually refers to a heavy repair shop for steam engines, but that was not the case at Hillyard. The back shops there was a yard containing 11 tracks where the carmen repaired bad order cars in the open air. The back shops did not have a shop building where repair work could be done inside. Working at the back shops during the winter time was cold, slippery, and brutal work for the carmen.

Spotting the back shops was a tedious undertaking. Each car was spotted individually, and separated from the next by 10 to 15 feet. If the hand brake worked, it was set. If the hand brake did not work, then the car was chocked in both directions to assure that it would not move.

Carmen working at the back shops performed running repairs and heavy repairs. Running repairs were light repairs to cars identified as bad order in the west yard, train yard, or east yard. Running repairs were made on both loaded and empty cars. Since the cars were in revenue service, every effort was made to get them repaired in one day.

Heavy repairs were more extensive than running repairs. Heavy repairs could be repair of damage caused in a derailment, replacement of boxcar linings, replacement of doors, side sheets, or slope sheets in hopper cars, or even rebuilding cars either in like kind or modifying them some way, like stretching 40-foot boxcars to 50 feet.

Cars that received heavy repairs were typically painted. The freight car Paint Shop was located west of the Burke Yard on the geographic east side of the back shop lead. The paint shop building was about 30 feet tall with a roof. The walls on two sides came down about 20 feet leaving the bottom 10 feet of the side walls open. There were no end walls. This building contained three tracks with room between all three tracks and the walls to paint cars.

The paint shop held three cars on each track with about 10 feet between the ends of the cars. The long axis of the building sat parallel with the end wall of the diesel shop, and the geographic east wall of the paint shop directly aligned with the geographic east wall of the diesel shop. Two tracks where the cars could be prepared for painting could be found beside the paint shop building on the Dogtown side.

Cabooses were repainted in a car shop building south of the transfer table and next to the back shop tracks. This shop building was separate from the paint shop.

At the west end of the back shops sat a track that once was one leg of a wye. By the 1960s, this track was the shifter track. Loads of lumber shifted beyond the end of a flatcar were spotted to the shifter track where the carmen would shove the load back to center the load on the car, a process known as 'adjusting the load.' Some loads shifted from side to side and leaned to one side of the flatcar. These loads were also straightened up and tied down on the shifter track.

Parts of the Wreck Train, including the Big Hook, Boom Car, Supply Car, and Diner, were kept on the track on the geographic east end of, and immediately adjacent to, the diesel shop. This track was chosen for its good access. Carmen could fuel and service the Big Hook after it was used, and could supply the diner when the Wreck Train was called out. 'Big Hook' is a slang term for the crane used to pick up and rerail cars and engines. Most wrecking cranes were also locomotive cranes, meaning they could move themselves, albeit slowly. The big hook was also known as the wrecker, another slang term based on its function of clearing derailed or wrecked equipment. When the Wreck Train was called out, it consisted of these cars, plus a few cars of track panels from the Burke Yard, and a pool caboose from the caboose track.

➻ The Diesel Shop

Shortly after the transcontinental line was completed in January of 1893, Hillyard was selected as the site of important equipment maintenance facilities including a 20-stall brick roundhouse with a 60-foot turntable, a brick machine shop, a brick storehouse, a brick car repair shop, and a brick paint shop.[4] In 1912 the Great Northern opened a massive new locomotive overhaul and maintenance shop built at a cost of about $750,000.[5]

In the early 1920s, the Great Northern wanted a fleet of new freight engines powerful enough to haul 5,000 tons over the Rocky Mountains. In June of 1924, Baldwin proposed a simple 2-8-8-2 engine. Great Northern modified the Baldwin specifications in some details and ordered four of them in January of 1925. Class R-1 engines 2030 to 2033 were placed in service between Cut Bank and Whitefish, Montana in October of 1925.[6]

During 1927 and 1928, Hillyard built 10 additional R-1 engines with a slightly higher boiler pressure of 225 pounds. Hillyard was called upon to build 16 improved versions, the R-2 class, during 1929 and 1930. Shop employment grew to nearly 800 employees during the period that the R-1 and R-2 classes were built.[7]

The Great Northern bought only diesel engines after World War II. As steam engines were displaced by diesels, steam repair work was progressively concentrated at Hillyard. While an ever-expanding volume of diesel repair work was performed at Hillyard, most diesel repairs on the system were done at the new diesel shop at Havre, Montana.

As dieselization of the railroad continued, it became apparent that additional facilities for heavy overhaul would be required at some point west of Havre. Early in 1954, President John M. Budd announced that contracts in the amount of $675,000 had been let to modernize the Hillyard facilities for diesel engines. The Erecting Shop of 1912 was gutted and rebuilt inside, converting it to a modern diesel shop and machine shop, with both functions performed in the single structure.[8]

Four brand new U25B engines, totaling 10,000 horsepower with the 2507 in the lead, departing Hillyard in 1964. These units were assigned to premier St Paul–Seattle trains 97 and 82 at the time. Compare with photos on pages 7 and 113. PHOTO BY GREAT NORTHERN RAILWAY, COLLECTION OF GNRHS ARCHIVE.

The Diesel Shop was the most important shop building during the 1960s. When the shop was converted to maintain diesels in 1954, the area previously occupied by tracks 1 through 3 was remodeled into office space, and the remaining tracks were renumbered. Old track 4 became new track 1, and so on.

In the steam days, each track or group of tracks in the shop was set up to make specific repairs, or to rebuild engines. The transfer table on the south side of the Erecting Shop was used to move engines into and out of the shop and from track to track inside the shop. The transfer table also was used to move boilers between the Erecting Shop and the Boiler Shop.

The transfer table continued to serve the Diesel Shop, providing access to renumbered tracks 1 through 20. As

TOP Hillyard transfer table at the back side the Erecting Shop, was installed to move engines and boilers between the Erecting Shop and the Boiler Shop, located to the right in this view. After the Erecting Shop was converted to the Diesel Shop and the Boiler Shop to the diesel engine paint shop, the transfer table was used to move engines between the shops. COLLECTION OF DAVID SNYDER.

BOTTOM In steam days the table was used to move engines from one track to another in the erecting shop and to move engines to and from the boiler shop. After the steam days the boiler shop became the location where diesel fuel tanks were steam cleaned inside and out. COLLECTION OF DAVID SNYDER.

in the days of steam, groups of tracks were equipped to perform specific functions. The transfer table was used to place engines on and remove engines from specific shop tracks. It was also used to move diesel units to the locomotive paint shop, which was then located in the old boiler shop building.

Seven tracks ran into the diesel shop building on the geographic north side. Tracks 1 through 6 were used to perform general maintenance on diesel locomotives. Elevated platforms adjacent to these tracks provided easy access to the engines. Track 7 featured a drop pit for dropping locomotive trucks out from under a unit.

All the tracks in the shop were served by three overhead bridge cranes. The term 'bridge' refers to a design featuring a wheeled framework that spans a distance. The bridge cranes all travelled perpendicular to the tracks for the full length of the shop. Next to the doors at the front of the diesel shop, and the next to the doors at the transfer table end, were two 100-ton cranes that spanned at least 50 feet. One 200-ton crane in the center of the diesel shop covered the rest of the shop floor. All were capable of lifting a complete diesel engine into or out of a unit. The 200-ton crane was used in the steam days for lifting boilers off and setting boilers onto the running gear of the largest steam engines, including the R-1s and R-2s.

The Gentry Track was located on the yard, or north, side of the Diesel Shop. It ran beside both the Diesel Shop and the old boiler shop all the way to the Store House building. Roundhouse forces often put outbound power on the Gentry Track because it was convenient and out of the way.

➻ Home Oil, the Old Rip Tracks, and the Old Tie Plant

From the lower yard office, an engine could run down the lead under the Francis Avenue Bridge, which crossed over the entire yard. At the bridge, a crew could either continue on track 15 to the caboose track and the bottom end of the yard, or they could line the switch towards the old tie plant, the old rip tracks, the WFE yard and shop, and the Home Oil/URM Spurs. To line the switch means to change the position of switch points, and thus the route through the switch. All of these tracks, including the customer spurs, were level with no grade and opened only to the west.

The old tie plant, three stub tracks that held 145 cars, was used for grain inspection and storage. Westward grain from drags west was moved to the old tie plant on arrival. After the grain was inspected, it was moved to tracks 13 or 14 in the train yard. While an engine was not usually specifically assigned to handle the grain, at least the equivalent of one engine per shift was involved in switching grain.

The five old rip tracks were now used for storing heavy bad order cars ultimately headed for the back shop. The term rip track(s) is short for 'repair in place' and refers to a physical location where running repairs are made to rail cars.

Diverging from the lead to the old tie plant was a long lead that ran geographic east of and parallel with WFE tracks. This track served the URM warehouse at the east end of the lead track. Another track diverged from the URM lead and turned 90 degrees to the right. Beyond the curve, this track split to serve both sides of Home Oil which received tank and boxcars of petroleum products. URM and Home Oil required a switch at least once a day.

WFE Yard and Shop

Hillyard was the only WFE shop on the west end of the Great Northern. WFE employees inspected, cleaned, repaired, rebuilt, and repainted refrigerator cars. The 11 tracks of the WFE yard and shop complex were railroad east of the old rip tracks.

For simplicity, we will use compass, not railroad, directions to describe the WFE yard and shop. Tracks lay on a north/south axis and were numbered 1 through 11; track one nearest the yard. The several shop buildings were located in the middle of the yard between tracks 5 and 6.

All empty refrigerator cars coming into Hillyard were switched to one of the four inspection and cleaning tracks on the east side of the WFE complex nearest the buildings, tracks 6 through 9. Most cars were inspected and cleaned in preparation for their next load. Light repairs were done on the inspection tracks as needed. When the inspections found cars in need of heavy repair, the cars were switched to the storage tracks, numbers 10 and 11 on the east side of the WFE yard. The inspection and cleaning tracks were later used for mechanical reefer repair as the ice reefer fleet was being phased out.

Heavy repairs and program rebuilding of the ice reefer fleet were done on the tracks west of the shop buildings and toward the train yard, tracks 1 through 5. About halfway into tracks 1 through 4, there were crossovers between tracks 1 and 2, 2 and 3, and 3 and 4.

On the extreme north end of the two west tracks, tracks 1 and 2, condemned reefers were stripped of all useable parts, shoved out to the end of these two extra-long tracks, and set afire. Burning of condemned reefers stopped sometime in the 1950s.

Parallel with and west of the west WFE lead track to tracks 1 through 5, were two double ended tracks that each held 13 reefers. These open-air tracks were paint tracks 1 and 2. Paint 1 was nearest the freight yard, and paint 2 was nearest the lead. A complete collection of car stencils was kept on racks located between the two paint tracks and toward the south end.

There were four work areas on the two tracks. Spot 1 was at the north end, and spot 2 was at the south end of Paint Track 1. Spot 3 was at the north end, and spot 4 was at the south end of Paint Track 2.

Cars were prepared to be painted, that is, primed in the days of wood cars or sandblasted and primed in the days of steel cars, at spots 1 and 3. The painters worked from south to north at each spot, and they worked on only one end and on the side facing the area between the two tracks at each spot. The painting and stenciling of one side and one end was done at spot 2 and spot 4 on the south portion of paint tracks 1 and 2, respectively.

The night switch engine filled spot 1 with raw reefer cars. At the beginning of the day in the 1960s they typically spotted eight to ten cars on Paint 1, six or seven at spot 1, with the balance at spot 2. Paint 2 would have six or seven cars: three or four in spot 3, with the balance in spot 4.

The paint tracks were equipped with a cable system to move cars not only along the track, but from track to track. While the painters were at lunch, a separate group of carmen used the cable system to pull all of the cars out of Paint 1 and onto WFE track 1. The cars that were painted and stenciled on one side and one end were then pulled into spot 3, at the north end of Paint 2.

Adding cars to spot 3 moved cars in spot 3 toward spot 4 for painting. Cars that were ready were moved from spot 3 to spot 4. Cars from paint track 1 that were ready to be painted went to spot 2, and those that still needed prep work went back to spot 1. When the paint crew came back from lunch, they could resume work on cars not completed at their spot, and new cars were in position to be prepared or painted.

At the end of the day there would be a group of painted cars in spot 4, a group of half-painted and half-primed cars in spot 3, a group of half-painted half-raw cars at spot 2, and a group of half-primed, half-raw cars, plus perhaps an entirely raw car or two, in spot 1. The switch engine that switched WFE each afternoon switched the paint tracks. The first step was to gather up a group of raw cars from the WFE yard and set them on the lead. Next, the crew pulled all of track 2, doubled over to and pulled all of track 1, then doubled over to the raw cars on the lead. Then they refilled spot 1 with raw cars, left the half-primed, half-raw cars in spot 2, set the half-painted, half-raw cars to spot 3, left the half-painted and half-primed cars at spot 4, and took the completely painted cars to the east yard to be weighed.

Spike Yard

The 'Spike Yard' was the name attached to the remnant of the former Spokane Falls and Northern (SF&N) main track between Hillyard and the end of track, then located near the site of the long-gone SF&N passenger depot on the north side of the Spokane River, near Division Street. The line crossed Division Street to enter a small yard on the west side of Division.

Hillyard switch crews worked daylight and afternoon 'spike yard' jobs Monday through Friday, serving 176 customers. Many customers on the spike shared a single industry track, and some even used the same spot. It was common for 7 to 10 customers to be on the same industry track, which required a lot of cutting cars into the industry tracks, which made for slow and complicated switching. The multitude of street crossings also slowed movement and switching on the spike. Each spike yard switch engine typically left Hillyard with 25 to 40 cars and returned with the same number. At times, an extra switch engine was called to make a trip down the spike on the midnight shift to clean up the switching left over from the afternoon before.

Yard Jobs at Hillyard

Having talked about the layout of Hillyard and how it worked, let's consider how many switch engine jobs it took to keep the place running and what names identified each job.

Five jobs worked all three shifts, seven days per week. The Transfer Job moved cars between Hillyard and Spokane Yard, pulling from and delivering to the OW interchange as required. The Speedway Job usually switched at the top end of east yard and the train yard. The West Yard Job worked the west yard and concentrated on the through trains. The East Yard Job worked the east end of the west yard and the train yard. Once in a while, the East Yard Job would make a few moves at the east end of the east yard. The Lower Yard Office Tramp Job worked wherever it was needed.

Monday through Friday there were additional jobs: an afternoon Shop Job, a day and an afternoon Spike Yard Job, and an afternoon WFE Job. Extra jobs were called as necessary to handle high traffic levels or recover from disruptions in the yard or on the line.

Transfers between Hillyard and Spokane Yard

Transfer crews moved cars between Hillyard and Spokane Yard. Spokane Yard was located downtown, immediately east of the passenger depot on Havermale Island. These crews went to work at Hillyard and delivered cars to Spokane Yard. At Spokane Yard, they picked up a cut of cars for Hillyard. Transfer crews usually worked all three shifts seven days a week and usually made two round trips per shift.

Transfers were usually built on the running lead at Hillyard, which held 52 cars, and consisted of cars for the Spokane Yard, the SC&P Yard, and the industries served by each yard. Cars for the Coeur d'Alene and Moscow locals went to Spokane Yard on the transfers, as did cars for the 'OW interchange tracks' which were located between Hillyard and Spokane Yard.

Transfer crews delivered cars to and pulled cars from the two OW interchange tracks located immediately west of Mission Avenue. The OW interchange tracks were so called because when they were built, the name of the other railroad was the Oregon-Washington Railway

TOP A locomotive crane, known colloquially as the "Hook," at Hillyard. The Hook, used to lift and rerail equipment, was the heart of the wreck train. GNRHS ARCHIVE.

BOTTOM The Hillyard-based Spokane Transfer Job shown here moved cars between Hillyard and Spokane Yard. GNRHS ARCHIVE.

& Navigation Company. By the 1960s, the O-WR&N still existed as a corporate entity, but its identity was overwhelmed by that of its parent, Union Pacific. The OW interchange tracks were the Union Pacific interchange tracks.

The OW interchange tracks could be reached only from the westward main track. Cars for the OW moved from Hillyard on the head end of a transfer job which set its OW cars to one of the OW interchange tracks and picked up cars from the other OW interchange track on its westward move to Spokane Yard. At Spokane Yard, the transfer crew switched any Spokane cars out of the OW interchange cut, added the Hillyard cars to the cut that Spokane Yard crews had previously lined up for them, and took all the Hillyard cars on the return trip. Not every transfer picked up cars from the OW interchange, since the UP usually delivered cars only once a day.

Among the hot loads to the OW interchange was aluminum from the Kaiser Aluminum reduction works at Mead to the Kaiser rolling mill at Trentwood, where the large ingots, called 'sows,' were reheated and rolled into sheet aluminum. The 14 flatcars used in this captive service were modified at the Hillyard car shops to hold 24 aluminum ingots which weighed 5,000 pounds each, or 60 tons of ingots per carload.

Both the UP and NP served Kaiser at Trentwood. The GN worked with the UP on this traffic because the interchange with the UP was much more convenient than with the NP. The ingots were still warm when we delivered them to the OW. GN delivered two or three loads of ingots to the OW six days a week. Other routine loads for the OW were twenty car blocks of dolomite limestone in ore jimmies that came to Hillyard on the Kettle Falls turn three days a week.

➻ Lead Rider and Bleeder

The Lead Rider and the Bleeder jobs were one-person switchman jobs.

The Lead Rider worked mainly in the train yard and the east yard. This switchman was not part of any particular switch crew. He would help any switch crew that needed help. His prime job was to tie hand brakes on the tracks as the cars were switched, and to make sure that there were enough hand brakes on each track to prevent cars from running out of the yard. He would generally ride a cut of cars into a track, set the hand brakes, and walk out to the top end lead to make his next move.

I worked as a switchman at Hillyard for a short time when I could not hold a brakeman job. One night I was called for the Lead Rider job. I reported for work to the Lower Yard yardmaster. He told me that the switch crew had a lot of wheat to switch out and that was why I was called for the Lead Rider job that night.

The switch foreman of the crew switching out a transfer from Spokane Yard with quite a bit of wheat in it told me to ride three cars of wheat into track 12 far enough to hold three more cars of wheat. I was to wait for the second cut of three cars to make a joint on the three cars of wheat that I was on. The foreman told me as soon as the second group of three cars of wheat hit me, to ride them to a joint about thirty car lengths down track 12. As soon as the three cars hit, I was on my way riding the hand brake between the first two cars to keep my speed down to about 3–4 MPH.

Everything was going fine until the cars I was riding got hit hard by another 10 cars of wheat. The impact almost knocked me off of the car I was riding. I would have ended up a mess of bloody rags if I had fallen from the moving cars. By the time I recovered and realized what had happened, the cars and I were going about 15 MPH in the dark. I tied three hand brakes, having to go over the top of the cars to get to the other hand brakes. I knew that I must be getting close to those cars down in track 12. I got off, and almost went down, because the cars were moving so fast. The cars travelled about three more car lengths before they hit the cars in track 12 with a deafening boom.

My heart was racing due to the adrenaline dump from the impact of the ten cars and running along the tops of the cars in the dark. It took me about 10 minutes to get my legs back under me. When I finally reached the Lower Yard Office, I told the yardmaster that if that switch foreman could not give accurate instructions, I was not going to work with him. The yardmaster told me that the crew had taken their engine to the diesel shop and tied up for the night.

The Bleeder's job was to help expedite the switching of trains 83 and 97. Once the train arrived and the engine was on its way to the diesel shop for fuel and service, the carmen would blue flag the train and inspect it. Four carmen inspected the train on both sides from both ends, which cut the inspection time in half compared with the usual case of one crew of two men inspecting the entire train. As soon as the carmen finished inspecting the train and the blue flags were removed, the Bleeder started to 'bleed' the air out of each car, beginning at the west end.

The Bleeder received a switch list that showed where to make the cuts behind the blocks of cars to be switched. When the Bleeder arrived at the first cut, he pulled the pin to uncouple the first cut of cars. As soon as the switch crew pulled the cut away, the Bleeder returned to bleeding air out of the cars until he reached the second cut. He waited until the switch crew came against the second cut, pulled the pin, and give the engineer a backup sign. This would continue until the entire train was switched.

Hillyard Oiler

In the late 1960s, the railroad was suffering many hot boxes on through freight trains. 'Hot box' is a slang term for an overheated journal bearing. Each journal bearing was located in its own journal box. If a hot box was not detected, it usually resulted in melting off the end of the axle, also called the journal. This virtually always resulted in a derailment. Brass journals have been replaced by roller bearings because roller bearings are far less likely to overheat and require far less routine maintenance. To rectify the hot box problem, the company installed an oiling station at the east end of the yard. The oiler sat on both sides of West 5 and 6. Every train arriving or departing the east end went through the oiler. Six carmen worked the oiler. Since it takes four individuals to cover one job for three shifts seven days per week, the oiler provided work for 24 people.

Arriving westward trains pulled through the oiler at about 3 MPH. The first carman opened the journal box lid. The second carman put about a quart of oil into the box. The oil hose was under pressure from a compressor pushing journal oil through the hoses from a 1,000-gallon tank. As soon as the carman squeezed the trigger, the oil ran into the journal box. The last carman left the journal box lid open on arriving westward trains only.

When the carmen inspected cars after they arrived from anywhere, one of the things they inspected was the journal boxes. The carmen left the journal box lids open while the cars remained in the yard. Departing westward trains were inspected by the carmen who closed the journal box lids while they were making their pre-departure inspections.

Eastward trains departing Hillyard pulled through the oiler at about 3 MPH. Most of the journal box lids were already open, having been opened as part of the inbound inspection, so the first carman opened relatively few lids. The second carman put oil into the box and looked to see that the brass journal bearing was properly seated. On occasion, the carmen would stop the train because a brass was cocked and not seated properly on the journal. To make a repair, the carmen jacked the car up at the journal that was cocked and re-seated the brass. When they were finished, they released the train to continue through the oiler. The third carman closed the journal box lid. The oiler reduced hot boxes drastically and immediately.

Air Brake Tests

A brake test is any test of the air brake system of an engine or train. A several step test of the engine air brake system was and is required before moving the engine from the roundhouse and after any change to the power consist.

There were and are two types of train brake tests: an initial terminal brake test, and a stub test. An initial terminal test was and is required when a train is made up at its initial terminal. All trains received an initial terminal brake test at Hillyard, as did all trains that originated at Wenatchee.

To perform an initial terminal brake test, the brake pipe is first charged to within at least 20 pounds of the intended brake pipe pressure, as measured at the rear of the train. The engineer makes a full service reduction, and the entire train is inspected to confirm that the brakes have applied on all cars, that the piston travel is not excessive, and that all of the brake shoes are in place and not worn beyond their condemning limit. This requires walking both sides of the entire train.

While the carmen or the brakemen are walking the train, the engineer makes a leakage test. The leakage test begins by cutting out the pressure maintaining feature before making a full service reduction on the train. Once the brake valve in the cab quits exhausting air, the engineer must note the brake pipe pressure displayed on his gauge in the cab, time 60 seconds, and again note the brake pipe pressure displayed on his cab gauge. The difference in the two pressures is the rate of leakage in the train line, which must not exceed five pounds per minute. The pressure maintaining feature must be cut back in at the end of the brake test and before departing.

The 'stub test' is a slang term applied in three somewhat different situations. The first is picking up a block of cars. In this case, the head brakeman must walk the set to inspect the cars being added to the train, and the rear end crew must confirm the set and release on the rear car.

The term stub test also applies to picking up a block of cars that another crew has air tested for you. In this case, the crew that made the test has walked the set, so the crew of the train receiving the cars does not have to walk them, but must confirm an application and release on the rear car.

The term stub test also applies if a crew sets out a block of cars. In this case, there are no new cars to inspect, but an application and release must be made and confirmed on the rear car of the train to assure the continuity of the brake pipe through the entire train.

➻ Runaways on the East End

Beginning at the Francis Street overpass, an engine moving east on train yard 15 came out on the train yard switching lead at the east, or bottom, end of track 15. Continuing east on the switching lead, you came to a facing point crossover to west 6, then a switch to the Standard Oil bulk plant which featured three tracks, with two unloading racks between the three tracks. Standard occasionally loaded cars. The Great Northern, for example, bought diesel fuel for Kettle Falls from this facility using its own tank cars to haul the fuel to Kettle Falls.

Continuing east beyond the Standard Oil tracks, there was a controlled switch to the 'Sump Track.' Beyond that, the train yard switching lead joined west yard track 6 to become the east end lead, which extended eastward to the main track. Eastward trains entered the main track by authority conveyed by the controlled block signal. Westward trains entering the yard passed the switch that split the train yard lead from west yard track 6 and continued on track 6 for about 15 car lengths to a series of switches where west yard tracks 1 through 5 diverged from west 6.

The controlled switch to the 'Sump Track' was facing point eastward. It was located at the bottom end of the train yard and was always lined for the Sump Track unless a train was arriving or departing the yard. The Sump Track was there to catch runaway equipment. Remember, the yard was downgrade to the east at about .6%. When cars ran out of the west yard or the train yard due to insufficient hand brakes, they ended up on the dirt pile at the end of the Sump Track.

I saw cars in the sump several times. Those cars on the dirt pile and in the end of the Sump Track served as a constant reminder of how dangerous it was to work at Hillyard Yard.

I saw a switch engine on top of this dirt pile twice in the years I worked at Hillyard. The first time was when I was called as a brakeman for a Drag West to Wenatchee for 5:00 PM. I showed up at the yard office and was getting ready to go get our power and get on the train, when the yardmaster hollered on the intercom that West 4 was running out. My conductor, Edward 'Silky' Foster, said, "Hey, that is our train."

We drove our private automobiles to the east end of the yard, and there sat the switch engine on top of the dirt pile with the rear end of our train attached to it. My good friend Michael Downing, who I grew up with as a kid in Hillyard, was the fireman on that switch engine. Mike told me later that the yardmaster told them to catch West Four as it was running out. Mike said that as they started up West Four, he could see dust rolling out from under the cars. Mike told the engineer, Clifford Daub, that the cars were going too fast and he was getting off. Mike got off as Cliff continued up West Four a short distance and then reversed direction.

The cars soon coupled into Cliff and the switch engine. The speed tape showed that the engine instantly went from 10 MPH to 20 MPH. Shortly before the cars made this violent impact, the last switchman bailed off, which left poor old Cliff all alone for the ride of his life. Cliff jumped off just before the switch engine and about

40 cars hit the dirt pile. The Chewelah Turn was sitting at the block at the east end of the yard waiting for a signal to enter the yard. The crew saw Cliff hit the ground and bounce like a rubber ball, hitting the ground at least twice before rolling up against a cyclone fence.

An operating officer took Cliff to the hospital. Cliff was lucky; he sustained only bumps and bruises. It was a good thing that Cliff got off the engine since there ended up being about four feet of dirt inside the cab. Cliff would have undoubtedly been more seriously hurt, or perhaps killed, if he had decided to ride it out. This delayed our departure until about 10:00 PM.

The second time I saw a switch engine on top of the dirt pile was after the BN merger, when a former NP engineer, Neil Corrin, was called to work the east yard switcher. Neil was one of those promoted NP firemen who had not been working as an engineer. When the merger came along, he found himself working as an engineer, but he did not have the experience that he needed to do the job well.

Their first move was to pull some wheat out of track 14 and put it into track 13. The loaded cars of wheat were heavy, the pull was down grade, and as always, the car's air brakes were long since bled off. This meant that the only working brake was that on the engine. The switchmen told Neil that he needed to pull out very slowly so the wheat would not get away from him coming out of track 14. Neil did not do that; he just pulled the wheat out. When he tried to stop, he was already going too fast. Next thing he knew, he, the engine, and the wheat were sitting on top of the dirt pile.

Years later, when he and I were working the Newport Local, Neil told me that he figured that he and the crew were done for the day. The messenger came down, picked them up, and took the crew to the diesel shop, where they received another engine, and they went back down to finish their work. Neil said that every time they pulled east, he saw that switch engine sitting on top of that dirt pile like a monument and a constant reminder of the first move of the day. Neil also told me that he went home that night and poured himself about three fingers of rot gut whisky in a glass, and sat in his favorite chair, where he sipped and shook.

Runaways on the West End

West of Wellesley Avenue the main track descended to the west at 1% for the first mile, then progressively less steeply to the passenger depot on Havermale Island.

Both runaways that I know about on the west end of Hillyard featured engine 620, which was modified with dual controls, one set on each side of the cab. The air brakes on this unit were known to fail once in a while without warning. Despite the efforts of the roundhouse crews, the company did not resolve the brake failure issue on this unit until after the second runaway.

Engineer George Kubes was doubling over a large cut of wheat at the west end for the afternoon Drag West. George got a little too far over the hill at Wellesley Avenue and could not stop, because the brakes failed.

George and the cut of wheat ran out of control down the grade to downtown Spokane. They went over the Howard Street crossing immediately west of the depot at about 60 MPH. The crossing lights did not come on until he was about 10 car lengths beyond Howard Street, according to George. None of us could believe that George went over the Howard Street crossing and never hit an automobile, and that he did not derail on the bridge over the Spokane River between Howard Street and Monroe Street at the west end Havermale Island. There was a 20 MPH speed limit over this bridge, which was all on an S curve with no super elevation. One of the curves was a bit sharper than 10 degrees, a very sharp curve, and the reason for the 20 MPH speed limit. A derailment at speed on this bridge would have resulted in about a 150-foot plunge into the river.

The operator at the Fort Wright Interlocker lined George up the hill toward Wenatchee. A switch engine at Spokane Yard was instructed to chase George as soon as he went by. As the switch crew approached Fort Wright, they called George on the radio to tell him that they were chasing him. George told them that they better stop and go the other way, as he was now running away down the Fort Wright hill because there were no brake shoes left on the engine to stop with. The switch engine stopped, reversed direction, and continued talking to George as they both moved east toward Spokane. As George approached them, the switch crew matched speeds as they came together, finally stopping George and his wheat in downtown Spokane.

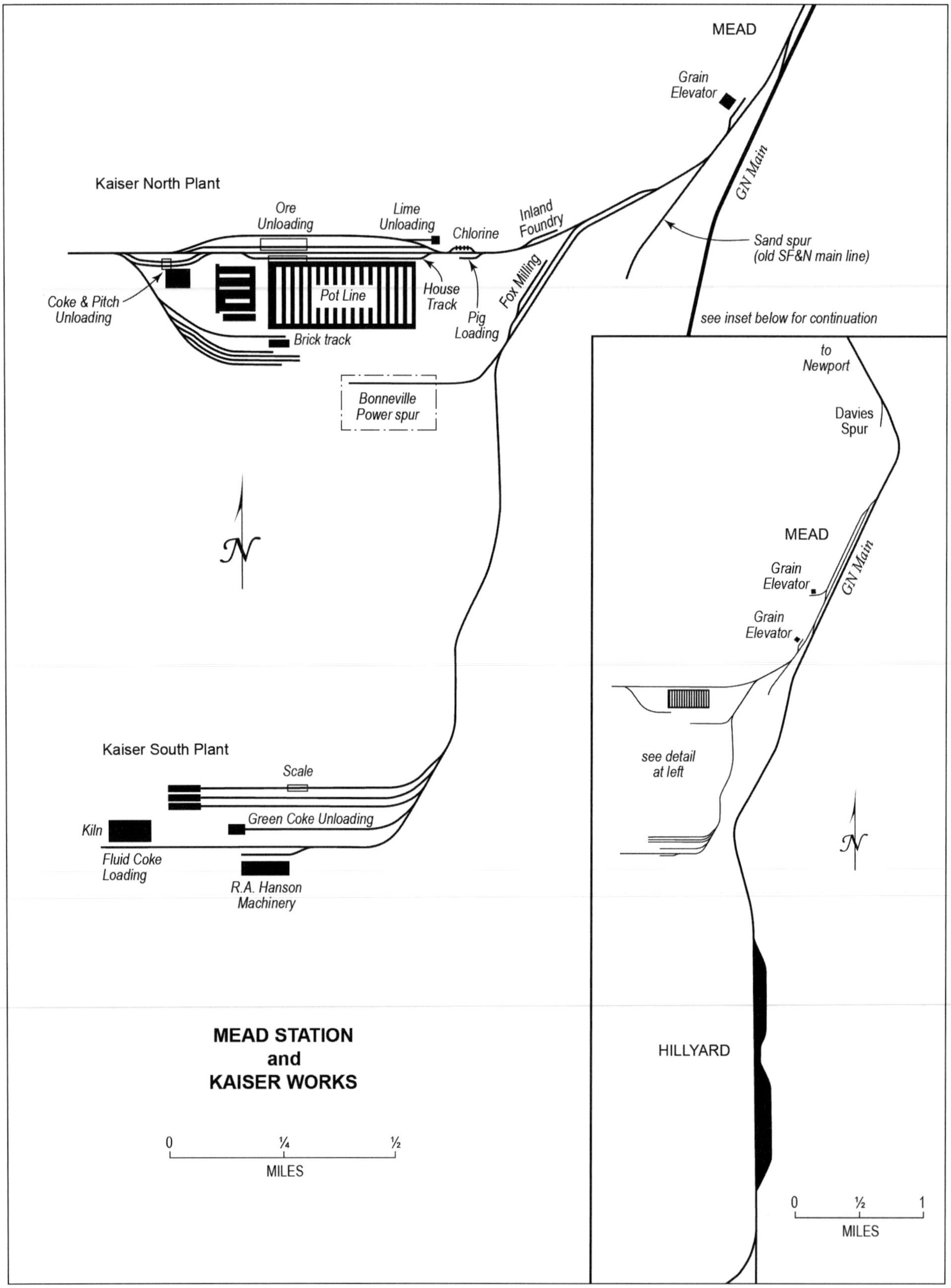
MEAD
Grain Elevator
GN Main
Kaiser North Plant
Ore Unloading
Lime Unloading
Chlorine
Inland Foundry
Sand spur (old SF&N main line)
Coke & Pitch Unloading
Pot Line
House Track
Pig Loading
Fox Milling
Brick track
see inset below for continuation
Bonneville Power spur
N
to Newport
Davies Spur
MEAD
Grain Elevator
GN Main
Grain Elevator
see detail at left
Kaiser South Plant
Scale
Green Coke Unloading
Kiln
Fluid Coke Loading
R.A. Hanson Machinery
HILLYARD
MEAD STATION and KAISER WORKS
0 ¼ ½
MILES
0 ½ 1
MILES

George was done for the day. He did not come back to work for about nine months. It took him that long to deal with anxiety attacks brought on by this experience.

The second run away of the 620 involved engineer Harry Howard; the brakes failed again and this time things did not go well. Harry ran into the Transfer Job's engine while the crew was doubling their train together at the east end of Spokane Yard. Harry hit the transfer engine when they were on the bridge over the Spokane River, about a third of a mile west of Hamilton Street, damaging both units. Both engineers went to the hospital with minor injuries.

Both engines were repaired at the diesel shop. After Harry Howard's runaway, the 620 was rebuilt with a low nose on the short end, and the dual controls were removed. The new low nose resembled the low noses on the then new GP 30 and 35 models. A bulletin was posted after the second runaway that required the Hillyard operator to line the track leaving Hillyard for the Spike Yard line during all double over moves by switch engines.

➻ The End of Hillyard

Hillyard was doomed the day the Burlington Northern merger finally took place. Once the Latah Creek and Sandpoint connections were completed, the company shifted all former Great Northern traffic to the Northern Pacific line through downtown and to Yardley Yard. After the on-duty locations of the Mead Turn and the Kettle Falls Turn were moved to Yardley, Hillyard Yard served no purpose.

The Northern Pacific owned mechanical facilities at Parkwater, adjacent to Yardley. The diesel shop was closed and fuel and inspection functions were transferred to Parkwater.

Today, everything is gone from Hillyard except for the main track to Dean and Kettle Falls, a single siding, and a handful of industries. Standard Oil is now Holly Distributors, which receives 20 to 40 tank car loads per week. Pasta USA, whose track comes off the old Safeway Spur, receives airslide design covered hopper cars of flour. Safeway no longer does business with the railroad at Hillyard. The Time Oil Spur is still operable, but Time currently does no business with the railroad. The Black Line is still in operation and receives a few cars of asphalt. The Washington State Department of Transportation is poised to destroy the site of the yard by building a new highway through it.

➻ The Mead Turns

During the late 1960s the company operated two Mead Turns. These were road jobs that went to work at Hillyard and switched the Kaiser Aluminum reduction plant at Mead, about four miles east of the yard. The Mead Turn worked Monday through Saturday called for 6:00 AM, while the Night Mead Turn worked Monday through Friday called for 4:00 PM. Most of the time, the night job left the yard immediately after the day job arrived, and always with a different engine.

I occasionally worked as brakeman on the Night Mead Turn off the extra board, managed to bid the job in 1969, and held it well into 1970. The aluminum reduction works at Mead and Malaga were the dirtiest places that I ever worked due to all of the coke, alumina ore, and dust flying around. When I got home, I headed right for the shower and changed all my clothes. I thought once in a while about the working conditions inside the aluminum plants. I never saw any vegetation growing inside these plants, not even weeds! Now if weeds will not grow, in my book that meant that the soil contamination was bad, and we were breathing the dust and fine particles from this soil floating around in the air. No one seemed to address these conditions, and I often wonder what the long-term effects were on anyone who spent several years working these jobs under those conditions.

The Kaiser Aluminum reduction plant at Mead required a lot of switching. Its most important raw material was alumina ore, which moved in 40-foot single door boxcars, the same type of car used to haul grain at the time. The ore that Kaiser used at Mead was transloaded from ships to rail cars at some point on the Gulf coast since the alumina ore came to us in trains from Laurel, Montana. The loaders lined the bottom portions of the sides and ends inside the car with a heavy paper to prevent the alumina ore from running through the often broken inside lining of the car and getting trapped in the walls, or worse, escaping from the car completely. Once the car was lined, the loaders applied a fiberboard door across the bottom three quarters of each car door. The temporary door was secured in place with steel banding. This door was very much like the wooden grain doors used in grain service, but was made of steel and fiberboard so it was a single trip door, unlike grain doors which could be returned and reused. This process was known as 'coopering.' Once the cars were coopered, they were loaded with about 60 tons of dry powdered alumina ore and shipped to Mead.

Alumina ore came to Mead in multiple car blocks that were set out by the through trains at Mead rather than bringing it into Hillyard. Mead included two set out tracks parallel with the main line. Even today both tracks are white with alumina ore.

Kaiser also received three kinds of petroleum coke and four kinds of pitch, all used to make the carbon electrodes that are consumed in the aluminum smelting process. Most coke, by tonnage, is coal that has been cooked in the absence of air to drive off the moisture and volatile hydrocarbons. Coke is also derived from petroleum. Petroleum coke is the solid material left over after all of the liquid fractions of petroleum oil have been cooked off in the refining process. Kaiser used only petroleum coke, but referred to it simply as coke.

Casper coke came from Casper, Wyoming. Casper coke and calcinated coke (petroleum coke that has been heated to cause thermal decomposition other than melting) came in CNW open top hopper cars.

Green coke from Billings, Montana, was a very fine, very black powder that arrived in 70-ton capacity SHPX marked covered hopper cars. Kaiser ran this green coke through a giant kiln at the former Pacific Alloys plant, which they called the south plant. Kaiser heated the kiln with natural gas for three days before they could run a batch of green coke to make fluid coke. Once the fluid coke, which was really solid material of small particle size, was coming out of the kiln, Kaiser could shut off the natural gas, and the kiln would continue to run hot enough without the gas. Evidently the green coke released sufficient light hydrocarbons to keep the kiln fired. Kaiser held their fluid coke in storage tanks which allowed it to cool off somewhat.

Fluid coke was loaded from the storage tanks into any of five or six old, 50-ton, GN covered hopper cars used for intraplant shuttle service. In the winter, loaded fluid coke cars were nice hand warmers. The loads went to Coke Track 1 for unloading.

All types of coke were unloaded on track Coke 1, and the pitch on track Coke 2. These tracks ran through a shed that was open on each end and covered about 100 feet of each track. Both tracks ran over pits that were one car length long.

A car shaker on Coke 2 attached to the top of the hopper cars to shake from the car any pitch that froze to the sides and end sheets of the car. Open top pitch cars needed to be thawed in the winter. The plant employee who unloaded the coke and pitch placed open low flame propane burners under the hopper doors to thaw the ice that had formed in them. Sometimes they thawed too long and began to melt the pitch.

One type of pitch was in the form of lumps about three inches in diameter. Another looked like it had been melted and poured onto a cold surface. This pitch looked like slate. The third kind was 'pencil' pitch. It was about the diameter of your finger. It looked like it had cooled in a mold. Pencil pitch shattered if handled. These three varieties of solid pitch arrived in CNW open top hopper cars. The fourth kind of pitch came in tank cars that we spotted to the west end of the house track, inside the building at spot 32-A. That spot featured access to plant steam, so the tank car could be hooked up to the steam to liquefy the pitch. These were insulated and jacketed cars, either with steam pipes inside the tank, or with half oval steam coils on the outside of the tank.

Kaiser also received carloads of firebrick, lime, and chlorine. The firebrick came in boxcars which were spotted to track 3, which diverged from track Coke 2. The single car brick spot was adjacent to a building. Some days we spotted a brick car two or three times per day. Lime in 70-ton covered hoppers for the mill sewage plant spotted inside a building served by a spur off track Ore 2. We spotted a car of lime only once in three or four months.

The chlorine tank car unloading site featured two spots on a single track with a switch on both ends and a fixed bumper permanently placed between the car spots. There was a derail at each end of the track, normally lined and locked against us coming into the track. When the mill wanted a switch, about once a month, they would unhook the empty car and unlock the appropriate derail to give us access to the car that they wanted us to pull. This track design was used so that the plant could always have one car hooked up and feeding the mill while the other side was switched. The elaborate protection was to minimize the chance of a chlorine leak due to us pulling or bumping a car that was hooked up and causing a release of the highly toxic chlorine gas.

Unloading the alumina ore cars was a slow process that involved several moves for us. Kaiser could unload 15 or 16 cars per shift, but the unloading track would hold only 12 cars at a time. This meant that both Mead Turn jobs spotted alumina ore loads at least twice per shift.

Kaiser used a 'tilt table unloader' to unload their boxcars. The unloader was located on Ore 2, a through track with a winch that could pull a car to spot on the tilt table. Once a car was spotted, coupler grabbing devices attached to both ends to hold the car in position. One car door was opened and a rectangular shaped funnel was placed against the car at the door. Hydraulic saw blades in the funnel punched through the paper and cut the metal bands. The tilt table rolled the car about 20 degrees toward the funnel. Then it raised one end of the car about 70 degrees, and then raised the other end, to flow the alumina ore out of the car, into the funnel, and into the plant. After this unloading cycle, the tilt table was returned to straight and level and the coupler grabbers were released. The car was winched off the tilt table with the ripped up temporary car door still in place.

The capacity of the track beyond the tilt house was about 30 cars. We pulled the empty cars out at the end of our day. The empty cars went to Ore 1 where Kaiser employees removed all of the doorway protection and the paper lining, which was rolled up and left in the doorway of the car. This seemed to be the job that Kaiser would rob people from to keep other things in the plant running. At times, Kaiser held as many as 100 empty cars, stuffed everywhere, waiting for them to strip the coopering material. Kaiser's delay in stripping the coopering material created poor car utilization for the railroad, and big demurrage bills for Kaiser. Demurrage is a charge assessed against shippers and consignees for detention of rail cars in excess of the free time allowed by tariff.

After the coopering material was stripped, we respotted the cars for a second run over the tilt table to get the last of the alumina ore out of them. The debris was thrown into a dumpster beside the track immediately before the car went through the tilt table the second time.

One day, Kaiser became concerned about leakage from their alumina ore cars. Kaiser demanded that the railroad weigh every car using the scale at the South Plant, the former Pacific Alloys plant built during World War II. The best our power could do was to shove 12 cars up the hill to the scale. It took an hour to shove a cut up there and weigh the cars one by one. Kaiser employed a qualified weigh master, so we did not incur much delay waiting for a weigh master. Only the Second Mead Turn weighed loads of alumina ore. Some nights the job spent all night weighing cars when not doing something else more important. Often there were so many loads on hand that we were forced to return cars to the set out tracks along the main track at Mead after weighing them. Weighing boxcars of alumina ore was a pain in the posterior. I hope the company charged them for the extra switching. The weighing continued until Kaiser decided that leakage was not a serious problem.

Kaiser shipped its product, aluminum ingots, to customers beyond the Spokane area by rail. Kaiser used boxcars for the relatively small aluminum ingots called 'pigs.' Ingots were loaded on the "House Track' which was immediately adjacent to and parallel with the north wall of the Pot Line building. Kaiser also loaded 'sow cars'; flatcars with special restraining devices used to move large 'sow' ingots via the Union Pacific to Kaiser at Trentwood. After the BN merger, Kaiser shipped molten metal to Trentwood in specially designed 'pot trucks' to save the cost of reheating the aluminum. Each pot truck was a tractor with a trailer that carried two pots.

Another customer, Inland Foundry, received coke in hopper cars on a private spur off the lead to the North Plant. Inland used an under-track augur to transloaded their coke into trucks for the short haul to their nearby foundry.

At the end of our day, the Mead Turn brought everything out of Mead to Hillyard. Empty alumina ore cars went to the washout tracks where they were washed out with water. Once washed out, the cars were ready for loading grain, lumber, or anything else that was shipped in 40-foot boxcars.

Kaiser at Mead used a tilt table like this to unload bulk alumina from box cars. It could lift each end of the car and roll the car from side to side, causing of the fine-grained alumina to flow from the car. PUBLICITY PHOTO FOR GREAT NORTHERN TRAFFIC DEPARTMENT, COLLECTION OF GNRHS ARCHIVE.

Kaiser and the Burlington Northern converted Kaiser's alumina ore traffic from boxcars to covered hopper cars in the 1970s. Kaiser unloaded the new 100-ton covered hoppers at an existing covered pit on Ore 1. The pit was long enough to hold two cars, both of which could be unloaded at one time. This did wonders for our productivity, in fact, the change to covered hopper cars allowed the company to get by with a single Mead Turn. The use of covered hoppers eliminated the need to wait for Kaiser to strip the cooperage material from the empty boxcars, which improved car utilization and reduced demurrage bills. The loaded covered hoppers came from Everett, as did loaded covered hopper cars for Reynolds Aluminum at Conkelley, Montana.

Also in the early 1970s, green coke from Billings, Montana, moved in new 100-ton capacity SHPX covered hopper cars. After the new alumina ore cars were introduced, Kaiser developed the habit of 'borrowing' the railroad's empty alumina cars for a day to make the intra-plant fluid coke move. Kaiser was careful to borrow any particular car for only one trip and quickly unloaded and released such cars to avoid demurrage charges. Kaiser released the old 50-ton GN covered hopper cars that it had previously been using.

Burlington Northern located a new customer at Mead. Fox Milling was served by a new spur parallel to the lead to the South Plant. Fox received bulk grains in covered hopper cars. They shipped feed to local markets by truck and to distant markets by covered hopper cars.

In the 1970s, I was working as conductor on the Mead Turn with Rick Miller and Forest Markham, both former NP trainmen, as my brakemen. Rick was the swing man. Forest was the head brakeman, and that was about all Forest could handle. Every day, the crew made the same basic moves to switch Kaiser Aluminum. Forest never seemed to catch on to what went where. I spent a lot of effort to keep track of Forest; he would get lost at the drop of a hat. I think he just did not try or care.

Forest's philosophy seemed to be, "If I do not know, then I cannot be held responsible." That worked until one day on the Whitefish chain gang pool. He was the head brakeman when the engineer he was working with ran an absolute stop signal. Forest told the officials his philosophy at the investigation when they asked about what had happened. The company gave Forest 30 days off without pay to reconsider that philosophy.

Rick was going on two weeks' vacation starting Monday, and he and I were talking about where he and his family would be going. All of a sudden, Forest pipes up with, "Well, you are sure going to get your tail worked off for the next two weeks with Rick not being here, with all the extra board brakemen having to work the list, HA HA." This smart aleck comment, combined with my knowledge and experience with Forest's lack of ability, caused me to tell Forest that he would be the swing man for the next two weeks. Forest snapped back that he was the head brakeman. I informed Forest that the conductor can place his brakeman as he sees fit, and that he would be the swing man for the next two weeks.

Monday morning came, and Forest was the swing man. It was a long day for Forest. My extra board brakeman and I basically did the work while Forest walked himself to death trying to read the list and figure out what to do. He was in a nervous sweat all day long. By the end of the day, Forest was extra dirty, dead tired, and a nervous wreck. I told Forest that in the future, every time Rick was off for vacation, off sick, or off for any other reason, he would be the swing man. I also told him that if Rick bid off the job, he would be the permanent swing man.

Well, the next morning, guess what? No Forest! I got two extra board brakemen. Both men had worked the Mead Turn several times, so it was a good day. The third morning, when I got called, I asked the crew clerk who my brakemen were. He told me that Pat McCarthy had marked up on Rick's temporary vacancy, and I had one of the extra board brakemen from the day before. I asked what happened to Forest. He said that Forest took two weeks' vacation. "Payback is hell," I thought. About a month after Rick came back from vacation, Forest bid in another job.

➻ The Priest River Turn

The Priest River Turn was established in the late 1960s to relieve the Newport Local and the Bull Local which had become overburdened due to increased business and reduced hours of service. The Priest River Turn worked out of Hillyard called for 10:00 PM Monday through Friday. This job headed east on the main line to Newport, Washington, 43 miles east of Hillyard. The turn cleared up for No. 31, No. 32, and No. 28 every trip.

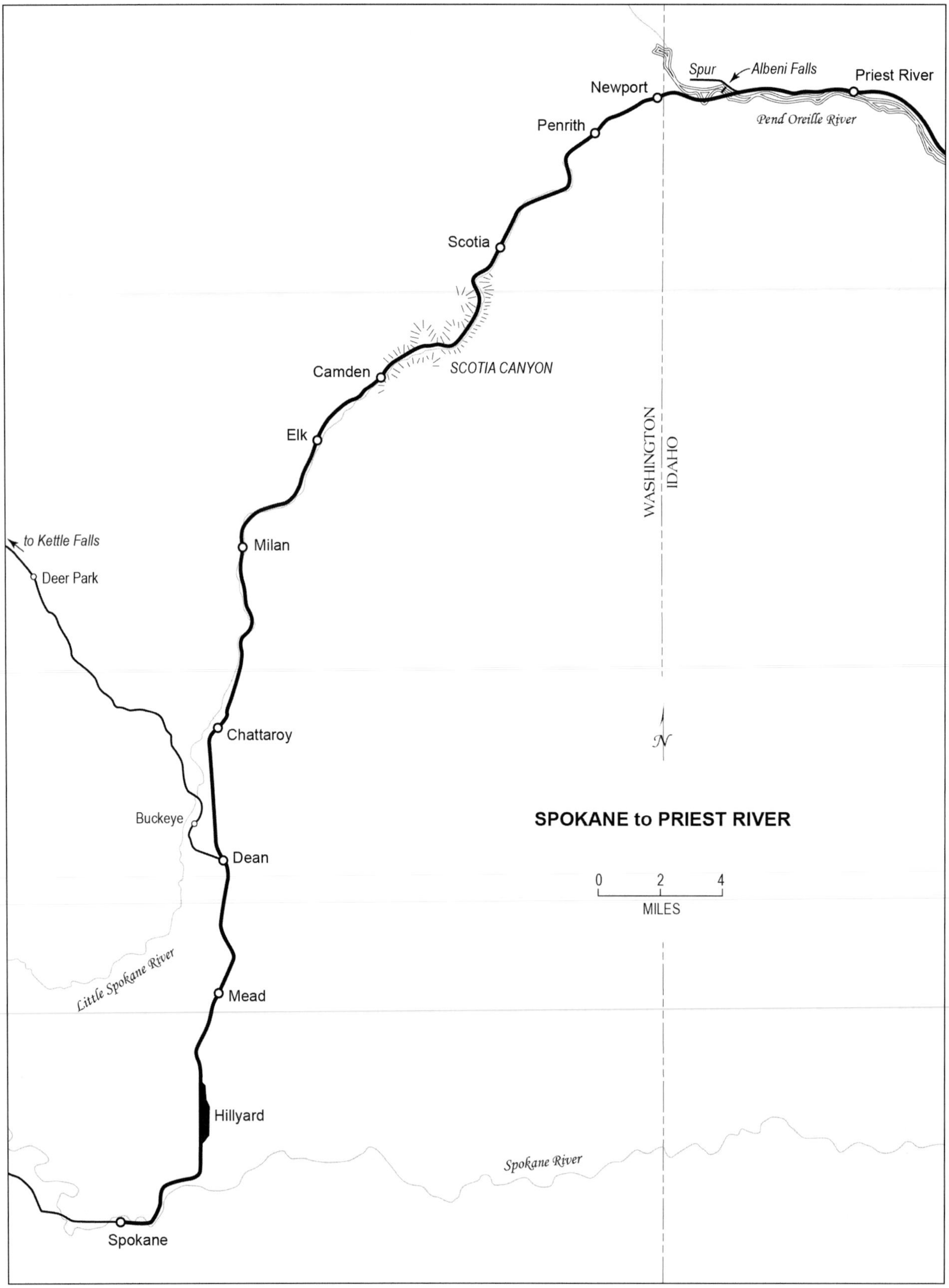
Spur
Albeni Falls
Priest River
Newport
Penrith
Pend Oreille River
Scotia
Camden
SCOTIA CANYON
Elk
WASHINGTON
IDAHO
Milan
to Kettle Falls
Deer Park
Chattaroy
N
SPOKANE to PRIEST RIVER
Buckeye
Dean
0 2 4
MILES
Little Spokane River
Mead
Hillyard
Spokane River
Spokane

Train No. 31, the westward Empire Builder, was due to pass Hillyard at 11:01 PM, while No. 32, the eastward Empire Builder, was due by at 11:25 PM. If they were on time, the local stayed in the yard until they were both by. Train No. 28, the eastward Western Star, was due to leave Hillyard at 6:45 AM and Newport at 7:35 AM.

Our first stop was at Camden. The customer at Camden loaded pulpwood in 40-foot drop bottom gondolas spotted on the industry track.

At Newport, we received the switch list for Newport and the Diamond National lumber mill at Albeni Falls Spur, 2.7 miles east of Newport. The main track crossed the Pend Oreille River shortly upstream, or east of, the Albeni Falls dam, which was located in a narrow and steep walled canyon. Our bridge was located at a particularly narrow point where the canyon was only about 200 feet from rim to rim. The Albeni Falls Spur left the main line immediately east of the bridge. The spur opened to the east and ran west about a mile and a half into the Diamond National lumber mill. We switched the lumber dock and the chip track pulling five to seven box car loads of lumber and four or five loads of wood chips per night. Diamond National also owned a separate stud mill at an intermediate point on the spur. The stud mill generated two or three boxcar loads of 2 × 4 studs every night. The job was bulletined to Priest River so we could switch Diamond National, but we never went to Priest River.

After switching Diamond National, we returned to Newport to receive a second set of switch lists. One or two of the loads from the mill usually went to the Milwaukee (Chicago, Milwaukee, St. Paul and Pacific Railroad) transfer, which was also our source for empty MILW cars for the mill. Newport included a pulp wood spur, which loaded two or three 40-foot drop bottom gondolas per day. The pole yard at Newport loaded two or three loads of treated poles, used to build telephone and electric lines, each week. We put the eastward cars together for the Bull Local to pick up later and lined up the west cars to go with us.

We went to eat after doing all the switching at Newport and started back toward Hillyard after beans. About this time of day, the eastward trains began to run. Train No. 28, the eastward Western Star, was due to leave Newport at 7:35 AM. We usually cleared up for No.

An Extra West heading in to West Yard track 5. West 6 is to the right and the next track to the right is the South Lead of the Main Yard. PHOTO BY DALE JONES.

28 at Newport. The first east freight train was usually the Bull Local. We usually waited for the Bull Local to go by at the Albeni Falls main track switch or at Newport. The next train was usually No. 490, a second class train. The Priest River Turn usually met No. 490 at Scotia, 7.8 miles west of Newport, or at Camden, 6.6 miles west of Scotia. Sometimes the local could make it all the way to Milan if the dispatcher gave us enough time to get to Milan on a run late order against No. 490's scheduled time.

Our first work on our trip back was to pick up the loads of pulpwood at Camden. The next work was at Davies Spur, west of Dean on double track, where the shipper loaded one or two loads of silica rock per night in 40-foot drop bottom gondolas. The spur opened to the west, so we dropped the empty gondolas into the spur, putting the engine down the main track. The term 'drop' refers to a move in which one or more cars are accelerated, usually by the engine, and cut off in motion. The engine goes into one track and the cars go into another. The crew then pulled the track, setting the loads to the main and spotting the empties to the loading conveyer. Then we grabbed the loads of rock, reached back and coupled into the train, and shoved the rock to Mead, which was only about a mile away. We cut the engine off train about 10

Until Washington's full-crew law was repealed, all freight trains of more than twenty-five cars stopped at Newport to drop off or pick up the legally required extra brakeman. COLLECTION OF JOHN E. LANGLOT.

car lengths short of the west switch at Mead, kicked the loads of rock up the main track, put the engine into the storage track, and let the loads of rock roll back downhill to the train with a brakeman on the hand brake, completing a gravity dutch drop. After a stub air test, we were off to Hillyard where we put our train into a track designated by the yardmaster, took the engine to the house, and tied up, usually at about 12 noon.

The Newport Local

The Newport Local, based at Newport, Washington, served Newport to Bonners Ferry, Idaho. The following description is based on the early 1960s duties and work of the Newport Local. When the Priest River Turn was later established, the Newport Local was moved to Sandpoint, renamed the Sandpoint Local, and its territory shortened to Priest River to Bonners Ferry.

Newport was only about an hour from Spokane, but for those who lived in the Spokane Valley, the drive was much shorter. I remember some of the men saying that they could drive to Newport quicker than they could drive to Hillyard, especially during heavy traffic hours.

The Newport Local went on duty at Newport at 6:00 AM. Our first move was to get any cars for Diamond National from the Milwaukee interchange track and line up our cars for Diamond National. Diamond National Lumber Company was located on the Albeni Falls Spur. We usually waited at Newport for the Bull Local to set out cars for us. The Bull Local usually arrived shortly after 7:00 AM and made its set out after No. 28 left at 7:35 AM.

We usually followed No. 28 and the Bull Local to the Albeni Falls Spur. The Albeni Falls Spur ran over a hill to the Diamond National mill. We switched Diamond National and took the loads with us to Priest River.

The Bull Local set out our Priest River cars at Priest River. We switched the lumber mills at Priest River and took all of our cars to Sandpoint, but left any MILW cars at Priest River to keep them out of the way. Like most mills in the Pacific Northwest, the mills produced lumber, which they shipped in boxcars or on flatcars, and wood chips. The vast majority of the lumber went east, but all of the wood chips went west.

The Sandpoint depot was located about 45 car lengths east of the west siding switch. The siding lay on the north side of the main track. The depot, wye, a three track yard, and the associated connecting tracks were located

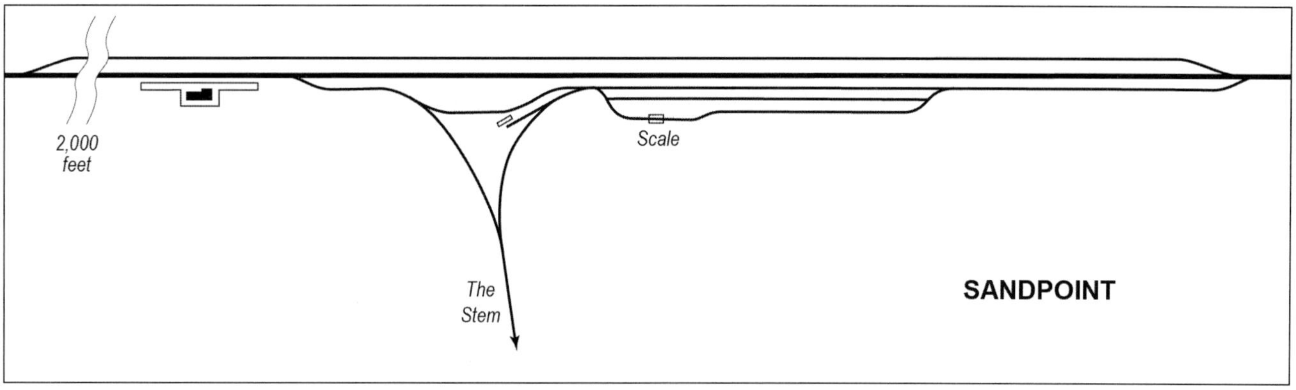

on the south side of the main track. The tail of the wye became 'The Stem' and extended geographic east-southeast for about a mile and a half to a connection with the Northern Pacific. The stem passed two pole yards on the east side of the stem and a lumber yard on the west side that were served by spur tracks off the stem. The stem crossed the Spokane International Railroad, which was then and is now part of the Union Pacific, at grade. There was an interchange track between the GN and the SI near the crossing. The GN also interchanged with the NP at Sandpoint. The NP left cars for us immediately on their side of the SI crossing, and we delivered their cars to the same location. Both of these were very low volume interchanges.

At Sandpoint, we pulled our train past the depot on the main, headed into track 1, continued past the wye, pulled into yard track 1 or 2, whichever was open. We set all of our pickups towards the scale, which was on track 3, and sloughed any Sandpoint cars to join the others already on track 1 or 2. Next, we ran west on the main track to the west end and switched out the flatcars that we needed to spot to customers on the stem, pulled the cars past the west leg of the wye switch, shoved east on the west leg of the wye, and then onto the stem. We pulled and spotted each pole yard and the lumber yard as ordered. The pole yards shipped six or seven flatcars of power poles a week. Next, when necessary, we reached down the stem and interchanged with the Spokane International and the Northern Pacific at the far end of the stem track.

We came back on the west leg of the wye and shoved the interchange cars and loads of poles and lumber into the Scale Track. We weighed all lumber and pole loads so that the agent could make his waybills with the weight data in hand. We spotted each car on the scale, and cut away from the car being weighed to eliminate any weight transfer through the couplers. The clerk weighing the cars rang the bell when he finished weighing each car. We then shoved the car off the scale, stopping the next car on the scale to be weighed. After the weighing was done, we set any cars for the west aside for pick up on our return trip. Switching done, we connected all the air hoses, left the weighed loads, which were all destined eastward, on track three, ran east on the main track, got back on our train, and headed east.

At Colburn, about eight miles east of Sandpoint, we switched a big saw mill that shipped three or four boxcars of lumber and two or three loads of wood chips per day. At Naples, we switched another saw mill. Six and a half miles east of Naples was Moravia Spur, where we picked up three or four loads of logs on log flatcars each day and spotted empty log flats in their place. The logs went to Hillyard, and then to a mill west of the Cascade mountains.

Bonners Ferry, five miles east of Moravia, was our turn back point. There was a very large saw mill to switch at Bonners that was always good for three to five loads of lumber and three or four loads of wood chips each day. There was an interchange track with the Spokane International at Bonners. The UP supplied empty lumber boxcars for us to spot at the lumber mill and return to them loaded. The E. Smith grain elevator and

Selkirk Seed, both served by the house track, were each good for two or three boxcar loads of grain each week. Before leaving Bonners Ferry we made two blocks of cars, one east and one west. The west cars went against our caboose. The east cars went to the head end of our train.

During late morning to early afternoon, the Newport Local returned to the yard at Sandpoint and weighed the additional eastbound loads. We took the cars to be weighed to the west end of track 3 and began to weigh the new loaded cars. We continued this process until the few loads were weighed. Now we coupled all the cars back up, connected all the air hoses, and left the weighed east loads on track 3 for the Bull Local to pick up the next morning. If we weighed a west load, we put it to our train.

We switched chip cars at Priest River on our return trip because the chip spur opened to the west and brought chip loads and any MILW cars to Newport. We set our handful of westbound cars to the storage track for pick up by the westbound Bull Local, got our caboose, spotted it, and tied it down. Finally, we switched Diamond National a second time. Those cars, and an occasional east load from the Milwaukee, went to the east pickup for the Bull Local in the morning. East pickup made, we delivered any MILW cars to their interchange track, tied the engine down, and were done for the day.

Endnotes

1 Train Briefs used as basis for discussion of blocking and switching are: No. 97 Revised 12/1/70, No. 83 Revised 10/13/70, No. 82 Revised 1/20/71, and No. 88 Revised 1/28/71.

2 Staffan Ehnbom, email December 14, 2011.

3 *The Official Guide of the Railways,* New York: National Railway Publication Company. December 1968.

4 Great Northern Railway, *Hillyard and the Great Northern Railway 1892–1954,* Great Northern Railway, November 1954.

5 Great Northern Railway, *Hillyard and the Great Northern Railway, 1892–1954.*

6 Kenneth R. Middleton and Norman F. Priebe, *Steam Locomotives of the Great Northern Railway* (Geneva IL: Great Northern Railway Historical Society, 2010), 227–28.

7 Great Northern Railway, *Hillyard and the Great Northern Railway 1892–1954.*

8 Great Northern Railway, *Hillyard and the Great Northern Railway 1892–1954.*

4. Spokane Jobs

Spokane Yard

Spokane Yard was located immediately east of Havermale Island on the north side of the double track main and south of the Spokane River. Spokane Yard was about 2,000 feet long, centered on MP 1477, and between bridges 269 and 270.

The yardmaster managed switch engines that worked in three physical areas: Spokane Yard, the passenger depot on Havermale Island, and the SC&P Yard. The yard worked two jobs each shift, seven days per week: the Top End Job, and the Coach Job. These jobs switched freight cars at Spokane Yard, switched the Freight House, the Team Tracks, and downtown customers. They also switched passenger trains and passenger cars at the depot.

Spokane Yard contained seven double ended tracks, plus one stub track opening to the east. The stub track was closest to the river and was used for coal unloading. Coal was unloaded from hopper cars and trucked to consumers. In the past, another track had run down to the river. Logs were dumped into the river and floated down stream to the sawmill that was right downtown in the early days. The log dump track was removed years before I started on the railroad, but you could still see where the ties had once been.

The Spokane Freight House was located across the main tracks from Spokane Yard with the building itself at the west end of the complex. The freight house was the loading, unloading, and sorting center for less than carload traffic in the Spokane area on the Great Northern. This was a very busy facility boasting five tracks, each 14 cars long. When I started in 1960, the LCL freight business was still strong enough that the freight house was spotted full at least once a day. Cars were spotted with the doors of the boxcars lined up with each other so that the freight depot crew could work through the cars near the building to cars on the tracks away from the building.

The freight house was spotted between 12:01 AM and 6:30 AM Monday through Friday. Blue flags to protect the freight house workers went up at 6:30 AM. At 11:00 AM, the blue flags were dropped from one or two of the tracks farthest from the building for about half an hour to allow some loads to be pulled and additional cars to be spotted. The flags were dropped again at about 4:30 PM so that the loaded cars could be pulled. A midnight crew spotted the new loads, empty cars for loading, and respotted any part loads. The other tracks near the freight house were blue flagged during daylight hours but left available for switching between about 4:30 PM and 6:30 AM.

A piggyback track with a ramp on the end was located behind the freight house. 'Piggyback' is a now obsolete slang term for intermodal service. Trailers were backed the full length of the cut of flatcars to load them. This practice was known as 'circus loading,' since the technique was that traditionally used by circuses to load and unload their wagons at each town on their tour.

A dock track and a team track were located behind the freight house. The team track was a track open to the public for unloading and loading boxcars. The dock track was also open to the public to load and unload both flatcars transporting machinery and boxcars at a loading/unloading dock.

A bilevel (two tier) auto unloading device sat at the end of a stub track. This device was not set up for the much more common trilevel auto racks. Trilevel auto racks were taken out to Clark Equipment on the SC&P

TOP Spokane Yard was located just west of the Spokane passenger depot, whose tower can be seen in the distance. Three GP units without dynamic brakes, today's Moscow local power, sit in the pocket track adjacent to the double-track main line in 1969. The building in the background is the Freight House. PHOTO BY DALE JONES.

BOTTOM Spokane Freight House had five tracks, each of which could hold fourteen cars. Freight Houses handled Less than Carload merchandise traffic nationwide. Cars billed to Spokane contained products for Spokane and for stations tributary to Spokane. PHOTO BY NORM HOCHHALTER.

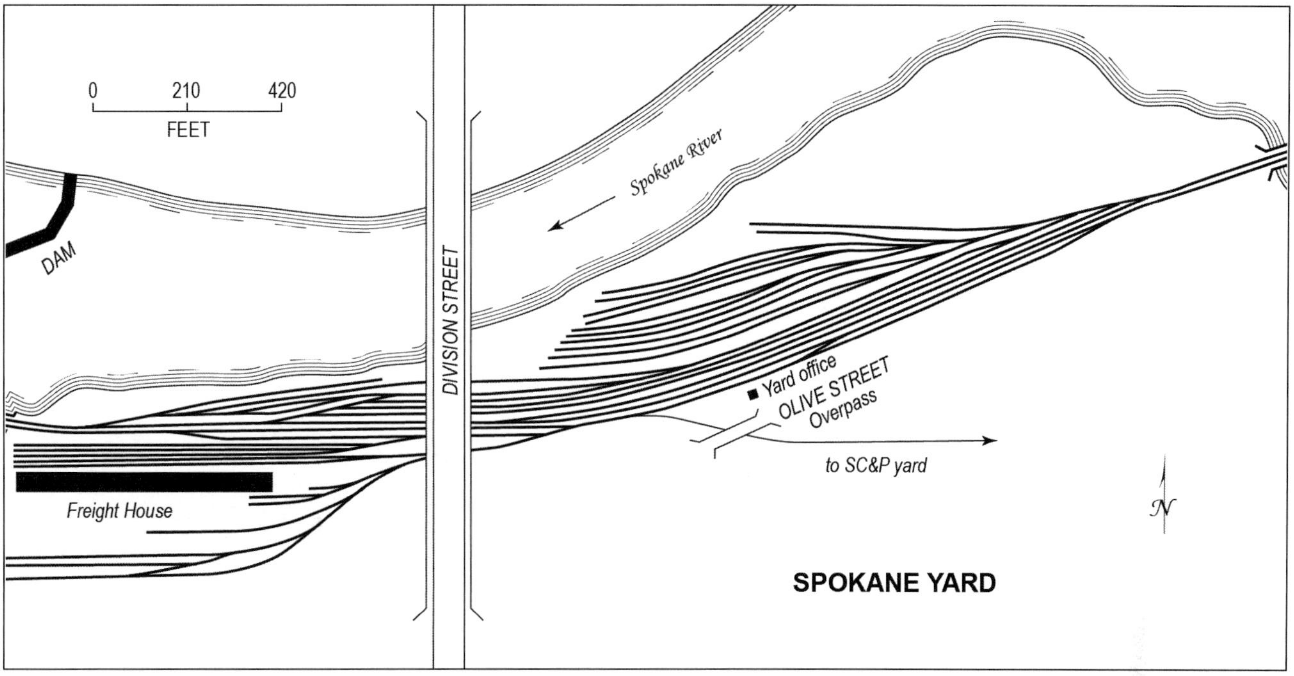

line, where a three-tier auto unloader was located. When the switch engine took these trilevel auto racks out to Clark Equipment, they passed under the Union Pacific's overpass near the SC&P wye. When trilevel auto racks were loaded with Ford four-wheel drive pickups, they did not clear the UP overpass, shearing off the tops of the cabs on the pickups. The company destroyed ten pickups on two different cars before somebody figured out what was happening. After that, trilevel auto racks were given to the Northern Pacific at the SC&P Yard via the NP transfer track. The NP took them to the south 40 tracks at Yardley, where the Convoy Company operated a trilevel auto rack unloading device. After the BN merger, the auto racks were given to the Milwaukee for unloading, because Convoy had moved to the Milwaukee Yard where they enjoyed sufficient room to unload and store new autos until they could be delivered to the car dealers.

Switching The Passenger Trains

Spokane Yard crews and engines switched the passenger trains at the depot and moved mail cars between the trains and the Spokane Mail Terminal. The Mail Terminal was about a quarter of a mile east of the east end of Spokane Yard and one block west of Hamilton Street. Both Spokane Yard switch engines switched the passenger trains.

The passenger depot was located on Havermale Island, literally in the middle of the Spokane River, between bridges 270 and 273, a distance of .26 miles. The depot was also located near the middle of a segment of double track that extended from the east end of the high bridge over the Spokane River, bridge No. 274, to the west end of Hillyard. The brick depot building was south of the tracks. Between the depot and the main tracks, there was a track called the 'Depot Track.' Before the Spokane Mail Terminal was built, the Depot Track

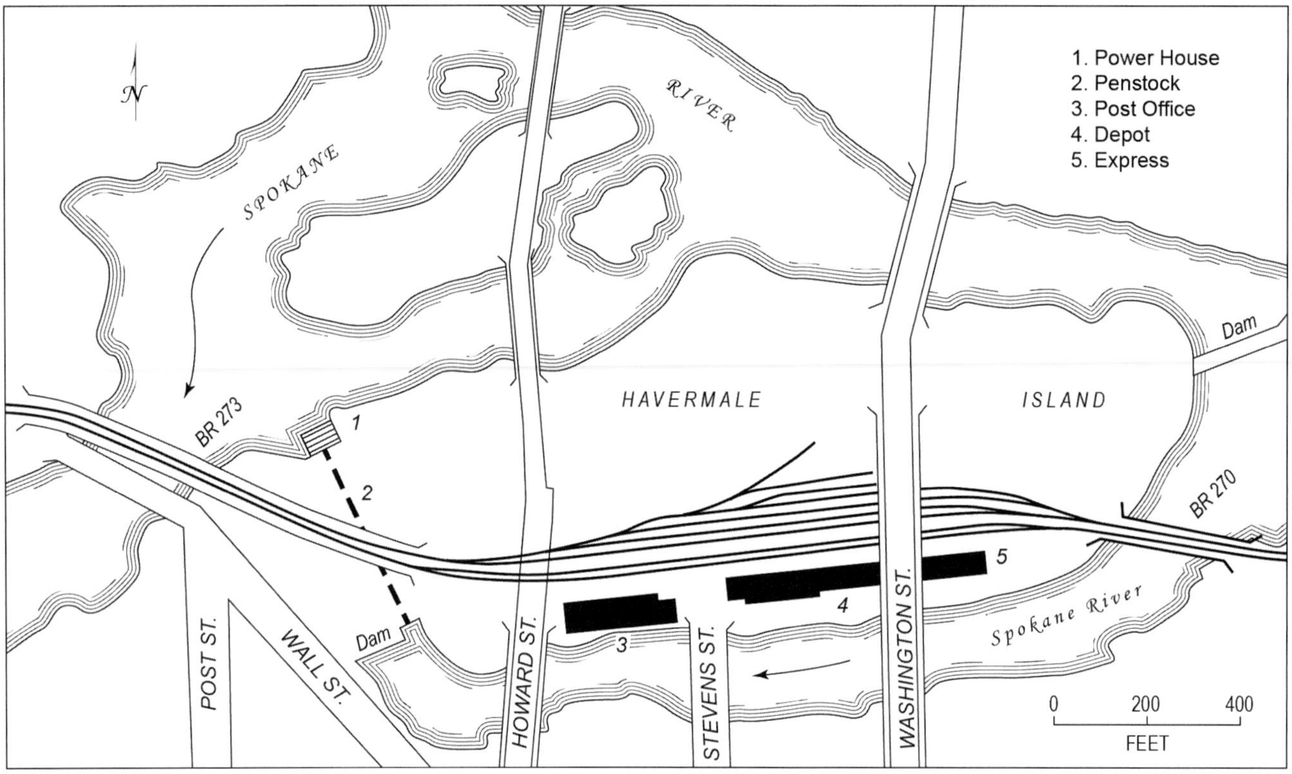

was extensively used to hold baggage and mail cars that mail was transferred to and from.

Moving away from the depot, the next pair of tracks was the eastward and westward main tracks. Tracks Depot 1 through Depot 5, numbers increasing as the tracks became further away from the depot, were situated north of the main tracks. A stub track north of Depot 5 often held a tank car of fuel oil for the depot furnace, and always held an ice service reefer containing ice for passenger trains. Beyond the main tracks, a wood surface crossing about 60 feet wide was centered on the clock tower, which was in turn centered on the south wall of the depot. At each end of the crossing, depot tracks 1 through 4 were equipped with fittings that allowed steam, yard air, and electricity to be connected to cars. In the late 1960s, the usual track for spotting Great Northern business cars, or 'A cars,' reflecting the first character of their car number, was Depot 2.

Train arrival and departure times that follow are taken from Kalispell Division Employee Time Table No.110, effective November 27, 1966. The times are typical for the 1960s but may have varied by a few minutes under different Employee Time Tables.

➻ A Day of Passenger Service at Havermale Island

➻ **5:40 AM** SP&S train No. 4 arrives from Portland. This train was timed to make connection with Northern Pacific No. 2, the eastward Mainstreeter, at Pasco in the dark of night and with Great Northern No. 28, the eastward Western Star, at Spokane. The SP&S sold through tickets to points east of Pasco and Spokane via their No. 4 and either NP No. 2 or GN No. 28. SP&S No. 4 usually arrived on the westward main or Depot 1. The power cut off and was taken to Hillyard. When SP&S train

Great Northern's Spokane passenger depot was located on Havermale Island, as shown clearly in this photograph taken from Union Depot. GNRHS ARCHIVE.

Bridge 273 was west of the west end of Havermale Island. This photo, looking east up the Spokane River, clearly shows why Spokane was originally named Spokane Falls, even despite being partially dammed to generate power: the river drops 140 feet in only one quarter of a mile here. Washington Water Power's brick power house is the large building to the right. This photo was taken from the Monroe Street Bridge and shows both the Post Street Bridge and Bridge 273 with a westward train on it. DAVID EMERSON COLLECTION, PNRARCHIVE.ORG.

No. 4 arrived, a switch engine was waiting at the depot to switch both it and No. 28.

➻ **SWITCHING** The cars that were continuing on train No. 28, one coach and one Pullman, were switched out of SP&S No. 4 and set aside to await the arrival of No. 28. The SP&S RPO, mail car, crew-baggage combination car, one coach, and the buffet-lounge car turned at Spokane. They were set over to an open depot track for the moment. Great Northern crews transferred mail from the mail car of SP&S No. 4 to No. 28 and the remainder went to the post office by truck.

➻ **6:00 AM** Train No. 28, the Western Star, arrives from Seattle.

➻ **SWITCHING** The one coach and one Pullman were cut into the Western Star from the rear. Since the coach went against the coaches in No. 28, and the sleeper went with the sleepers, two cuts were required in the passenger portion of No. 28. In addition, a car or two of mail from Spokane plus a car of mail from Portland were usually added to the rear end of No. 28, cut in ahead of the rider car which featured a space for the flagman to ride the rear of the train. Switching No. 28 thus involved a total of three cuts.

Tuesday through Saturday, No. 28 brought back to Spokane the RPO and the crew-baggage car that had gone west on No. 5 two nights before. They were always near the rear end of No. 28. The crew-baggage car often contained Seattle to Spokane mail. If there was a third car of Spokane mail on No. 28, it was next to the crew-baggage and RPO cars for No. 5 so that they all could be cut out of No. 28's train as one block.

➻ **6:30 AM** Train No. 28 departs.

➻ **ADDITIONAL SWITCHING** After No. 28 departed, the RPO, the baggage car, and any additional mail cars off No. 28 were spotted at the Mail Terminal. When mail volume was high, the mail car of SP&S No. 4 was taken to the Mail Terminal to be loaded to go west on SP&S No. 3 that evening. The RPO and baggage car were loaded at the Mail Terminal during the weekdays for the next train No. 5.

After No. 28 departed, the remaining SP&S cars were taken up to the SC&P Yard and around the SC&P wye which turned the cars around for their return trip to Portland that night. After the SP&S passenger cars were returned to the depot, they were set into Depot 1 where they were hooked to steam and electric power and were cleaned and serviced. They stayed on Depot 1 until that night.

➻ **2:15 PM** Train No. 27, the westward Western Star, arrives.

➻ **SWITCHING** A coach and a sleeper were switched out of the Western Star and set over to Depot 1 with the clean SP&S cars to make up SP&S train No. 3. The basic moves were the same for switching No. 27 as they were for No. 28, except that cars were cut out of No. 27. A car or two of mail was usually cut out from the rear of No. 27 ahead of the rider car.

➻ **3:00 PM** No. 27 departs.

➻ **ADDITIONAL SWITCHING** Before returning to Spokane Yard, the switch engine lined up the cars for SP&S train No. 3 on Depot 1. Mail cars off No. 27 for the Mail Terminal were spotted to the Mail Terminal after No. 27 departed.

➻ **SWITCHING TRAIN NO. 5** Spokane Yard engines also made up Great Northern mail train No. 5 Monday through Friday nights. About 6:00 PM, the Spokane yardmaster gave a switch engine a list of the Mail Terminal. The switch engine went east to the Mail Terminal, got the loaded RPO car and baggage car that arrived on No. 28, and usually two or three express boxcars full of mail, and brought them to Havermale Island.

The RPO car and baggage cars would become the head two cars of No. 5. The storage mail cars were lined up in station order and would become the rear of train No. 5. Hot loads in roller bearing equipped boxcars, delayed due to being bad ordered and which would be late in making their delivery date, came down from Hillyard on a transfer. Hot loads from the freight house and piggyback loads for Seattle from the piggyback ramp were added to the west end of the storage mail cars.

The first piggyback flats the Great Northern owned were 50-foot flatcars with friction bearing journals converted to piggyback service. Because No. 5 operated at passenger train speeds, only roller bearing equipped cars were allowed on the train. When new 85-foot piggyback flats with roller bearing trucks came out in 1960, they were allowed on train No. 5, which added to the revenue for No. 5's train.

The RPO and baggage car were spotted on Depot 2 or Depot 3, and in cold weather the carmen hooked up the steam lines to get the cars warm. The rest of the train, which did not need heat, was usually set to Depot 5, which did not have heat, while the cars were accumulated and lined up.

About 8:00 PM, the switcher pulled the RPO and baggage cars for No. 5 out of Depot 2 or Depot 3, picked up the rest of the train, and set everything over to the Depot Track, which set train No. 5. The switch crew spotted the west end of the RPO car to the steam and yard air lines. In cold weather, the carmen hooked up both lines, hung their blue flag on the cars, and connected the RPO to the depot steam line.

From the head end No. 5 carried: the RPO car, the crew-baggage, hot freight loads, storage mail and/or baggage cars of mail for Seattle, a storage mail car for Everett, and a storage mail car for Wenatchee. There were at least two express boxcars of mail on the rear on the train leaving Spokane. One set out at Wenatchee and one set out at Everett. At Wenatchee, a switch engine picked the storage mail car off the rear of the train and set it behind the depot for the Wenatchee baggage man and a post office contractor to unload. At Everett, the rear storage mail car was also picked off the rear of the train by a switch engine.

After the train was made up and sitting on the Depot Track, the Postal Service made a final delivery, by truck, to both the RPO and the baggage car of mail sorted after the cars left the Mail Terminal.

When the road crew arrived with the power from Hillyard, they were usually required to wait for the carmen to pull down the blue flag. As soon as they did so, the power backed onto the RPO car. The carmen re-hung the blue flag and hooked up the stream line, the brake pipe, and the signal air. As soon as the brake pipe was charged with air, the carmen made the air test and took down their blue flag. Our final wait was for the station baggage men to finish loading our baggage car with packages for Ephrata, Wenatchee, and Everett, and the RPO car with sacked first class mail.

➻ **9:30 PM** Train No. 5 departs.

➻ **9:40 PM** SP&S No. 3 departs for Portland, usually leaving from Depot 1. When mail volume was high, the mail terminal would load the mail car off SP&S No. 4 in the morning to go west on SP&S No. 3. This car was pulled in the early evening with cars for GN No. 5. SP&S No. 3 was timed to connect with NP train No. 1, the Mainstreeter, at Pasco. The engine crew brought the power from Hillyard while the train crew went to work at the passenger depot.

➻ **10:00 PM** SP&S train No. 2 arrives from Portland. The SP&S also sold through tickets to points east of Pasco and Spokane via their No. 2 and either NP No. 26 at Pasco or Great Northern No. 32, the eastward Empire Builder, at Spokane. When SP&S train No. 2 arrived at Spokane, a switch engine was waiting at the depot to switch both it and No. 32. The SP&S engine crew took their power to Hillyard.

➻ **SWITCHING** The cars that were continuing east on train No. 32, one 48-seat coach, a dome coach, and one Pullman, were switched out of SP&S No. 2 and set aside to await the arrival of No. 32. The crew-baggage

combination car, one coach, and the diner did not go onto No. 32, but were switched to line them up for their return trip to Portland.

➻ 10:40 PM The eastward Empire Builder, No. 32, arrives.

➻ SWITCHING No. 32 was switched from the rear end. The sleeper went to the rear of the train with the rest of the Pullman cars. The 48-seat coach and dome coach were cut in ahead of the Dining Car. If No. 32 carried an observation car that night, then the switcher picked the observation car off the rear of the train first to cut the sleeper in ahead of the observation car. In the later years of the Great Northern, the observation cars were replaced by the Big Dome cars which were placed right behind the diner and ahead of the Pullman sleepers.

➻ 11:10 PM No. 32 leaves.

➻ 11:15 PM Five minutes after No. 32 was scheduled to depart, the westward Empire Builder, No. 31, arrives.

➻ SWITCHING As soon as the carmen cut the steam joints between the cars and pulled down the blue flag, the switch engines started to switch the cars out of No. 31 for SP&S No. 1. The sleeper was cut out of the rear of the train where it had been with the rest of the Pullman cars. The 48-seat coach and dome coach were cut out from their positions ahead of the Dining Car. These cars were immediately folded into the cars recently received from SP&S No. 2 to make up SP&S No. 1.

➻ 11:40 PM SP&S No. 1 departs Spokane for Portland. The engine crew brought the power from Hillyard ahead of No. 31.

Switching #27 at Spokane was scheduled to take thirty minutes. As required by the labor agreements, the road crew could not do this work; a yard crew and engine were required. GNRHS ARCHIVE.

➻ 11:45 PM Train No. 31 departs Spokane for Seattle.

Because of the quick turn of their equipment at Spokane, SP&S No. 1 and No. 2 required only one set of three cars to protect both trains. Running repairs, deep cleaning, and servicing were done during the eight hours that the equipment was in Portland. SP&S No. 3 and No. 4 required two sets of cars. One set of equipment left Portland within minutes of the time the other set left from Spokane. The equipment at Spokane was turned, cleaned, and serviced while the same was done to the other set in Portland. Running repairs to both sets of equipment were done in Portland.

Train times were very busy times at the Spokane depot. Depot baggage men worked the RPO car and baggage car loading and unloading bags of mail and passenger baggage. Carmen cut steam lines and air hoses so the trains could be switched and reconnected them after the switching was done. Carmen also inspected the trains during the air brake test before the train departed. A crew from the Hillyard diesel shop was there to inspect the power and to handle any small problems with the power. They filled the boiler water tanks and cleaned the windshields as needed.

Both the carmen and the diesel shop crew put blue flags on the train to protect themselves while they were working. Some of the work was done while the switch crews were waiting to switch the train; the rest was finished after the switch crew finished and the train was back together.

All of the passenger equipment of these trains was washed at Spokane, weather permitting. Washing was done by a flatbed truck equipped with tanks, pumps, and hoses. One man drove the truck along at about 1 MPH, one sprayed the equipment with soapy water, two brushed the sides and ends of the dome cars and the car sides from roof to floor, and one rinsed everything off. This process took about 15 minutes per side.

This passenger train switching took quite a bit of time away from switching the industries in the Spokane and SC&P yards. All Spokane Yard switch jobs switched passenger trains. Based on an average of one and a half hours per GN passenger train, and four trains, the passenger trains absorbed at least six hours of switch engine time per day. Taking SP&S No. 4 around the wye also took about an hour if there was no congestion, or one and a half hours to two hours with congestion, including time to get back to Spokane Yard. There would be at least three trips to the Mail Terminal; deliver off No. 28, get cars for No. 5, and get cars for No. 27. At an hour each, that is another three hours per day. Switching to make train No. 5 took about one and a half hours. The total passenger train time spent by Spokane Yard switch engines was thus six hours switching the passenger trains, plus one and a half hours taking No. 4's equipment around the wye, plus three hours delivering and fetching mail, plus one and a half hours switching train No. 5 for a total of 12 engine hours per weekday. That is 25% of the total work time of two engines that worked all three shifts.

➻ The SC&P Yard

The former Spokane, Coeur d'Alene & Palouse Railway Company (SC&P) freight yard was located immediately east of downtown Spokane, parallel with and north of Trent Avenue. The SC&P Yard was south of and about 25 feet higher than the Great Northern's Spokane Yard, down beside the Spokane River. The two yards were connected by a transfer track about 1,600 feet long. About 1,200 feet of the transfer track ran on a continuous up grade through 'the hole,' actually a deep rock cut, to the SC&P Yard.

Leaving the SC&P Yard eastward, the SC&P main track crossed the meandering Spokane River twice on its own bridges. The line then split at the Inland Junction wye. The right leg of the wye went to Moscow. The Coeur d'Alene line took the left leg, crossed the UP main track at grade, and then headed east to Greenacres and Coeur d'Alene.

Cars for the SC&P locals and the SC&P switch engine came to Spokane Yard on transfers from Hillyard. Spokane Yard crews switched cars for the SC&P Yard into a track in Spokane Yard.

A SC&P Yard job worked Monday through Friday, both daylight and afternoon shifts. The day job made up the Coeur d'Alene and Moscow locals, and served freight customers along the former SC&P lines in Spokane. When the daylight SC&P switch engine went to work at 6:00 AM, they went down to Spokane Yard, picked up their cars for spotting at the SC&P Yard,

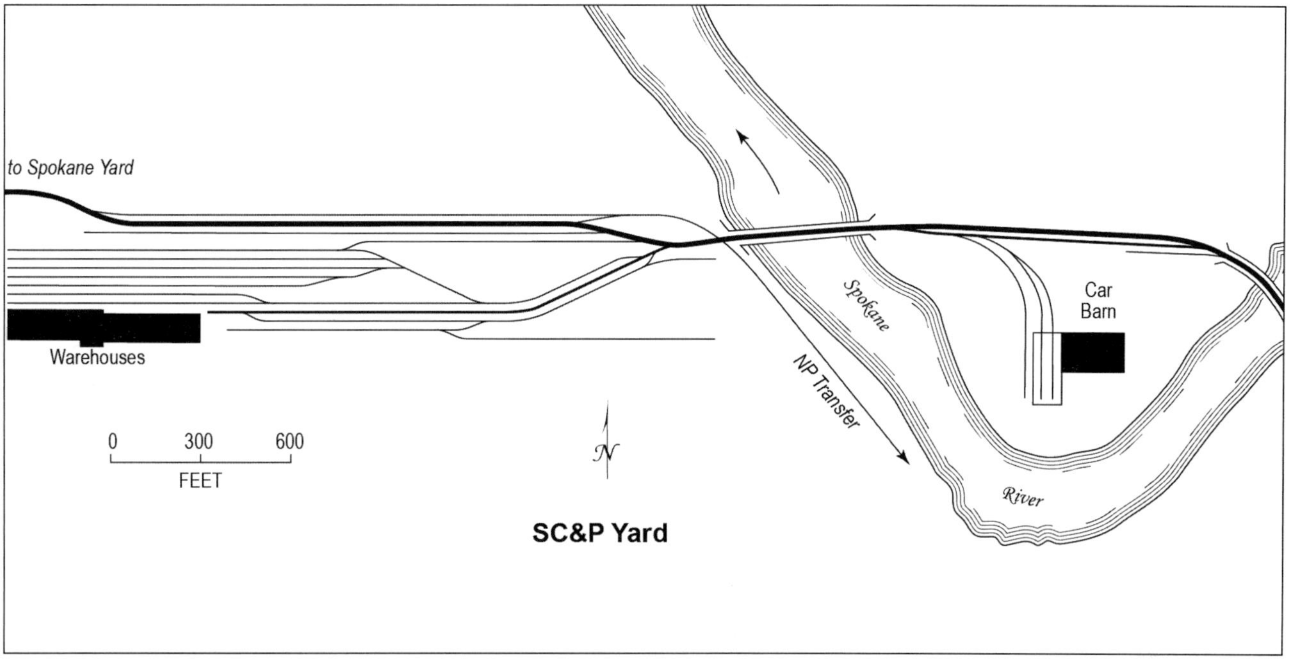

LEFT The hole track between the Great Northern main tracks at Spokane Yard and the SC&P Yard. The Spokane Yard yard office is atop the cut to the left of the Hole Track. PHOTO BY NORM HOCHHALTER.

and those for the two SC&P locals, and pulled them up through the hole to the SC&P Yard. This connection was so steep that coming down, every engineer laid a trail of sand on the rail to make sure he got sufficient traction to stop short of the main track. The afternoon SC&P Yard job switched the industries adjacent to the yard. On the rare occasion when the two SC&P switch engines did not complete all of the work, an extra engine was called to finish their work and then help with the switching in Spokane Yard.

The SC&P Yard served several industries. At the SC&P Yard itself, there were small businesses which leased portions of the old SC&P freight house to receive and ship their loads. Just east of the Trent Avenue crossing, Pacific Hide and Fur shipped scrap metal in gondola cars and cattle hides in boxcars. After the SC&P line crossed the Spokane River on the first bridge, the main track ran parallel with Trent Avenue. Here was the private track for the Taylor-Edwards warehouse for appliances and household goods. Joey August Beer and Wine distributors leased some space from Taylor-Edwards and received boxcars of beer and wine on this track. About a third of a mile from Taylor-Edwards, and after crossing the second bridge over the river, there was the Roundup Grocery Distributors warehouse with nine doors for unloading boxcars. Roundup always got a full spot of boxcars and was switched at least once a day, six days a week. Roundup was later bought out by URM.

Immediately after the Burlington Northern merger, the Moscow Local, which switched the former Vera line along Sprague Avenue, was pulled off, and the traffic in the Palouse region was then handled via the former Northern Pacific P&L branch. The SC&P switch engine then handled the former Vera line, a three hour round trip.

The afternoon SC&P switch engine came on duty at 2:30 PM. They switched out their cars for the Coeur d'Alene line between Spokane and Millwood, as this was all within yard limits, and they served the industries in this area. The afternoon SC&P switch engine started out by switching Centennial flour mill, which took a full hour on some days, and the Long Lake lumber mill about a half mile east of Centennial. Switching the Long Lake mill took at least an hour. Next stop was normally Clark Equipment out near Felts Air Field. Flatcars loaded with steel and aluminum for fabricating truck trailers were unloaded and the empties were returned to the SC&P Yard and redistributed to other shippers. After Clark Equipment, it was on to Millwood where they would set out to and pick up cars from the Inland Paper Company. Inland is owned by the Cowles Publishing Company, which owns the *Spokesman-Review* newspaper. Inland Paper Company worked a private switch engine, so this was just a pick up and set out move. They headed back to the SC&P Yard after Inland Paper. This trip to Millwood and back took four to five hours, depending on the amount of switching required.

The SC&P Yard jobs also interchanged a few cars with the Northern Pacific. Most of the NP interchange traffic was cars in reciprocal switch service, that is, cars that arrived or departed Spokane on one line but were spotted to a customer on the other. The transfer track was the first switch out of the SC&P Yard proper on the way to Coeur d'Alene or Moscow and ran up hill to the Northern Pacific. The transfer track entered the NP on their lead between the Erie Street Yard and the NP passenger depot. Transfer cars were shoved up the transfer track and left on the transfer track just to clear the NP lead track.

➻ The Moscow Local

Hillyard train crews worked both locals based at the former SC&P Yard. Each morning the local crews got their engine from the lead between the freight house tracks and the hole at Spokane Yard. Their first move was to take the power through the hole to the SC&P Yard to get their trains.

The Moscow Local worked six days per week. They went on duty at 7:00 AM Monday, Wednesday, and Friday at Spokane, and returned from Moscow on Tuesday, Thursday, and Saturday. Until 1952, the Moscow line occupied its own right of way as it headed generally southeast, ascending the side slope of Spokane's South Hill, passing through prosperous residential neighborhoods on a 2% grade for seven miles to the top of South Hill.

The 1057.5 foot long Rock Creek Bridge, which included trestle approaches on both ends of a Howe Deck Truss bridge, was located about three miles north of Mount Hope, and needed to be replaced by the early 1950s. For years, all freight trains were required to stop before proceeding over the Rock Creek bridge, and the speed of passenger trains was restricted. In its final few years, the Great Northern was so worried about the condition of the Rock Creek Bridge that an inspector was required to inspect the bridge before and after any train went over it.[1]

To avoid spending $520,000 to repair the Rock Creek Bridge and several large trestles between Spokane and Mount Hope, the Great Northern secured 32.2 miles of trackage rights on the Union Pacific between Spokane and Fairfield. These rights extended between the point in Spokane where the Coeur d'Alene line crossed the Union Pacific at UP Tower, and a point near Fairfield shown in our timetable as 'UPRR Junction.' UP Tower was a few hundred feet north of the UP crossing of the NP main track.

The rerouted Moscow Local left the SC&P Yard, took the left leg of the wye at the Inland Junction, and joined the UP branch main track at UP Tower. This branch was the Union Pacific's original route into Spokane. The Moscow Local crossed the two Northern Pacific main tracks at grade and ran to Dishman. At Dishman there was a switch to a segment of the former SC&P Vera Line about half a mile long along the side of Sprague Avenue. By the 1960s this short track, once an alternate route between Spokane and Coeur d'Alene, was an industry track that served five customers. The Moscow Local worked the industry track as required on the way out by heading into the UP siding and leaving our train on the siding. Switching these five customers added about two hours to the Moscow Local's day. We brought the pull cars with us, set them out at Waverly, and picked them up the next day on our return trip.

Beyond Dishman, the Moscow Local continued on the UP through Manito, a junction point between the Milwaukee and the UP and one end of MILW trackage rights through Spokane on the UP. From Manito, we went another 15 miles on the Union Pacific to UPRR Junction, about 250 feet past the UP depot at Fairfield. While our timetable called this switch UPRR Junction, the UP called it West Fairfield. Whatever name it was called, it was where the Moscow Local left the UP and returned to our own railroad.

In 1952, the Great Northern built a new connection extending 2.6 miles between UPRR Junction and West Fairfield (GN), a new junction on the former SC&P main between Mount Hope and Waverly. West Fairfield was almost due west of the UP depot at Fairfield.[2] The first mile of the Great Northern connection used the right of way of the former UP Waverly branch (1899–1913), while the rest of the line was on a new right of way. Service via the new GN route began on September 17, 1952.

The old line between Inland Junction in Spokane and Mount Hope was then abandoned, eliminating 22.87 miles of track. The rail was removed and the high bridges were torn down. The former SC&P main line station of Mount Hope was left stranded on an industrial spur that began at West Fairfield, seven miles from Mount Hope.

Spring Valley was the junction between the line to Moscow and a separate subdivision to Rosalia, Manning, and Colfax. The line to Colfax was shortened up to Manning after the tunnel between Manning and Colfax was declared structurally unsafe in 1967. The Great Northern gave the very modest business at Colfax to the Union Pacific, which owned trackage in Colfax and in three directions from Colfax.

The Moscow Local handled mostly grain, which in the 1960s moved in nominal 50-ton, 40-foot boxcars. Every station featured one or two or three small

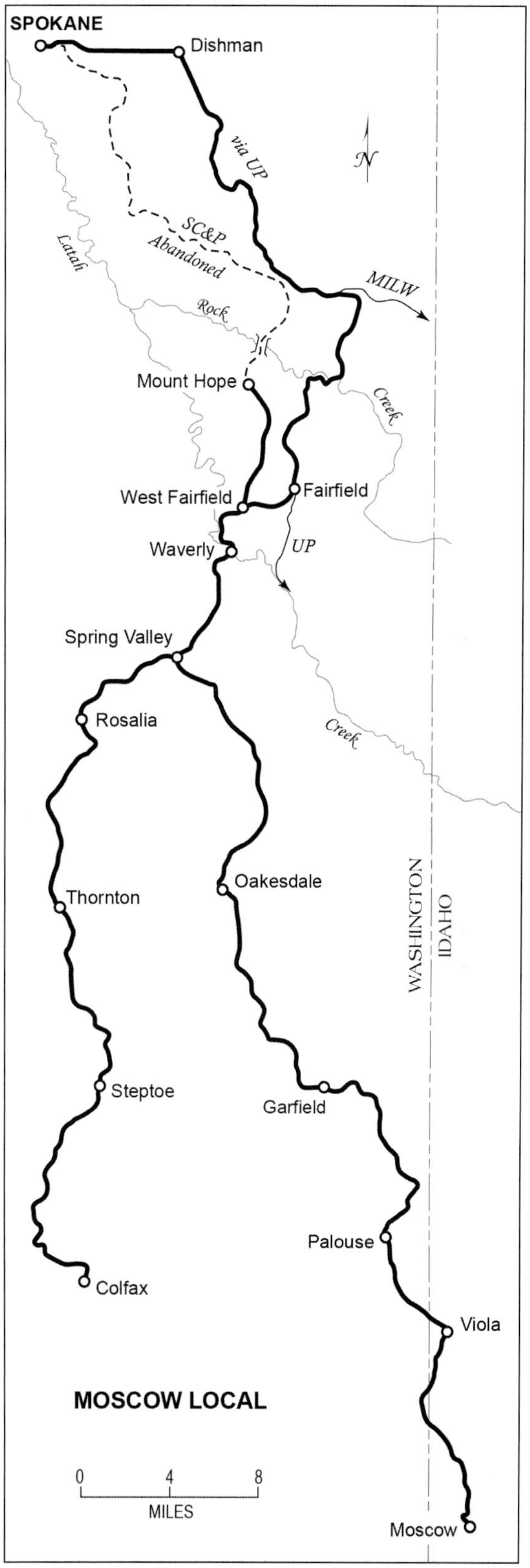

grain elevators designed to load one to six boxcars at a time. Since grain moves strongly in the fall and winter, and slowly or not at all the rest of the year, traffic on the Moscow Local was quite seasonal. During the fall and winter wheat shipping season the Moscow Local brought in 40 to 50 loads of wheat, but in the summer, it was just a handful of cars.

Several stations served customers who unloaded dry fertilizer from boxcars or covered hoppers. Most of the fertilizer customers also unloaded tank cars of anhydrous ammonia or ammonia solutions. During the spring fertilizer season, which was the off season for wheat, the Moscow Local brought in as many as 10 empty tank cars that last contained ammonia unloaded at several stations on the line. Inbound shipments of seed wheat moved in the late summer and early fall for the planting of winter wheat. Other seed grain moved inbound for planting in the spring. The local also handled a way freight car for the different stations.

The only relatively stable traffic all year round was the lumber interchanged off the Washington Idaho and Montana (WI&M) at Palouse. We shoved empty lumber cars down the interchange track to the WI&M and they shoved loads of lumber to us. Regardless of the season, the Moscow local always brought in six to 10 loads of lumber.

When the Moscow Local returned from Moscow on Tuesday, Thursday, and Saturday around 5:00 to 7:00 PM, they pulled their train down the transfer track between the SC&P Yard and Spokane Yard, left the train and power right there, and tied up. One of the Spokane Yard switch engines would later pull the train out of the transfer track, cross over both main tracks to the Spokane Yard, and switch out the Moscow Local.

Power on the Moscow Local was GP 7 and GP 9 units, one in the summer and two in the fall and winter. If the midnight transfer job needed more power to get a heavy cut up to Hillyard, they would take the Moscow power for their own use for one trip. If the Moscow Local power needed fuel and/or sand, the transfer crew would take it to Hillyard and return the power on their second trip to Spokane. Even if the midnight transfer crew did not need the power, they took the Moscow power to Hillyard for fuel and sand, or to change units if necessary, on the weekend and once during the week.

THE COEUR D'ALENE LOCAL

The Coeur d'Alene Local worked out of the former SC&P Yard on duty at 9:00 AM, Monday through Friday, making a round trip to Coeur d'Alene, Idaho each day. The Coeur d'Alene Local served the lumber mills between Greenacres, Washington and Coeur d'Alene, Idaho.

The Coeur d'Alene Local's first and last stop each day was Quickie Box at Greenacres, between Spokane and Spokane Bridge. In the morning, we usually delivered one or two loaded boxcars of lumber and got one or two loads back out each afternoon. Quickie bought boxcars of grade three and better 1 × 6s and 1 × 8s. They ran this lumber through their plant, cut out the bad spots, and glued the boards together to make prefabricated furniture and casket shook.

The SC&P and the Milwaukee Road originally operated separate lines to Coeur d'Alene. Since the GN and the MILW were each running only one local a day to Coeur d'Alene, it made sense to consolidate the lines so that they would not have to maintain two lines. In 1945, the GN and the MILW made a deal for the GN to use the MILW between Spokane Bridge and Post Falls, and the MILW would use parts of the GN line beyond Post Falls. Beyond the beginning of the MILW branch at McGuires, both railroads enjoyed equal access to the customers on this joint facility portion of the line.

The GN abandoned its line between Spokane Bridge, MP 18.89, including its Spokane River Bridge, and MP 23.32, almost to Post Falls, in favor of using the MILW line. At Great Northern MP 23.32, both carriers used the GN line through Post Falls to MP 27.26, where both carriers returned to the MILW line through Huetter to Great Northern MP 29.56 at Atlas, where the joint route returned to the GN. The MILW had originally separated from the GN east of Gibbs and operated over their own line their yard in Coeur d'Alene.[3] By the 1960s, the MILW yard was gone and the MILW used our yard and main track to access Potlatch Forest Industries (PFI) at Rutledge. The MILW timetable and dispatcher governed operations on the joint line between Spokane Bridge and Gibbs. Our timetable governed on our line for the 1.1 miles between Gibbs and Coeur d'Alene depot. Yard limits extended from about one mile west of Huetter into Coeur d'Alene and out to Rutledge, which was about one mile east of the GN Coeur d'Alene depot and

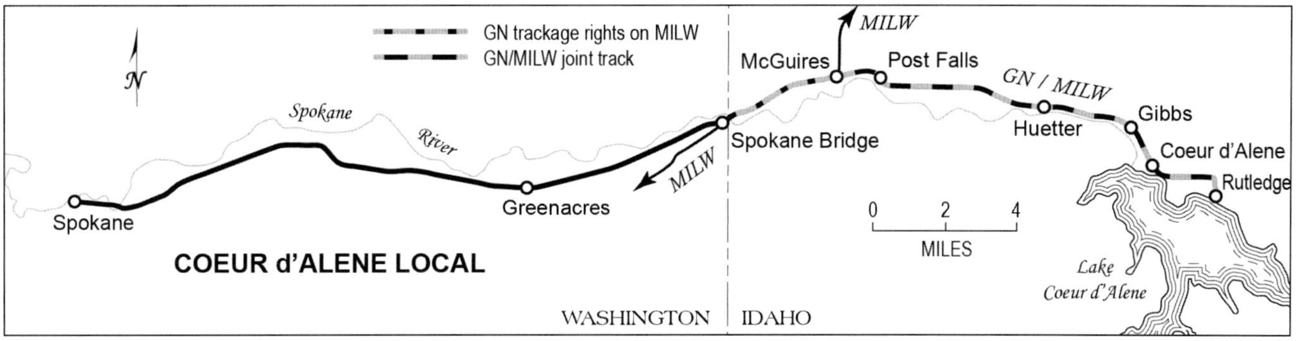

yard. All moves within yard limits were at restricted speed.

On the Great Northern between Spokane and Spokane Bridge, 18.8 miles, we ran as an extra east. At Spokane Bridge, our conductor registered, the head brakeman opened the switch and pulled out onto the Milwaukee branch main, and the rear brakeman lined the switch behind us. Our Coeur d'Alene Local operated as second class train No. 95 on the Milwaukee from Spokane Bridge to McGuires. At McGuires the Milwaukee's line split. The other MILW line went north to Newport and Metaline Falls. Our conductor registered again at McGuires. We entered the MILW branch to Coeur d'Alene and lined the switch behind us before departing for Post Falls.

The first customer beyond Spokane Bridge was at Post Falls: the lumber mill owned by Georgia Pacific, later Louisiana Pacific. Georgia Pacific was good for one to three flatcars of lumber a day.

Diamond National at Huetter shipped one or two loads per week off the loading dock. The Milwaukee received most of the lumber business here. Two man teams at Diamond National loaded boxcars by hand. Diamond National later put in a flatcar track. After that, the GN got four to six flatcar loads per week.

The Northern Pacific's Coeur d'Alene branch lay 150 feet or so north of the GN/MILW joint line at Huetter, and both were headed more or less compass east toward Coeur d'Alene. There was a NP transfer track about one tenth of a mile east of Huetter. The NP local occasionally came through the NP transfer track and used the joint line to spot an empty car or pick up a load at Diamond National.

On arrival at Huetter, our conductor called the agent at Coeur d'Alene on the telephone to find out which of the cars in our train were for Diamond National, Northwest Timber, and PFI at Rutledge. We then switched out our train to put the PFI cars against the engine. If our train included a flatcar to spot at Northwest Timber, it went against the engine with PFI cars behind. If our train included cars for Diamond, we spotted them.

The next customer was the Atlas Tie sawmill located immediately east of the NP transfer track. The joint line returned to the SC&P at the west end of Atlas. Because of the way the switches opened, we switched Atlas Tie on our way back to Spokane.

The next station was Gibbs, about one mile east of Atlas Tie. Northwest Timber, one of the largest mills in the Coeur d'Alene area, was located at Gibbs. The Union Pacific, formerly the Spokane International, also operated a branch to Coeur d'Alene. The UP passed under the NP between the NP transfer track and Northwest Timber. All four railroads directly switched Northwest Timber. The UP ran along the south side of the mill immediately north of the SC&P line. Union Pacific served a two or three car long dock track inside the mill and a chip track at the southwest corner of the mill.

The UP then continued east for about half a mile and passed under the SC&P. The UP rose back to the general level of the ground over the next half mile, crossed the tail of our Coeur d'Alene yard wye at grade, and continued to Coeur d'Alene as the farthest south of the original four lines into town.

At Northwest Timber, the SC&P was parallel with and south of the Union Pacific. Our spur opened toward Coeur d'Alene, crossed the UP, and split. One track

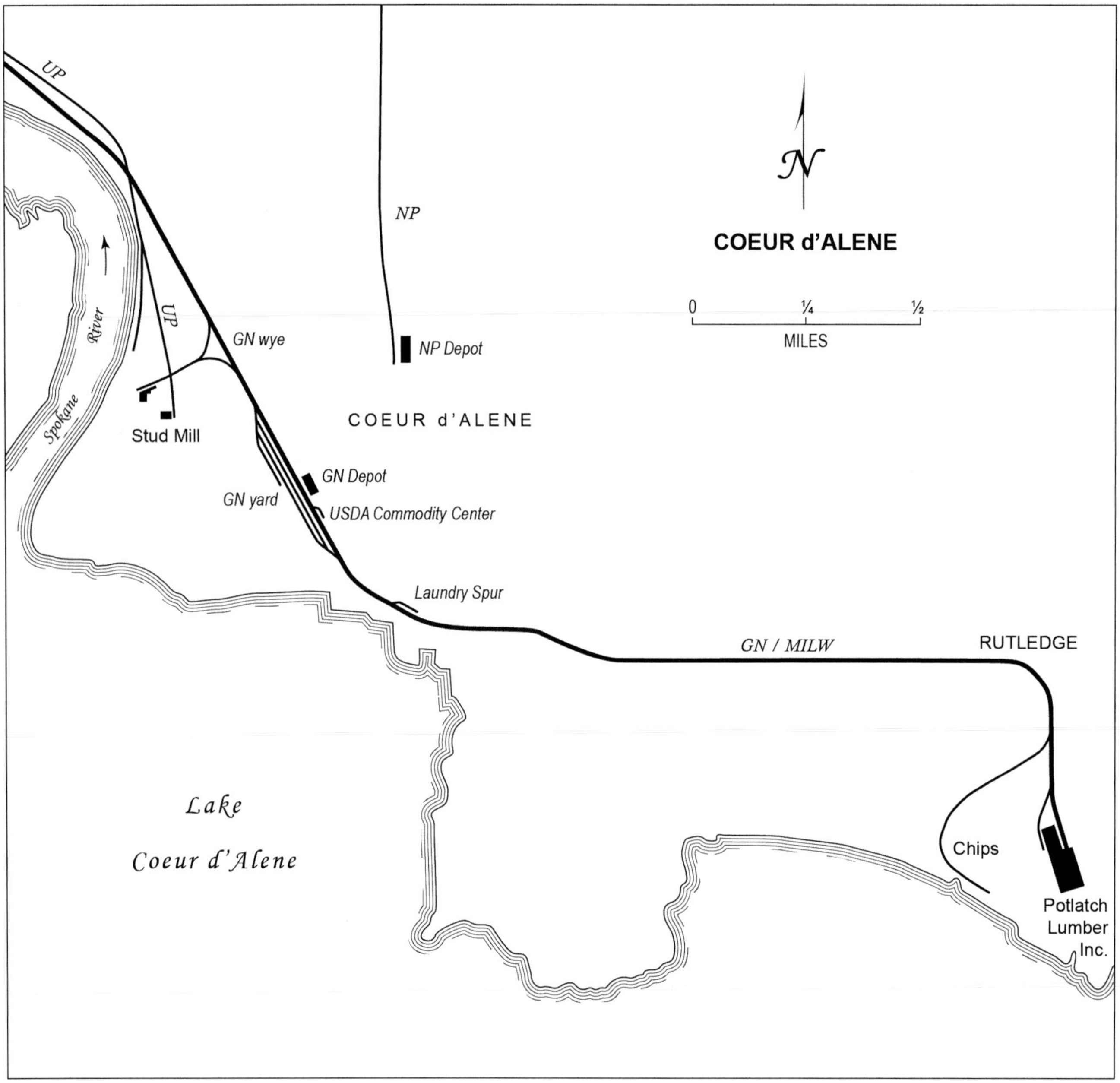

became the outside flatcar track located about 150 feet east of the mill building. The other ran to the north along the east wall of the mill. North of the mill, a trailing point switch gave access to our dock track, which entered the building from the north to serve a six or seven car long inside dock track at the east end of the building. We switched Northwest Timber's flatcar track on our way east and the inside dock track on our return trip.

The Northern Pacific served Northwest Timber by a spur that came off their branch main track, which was north of the mill. The NP spur ran downhill and to the south for about an eighth of a mile to a flatcar loading track called Blackwell flatcar track. The NP track continued to the mill and ran into a loading dock track inside the building about 150 feet west of our dock track. The NP got only two to three cars a week from Northwest Timber.

There was a two or three car long interchange track where the UP crossed our spur to Northwest Timber. About once a week we got an empty boxcar from the Union Pacific transfer on our way east, took it out to Rutledge, and spotted it on the lumber dock at PFI. After switching Northwest Timber's flatcar track, we continued east to our yard at Coeur d'Alene. Track 1 was the siding, track 2 was double ended, but track 3 was a stub track.

At Coeur d'Alene we headed the train into track 1 after cutting our caboose off on the main track short of the yard. We left the rear of our train on track 1 and held on to the PFI cars and any loads of coal. Next, we dug out any PFI cars from yard track 2, set all the PFI and coal cars to the main track, and put the loads from Northwest back to the cars on track 1. We coupled to the PFI cars on the main, shoved back to get the caboose; pulled ahead and entered track 1 at the intermediate crossover. While all this was going on, the conductor got a PFI list from the agent at the depot.

We went to eat, as this was the one time in the day that we had time to eat. The Milwaukee local ran ahead of us, so we used the lunch break to wait for them to come back from PFI at Rutledge. After the Milwaukee local returned, we went to Rutledge not earlier than 2:30 PM. PFI wanted us there at shift change time which was 3:00 PM. The trip to Rutledge took us right down the residential streets of Coeur d'Alene. We were required to stop at all the stop signs and to flag our way across each intersection.

At Rutledge we opened the gate, pulled in, dropped our train by the engine, and stopped the train just to clear the track that the engine was on. This was an easy downhill drop. The engine then came against the caboose and empty boxcars and shoved down toward the lumber dock. We set the caboose to the woodchip track, talked with the PFI loading foreman about how he wanted the dock track lined up, and then switched the lumber dock. PFI usually shipped three or four loaded boxcars of lumber per day via the GN, but we did not get any wood chips out of PFI. The woodchip buyer was located on the Milwaukee, so they got the chips. We picked the caboose off the chip track, pulled out of PFI, closed the gate behind us, and proceeded back through the streets of Coeur d'Alene to the yard.

On our return from Rutledge, we spotted a hopper car of coal to the laundry using their short spur or pulled an empty. The laundry used about two carloads of coal each month well into the 1970s.

Back at the yard, we left our train on the main track and got the list the agent left at the section house. We switched the one customer at the yard, the USDA commodity center, when and as directed by the list.

Now we did most of the switching to line up the rest of our day. The cars from Rutledge were on the main with the caboose. This would be the rear of our train leaving Coeur d'Alene.

The cars previously brought into town, both loads and empties, were on track 1; loads on the east end and empties on the west end. Track 2 held slough cars, but we could use it during our switching, and stub track 3 was also available for us to spread cars into.

We came against the west end of track 1, made a cut behind the empties and switched out the empty cars from both track 1 and track 2. Double door boxcars for DeArmond went to track 3. Empties for Atlas Tie went against the loads on track 1 and then empties for Northwest Timber at Gibbs went against the Atlas cars on track 1. Any empty cars left over went into track 2 with any other empties previously left in track 2.

DeArmond was located on the trail of our wye at the west end of the Coeur d'Alene yard on the south, or river side, of our line. We switched DeArmond through the west leg of the wye. The Union Pacific crossed the tail of our wye before our spur entered the DeArmond mill, so we flagged our way across the UP and they flagged us. We went to DeArmond as a light engine, that is, an engine with no cars, because the steep grade down the tail of the wye made a very hard pull with the cars out of the mill. We shoved all the cars we pulled, loads and empties, to a joint on the cars on the main track. As one brakeman made the joint and lined the air hoses, the head brakeman cut the engine off and brought it into track 3, picking up the new empty cars for DeArmond. We doubled the new empty cars to the old empties on the main track, made a cut behind the last empty or part load, returned to the wye, and shoved down the west leg of the wye to spot the mill. DeArmond was always good for three or four 40-foot double door boxcars full to the roof with bundles of 2 × 4 and 2 × 6 studs.

BN engine 988, formerly GN 188, crosses the Spokane River as the Coeur d'Alene Local approaches the SC&P Yard in Spokane. She is an EMD model NW 5, one of ten built in 1946 to power local and branch line trains in Minnesota and North Dakota. DAVID EMERSON COLLECTION, PNRARCHIVE.ORG.

After spotting the stud mill, the power came against track 1, the empty cars to be spotted at Northwest Timber and Atlas Tie with the loads previously brought to town behind them, doubled all of them to the main to set our train, made an air test, and departed.

After Coeur d'Alene, our usual first stop was Gibbs, to pull the loads and spot or respot empty boxcars to Northwest Timber's dock track. Northwest Timber's dock track at Gibbs was good for two or three loads of lumber each day.

About once a week we set a loaded boxcar from PFI to the Union Pacific transfer. We dropped the loaded car by on our main, picked it up, and shoved it onto the UP transfer at Gibbs before switching the dock at Northwest Timber. The only reciprocal switching service on the Coeur d'Alene line was our switching of UP cars to and from PFI.

The next customer was Atlas Tie, which shipped one or two loads of lumber per day off the dock track. After gathering up all our cars, the local left Huetter with 17 to 20 loads every day of the week. We ran by Post Falls having switched Georgia Pacific on the way out.

Our next stop was McGuires, where we entered the Milwaukee line from Newport and registered again, this time as MILW No. 96, an eastward third class train. At Spokane Bridge, the conductor registered that No. 96 had arrived at Spokane Bridge, and from there to Spokane we became a GN Extra West, again displaying white signals. Our last stop was Quickie Box at Greenacres for the final switch of the day, picking up the loads and empty cars.

When the Coeur d'Alene Local came in about 9:00 PM, it pulled down into the hole unless the Moscow Local's train was still in the hole. In that case we just pulled our train into the SC&P Yard and left the engine and train right there. At Spokane Yard, cars off the Coeur d'Alene local were put with other cars for the Hillyard transfer job.

The engine off the Coeur d'Alene Local, GN 188, an EMD model NW 5 unique to the GN, went to Hillyard for fuel and sand on a weekend transfer.

Traffic between Spokane and Hillyard

Traffic to and from Spokane in the 1960s was very significant to the Great Northern. Start with 50 to 60 cars per day to and from the freight house, which is actually a low count since some cars were loads in and loads out. Spokane customers served by the SC&P switchers plus the Coeur d'Alene Local amounted to 50 to 60 cars every weekday. The Moscow local returned to Spokane with 20 to 30 cars three days per week, and in the grain season the Moscow Local was 50 to 60 cars per trip. Call the Moscow Local 125 loads per week, or 25 per day, on an annual average basis. Spokane Yard thus generated an average of 55 cars at the freight house, plus 55 from the SC&P Yard and Coeur d'Alene, plus 25 from Moscow, or 135 cars per day five days per week. Another 20 to 30 cars were interchanged with the Union Pacific six days per week, so the total averaged about 160 cars each way per week day at Spokane Yard. It is no wonder there were six transfer round trips per week day between Hillyard and Spokane!

Customers at Hillyard added 20 to 30 loads, plus 60 to 80 cars of Spike Yard traffic per week day. The locals that worked out of Hillyard, the Priest River, Chewelah, Kettle Falls, and Mead Turns between them brought in 120 to 180 cars per day; Hillyard thus generated 240 to 290 cars per day, excluding the West Local from Wenatchee arriving at Hillyard on Tuesday, Thursday, and Saturday.

Adding this all up, it amounts to 360 to 450 loads per week day into and out of through trains at Hillyard, say an average of 410 cars per week day. This traffic split about 70% east and 30% west. That means there were about 290 eastward cars new to the system to move east from Hillyard each day. In addition, there were about 150 cars per day for the east off the SP&S. This was why the company ran second and third sections of No. 88's train running as second or third section of the Time Table second class train 492, and why 490's schedule often ran in sections east of Hillyard.

Endnotes

1 Clive Carter, *Inland Empire Electric Line* (Coeur d'Alene ID: Museum of North Idaho, 2009), 205–206.

2 Clive Carter, *Inland Empire Electric Line*, 205–206.

3 Clive Carter, *Inland Empire Electric Line*, 202.

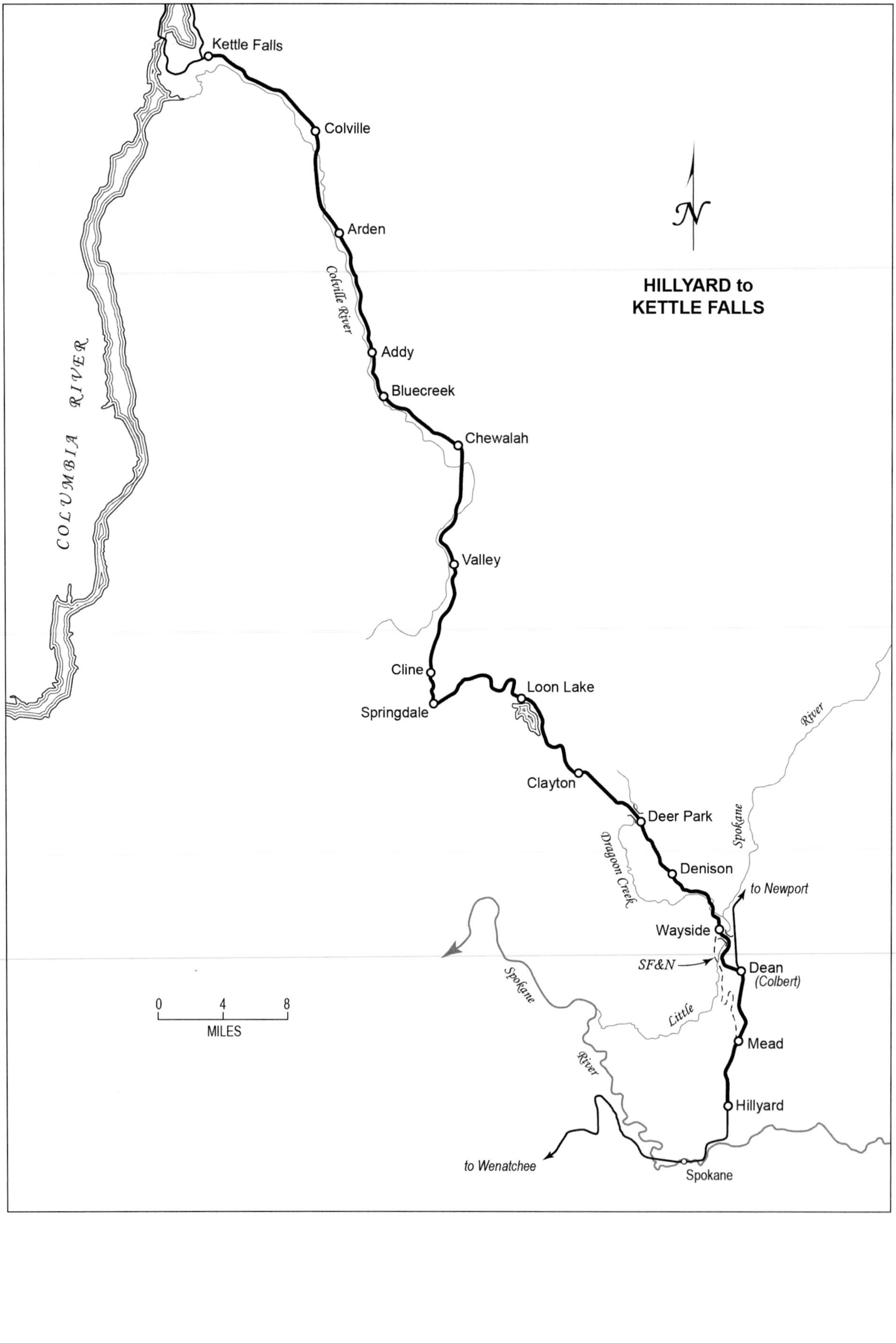

HILLYARD to
KETTLE FALLS
N
Kettle Falls
Colville
Arden
Colville River
Addy
Bluecreek
Chewalah
Valley
Cline
Springdale
Loon Lake
Clayton
Deer Park
Dragoon Creek
Denison
Spokane River
to Newport
Wayside
SF&N
Dean
(Colbert)
Little
Spokane River
Mead
Hillyard
to Wenatchee
Spokane
COLUMBIA RIVER
0 4 8
MILES

5. Kettle Falls Jobs

➻ Introduction

The Kettle Falls branch left the main line at Dean, 9.1 miles east of Hillyard. This chapter describes the locals that worked the Kettle Falls line, which split at Kettle Falls into the Republic branch and the Nelson branch.

➻ The Chewelah Turn

The Chewelah Turn went on duty at Hillyard at 6:00 AM Monday through Friday. The Chewelah Turn ran to Chewelah, an intermediate point on the line to Kettle Falls, and returned to Hillyard in one shift. This portion of the Kettle Falls branch was built by the Spokane Falls and Northern (SF&N) in 1889, three years before the Great Northern reached Spokane.

In 1899, very soon after securing control of the SF&N on July 1, 1898, the Great Northern built a new connection extending 3.62 miles from its main track at Colbert, later renamed Dean, to Wayside on the SF&N. The connection descended to and crossed the Little Spokane River. Beyond the river. the line turned to the right and joined the SF&N at MP 17.2, just south of the south switch of Wayside. In 1899, a second new connection at the west end of Hillyard brought SF&N trains to and from the Great Northern main track. The two new connections enabled abandonment of about 14 miles of the SF&N between Hillyard and Wayside.

After building the connections, the Great Northern resurveyed and reset mileposts on the Kettle Falls line using the junction at Dean as the starting point for mileposts. Chewelah was at MP 50, so it was 59 miles from Hillyard to Chewelah, which meant the crew ran 118 miles per day on the Chewelah Turn.

Two short segments of the former SF&N main track, which lay north of GN between Hillyard and Dean, were retained and connected to the GN trackage. Davies Spur left the GN main 1.5 miles east of Mead, ran over to the SF&N alignment, and dead ended at a small lumber mill at Dead Man's Creek. The second segment was off the siding at Mead. A switch at the west end of Mead ran to the Kaiser Aluminum plant. Partway to the aluminum plant, the Kaiser switch veered off to the north and continued up the hill to Kaiser. The track off the straight side of the Kaiser switch was on the former SF&N main track. It ran west for about a quarter of a mile to serve a company that loaded a car a month, covered hoppers filled with what the waybills called 'earth.'

From Hillyard to Dean, the Chewelah Turn was on double track constructed during the summer of 1922[1] with single direction ABS signals on each track. The switch to enter the Kettle Falls branch was located about 500 feet east of the end of double track. An operator was on duty at Dean 24 hours a day. The operator took train orders from the dispatcher and hooped them up to both eastward and westward trains. He also controlled the interlocked switch and signals at the end of double track as directed by the dispatcher, but the switch to the Kettle Falls branch was a hand throw switch. Coming off the branch at Dean, the crew checked with the operator to see if it was OK to enter the main track at Dean.

The Chewelah Turn switched Denison, spotting empty gondola cars for pulpwood loading on the way to Kettle Falls, and picking up the pulpwood loads on the way back.

Next was the Deer Park Lumber Company mill about half a mile north of Deer Park. The Great Northern main track ran north/south at Deer Park Lumber, whose pond and mill was located on the east side of main track. The log pond was north of mill, and all other tracks were south of mill. Our main track switch opened to the south; the

Dean Interlocker with an eastward train approaching. The train order board is clear in both directions. PHOTO BY DALE JONES.

mill main track extended to the north. The log pond spur diverged from the mill main and continued north to run along a piling wall at the edge of the log pond.

A short run around track was located parallel to the mill main and south of the mill buildings. A double-ended chip and sawdust loading track ran beside the runaround and opposite the mill main track. Wood chips and sawdust, two separate materials, were blown from the mill to the cars through metal pipes. This is the only mill I ever saw that loaded chips and sawdust into 40-foot boxcars. The mill hands installed grain doors in the boxcar doors and loaded the cars using a separate chute for each material. Deer Park Lumber's loading track was located at the far north end of the mill main track and beside the building. Empty boxcars spotted to the doors in the side of the building. The lumber dock switch opened to the north.

We worked Deer Park Lumber on the way out and on the way back. In the morning, we left the train on the main track in town, brought cars for the mill with us, and pulled through the runaround track. From there, we pulled the chip and sawdust track, spotted the track with empties from Hillyard, and sloughed any loaded cars we pulled to the runaround, along with any excess empty cars for the mill. Then we switched the lumber track, again sloughing loads to the runaround. As our last move, we pulled empty log flats from the log track, shoved them north on the main, let them roll by the engine by the force of gravity, and then we shoved them into the siding back at Deer Park for the Kettle Falls Turn to pick up.

On the return trip to Hillyard in the afternoon, we switched the chip and sawdust track again and took all the loads with us. The mill shipped five or six loads of lumber and three to five carloads of chips and sawdust per day.

At Loon Lake, we spotted empty pulpwood gondolas on the way out and pulled the loads on the way back. The next customer was North American Non Metallics, served by a spur located two miles south of Valley. The spur opened to the north, so we switched North American on our northward trip. This customer shipped one load per day but had space for two empty cars.

At Chewelah, the train pulled up to the depot, where the conductor got the switch lists from the agent and the crew went to the restaurant to eat. After lunch, we switched the industry track at Chewelah, where Northwest Marble Products produced crushed marble rock shipped in open top hopper cars. Fantasia Feed received a load on occasion. For the Magnesium plant at the south end of town, we spotted a load of coal about twice a week, pulled one or two loads of magnesite a day, and spotted empty cars for loading. This customer shipped five to six loads per week of magnesite in bags in boxcars.

Deer Park depot surrounded by snow. PHOTO BY LOREN GUENTHER.

The turn switched the Lane Mountain Sand plant at Valley on the return trip. Lane Mountain shipped mostly glass sand for wine bottles in covered hoppers, but they also shipped traction sand. Most of Lane's traction sand was purchased by the Great Northern, and later by the Burlington Northern, for their engines. Railroad sand was shipped as far away as Interbay in company sand service covered hopper cars.

Lane Mountain also shipped boxcars loaded with paper bags marked 'Traction Sand.' The sand was sold at auto parts stores in the fall of the year for added weight in your car trunk, or the back of your pickup.

Lane Mountain shipped sand for filtering water in public water systems in covered hoppers, unusually in a C-4, a nominal 70-ton covered hopper with 1958 cubic feet capacity. Sometimes they would use a nominal 70-ton car with 3215 cubic feet capacity. On occasion, the car distributor would supply a C-6, a nominal 100-ton car of about 4750 cubic feet. Lane Mountain had to be careful not to overload the higher volume cars, as they were designed to haul grain, which is not as dense as sand.

From Valley, the line was up the hill. We stopped at Cline siding and switched Springdale Lumber Company, pulling one or two flatcar loads of lumber and spotting one or two empties. South of Cline about 500 feet was the Allied Mineral spur. Allied loaded covered hoppers full of a very fine gray material which they called 'earth' on the waybill. Out back behind the processing plant sat big piles of this material, trucked in from somewhere. The 'earth' looked like it had been scraped off some dry lake bottom in slabs and chunks. Allied took almost a full week to load one covered hopper car.

➸ THE KETTLE FALLS TURN

The Kettle Falls Turn reported for duty Sunday–Friday at Hillyard at 9:00 PM. The Turn ran from Hillyard to Kettle Falls and returned to Hillyard in one shift. Kettle Falls was 90.9 miles from Hillyard, which meant the crew covered 182 miles per night. This job did very little station work. Frankly, there was no time. Our mission was to take empty cars to Kettle Falls to supply the locals there and to bring the loads accumulated at Kettle Falls back to Hillyard.

The Kettle Falls Turn picked up empty log flats at Deer Park that the Chewelah Turn pulled and left on the siding. En route we traversed 'Bellyache Springs Curve,' located at MP 68.5, is the site of a very cold spring that railroad construction crews used for drinking water. There must have been something in the water that contaminated it, because the whole construction crew got bellyaches after they drank from the spring.

In the early 1960s, our next stop was Arden, about 15

Company sand cars like this were loaded at Valley Sand in Valley, Washington, and spotted at engine terminals in Washington, Oregon, Idaho, and Montana. From the car, dry sand was conveyed pneumatically into a sand tower and dispensed by gravity to locomotives. Sand was and is applied to the rails by the engineer to increase traction when required. GNRHS ARCHIVE.

miles north of Chewelah, to switch the Arden Lumber mill. Arden shipped four or five boxcars of lumber and two or three loads of wood chips per night. Hillyard blocked cars for the lumber mill at Arden and placed them on the head end of our train. After Arden, our next stop was Kettle Falls.

During the 1960s, Great Northern time table directions were east and west. 'Eastward' was from Hillyard to Kettle Falls, and 'westward' was from Kettle Falls to Hillyard. The yard at Kettle Falls lays basically geographic east and west. The Great Northern time table directions at Kettle Falls were opposite compass directions.

The Nelson Local and the Republic Local worked their respective branches out of Kettle Falls. The Nelson Local ran eastward by time table from Kettle Falls to Nelson and returned westward. The Republic Local, however, ran 'timetable west' from Kettle Falls to Republic and returned eastward, despite the fact that they both left Kettle Falls yard in the same direction.

After the BN merger, when the Kettle Falls Turn ran out of Yardley, the time table direction was changed from eastward to Kettle Falls to westward to Kettle Falls. The reason for the change was that when the Kettle Falls Turn left Yardley, the train headed west down the old main to Napa Street Junction where it diverged to Hillyard, Dean, and Kettle Falls.

In December of 2004, the time table direction was changed again; this time to north and south, northward to Kettle Falls and southward back to Yardley. I was working the second Kettle Falls Turn when this

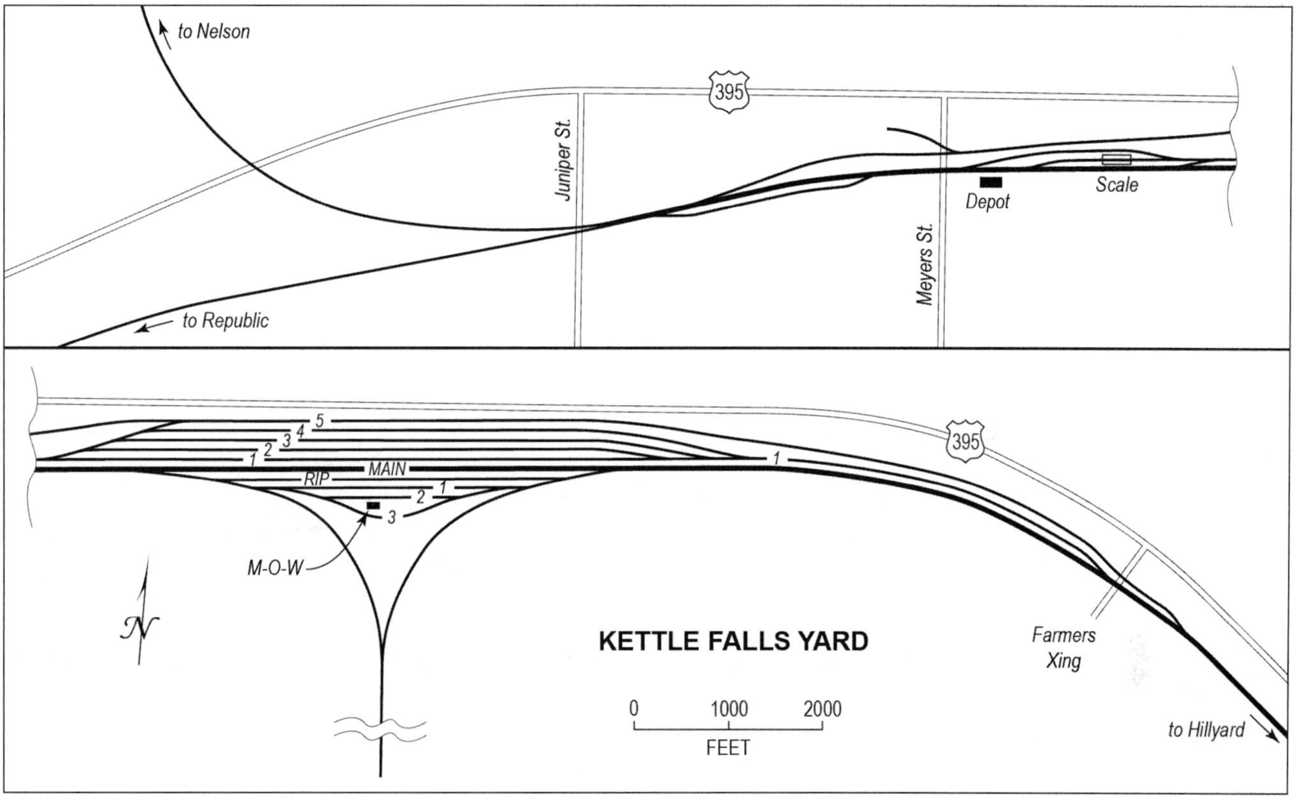

last change in time table direction was made. After this change, the Quirk Turn, formally the Nelson Local, and the San Poil Local, formally the Republic Local, both ran northward leaving Kettle and southward back to Kettle Falls. This was a return to the former SF&N direction convention, though I doubt anyone knew or cared.

The following description uses early Burlington Northern timetable directions, which most closely match actual compass directions at Kettle Falls.

The yard at Kettle Falls consisted of five tracks on the north, or right, side of the main track, facing west. The first track our train encountered was track 5, the longest track in the yard. It held about 60 cars of average length. A farmer's private crossing was located about 10 car lengths from the east end. If the track was full, we were required to cut the crossing. The switch to track 1 was located in the main track immediately west of the farmer's crossing. Track 1 lay adjacent to the main track and held about 45 cars.

Tracks 4 through 2 diverged from track 1. In an unusual arrangement, track 4 was the first track to diverge from the east end of track 1. The switch to track 4 was about 10 car lengths west of the one track switch off the main track. Track 4 held about 30 cars. Track 3 was the next track to branch off of track 1. Track 3 held about 25 cars. The last track to branch off of track 1 was track 2; it held about 20 cars.

Tracks 1 through 5 came together at the west end of the yard on a single lead track. West of the switch between the lead track and track 1, a switching lead extended west. The west switching lead also functioned as the scale track. The west switching lead extended west to a point immediately east, or short of, the depot, which was located about 200 feet east of the Meyers Street grade crossing and on the south side of the main track. The depot was about 750 feet west of the crossover. Immediately west of the switch between the lead and track 1, there was a facing point, in the westward direction, crossover from the main to the lead. The crossover provided access from the west switching lead to the yard, to the main track, to the wye, and to the rip track and the engine tracks which were all located on the south side of the main track east of the crossover.

Meyers Street was the busiest street crossing in town. It connected the highway, which is located north of the railroad, with the town of Kettle Falls, south of the railroad. West of the Meyers Street crossing was a short double ended track for holding track material and track machinery like tie tampers and ballast regulators. This track was located on the south side of the main track and between the two grade crossings. Juniper Street was about 600 feet west of Meyers Street.

The junction switch between the Nelson line and the Republic line was located west of the Meyers Street crossing and about 130 feet east of Juniper Street. The Nelson line veered to the right and descended towards Evans on a light grade; the Republic line ran straight ahead and immediately started to drop down a steep 1.5% grade towards West Kettle and the Columbia River Bridge.

Between the two road crossings, a switch diverged from the main track to the north side. This was the west end of the industry track. The industry track crossed Meyers Street and connected to track 5 immediately east of the point that the yard lead turned toward this switch. A grain elevator sat beside the industry track between the two crossings. An old warehouse, no longer used, sat beside the track east of Meyers Street. When I hired out, the cabooses were kept on the east end of the industry track between the warehouse and where the industry track tied into track 5.

The switching lead/scale track was only about 15 car lengths in the clear between the crossover and the main track switch at the west end. The lead included a track scale, which was used to weigh cars. The scale featured 'live' rails and 'dead' rails. 'Live' rails were supported by the scale mechanism and were used to weigh cars; 'dead' rails bypassed the scale mechanism. The dead rails were right next to the live rails. There was a pair of switch points on each end of the scale so that a crew could use the live rails on the scale to weigh loaded cars, or use the dead rails for all other moves. The dead rails were used to avoid working the scale mechanism unnecessarily and to keep the heavy engines off the live rails of the scale.

The west switching lead/scale track was the most heavily used track in the entire yard. This caused heavy wear on the switch points on both sides of the scale, for which they required constant maintenance.

After a series of derailments at the points of the track scale, the company built a new switching lead from a point on the scale track east of the scale to the main track. The west switch of this new track was located in the main track between the depot and Meyers Avenue. The new switching lead passed behind the scale house and eliminated the heavy traffic over the scale.

The switch to the west leg of the wye was about three car lengths east of the main track crossover switch. The first switch on the west leg of the wye was the Rip Track, which lay adjacent to the main track and held about 15 cars. The next switch off the west leg of the wye was Engine Track 1. Engine Tracks 2 and 3 branched off Engine Track 1. Off the engine tracks, there was a switch to a spur track that ran behind the two diesel fuel tanks and storage buildings. This track was used to store maintenance-of-way equipment like the Snow Dozer, water tank car, and company material flats of rail and track angle bars and tie plates. The Rip Track came back to the east end of the wye. The engine tracks and the material track came together and rejoined the wye at a second switch off the east leg of the wye. The tail of the wye held 8 to 10 cars. The tail of the wye was kept clear so that the Kettle Falls Turn could wye their engine at night.

The outbound Kettle Falls Turn was always made up on track 5. Track 1 was generally left clear for the inbound Kettle Falls Turn to put their train. Normal practice for making the turn at Kettle Falls was for the rear brakeman to drop off at the east end of track 5 and to walk the train connecting the air hoses, checking that the angle cocks were open, and assuring that no hand brakes were set on any of the cars, a process known as 'lining the air' to the farmer's crossing.

If our inbound train was going to be a tight fit in one track, the rear brakeman would climb up the three ties that supported the gate at the farmer's crossing so that he could signal the head brakeman by hand lantern to stop his shove before he ran through the switch between one track and the main track. When the head brakeman stopped his shove, he cut the engine off, dumping the

Kettle Falls depot was an important communications center. Crews received train orders, switch lists, and waybills from the operator at the depot. PHOTO BY LOREN GUENTHER.

air. The rear brakeman could hear the air dump, which told him that the shove was done and he could go back to lining up the air on track 5. He would end up at the caboose.

Meanwhile, the head brakeman pulled the entire train past the west switch of the lead/scale track, shoved past the scale and up the lead into track 5, where he coupled the caboose to our outbound train and uncoupled the inbound train from the caboose. The head brakeman pulled out the lead to clear the switch to track 1 and shoved the inbound train into track 1 while watching the rear brakeman if there was any concern about whether or not the train would fit in this track. In the rare event that train would not fit in track 1, the head brakeman left the excess cars on the rip track between the wye switches.

The head brakeman ran the engine around the wye so the lead unit was now headed east. It was quicker and easier to go around the wye than to change ends on the engine. The other reason we went around the wye was to keep the F unit that typically was the lead unit out of Hillyard on the head end. F units were much more comfortable in the winter, since the weather stripping on GP units allowed a lot of cold air into the cab. We took the engine to the east end of the yard, backed in, coupled into the train, coupled the train together at the farmer's crossing, cut in the air, and pumped up the train with air for the air test. If our train included logs from Evans on the Nelson line, they were on the head end of our train from Kettle Falls to spot at Deer Park Lumber.

The conductor dropped off the caboose when it first went by the depot. He turned in his train consist and waybills and received the paperwork and train orders for our outbound train. He walked to the caboose while the brakemen were making the air test.

Many nights on the Kettle Falls Turn, both as a conductor and brakeman, we would find that the only track open was the main. To deal with this situation, Gene Sponcler and I invented the 'Kettle Falls Double Shuffle.'

The double shuffle began by pulling the whole inbound train west on the main track past the yard. As the train moved west on the main track, the rear brakeman dropped off at the east end of track 5 and walked the outbound train lining the air. If the head end of our outbound train was on track 1, the rear brakeman would line the air and check angle cocks and brakes on both tracks 5 and 1 at the same time for about 15 car lengths where tracks 1 and 5 were side by side on the east end of the yard. Where tracks 1 and 5 separated, I worked west on track 1, which usually held a short cut, then returned to track 5 and resumed checking the outbound train.

As the inbound train moved west on the main, we always made sure to head up the Nelson line, to avoid the steep grade of the Republic line. When the caboose went by the depot, the conductor dropped off, went to the depot, borrowed the night operator's car, and drove down the highway to protect two road crossings when we would shove the inbound train east on the main line. While this was happening, the head brakeman gently shoved our caboose to a joint on the rear end of our outbound train on the east end of track 5 and then cut the train away from the caboose.

The head brakeman and engineer pulled the inbound train out of track 5 and shoved it east on the main. The head brakeman rode the east end of the shove until it approached the east switch to track 5, where the brakeman dropped off to handle the switch. While the engineer was shoving blind to the east on the main track, the conductor protected the Riverview Lane and the Boy's Ranch crossings as the east end of the train approached each crossing. The engineer stopped his shove when the engine was east of the east switch to track 5.

The head brakeman lined the switch, then got on the engine as it moved west pulling the inbound train into track 5. The head brakeman coupled the engine to our outbound train, made the joint at the farmer's crossing if necessary, cut the air in, and began to charge the train.

By the time the rear brakeman arrived at the caboose, the air was usually coming through the train line. He would check the air gauge to confirm that the air was coming through to the caboose. When the gauge showed at least 75 pounds in the outbound train, he radioed the engineer to shove our outbound train westward out of track 5 to the main track while pulling our inbound train into track 5.

After protecting the crossings during the eastward shove of the inbound train, the conductor drove back to the depot, returning the operator's car. Then he lined the main track switch for the switching lead and moved into position to flag the Meyers Street crossing near the depot when the crew shoved the outbound train out of the west end of the yard on the main track. The rear brakeman protected the Juniper Street crossing by blowing the caboose whistle with one hand while holding his lighted lantern in his other hand to warn errant motorists. The conductor walked back to the depot to turn in his inbound wheel report and waybills, and to get the outbound wheel report, waybills, and train orders for the return trip to Hillyard. He got on the caboose when the crew stopped the train with the caboose on the main track in front of the depot to begin our air test.

Shoving out of the yard sounds simple enough, but we were handling a fully charged inbound train of mostly empty cars behind the engine and not fully charged loads of the outbound train ahead of the engine. If the train went into emergency, that would tear the train in two, because the empties would stop "right now," but the loaded cars would not stop as quickly. The loads would run out and tear the inbound train in two or three pieces. The name of the game was slow and easy to avoid tearing the train in two.

Another consideration was that our power was pulling the empty inbound train uphill into track 5 and shoving the heavy outbound train on basically flat track. Once the rear of the outbound train got past the junction switch towards Nelson, the grade broke downward. The slack would run out of the loads on the down grade. If the engine made a sudden stop while the slack was running out, it could tear the train in two. The grade break reinforced the 'slow and easy' nature of this move.

The head brakeman cut the inbound train off at the west end of track 5. After the inbound train was cut off, we continued west until the entire outbound train was on the main track, and then brought the train eastward on the main track. The crew stopped on the main beside the yard with the caboose at the depot to make our air test, since it was clear of grade crossings and was a good place to walk, even in the dark.

The last thing to deal with in the Kettle Falls shuffle was that when the yard was plugged like this, some of the cars on the east end of track 1 were for the head end of our outbound train. In this case, we stopped short of track 1, cut the engine off, picked up the loads off track 1, doubled them to our train, lining the east switch of track 5 for the main in the process, and made our air test. If there was no need to make a pick up out of the yard, the head brakeman would walk to the east switch of track 5 and line it for the main. With the switch lined and the air test done, we were ready to depart for Hillyard.

When I first worked the Kettle Falls Turn as a brakeman in the late 1960s, doing the shuffle was rare. Later, as traffic increased, we did the shuffle about once a week, most often on Friday, as shippers did all they could to get their loads out by the end of the week. A night with a double shuffle took about an hour and a half from arrival to departure.

Not Always a Good Trip

I do not know how many times a crew would be having a good trip when out of the blue something would happen. We would be involved in a grade crossing accident, or have a derailment, hit a rock slide, or find a switch open.

I encountered an open switch on the Kettle Falls Turn. The train suffered no damage, but it was exciting enough to make my heart skip a few beats. Gene Spencler and I were braking together. Our conductor was Scotty Campbell and the engineer was Jimmy Wiles.

Jimmy was one of the best engineers I ever worked with. Nothing ever got by Jimmy. I do not know how many times Jimmy would say, "something is not right back there," and sure enough, the brakemen would find something wrong when we inspected the train and track.

It was my week to be the head brakeman and Gene's week to be the rear brakeman. The Kettle Falls Turn was headed north, coming down the hill from Loon Lake to Valley, which is about 18 miles of 1% grade. The train had just left Springdale with five units, an F 7 as the lead unit, and 50 to 60 cars. Jimmy previously set about three pounds of air using the feed valve, and was in about throttle two, pulling the train down the hill. Engineers often chose not to use the dynamic brake to hold the train's speed on this hill. The line is full of curves as sharp as ten degrees. That much curve bind can stretch out a descending train with a lot of empties, but when the rear hits the tangent track, the slack runs in. This line is so crooked, crews had called it 'the Snake' for decades. When I started on the railroad, men holding seniority on the former Marcus Division were referred to as 'Snakemen.' The result of the sharp curvature was a constant run in and run out of the slack. A combination of feed valve braking and a light throttle made for a smooth descent. Both head and rear end crews could safely drink their coffee, the caboose crew could safely move about in the caboose, and the equipment did not get beaten up by repeated slack run out and run in.

Feed valve braking is a braking method in which a very light set of the train air brakes is made by adjusting the feed valve from its normal setting to a setting three or four pounds below normal. The feed valve kept the pressure in the train line at the setting of the feed valve. Feed valve braking was never recognized by the company as a proper braking method, nor was it found in the *Air Brake and Train Handling* rule book. It relied on a leaky train line to lightly apply the brakes and sometimes left brakes set on the rear portion of the train after the feed valve had been reset.

We rounded the curve approaching the 400-foot long Allied Mineral Spur at 25 MPH in this happy condition when Jimmy dumped the air. The switch was lined for the spur. As luck would have it, there were no cars spotted on the spur. Jimmy was applying as much independent engine brake as he could without sliding the wheels. Neither of us thought the train would get stopped soon enough. As the lead unit approached the end of the track I kept waiting to feel the lead unit going on the ground. This was a very long ride; either your mind speeds up or time slows down when you are suddenly riding to the end of the world.

The train stopped without any hard thuds. I got out to take a look and discovered that the lead unit was more than halfway through the dirt pile at the end of the track. The lead unit was still on the rail, but there were only about 18 inches of rail left in front of the lead wheel on one side of the engine. I gave Jimmy a sign with my lantern to back up really easy. Jimmy and I sure were glad that we got stopped, because just beyond the dirt pile was a drop of about 25 feet at about a 30-degree angle that would not have been fun to go down in the F 7. Jimmy and I were positive that because the rail on one side ended before the other side, the F 7 would have rolled onto her side.

The FBI went to work and the very next day a 13-year-old lad was in custody. As usual, the switch lock had been broken open with a rock. I thank the good Lord that the general public did not know how easy it was to force those old-style switch locks open by hitting them with a rock or a hammer.

Another time Gene and I were working the Kettle Falls Turn. I was the rear brakeman that week. Gene was putting the caboose to track 5, but he had been delayed due to a small herd of horses running around the west end of the yard. When he finally got the caboose coupled on track 5, the horses were trapped on the south side of the inbound train sitting on the lead. Something spooked the horses and they ran through the yard between tracks 4 and 5. I was connecting the air hoses on our outbound train and wondering why Gene had not coupled the caboose on yet. When I was almost to the caboose, Gene started hollering at me that a herd of horses was coming toward me between track 4 and track 5. I stepped between two cars and waited. I kept peeking around the corner of that car, looking for the horses. Finally, here they came. I think I counted six horses but I was not sure they were all past me, so I waited a little longer. Finally, I returned to lining the air, while still looking for more wild horses. If I had not been clear of that three and one-half foot space between tracks 4 and 5, I probably would have been trampled to death.

➻ The Nelson Local

The Nelson Local, the Republic Local, and the Kettle Switch Local worked out of Kettle Falls when I hired out in 1960.

The Nelson Local made three round trips to Nelson, British Columbia, each week. It was 104 miles between Kettle Falls and Nelson, including 5.5 miles on the Canadian Pacific. The Local went on duty at Kettle Falls at 6:00 AM Monday, Wednesday, and Friday, and at Nelson at 6:00 AM Tuesday, Thursday, and Saturday. In the 1960s the Nelson Local ran timetable east from Kettle Falls to Nelson and returned westward.

The local crew made up our own train at Kettle Falls, which took about an hour to hour and a half. The Kettle Switch Local (a switching job at Kettle Falls) had previously switched out yesterday's cars for our train and left them in one of the yard tracks, but they did not block the cars in station order. Cars for us on this morning's Kettle Falls Turn were in random order in the train from Hillyard, which was typically in track 1. We spread the yard track, then dug our cars out of this morning's train and spread them. Then we doubled the spread cars together to block our entire train.

Our train included cars to spot on line between Kettle Falls and Troup Junction and interchange traffic for the CP at Nelson. After blocking our train, with CP cars against the caboose, and doubling it together in station order, we went to breakfast while the clerk and agent prepared the customs papers at the depot. After breakfast, we made our air test. By the time the air test was done, the paperwork was ready and the train could depart.

Two or three times a month our first stop was 10 miles out of Kettle Falls at the station of Evans to spot the empty log flats the Chewelah Turn had pulled from Deer Park Lumber. The typical spot was 10 to 15 empty cars and the loaded pull was the same. They generally loaded whatever we spotted.

Janni Spur, 30.6 miles east of Kettle, opened to the west. We dropped 40-foot drop bottom gondola cars into the spur. This was an easy gravity drop since it was downhill into the spur. Traffic from Janni was three to four loads per week of marble rock crushed to gravel size.

At Northport, the conductor got the switch lists from the agent and we did the switching. Northport included a pole yard two lumber mills to switch. The pole yard generated one or two loads of poles per trip and the two lumber mills combined generated four to six loads of lumber per trip.

The Nelson Local went through American customs at Northport. The brakemen opened the doors of all of the empty boxcars so that the customs inspectors could look inside to check for stowaways trying to cross the border into Canada. American inspectors also checked the paperwork on all loaded cars going into Canada to make sure everything was in order. When the paperwork was incomplete or wrong, we set the offending car(s) out at Northport until the proper paperwork could be obtained, which meant the next trip or longer.

After clearing customs, we headed to Waneta, British Columbia, 10.9 miles east of Northport, and less than one mile north of the International Boundary, at an elevation of 1,359 feet. Here, both American and Canadian immigration inspectors checked the train for stowaways, and the Canadians checked to see if all of the crew were U.S. citizens. They also checked the U.S. export documents.

Canada's flagging rules were different. In Canada, even on our own railroad, when a train hit a set of torpedoes, the crew was required to stop and replace the torpedoes that the train had just set off. This was not required under the Great Northern's flagging rules. The Canadian flagging rules were the law, which is why they applied on our railroad. In Canada, the distance the flagman went back to flag a train was determined by the percentage of the descending grade that your train was on. The steeper the grade, the farther back we went to flag.

Shortly beyond the International Boundary, the line crossed the Pend Oreille River. Boundary Dam was located in the Pend Oreille River just upstream of the railroad. The railroad was so close to the dam that if water was being released over the spillway, we could feel the spray as the water cascaded to the river below. The parallel highway bridge is immediately downstream from our railroad bridge and immediately upstream of the confluence of the Pend Oreille and Columbia Rivers.

The Dam Spur, immediately east of the bridge, was built to bring in material to construct the dam. When I worked the Nelson local, the Dam Spur was used as a

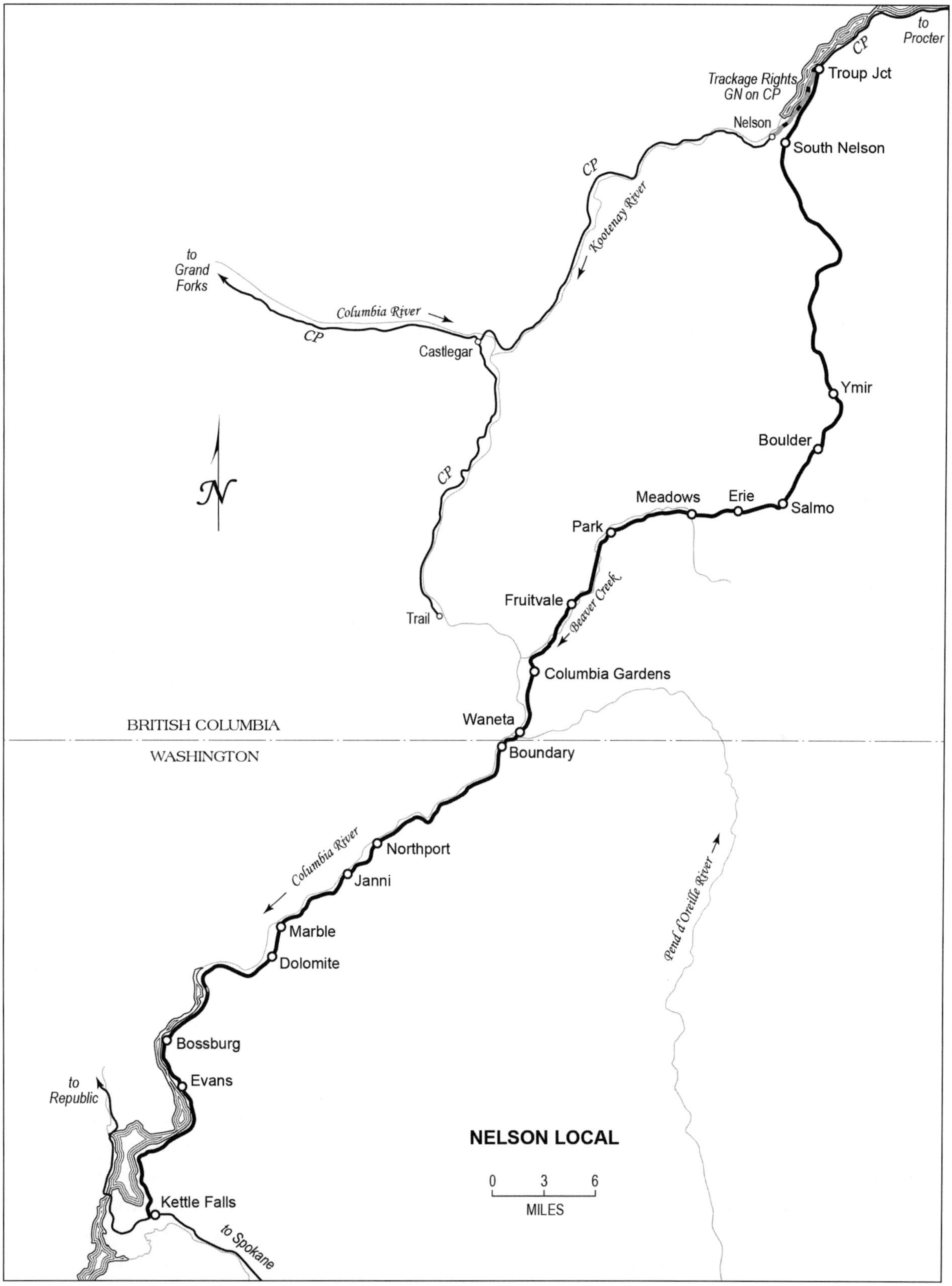

to Procter
CP
Troup Jct
Trackage Rights GN on CP
Nelson
South Nelson
CP
Kootenay River
to Grand Forks
Columbia River
CP
Castlegar
CP
Ymir
Boulder
Meadows
Erie
Salmo
Park
Fruitvale
Beaver Creek
Trail
Columbia Gardens
Waneta
BRITISH COLUMBIA
WASHINGTON
Boundary
Columbia River
Northport
Janni
Marble
Dolomite
Pend d'Oreille River
Bossburg
Evans
to Republic
NELSON LOCAL
0 3 6
MILES
Kettle Falls
to Spokane

transload point where lumber trucked down from Canada was loaded onto flatcars. The spur held about nine cars, but a spot of three to five cars per trip was typical. We put the empties in on the eastward trip and picked up the loads the next day on the way back to Kettle Falls.

About a mile beyond the Dam Spur, the line started up the hill, on a 1.6% compensated grade through Beaver Creek Canyon, which extends a little over nine miles between the Columbia River and Fruitvale, British Columbia. As the line, which was full of curves as sharp as 10 degrees, proceeded up through Beaver Creek Canyon, the creek kept getting deeper in the canyon since the line climbed more steeply than the creek did. About half a mile below Fruitvale, the grade broke to about 0.75% and Beaver Creek ran under the tracks and spilled down to the bottom of the canyon at about a 70-degree angle.

Beyond Fruitvale, elevation 1,984 feet, the grade was almost flat for three and a half miles and then ascended irregularly to a false summit at Erie, elevation 2,337 feet. The line then descended to Salmo at elevation 2,183 feet and ascended again from Salmo to Apex at grades not exceeding 1.6% compensated. Apex, aptly named, was the highest point on the line at 3,036 feet. From Apex, the grade descended for 11.6 miles, most at 2.5 percent grade, compensated for curvature, down to Troup Junction at elevation 1,777 feet. This descent contained many curves of up to 10 degrees, with a few of 14 degrees in the final mile.

At least once in the round trip, we would stop near Apex and get drinking water for the crew in both the engine and the caboose. There was a spring there, and some section men affixed a galvanized pipe into the spring and blocked up the other end so crewmen could walk right up to the pipe and fill our water jugs with the best spring water I ever tasted.

One Friday I was called off the conductors' extra board for a work train out of Northport to take some air dump cars loaded with riprap up Beaver Creek Canyon to repair a slip out. The roadmaster took us by road to Northport, where we picked up the engine, ten air dump cars loaded with riprap, and a flatcar loaded with a Caterpillar bulldozer and a fabricated steel ramp to unload and load the bulldozer. After customs at Waneta, we left the loads of riprap in the siding at Waneta and shoved the flatcar with the bulldozer up the hill into Beaver Creek Canyon to the slip out.

While the operator was unloading the bulldozer, the train and engine crewmen all went and looked at the washout. It had been raining for several weeks, which had saturated the roadbed under the track. The roadbed had slipped out as far back as the end of the ties. The head wall of the slip out dropped straight down for about 25 feet. The hole was about 100 to 150 feet long. I did not think that 10 loads of riprap would make much progress against this hole, but nobody cared about my opinion so I kept it to myself.

It took the B&B guys and the operator about an hour to get the bulldozer off the flat. This excessively long time to unload occurred because the B&B foreman did not bring enough blocking material to properly crib up the ramp that the bulldozer came down, and because the ground was very soft. They finally got the bulldozer on the ground, but it was starting to get dark, so the bulldozer operator and the B&B foreman decided to call it a day and start fresh in the morning. My crew took the engine and the empty flat back to Waneta and tied the engine down.

The roadmaster took us to the motel at Fruitvale, and we were back on duty at 6:00 AM. After breakfast, we headed for Waneta, picked up the engine, and shoved four loads of riprap up the hill to the washout. When our train arrived at the slip out, the operator was just starting up the bulldozer, so we walked up to the washout and found that things had gotten much worse overnight. Now about 150 feet of rail and ties was hanging across the void. There was nothing but air underneath the track, and the hole was about 50 feet deep directly under the track.

The bulldozer operator was ready to start to push the riprap into the hole. I moved the first car of riprap as close as I dared to the edge of the hole and dumped the riprap on the ground next to the track. Then I moved the air dump cars and engine back far enough to give the operator room to work. About this time, I asked myself, "What is going to keep this riprap from going clear to the bottom of the canyon?" My question was answered when the operator started to shove the riprap over the edge of the hole. The riprap went down the side of the canyon, picking up speed as it went, sometimes flying 100 feet between impacts with the ground. A couple of

The Nelson Local with a SD 9 and a GP 9 on the Beaver Creek Bridge in the late 1960s. Both units are in the "simplified paint scheme" introduced in 1962. PHOTO BY LOREN GUENTHER.

boulders went right through 8- to 10-inch diameter trees without even slowing down. Everyone stood there looking at all this riprap splashing into the creek some 500 feet beyond the toe of the slope. It was real quiet for a long time until someone finally said, "Well, back to the old drawing board."

The B&B foreman figured out that until they placed some cribbing down in the hole, he did not need a train crew. This was Saturday afternoon, and he figured it would take about two days to just get the cribbing ready to move up to the site. We were taken back to Yardley and released to the extra boards. The line through Beaver Creek Canyon was shut down for about three weeks. While our line was being repaired, the Canadian Pacific served our customers beyond the slip out. We delivered cars for our isolated stations to the CP at Grand Forks and received cars from those stations at Grand Forks.

At Fruitvale, there were two lumber mills, and one of the mills loaded chip cars. These mills shipped a couple of loads of chips and three to five loads of lumber per trip. The next stop was Hearn Brothers mill at Parks, which loaded lumber into boxcars at their loading dock. Parks was good for one to three loads of lumber a week. From Parks, it was usually a straight run to Salmo.

At Salmo, we spotted empty gondolas for lead and silver ore at the three different ore docks in town. This ore went to Kettle Falls and Hillyard and was interchanged to the UP at Spokane. The most likely destination for this ore was the Bunker Hill smelter at Wallace, Idaho.

A solid bottom "mill gondola" spotted for ore loading at Salmo, British Columbia. Note the ramp behind the car. Dump trucks drove up the ramp, backed onto the elevated apron bringing it to about level, and then dumped their load into the car. PHOTO BY MIKE BARONE.

Some of the lumber loads from Fruitvale, Parks and Boulder went to Nelson as interchange business with the Canadian Pacific, and some went to Kettle Falls and Hillyard to go east or west. The Canadian Pacific put empty CP boxcars into our train at Nelson to handle CP traffic from these three locations. We left the lumber and ore loads going to Hillyard at Salmo and picked them up on our return trip.

After switching Salmo, it was time to eat. The only place to eat was a Chinese restaurant. I cannot remember the name of the restaurant, but the owner's nickname was Charlie, so we called the place 'Salmo Chuck's.' Chuck came out of the kitchen to take our orders but he did not speak English very well, so I never knew what I was going to get for dinner or even if it would be edible. Sometimes when I looked at my plate I could not recognize anything on it. After dinner, the crew stopped by the grocery store to pick up something to eat the next morning between Nelson and Salmo since there were no restaurants close to the hotel at Nelson. The last move at Salmo was to get train orders from the Canadian Pacific dispatcher. The CP dispatcher transmitted orders for our run from Troup Junction to Nelson to the Great Northern agent at Salmo.

Beyond Salmo, the turn usually stopped at Boulder, about three and one third miles east of Salmo. The mill at Boulder loaded two or three cars of lumber a week.

The next station was Ymir. I never stopped at Ymir in all the times I worked the Nelson Local. The only thing I remember about Ymir was the hotel; it was painted purple with lime green trim, and it was the first thing crews saw approaching Ymir.

The trackage arrangement at Troup Junction was unusual. The main came down the mountain on side hill construction. At the bottom of the mountain the original Nelson & Fort Shepard line made about a 180-degree left hand turn that took the line from being headed more or less compass east to headed more or less compass west ending on a dock in Kootenay Lake, where traffic was interchanged with steamboats. In 1895, the line was extended through another 90 degrees of left curve, and about five miles of line was built toward, but not all the way to, Nelson.

When the Canadian Pacific built their line between Nelson and Proctor in 1902, it passed through Troup. By agreement, the CP purchased the GN line between Troup and Nelson, incorporating it into its new line and giving the Great Northern access to Nelson proper over the now CP line, creating Troup Junction.[2]

The arrangement of Troup Junction favored the CP. The CP main line passed through along the base of the mountain tracing a lazy 'S' curve. The GN main off the mountain joined the CP in the middle of the 'S,' with the switch opening to the east, toward Proctor and Crows Nest Pass and the opposite direction from Nelson.

A wye on the lake side of the CP main allowed us to get turned around for the trip to Nelson. The tail of the wye was too short to allow us to turn the whole train, so we were required to make some extra moves to get turned around. The GN main track switch joined the CP main track just west of the east switch of the GN wye. The west switch of the wye was about 35 car lengths west of the GN main track switch and around the bottom curve of the 'S.'

Before a GN train could enter the CP main line at Troup Junction we stopped short, went to the phone, talked to the dispatcher, and got permission to occupy the CP main. The Canadian Pacific train orders provided at Salmo were often conditional; that is, they

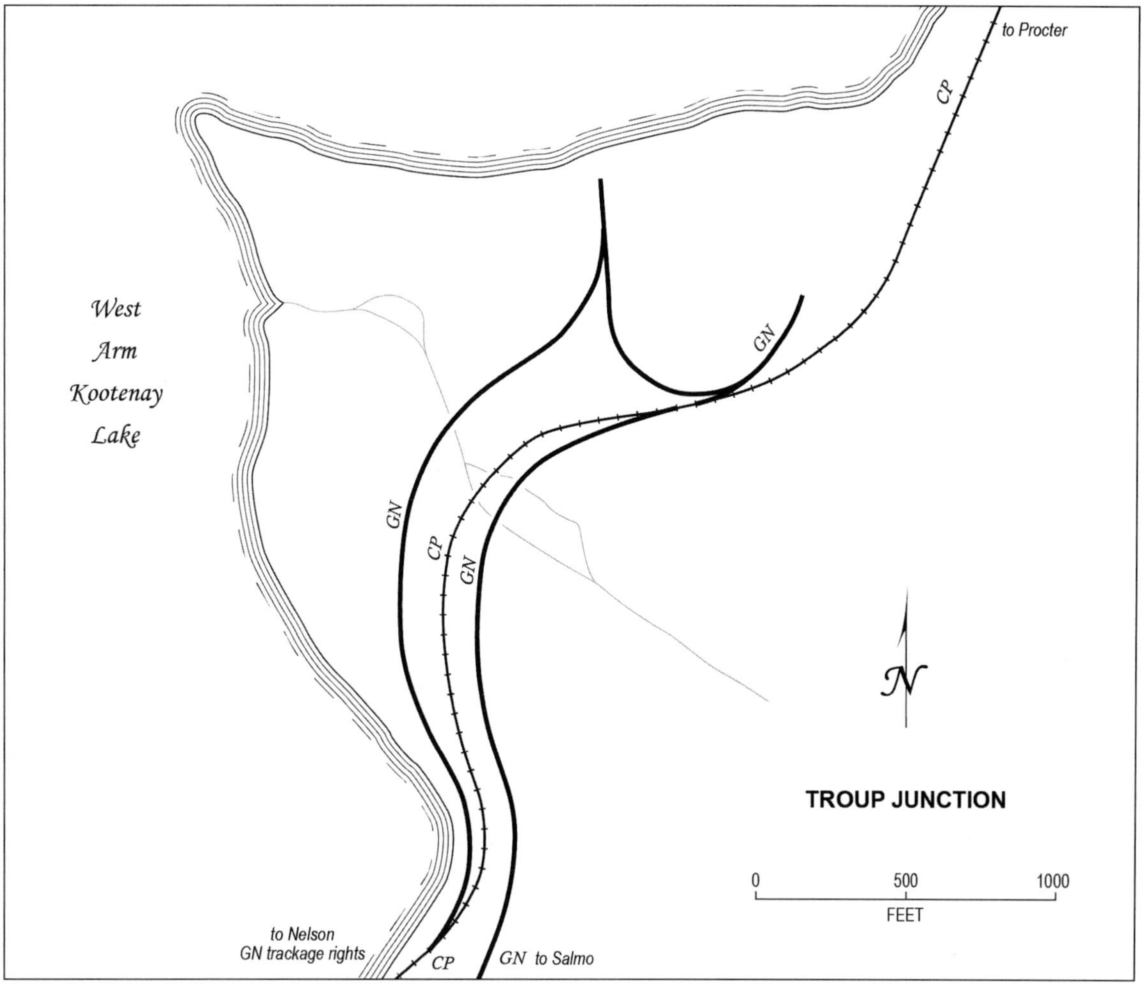

included the phrase "after the departure of extra NUMBER west (or east)." The head brakeman contacted the CP dispatcher to determine whether or not the other train was by. He called every trip, regardless of what our orders said, as directed by the Special Instructions. Even if our orders showed no opposition, things could have changed after they were issued, so checking with the CP dispatcher was an important safety procedure. Our conductor registered at Troup Junction. Sometimes we were required to wait for a westward CP train to go by.

Once the head brakeman got the OK from the CP dispatcher to enter his main track, the brakeman lined the switch and our train rolled out onto the CP main. We stopped and cut off our caboose just to clear on our main track, pulled out to clear the switch, stopped, shoved our train west on the CP main, and left it between our main track switch and the west switch of the wye with room to hold our caboose on the east end. The engine then grabbed our caboose off our main, shoved it to a joint with our train, cut off, and then started around the wye.

Troup Junction featured the only wye that I ever saw with two tail tracks. When our engine moved eastward on the CP main, we passed our main track switch in a trailing point move and came to a facing point switch that gave access to our wye. The two switch points were only about 15 feet apart. Our track beyond the facing point switch extended to the east more or less parallel with the CP main, and at first glance would be taken for a simple spur off the main. This track was not just a spur track; it was actually the east tail track of our wye. The trailing point switch to the east leg of the wye diverged from this east tail track. The switch for the east leg of the wye was about five car lengths east of the fouling point of the switch off the CP main track. The arrangement at Troup Junction was unique in that the first switch one encounters in a wye is trailing point from a vantage point on the main track between switches. Having the trailing point wye switch at Troup Junction placed in the spur track rather than in the CP main track created the unusual second tail track.

The east tail was the result of the track changes made when the CP main was constructed. The original GN alignment here was the beginning of the long turn back curve to the left. The top of CP's 'S' curve to the left began just east of the paired facing point switches. The two roads doubtless agreed that rather than CP installing a low angle crossing for the GN, the CP would install the two facing point switches, probably at CP's expense and ongoing maintenance since the GN had been there first. CP could then build its line through the area while GN operations to the lake dock and beyond continued uninterrupted around the long curve to the lake. When the CP's line was complete between Troup Junction and Nelson, the GN built the wye, placing the east switch in the original curve, part of which became the east tail track and abandoned the balance of turn back curve and the track beyond. Most of the east tail track was at an elevation of about three or four feet below the CP main.

The east tail track could hold two GP units and a snowplow in the clear east of the switch to the east leg of the wye. The extra length provided us with a place to leave a snowplow rather than take it into Nelson. The CP probably wanted an outrageous switch charge to switch and turn the plow at Nelson, so the GN just left the east tail track long enough to accommodate the plow.

In the winter, we would cut the Snow Dozer type snowplow off in the east tail and set a hand brake on the plow. The plow used electricity supplied by an extension cord plugged into the engine to run the headlight and used air pressure from the main reservoir of the engine to move the bat wings, the front cage, and the flanger. Main reservoir pressure was about 160 pounds per square inch.

After leaving the plow, we threw the wye switch and backed around the east leg of the wye toward the second, or north, tail of the wye. The north tail was a normal tail track and it ran straight almost to the shore of Kootenay Lake. There was about five car lengths of room between the switch and the pile of ties at the end of the tail track. We lined the switch and proceeded onto

Engine 221, an Alco RS-3 built in May of 1950 at Troup Junction. The style and placement of the road name is as built. PHOTO BY LOREN GUENTHER.

the west leg of the wye crossing the creek for the second and third time. The west leg was about 30 cars long. After an initial curve to the right, it curved more gently to the left and broadly followed the curve of the CP at the west end where it brought us back to the CP main. We lined the CP main track switch to bring the engine out on the CP main, closed the switch and ran back to our train. We coupled onto the head end of our train, which had been the rear end leaving Kettle Falls, cut in the air, made a quick stub air test, and departed.

Recall that prior to 1960, extra trains were required to display of two white flags by day and two lights of the same color at night. The Canadian Pacific required the display of both flags and lights until the late 1960s. On the Canadian Pacific between Troup Junction and Nelson, the Nelson Local was an extra train, so we displayed both white flags and white class lights while on the CP.

The creek at Troup Junction ran under the CP main track and then split into two channels, with one running under the east leg of the wye and into Kootenay Lake. The other channel split again before it ran under the west leg of our wye at two locations on its way to Kootenay Lake. Late in the fall of the year, as the engine crossed the creek three times while going around the wye, I saw hundreds of Kokanee Salmon with their

black heads and bright red bodies swimming up the stream to spawn. With all the birch, alder, and cedar trees and sword ferns running all the way throughout the wye and down to the lake, this was one of the prettiest spots on the railroad, and one of my favorites.

The CP dispatcher also gave us a head in when we got permission to occupy the CP main. When our train arrived at Nelson, we headed in to the designated yard track, cut the engine off, took it to the roundhouse, and tied up. We were required to tie up by 10:00 PM under the hours of service law, and we generally made it with not much time to spare. Leaving Nelson Yard, we had to walk up six flights of stairs to get to the hotel. After switching cars and shoveling snow out of switches all day the last thing anybody wanted to do was to climb six flights of stairs. After checking into the hotel, we washed up and went down to the bar for some broasted chicken and a schooner of beer. Then it was off to bed since it was now 11:00 PM and the desk clerk will be knocking on the door at 5:00 AM.

We were on duty at 6:00 AM. The CP switch engine made up our train, so all we needed to do was bring our engine out of the roundhouse, get on our train, pump up the air, and wait for the carmen to make the air test. Our train out of Nelson was about 15–20 cars. The head end was made up of interchange cars from the CP to the GN, while the rear end was empty CP boxcars for lumber loading at Boulder, Parks, and Fruitvale. Remember that the ends would get flipped at Troup Junction, putting the through cars against the caboose and the shorts on the head end, as they should be. The Nelson Local was usually on the move by 6:30 AM.

Some mornings it was 'hurry up' at Troup Junction because the CP dispatcher gave us only a short period of time to occupy his main track. In the time allowed, the crew pulled the train past our main track switch, shoved our caboose up our main track just to clear the CP main, and cut it off. Then the engine pulled the train east to clear the GN main track switch and shoved our train west on the CP main, stopping short of the west wye switch but clearing the switch to our main track. We then grabbed our caboose from our main and shoved it to a coupling on our train.

After all that, the engine ran around our train by going around the wye, picking up the snow plow if it was winter time. After going around the wye, the engine was on the Nelson end of the train. The power coupled to the train, made our air test, and shoved east on the CP main past our main track switch. After lining the main track switch, the train started up our line, stopping just in the clear so that the rear brakeman could line the switch for the CP main. The conductor signed the train register and reported by phone to the CP dispatcher that the Nelson Local was clear of the CP main track after the rear brakeman lined the switch for the CP.

When the crew could not get in the clear of the CP main track within the prescribed time, working against a westward CP train, we were required to flag that CP train. CP trains received a train order at an open station east of Troup Junction to wait for us at the next station east of Troup Junction until a designated time. I could not believe how closely the CP trains arrived to the time our orders allotted us to get in the clear at Troup Junction. If it proved impossible to get in the clear by that time, then the GN crew had better be out flagging that train about five minutes before the clear up time the dispatcher had given us, because that train would be there for sure. The CP dispatchers were good; they treated us well and usually gave us every break they could.

Running time from Troup Junction to Apex, 11.6 miles, was about one hour and 25 to an hour and 40 minutes. I can still remember grinding up the hill at 8 to 10 MPH on many occasions with a single EMD SD 7 or 9 or a pair of GP 7 and/or 9 units. The first few trips I made to Nelson, the job got an SD unit for power. They rode smoothly on those big three axle trucks and would walk right up the hill, but very slowly. Later, the usual engine was a pair of geeps. Since the pair of geeps produced twice the horsepower of a single SD, the geeps were twice as fast with any given tonnage. With a heavy train, the GP-7s or 9s could make 12 MPH versus 6 or 7.5 MPH with a SD-7 or SD-9 respectively.

Running time from Apex to Salmo was about 45 minutes. It took about three hours 45 minutes to four hours from our on-duty time of 6:00 AM to get to Salmo without any stops.

The first thing we did at Salmo was go eat. Oooooo, so wonderful, back to Salmo Chuck's for breakfast! After breakfast, we switched out the loads, spotted and respotted the empties, and departed about 11:00 AM for

Nelson Local with BN 1804 and BN 1806, both former Great Northern units, arriving Nelson as a caboose hop. PHOTO BY MIKE BARONE.

Parks and Fruitvale, switching each station as the train proceeded west. By the time the turn left Fruitvale and started down through Beaver Creek Canyon, our train included 20 to 30 cars, and the time was about 3:00 PM. The running time from Fruitvale to Waneta was just over an hour since the speed limit through Beaver Creek Canyon was 10 MPH.

Our next stop was the Dam Spur where we pulled two to four loads. To pick up at the Dam Spur, the head brakeman cut our train off short of the spur, switched out the loads setting them to the main line, and respotted any empties. He then picked up the loads ahead of the engine, cut the air into the loads, and reached back to pick up the train.

At Waneta, we cut the train off short of the road crossing and the siding switch, shoved the lumber loads down the main track, cut them off between the siding switches, and ran the engine around the cars by running through the siding to get the loads behind the engine. We then made a joint on the cars, shoved them back to the train, and pulled the train ahead to the customs and immigration offices for both the United States and Canada to inspect the train for stowaways and to check the crew. By the time the switching and customs formalities were done at Waneta, it would be between 4:00 to 4:30 PM.

Running time to Northport was about 40 minutes. The American customs inspectors required us to let them finish their inspection of the train before doing any switching, so we went to the restaurant to eat before switching Northport. Northport took a little longer to switch than most towns with just a few industries since they were spread over about a half a mile and all movements over the yard tracks were at 10 MPH.

When the switching was done, we made our air test and departed for Janni spur. We pulled whatever they had loaded. Our last stop was at Evans to pull the log loads, and then it was off to Kettle Falls with an arrival of about 8:30 to 9:00 PM. The Switch Local crew usually told us to head down the main track, cut the engine off to clear the far leg of the wye, and take the engine to the house, which was between the wye switches. Tying the engine down was the end of our day.

➸ The Republic Local

When I first went to Kettle Falls in 1960, the Republic Local worked the 80.7 miles from Kettle Falls to Republic and returned the same day on Monday, Wednesday, and Friday. On Tuesday and Thursday, the Republic Local crew, engine, and caboose made a turn to Dolomite to serve the limestone mine located off the east end of Dolomite siding on the Nelson line. The Republic job was a daylight job, going to work at 8:00 AM at Kettle Falls.

As soon as the Nelson Local departed from Kettle Falls, the Republic Local crew brought our engine out of the house, up the main line to the west end of the yard, and started to build our train. We fanned our cars out in the yard tracks and the main, blocking the cars by station. Then we picked them up in station order and set them to the main track against the caboose and the cars for Republic and San Poil. The brakemen opened all the doors of empty boxcars at Kettle Falls so that when the train went through customs, the inspectors could look inside each car. As soon as the conductor got our train list, waybills, and customs paperwork in order, and the rest of the crew completed our air test, the train departed for Republic.

Once in a while there would be an empty lumber boxcar or a load of company material for Dulwich, Barstow, or Orient, but the train usually ran straight to the border at Laurier, Washington, across from which on the Canadian side was Cascade, British Columbia. After clearing the joint U.S. and Canadian customs, the train headed for Grand Forks, but first the line ran through a Doukhobor settlement.

The Doukhobors were people of Russian descent who left Russia to escape religious persecution by Russia's nineteenth-century czars. They ended up in this far corner of Canada, settling in the Grand Forks and Castlegar areas. It was common to see the Doukhobor women out working in their gardens with only a big straw hat on their heads . . . and nothing else. They were just out there in the buff. The Doukhobors were not popular with the citizens of Grand Forks due to their tendency to burn their own people's homes or barns if they felt that someone was holding back on their contribution to the community store house. The English heritage citizens of Grand Forks and Castlegar did not mix well with the Russian Doukhobors.

The Republic Local usually got a load or two of lumber from the CP transfer at Grand Forks and usually set a couple of empties to the CP transfer. The tail of our wye connected directly with the tail of a CP wye. This joint tail track of the two wyes was our interchange track with the CP. Off the tail of our wye there was a spur where the black slag from the Granby copper smelter, which shut down in 1919, was loaded. Trucks brought the slag from the long-abandoned Granby smelter site on the other side of town to the spur. The shipper used an auger from the ground to the top of the covered hoppers to load the slag into 100-ton capacity covered hopper cars. The slag moved to United States Navy shipyards in Bremerton and San Diego for use in sandblasting. The Navy found that the very hard slag lasted much longer than sand in sandblasting.

Our next stop was at Carson, British Columbia/Danville, Washington to go through customs again. Any loaded boxcar that came into Canada at Laurier that was going through Canada and back into the U.S. was required to have a customs seal put on the car at Laurier. That customs seal was removed at Carson/Danville by the U.S. and Canadian customs officers. When released, we departed for Curlew.

At Curlew we set out some log flats for loading and then headed for Republic. We stopped at Curlew on our return trip to pick up loaded log flats. At the north end of Curlew Lake, the track crossed a wood pile trestle about 650 feet long. We ran by San Poil spur, to be switched on the way back since the spur was facing point going to Republic.

At Republic we cut our train off on the main between siding switches, took the engine around the wye, and stopped at the depot to get the switch list for Republic and the lumber mill at San Poil. The only traffic the Great Northern received at Republic was one solid bottom gondola per month. This gondola spotted on the house track just east of the depot. The Knob Hill gold mine spent about a week welding all the drain holes closed so that the high-grade concentrate would not

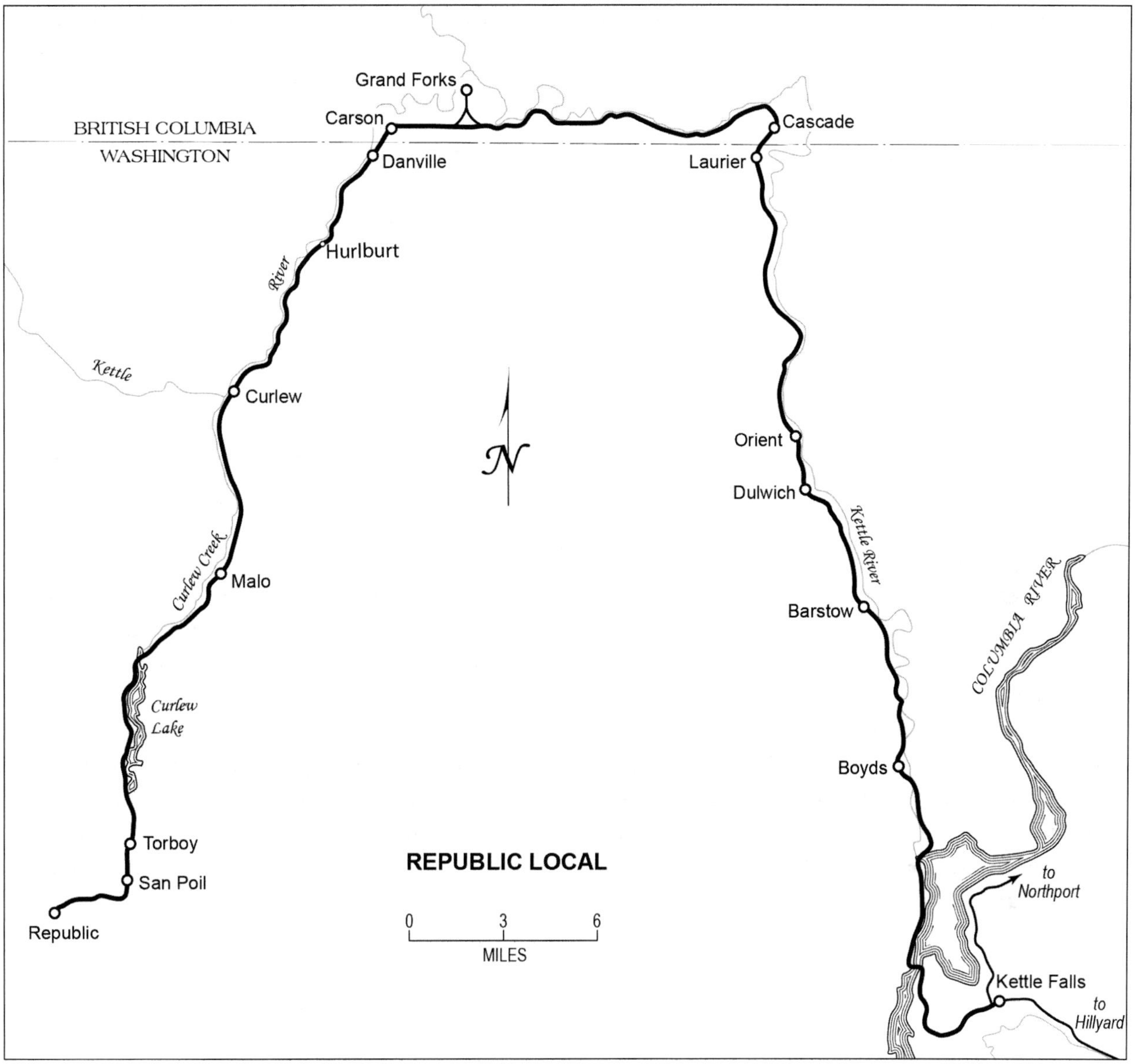

leak out. Before leaving Republic, we switched out our inbound train to line up the cars to be spotted at the San Poil mill and to put the caboose to the rear. If today's train included excess cars for San Poil, we left them on track 2, which lay parallel with the siding. The empty cars usually moved to the San Poil mill on the next trip. After switching out our train, we made an air test and departed for San Poil.

At the San Poil Lumber spur, the crew cut the caboose off on the main track to hold six to eight cars. Holding on to the empty cars, we went into the spur and made a joint on the cars. It was always necessary to gather up the track because the lumber loaders always rolled one or two loaded cars past the end of the lumber loading dock. The brakemen connected the air hoses as the engine gathered up the track. In the early 1960s, all loads of lumber at this mill were hand loaded into 40 and 50-foot long boxcars.

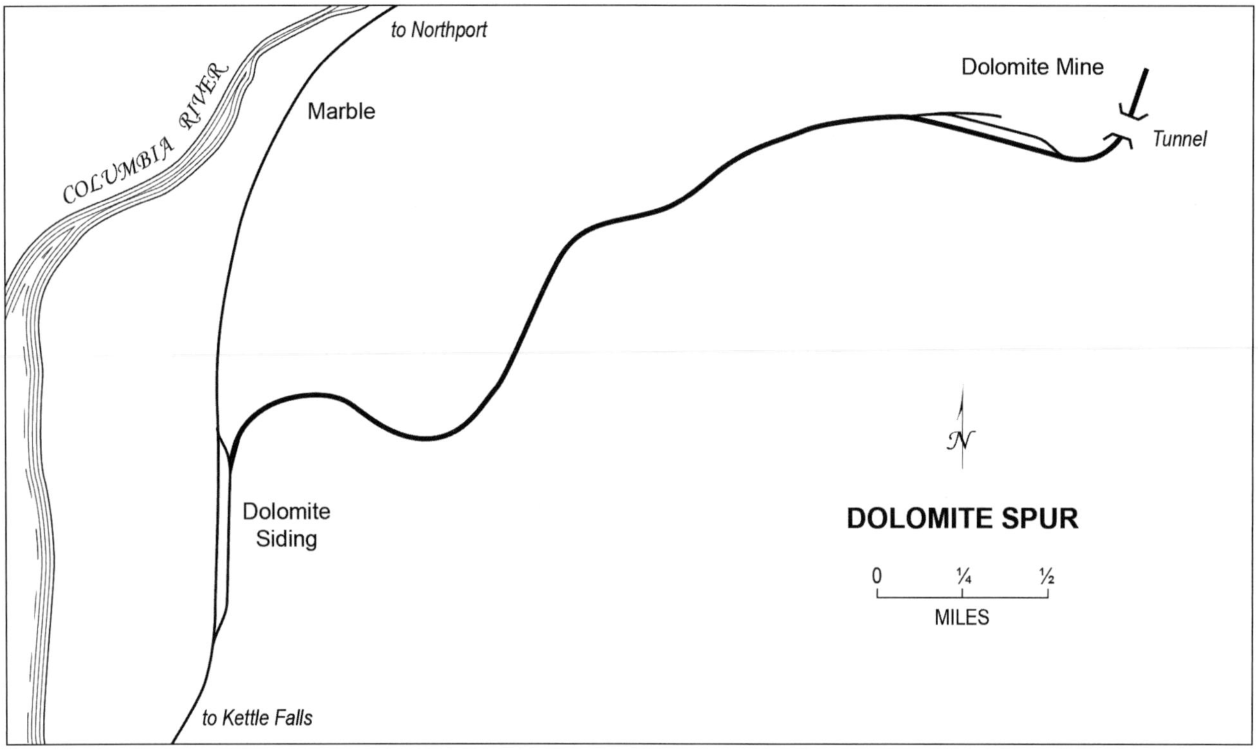

In later years the San Poil mill started to load chips. A few years later, after Biles-Coleman at Omak on the W–O line started to load bulkhead flatcars of lumber, the San Poil mill also began to load bulkhead flats. This complicated the switching since everything was on one track. The boxcar lumber dock was first in. Next in was the chip loader. The mill crew loaded the bulkhead flatcars on the far end of the track, which was extended to provide room for the flats. The walkway along the chip loading spot and the adjacent bulkhead flatcar loading spot was a big muddy mess.

Sometime in the 1980s, the San Poil mill received a federal grant to rebuild and expand the mill, since the area suffered from high unemployment. This helped the mill, and really helped with the unemployment problem in the Republic area, but they did not improve the messy areas we were required to work in. Traffic from San Poil expanded to 10 to 12 loads per trip in the 1980s and most of the lumber was shipped on center beam flats rather than boxcars.

During the 1980s, the Republic Local was bulletined to make three round trips per week to Republic, staying overnight in Republic. By this time the mill at Midway was trucking lumber to Curlew and loading 85-foot center beam flats cars at Curlew. This Canadian lumber amounted to about eight to 10 loads per trip. Between the increase in lumber traffic and the increase in shipments of smelter slag from Grand Forks, the car count of the Republic Local had tripled from the early 1960s, but the tonnage increased even more than that due to the use of the bigger cars.

Back in the 1960s, before the increase in business on the Republic line and when the local was making only three one day turns per week, the Republic Local crew made a Dolomite Turn on Tuesday and Thursday. The Dolomite Turn served the limestone mine located off the east end of Dolomite siding, 24.5 miles east of Kettle Falls on the Nelson line. Dolomite is a species of limestone with high magnesium content.

The spur to the mine ran eastward up the hill from the east end of Dolomite siding on a 1.75% average grade for about 3.75 miles to a run around track that held 22 ore cars. The ore cars were the 24-foot long iron ore 'jimmies.' A spur off the west end of the run around could hold three 40-foot drop bottom gondolas. This was the AS&R Spur, which stood for American Smelting & Refining. The cars we spotted here were loaded with lead and zinc ore that went to the coast, probably to the ASARCO smelter at Tacoma.

At Dolomite, the train stayed on the main track to the east end of the siding and backed into the siding to clear the switch to the Dolomite Spur. It was quicker to run up the main to the east end and shove back than it would have been than to head in, stopping twice, running slowly through the siding, and then stopping to line the switch to the spur at the east end. The rear brakeman restored the main track switch for the main and opened the spur track switch which was directly in front of us as the train sat on the siding. The train then pulled up the hill to the run around track.

At the top of the hill the engineer stopped and the head brakeman removed the derail that was located about 200 feet west of the west switch of the run around. The track on top of the hill was on a slight down grade to the west. The derail was there to protect us in case any cars got away from the shipper's loading crew, for they would certainly have run away once they hit the steep part of the hill.

The engineer pulled the train into one of the tracks between the switches, either the run around track or the main track, whichever way the switch was lined. We then cut the engine off the train, ran it ahead to the loaded ore jimmies, and coupled into the head car.

Immediately past the east switch of the run around track, the spur went around a curve to the left and entered a cut. The walls of the cut grew higher until we reached the first of the loaded ore jimmies, about 10 cars west of the tunnel portal, which was about 700 feet east of the east run around track switch. An "Engine Stop" sign sat right at the mouth of the tunnel. The reason for the stop sign was that the tunnel ceiling was too low to clear the engine and the cupola on the caboose. In fact, the tunnel was just high enough to clear the tops of the ore cars.

The shipper's loading equipment was on the far end of the tunnel. Dolomite rock was stored in any of four elevated loading bins. The loading crew loaded two ore jimmies at a time. The shipper's track, and the track through the tunnel, lay on a slight down grade toward the run around track. This grade made it easy for the loading crew to roll the loaded cars downhill using the hand brake to control the speed and stop their two car cuts. The hand brakes were set on the first two cars, plus another seven or eight cars scattered throughout the cut. We found it necessary to connect the air hoses between every other car, which is how we knew that the men loading the ore jimmies rolled them down two cars at a time. As the brakeman walked back toward the engine after connecting the air hoses, he released the handbrakes on the entire cut.

The practice was to always cut the air into the loaded cars and charge them with air right where they sat. When the air gauges on the engine showed that the air was equalizing, and the engineer could hear the air flow through the feed valve slow down, he began to creep down toward the main or the run around track, whichever was clear. We stopped the loaded ore jimmies between switches, set some hand brakes, and cut away from the loads.

Then we ran the engine past the switch and lined the switch towards the caboose and the empty ore jimmies. A brakeman made a joint on the caboose, cut the air into the caboose and the empty cars, and shoved towards the tunnel. We stopped just over the east run around switch, tied some hand brakes on the empty ore jimmies, and cut away from the ore jimmies while hanging onto the caboose and any empty gondola cars for the AS&R Spur. We then pulled down into the open track and cut the caboose and any gons off, setting the hand brake on the caboose. Next, we went down to the west end, came against the loads, and cut in the air. When the air released, we shoved to a joint on the empties and cut in the air.

The brakeman at the joint between the loads and the empties then gave the engineer a "come ahead" sign and climbed in between the last empty car and the first load while the engineer shoved both empties and loads towards the tunnel. The brakeman was required to ride the end of a car, between the cars, because there was not enough clearance between the side of the cars and the tunnel walls to clear a man on the side of the cars. The engineer shoved into the tunnel until he was at the "engine stop" sign. He did not move until the rear brakeman walked out of the tunnel and gave him a backup sign.

This shove was done with no signs after the rear brakeman gave the engineer that sign to come ahead after making the joint on the empties with the loads. When the engineer stopped at the engine stop sign, the first two empty ore jimmies were spotted under the first loading hopper. The rear brakeman closed the angle cock on the rear load, tied some hand brakes on the empty cars, pulled the pin lifters on both cars between the loads and the empties, and walked through the tunnel to the engine. This was all done without the aid of a radio or hand signs and would not be allowed with today's rules. Portable radios were not available on the railroad at this time. After the brakeman came out of the tunnel, he gave the engineer a backup sign. We backed down the clear track with the loaded ore jimmies and cut them off to clear the other track.

If there were loads to pull from the AS&R Spur, and/or empties to spot there, now was the time to switch the AS&R Spur. If there were loads to pull, we ran in and pulled the loads out of the spur, coupled them to the caboose, and cut in the air. If our train included any empty gondolas for the AS&R Spur they were against the caboose leaving Kettle Falls and they would now be on the other end of the caboose from any loads and from the engine. To spot the empty gons, we backed the engine, any loaded gons, the caboose, and the empty gons over the AS&R switch, shoved the empty gons to spot, tied the hand brakes, cut the cars off, and came out of the spur.

Our last move was to shove the loaded gons and caboose up the clear track over the switch at the east end and cut them off. After cutting the engine off, the head brakeman stopped the engine just beyond the east switch and lined it for the loaded ore jimmies. The head brakeman took the engine down to the west end, threw the switch, and coupled to the loaded ore jimmies. The rear brakeman, meanwhile, bled the air from the brake reservoirs of the caboose and any loaded gons so that they would roll down onto the east end of the loaded ore jimmies. The rear brakeman controlled the speed of the gons and caboose using the hand brake on the downhill end of the cut.

The engineer pumped the train up with air until the cars quit singing and the air gauge in the caboose held at 90 lbs. Only then would the brakemen signal the engineer to set the air. The two brakemen walked the set checking every car to make sure all the brakes were working. Each ore jimmy provided only 1,000 cubic feet of capacity, but that much dolomite weighed 75 tons, so the gross weight per car was 95 tons. The 20-car cut weighed 1,900 tons and was only 480 feet long. A runaway train on the grade would have been too exciting for words and could have been fatal. Years before I hired out, two loaded ore jimmies got away from the loading crew at the mine and came down the hill. About a half mile below the run around track there was a pile of dolomite strewn over 100 feet. The dolomite was about 75 feet from the track, showing where the loaded jimmies came back down. That pile of dolomite was a constant reminder that it could be a fatal mistake to short cut our air test.

While he walked the release, the head brakeman always set up about eight retainers on the head end for the trip down the grade, which exceeded 2.5% for over half a mile. Retainers allow the engineer to release the air and recharge the train line and the auxiliary reservoirs on the cars, because cars with the retainer set up will not immediately release. With the retainers set up, the usually quick release of the brakes took place very slowly. The retainers thus retained the air in the brake cylinder and kept the brakes applied, which allowed the auxiliary reservoirs on the cars to be recharged with the brakes still set.

This was in the days before the GP units were equipped with the pressure maintaining feature. Pressure maintaining is a feature of all 26-L brake valves, and certain modified D-24 and DS-24 brake valves. It provides for maintaining normal service brake pipe pressure to compensate for brake pipe leakage during a non-emergency brake application. The pressure maintaining feature allowed the discontinuance of retainers in some situations.

Our engineer set some air in the train and began to pull the train against the air. He slowed down to a crawl by just backing off on the throttle so the rear brakeman could line the derail to the derailing position. After the rear brakeman lined the derail back and jumped on the caboose, the engineer would widen on the throttle and pull the train down the hill. If the engineer got a good set of air on the air brakes, he could pull the train down the hill in throttle one or two. This is another example of power braking.

At Dolomite siding, the head brakeman dropped off

at the switch and knocked the retainers off as the engineer pulled the train by him. The engineer notched out on the throttle to keep the train moving as the grade leveled off, and then reduced the throttle as the number of retainers in the train was reduced. When the engineer pulled the train past the switch, we stopped, lined the switch for the siding, and opened the main track switch on the east end of Dolomite siding. We then shoved out to the main, stopped, lined the main track switch for the main, and were off for Kettle Falls.

The loaded ore jimmies of dolomite went to Hillyard on the Kettle Falls Turn. The transfer job between Hillyard and Spokane Yard set them out on the OW interchange track. Since the name of the company that operated the Dolomite mine in 1970 was Spokane Portland Cement, I suspect now that they were the consignee and that their cement kiln was in the Spokane Valley east of Spokane and served by the Spokane International line of the Union Pacific.

Dolomite station and spur were both built in the spring of 1943 to reach the dolomite deposit, not for the limestone, but for the magnesium in the limestone. During WWII, magnesium was a strategic material used to strengthen the aluminum used to build airplanes. Between 1941 and 1943, 15 magnesium plants were built in the United States, 13 by the government. AFE 65351, which provided for the siding and the beginning of the spur, says that the balance of the track was to be built by Electro-Metallurgical Company, which expected to ship 30 cars per day to their plant at Mead, which I knew as the Pacific Alloy plant near Kaiser Aluminum. The dolomite evidently did not work well in the Mead plant, or sufficient magnesium was produced by the other plants, because by January 1 of the next year, the quarry was owned by Spokane Portland Cement.

The Kettle Switch Local

The Kettle Switch Local went to work at 12 noon Monday through Saturday. The first thing this crew did was switch out the yard. The remains of the inbound Kettle Falls Turn were scattered about the entire yard. The Kettle Switch Local separated the cars from the inbound Kettle Falls Turn for the Nelson and Republic locals, and left those cars in separate blocks on tracks 2, 3 or 4.

The Kettle Switch also switched out their own cars as they cleaned up the yard. They lined up cars for Boise Cascade at West Kettle and for Matinees Lumber at Boyds on the Republic branch, and for Colville and Arden, which were east of the yard, toward Hillyard.

The Kettle Switch served Boise and Matinees first. Boise received two or three loads of veneer, the wood peelings used to make plywood, from the Kettle Falls Turn in boxcars that were not equipped with doors. The door openings on one side of the car featured four 6" × 6" posts bolted vertically in the door, while on the other side the four posts were removable. All the loads of veneer had to be turned so that the removable posts were on the dock side in the building for unloading at Boise Cascade. The Kettle Switch turned the cars by taking them around the wye. Boise shipped five or six boxcars of plywood and three or four loads of wood chips per day. Matinees shipped two or three loads of lumber and about one car load of chips per day. When the Kettle Switch got back to Kettle Falls, they weighed the lumber and plywood loads in their train and shoved it all into track 5, grabbed the cars for Colville and Arden, and headed east.

We weighed all the loads except the wood chips because most freight rates were on a weight basis. The cars were weighed so the company knew how much to charge the customer for moving each car. The rule in those days was to weigh cars as near as possible to the origin point. Cars were weighed one at a time, uncoupled. This slow process was due to the design of the scale and concern about weight transfer through the couplers if the cars were coupled.

At Colville, the job switched the Vaagen Brothers saw mill for both lumber and wood chips. Once in a while we got an inbound boxcar for the feed store. The Kettle Switch then departed for Arden and switched the saw mill there. The mill at Arden changed names twice while I worked the Kettle Falls line. In the late 1980s, Plum Creek purchased the mill, and in the 1990s Stimson Brothers purchased the mill. The Arden mill was always good for five or six box or flatcars of lumber in about any combination, and two or three loads of chips per day.

When I hired out in 1960, and for most of that decade, the Kettle Falls Turn switched the saw mill at Arden. With the increase in business combined with the hours of service being shortened from 16 hours to 14, and two years later coming down to 12 hours, the Kettle Falls Turn did not have time to switch Arden, so Arden was added to the duties of the Kettle Falls Switch.

The Kettle Switch came back from Colville with 14 to 18 loads of lumber and wood chips. The crew weighed all the lumber and plywood loads using the track scale and set them to track 5 along with the loads of wood chips. After the weighing was done, the crew went to eat and wait for the Nelson or Republic locals to arrive.

The Nelson Local usually arrived first. By the time they arrived, our engine was on the West Yard Lead or in the west end of a yard track. When the Nelson arrived, our conductor told them to head down the main line, stop, and cut their caboose off west of the scale track switch. When the rear car was east of the scale track switch, we stopped them, and they cut their engine off the train. They would then slip into the east end of the wye and tie up on one of the engine tracks that extended between the two legs of the wye.

After the Nelson Local cut off their train, our engine went west on the scale track and got their caboose off the main. We then ran east on the scale track and the switching lead into track 5 and set the caboose into the east end of the industry track that ran off track 5 westward towards the crossing. In the 1990s, the caboose track was moved to one of the engine tracks so that the chemical toilets could be serviced.

After putting the Nelson Local's caboose away, we bled the air from the cars in their train and weighed all the loads except the wood chips. Wood chips moved on per car rates, so they did not have to be weighed. I know that some of the chip cars were overloaded because I saw water running out of the bottom of the cars from snow that was falling when the mill loaded the chip cars. I mean running in streams out of the bottom of the car. By the time I could hold the Kettle Switch, our work day was down to 12 hours by federal law. I still remember weighing cars at 11:00 PM when our hours of service expired at 12 midnight. Many, many times we worked right up to the last minute.

When the Republic Local arrived, it was the same routine. Put the caboose to the caboose track and weigh and switch the loaded cars and continue building the outbound Kettle Falls Turn on track 5. Shorts for the Kettle Falls Turn to set out on line, like logs from Evans for the mill at Deer Park, went on the head end of the outbound train at Kettle Falls. The Kettle Switch usually set the shorts to the east end of track 1. If the outbound train was short enough, our crew would double the shorts to the east end of track 5.

Sometime in the 1990s, the BN finally convinced the Canadian government to allow it to abandon the Nelson line beyond Salmo. Later, the BN sold the line from Columbia Gardens, 3.8 miles beyond Waneta, to Salmo for operation by a lumber mill controlled short line. A couple of years after the sale to the short line, the line between Columbia Gardens and Salmo was removed and sold for scrap. About the time of the sale, Consolidated Mining & Smelting Company of Canada (Cominco), the owners and operators of the Trail, British Columbia smelter, built a transloading facility at Quirk, just across the border in Canada to load tank cars with sulfuric acid and molten sulfur. Sulfur and sulfuric acid are shipped from Quirk to this day.

The Republic line was removed between San Poil and Republic in the early 1990s after the shipments of ore concentrate from Republic ended. Vaagen Brothers at Colville bought the San Poil mill. In 2004, the mill at San Poil closed forever, and in 2007 the track was removed from about 200 feet west of the west switch at Danville, Washington to San Poil. Today the mill at Midway, British Columbia is gone, and the line again has been cut back to Grand Forks. If not for the black slag still being shipped out of Grand Forks, I think the line would be removed all the way back to West Kettle Falls. It is sad to think that this entire railroad is now gone.

Endnotes

1 Duane Becker, *The Great Northern Railway, Priest River, Idaho to Hillyard, Washington 1890 to 1920*. Great Northern Railway Historical Society Reference Sheet No. 376, June 2012, 20.

2 Roger G. Burrows, *Railway Mileposts: British Columbia Volume II: The Southern Routes from the Crowsnest to the Coquihalla* (North Vancouver BC: Railway Milepost Books, 1984), 48.

6. The Main Line West of Hillyard

Introduction

This chapter will cover chain gang, or through freight, service and then will move to a discussion of through freight operations west of Hillyard. Specific trains, the work they did, and the blocks of traffic they carried in the last decade of the Great Northern are reviewed in detail. The East Pig and train Number 5 are also discussed.

Chain Gang

I previously mentioned 'through freight,' or 'chain gang' service. These were also known as 'pool jobs.' The East Chain Gang Pool protected, that is, served as the source of crews for, the main line traffic to Troy, Montana, while the West Chain Gang Pool protected the main line traffic to Wenatchee. 'East' and 'West' refer to the direction each pool covered from Hillyard. At any given time, there were a fixed number of train crews and engine crews in each pool.

At Hillyard, the train crew and the engine crew completed their days and separately advised the crew caller of the time they went off duty. The crew caller then placed each crew at the bottom of the chain gang call list, noting the time off and the earliest time that he could call them. In the early 1960s, the minimum rest time was eight hours, unless a man had previously worked a full 16 hours on duty. If a man had worked 16 hours, he was required to get 10 hours of rest. For this reason, tie ups at 15 hours, 55 minutes were the norm.

When the Hillyard crew caller was advised that a train would be ready to run and when, he called a train crew and an engine crew for that train. The crew called was the one 'first out,' that is, at the top of the caller's list. Train crews were assigned together, for example, conductor Langlot, and brakemen Smith and Jones. Engine crews were also together, engineer and fireman, but the train crews and engine crews were assigned separately. The reason for this was that there were always more engine crews in the engine pool than there were train crews in the trainmen pool. The Hillyard crew caller also filled the jobs of men who laid off with men from the appropriate extra board.

Earl Currie provided the following explanation of the origin of the term 'chain gang':

> The term chain gang came into use because of the irregular nature of through freight service in which employees can have no set times, or even days of the week for going to work. Many of the trains they handle are not operated on a set schedule, so a group of crews must be available for call whenever the company decides to run such trains.
>
> Most railroads also man their scheduled trains with chain gang crews, even though these trains do operate on a schedule rather than as needed basis. In that way, they have the flexibility to consolidate or annul scheduled trains on a day by day basis, depending on the volume of business available each day. Having crews assigned to scheduled merchandise trains is restrictive and does not give railroads the flexibility they like to have in managing the number of trains to be run, and when to run them.
>
> The term chain gang has the connotation of prisoners working in the fields or on a construction job in which they are chained together and cannot escape from the work. Likewise, on a railroad's chain gang, a man cannot get away from having to be ready for a call to work at almost any time. It is difficult for employees and their families to plan for activities outside of work because they never know how much time they will have off duty

> between trips or when they will return home. They are wedded to the railroad. The railroad is their way of life, and almost their whole life, when they are in the chain gang or on the extra board. Men are chained to the railroad and its whims, its ups and downs, and the always changing lineup, the current list of trains that the railroad plans to run.
>
> Since crews work on a first-in, first-out basis, crewmen must be constantly looking to see where they stand in the rotation to make sure they do not miss a call. The lineup often changes unexpectedly. A man may think he will be called in eight hours, but something changes and the call comes much sooner. If that man failed to stay close to the telephone, he may miss a call and a trip, lose earnings, and be in trouble with the boss.

The chain gang used to be a young man's game. Chain gang jobs were relatively easy, paid well for the time involved, and there was a good spirit of camaraderie among the crews. The guys in the chain gang looked forward to the day when they would be able to hold a regular job in passenger service or scheduled local freight service. Today, there are few such jobs available, and most employees will spend their careers in chain gang service.

When I started on the railroad, the state of Washington enforced a 'full crew law' which mandated that if a train on the main line exceeded 24 cars, then a third brakeman was required. In the east pool, the third man worked to Newport, Washington, got off, and worked the next train back to Hillyard.

In the west pool, the third man was on for the entire trip. When the train to be handled by a chain gang crew exceeded 24 cars, as was the usual case, the required third man was called off the Hillyard extra board. At Wenatchee, the third brakeman might not come back to Hillyard with the same crew that he worked to Wenatchee with. The most common reason was that his crew worked back on the East Pig, which often required only two brakemen. In this case, the third brakeman would work back to Hillyard on the next available train over 24 cars, and the third brakeman who came to Wenatchee with that conductor stayed in Wenatchee. The unused third brakeman in Wenatchee usually got balanced out by one of these three methods: filling up a short crew that arrived on train Number 5 when they returned on a long train; working back on the East Pig even if not required by law; or being deadheaded back to Hillyard. Washington State voters repealed the full crew law on November 8, 1966.

At the 'away' terminal, the crew caller kept a list of crews in town and when they were rested. The away crew callers were generally spared the need to deal with layoffs since a crewman at Wenatchee or Troy wanted to go home. They would work back to home unless they were very sick, seriously injured, or dead.

An important disadvantage to chain gang service is that you never knew when you would go to work and when you would get back. Your social life and your body clock were both a total mess. When I first started to work the west end chain gang, the lineup information that let us predict when we would be going to go to work was pretty good, which made chain gang more livable.

When things went wrong in through freight service, like when the train broke in two, the easy ride was over. The most common cause of a break in two was a broken coupler knuckle. Replacing a broken knuckle was and is hard work. The only question was how hard and in what weather. In the full crew days, replacing a knuckle sometimes meant two men putting a broom handle through the hole in the knuckle and walking a replacement knuckle up to the break in the train over rough ground. Then we had to figure out how to pass signs to the engineer to put the train back together. The arrival of the portable radio took most of the misery out of passing signals.

I replaced knuckles by myself after they pulled the brakeman off in through freight service, and at 55 years of age it was not fun. Knuckles are heavy. A type E knuckle weighs about 65 pounds, and an F weighs about 75 pounds.

Starting from the engine cab with the engineer since we were no longer using a caboose, I walked back, inspecting the train to see what was wrong. At the broken knuckle, I looked to see what type it was, E or F, called the engineer, and told him what type was needed. The two types are not interchangeable. He went through the units to find the correct type of knuckle. He threw it off, leaving a burning fusee by the knuckle, and pulled the train ahead with me hanging on a car until I stopped him using my portable radio. If the knuckle was out of the rear car of the cut, I put the knuckle in, shoved back to the train, coupled the train together, stretched the coupling, cut in the air, and walked back to the head end. If the broken knuckle was in the first car on the rear portion of the train, I loaded the knuckle onto the rear car of the cut, hanging it on the truck side frame. I would then have the engineer shove back, always stopping well short of making a joint to provide room so that I could safely replace the broken knuckle.

Replacing the knuckle is the hard part. You have to lift the knuckle and place it in the coupler body, and you must keep the pin lifter all the way up to get the knuckle into its final position. There are two ways to keep the lifter up to slide the knuckle into place. One is to borrow some wire off a farmer's fence to wire the pin lifter up. The other is to tear off a piece of rotten fence post to prop the pin lifter up. Imagine doing this in the winter with a couple of feet of snow on the ground, and you can see that chain gang was not all it was cracked up to be at times.

Another problem that happened on occasion was having two air hoses that hung a little too low. The air hoses would hit the crossing planks between the rails at a road crossing, bounce up, and come apart, causing the train to go into emergency stop. Under these conditions, if you did not have any nylon ties to tie the air hoses together, then you looked around for some good old fence wire. Some of the guys carried wire in their pockets for just this reason.

➸ Eastward Trains

Eastward symbol freight trains No. 82 and No. 88 originated daily at Balmer Yard in Seattle, also known as Interbay, and ran to Union Yard in Minneapolis. These symbol train numbers were not traditional GN numbers, but were CB&Q numbers adopted by GN in 1963 in anticipation of the BN merger. Most days there was also an extra east, or Drag East, from Balmer to Wenatchee, and from Wenatchee to Hillyard.

Train No. 82, the hottest eastward train, left Balmer Yard at 12:01 AM carrying only 'Gavin and beyond' traffic and, except for empty auto rack and auto parts cars, the train was all loads. Gavin was the name of the hump yard located at Minot, North Dakota. At Everett Junction, No. 82 picked up only loads for Gavin and beyond. In the late 1960s, it ran with three SD-45 or U-33C units for power and was limited to 3,600 tons east of Everett without a helper.

Wenatchee filled No. 82 with perishables in mechanical refrigerator cars, aluminum from the Alcoa plant at Malaga, and lumber traffic, all Gavin and beyond. No. 82 was expected to arrive at Wenatchee at 7:00 AM and to depart at 7:30 AM. Normally a main line crew change was made at the Yard Office downtown.

During the last years of the Great Northern, No. 82 often picked up fruit in mechanical refrigerator cars and intermodal trailers from the West Yard at Wenatchee. Other times the Wenatchee fill was added at Appleyard, two miles east of the yard office. The fill was cut in just ahead of the caboose since filling from the rear minimized disruption to the train's brake system. Because the ruling grade east of Wenatchee was only 1%, No. 82 generally had enough power to take all the Gavin and beyond traffic that Wenatchee generated each day.

Train No. 88 left Balmer Yard at 2:00 AM carrying blocks to Gavin Yard and beyond, Hillyard, and Wenatchee. Leaving Balmer, the blocks were arranged with Gavin cars on the rear, Hillyard in the middle, and Wenatchee cars on the head end.

Refer to the following legend to identify the blocks. Switching is based entirely on destination blocks.

➸ *Capital letters indicate destination block, small letters indicate origin of the block.*

B	*Balmer Yard (Seattle)*
E	*Everett*
G	*Gavin*
H	*Hillyard*
W	*Wenatchee*

➸ *Other characters:*

CAB	*Caboose*
ENG	*Engine*
>	*Direction of travel*

Block diagram of No. 88 leaving Balmer Yard.

CAB Gb Hb Wb ENG>

At Everett Junction No. 88 picked up cars blocked for Wenatchee, Gavin, and Hillyard.

Block diagram of Everett Junction where cars are blocked as shown, east is to the right.

He Ge We

When making the Everett pick up, the road crew held onto the Wenatchee block. This put the Wenatchee and Hillyard blocks together but left the Gavin block from Everett and the Gavin block from Balmer separated by the Hillyard block. Train was blocked as shown below leaving Everett Junction.

CAB Gb Hb He Ge We Wb ENG>

Train No. 88 was also predominately loads, with only empty intermodal cars routinely handled. No. 88 was limited to 6,500 tons east of Everett with a helper over the Cascade mountains. The objective at both Balmer Yard and Everett Yard was to use No. 82 and No. 88 to move as much traffic for Gavin and Hillyard as possible. Empty cars, overflow cars for Wenatchee, and overflow cars for Hillyard and points short of Gavin moved from Seattle and Everett on the daily Drag East.

Number 88 was the fruit train. It took the bulk of the eastward fruit, that moving in ice cooled cars, from Wenatchee. Most of the fruit was Gavin and beyond; all fruit shorts went in the Hillyard block. Wenatchee always filled No. 88; first with fruit, then with lumber and aluminum. Wenatchee was allowed two hours to remove its cars from the head end, add its traffic and rearrange the train to minimize switching at Hillyard by getting the Hillyard block to the head end of the train.

Please follow along as we take you through the switching of train No. 88 at Appleyard. Refer to the following legend to identify the blocks.

- *Capital letters indicate destination block, small letters indicate origin of the block.*

B	*Balmer Yard (Seattle)*
E	*Everett*
G	*Gavin*
H	*Hillyard*
q	*Quincy*
W	*Wenatchee*

- *Other characters:*

P	*Perishable*
CAB	*Caboose*
ENG	*Engine*
>	*Direction of travel*

The inbound train is the same as it was leaving Everett Junction as shown below.

CAB Gb Hb He Ge We Wb ENG>

Appleyard switch crews pre-blocked cars for both Hillyard and Gavin. Since the perishables came from the ice dock, these blocks were most often made up in the low numbered tracks, usually 3 through 6.

HPw Hw

GPw Gw

Number 88 was yarded at Appleyard, usually in one of the high numbered tracks, 9–12, with the rear end hanging west on the W–O main as necessary.

An east end switch crew removed the cars for Wenatchee, We Wb, and set them into a convenient yard track.

A second cut from the east end was required to get the Hillyard cars out from behind the Gavin cars from Everett. The Hillyard cars were set over against the Hillyard cars that Wenatchee planned to add to the train.

HPw Hw Hb He Ge

Then the switch engine cut off the Hillyard cars but held on to Gavin cars from Everett and set them back against the Balmer cars for Gavin to create a single Gavin block.

CAB Gb Ge

Note that the Gavin cars from Balmer have not moved.

Then the Hillyard cars were doubled back to the head end of the train.

CAB Gb Ge HPw Hw Hb He

The Gavin perishables, plus any lumber and aluminum fill, went on the rear in a single move from the west end. This was done by picking up the caboose from the rear of the train, coupling the caboose to the Gavin fill from Wenatchee, and doubling everything to the rear of the train.

CAB GPw Gw

Departing Wenatchee, the train was blocked from the caboose forward; perishables Gavin and beyond, non-perishables Gavin and beyond, and Hillyard including perishable shorts, other main line shorts, and Laurel–CB&Q cars.

CAB GPw Gw Gb Ge HPw Hw Hb He ENG>

If the train arrived too late, Wenatchee did not have time to make all of its moves. Wenatchee would remove its cars, add its traffic, and try to run the train on time which meant leaving the Hillyard block buried for Hillyard to dig out.

No. 88's power was almost as good as that on No. 82. Tonnage eastward from Wenatchee was limited to whatever that day's power could handle on the 1% grade of Trinidad Hill from Columbia River to Quincy. No. 88 usually ran with four axle units, five of which were good for about 6,500 tons up Trinidad Hill. The only Hillyard cars usually added were fruit shorts. Train No. 88 left Wenatchee behind No. 82, say, 10:00 AM to noon. Train No. 88 picked up the spuds at Quincy.

Balmer Yard also made a Drag East for Wenatchee, a block of cars for Wenatchee and a block for Hillyard. The Drag East picked up another block of cars for Wenatchee and Hillyard at Everett. East of Everett, the Drag East was limited to not over 6,500 tons as helper train. Power for the drag was whatever the Interbay roundhouse foreman could scrape up. F units dominated both the drags and as helpers, six on the point and four cut into the train were required for 6,500 tons, 650 tons per unit. GP 7 and GP 9 units could and did substitute on a 1 for 1 basis.

The Drags East were Wenatchee's source for empty wood chip cars and for empty gondola cars to protect the gold concentrate loadings. The most important loads off the Drags East were alumina for Alcoa. Tank cars of gasoline, diesel fuel, and propane also arrived on the Drags East.

Wenatchee switched the drag at Appleyard, removing its cars. The Hillyard cars from the west continued, and all available Hillyard cars were added to the drag. If things worked out, Wenatchee got all its Gavin and beyond cars onto No. 82 and No. 88 so that the Drag East was all 'east shorts,' that is, cars for points short of Gavin Yard.

An interesting move through Wenatchee was DODX tank cars of jet fuel from Standard Oil at Mukilteo to Fairchild AFB just west of Spokane. Mukilteo was a transload and storage facility that got its product by ship from Richmond, California or El Segundo, California. These were old specification ICC 103 riveted tank cars with domes of 12,000-gallon and 100,000-pound nominal capacity, small cars by the late 1960s. They were notorious for hot boxes since they were held empty at Mukilteo where rainwater could get into the journal boxes and float the oil out.

The jet fuel loads usually moved in and out of Wenatchee on the Drag East in blocks of 10 to 15 cars that were set out at Fairchild. The West Local would spot the cars at the Deep Creek storage facility, inside Fairchild Air Force Base. After the Air Force closed Deep Creek and moved the fuel storage to the north side of the base, the Air Force had an engine that, by agreement, could come out on our track and take the cars onto the base and spot them. If Fairchild was low on fuel, I have seen jet fuel moved on train No. 82 with instructions that it be set out at Fairchild "without fail" per the message from the Chief Dispatcher.

Wenatchee did not block the Drag East; it was totally switched out at Hillyard. The Drag East often picked up non-perishable traffic from Quincy. It was usually called for about 7:00 PM at Wenatchee, which put them out of town about 8:30 PM after No. 27 cleared, after No. 32 went ahead of the extra east, and after the Alcoa Local left town. Power was whatever was available, mostly a combination F 7, GP 7 and GP 9 units. Five of them were good for 6,500 tons, which was the limit going up Trinidad Hill.

MINNEAPOLIS-LAUREL-SEATTLE-PORTLAND-VANCOUVER, B.C.								
No. 97	No. 79	No. 81	No. 83	STATIONS	No. 82 Forwarder	No. 88 Fruit Spl.	No. 78	No. 98
2.30AM-1	....	6.00AM-1	11.30AM-1	MINNEAPOLIS (Union Yard)	11.00AM-3	8.00AM-4	....	11.59PM-4
....	....	LV 4.00PM-0	....	.... SIOUX CITY	ARR 6.00PM-3	ARR 6.00PM-4	....	ARR 6.00PM-5
....	....	8.45AM-1 9.30AM-1	2.15PM-1 2.30PM-1	.... WILLMAR	5.30AM-3 4.30AM-3	3.45AM-4 2.15AM-4	....	7.30PM-4 5.30PM-4
7.20AM-1 7.25AM-1	....	11.40AM-1 12.01PM-1	4.45PM-1 4.55PM-1	...... BRECKENRIDGE	2.10AM-3 2.00AM-3	11.15PM-3 11.00PM-3	....	2.30PM-4 2.00PM-4
12.40PM-1 2.00PM-1	....	7.00PM-1 3.00AM-2	11.00PM-1 2.45AM-2	... GAVIN YARD (Minot) ...	8.00PM-2 5.00PM-2	4.00PM-3 1.00PM-3	....	7.00AM-4 3.00AM-4
4.30PM-1	....	7.15AM-2	6.30AM-2	.... BAINVILLE	12.01PM-2	6.00AM-3	....	6.30PM-3
9.30PM-1 9.50PM-1	....	1.30PM-2 5.00PM-2	12.30PM-2 12.50PM-2	.... HAVRE	6.45AM-2 6.15AM-2	9.00PM-2 8.00PM-2	....	9.00AM-3 7.30AM-3
....	12.01AM-1	....	....	.... LAUREL	....	....	10.00AM-3	....
....	8.00AM-1 11.00AM-1	....	....	...... GREAT FALLS	....	....	11.45PM-2 9.00PM-2	....
....	5.00PM-1 6.00PM-1	10.00PM-2	....	.... SHELBY	....	3.30PM-2	5.30PM-2	....
4.15AM-2 4.30AM-2	3.00AM-2 5.00AM-2	5.00AM-3	9.30PM-2 9.50PM-2	.... WHITEFISH	11.15PM-1 10.45PM-1	8.30AM-2 6.00AM-2	9.30AM-2 8.00AM-2	8.00PM-2 6.00PM-2
10.15AM-2 10.45AM-2	1.00PM-2 TOFC 5 9.15PM-2	....	5.00AM-3 8.00AM-3	... HILLYARD (Spokane) ...	3.00PM-1 1.00PM-1	7.00PM-1 5.00PM-1	8.00PM-1	6.30AM-2 4.00AM-2
2.45PM-2 3.00PM-2	....	....	2.30PM-3 3.30PM-3	...... WENATCHEE	8.30AM-1 8.00AM-1	11.00AM-1 4.00AM-1	....	10.00PM-1 6.30PM-1
8.00PM-2	5.00AM-3	....	10.00PM-3	.. INTERBAY (Balmer Yard) ..	3.00AM-1	8.00PM-0	....	11.00AM-1
7.00AM-3	....	....	7.00AM-4	.... VANCOUVER, B. C.	5.00PM-0	9.00AM-0	....	....
SPS 2/275 11.15AM-2	SPS 1/275 7.00AM-3	....	SPS 1/275 7.00AM-3	.... HILLYARD	SPS 190 11.30AM-1	SPS 190 11.30AM-1	....	SPS 186 12.01AM-2
9.00PM-2	9.00PM-3	....	9.00PM-3	.... VANCOUVER, WN.	9.00PM-0	9.00PM-0	....	6.30AM-1
10.00PM-2	10.00PM-3	....	10.00PM-3	.... PORTLAND	7.00PM-0	7.00PM-0	....	....

Schedules shown herein are not guaranteed and are subject to change without notice, except on fresh fruits and vegetables from concentration points Wenatchee and east thereof in the states of Washington and Idaho, moving on No. 88, fourth morning arrival (at 9:00 AM) to our connections at Twin Cities only is guaranteed.

No. 79 connects with CB&Q No. 75 & CB&Q No. 77 at Laurel.
No. 78 connects with CB&Q No. 78 and CB&Q No. 188 at Laurel.
SPS No. 275 connects with GWP at Wishram for Oregon and California.
No. 82 and No. 88 connect with CB&Q No. 82 at Minneapolis.

2

System Freight Schedules. For many years, the Great Northern published these system freight schedules in the Official Guide. Used for marketing purposes, the train numbers and schedules were also provided to customers. COLLECTION OF JOHN E. LANGLOT.

WESTWARD TRAINS

Train 97 was the hottest freight train on the Great Northern. It carried less than carload (LCL) and carload merchandise traffic interchanged from the eastern lines at Chicago, and TOFC and forwarder cars loaded at Chicago to Seattle and Portland. Forwarder cars were carloads of less than carload merchandise gathered and shipped by freight forwarders to their own facilities at Seattle and Portland for local delivery. This traffic was both high rated and truck competitive, a double incentive to priority handling.

The Burlington served the large freight forwarders Merchants Shippers Association and Universal Carloading at Chicago, plus the smaller forwarders Washington-Oregon Shippers Co-Operative (WOSCO), and Terminal Freight Carriers Association (TFCA), a subsidiary of Sears that also handled freight for Boeing. The Burlington also received a large volume of forwarder and LCL traffic at Chicago from the New York Central, Pennsylvania, and Erie railroads.

The Northern Pacific, Milwaukee, and Chicago and North Western–Union Pacific also provided service between Chicago and Seattle. The traffic that No. 97 was designed to handle was very service competitive. Since this traffic was of high value, customers were very sensitive to transit time and reliability, and customers routed the traffic based on who provided the best service. The Burlington had an advantage in that the forwarders loaded their cars at facilities located on the Burlington. Burlington and GN freight traffic salespeople solicited carload traffic moving from the east based largely on the reliably fast schedule established for No. 97 from Chicago to St. Paul and Seattle. Burlington and NP freight traffic sales people also solicited carload traffic from the east for NP No. 603 from Minneapolis to Seattle.

No. 97 departed Cicero Yard in suburban Chicago at 10:30 AM with Chicago origin forwarder cars pulled the evening before and the day's interchange traffic from the eastern lines. Power in the 1960s was typically three of the newest available GP units, that is, GP 20, 30, 35, or 40 models. This power provided about two horsepower per ton of train weight, which allowed fast running over the nearly flat Burlington route. The train was blocked as follows from the head end: Gavin and beyond, short of Gavin but beyond Union Yard, Twin Cities industries and interchange, Laurel (NP) and beyond, and stations short of Laurel. The train was filled out on the rear to a total of about 6,000 feet with empties blocked by ownership, GN or NP, that were generally set out at the Burlington's Dayton's Bluff Yard in St. Paul. No. 97 arrived at Union Yard in Minneapolis at 9:00 PM where the Burlington delivered cars to the GN. The Burlington delivered to the NP at NP's Park Junction Yard at the same time to avoid favoring one parent or the other.

Train No. 97 leaving Hillyard. Lead unit No. 438 is a 3600 HP F 45, a model introduced by the Great Northern. The wide car body allowed crewmen to move within the car body, as opposed to on outside walkways—a big improvement in the winter on the northern plains. This unit, delivered the summer of 1969, was one of the last bought by the Great Northern. Three F 45s or SD 45s in any combination, a total of 10,800 HP in three units, was the usual power for No. 97 in the late 1960s. PHOTO BY DALE JONES.

Great Northern Railway Condensed Freight Schedules No. 17, dated June 1, 1969, shows No. 97 scheduled to depart Minneapolis at 2:30 AM. The Northern Pacific counterpart, No. 603, left a bit earlier and seldom exceeded 40 cars west of Livingston, Montana, a reflection of the longer route and generally more adverse grades that the NP faced. In contrast, a Burlington Northern train brief dated December 1, 1970 showed that BN No. 97, which took the former GN route across Montana, was limited to 100 cars from Chicago to Gavin, and 80 cars west of Gavin.

No. 97 was fast: 43 hours and 30 minutes from Union Yard in Minneapolis to Balmer Yard in Seattle. Number 31, the Empire Builder, was scheduled for 37 hours 30 minutes from St. Paul to Seattle, so No. 97 was only six hours slower than the Builder despite scheduled stops at Gavin (1 hour and 20 minutes for switching and inspection), Havre (20 minutes for inspection), Hillyard (30 minutes for switching and inspection), Whitefish (15 minutes for inspection), and Wenatchee (15 minutes for switching), a total of 2 hours, 40 minutes.

Great Northern management monitored the performance of No. 97 very closely and was able to check its performance against NP No. 603 at Casselton, North Dakota, about 20 miles west of Fargo where the GN and NP main lines crossed. The crossing was protected by a manned interlocker staffed by a GN employee. As long as No. 97 passed Casselton not more than four hours after NP No. 603, No. 97 could beat No. 603 to Seattle.[1]

Hillyard to Wenatchee, 176 miles, was scheduled to be covered in four hours. The first 7.5 miles to Fort Wright passed through the city of Spokane and took 20 to 25 minutes to traverse. Fort Wright was the start of the climb up the 1% grade to Fairchild with a track speed restriction of 35 to 40 MPH. Most days, No. 97 had enough power to make at least 30 MPH over this segment. Once by Fairchild, it was mostly downhill to Wenatchee with a 60 MPH speed restriction, which most engineers exceeded by 5 or 10 MPH most of the way. The 25 MPH restriction around the horseshoe curve in Lynch Coulee and the 25 MPH restriction around the two curves on each side of the Columbia River Bridge at Rock Island were faithfully observed.

No. 97 was through Wenatchee early in the afternoon. During the late 1960s, with three SD 45 units, it was limited to 3,600 tons and ran single, that is, without helpers, over Stevens Pass. Tonnage limits west of Wenatchee for No. 97 and No. 83 were lower than east of Wenatchee. Wenatchee often reduced No. 97 to 3,600 tons. The reduction was usually made at Appleyard from the rear with the train sitting on the main track. Power from No. 97 was inspected, fueled, and serviced at Interbay roundhouse in Seattle to prepare it for service on No. 82.

Train No. 83 normally arrived and departed Wenatchee in the afternoon after No. 97. Number 83 was a helper train limited to 6,500 tons over Stevens Pass. Wenatchee often reduced No. 83 to the 6,500-ton limit, always at Appleyard. The preferred move was from the rear while the train held the main, but it could be done within Appleyard if there was other traffic on the main, which was rare. If No. 83 arrived at Wenatchee ahead of No. 97, it was usually yarded at Appleyard and called to depart behind No. 97. Since No. 97 ran without helpers over the Cascades, by holding No. 83 in Appleyard, No. 97 was not delayed due to No. 83 cutting helpers in or out.

Wenatchee got a Drag West almost every morning from Hillyard. During the 1960s, the inbound Drags West were Wenatchee's source of empty reefers, which were cleaned by WFE at Hillyard. Drags West also brought empty lumber boxcars, empty boxcars and flatcars for Alcoa, loads of pitch and coke for Alcoa, and the occasional load for Keokuk at Rock Island, for the W–O Local, the Grotto Local, or Wenatchee proper.

Through traffic on the Drag West included wheat from points east of Hillyard and wheat picked up between Espanola and Quincy. The wheat went to Seattle and Tacoma. The drag also handled wood chips and pulpwood from Hillyard. The balance of the train was mostly empty cars for Everett, Seattle and Tacoma.

Wenatchee built its Drag West at Appleyard from the through traffic that came in on the inbound Drag West plus the reductions from No. 97 and No. 83. The Drag West also handled westward traffic off the locals that terminated at Wenatchee, mostly wood chips for paper mills at Bellingham, Everett, Tacoma, and Longview, and empty alumina cars from Alcoa. The Drag West, or yard drag, ran almost every day, and was usually called for 4:00–5:00 AM. The call was timed to allow the drag to use the helper power that came east with No. 88. The Drag West was a 6,500-ton helper train with whatever power was handy. Again, F units dominated.

Two sets of helper power and three helper crews were assigned at Skykomish in the 1960s. The availability of helper power and crews controlled the capacity of the railroad over the Cascade mountains. Helpers were always cut in or out at Skykomish and were usually cut in or out east of the mountain at Cashmere. Helper power rarely came to Wenatchee to swap units. The crew was paid for an extra 100 miles if they went to Wenatchee since Wenatchee was beyond the bulletined limits of the job.

The first helper crew call was for No. 88 and the Drag West. They cut into No. 88 at Skykomish, then helped it to Cashmere where they cut out of No. 88 to wait for the Drag West which it helped from Cashmere to Skykomish.

The second helper crew was called based on No. 83's expected departure time from Wenatchee. The helper crew ran light engine to Cashmere, helped No. 83 over the Cascades, and cut out at Skykomish where they tied up. The call time of Drag East at Seattle was chosen so that it met westward No. 83 at Baring, the first siding west of Skykomish. This timing allowed the third helper crew to cut the helper engine into the drag at Skykomish without having the other train in the way. The third crew helped the drag to Cashmere and returned light engine to Skykomish.

This general plan was of course varied from day to day if No. 97 or No. 82 was so heavy as to require help, and to handle additional trains above and beyond those described, such as a grain Drag West in the fall and winter.

The Burlington Northern moved the helper power and helper crew home terminal to Wenatchee in 1974. BNSF does not now, in 2018, operate helpers over Stevens Pass. Heavy trains over Stevens Pass now use 'Distributed Power.' Distributed Power is usually three units on the head end of the train and two unmanned units controlled by radio from the lead unit on the rear. Like the old manned helpers, distributed power is necessary to limit the drawbar pull of the lead units on heavy trains.

One Sunday in the full crew days, I was working the brakeman's extra board at Hillyard and caught a trip to Wenatchee on train No. 83. Our train included 10 cars of cattle for Quincy that we were required to unload. No. 97 was called about an hour behind us. The General Yardmaster at Hillyard made a point of rubbing it in, saying, "I made sure that you are going to get run around" to my conductor.

By the time we got out of Hillyard, No. 27, the Western Star, was about an hour behind us, and No. 97 would be right behind No. 27. We were sure to get run around if we made our normal moves: head into the siding, cut off the power and the stock, come out the west end of the siding, shove east on the main and then into track 8 to unload the stock. There was no way to unload the stock and get back on our train ahead of No. 27, and the worst thing we could do was delay No. 27, the mail train, which was scheduled to stop at Quincy. We talked about this all the way to Quincy and came up with a plan. The fireman, Harry Howard, and brakeman, Willy Quinton, would unload the stock at Quincy if the Spud Local left their engine on track 8 as they usually did on Saturday night. The local did not work on Sunday.

Well, the Spud Local's engine was parked on track 8 all by itself, so plan A went into action. We stayed on the main track, slowed down, and Harry dropped off. He ran over and got on the Spud's engine. Willy dropped off to make the cut behind the stock and I stayed on the rear unit of our power. Willy made the cut behind the stock cars, gave us a sign to pull ahead, and stopped us just west of the west switch to track 8. Willy opened the switch while I bottled the air and cut our power away from the stock. Harry came out of track 8, Willy made a joint on the stock, cut in the air, and they pulled the stock into track 8 heading for the stock chute. I gave our engineer a backup sign, stopped to line the track 8 switch back to the main, brought our power back to the train, made and stretched the joint, and cut in the air. My work done, I went back to the cab of the lead unit where I waited for the caboose crew to confirm by radio that the air was releasing. As soon as the air released, No. 83's train was gone.

Fifteen minutes or so later, as we were going around the horseshoe curve in Lynch Coulee east of Trinidad, Karl P. Buschmann, the operator at Quincy, called us on the radio. He said that the dispatcher said to head in at Trinidad, cut our power off our train, come back to Quincy, and unload the stock. We told Karl that the stock was unloaded and for him to drive down and check before he talked to the dispatcher again. Willy said later that Karl came down and looked around the end of the stockyard fence. Willy put his finger to his lips and said, "Shhhh." Karl responded in his German accent, "Me thinks it's too late already."

Willy and Harry unloaded the stock, walked up the depot, and caught No. 27 to Wenatchee. We headed in at Appleyard, ran through the yard, came up the W–O main, and stopped opposite the yard office. No. 27 went by on the main as our head end came out of the west end of Appleyard and started onto the W–O main. Willy and Harry were at the yard office when the engineer and I walked in. We did not get run around that day.

➻ The East Pig

The West End Pool between Hillyard and Wenatchee included two very fast runs, the East Pig and train No. 5.

During January of 1959, the Great Northern instituted an eastward piggyback train from Seattle to Spokane, which quickly became known as the 'East Pig.' This was very early in the modern piggyback era. When it was introduced, the train generally carried two to four piggyback flatcars carrying truck trailers, an express boxcar or two, and a dozen or so ordinary looking freight cars of LCL or time sensitive carload freight for Spokane.

The East Pig left Balmer Yard about 7:00 PM Monday through Friday, was by Monroe about 8:40 PM, was through Wenatchee about 12:30 AM, and arrived at Spokane about 5:00 AM. On some nights shortly after the service was introduced, the piggyback business was so modest that the train carried no trailers. When the train was very small, the Great Northern did not make any net income off this train. To management's credit, they continued to operate the train on a fast timing. The fast time was a market requirement; the company was trying to retain and capture traffic by enticing shippers with overnight service from Seattle to Spokane in trailers or in boxcars in competition with overnight truck service.

Between 1958 and 1961, the Great Northern converted about a hundred 54-foot long flatcars into piggyback flats that carried a single 40-foot trailer. These cars were a low-cost way to test the market, but they were not very efficient due to the high tare weight of the cars.

In the mid-1960s, the company managed to build the East Pig up to about 40 cars. This kept the train light enough to make good time and to operate over the Cascades without a helper. By the late 1960s, several trailers were moving each night on 85- and 89-foot long piggyback flats that carried two 40-foot long trailers.

I worked the East Pig from Wenatchee to Hillyard in the late 1960s. Our power was sometimes the power from the previous night's No. 5, and sometimes freight service GP 9s, and later, GP 20s. Our usual call was for 2:00 to 3:00 AM at Wenatchee. Crews changed at the yard office. The train most often arrived at Wenatchee shortly behind No. 28, the Western Star. In that case, the East Pig would be on the main track. If the East Pig was a bit late, then it was close to the arrival time of No. 31, the Empire Builder. In this case, the East Pig was headed in at Olds Junction and arrived on the W–O main. The Spokane crew took the train down the W–O main, went through a clear track at Appleyard, and returned to the main track at Switch 1 at the east end of Appleyard.

Since the East Pig was not a scheduled train, our clearance often read something like "C&E Extra 2005 East" and we would have an order to run extra from Wenatchee to Fort Wright. C&E is the rulebook approved abbreviation for 'Conductor and Engineer.' Some times when the Western Star was late the dispatcher ran the East Pig as First No. 28, rather than an extra. Other times, when the East Pig was going to follow No. 28 out of Wenatchee, the East Pig ran as Second 28. In either case, First 28 would carry green signals for Second 28. What happened on any given morning depended on how the East Pig and No. 28 were running and what seemed to us the whim of the dispatcher.

Whether we were on the main line or on the W–O main, the East Pig usually got a fill at Appleyard. If the East Pig was on the main, then we would stop the caboose just east of crossover No. 3 at the west end of Appleyard. A switch engine would come out of the yard through the crossover, pluck the caboose and the cars for Spokane Yard off the rear end, shove into the yard and grab the Wenatchee pick up, which consisted mostly of fruit in trailers on flatcars, and put the train back together. This move usually took about 20 minutes to accomplish. If the East Pig ran through Appleyard it typically used track 13, which was generally left clear. The switch engine made the same moves, but they were shorter since we were in the yard. The Wenatchee pick up was cut into the train ahead of the Spokane set out, so that when the East Pig arrived at Spokane, the switch crew could set the Spokane cars over as a single block.

After picking up the Wenatchee fill, the road crew made a stub test on the whole train as the switch crew had already air tested the fill. When the East Pig left Appleyard, we were off for Spokane, meeting No. 31 perhaps at Wenatchee or Appleyard or even as far east as Quincy, depending on our progress and whether or not No. 31 was on time. After we met No. 31, the railroad was pretty much ours as any westward freight trains were usually in the siding for us.

At Spokane, the Spokane yardmaster usually instructed us to cut our caboose off on the main and then pull ahead to clear the crossover. The switch engine would come through the crossover and pull the Spokane set out off the rear of our train. One of the boxcars often contained Rainier Beer for Joey August Distributors that went up to the SC&P Yard to be spotted for unloading. Some of the boxcars were LCL loads that were spotted at the freight house right away for unloading by the freight house crew that went to work at 8:00 AM. After the Spokane set out was done, the East Pig backed up, coupled to our caboose, cut in the air, made a stub test, and headed for Hillyard.

At Hillyard, the yardmaster usually gave us a head in off Two Lead to the lower yard office, power to the house. Typically, the switch crew immediately came against the caboose and began to switch our train out. Some of our train would be put on the rear end of No. 490, which would be leaving within an hour or two. This always included most of the fruit in trailers on the flatcars from Wenatchee.

➻ Train Number 5

The East Pig was joined by a new mail train, No. 5, from Spokane to Seattle effective May 22, 1960. Number 5 was created as a result of changes in the passenger service through Spokane, which is summarized below.

As of late 1945, the Great Northern operated two pairs of first class trains through Spokane. The 'Empire Builder,' number 1 westward and 2 eastward, between St.

Paul and Seattle, was the premier passenger train of the Great Northern, dating to 1929. The Burlington handled the Empire Builder equipment between St. Paul and Chicago as their train numbers 49 and 44. To the public, it was a single train between Chicago and Seattle.[2]

The 'Fast Mail,' trains 27 and 28 between St. Paul and Seattle, had operated over the Great Northern for decades. The Fast Mail carried a Railway Post Office car, several storage mail cars loaded with mail, and several baggage and express cars of express traffic. Numbers 27 and 28 also and carried coaches and a sleeping car between St. Paul and Spokane. This passenger service on the Fast Mail was the remnant of 'Oriental Limited,' number 3 and 4, the secondary St. Paul/Seattle passenger train, which was discontinued during the Great Depression.[3]

The Empire Builder was re-equipped with new streamlined cars and diesel locomotives in February of 1947 and was shown in Employee Time Tables as 'Streamliner' until 1955. The Oriental Limited was also re-established between Chicago and Seattle in February 1947, taking back its traditional numbers, 3 and 4, and using the heavyweight equipment previously assigned to the Empire Builder. In 1951, the Empire Builder received entirely new sets of streamlined cars. The 1947 cars were reassigned to the Oriental Limited, which was renamed the 'Western Star,' also in 1951. During the summer of 1951, trains 27 and 3 left Spokane at 7:00 PM and 9:35 PM respectively. Trains 4 and 28 left Spokane at 7:40 AM and 8:30 AM respectively.

To reduce costs in the face of declining revenue, trains 27 and 28 were discontinued west of Spokane effective October 15, 1953. West of Spokane, train 3 carried the through Seattle cars from train 27, a Railway Post Office car, two storage mail/express cars of mail from New York City (via the Milwaukee Road between Chicago and St. Paul), and other cars of mail and express traffic that had previously moved on trains 27 and 28.[4] The mail and express cars from No. 27 were placed behind the passenger cars of train number 3, which during 1954 left Spokane at 9:00 PM and arrived at Seattle at 5:00 AM. Train 4 from Seattle handled through St. Paul mail and express cars into Spokane that became the core of train 28 east of Spokane.

Effective September 25, 1955, the Western Star and the Fast Mail were consolidated west of Minot, North Dakota, as trains 3 and 4. During the summers of 1956, 1957, 1958, and 1959, however, mail trains 27 and 28 operated between St. Paul and Spokane.[5] We believe this was to allow the longer, heavier summer Western Star passenger trains required to serve summer season only passengers to and from Glacier National Park.

During the Christmas season, when mail volume was very heavy, trains 3 and 4 were operated in sections between St. Paul and Seattle: a 'Passenger Section,' and a 'Mail and Express Section.' The Mail and Express section was a return to the Fast Mail in that if carried the traditional Railway Post Office car, several storage mail cars, and several cars of express traffic.

On June 10, 1956, the train numbers of the Empire Builder between St. Paul and Seattle were changed from number 1 westward and 2 eastward to number 31 westward and 32 eastward. On the same date, the Burlington also changed its train numbers for the Builder between Chicago and St. Paul to 31 and 32. These train number changes were made in anticipation of the merger between the GN, NP, Burlington, and SP&S then under study.[6]

To further reduce costs in the face of a continuing decline in passenger revenues, the Western Star and the Fast Mail were consolidated between Saint Paul and Seattle as trains 27 and 28 effective May 22, 1960. Coincident with the consolidation, the route of the Western Star was changed from via Grand Forks to the shorter and faster New Rockford cut-off in North Dakota and to the main line in Montana, rather than the longer and slower detour though Great Falls. Number 27 now left Spokane at 3:30 PM and arrived at Seattle at 11:30 PM, five and one-half hours earlier than number 3 had previously.[7] This version of the Western Star was long and heavy, with 25–30 cars between St. Paul and Spokane.[8]

Revenue from handling the mail was important to the railroads, and rail service was important to the Post Office. The Post Office had built its Spokane to Seattle service around the previous schedule of train No. 3. The 3:30 PM departure of No. 27 from Spokane was too early for that day's Spokane mail to make the train. The Post Office probably also determined that shifting this mail to the 7:45 AM arrival of No. 31 at Seattle did not allow sufficient time to get Spokane mail sorted and out to the

Seattle letter carriers that day. The Post Office doubtless demanded restoration of the old schedule, but that was not possible since changing the schedule at Spokane would have required changing the schedule all the way back to Chicago. The solution was to add first class train No. 5 from Spokane to Seattle, effective May 22, 1960.

Train Number 5 left Spokane on the previous time of train No. 3, 9:15 PM. No. 5 was very fast, 15 minutes faster than No. 3's time from Spokane to Wenatchee, and 40 minutes faster from Spokane to Balmer Yard. No. 5 was faster from Spokane to Balmer Yard than both No. 27 and No. 31.

Creation of No. 5 required two sets of passenger units geared for higher speed than freight units and equipped with steam boilers to supply steam to heat the RPO and baggage cars that were right behind the power. The previously established East Pig had unbalanced engine utilization. By creating No. 5, the passenger units it required could return to Spokane on the East Pig. This released the previously assigned freight units from the East Pig and utilized surplus passenger units on both the East Pig and No. 5.

No. 5's power was generally passenger F units arranged A-B, A-B-B or A-B-A. An A unit is one with a cab; a B unit is a booster without a cab. The power depended on what was available at Hillyard and the tonnage of that night's train. No. 5's train length varied from 15 to 25 cars per night. With a short train, No. 5 usually got two units; a long train typically got three units. The train crew rode in the baggage car.

Since No. 5 was manned by chain gang freight crews, the entire crew reported to work at Hillyard. I was occasionally called for No. 5 off the brakeman's extra board, on duty at Hillyard at 8:00 PM. A typical run of No. 5 went about as follows.

Since I was the head brakeman, I walked over to the diesel shop with the engine crew to get the power. We came up the lead and picked up the rest of the crew. The conductor handed the engineer the clearance with any track condition orders between Hillyard and Spokane, and off we went.

We stopped at the Spokane Yard Office to pick up the wheel report and waybills for our train. At the passenger depot, the conductor got off and went inside to get our clearance. The clearance gave our lead unit the authority to run on No. 5's schedule. The conductor also got any track condition orders required for that trip. Our conductor registered our arrival as an extra west and registered us out as No. 5, showing the engine number, names of the crew, and loads, empties and tons.

While the conductor was handling the paperwork, the crew ran the power to the west end of the depot, crossed over to the eastward main, and backed toward our train which was usually on the Depot Track, stopping short of the head car with the blue flag on it. We often waited a few minutes for the carmen to cut off the depot steam line, the yard air (compressed air from a stationary source piped to various outlets), and to pull down their blue flag before the power could come against our outbound train. While we were waiting, sacks of mail and packages were loaded into the RPO and the baggage cars from depot baggage carts by the depot baggage and mail handling crew. As soon as the blue flag was down, I made a joint on the train and stretched the joint. The carmen then hooked up the steam line from the engine to the RPO car and cut the steam into the train. Next, they hooked up the hoses for the brake pipe and the signal air and cut in the air for both air lines.

The signal air was a line of communication between the baggage car and the engine. When the carmen were done with the air test, and the depot mail crew was done loading packages and mail, and it was time for us to depart, the conductor instructed a brakeman to signal the engineer to depart. He pulled the signal air handle twice to give the engineer the signal to proceed. This signal air blew a whistle in the cab of the lead unit, and the two blasts on this whistle told the engineer to proceed. The engineer would respond with two blasts on the engine whistle, and start the train.

No. 5 was scheduled to meet No. 32 on the double track between Bluestem and Lamona. If both No. 5 and No. 32 were on time, they met just west of Harrington.

During the Christmas season, No. 5 was often late out of Spokane. Westward trains were superior to eastward trains of the same class by the Time Table. Absent the dispatcher's intervention, No. 32 would have to wait for No. 5 at the end of double track at Bluestem. In the usual case when No. 32 was on time, the dispatcher would issue a train order giving No. 32 rights over No. 5 between Bluestem and Fort Wright. The rights over order avoided No. 32 having to wait for No. 5 at the end of double track at Bluestem and required No. 5's crew to figure out where to clear up for No. 32, and then do it.

When No. 5 needed to clear up for No. 32, No. 5 would usually meet No. 32 at Espanola or Edwall. In this case, when the train was about five miles east of meeting point, the conductor would tell the brakeman to signal the engineer using the signal air. The brakeman would then give two short blasts on the signal whistle signifying that we were approaching a meeting or waiting point. The engineer would acknowledge with two blasts of the engine whistle. The signal air was used in passenger service to allow the conductor to communicate with the engineer. By the late 1960s, it was a carryover from days before radio communication, but it was still well suited to its purpose and reduced radio chatter.

After No. 5 met No. 32, the railroad was ours. Our only stop short of Wenatchee was at Ephrata.

A few times I was head brakeman on a freight train that met No. 5 at Odessa and gave No. 5 a roll by there. No. 5 picked up and delivered the mail at speed at Odessa. A Post Office employee was sitting near the crossing waiting for No. 5 with his automobile's headlights turned on so the RPO clerk knew where to throw the sack of mail. The Post Office employee had previously hung a sack of mail up in the mail crane for the RPO car to pick up. I kept my lantern on that sack of mail hanging in the crane. No. 5 went by at about 80 MPH. I watched as the sack of mail was snatched into the RPO car, while at the same time a cloud of dust appeared in the headlight beams. When the dust settled, the fellow waiting retrieved the sack of mail that the RPO clerk had thrown off the train.

Train No. 5 arrived at Ephrata at 11:20 PM. The train crew unloaded sacks of packages and mail onto baggage carts brought to the side of the train by the operator and the clerk. Ephrata usually received half to three quarters of the fully loaded baggage car. In addition, we loaded a small amount of bagged mail for the coast into the baggage car. Our Spokane crew got off at Wenatchee, and the Seattle crew got on. They unloaded the mail sacks for Wenatchee and loaded mail sacks for Everett and Seattle. A switch engine picked off the rear car, an express boxcar of bulk mail for Wenatchee.

At Seattle, the RPO and baggage cars off the morning's No. 5 returned to Spokane on the rear end of No. 28, the Western Star. These cars were taken off at Spokane in the morning and spotted to the post office for that night's No. 5.

➻ The 490 Series Second Class Trains

Beginning in the 1930s, regular, or Time Table scheduled, freight trains gradually fell out of favor and were discontinued on many railroads. All freight trains were then run as extras. The most common exceptions were on branch lines where local freight trains were often carried in Time Table schedules.

Another notable exception for many years was the practice of carrying two or three eastward, but not westward, second class freight schedules on Great Northern main line subdivisions between Wenatchee and Bainville, Montana, a distance of almost 1,000 miles. These schedules usually were numbered 490, 492, and 494, but other, similar numbers were also used from time to time. This practice began during WWII and continued until made unnecessary by Centralized Traffic Control in the 1970s and 1980s.

During the 1960s the 490 series schedules published in Employee Time Tables were intended for convenience in dispatching. Dispatchers could, and did run, any train they wished on these schedules, or as a section thereof. Conductor John Langlot describes the procedure:

> Symbol freight trains 82 and 88 operated as extra trains from Balmer Yard to Wenatchee, but often ran as Nos. 492 and 494, the second class schedules from Wenatchee to Hillyard.
>
> Train and engine crews called at Wenatchee for train 82 often discovered, upon reporting for duty, that they received a clearance and train orders addressed to "C&E No. 492." No. 88's crew at Wenatchee might find their clearance and orders addressed to "C&E No. 494." Occasionally additional trains were also run, and depending on the time of day, any of these trains could very well be run as a "Section" of No. 494. Once in a while, when both fruit and potatoes were in high demand on the eastern market, there would be enough business out of Wenatchee to originate a second section of No. 494 at Wenatchee.

The Fort Wright interlocking tower in a view to the west. The "rods" to the right of the track indicate that Fort Wright is an "armstrong" plant with man-sized interlocking levers in the tower. When moved, the levers moved the rods connecting to the main track switch to the SP&S and the three signals that control movement over the switch. The switch east of Bridge 274, at the west end of the double track to Hillyard, was electrically controlled from Fort Wright. PHOTO BY DALE JONES.

Train No. 27 at Fort Wright. The tower is hidden behind the train but is located at the train order signal. The switch to the Spokane Portland & Seattle `main track, curving away to the right, is under the middle of the train. The rear of the train is on Bridge 274 over Hangman (later Latah) Creek. COLLECTION OF JOHN LANGLOT.

This worked quite well. By the time "No. 82's train" left Wenatchee they were late on No. 492's schedule, so No. 82's train incurred no delay by running on No. 492's schedule to Hillyard. The same thing applied to No. 88's train running on the schedule of No. 494.

Between Fort Wright and Hillyard no second class trains were shown in the Employee Time Table. This segment was all yard limits. By rule 93, switch engines did not have to protect against extra trains, but they did have to protect against the schedule of first and second class trains. By not showing any second class trains between Fort Wright and Hillyard in the Employee Time Table, switch engines did not have to protect against them. When a crew ran as No. 492 or No. 494 from Wenatchee to Fort Wright, at Fort Wright they received a clearance with and order making the train an Extra East from Fort Wright to Hillyard. The crew was required to turn on the class lights and make sure that they displayed the color white.

As long as trains were available to operate on these eastward second class schedules, the dispatcher did not have to issue nearly as many running orders, right of track, or meet orders. All that was necessary was to issue a clearance at Wenatchee, or Hillyard, to "C&E No 492." If westward extras were on the road at the time, they took siding for No. 492 or No. 494 on the Time Table schedule for those trains, unless otherwise instructed by a "wait" or "meet" order involving the scheduled train.

From Hillyard to Troy the Time Table schedules for second class trains were No. 490 and No. 492. No. 490 was scheduled to leave Hillyard at 6:00 AM and No 492 was scheduled to leave Hillyard at 4:00 PM daily. The operating rules provided that schedules were useful for up to 12 hours, or more precisely that if a scheduled train became more than 12 hours late, then it lost its schedule authority and could no longer proceed on that schedule.

If 82's train was called at its normal time of 4:00 PM to 6:00 PM, the dispatcher would run it on 492's schedule. Train 88 typically ran as second 492, leaving Hillyard between 7:00 PM to 9:00 PM.

With all the lumber mills in the Spokane and Coeur d'Alene area, plus the large amount of lumber and other east bound business coming into the system at Hillyard, the company ran third sections of No. 492 from about Wednesday through Saturday morning. Once in a while there was even a fourth section of one of these schedules. No. 490 was often used late in the week to run the previous day's overflow traffic.

By using the second class schedule 492 for trains 82 and 88, and utilizing schedule 490 for the overflow train that originated at Hillyard after 6:00 AM, the dispatchers did not have to put out flat meets with the westward extra trains. If a train was ready to leave Hillyard shortly after the scheduled leaving time of one of the 490 series trains, the dispatchers would run the train on the published schedule. The Time Table schedules dictated the meeting points. The crew of any opposing Extra West was required to figure out where to clear the 490 series train. The dispatcher did not have to put out any additional train orders.

If a train was ready to go significantly later that the scheduled departure of one of the 490 series trains, the dispatcher would also put out a run late order addressed to the 490 series train and to westward extra trains. The run late order set back the scheduled departure times at all stations by the amount of time specified in the order. The crew of any Extra West would have to determine where to clear the late running 490 series train. Use of the 490 series schedules made determining the meeting point the responsibility of the westward extra train working against the schedule or run late times of the eastward second class train(s) that they were going to meet.

From Troy to Cut Bank, Montana the Time Table schedules were; No. 490, No. 492, and No. 494. Symbol train No. 88 usually ran as No. 494 east of Troy since they were a better fit to No. 494's published schedule.

The reason for more second class train schedules east of Troy was to handle the east bound lumber business from main line stations east of Troy. The Bull Local picked up lumber from Newport, Priest River, Sandpoint and Bonners Ferry, Troy and Libby. The Bull Local always made a big lumber pickup for the east at Libby that the Libby Logger switched out from the J. Neil's Lumber mill at Libby. More lumber traffic originated at Whitefish and Kalispell. The Whitefish area easily produced thirty-five to fifty loads of lumber per day plus other high revenue loads, like aluminum from the reduction plant at Conkelley, for the east.

One final point; run late orders could be and were used on occasion for first class schedules like No. 5, 31, 32, 27, and 28. For example, the evening Drag East out of Wenatchee was required to be in the clear of the main line five minutes before No. 5 was due out of a station, say Odessa at 10:35 PM. Whether the drag was running as an extra or as the second section of No. 494, he was required to be in the clear of the main track at Odessa by 10:30 for No. 5.

If the Drag East held a train order stating "No. 5 run 20 minutes late between the end of double track Lamona and Odessa" then No. 5 could not leave Lamona until 10:45 PM and Odessa until 10:55 PM. The run late order granted the drag an additional 20 minutes to advance against No. 5. The drag would have to be east of Lamona on the double track no later than 10:40 PM or would have to be clear of the main track at Odessa at 10:50 PM. If no further run late times were listed on this order, then No. 5 was figured to be on time after they left Odessa and the engineer of No. 5 would make every effort to recover the lost time once they were by Odessa.

During the Christmas season in the 1960s, the Great Northern always ran a second section of trains 27 and 28 to handle the overflow mail and Christmas holiday packages. These second sections of No. 27 and 28 handled mail and packages only, no passengers. The second sections of No. 27 and No. 28 were generally put on about two weeks before Christmas and were pulled off on Christmas day.

I remember several occasions waiting in a siding for a regular train like No. 492 and when they went by, they were displaying green signals and would whistle signals, one long and two shorts, signifying that they were carrying signals for a following section. We were required to whistle two shorts to acknowledge the 'long and two shorts,' or the train carrying green signals was required to stop, if necessary, and find out why we failed to acknowledge their display of green signals. This made the operation safe by assuring that the crew of the inferior train saw the green signals.

This was the way it was when I hired out; these practices were just accepted. We did not think a thing about it. Eastward second class schedules like 490, 492, and 494 were printed in the Time Table in the same manner as first class trains in both directions. Crews on westward extra trains would automatically consider the schedules of those superior first and second class trains. In fact, crews thought about the first and second class trains no matter where they were, or which direction they were going. It was simply common practice under the rules, which required extra trains to clear the time of all regular trains in the opposite direction and of first class trains in both directions.

Retired train dispatcher Mr. David Sprau explains the dispatchers' viewpoint:

The difference between a Time Table schedule and an actual train of the same number is often misunderstood. A Time Table schedule exists only on paper. It can be likened to a published 'greased skid,' upon which any engine, with any kind of cars, and perhaps a caboose, could be placed. A 'clearance' form issued to a regular train at its initial station on a Time Table subdivision gave the crew of an engine permission to operate on a schedule published in the Time Table. Once a clearance was issued, the crew of the train receiving that clearance was authorized to operate the designated engine on the schedule indicated. When the scheduled departure time rolled around, off they went.

In actual practice, a passenger train, such as the 'Empire Builder,' was normally run on the first class Time Table schedule, No. 31 or No. 32, intended for it. Freight trains were similarly operated on schedules of lower class, or more often in later years, not shown on the Time Table at all, but instead run as 'extras.' In everyday conversation around dispatching offices, railroad stations, yard offices, and other places, but never in train orders, these extra trains were often referred to as "No. 97," "No. 83," or some similar number because the particular train was loosely adhering to unofficial schedules advertised by the Traffic Department. When it came to operating documents, such as train orders, clearances, and train register books, such trains were properly referred to as 'Extra 2508 West.'

I liked this system because a dispatcher could get pretty busy as morning approached. Consider No. 82's train, which often stopped at Wenatchee only to change crews. Before one knew it, No. 82's extra off the Cascade Division would be coming into Wenatchee needing orders for the trip to Hillyard. To run No. 82's train as an extra often required issuing two or three orders immediately, arranging meeting points with westward trains, plus an additional running order before a clearance form could be issued. Sometimes this involved dropping everything else and hurriedly issuing 'meet,' 'right of track,' and/or 'wait' orders involving every single westward extra train that might be coming during the next several hours. With the second class schedule system, there was no need to do any of that. I could simply issue No. 82's train a clearance as "No. 492" at Wenatchee. If meets were necessary, most of them could be issued later, at other stations as convenient, and after I could see how both trains were running. The dispatcher cannot do that with opposing extras; right of track or meet orders were required to be established before issuing opposing running orders.

One last word about the flexibility of Time Table schedules. Under unusual circumstances, such as when a foreign railroad detoured their trains over the Great Northern, or when communications failure left a dispatcher with no other method, almost anything could, and occasionally would, be run on any convenient, available schedule. This included work trains being run on, or as a section of, a first or second class schedule, and passenger trains run on schedules normally assigned to other passenger trains, or even as extras.[8] The fact that these kinds of things were not everyday occurrences did not preclude the dispatcher's ability to do so under the rules.

The operating rules were very specific about the sequence in which orders for more than one train were addressed, and required that they be repeated in the same sequence as they were addressed. By rule and practice, orders were transmitted simultaneously to the operators at the stations where each train was to receive them. Each operator then repeated the order back to the dispatcher. Following correct repeat, the dispatcher would respond with "Complete," the time, and the superintendent's initials. The order was then considered complete and could be delivered to the train(s) it was addressed to. In later years, the chief dispatcher's initials were used, and still later the initials of the individual dispatchers.

It would not do for a train order instructing the Empire Builder, "No. 31 WAIT AT EPHRATA UNTIL 701AM FOR EXTRA 734 EAST" to be addressed and made "complete" to the eastward extra before issuing it to No 31. This order restricts No. 31 and gives Extra 734 East additional time to run to Ephrata. If the order was issued first to Extra 734 East, and communication were to fail, as it often did, immediately after the train order was given a complete time by the dispatcher, then Extra 734 East would utilize that wait time and run to Ephrata for a No. 31 that had not received a copy of the restricting order! This series of events would create a lap of authority and set up a possible head on collision. However, if the order was properly addressed first to No. 31 and then the wires failed, the worst thing that could happen is No. 31 would wait at Ephrata until 7:01 AM for a train that did not have a copy of the order and therefore made no attempt to reach Ephrata.

Remember the earlier statement regarding opposing extras needing to have their meet or right of track orders established before their running orders could be issued.

> This and other important requirements of train order dispatching, including addressing train orders restricting the movement of a train to that train first, and addressing secondarily trains that would be relying upon that information to advance, was important because of the provision in the operating rules that allowed operators to issue 'wire failure' clearances to trains in cases where they held orders for those trains, but communication failed.
>
> When operators issued 'wire failure' clearances, they were required to include only train orders previously made 'complete' at their station. If communication failed while an operator was repeating an order, it became a 'holding order' of indefinite duration, for the train addressed at that station. As a practical matter, indefinite duration meant until communication was restored.

John Langlot concludes: these rules, of such apparent complexity, but actually quite simple once the system was understood, were created when real time communication between the dispatcher and the trains in his territory was impossible. They evolved over several decades in an ongoing process aimed at safely moving more trains with less delay. The saying that "The rules are written in blood" was no exaggeration. By the time Dave and I worked with them, they had evolved to the point that it was possible to work safely under them provided that everybody paid attention to what they were doing.

I truly miss this 'old time' railroading. Railroaders in the 1960s were required to know the operating rules, the safety rules, the Time Table, their train orders and their role in the moves that were being made. We always needed to be on our toes. Operating jobs, in particular, were heavily laden with responsibility for thinking carefully about everything you did. Fortunately, there were living, breathing people with us on the crew to help watch our backs. Figuring out whether or not you had enough time to run to the next station, and the adrenaline rush when you made the decision to go against a superior train on short time, added to the excitement of the job. Railroading was not for the incompetent, nor for the faint of heart.

Endnotes

1 Discussion of Burlington No. 97 based on Earl Currie emails dated November 19, December 3, and December 7, 2016.
2 John Strauss email December 4, 2016.
3 Dave Sprau email October 27, 2016, citing 1936 public passenger timetable.
4 John Strauss email November 2, 2016, based on public passenger timetables and personal recollection.
5 Dave Sprau email October 27, 2016, citing multiple Employee Time Tables.
6 John Strauss email December 4, 2016.
7 Chuck Hatler, The Western Star: Train of Many Routes, Reference Sheet 368, June 2011, GNRHS.
8 John Strauss email November 2, 2016, personal recollection.
9 In the legendary wreck of "Fast Mail" train No. 27 at the Foss River Bridge east of Skykomish on March 7, 1945, few people are aware that No. 27's schedule on that day had been annulled for reasons lost to posterity, and the train that wrecked was actually running as "Third 1."

7. The Main Line East of Hillyard

Introduction

This chapter will cover the main line east of Hillyard with emphasis on how the Great Northern operated sections of scheduled trains in this territory. In addition, I will recall some of the 'colorful characters' I worked with over the course of my career.

Through Freight Service East of Hillyard

Number 82 was switched at Hillyard to fill to tonnage with time sensitive freight from Portland and Spokane for Gavin Yard and beyond. The Traffic Department advertised 54 hours from Balmer Yard to Union Yard in Minneapolis. That pace did not allow time for extensive switching at Hillyard, and No. 82 usually departed about two hours after it arrived each day. No. 82's train usually operated as the first section of No. 492 leaving Hillyard between 5:00 PM and 7:00 PM.

Number 88, the fruit train, carried fruit from Wenatchee and spuds from Quincy, plus lumber and paper products from Seattle and Everett, and was allowed 69 hours from Balmer to Union Yard. The switching of No. 88 at Hillyard was more complex than that of No. 82, and it took longer, typically two hours. Cars for Hillyard were removed. Traffic from Spokane, Portland, and fruit off the SP&S was added to the appropriate destination blocks. No. 88's train usually operated as second No. 492, leaving Hillyard between 7:00 and 9:00 PM. If there was a second No. 88's train, it usually operated as third No. 492, about an hour behind second No. 492.

In addition to switching eastward trains 82 and 88, Hillyard originated several eastward trains from traffic received off the branches and from Spokane proper. If there was more traffic than trains 82 and 88 could handle, the overflow traffic usually made a second section of 88's train. Many days during the winter fruit and spud season there was a third 88.

Wednesday through Saturday, the first eastward main line train out of Hillyard after midnight would actually be the last section of No. 88's train, which usually ran as the last section of the previous day's No. 492. This train was made up from local business, particularly aluminum from the Kaiser Mead reduction plant and lumber from the Kettle Falls, Coeur d'Alene, and Moscow locals.

After the last sections of No. 88 of the previous day, the first eastward train out of Hillyard was the Bull Local, called for 5:00 to 6:00 AM. Next was train No. 490 made up of loads and empty cars on hand at Hillyard headed for Havre, Montana, and stations east of Havre, usually called for 8:00 to 9:00 AM. If the Bull Local made a trip on the Kootenai Valley (KV) branch, No. 490 usually passed Bull Local at Bonners Ferry; if not, then No. 490 often chased the Bull Local into Troy.

Traffic to the Burlington at Laurel was handled east of Hillyard in one of two ways. During the spring and summer, when the wheat was not moving strongly, Hillyard did not generate a full eastward train to the CB&Q. Laurel traffic moved in block in the 490 dead freight, or in the trailing sections of No. 88's train. Laurel and Great Falls traffic was set out at Whitefish or Cutbank, which would originate a train No. 78 for Laurel. During the busy season for wheat, Hillyard received enough returning empty wheat cars to originate a train No. 78, and would do so. On the days it operated, No. 78's train was usually called after the first section of No. 88's train.

In addition to No. 97 and No. 83, the other westward symbol train out of Troy, Montana was No. 79, which

WESTWARD									SECOND SUBDIVISION								EASTWARD		3
Station Numbers	Car Capacity		FIRST CLASS					Distance from Troy	Time Table No. 110 Effective November 27, 1966 PACIFIC STANDARD TIME	Telegraph Calls	Distance from Fort Wright	SIGNS	FIRST CLASS				SECOND CLASS		
	Sidings	Other Tracks	1 S. P. & S. No. 1	31	45 S. P. & S. No. 3	5 TOFC	27						46 S. P. & S. No. 4	28	2 S. P. & S. No. 2	32	490	492	
			Daily	Daily	Daily	Daily Ex. Sat.	Daily		STATIONS				Daily	Daily	Daily	Daily	Daily	Daily	
01736	279	451	....	L 8.05Pm	....	....	L11.08Am	0.00	TROY ★	UX	142.08	RDNPBK XIYW	....	A 9.37Am	....	A 2.15Am	A10.00Am	A 8.00Pm	
01742	140	20	....	8.15	....	....	11.16	6.69	6.69 YAKT	....	135.39	P	....	9.27	....	2.02	9.40	7.50	
01749	126	23	....	8.26	....	....	11.26	13.49	6.80 LEONIA	....	128.59	P	....	9.18	....	1.52	9.25	7.38	
01768	130	11	....	8.46	....	....	11.46	27.00	13.51 CROSSPORT	....	115.08	P	....	8.58	....	1.32	9.02	7.13	
01767	116	177	....	8.56	....	....	s11.56	31.31	4.31 BONNERS FERRY ★	BY	110.77	DNPVY JW	....	490 s 8.47	....	1.26	28 8.47	7.01	
01778	116	38	....	9.10	....	....	f12.08Pm	42.68	11.37 NAPLES ★	....	99.40	PW	....	f 8.36	....	1.13	8.28	6.38	
01786	198	33	....	9.19	....	....	12.16	50.07	7.39 ELMIRA	....	92.01	P	....	8.28	....	1.05	8.15	6.25	
01793	122	11	....	9.26	....	....	12.23	56.88	6.81 COLBURN	....	85.20	P	....	8.21	....	12.57	8.05	6.15	
61903	105	391	....	9.35	....	....	s12.34	65.23	8.35 SANDPOINT ★	S	76.85	DNPVY ZW	....	s 8.12	....	12.48	7.52	6.02	
61917	124	16	....	9.50	....	....	12.48	78.58	13.35 LACLEDE	....	63.50	P	....	7.54	....	12.33	7.32	5.40	
61921	68	42	....	9.55	....	....	12.53	83.29	4.71 THAMA	....	58.79	P	....	7.49	....	12.27	7.25	5.32	
61925	67	105	....	9.59	....	....	s12.59	86.83	3.54 PRIEST RIVER	NC	55.25	DP	....	s 7.45	....	12.23	7.19	5.25	
61931	120	242	....	10.08	....	....	s 1.11	93.40	6.57 NEWPORT ★	NR	48.68	DNPVW	....	s 7.35	....	12.15	7.08	5.10	
61939	126	4	....	10.17	....	....	1.19	101.19	7.79 SCOTIA	....	40.89	P	....	7.22	....	12.06Am	6.55	4.55	
61946	117	25	....	10.25	....	....	1.26	107.78	6.59 CAMDEN	....	34.30	P	....	7.15	....	11.58	6.45	4.45	
61953	121	31	....	10.34	....	....	1.35	115.07	7.29 MILAN	....	27.01	P	....	7.07	....	11.50	6.35	4.35	
61963	....	52	....	10.47	....	....	1.47	125.45	10.38 DEAN	SF	16.63	DNPXJI	....	6.56	....	11.37	6.20	4.20	
61968	....	171	....	10.54	....	....	1.53	129.68	4.23 MEAD	....	12.40	P	....	6.50	....	11.31	6.11	4.11	
61972	....	3519	....	11.01	....	....	f 2.00	134.57	4.89 HILLYARD ★	HU	7.51	BRKDNP TWOIXZY	....	f 6.45	....	11.25	L 6.00Am	L 4.00Pm	
....	....	....	....	11.08	....	....	2.08	138.16	3.59 U. P. R. R. Cross'g	....	3.92	PIMVX	....	6.35	....	11.15	....	....	
61977	....	621	L11.40Pm	A11.15 L11 45	L 9.40Pm	L 9.15Pm	A 2.15 L 3.00	139.34	1.18 SPOKANE ★	Q	2.74	RKDNPO BXVZW	A 5.40Am	L 6.30 A 6.00	A10.00Pm	L11.10 A10.40	....	....	
61980	68	37	A11.45Pm	A11.50Pm	A 9.50Pm	A 9.20Pm	A 3.05Pm	142.08	2.74 FORT WRIGHT ★	FW	0.00	IDNP YXVR	L 5.30Am	L 5.53Am	L 9.50Pm	L10.35Pm	....	....	
			.05 32.88	3.45 38.15	.10 16.44	.05 32.88	3.57 35.96		Time Over Subdivision Average Speed Per Hour				.10 16.44	3.44 38.05	.10 16.44	3.40 38.75	4.00 33.64	4.00 33.64	

ABS

DOUBLE TRACK

WESTWARD	THIRD SUBDIVISION		EASTWARD		
Station Numbers	Capacity of Tracks	Distance from Columbia Falls	MOUNTAIN STANDARD TIME Time Table No. 110 Effective November 27, 1966 STATIONS	Telegraph Calls	SIGNS
01593	240	0.00	COLUMBIA FALLS ★	CF	JDNPYX
61605	44	5.46	5.46 LA SALLE	....	P
61617	427	14.40	8.94 KALISPELL	K	DNP JWYXZ
61625	Yard	24.85	10.45 SOMERS	....	PX

WESTWARD	FOURTH SUBDIVISION		EASTWARD		
Station Numbers	Capacity of Tracks	Time Table No. 110 Effective November 27, 1966 PACIFIC STANDARD TIME STATIONS	Distance from Bonner's Ferry	Telegraph Calls	SIGNS
61826	15	PORT HILL	25.95	....	....
01767	177	25.95 BONNERS FERRY ★	0.00	BY	DMNPYJV

The Kalispell Division Employee Timetable page showing main line between Hillyard and Troy. COLLECTION OF JOHN E. LANGLOT.

originated at Laurel, Montana and terminated at Spokane. No. 79 handled traffic from the CB&Q and export grain from Montana. This train handled the Alcoa alumina, the Kaiser alumina, coke, and pitch plus heavy loads of grain. No. 79 usually was about seven to eight thousand tons, which was a very heavy train in those days. No. 79 typically arrived Hillyard Wednesday through Saturday. Since the train was consistently heavy and made up of low priority traffic, the operating plan for No. 79 seemed to be to accumulate traffic to make a full tonnage train.

In addition to the symbol freights 97, 83, and 79, there were always time freights on the line up west of Troy, Montana. These were low priority trains that were operated as needed and when able. The lineup often included four or five such trains; if two of them showed up in a day it was a bit of a surprise. Some of these trains came up from the CB&Q, and some came from the eastern part of the Great Northern. They consisted of empties and dead freight such as grain. Basically, they moved anything and everything the yardmaster wanted to get out of his yard. Lineups at Troy sometimes showed a 'sod buster' for a low priority westward train.

West of Hillyard, low priority trains were called 'drags,' but the term 'drag' was not used east of Hillyard. The reasons for the different nomenclature are lost in the fog of history.

When 97 and 83 were closely approaching at Troy, any time freight in the vicinity was headed in and doubled over in the yard to be run after 97 and 83 departed. This avoided the possibility of delay to 97 and 83, and the dispatcher having to figure where to have the time freight head in to be passed. As a side benefit, this practice also avoided having the crew on the time freight get run around.

Time freights were always yarded at Hillyard in the West Yard. The train was tied down with about 10 hand brakes on the rear end, and the power would go to the diesel shop. The typical head in from the yardmaster would be, "Head in to West Two, tie it down, power to the house." They were switched on all three shifts from both ends of the yard when the engines were not otherwise engaged, but it could take as much as 24 hours to completely disassemble any particular time freight. Some of the cars went to the grain inspection tracks at Hillyard, some went on a drag west to Wenatchee, some went on a SP&S drag west to Wishram, and Vancouver, Washington, some went to the Hillyard and Spokane locals, and a few went to Hillyard and Spokane customers.

All export grain was inspected at Hillyard. The grain was switched to the Old Tie Plant for inspection. Once the grain was inspected, it was moved to train yard tracks 13 and 14. When it was called for on the coast, to Portland, Vancouver (Washington), Kalama, Longview, Tacoma, or Seattle, the grain was switched out by individual car number, and into a drag west for Wenatchee and Seattle or Tacoma, or into a SP&S drag west for Vancouver from which it went to Portland or one of the lower Columbia River ports.

When the grain was running heavy, the Drag West out of Hillyard carried a large block of grain on the head end leaving Hillyard and would pick up more grain on the way to Wenatchee. The Drag West picked up blocks of grain pulled from individual elevators and aggregated for the Drag West by the West Local. Odessa, Wilson Creek, and Quincy were favored stations for the West Local to leave a grain pick up.

This often resulted in a drag west into Wenatchee that could easily be made into an all grain extra west out of Wenatchee. Hillyard typically made their drags west with a block of cars on the rear for Wenatchee. This allowed the cars for Wenatchee to be taken off the rear end at Appleyard by the switch crew while the inbound crew cut the power off, ran up the W–O main to the yard office, and tied up. If the inbound drag was to be split, the Appleyard crew would next set all of the non-grain traffic over to another track to be run as a second extra west. If a Seattle crew was immediately available, they would back down the W–O main to their train, make a stub test, and depart Wenatchee as an all grain train.

When the grain was moving and empty reefer cars were in high demand, on some days the company ran two drags west to Wenatchee; the first one called at about 3:00 PM at Hillyard and another called for 11:00 PM plus a couple of drags to the SP&S per day.

The Bull Local

The eastward Bull Local originated at Hillyard. It was a straight away local that switched the industries at Priest River, Naples, and Bonners Ferry at times when other local service did not cover these stations. Since it seemed like every new trainmaster had to reinvent the wheel, duties were periodically shuffled among local jobs. The Bull Local operated six days per week between Hillyard and Troy, Montana. The Spokane crew tied up at Troy and a Whitefish crew took the train to Whitefish.

If a crew caught the Bull Local eastward, odds were they would come back on a through freight. Conversely, if a crew went east on a through freight, they might catch the Bull Local on their next trip. Nobody liked the Bull Local because it was slow, made many set outs and pick-ups, and the crew was sure to get run around twice on an eastward trip and probably once on a westward trip.

Nobody liked to get run around, because it reduced our earnings. Crews were called out of Hillyard, Troy, and Wenatchee on a first in, first out basis. Some guys spent a lot of effort whining about getting run around, but it happened to everybody with about the same frequency, so in the long run no one was hurt in terms of earnings. At least the Bull Local was a daylight trip.

The mission of the eastward Bull Local was to serve customers between Hillyard and Whitefish by delivering loads to customers, but more often delivering empty cars for loading, and picking up loaded cars moving eastward from customers and stations. The Bull Local was also used to move cars for Whitefish and beyond to Whitefish. Hillyard switch crews blocked the train station order with the Whitefish cars on the rear. Whitefish switched the train and forwarded east traffic, in block, by a variety of trains including another straight away mainline local beyond Whitefish. The eastward Bull Local was routinely called for 5:00 AM at Hillyard and it operated as an extra train.

The conductor picked up his train orders and 'train consist,' which is a list showing the cars in standing order starting with the caboose and ending with the car next to the engine, and the waybills for each loaded car. Today's train has 21 loads, 48 empties, 2,540 tons, and is 3,520 feet long, excluding the engine. Our engine today is three F 7 units. The Bull Local typically got three or four F 7 and/or GP 7 or GP 9 units drawn from whatever the roundhouse foreman had available at the time.

The Bull Local included a boxcar of way freight on the head end of the train. This car came out of the freight house at Spokane Yard and contained LCL freight for the stations on line. The bulk of the train consisted of cars for Newport, Priest River, Sandpoint, Bonners Ferry, Troy, and cars for stations east of Troy all the way to Whitefish. A final block of cars on the rear of the train was for Whitefish and stations east of Whitefish as far as Havre, Montana. Hillyard blocked these cars in station order. Whitefish thus was required to switch out only the head end of the Bull Local, add their cars, and fold it back together.

All West Yard tracks plus the low numbered tracks in the Train Yard were equipped with yard air. Trains were connected to the yard air to partially charge the air brake system, which greatly reduced the time needed to pump up the air before making an initial terminal air brake test. Yard air was particularly helpful to trains made up from cars in the yard.

The road crew brought the power out of the house, ran down the east end of the yard, and backed toward the train. The carmen usually attached the yard air about 20 cars or so into the Bull Local. A carman was usually on hand to disconnect the yard air after the head brakeman coupled the engine to the train, cut the engine air into the train, and walked back knocking the hand brakes off the train. The swing brakeman walked forward knocking off any handbrakes. The two brakemen met and walked to the head end. At the same time, the carmen made the air test. When the air test was complete, the Bull Local would depart about 6:00 or 7:00 AM.

Our usual first stop was Camden to spot empty gondolas for pulp wood loading. To make the Camden set out, we were required to head in to the siding, stop the train short of the industry track, make a cut behind the gondolas, spot the gons on the industry track, get back on our train, release the air, and pull to the east end of the siding. Next, we switched the little mill at Penrith Spur. West loads came to Newport for a west pickup, while the east loads stayed in our train.

At Newport, we unloaded way freight, always made a set out for the Newport Local, and made a pickup from the Newport Local's work from the day

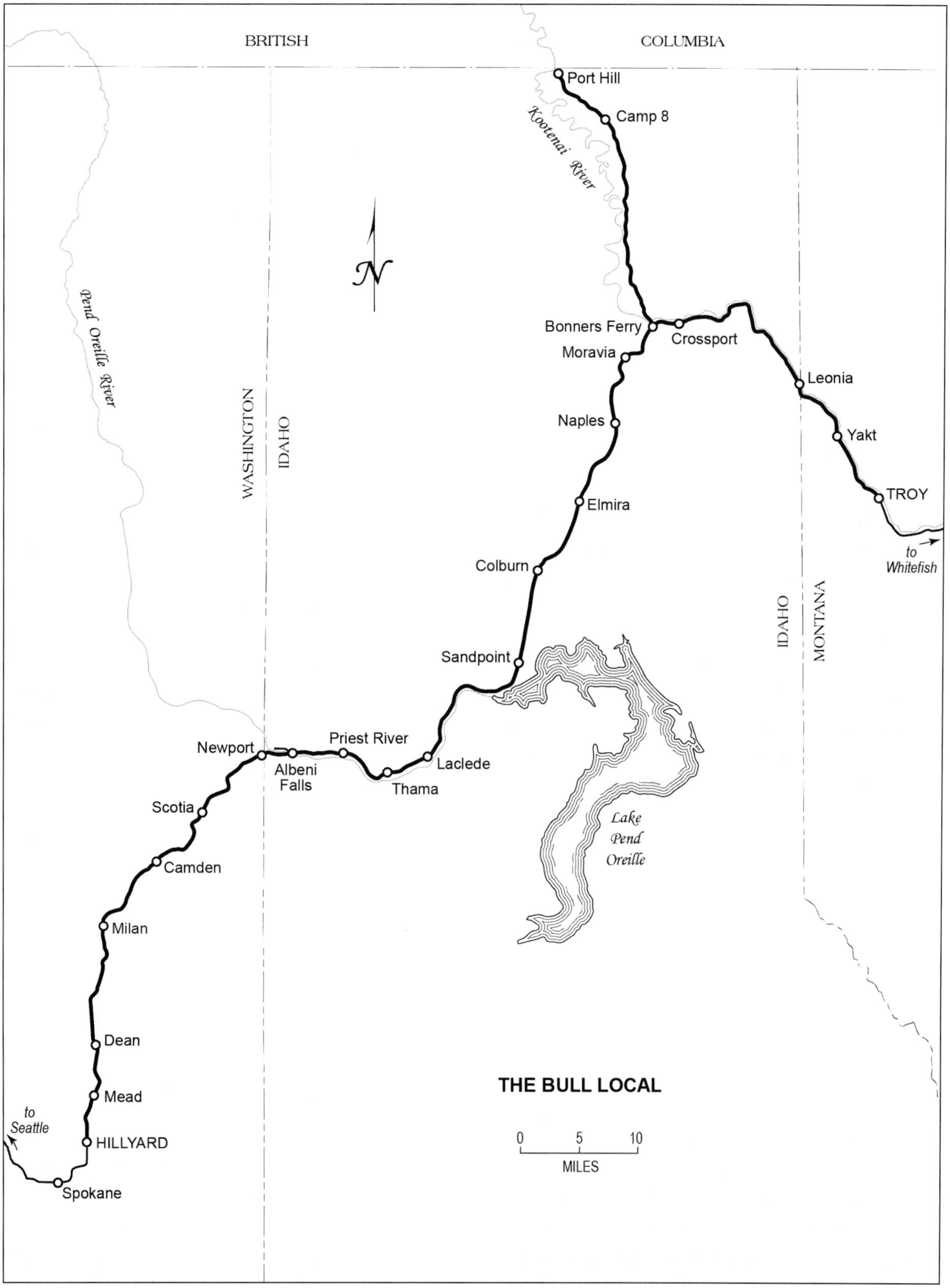
BRITISH
COLUMBIA
Port Hill
Camp 8
Kootenai River
Pend Oreille River
N
Bonners Ferry
Crossport
Moravia
Leonia
Naples
Yakt
WASHINGTON
IDAHO
Elmira
TROY
to Whitefish
Colburn
IDAHO
MONTANA
Sandpoint
Newport
Priest River
Albeni Falls
Laclede
Thama
Scotia
Lake Pend Oreille
Camden
Milan
Dean
THE BULL LOCAL
Mead
to Seattle
HILLYARD
0
5
10
MILES
Spokane

before. Our set out included the west cars from Penrith, and cars for the Newport Local to spot at Newport and at the Diamond National Lumber mill on the Albeni Falls Spur. We usually cleared up for No. 28 at Newport. In that case, we headed in to the siding and the rear brakeman lined the switch back for the main track behind us. We pulled down the east end of the siding and stopped at the depot. The head brakeman went to the depot where he gave the agent a list showing what we had set out, and got a switch list from the agent for our pickup off the industry track, adjacent to the siding.

After No. 28 departed, we lined the east end siding switch for the siding, made our pickup off the industry track, and set out our cars for the Newport Local in their place. We doubled the pickup to our train, made an air test on the pickup, and headed out of the siding for our next work at Priest River. The Newport Local told us to hurry up and leave, and that they would line the main track switch back for us when they came over to get the cars we had set out for them in the industry track. The east switch at Newport was the only siding switch between Hillyard and Troy that was not a spring switch.

On the way to Priest River we went by Albeni Falls Dam across the Pend Oreille River and ran along the river. Diamond National Lumber Company was located on the Albeni Falls Spur on the north side of the river, about three miles east of the Newport depot. Albeni Falls Spur opened to the east and extended about one mile over a hill to the lumber mill. The Newport Local switched the mill on their eastward trip. The Newport Local could not take the Priest River cars into the mill with them because they would have too much tonnage to get in and out of the mill with the grades on the Albeni Falls Spur.

At Priest River, we set out cars for the Newport Local to spot to a lumber mill at Priest River. The constraints at Albeni Falls were the reason why we set out the Diamond National cars at Priest River rather than at Newport. Between Priest River and Laclede, the line ran alongside the beautiful Pend Oreille River.

Our next stop was Sandpoint. We always made a set out and a pickup at Sandpoint and often did some switching and spotting of cars. We headed into the siding, dropped the head brakeman at the Baldy Mountain Road crossing to cut the train to clear the crossing and behind the Bonners Ferry cars, while holding on to the Sandpoint set out and the Newport pickup, which was right behind the engine. Behind the cut, the remainder of the train was for Whitefish and Troy, in that order, from the rear. This left the caboose in the clear at Sandpoint, so that everything would fit into the siding during our stub test just in case we met another train before we departed.

We came out of the east end of the siding, shoved west on the main track and into the Sandpoint Yard, which was located on the opposite side of the main from the siding. We set the Bonners Ferry cars into the one clear yard track, set the Sandpoint cars to the yard track that already held a few Sandpoint cars, and set the loads from Newport to the Scale Track. As part of their previous day's work, the Newport Local built a block of eastward lumber and pole loads, weighed them, and left them on track 3, the Scale Track, for us to pick up. A few of the cars we picked up at Newport and set to the east end of track 3, those from the second pull at Diamond National and off the Milwaukee, needed to be weighed. Our Sandpoint set out included cars for the mills at Colburn and Naples, plus empty log flatcars for Moravia. The Newport Local would pick these cars up later in the day and spot them to the customers on their way to Bonners Ferry.

By this time, our conductor and rear brakeman had picked up the switch list and waybills at the depot and walked east to the yard. We often got a switch list from the agent telling us to pull loads of poles to go east from the two pole yards that were located off the 'stem' track, which was also the tail of the wye. In this case, we ran down the main track to the west end of the yard and dug out any flatcars to be spotted to the pole yards. We took the flatcars past the west leg of the wye switch, shoved east on the west leg of the wye, and onto the stem. Today we switched both pole yards picking up four loads of poles, two out of each pole yard, and spotted the empty flatcars as ordered.

We came back the west leg of the wye and shoved the loads of poles into the Scale Track against the loads already there, pulled them all past the scale, and began to weigh the loads we had added to the east end on the scale, one at a time. We continued this process until all of the new loads on the east end were weighed. We then got all the cars on the east end of Scale Track

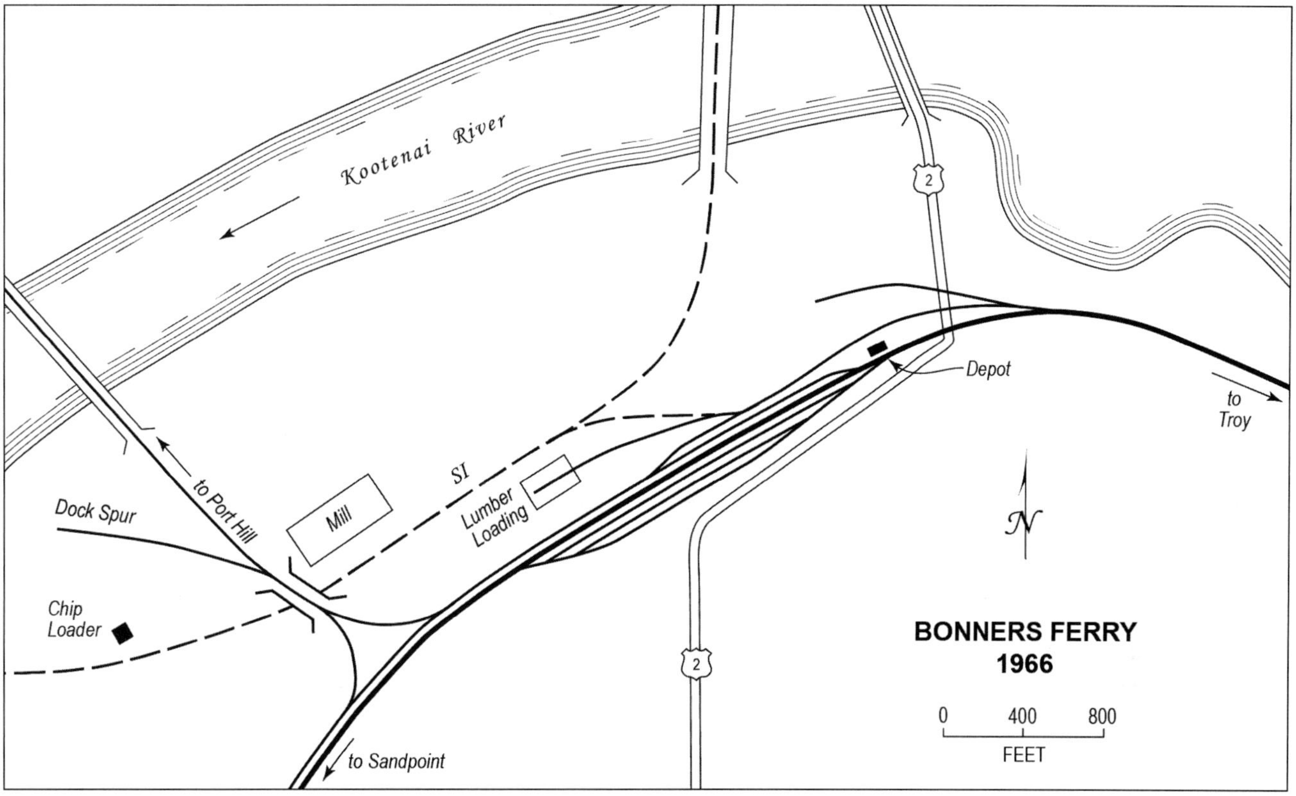

back together and shoved them east of the scale. Then we weighed the few cars from Sandpoint that were on the west end. Weighing done, we got all the cars on the Scale Track back together and cut away from them. We got permission from the dispatcher to use the main track, and ran to the east end of the yard where we coupled into the track with the cars for Bonners Ferry, doubled them to the east loads on track 3, and then doubled everything back to the train on the siding.

The reason we brought the cars for Bonners Ferry over to the yard was because the cars we picked up at Newport and Sandpoint were going to points east of Whitefish. These cars needed to be cut into the train sooner or later. By bringing the Bonners Ferry cars to the yard at Sandpoint, the cars for Whitefish and beyond fell together, and any pole loads, which were likely to shift, were buried in the train. By putting the Whitefish and beyond cars together at Sandpoint, we could do the rest of our work without handling the loads we picked up at Sandpoint at every other stop short of Bonners.

At Bonners Ferry the siding, depot, house track, industry track, interchange track, and the wye were all located on the north side of the main track. The yard was located south of the main track. The Bull Local headed into the siding, made a cut behind the Bonners Ferry cars, pulled them out on the main, then shoved west to put the set out into the house track behind the depot. By the time this was done, we could pick up the conductor and rear brakeman who were walking toward the depot, which was east of the east siding switch.

We switched the lumber dock, which was located off the House Track, pulling two or three loads of lumber and spotting two or three empty cars for lumber loading. Many days we delivered a boxcar of lumber from the lumber dock to the Spokane International transfer and/or picked up an empty boxcar off the SI transfer to spot to the lumber dock. The lumber cars we pulled went east, so we put them to the head end of our train.

We occasionally spotted one or two boxcar loads of feed, or pulled an empty or two, at the combined feed store and grain elevator. The grain elevator loaded grain in season. Some days we spotted an empty boxcar or pulled a load of grain. Empty boxcars that last contained feed and loads of grain usually went west, so we set them first out on the west end of the house track for a west pickup.

During the wheat shipping season, the Bull Local often made a trip up the Kootenai Valley branch line that left Bonners Ferry off the tail of the wye located at the east end of Bonners Ferry siding. If we planned to go up the KV line after the industry switching, we put the pull cars onto the head end of our train and pulled the entire train east to beyond the east switch of the wye. Then we shoved west and set the caboose onto the east leg of the wye. Then pulled the train east, lined the east wye switch for the siding, and shoved our train back into the siding, stopping well west of the west wye switch. We needed to shove the train far enough west so that when we came back from the KV line, the engine and KV wheat loads would fit between the train and the west switch of the wye.

We used only one unit, and it was required to be a road switcher type like a GP 7 or GP 9, to make our trip up and down the KV line. If, as was common, a road switcher unit was not on the point, then we switched one out and put the rest of the power back on the train to keep the train fully charged. If we did not keep the train charged, when we returned and were ready to proceed east, we were required to make a full terminal air brake test.

With our GP unit dug out, we got the caboose off the east leg of the wye, pulled out onto the main track, and went to east end of the yard. We went into the yard and gathered up our empty boxcars for wheat loading. Next, we pulled our Port Hill train east onto the main track and shoved the cars and caboose west into the house track, cutting them off to clear the main track switch at the east end. Then we came out onto the main and ran west on the main and siding to the west end of the house track. Completing the run around move, we backed onto the train, made our terminal air test, and waited for the conductor to come out of the depot with our train orders for the KV line. Leaving the house track, we lined the switch for the siding and took the west leg of the wye to head for Port Hill, lining the wye switch behind us for the siding.

While the brakemen were getting the train together, the conductor received new orders. One such order annulled our running order from Hillyard to Troy so that the dispatcher would not be 'stuck' with a running order on his main line held by our train, which would be long lost on the KV branch. Another new order was a work order that authorized us to move in either direction with the GP unit between Bonners Ferry and Port Hill.

The usual KV line trip took 15 to 20 empty boxcars, spotting empty cars on the way up and picking up loads of grain on the way back. This was in the days of loading grain in 40-foot B2 boxcars with a single six-foot wide door on each side. Very seldom did we have to go all the way to Port Hill, which was 25.95 miles from Bonners Ferry and adjacent to the International Boundary. Most of the time, Camp 8, 19.74 miles north of Bonners, was our turn back point. A trip to Camp 8 was two hours up and two hours back since this was all on 10 MPH track. With switching, a round trip to Camp 8 usually took five or six hours.

Upon our return to Bonners Ferry we took the west leg of the wye, stopping to uncouple the caboose on the tail of the wye. We then shoved east on the siding and into the house track to deliver our conductor to the depot. The operator told the dispatcher that we were back. The dispatcher gave us authority to occupy the main track at Bonners Ferry, annulled the work order on the KV, and gave us a new running order to Troy. Once we got a hand sign from the conductor to occupy the main track, the power shoved the loads east onto the main track, pulled them to the west end of the yard, and shoved the wheat into the Bonners Ferry yard for the westward Bull Local to pick up. We came back and pulled the caboose to the east leg of the wye to clear the siding.

Then we usually switched our single unit back into the power consist and air tested it. We could not tack the GP unit onto the head end unless it was our lead unit out of Hillyard, because both our old and new running orders were addressed to our lead unit from Hillyard. The addressed unit was the one anyone we would meet was looking for to identify us, and it was required to be the lead unit.

We made a stub air test on the pickup while the conductor was up at the depot getting train orders for our trip to Troy. Once the air test was done, we pulled the train east, picked the caboose off the east leg of the wye, and the conductor gave a copy of the new orders to the engineer, we could depart for Troy.

All freight trains changed crews at Troy. If the Bull Local was to change crews at the depot, then the operator would tell us to head into the siding. The outbound crew would do the station work at Troy from the siding before they departed. If the dispatcher decided to run the train later, we were usually told to head in to track 2 and double the head end of the train into track 3.

The westward Bull Local was called early in the morning at Whitefish, Montana. The crew worked their way toward Troy picking up, setting out, and spotting cars at places like Stryker, Fortine, Eureka, and Rexford. At Libby, they picked up several carloads of wood chips for the west plus an occasional car of lumber for California.

Sometimes the westward Bull Local crew changed immediately at Troy, while other times the train would be headed in to the yard and run later due to heavy eastward traffic or a shortage of rested crews. Again, the outbound crew would pick up, set out, and spot cars for Troy. After switching at Troy, we could depart for Bonners Ferry.

At Bonners Ferry, the westward Bull Local set out any cars for Bonners on the house track or into the yard, and picked up the west loads. Very seldom did we spot cars at Bonners on the trip west; we routinely picked up westward loads of wheat off the KV line, plus logs from Moravia and lumber from Naples that the Newport Local left for us. The pickup at Bonners Ferry ranged from 10 to 30 cars. The large pickups always included grain off the KV line. Pickup made, we headed west.

At Sandpoint, the Bull Local picked up 15 to 20 west loads that the Newport Local had pulled from customers at Naples and the Pack River Lumber Company at Colburn. On occasion, we made a small set out at Sandpoint.

At Newport, we stopped and made our pick up from the storage track. The storage track was located on the north side of the main at the east end of Newport, while the siding was on the south side of the main and west of the storage track. The Bull Local picked up the chips that the Newport Local switched out of Hedlund Lumber Co. at Priest River. There was also an occasional west load of lumber from Hedlund or the other lumber mills at Priest River or Diamond National Lumber at the Albeni Falls Spur. West loads of poles from Sandpoint, plus pulp wood loaded in 40-foot drop bottom gondolas off the pulp wood spur at Newport were included in the Newport pickup. Our last usual stop was at Camden to pick up pulp wood in gondolas.

Once in a while symbol train No. 79 was terminated at Whitefish and its alumina ore loads put on the Bull Local for set out at Mead. In this case, we made a cut behind the 20 or so cars of alumina ore to be set out and set them over onto the storage track. We came back out with the Newport and Bonners Ferry pickups that were behind the engine, backed on to our train, made a quick set up and release air test, and headed for Hillyard.

At Hillyard the yardmaster generally told us to head in to the west yard, tie the train down, and take the power to the house. The inbound Bull Local was not blocked when it got to Hillyard because both Spokane and the Whitefish crew picked cars up to the head end. The Bull Local was a jumbled mess that needed to be completely switched. Some of this train went west to Puget Sound points via Wenatchee, and some of it went to Vancouver, Washington via Pasco on the SP&S.

➻ Scotia Canyon and Kootenai Canyon

Between Hillyard and Troy the main line passed through two notable canyons, Scotia Canyon and Kootenai Canyon.

Scotia Canyon extends about four miles between Camden and Scotia. It was part of a minor flood channel during the Spokane Floods of the most recent ice age. The canyon is now occupied by Scotia Creek and the Little Spokane River. Scotia Creek is an unimpressive stream that originates at a small lake only a couple of miles southwest of the Newport depot. Scotia Creek feeds a series of lakes known as Chain Lakes. The Little Spokane flows out of the last of the Chain Lakes. The Great Northern followed Scotia Creek and the Little Spokane downstream, westward, from Scotia Creek's origin to Chattaroy, about 25 miles. The bedrock is hard granite or well-cooked hard metamorphic rock for this

TOP Train No. 28 crossing the bridge over Scotia Creek west of Scotia. Lead unit, number 333, is one of eight SDP 45s built in 1967 and delivered in the new Big Sky Blue paint scheme. The trailing unit is an SDP 40 built in 1966. PHOTO BY DALE JONES.

BOTTOM Extra 2531 East with engine 2531, a General Electric model U33C, and an unidentified GP 20 have just exited the eastern most tunnel in Scotia Canyon. Chain Lakes is in the background. The train is probably the Bull Local with much more modern power than usual this day. PHOTO BY DALE JONES.

entire distance.[1] The rock walls extend upward for 200 to 300 feet above the roadbed.

On July 23, 1906, passenger train number 3 derailed as it emerged from the west portal of tunnel 11. Engine number 930, its tender, the mail car, and the baggage car were totally submerged in Chain Lake. The smoking car was partially submerged and a coach was turned on its side on the embankment. Nine people were killed.[2] Some survivors claimed that the train was running faster than normal.[3] The distance the engine traveled on its side is consistent with that claim.

The original construction of 1892 featured one tunnel and three bridges near Chain Lake. A line change in 1927 replaced one bridge with a new tunnel, tunnel 10.4, to reduce both length and sharpness of the curves. A line change in 1945 replaced the original tunnel number 11 with a new and longer tunnel 11, again to reduce curvature and increase speed.[4] During the 1960s, the freight speed limit through the canyon was 45 MPH.

The Great Northern main track is located on the south flank of the Kootenai Canyon from the east end of Crossport, a siding four and one-half miles east of Bonners Ferry, 20.3 miles to Yakt, Montana. Track speed is limited to 30 MPH between Crossport and Yakt. The canyon was cut by the Kootenai River. The Purcell Mountains are north of the river, and the Cabinet Range is to the south.

The rocks in the canyon are mostly Precambrian rocks of the Belt Formation. They are at least 570 million years old and could easily be one billion years old. Long after the rocks were deposited, they were heated and compressed, becoming low grade metamorphic rocks, which are harder than the original sedimentary rocks, but still not particularly solid. In addition, the rock weathers to a 'rotten' condition. In some places, the canyon walls rise as much as 300 feet at a very steep angle. Rock slides are a constant danger in Kootenai Canyon. Rain, snow, and freezing weather increase the chances of rock falls and rock slides.

For example, about 11:00 AM on June 27, 1942 train First 460, engine 2013, a class N-3 2-8-8-0, with 103 cars and 5,000 tons hit a rock slide at MP 1361, measured from St. Paul, about half a mile east of Crossport Rock Quarry spur. The rock quarry belonged to the Great Northern and was shown as a business track in the Time Table. The head end crew members, engineer Al Simpson, fireman Charlie Krupa, and head brakeman Al Ballard, who jumped from the engine before impact all lived, as did the rear end crew of conductor Ray Fifer and rear brakeman George Hebron. Six hundred sheep were killed.

Author Langlot's father, John H. Langlot, and Julius Ryan were two of the brakemen called off the extra board for the Hillyard wrecker to clean up the derailment from the west end. The Whitefish wrecker was called to work the east end. John H. said that they stacked the dead sheep up, poured stove oil on them and set them on fire. The sheep did not burn well and the air was full of thick rancid smoke that hung in the canyon air for days. One night the crew went to the cook car for dinner to find that the cook had prepared lamb stew; there was talk of hanging the cook.

Al Ballard gave the photo to Tom Ryan, son of Julius Ryan, since Al knew the photo would be thrown away and the story lost with his passing. Tom went into engine service on the GN and retired from BNSF as an engineer. Tom gave the photo and the story to John Langlot.

By the time I arrived on the scene in the 1960s, the places where rocks were expected to slide or fall were protected by slide fences. Slide fences were, and are, coarse wire mesh fences attached to electrical connections on both ends of each section of fence. If snow, rocks, or trees came down the slope, the slide fence would be displaced, which would unplug the electrical connections and set the lineside automatic block signals to red. Trains could go past the red block signal, but no faster than the restricted speed, so they could and would stop short of any slide.

Now and then we get a reminder that Mother Nature is still alive in Kootenai Canyon. On January 1, 2020 a westward freight train moving through Kootenai Canyon on clear signals hit a slide at Milepost 1365, immediately west of the west switch at Katka. The lead unit ended up entirely in the swiftly flowing river, the second was nearly perpendicular to the roadbed, and the third stayed on the roadbed with at least one car derailed behind it. The crew, trapped in the partially flooded engine cab, were rescued by members of the Boundary County Sherriff's Office Rescue Team.

By placing very large air bags under the lead unit, it was floated off the river bed and pulled across the river to a sand bar on the north side, where it was cut up for scrap.

Crossport Pit, at the west end of the canyon, featured a vertical wall of rock extending about 200 feet above the grade. The exposed wall was about 600 feet long, extending to the south from the main track at about a 60-degree angle. The hard rock was a gray colored igneous material forced into the seams in the surrounding rock. Great Northern built a spur track along the base of the talus slope, which it excavated and used for rip rap in the canyon and as needed to the east and west.

The derailment of train first 460, engine 2013, class N-3, in Kootenai Canyon near milepost 1361 on June 27, 1942, illustrates one risk associated with locating a rail line in a canyon: rockfalls, which are quite capable of derailing a train, as shown here. PHOTO BY AL BALLARD. COLLECTION OF TOM RYAN.

Ditching in Kootenai Canyon

During the summer of 1999, I was conductor of a work train ditching along the roadbed between Sandpoint, Idaho and Troy, Montana with the Georgetown Slot Train. The slot train was 13 gondola car bodies joined together by draw bars, and sharing a truck between adjacent car bodies. The whole train was open from end to end. Steel plates welded to the bottoms and sides at the end of each car body slid back and forth against the adjacent car body as the car bodies went around curves. The slide plates allowed the gondola bodies to go around curves without binding and without spilling any of the material. The gondola bodies on each end are equipped with a set of trucks and conventional couplers at the outside ends along with removable car ends. The proper name for this multi-unit car was an articulated gondola. A track hoe inside the train could move freely from end to end. It excavated the ditch and put the spoils in the car.

On January 1, 2020, a westward train hit a slide near the west end of Katka, milepost 1365, putting the entire lead unit in the Kootenai River. The crew was rescued by members of the Boundary Search and Dive Rescue Team using their Marine 1 rescue boat. BNSF employee Adam Reeves was one of the first two team members to respond. Adam broke a window and got the crewmen out of the partially flooded cab to a position of relative safety on top of the engine. PHOTO BY IDAHO STATE POLICE.

Kootenai Canyon, which extends 20 miles from a point about a mile east of Crossport, Idaho to Yakt, Montana, requires a lot of ditching due to the generally steep slopes above the railroad, which is built about 20 feet above the normal level of the river. The ditches are there to intercept the water runoff from the slopes above the railroad and convey the water to culverts or bridges under the roadbed. Our preferred on-duty point was Bonners Ferry, which had sufficient track to hold the train when we were not using it and a depot where we and the Roadmaster could meet each morning to plan the day's activity and advise the dispatcher by phone what we wanted to do. Troy was the next place to the east with a depot and tracks available to hold the train.

Between Katka and Leonia, we encountered several spots where the rock was very soft and unstable. We were ditching at the west end of the siding at Leonia one day when a rock about the size of a Volkswagen Beetle started to roll down the slope from about 200 feet above us on about a 45-degree angle. We were about ready to run when the rock broke in half the first time it rolled over. Each time the pieces of rock rolled over they broke in half again. By the time they reached the bottom of the slope, the pieces were about the size of a basketball. By the time this slide stopped, it was up tight against the trucks under our train. There was no way the track hoe operator could reach the debris that was under the side of the train.

Mark May, the section foreman in charge of us, said, "What do we do now?" We talked it over and decided that as soft as this rock was, maybe if we moved the loaded train very slowly it would just push the rocks out of the way. We started to move the train, and the trucks shoved and broke the rocks up into very small pieces. We were able to move back far enough to cut the caboose off so that the operator could work over the end of the car with his bucket. He shoved the debris to the side where the ditch should be, and then picked the muck up and load it into the gondola.

There was a lot of other work going on between Bonners Ferry and Troy that summer. To reduce congestion and delay, we moved our train and on duty point to

A westward BNSF stack train emerges from Kootenai Canyon in the last rays of sunlight on October 27, 2018, at the site of the Great Northern's now abandoned Crossport Pit. A spur track ran along the bottom of the face of the rock wall, which was worked to supply rip rap and ballast for many miles in each direction. PHOTO BY BRUCE KELLY.

Troy and concentrated on ditching between Troy and Leonia. Because suitable lodging was not available in Troy, we continued to stay at the Kootenai River Inn and Casino at Bonners Ferry, about 30 miles from Troy. One evening, as I was driving myself and the crew back to Bonners Ferry, we could see that the sky to the west was very black, so we knew that a storm was coming our way. When we headed to bed, we were actually in a cloud burst. I looked out the glass sliding door of my top floor room, and it was raining so hard that I could not see the Kootenai River, which was only about 50 feet away. This hard rain continued most of the night; several times the sound of the rain beating on the roof of my room woke me up.

At the morning meeting at the Bonners Ferry depot, we were instructed to drive to Troy and work westward to check the canyon for mud and rock slides. The diesel electric crane was between Troy and Yakt, working to clear debris from the upstream side of the bridge over a creek that was now running like a raging river before the high water could take the mainline bridge out. I copied joint Track and Time with the diesel electric crew and proceeded from Troy to the bridge where we saw that trees 20 to 30 feet long and brush were piling up at the bridge. We waited until the crane had cleared enough material from behind the bridge to at least temporary alleviate the problem.

We both headed to Yakt, where the crane headed into the siding to let us by. After we cleared the siding,

I called the dispatcher and gave up my joint track and time and we headed toward Leonia, cleaning up small slides along the right-of-way. The rain continued to fall very hard, and it took us about two hours to reach Leonia, which is a bit less than seven miles from Yakt. By this time, the slot train was about half full of mud, rocks, brush, and parts of dead trees.

At Leonia, where the Idaho–Montana state line passes through the middle of the siding, we continued west on the main track to evaluate the conditions, and were soon in shock at what we saw. The canyon wall along the entire Leonia siding was a giant waterfall, and it had flooded the siding. The water was slowly running through the main track toward the Kootenai River. I contacted the dispatcher and asked him to clear the signal at the east end of Leonia back toward Yakt, and then head us into the siding so we could clean up the mess. I also advised the dispatcher of the conditions at Leonia and said that we would be here ditching for two or three hours. He said the railroad was ours, as the west end of the new siding at Katka was washed out, and the other work train was loading rip rap at Crossport Pit to fill that hole.

We ditched all along the siding to restore the ditch so that the water would run off toward both ends of the siding. By this time, the train was full and we needed to find a place to unload it. I contacted the dispatcher and had him line us out of the siding at Leonia and west down the canyon. As we crossed over the Boulder Creek Bridge, we found the same tree debris problem was occurring there as at the creek between Troy and Yakt. I again called the dispatcher and informed him of the conditions at Boulder Creek, and the crane operator, Scott Granger, responded and said he had cleared up the first mess and was headed our way. The dispatcher had us both copy joint Track and Time between Yakt and Katka, and we continued to work our way toward Katka.

The first order of business was to find a spot on the river side of the roadbed that needed widening, to unload the slot train. We found a spot about a mile west of Leonia, unloaded, and then resumed ditching to the east switch at Katka. By this time, it was about 4:00 PM and the line at the west end of Katka was still not back in service, but the other work train was resetting the west switch. We contacted the crane operator and informed him we were headed east, and Scott responded that he was just about done cleaning up the mess at Boulder Creek. We stopped and unloaded the train again, and proceeded to Leonia. By the time we arrived at Leonia, Scott was sitting in the clear on the west end of the siding. We stopped on the main and Scott brought the crane out of the west end of the siding and coupled to our engine. Scott shifted the crane out of gear, and we headed to Troy with the crane in tow. We headed in at Troy, put the train away in the yard, and motored to Bonners Ferry.

While we were headed to Troy, the head of the Maintenance-of-Way Department for the entire railroad called on the radio from Fort Worth, Texas, and asked the Roadmaster, Arnie Olson, for a report of the conditions in the canyon. We all listened to Arnie's report. At the end of Arnie's report, the big boss asked Arnie, "What could you have done to prevent this situation?" Poor Arnie was speechless. How could he explain Kootenai Canyon to a Frisco flatlander? It was all I could do to refrain from picking up the radio handset and saying "TALK TO GOD!"

Later that summer, we were ditching with the slot train between Bonners Ferry and Leonia. This particular day we planned to begin ditching from the new siding at Katka, east of Crossport, and work eastward toward Leonia. When we arrived at Katka, we were held west of one area that was a chronic slide problem due to soft rotten rock that kept sloughing off the face of the rock wall above the track. Two scalers the company had hired were hanging from cables and swinging back and forth, prying giant slabs of rock off the face of the wall. Some of these slabs must have weighed two or three tons, and when they hit the bottom they broke into hundreds of pieces. The company obviously figured it was better to bring the rock down at its convenience rather than have it fall on the track or a train. The scalers were two brothers who got $500 per hour for their work. We waited about two hours before we could pass. We all agreed that we would not change occupations with the scalers.

➸ Colorful Characters

Blue collar workers built this country. Their blood, sweat, and tears made America the great country it is today. This is particularly true of the railroad industry.

Railroads hired their blue-collar work force in cities and small towns all across the United States and Canada, and from all social levels. In the early years, railroad operating jobs involved long hours of hard work which took its toll on these men both physically and mentally.

Between 1865 and 1940, millions of men migrated to this country. Many of them struggled to speak English and in many cases their education was extremely poor. Some of these men, and many of their sons, found their way into the railroad craft jobs including in engine, train, and yard service, the car shops and the roundhouses. Immigrants were particularly likely to work in construction camps and on section gangs. One thing is for sure, the huge majority were devoted to the company and to their jobs. They worked long days, day in and day out, for months at a time. In case of emergencies, they worked for weeks at a time, often with very little sleep.

In engine service, one started out as a fireman. The fireman's basic job was to keep the fire in the fire box hot enough to produce adequate steam for the engine to pull the train. This was largely a matter of shoving coal while standing on a heaving deck; it was backbreaking work. My father, who hired out on the Great Northern in 1929 as a brakeman, told me that on a hard pull with maximum tonnage, both the fireman and the head brakeman would work shoving coal into the fire box to keep the steam pressure high enough to pull the grade. The gateway craft in engine service did not take much brain power, just a strong back and a lot of muscle. Most men with a decent education or better prospects sought employment elsewhere.

During World War II, many railroad men in all the crafts and in operating management positions entered the military services. This loss of labor, combined with the huge increase in traffic associated with World War II, forced railroads all over the country to hire men in all crafts who were too old to fight to keep the railroad running. A good portion of these men were hired in engine service as firemen. By this time, Great Northern steam engines on the west end were burning oil, and the first diesels were just coming into service, so the physical demands were not as daunting as with coal firing. Very few of this group ever became good engineers. They were too old to acquire the skills and the touch of running engines pulling longer and heavier trains. Most of them bid in switch engines in their later years rather than work the chain gang pools, where they would be running long, heavy, and fast mainline trains.

As the workload increased and became more difficult after the war, the older brakemen and switchmen hired during WWII would mark up only on a job that they could handle. They could handle a local that switched 20 or 30 cars a day at two or three towns, but not the Spud Local out of Quincy which got 15 to 20 switch lists, averaging 20 cars per list, each night, on which the conductor and swing man needed to keep track of every car in their minds.

The W–O locals during fruit season were challenging jobs. Crews on these locals were spotting reefers all night long and double spotting on some storage tracks. Double spotting means spotting two cars on parallel tracks, with the car doors aligned so that the customer can load, or unload, the car farthest from his facility by moving his product through the car nearest his facility. On the W–O, the crew often lined up the reefers that the customer ordered, and that the agent selected, to specific doors on the industry track. This was time consuming and complicated switching. We usually held three or four switch lists each for Chelan and Pateros, two for Brewster, two to three each for Okanogan and Tonasket, five or six for Omak, and three or four for Oroville. Granted, there were short breaks between stations, but this intensive switching went on all night long, night after night, for up to 16 hours. Some brakemen could not handle the pressure. Here again, water seeks its own level.

One of the most colorful characters I ever met was a Great Northern engineer named Maynard Young, who was a fireman when I hired out in 1960. Maynard was a real nice guy, a gentle giant. He was about six feet seven and weighed about 260 pounds, which was a big man in those days. I really liked Maynard; he was always kind and considerate of others. He was not too graceful on his feet, so he was kind of like a bull in a china closet. If something got knocked over or broken, Maynard was probably the cause.

When I was working the Wenatchee chain gang freight pool as a conductor, I always asked the crew clerk who my engineer would be. One day, Dick Lyonnais told me that it should be Maynard Young, but Dick was still trying to find him. About 10 minutes later, as I was getting ready for work, the phone rang. It was Dick. He told me that Maynard would be a little bit late; he had suffered a minor accident and would be a while getting the bleeding stopped. Dick told me that Maynard told him that he was putting in new basement stairs and was down in the basement when the phone rang. Since there were no stairs, Maynard was forced to climb up a ladder and out a basement window, run around to the front door, go into the house, and answer the phone. When Maynard ran into the kitchen to grab the phone, he slipped and fell down the hole in the kitchen floor where the stairs to the basement used to be, landing on his head on the concrete basement floor. Now this would probability kill you and me, but obviously not good old Maynard. I reported for work at Yardley. About 10 minutes later Maynard came in with a big gauze patch taped to the top of his forehead. Maynard did allow that his head hurt a little bit. I rode the caboose to Wenatchee; the trip was routine.

Another time I was working the Wenatchee pool with Maynard as my engineer. I was in the yard office when I noticed that Maynard wore a brand-new pair of shoes, but they were smeared with white paint. Now, Maynard was a bachelor. I asked him what happened to his new shoes. Maynard told me that he was painting the bathroom door on a couple of saw horses in the living room when he accidently kicked the gallon can of paint over, spilling it all over his shoes and the living room carpet. Maynard told me that he mopped the paint up the best he could with rags. He went on to say, "You know, the vacuum cleaner makes a funny sound when it goes over that spot." What more can I say!

Another time I was called to deadhead to Wenatchee in chain gang freight service. When I arrived at Yardley, Dave Johnson, my engineer, came up and said that we could take Maynard's Wenatchee car to Wenatchee for him rather than ride the bus with four other deadhead crews. My two brakemen and I told Dave that would be great. Then Dave said that we would have to wait for Maynard to bring a trunk key out for the car so we could put our grips in the trunk. Right then I started to have second thoughts, but Dave was a pretty sharp guy, and he probably thought nothing could go wrong. I decided that if Dave was happy, I would be happy. Foolish me!

Finally, Maynard showed up and jumped out of his car. I noticed that Maynard's right hand was all bandaged up, so I asked Maynard what happened to his hand. Maynard said, "It's been one hell of a day," which was a common phrase on the railroad. As Maynard was saying this, he walked to the trunk of his Wenatchee car and jammed the key into the lock on the trunk with his left hand. The key went into the lock crooked. Instead of pulling the key back out, Maynard whacked the key open handed with his left hand. This punched a hole in the palm of his left hand and broke the key off in the lock. One of my brakemen ran to the yard office and brought back some paper towels for Maynard to wrap his left-hand in. So here we are going to Wenatchee in Maynard's two door car: four of us and our grips all crammed into Maynard's car like sardines. As we left, I looked at Maynard standing there. He was a sight with both hands now wrapped up from that day's injuries. Maynard was right; it was one hell of a day.

Later I was working with Maynard in the Wenatchee pool after the company pulled the brakemen off through freight trains, so it was just Maynard and me on the train. We were westward coming into Edwall when, without warning, the overspeed whistle started to blow in the engine cab. All the wheels on the lead engine were spinning and the speedometer showed about 90 MPH. If the engineer does not get the speedometer to drop back where it belongs in a short period of time, the overspeed will dump the air, putting the train into emergency. That could derail the train. The overspeed whistle has a very high pitch and is very loud. Believe me, it will make your eyes cross.

I instantly looked over at Maynard, and I could tell that he did not hear the overspeed whistle. I jumped across the engine cab, reached over the control panel, and shut the throttle off. Maynard looked a little put out until I pointed to the speedometer. Maynard then realized what had happened. He applied the engine brakes just a little bit to get the wheels to quit spinning, and the overspeed whistle finally stopped blowing. Nothing was said until we started down the hill west of Bluestem. Maynard turned on his overhead cab light and thanked me for keeping the air from going into emergency. He told me that he was so deaf after working in engine service all these years that he could no longer hear high pitched sounds. I can relate to this as now I have trouble hearing high pitched sounds myself.

One of the conductors who worked the west end chain gang when I was working as a brakeman off the Hillyard extra board was Louis Payton, called Bud. Bud was very opinionated and thought he was a cut above the rest. His nickname was "Lord Louie." One night, Bud and George Rasmussen, another conductor, had been out for the evening in Wenatchee, and were on their way back to the Columbia Hotel in Bud's car. They attracted the attention of a couple of Wenatchee police officers who tailed them back to the hotel. Rumors have it that Bud was a little over the speed limit that night. Bud and George walked into the lobby of the Columbia Hotel while the police followed them into the lobby and stood by the door. Lord Louie could not stand this, so he turned around and gave the officers the finger. Bud and George immediately found themselves under arrest. Bud and George were both required to post bail and later went to court. Rumor had it that it cost them about $250 each to get out of this little mess. From that day forth, Bud Payton was known as "Goldfinger."

Conductor Francis Coppay followed my father on the seniority list, both hiring out in September of 1929. Most of us younger men called him Frank, but the older men called him "Frenchie." Frank was of French descent and was only a little over five feet tall. Frank was a sharp dresser and neat as a pin, with not a hair on his head out of place right down to his pencil line mustache. His bib overalls were always ironed, complete with a crease ironed down the front of the legs of his overalls, thanks to a diligent wife.

Frank's rear brakeman was Paul Watts. When they left town, it was Paul's job to man the radio while the caboose approached the point where Frank was going to board it. At Hillyard or Wenatchee, we would hear Paul on the radio giving instructions to the engineer about how far the train needed to go to pick up Frank as they pulled out of the yard. Paul would say over the radio, "Ten cars to the little leader," then in a moment or two, "Five cars to the little leader," then "Three cars" followed by "Two cars" and then "One car." After a short pause, Paul would say, "Highball, the little leader is on." Everyone got a kick out of this routine, no matter how many times we heard it. The irreverent reference to his conductor, as well as Paul's sports announcer style of delivery, always struck our funny bones.

Traditionally, the conductor made out and signed the time slip for the trainmen, and the engineer did the same for the engine crew. Trainmen's slips were green, while enginemen's were red, so the timekeepers could separate them by color. The timekeepers specialized by craft since the operating agreements were different. The BN decided that they could cut the number of pieces of paper in half and reduce the timekeeping staff by consolidating the time slips. This meant that the conductor now filled out one slip for everyone, which was not a big deal but it did lead to a couple of now humorous incidents.

The first involved engineer Dean Abbott on a round trip to Whitefish. He told me in no uncertain terms that I was NOT to put any of his information on the time slip. He would do it himself. When we got back to Yardley, I had the time slips partially completed. He filled out his portion of the going and return trip time slips. After he was done, he got up and I asked him if he was done. He said, "Yup." I asked if I could mail them. He said "Yup," and walked out. I looked at the slip and found that he had not signed it as required. I called the Spokane Timekeeper, Dick Lyonnais, and told him the story. Dick told me to turn the slips in. The brakeman and I would get paid, but Dean would not. I never heard a word about it, even though Dean was shorted two days' pay and had to go to the crew office and sign his portion of the time slip for that trip.

Another time I was the conductor going to Wenatchee. We had a fireman this trip. As usual, I asked each man for his stamp so that I could stamp the time slip. Each stamp showed the man's name and employee number. The fireman decided that his stamp was too clogged with hair and debris to make a clear stamp so he went to the rest room to clean it up by washing it out under flowing water. He returned to the crew room, poured the pad in the tray side of the stamp full of ink, put the stamp in the ink, and laid the bare stamp in my hand, saying to himself, "Now why did I do that?" Since he had over-inked the stamp and did not blot it to remove the excess ink, my palm quickly began to turn black. Without thinking, I picked the stamp up by the handle, stamped his forehead, and said, "Now maybe you will remember not to do that again." He stood there with a shocked look on his face said, "I guess I will remember not to do that again." I agreed. We both spent time in the restroom trying to remove the ink.

After the incident involving Maynard's Wenatchee car, as we drove away from Maynard with his bleeding hands, Dave Johnson said that he was going to hate to see all of the 'colorful characters' retire from the railroad. Dave said it was sad to see this era come to a close so soon. I have to agree with Dave. Their retirements took some color out of our lives. I surely miss them and feel the loss of not being able to enjoy their ethnic backgrounds and entertaining humor in the days to come.

Endnotes

1 David D. Alt and Donald W. Hyndman, *Roadside Geology of Washington* (Missoula, MT: Mountain Press Publishing, 1984), 36–39.

2 Duane Becker, *The Great Northern Railway, Priest River Idaho to Hillyard, Washington 1890 to 1920*, Reference Sheet 376, June 2012, GNRHS, p. 15.

3 Email from Duane Becker, September 3, 2016.

4 Duane Becker, *The Great Northern Railway, Priest River Idaho to Hillyard, Washington 1890 to 1920*, Reference Sheet 376, June 2012, GNRHS, p. 2–3.

8. Locals West of Hillyard

Introduction

This chapter describes the locals that operated west of Hillyard. The West Local/Quincy Turn was a main line local based at Hillyard that went west to Wenatchee or Quincy one day and returned to Hillyard the next day. The Beet Local and the Quincy Spud Local were seasonal jobs on duty at Quincy to handle sugar beets and potatoes respectively. The Alcoa Local was based at Wenatchee. It was established to serve the large Alcoa Aluminum reduction works located between Malaga and Rock Island but was bulletined to Ephrata.

Two branch lines were associated with Wenatchee. The Mansfield Branch extended from the main line station of Columbia River, 16 miles east of Wenatchee, another 60.3 miles to Mansfield. The Mansfield branch was a once a week grain line that operated most weeks. The train crew for the Mansfield was whichever chain gang crew happened to be first out at Wenatchee at about 4:00 AM Sunday.

The Wenatchee–Oroville line, or W–O, was the westernmost branch line that Hillyard trainmen worked. The W–O left the main line at Olds Junction, 2.7 miles west of the Wenatchee depot, and followed the Columbia and Okanogan Rivers to Oroville. Beyond Oroville a remnant of the Vancouver line occupied the Similkameen River Valley to Keremeos, British Columbia. A local crew at Oroville operated the Keremeos Turn to Keremeos.

The West Local

During the early 1960s, the West Local worked from Hillyard to Wenatchee six days a week, out one day and back the next, making three round trips each week. The West Local was on duty at 6:00 AM at Hillyard and at Wenatchee the next morning. The West Local did all the switching between Hillyard and Wenatchee, except for Alcoa.

The West Local served Fairchild Air Force Base and Geiger Field, the Air National Guard air base, which was adjacent to and west of Fairchild Air Force Base. The National Guard then shared the airfield with the commercial airlines serving Spokane. The Spokane International Airport today is listed as GEG, which stands for Geiger.

On arrival at the railroad station of Fairchild the crew opened the switch, headed in, and lined the switch back. Then we pulled up to, but stopped short of the switch into Geiger Field, and set several hand brakes on the train to make sure it would not run away down the hill to Fort Wright and Spokane if the air leaked out of the brake cylinders. While Hillyard made our train up with the Fairchild cars on the head end, they were in random order within the block, so we spent half an hour lining up cars at Fairchild for Fairchild AFB and Geiger to minimize switching on the bases.

If the Drag East set out a block of tank cars loaded with jet fuel on the storage track at Fairchild, we would find them and line them up to spot at Deep Creek. Traffic for Geiger Field was usually five to ten cars per trip. Among other things, Geiger received boxcar loads of munitions including Class A Explosives, which were capable of detonation, airplane parts, and a variety of supplies.

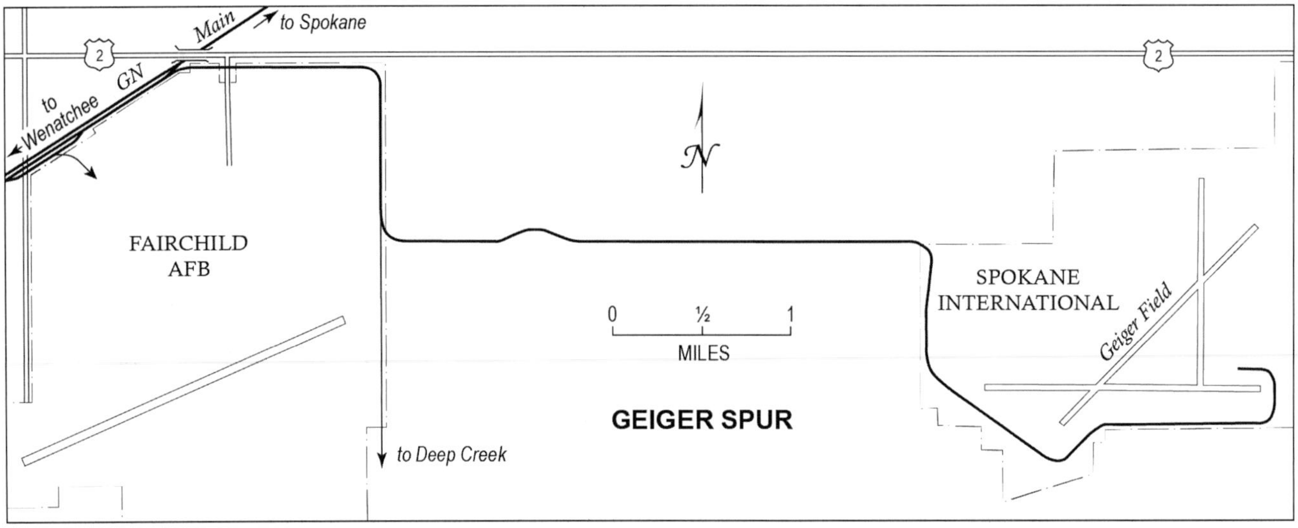

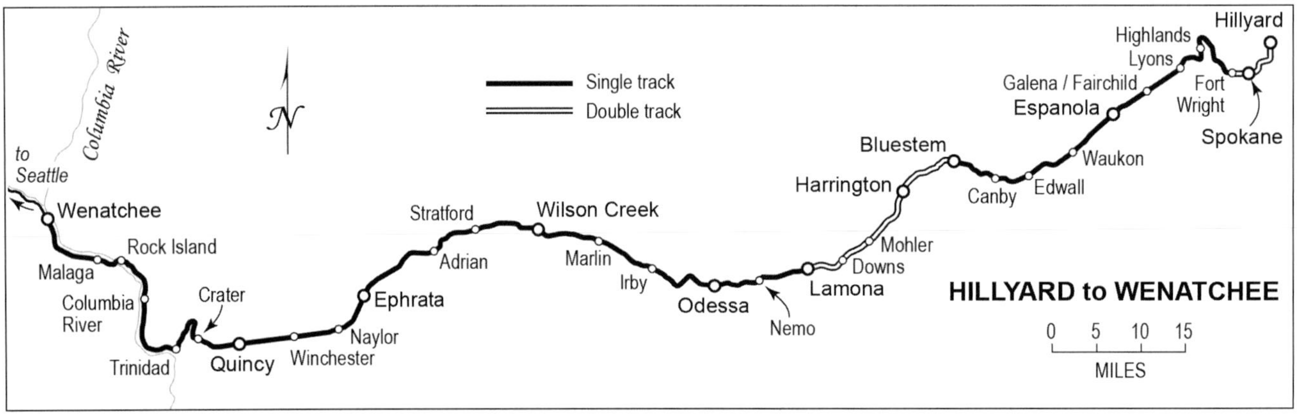

While the route was not very long in distance, only some 9.3 miles, most trips into Geiger Field took about four hours. The time on the spur itself was usually at least three hours per round trip. There was a 10 MPH speed limit on government track, so travel time exceeded two hours. The spots were spread out along at least a mile of track, so the switching on the bases often took an hour, and sometimes more. The worst thing about a trip to Geiger were the gates, which had to be shut as soon as we cleared them.

The first gate was located on the north side of Fairchild Air Force Base. About 1,000 feet later we came to two sets of gates, one on each side of the main entrance road into Fairchild Air Force Base. In addition to the gates, we had to flag the automobile traffic on the road. The next hurdle was the Fairchild AFB runway, which was protected by a traffic light that was always red. We were required to stop and blow the whistle to let the control tower know we were waiting at the red light. If no airplanes were taking off or landing, the light would go green and we could cross the end of the runway. After clearing the runway, we encountered another gate to

Extra 208 East, the West Local, switching at Quincy, circa 1953. Engine 208 is a RS-2 delivered in August 1949. Several RS-2 and RS-3 engines were assigned to Hillyard for maintenance Seven were used at Wenatchee as switch engines and as power for local trains originating at Wenatchee during the 1950s. Display of white flags to indicate an extra was not required after December 1, 1959. GNRHS COLLECTION.

leave Fairchild Air Force Base. There was a fifth and final gate just before we entered Geiger proper.

At Geiger, we delivered materials to the Air National Guard, ranging from food for their cafeteria to parts for their motor pool vehicles and airplanes. The National Guard got Air Force hand-me-down equipment, so their maintenance work was a little heavier than normal. After spotting Geiger, we walked across the highway, which is now I-90, and ate. If this seems early in the day to eat, remember: the crew had been on duty for about five hours by now and there were no other places along the way to eat. After beans, we headed back to Fairchild, opening all five gates and closing them behind us.

Back at Fairchild we separated the east cars from the west cars. Those going our way came with us and the others were left to be picked up the next day. During the fall and winter wheat shipping season, a trip to Geiger put us right at the limit of what we could do and still get tied up in 16 hours.

The Air Force later installed a new fuel storage facility near the north edge of the base. By agreement with the railway company, the Air Force's Fairchild switch engine could come out their gate, pull the loads of jet fuel out of the west end of one of the storage tracks, and shove them east to spot at their new fuel storage facility. By agreement, they could also place empty tank cars on a storage track.

The bulk of the West Local's work was spotting empty boxcars for grain loading and pulling the loads from the stations on top of the Columbia Plateau. The wheat started to move around the middle of August.

West Local switching at Ephrata with GP 9 693, probably between 1964 and 1970. The company removed all of the RS-2 and RS-3 engines from Hillyard to parts unknown about January 1, 1964. Two had been sold to the SP&S in 1959, and two more in 1963. The oldest group, built in 1947, was just over fifteen years old by 1963. Railroad equipment loans ran for fifteen years, and doubtless required that the railroad pay the bank if it sold a unit financed by the loan. The Great Northern traded in all of its Alcos for credit against new General Electric units between 1963 and 1968, very soon after each loan was paid off. GNRHS ARCHIVE.

At the beginning of the season, most of our empties were alumina ore cars off the Hillyard washout track. Once the export elevators were unloading lots of grain, Wenatchee would give us 20 to 30 empty boxcars to spot on our eastward trip. Regardless of where the empty cars came from, we spotted them to the elevators as required. This export grain was all single car business. A typical spot, or pull, was something in the range of two to five cars per elevator. Some stations supported a row of elevators alongside the industry track.

The West Local pulled cars of wheat headed for export at Puget Sound and lower Columbia River ports from individual elevators and built blocks for pick up by a Drag West. Odessa, Wilson Creek, and Quincy were favored stations to leave a grain pick up. Building grain pickups saved us time since we avoided dragging excessive tonnage to our final terminal. Building blocks of grain saved the drags time since they avoided picking up a few cars at every station with a grain elevator. The wheat moved heaviest after the harvest and into the winter. Farmers needed cash to pay off their bank loans and to live on, but they also wanted to sell for the best price. If prices were good in the fall and winter, the wheat moved briskly, but if the price was down, the farmers tended to hold their wheat into the spring or summer while hoping the price would improve.

In the fall, our customers received boxcar loads of seed wheat in bags from the east. In the spring and fall, we spotted hopper cars loaded with dry fertilizer and loaded tank cars of anhydrous ammonia and ammonia solutions, both used as fertilizer, and pulled the empty cars at the major stations like Edwall, Harrington, Odessa, and Quincy. The local also got occasional flatcar loads of farm machinery from the east to spot through most of the year, plus a peddler car of way freight from Spokane each westward trip.

About the time of the Burlington Northern merger,

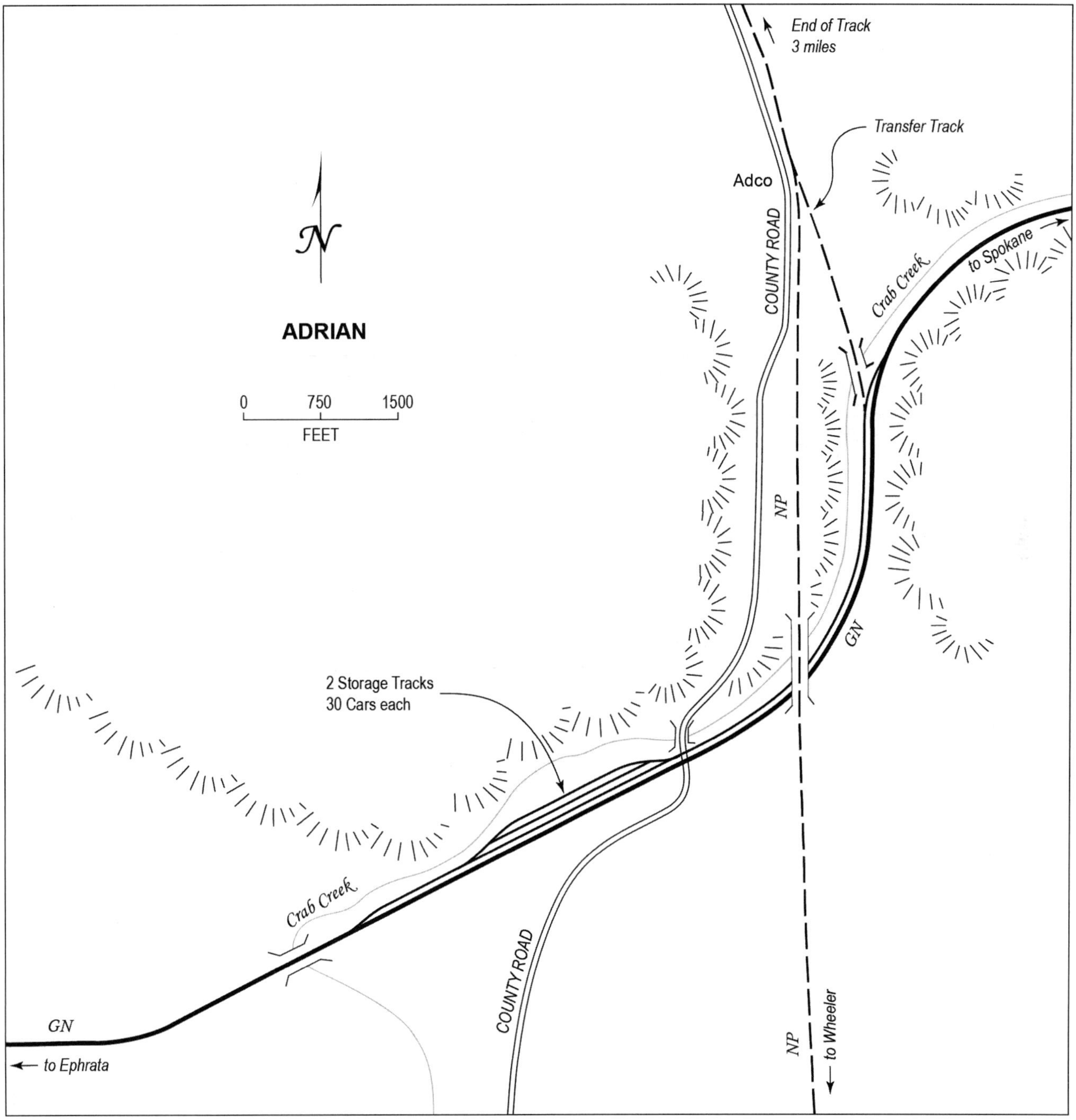
ADRIAN
0 750 1500
FEET
End of Track
3 miles
Transfer Track
Adco
COUNTY ROAD
Crab Creek
to Spokane
NP
GN
2 Storage Tracks
30 Cars each
Crab Creek
COUNTY ROAD
GN
to Ephrata
NP
to Wheeler

the West Local was shortened up to turn at Quincy and renamed the Quincy Turn. The pattern of west one day, east the next continued. Since the Alcoa Local had long been bulletined between Wenatchee and Ephrata, someone figured out there was no reason to have the West Local run the extra 30 miles between Quincy and Wenatchee each day.

➻ The Beet Local

One morning in 1968 or '69, at about 4:30 AM, I received a call to work the Beet Local at Quincy. I was to report for duty at Hillyard by 6:00 AM and I would be on the beet job for not less than 10 days. I needed to pack enough clothes for 10 days, eat, and get to work in one hour and thirty minutes. Except for the clothes, the 90 minute call was a routine occurrence when working the extra boards.

The crewmen: conductor, engineer, fireman and three brakemen, were all called off the extra boards. The job was a new assignment, so we would protect the job for 10 days, the life of the bulletin. Once the bulletin closed and the positions were filled with the highest bidders, we extra board people would be released and sent back to Hillyard as soon as the man who bid in our specific position was awarded the job and marked up to protect the assignment.

The Beet Local was established every year after the beets froze, since freezing raised the sugar content in the beets. The Beet Local usually worked for a month to six weeks until all of the beets stored on line were gone. The sugar beets were harvested and laid up in long windrow piles on the ground. The big piles of sugar beets at Quincy and Winchester were about 300 feet long by about 150 feet wide at the base and 30 to 40 feet high.

Our instructions were to run caboose hop from Hillyard with two GP 9 units and a caboose to Adrian, pick up 40 empty gondola cars, take them to Winchester, and spot them for sugar beet loading. There were two storage tracks beside the west end of the GN siding at Adrian; during the sugar beet season they were used as interchange tracks with the Northern Pacific. As instructed, we picked up the 40 empty gondola cars, made an air test, and proceeded to Winchester. This was in the days when 16 hours was the maximum allowed hours of service.

Northern Pacific's branch line crossed over the Great Northern main track, siding, and Crab Creek on a long timber trestle about 60 car lengths east of our west siding switch at Adrian. Near the east end of our siding, the NP transfer track opened to the west, turned to the north and ran uphill to the NP, ending at the switch to the NP branch main.

The NP line was their 'Central Washington' branch, and they called their station Adco. The CW was built from Cheney to Coulee City in 1889 and 1890, extended to a connection with the GN at Adrian/Adco in 1903, and extended on to Connell by 1910. The Central Washington was built as a grain line, and it did a good business in cement and steel when the U.S. government was building the Grand Coulee Dam in the 1930s. By 1968, the line was abandoned between a point about three miles east (geographic north) of Adco and Coulee City.

Beet gondolas were loaded on the east end of the industry track at Winchester. The site is occupied by a cannery today. At Winchester, we found 20 gondolas loaded with beets on spot. We cut our train off about 25 car lengths east of the east switch, reached in, gathered up the 20 loads of beets, and set them over to the old siding. The old siding was no longer used to meet trains because it was too short, so we could use it to hold beet cars.

Then we went back, coupled into our train, and pulled the 40 empty gondolas into the industry track. As we pulled into the industry track, we stopped and cut our caboose off just to clear the main track. The caboose was then sitting on the switch between the siding and the industry track. We pulled the gons into the industry track, spotting the east end of the 40 empty gons for loading with the balance hanging to the west. We cut the engine off, ran the engine out the west end of Winchester, came east on the main track to the east end, headed into the inside tracks, and stopped just short of the caboose.

About an hour later, the beet loading crew loaded the 10 cars on spot and needed a switch. We coupled into the caboose, coupled into the newly loaded gons, and pulled the whole cut eastward, spotting the next 10 empty gons. We made a cut behind the last load and shoved the loads to a joint on the 20 loads of beets on the old siding. We repeated this process two more times. After spotting the last 10 empty gons on the industry track, we set the final cut of loads over to the siding and hung on to our caboose. We went east to the main track then shoved west, caboose first, running to Quincy as a caboose hop. At Quincy, we tied up on our 16 hours.

The next morning, we received a message from the chief dispatcher to run to Winchester, wait for the loading crew to finish loading the last 10 cars, and take all 60 loads of beets to Adrian. At Adrian, we were to set the loads on the storage tracks and wait for the Northern Pacific to deliver some empty beet gons.

When we arrived at Winchester, the beet loading crew was finishing loading the last 10 gons. We cut our caboose off on the main, reached inside and picked up the 10 loads of beets, doubled them to the 50 loads on the old siding, doubled the 60 loads to our caboose, made our air test, and headed for Adrian with 60 loads of sugar beets.

At Adrian, we set 40 loads into storage track 1 and the remaining 20 loads into storage track 2. Then we sat and waited for the NP local to arrive with the empty beet gons. About 8:00 PM, our conductor, Frank V. Jones, went to the phone to talk to the dispatcher. The dispatcher told Frank to head for Quincy to avoid dying on our hours of service. We departed for Quincy, but had to wait quite a while at Naylor for an eastward freight train, and then made a mad dash to Quincy to clear for the eastward Empire Builder.

The next morning, we got a message from the chief dispatcher telling us to go to Adrian and wait for the NP's Wheeler Turn to deliver the empty gons. We waited all day at Adrian for the Wheeler Turn, which never showed up. Finally, at about 8:00 PM, we headed back to Quincy to tie up.

The sugar beets raised around Winchester and Quincy all went to the Utah and Idaho Sugar Company (U&I) sugar mill located at the NP station of Scalley, which was on a spur about a mile long that left the NP branch main at Wheeler and entered U&I from the north. The NP operated a Wheeler Turn from Pasco that worked the branch line north of Connell all year. The job usually turned at Wheeler after switching the sugar mill. The MILW also served U&I, their spur entering the plant from the south. Plant trackage was used by both railroads.

When the mill opened in 1953 it was projected to process 362,500 tons of sugar beets and consume 30,000 tons of coal and 21,000 tons of limestone during the season. The first year, the plant actually processed 262,500 tons of beets and produced 75,000,000 pounds, or 37,500 tons, of sugar. The beet consumption rate that first year was 2,000 tons per day. Over time, the plant was expanded to a capacity of 6,250 tons per day. In 1965, the plant processed 828,000 tons of beets to produce 230,000,000 pounds, or 115,000 tons, of sugar.[1]

During the beet and potato season, the NP added two jobs at Wheeler, a road switcher and a turnaround local to Connell.[2] During the season, the regular job handled the cars to and from Pasco. The turnaround local to Connell spotted empty cars to and pulled loads of beets from loading sites on the line to Connell,[3] delivered them, and switched the sugar mill. The seasonal road switcher also switched the sugar mill, pulled empty beet cars from U&I, ran to Adrian with the empty cars for the GN, and returned with loads of beets from the GN.

The usual operation at Adrian was that the NP train would back down the transfer track, stopping short of the GN. The conductor would walk to the GN dispatcher's phone to get permission to occupy our Adrian siding. After the NP local obtained permission, they shoved through our siding to our storage tracks, which were beside the west end of our siding. Each track held 48–50 cars. They set their caboose to the cut of loaded beet cars and set their empty gondolas to clear on the other storage track. Then they ran on the siding to the west end, coupled the engine to the loads, shoved east through the siding and up the transfer track toward their own main. In the process of shoving east, they lined the siding switches to the storage tracks back for the siding. Once the entire train was on the transfer track, they closed the transfer track switch and advised the GN dispatcher they were clear of his siding. Then they shoved onto their main track, lined the transfer track switch for the CW main, and pulled their loaded train to Wheeler.

On our third day, we got the usual message from the chief dispatcher to go to Adrian and wait for the NP local to deliver empty beet gons. Finally, on the third day, at about 7:00 PM, the NP local showed up with 207 empty gons.

Adrian was not designed to handle 207 empty gons, which is over 9,000 feet of cars. With our caboose east of our units, we shoved up the transfer track, stopped the NP local's engine at their switch, and made a plan. Their caboose did not have a radio, so we suggested that the NP local crew cut their engine off, pick up our caboose, and then get back on their train. They pulled ahead as our engineer talked to our brakeman in our caboose, who gave the NP engineer hand signs when it was time to stop his train. The NP crew cut their caboose off on the NP main just to clear the transfer track. The NP engineer pulled ahead far enough for us to couple to the gons with our units. Our brakeman cut the NP engine away from our caboose. Our engine started down the transfer track with the cars and our caboose picking up our conductor, Frank V. Jones, at the transfer track switch.

While we rolled down the transfer track and west on our siding, the NP crew picked up their caboose, followed us down the transfer track, and came out onto our siding. They coupled their caboose to east end of the loads of beets on one of the storage tracks, ran the power on the siding to the west end, shoved the track with the caboose onto the siding, then went west again, coupled into the other track, and shoved the other storage track full of beets to the cut of beets with the caboose. Then they shoved east on our siding, closed the east siding switch to the storage yard, shoved up the transfer track, closed our siding switch, and continued shoving to their main track. Once on their main, they headed back to Wheeler and the U&I sugar mill.

Frank said the dispatcher was not very happy with our 207 cars since our train would not fit in any siding. The dispatcher did not know what he was going to do with us. He was afraid that we would delay the eastward Empire Builder. We had to get rid of cars at Ephrata to avoid plugging Quincy tight. To expedite our planned moves at Ephrata, Frank put all three brakemen on the head end of the train at Adrian.

At Ephrata, we stopped on the main, the rear brakeman opened the east switch, and the train headed into the siding, and into the industry track. The rear brakeman walked a few cars east from the east switch, counting cars as he went. At 50 cars, he stopped us and made a cut behind 50 cars, leaving the rest of the train on the main east of the siding switch. The rear brakeman rode the rear car of the cut in, stopped us on the industry track clear of the siding, and set a couple of hand brakes on the east end of the cut. The rear brakeman then walked east, lining the industry switch back for the siding and the siding switch back for the main, restoring them to their normal positions. He continued east to head end of the remaining 157 gons and was in position to make the joint on the train and cut in the air when the engine returned.

Working as the swing brakeman, I dropped off the engine at the first road crossing. When the rear brakeman stopped us, I made the cut to clear the east end of first crossing. On my signal, the engine pulled the remaining cars ahead. I stopped them with the rear of the new cut just in the clear west of the crossing. Then I tied a couple of hand brakes on the cars on both sides of the crossing. The head brakeman made the cut to clear the second crossing, stopped the remaining cars clear of the second crossing, and tied a couple of hand brakes on the cars on both sides of the crossing.

The fireman had agreed to help with the ground work. He lined the derail so that the power could get by the derail on the west end of the storage track and pull the cars tight to the derail. He pulled the pin between the engine and the cars and reset the derail. The fireman also opened the siding and main track switches so the engine could get back to the main from the storage track. With the engine on the main west of the west siding switch, the fireman lined the west siding and main track switches back to their normal positions. Finally, he rode the second unit as the engine came eastward on the main track to blow the whistle and dump the air if necessary. The two brakemen who cut the crossings and tied their cuts of cars down got on the engine as it moved eastward to come against the train.

As soon as the air released, we were off to Naylor to meet the Empire Builder with minimal delay to both trains, and relieving the dispatcher's nervous tension about the meet. At Winchester we got rid of another 60 gons. We left the train on the main track east of the station, pulled the set out through the siding, and made a cut for a grade crossing. We left 50 cars in the siding and set 10 over to the industry track spotted for loading at the east end. That left 97 gons into Quincy. By the time we filled up the West Yard at Quincy, our day was done.

With this supply of empty cars, the beet loaders could load many cars quickly. We made two trips to Adrian each day with loads of beets for the NP. Every time the NP came over to Adrian to pick up the loads, they left some empty beet gons. The Beet Local kept the shippers fully spotted regardless of what the NP gave us by working off the excess supply of empty cars at Quincy and Ephrata.

The sugar beet crop was a big part of the agricultural economy in the Quincy area. When the U&I sugar mill at Wheeler closed, the sugar beet farmers in the Columbia Basin were forced to change crops, which caused some hardships on the former sugar beet growers. It took a couple of years to for the farmers to get back on their feet. I was told that the reason the U&I mill closed was low prices due to competition from corn syrup.

➻ The Quincy Spud Local

In late August of 1961, I was forced to the Quincy Spud Local because no one bid on one brakeman position. The Quincy Spud Local was a seasonal job established late each August that worked until the potatoes were gone late in November or the first part of December.

The Spud Local was one of the highest paying jobs on the division, and for me to get forced to it was a matter of dumb luck. The Spud Local was bulletined to make a round trip between Quincy and Ephrata, a total of 53.8 miles. The basic day was thus 100 miles, so each trainman earned 100 miles when he reported to work. The job worked 16 hours every night. The second eight hours was at time and a half, so each man earned an additional 150 miles, or 250 miles total, at the local train rate. In fact, the crew was on Initial Terminal Switch all night, so we could claim 200 miles of ITS instead of overtime, which gave us a total of 300 miles at the local rate for the night. Obviously, the conductor claimed the ITS.

The Spud Local went to Winchester, a 45-minute round trip, virtually every night. For that reason, we really should have claimed a combined ITS and FTS of 15 hours, or 187.5 miles, for a total of 287 miles for the night, not the 300 my conductor actually claimed. The payroll clerks in St. Paul never knew about Winchester, so they paid the 300 miles.

The Spud Local went to work at the Quincy depot at 4:00 PM and got our paperwork from the agent, Jim Burns. Jim's strongest expletive was "dad-gum-it." Jim was involved with the local firefighters and I think he spent some time at the local police department.

Jim Burns ran a tight ship. Some said he was hard to work for, but he just expected one to do his job. Quincy demanded an agent who knew what he was doing and possessed the ability to train and supervise others. While Quincy was a small-town station, it generated tremendous revenues for the Great Northern. Feed and diatomaceous earth originated at Quincy throughout the year. Outbound seeds, wheat, beets, and spuds ran heavy in the fall and winter. Quincy also handled the billing for Winchester, which generated significant traffic in sugar beets and spuds in season.

Since Quincy was a 24-hour train order station, an operator was on duty all three shifts. During the spud season, the company put two billing clerk jobs on at Quincy. One worked from 3:00 PM to 11:00 PM, and the second from 11:00 PM to 7:00 AM. The fact that the company put these two seasonal billing clerk jobs on is an indication of the sheer volume that Quincy handled. Each clerk produced up to 60 waybills per night. The sugar beet bills were mani-bills by which one waybill could cover the entire day's business from each loading site.

Billing in those pre-computer days was done on a typewriter. Waybills were typed in multiple copies, and the copies were distributed in a prescribed manner, including to the Revenue Accounting department in St. Paul. In addition to copying the data from the shippers' bills of lading onto the waybill form, the origin station determined the freight rate and calculated the freight charges. Determining the rate was an art in itself founded on reading commodity tariffs and applying a series of rate increases to the published base rate. Rating was exacting work.

Jim did not appear to be as busy as the operators or billing clerks. This was the way it seemed to be at most stations with an agent, operators, and more staff than most small stations. I noticed this at Quincy, Kettle Falls, Oroville, Sandpoint, and Troy, Montana. Despite not appearing to be busy, Jim checked the bill clerks' output and Jim himself checked the industries and the yard, took car orders from customers, applied cars on hand to his orders, ordered cars from the car distributor, kept the demurrage records, issued demurrage bills, collected freight revenues, deposited funds, and made up our switch lists.

Jim's big fancy brass spittoon sat next to his desk. One morning Jim came to work and the spittoon was

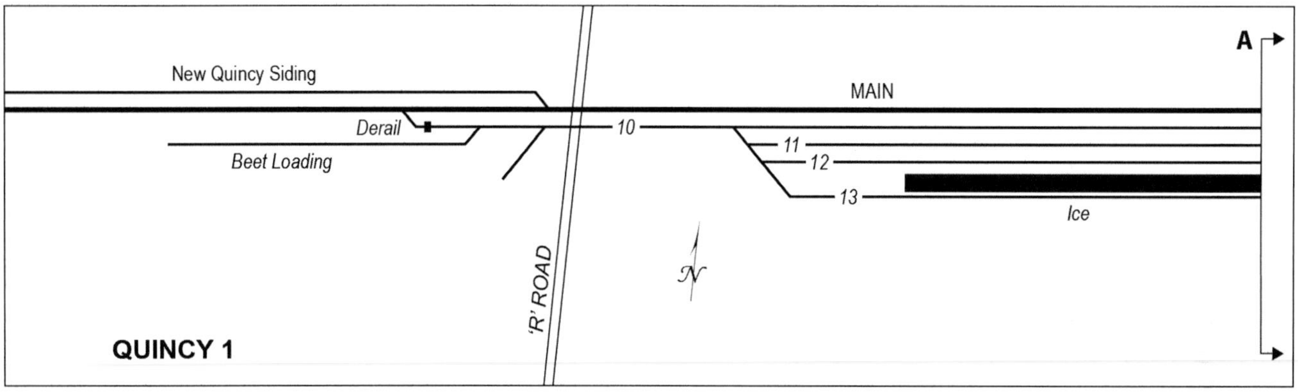
New Quincy Siding
MAIN
A
Derail
10
Beet Loading
11
12
13
Ice
'R' ROAD
N
QUINCY 1

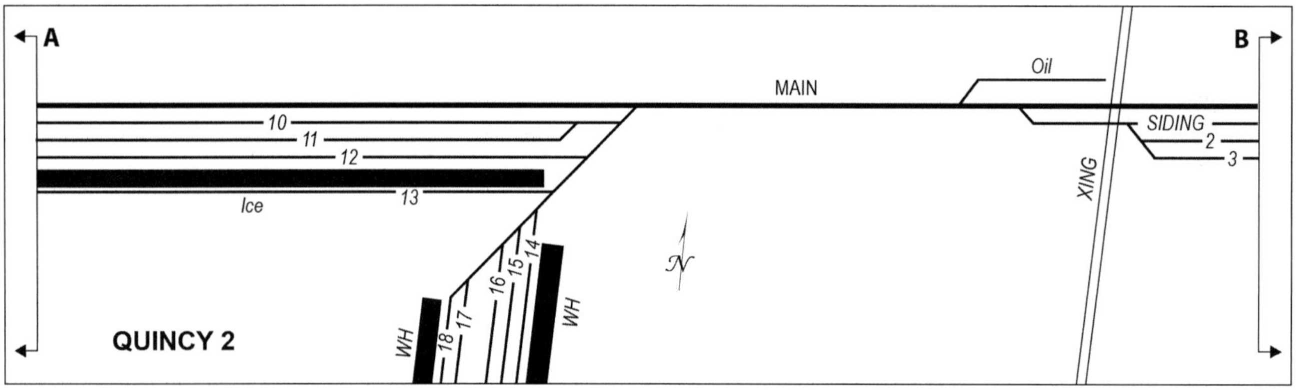
A
B
MAIN
Oil
10
11
12
13
Ice
SIDING
2
3
XING
14
15
16
17
18
WH
WH
N
QUINCY 2

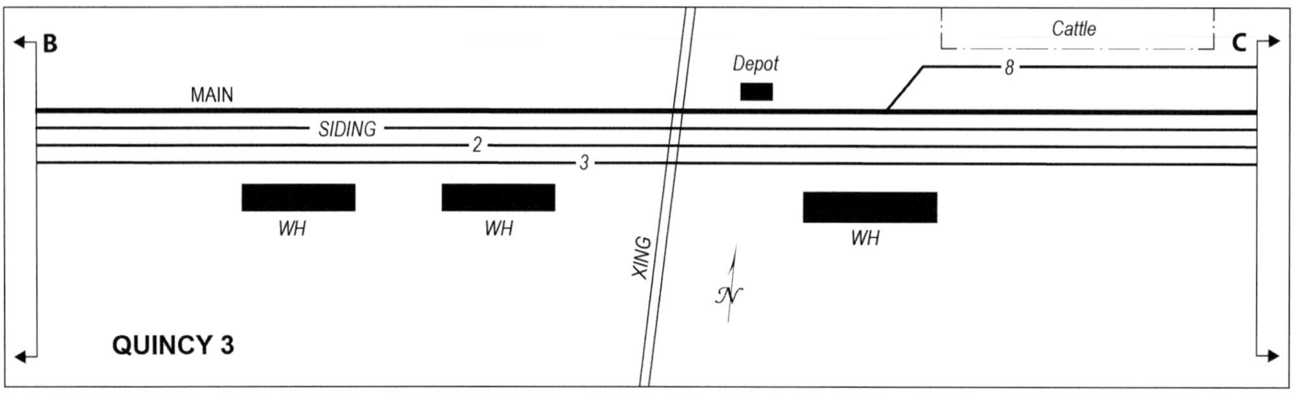
B
C
Cattle
Depot
8
MAIN
SIDING
2
3
WH
WH
WH
XING
N
QUINCY 3

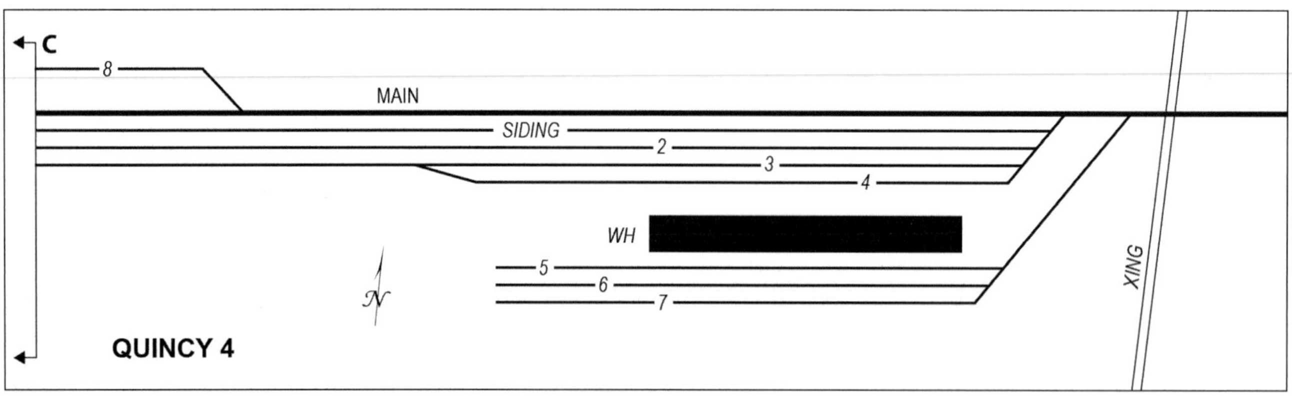
C
8
MAIN
SIDING
2
3
4
WH
5
6
7
XING
N
QUINCY 4

nowhere to be found. Two days later, lo and behold, the spittoon was discovered spiked to the peak of the Quincy depot roof. With the help of the section crew and a tall ladder, the spittoon was recovered. Jim took it to the local welding shop which brazed the spike hole shut, and Jim's spittoon was back in service.

Our switching centered on the West Yard, which was about half a mile west of the depot. The West Yard was on the south side of the main track and included tracks 10, 11, 12, and 13. The West Yard was constructed in the early 1950s to serve the new customers, particularly potato shippers, created by the Columbia Basin Project which brought irrigation water to 671,000 acres[4] of the otherwise arid Columbia Plateau. Track 10 was adjacent to the main track and was the first choice for receiving set outs and for making pickups due to its proximity to the main track and its longer length. The body of the West Yard was east of the Road R grade crossing, but the west end of track 10 extended west of the Road R crossing for about 20 car lengths. Westward trains made their set outs to track 10, leaving the cars between main track switch and Road R if possible. If not, they shoved across Road R, cut the crossing, and left the balance of their set out west of Road R. Track 11 was adjacent to track 10 and was used as a slough and switching track. Tracks 12 and 13 were the tracks farthest from the main track. The icing platform was between them, so they were the icing tracks.

In the early 1960s the Spud Local power came out of track 2 opposite the depot onto the siding, then onto the main track. It ran west on the main for about a quarter of a mile to enter the West Yard at a switch off the main. The east switch to track 10 was less than 10 car lengths east of the east switches for West Yard tracks 11, 12, and 13. Since 400 feet provides next to no switching lead, and since we switched from the east end of the West Yard, we had to get the dispatcher's permission to occupy the main track to do our switching. Getting permission was a source of irritation to us and to the dispatcher. Of course, if a train was approaching, permission would be denied, and we sat and waited.

The company installed Centralized Traffic Control (CTC) between Columbia River and Ephrata in 1967. CTC is a method of operation under which train or engine movements are authorized by controlled signals whose indications supersede the superiority of trains for both opposing and following movements. CTC allows the dispatcher, or control operator, to manage the movement of trains by controlling the position of junction and siding switches and related signals. Crews move their trains or engines, or not, based solely on the indication of wayside signals.

When CTC was installed between Columbia River and Ephrata, a new Quincy siding was built west of Quincy and on the north side of the main track. The east switch of the new Quincy siding was located immediately west of the Road R grade crossing. The east end of the new Quincy siding is almost flat. The west end starts downhill on a 1% grade where the main track breaks over the rim of the Columbia Plateau and begins its continuous descent to the siding of Columbia River, now renamed Albus in honor of BN Roadmaster Steve Albus, who was killed in a sport fishing accident on the Pacific Ocean. The new Quincy siding was 10,398 feet long and rated for 204 cars.

As part of the CTC project, the original siding near the depot was renamed the "old siding." More importantly for us, a connecting track was added on the south side of the main track between the west end of the old siding and the east lead of the West Yard. The switch into the West Yard from the main was left in place and a new switch was added on the new inside track to create a new crossover between the West Yard and the main track. The crossover was and is used by eastward trains to set out and pick up at the West Yard. The new connecting track/switching lead helped both the Spud Local and the dispatcher, since the local no longer needed to ask the dispatcher for permission to occupy the main track to switch the West Yard or to move from one end of Quincy to the other.

The conductor received our first batch of switch lists, covering the West Yard and the industry track, track 3, from Jim, and we took the engine to the West Yard. Our first move was to run west on the main track, and then east on the lead, to the west end of the icing platform, pull the empty ice service cars on spot, slough the empties to track 11, and respot the ice service loads to the west end of tracks 12 and 13. Ice service cars were old wood-sided reefer cars assigned to Columbia Ice & Cold Storage at Wenatchee and stenciled "Ice Loading Only." Ice came from Wenatchee in ice service reefers. The empties went back to Wenatchee for more ice. Quincy got ice about three times a week.

Because the icing platform at Quincy was supplied by rail car, the less than one car long west end of the platform was low, at car floor height, while the 27-car capacity icing platform to the east matched the reefer car roof height. Ice was unloaded on the west end, carried by a moving chain up a ramp, and then eastward on the high platform, from which it was loaded into the ice bunkers on each end of the cars. We left up to three excess ice loads hanging west of the unloading spot on the low dock. A winch beside each track enabled the ice car unloader to pull the next load to the platform, keeping the upper platform supplied with ice all night long.

Then we went to the east end and switched out the yard to get the dry reefers to be iced and spotted later that night. Dry reefers and empty boxcars generally came to Quincy as a set out from a Drag West, and today's new cars were in track 10. Dry reefers went into tracks 12 and 13 to be iced. WFE's ice crew came to work at 6:00 PM, so we needed to get the first batch of dry reefers spotted to both sides of the icing platform as soon as possible. Cars were iced before loading, so the reefers were cold when the customers opened them for loading the next morning.

Dry cars went to tracks 12 and 13 as directed by the agent's list of the West Yard, which was based on where they would go later in the evening. Reefers for the east end of Quincy, for Winchester and for Ephrata, went to track 12. WFE iced track 12 first to enable us to spot the east end of town and go to Winchester first. Potato customers served by tracks 4, 5, 6, and 7, at the east end of Quincy, loaded 10 to 15 cars per day between them. Reefers for the potato sheds near the West Yard went to track 13. Fortunately, most of the reefer cars were generic, so we did not have to spot them by individual car number.

After spotting the ice platform tracks we switched out the boxcars needed to spot tonight for dead freight. Customers served by tracks 3, 5, 6, and 7 loaded boxcars. The Spud Local often spotted empty boxcars for grain and diatomaceous earth loading on track 3. Celite shipped kiln dried diatomaceous earth in bags in boxcars. Diatomaceous earth is used for filtering a variety of liquids, and in cosmetics. I once saw a waybill for three cars going to Revlon, presumably to be made into face powder. The grain elevator and Celite were both on track 3, the industry track, at the south edge of the right of way. Track 2 was a storage track. It lay between Quincy siding and track 3. Track 2 was often used to hold extra boxcars for grain loading and for the Celite plant. If the list showed boxcars to pull or spot on track 3, we pulled and spotted that track, sloughing the pulls to the east end of track 3. Then we took the engine west on track 2, parked it opposite the depot, and went to eat about 7:30 or 8:00 PM. Dinner was our last stop until we went off duty at 8:00 AM.

After dinner, the conductor got the lists for tracks 4, 5, 6, 7, and Winchester from a clerk at the depot, and we went back to the West Yard to dig out and line up the cars to spot. If the icing crew was not finished icing the reefers on track 12, we would help them finish so that we could get on with our work.

As soon as the icing crew finished icing the reefers on track 12, we pulled the track, sloughed the two or three iced reefer cars for the Alcoa Local to a convenient track for them to spot later at Ephrata, gathered up the empty boxcars, and went to the east end of Quincy to switch tracks 4, 5, 6, and 7 which served several potato warehouses, a seed shipper, and a feed shipper. We pulled the loads, respotted any part loads, and spotted boxcars and iced reefers for loading the next morning. Tracks 4, 5, 6, and 7 generated 12 to 16 loads of spuds and dead freight that we left on the 5–6 track lead while we went to Winchester.

As the engine went by the depot headed for our switching on the east end, the conductor dropped off to get our train orders. If no traffic was close, he got them right away. After he drove to the east end with our train orders, we could head for Winchester with eight to ten iced reefers for loading. We never took the caboose with us to Winchester since it was a short trip, maybe 30 to 40 minutes, and having the caboose would slow us down by creating extra moves. The whole crew rode in the engine.

At Winchester, we dropped the iced empties into the west end of the old siding while putting the engine down the main. The engine reached into the old siding, coupled to the empties, went into the industry track with the empties, gathered up the loads of spuds, and set them to the old siding. We shoved the empties east and

The Icing Platform at Quincy was supplied with block ice from Wenatchee by "Ice Service" refrigerator cars, which were old reefer cars no longer suitable for revenue service. The ice service stencil is to the left of the car number. This photo was taken at Columbia Ice and Cold Storage Plant 2 in Wenatchee. GNRHS ARCHIVE.

spotted them at the requested doors as we went west on the industry track. Our last move was to go east on the main track, grab the loads off the old siding, and head back to Quincy with six to ten loads of spuds. The switching took about 15 minutes.

At the east end of Quincy, we dropped the cars from Winchester down the siding and took the engine inside to the loads of spuds and dead freight we previously left on the 5–6 track lead. We coupled into the loads, doubled them to the Winchester loads, doubled everything to the pulls from track 3 previously sloughed to the east end of track 3, and shoved everything through the siding to the West Yard, stopping at the depot to get the lists for tracks 14–18.

A big cattle feedlot was located on the north side of the main track just east of the depot. A cattle chute beside track 8 served the feedlot. The feedlot received carloads of cattle from the east on symbol train No. 83. Because cattle are a perishable commodity, the chain gang crew that took No. 83 west from Hillyard was instructed to stop at Quincy to unload the cattle. This meant spotting each car at the stock chute and waiting for the cowboys to unload each car. It took about an hour to unload eight to ten cars. The crew of No. 83 left the empty stock cars on track 8 for us to put in the east pickup. If we had stock cars to pull, we grabbed them from track 8 immediately after dropping the Winchester reefers down the siding, set the stock cars to the reefers, then got the dead freight off the lead and went to the West Yard.

After the feedlot closed in the late 1970s, Celite put in a big kiln to process the earth on the former feedlot site. Celite worked the earth both at the old plant on track 3 and the new plant on the former feedlot site, which is served by new track.

At the West Yard, we set the 20 to 26 loaded ice reefers into track 12 along the icing platform and sloughed the dead freight cars into track 11 for the moment. The icing crew then re-iced the loaded reefers, which had lost about one third of the initial ice due to cooling the car down and the doors on the cars being open while the customers loaded the reefers with sacks of potatoes. After setting the icing platform we came back and classified the dead freight, westward to track 11 and eastward to track 10.

The two large spud warehouses at the west end of town adjacent to and south of the West Yard worked days and afternoons loading reefer cars. We could not switch these warehouses until after 11:30 PM. The lead to the warehouses was an extension of the east lead of the West Yard, and the lead opened to the east. The buildings sat at a 90-degree angle to the main track with a wide-open area between tracks 16 and 17. The warehouses were located beside tracks 14 and 18. Tracks 15, 16, and 17 were located between tracks 14 and 18. Each track held eight cars. Tracks 14, 15, and 16 branched off the lead first and served the east warehouse. Tracks 17 and 18 served the west warehouse.

Both warehouses loaded all their tracks at the same time by loading through the cars on the near track. The loading crew at the warehouse adjacent to track 14 used three loading ramps at each spot. The first ramp was placed between the dock and the reefers on track 14. The second ramp extended from the cars on track 14 to the cars on track 15. The third ramp extended from the cars on 15 to the cars on 16. When the crew started to load spuds, they finished the partial loads on track 16 first. Then they loaded the cars on track 15 and loaded track 14 last. At the end of the day the reefers on 15 and 16 were loaded, while some of the cars on 14 were loaded and others were part loads. The part loads from track 14 went to track 16 each night to be finished loading first thing the next day. The same loading pattern was used on tracks 17 and 18.

We pulled the pre-iced reefer cars off track 13 and put the ones that would go to tracks 17 and 18 onto the 17–18 lead. Holding onto the pre-iced cars for tracks 14–15–16, we pulled the loads out of tracks 15 and 16 and set them towards the 17–18 lead to get them out of the way. Track 14 was a random mix of loads and part loads. Loads from track 14 went to the lead with the other loads, and the part loads went very carefully over to track 16, until the cars from track 14 had all been separated.

We spotted the far spot, spot eight, of track 14 first. This warehouse featured a continuous loading dock on the track side with spot numbers painted on the loading dock. We lined the doors of the reefers up to the spots. The spots were on 50-foot centers, so each car had to be cut away and its hand brakes set. Next, we shoved into track 15, again spotting the far spot, spot eight, first, and spotting the reefers on track 15 opposite those on track 14 so that the loading crew could drop a ramp between the two cars. Finally, we spotted track 16 the same way, with all the doors lined up across from each other from track 14 through track 16.

We put the loads out of tracks 14, 15, and 16 to the far end of track 13 to be re-iced. Then we went back, coupled to the empty cars on the 17–18 lead, and pulled tracks 17 and 18, setting the loads toward the 14–15–16 lead. If there were part loads on track 18, they went to track 17. Then we spotted tracks 18 and 17, first to spots along the loading dock and then to car doors to allow loading through. The loads from 17 and 18 went into track 13 to be re-iced.

It usually took us between two and two and a half hours to switch tracks 14 through 18 and get the 20 to 30 loads of spuds to the icing platform. The hard part of this was getting the doors on the reefers we were spotting lined up with the doors on the reefers on the adjacent track. If the alignment was off by more than a few inches, the loading crew could not drop the ramps in between the doors, which made the car and any beyond it unavailable for loading. If we did not have them spotted just right we were certain to hear about it from Agent Burns the next afternoon.

While the icing crew was topping off the reefers on track 13, we pulled the re-iced loads off track 12 and separated the east loads from the west loads. During the night, we wrote a big W or E with chalk on the side of the car by the pin lifter corners of each car, which saved us time when it came time to switch the east cars from the west cars. If our last pull included more cars than would fit on track 13, we would clear track 12 as described above, set the excess pulls into the east end of track 12, and then switch out the re-iced cars from track 12. East loads went to track 10 and west cars went to track 11. After the WFE crew re-iced the loads on track 13, or 12 and 13, we pulled them and separated east loads from west loads.

The Spud Local built a 30 to 50 car pickup for the east and a 10 to 20 car pickup for the west each night. We laced up the air hoses within each pickup but did not have the

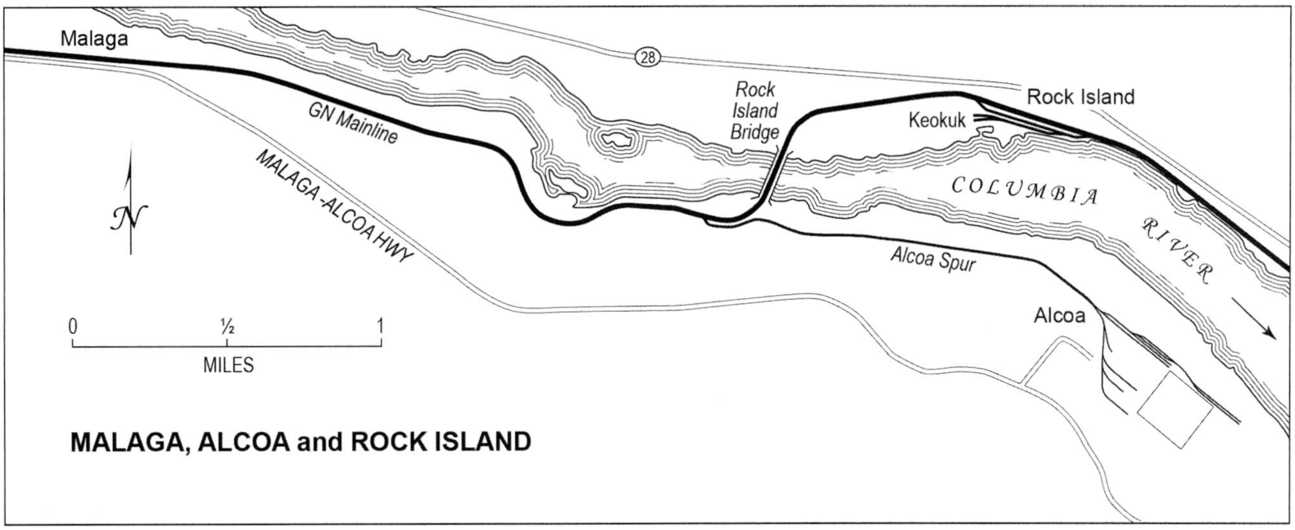

time or the room to block the east and west pickups in station order. This switching would be done at Hillyard and Balmer Yard in Seattle. Because we had separated the east and west dead freight before blocking the spuds, the east pickup was lined up with the spuds first out, with the dead freight behind. The west pickup was in reverse order. On the nights when we built a larger than usual west pickup, it was because a block of empty ice service reefers was headed back to Wenatchee for more ice.

Sometime around 5:00 AM the Alcoa Local arrived with loads of aluminum, silicon, and occasionally apples to go east in the east pickup, which the Alcoa crew cut into the pickup to maintain the blocking of perishables on the east end and dead freight on the west end. Some days the Alcoa Local brought loaded ice service reefers to supply the icing platform. The high portion of the icing platform was clear, so working from the east end, we spotted the ice loads on the west end of tracks 12 and 13 at the low platform for unloading, ending our long day's night. The Alcoa Local picked up its empty iced reefers from the West Yard and went to Ephrata to spot them. When the Alcoa came back from Ephrata, they dropped the spud loads onto the east end of the east pickup.

Wenatchee Locals

The locals that worked out of Wenatchee were a problem for both the men and the company. From our point of view, Wenatchee was a long drive from Hillyard, plus all the jobs in Wenatchee were night jobs, making them less attractive than day jobs.

More importantly, if a man bid in an outside job, his home terminal was where the job went to work, and the company would not pay expenses since he was working at his home terminal. If a man bid in a job at Wenatchee, as a practical matter he moved to Wenatchee. If that man wanted to move back to Spokane, he could only bid back and both moves were at his expense. If you bid in an outside job it was yours until you got bumped. The expense that a senior man would incur to move provided a measure of protection against getting bumped off the Wenatchee jobs, but the uncertainty was always there.

The preferred local in Wenatchee was the Alcoa Local. Older trainmen would bid in the Alcoa because it paid more than the W–O, and even though it worked nights, they were home every day. In the early 1960s enough brakemen lived in Wenatchee to fill one of the W–O locals. The W–O local with Sunday as a rest day was the better job between the two locals. Not enough brakemen lived in Wenatchee to fill the jobs on the W–O locals.

If nobody bid on an opening on a W–O local, the

company would force a brakeman to the job. Given the relative unattractiveness of jobs based in Wenatchee, the company found itself forcing the youngest brakemen, conductors, and engineers onto these jobs and calling crewmen off the extra board. The local jobs at Wenatchee required a higher degree of skill and knowledge than did chain gang jobs. Forcing inexperienced men onto these jobs slowed the crew down, and sometimes led to mistakes; the company absorbed the cost of these errors. Since the company paid mileage to and from the jobs when men were called off the extra board, filling them was more expensive than filling a Spokane job.

In the late sixties, the union and the carrier made an agreement that the Wenatchee locals would be put up for bid for every six months, and once a conductor or brakeman bid in the job, he was protected from being bumped for the following six months. An employee could bid these jobs and know he was protected for six months. The employee gained security and predictability. The company also gained, because the new agreement substantially reduced dead head moves to and from Wenatchee. The agreement was in place by the time I was working as a conductor on a regular basis. I did not have to serve any time as a conductor on the W–O locals. That did not hurt my feelings since I had spent so many years on these locals as a brakeman.

None of the Wenatchee jobs paid very well except for the Alcoa Local. The Alcoa paid well because its bulletined miles, based on turning back at Ephrata, was 104, compared to 137 miles for the W–O. Both jobs often worked 16 hours during the fall and winter, actually 15' 55" on the register. Since the basic day was 100 miles, the Alcoa crew went on overtime after 8 hours 15 minutes, while the W–O crew did not go on overtime until after they had worked 11 hours. A man on the Alcoa would earn 108 miles more per week than a man on the W–O, assuming they both worked 15' 55" for six days. That amounted to a bit more than two basic days per two week pay period on the Alcoa over that on the W–O. In the early ramp up and the late ramp down parts of fruit season, the W–O did not work the full 15' 55", which increased the differential in favor of the Alcoa. Summer earnings on the W–O were even less.

➸ The Alcoa Local

The Alcoa Local went on duty at Wenatchee at 7:00 PM Monday through Saturday, and was bulletined between Wenatchee and Ephrata. The Alcoa Local's prime job was to switch the Alcoa Aluminum reduction plant located east of Malaga and the Keokuk magnesium plant at Rock Island. I worked the Alcoa Local only when I caught it off the brakeman's extra board.

The Alcoa Local left Appleyard with cars for Malaga, Rock Island, Alcoa, Bon Spur, Trinidad, and the loaded ice service reefers for Quincy. Cars for potato loading at Ephrata came off the icing platform at Quincy.

At Malaga, there were a couple of fruit packing warehouses along track 3, the industry track. Track 2 at Malaga, the storage track, was used to hold cars that Alcoa did not want immediately, and was a place to stash cars for stations beyond Malaga. There was and is a siding at Malaga for meeting and passing trains.

After switching the fruit packing warehouses at Malaga, if necessary, we set any cars for the Keokuk smelter at Rock Island and for Bon Spur to the industry track to get them out of the way, and lined up our cars for Alcoa using the storage track and the siding. We blocked Alcoa cars in this order from the rear forward: box and flatcars for aluminum loading, then pitch, coke, chlorine, lime, and brick, then alumina ore on the head end. This done, we picked up the cars for Rock Island and Bon Spur on the head end and went east with the entire train. We stopped a quarter mile or so short of the Alcoa switch, cut off the Rock Island and Bon Spur cars and took them to Rock Island, leaving the bulk of our train on the main track.

Rock Island is located across the Columbia River from the Alcoa switch, so we crossed the bridge with our cars for Rock Island and Bon Spur. The silicon metal smelter at Rock Island consumed silica rock, coal, and wood chips, and shipped carloads of silicon metal. Since the smelter operated their own engine, we delivered cars for the smelter to track 2 and put any car for Bon Spur on track 1, from which we would pick it up on our eastward move. On our return to Wenatchee, we pulled everything the plant switcher set up for us on either track and took the cars to Wenatchee.

The switch into the Alcoa plant was only 750 feet or so west of the Columbia River Bridge. The Alcoa lead track

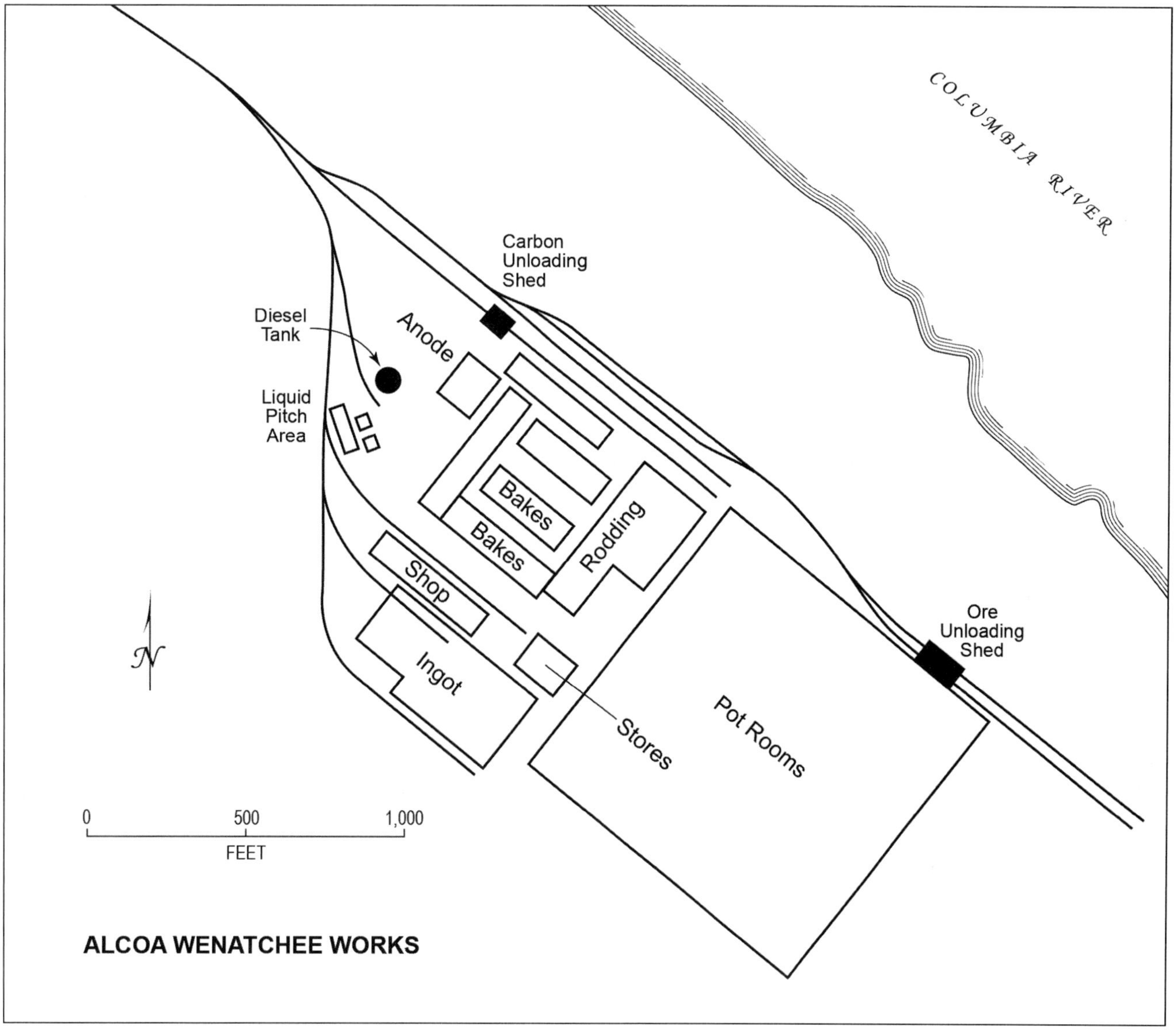

extended a bit over a mile from the main track switch to the plant. The grade on the lead was about 2.2% on both sides of the hill in and out of the plant. On dry rail, one GP 9 could pull only seven to eight boxcars loaded with alumina up the hill. These cars weighed 80 tons per car, so eight were 640 tons. As a point of comparison, a GP 9 was rated at 650 tons on the 2.2% grade over Stevens Pass. I recall that one frosty night we could pull only seven or eight loaded boxcars up the hill with two units!

Morrison & Knudsen Construction Company did the rock and earth work at the Alcoa plant in 1951. M&K made an offer to the Great Northern to reduce the grade down to virtually nothing for a nickel per cubic yard. This was an excellent offer as the line was built through solid basalt, and additional blasting would have been required to remove the additional rock. The GN did not accept this offer, which imposed excess operating costs on the company that continue to this day. This was a mistake. The Alcoa Local almost always got two units. If the track in and out of the plant had been built to the best reasonably attainable grade, the Alcoa plant could have been switched in one third of the time with one unit. The engineering of the Alcoa Spur was one of the few cases where Great Northern management did not adhere to J. J. Hill's policy of the best reasonably possible line, and they paid for it many times over.

The reason we cut the train off well west of the Alcoa switch was to get enough of a run at the hill to get our entire train into the Alcoa Spur and off of the main track to clear the early morning passenger trains and any Drag West that might appear. On our return from Rock Island, one brakeman dropped off at the Alcoa Switch, lined it for the spur, and put the derail in its non-derailing position. The engine continued west, coupled to the train, and brought it east with all possible speed. After the train got past the derail, the brakeman restored it to its derailing position, lined and locked the main track switch for the main, and walked east to the train, which had probably stalled on the hill.

The Alcoa Spur included an eight or ten car runaround track on top of the hill between the main track and the plant gate. Most nights we pulled the first cut of alumina ore up to the top of the hill, cut it off, ran back through the runaround track, grabbed the second cut of alumina, took it up the hill, coupled into the first cut of alumina, cut in the air, and started down into the plant with seven or eight cars ahead of us and seven or eight behind us. At the bottom of the hill, which was just inside the plant gate, we cut the trailing loads off and shoved the lead cut to one of the two alumina pit tracks. We gathered up the empty cars from both pit tracks and set them over to the adjacent third track, then set the loads on one of the unloading pit tracks and left the engine there. Another crewman then bled the air out of the trailing cut of cars and rolled them by the engine with a gravity drop into the other pit track.

Alcoa used alumina ore from three sources: Bauxite, Arkansas; Mobile, Alabama; and Point Comfort, Texas. Alcoa did not mix the three kinds of ore, so if one or more cars of alumina ore were delayed, the stragglers were set aside at Malaga until another shipment of that particular kind of ore came in. Alcoa used an auger on an arm that moved from one end of the car to the other to unload boxcars of ore. The auger pulled the alumina ore out of the car and discharged it outside the car door, where it fell through a grate into an under-track pit. With this system, Alcoa avoided the complex tilt mechanism and handled their boxcars only once. Switching boxcars of ore at Alcoa was much simpler than at Mead.

In the early years, alumina ore came in 40-foot boxcars. Sometime in the middle of the 1960s, the railroad converted Alcoa's inbound ore from boxcars to covered hopper cars. The hoppers could carry 100 tons, while the boxcars carried only about 60 tons. Using the hopper cars, only two cars were required to move the tonnage moved in three boxcars. The reduction in car count saved us considerable time at Alcoa.

After spotting the alumina cars we went back out the lead and brought in the rest of the Alcoa cars. Alcoa received loads of pitch and three kinds of coke used to make the carbon electrodes consumed in the smelting process, plus occasional carloads of lime, brick, and tank cars of chlorine. Alcoa got empty boxcars for loading aluminum ingots. The empties went to tracks 1 and 2 and came out as loads the next day or the day after. The local switched for hours, all at night, moving 30 to 50 cars a night into and 30 to 50 cars out of the Alcoa Aluminum plant.

When all the cars were gathered up, we had the caboose and any ice loads for Quincy behind the engine, followed by east loads of aluminum, followed by everything else. We brought them all out, stopped just short of the main track switch, tied the cars that would stay until our return trip to Wenatchee down securely with hand brakes, cut behind the last east load, and tied that cut, including the caboose, down. Then we took the engine east on the main and released the brakes on the loads of aluminum and the caboose so that they would roll out onto the main track.

Bon Spur was an oddball move. Bon Spur was a long spur, well over a mile, which began 5.33 miles up the Mansfield Branch. The Mansfield Branch began at the station of Columbia River. Bon Spur was built in 1952 to serve the Bonneville Power Administration, probably to unload material for power line construction in the area and for large electrical transformers for the substation, adjacent to the end of the spur.

For many years during the 1960s, the BPA kept an eight-axle depressed center flatcar loaded with a transformer on the curve near the end of Bon Spur. About once a month somebody was required to go up and move the car 8–10 car lengths and then return it to spot to lubricate the brass

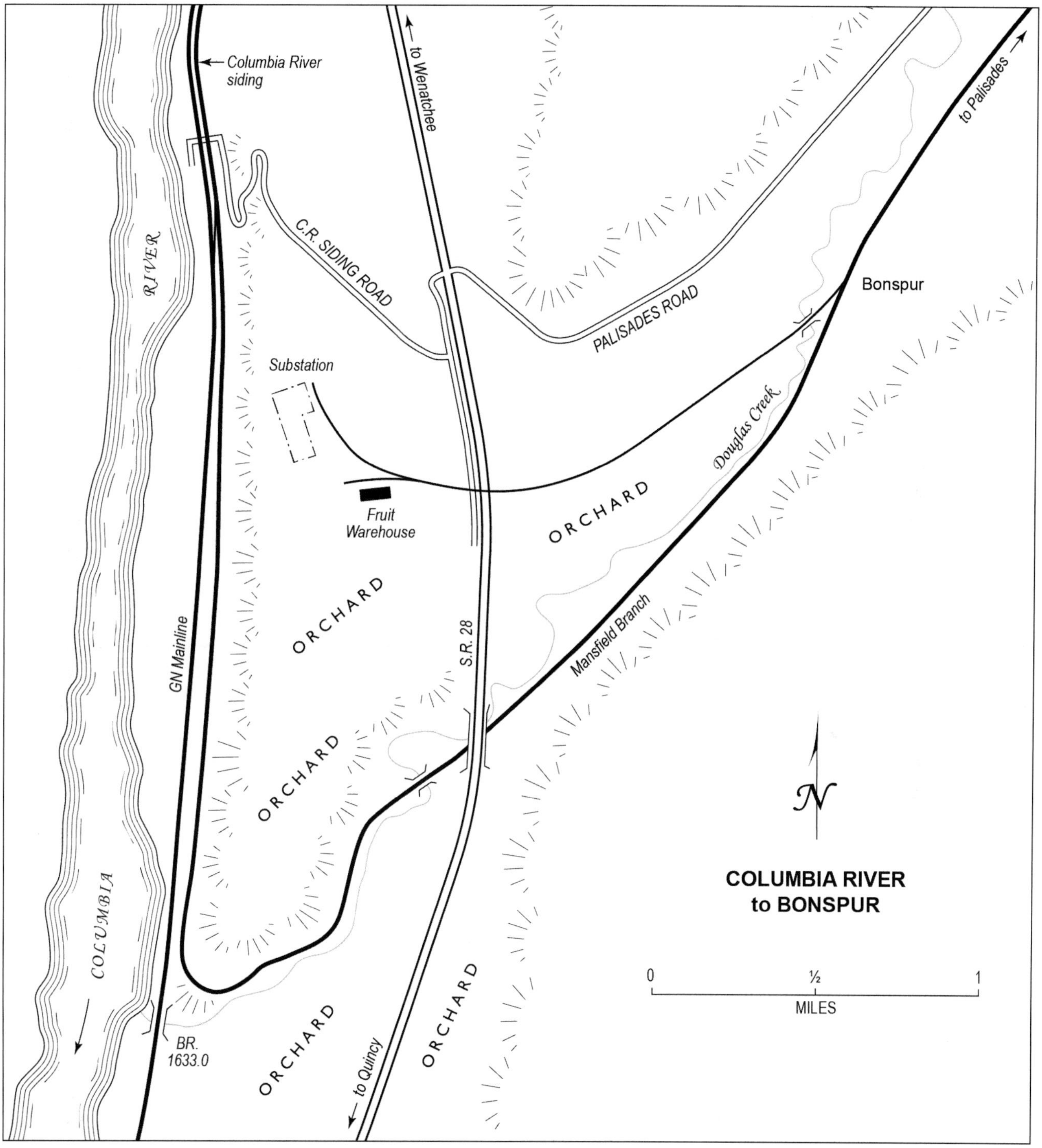
Columbia River siding
to Wenatchee
to Palisades
C.R. SIDING ROAD
PALISADES ROAD
Bonspur
RIVER
Substation
Fruit Warehouse
ORCHARD
ORCHARD
Douglas Creek
ORCHARD
GN Mainline
S.R. 28
Mansfield Branch
ORCHARD
N
COLUMBIA RIVER to BONSPUR
COLUMBIA
0
½
1
MILES
BR. 1633.0
ORCHARD
to Quincy
ORCHARD

journals of the car. We deliberately respotted the car to a location a few inches away from its original spot, supposedly so the axles would not take a permanent set. The dispatcher's office put out a two-page message every time we were required to fuss with this car.

By the 1960s, a small fruit shipping warehouse was built on a short spur that continued the tangent approach to the last curve of Bon Spur. The warehouse could hold only one car on spot at a time. Because of the way the branch and the spur were laid out, the fruit warehouse at Bon Spur could be switched only on the Alcoa Local's eastward trip. A trip to Bon Spur took at least an hour. This trip required us to secure the train in the Columbia River siding, travel 5.33 miles up the branch, and then back more than a mile up the hill and flag across the highway to get to the spot.

Every crossing of Highway 28 was a tense event. The road was posted for 55 MPH, but 70 was the normal speed. As our crossings occurred during the wee hours of the morning, no motorist ever expected to see us across his path. We always kept at least one fusee and a lantern in hand, did our flagging from the side of the road, and never lingered in the road lanes. Finally, every time we pulled a car from Bon Spur, one unlucky trainman was required to ride the leading end of the blind shove for the entire return trip back to Columbia River.

During the fruit season, the Alcoa Local usually did the transformer shuffle since they were up there anyway to switch reefer cars in and out. In the off season, when the Alcoa did not go up to Bon Spur, the Mansfield Turn did it on their way to Mansfield.

Leaving the Alcoa Local for a moment to finish the story of the transformer that sat on Bon Spur, in 1967, I bid in the Second Mead Turn that went to work at 4:00 PM, Monday through Friday. One afternoon, the conductor was told to wait at Hillyard for a hot car off No. 88, which turned out to be the loaded transformer car from Bon Spur. The car was to spot into the Bonneville Power Spur between the Kaiser Aluminum plant and the old Pacific Alloys plant which Kaiser then used to process green coke into fluid coke. The giant transformer on a well flat with two sets of trucks under each end of the car left Hillyard placed directly ahead of our caboose.

At Mead, we headed into the siding, closed the siding switch behind us, and passed over the eastward facing inside switch for the track into the plant. Then we opened the plant lead switch and shoved to the road crossing located just beyond the grain elevator. We flagged this crossing, got the traffic stopped, and shoved the entire train uphill and to the right towards the Kaiser Aluminum plant, just like every other night.

Alcoa Local at Rock Island has stopped to pick up empty cars from the Keokuk plant. COLLECTION OF JOHN E. LANGLOT.

This night, however, we shoved the caboose past the facing point switch to the Pacific Alloys main line, stopped, and cut the caboose off on the aluminum plant lead. Then we pulled back over the switch, threw it, set the car carrying the transformer to the Pacific Alloys main line, and cut it off. Next, we threw the switch, coupled to the caboose, cut in the air, and shoved the entire train toward the aluminum plant and past the Pacific Alloys switch.

We cut off the train, brought the engine over the switch, lined the switch, coupled to the transformer car, and cut in the air. I got on the leading end of the car and rode it up the hill to the Bonneville Power Spur switch. I gave the engineer a stop sign, got off the car when he stopped, lined the switch, got back on the car, and gave the engineer a sign to come ahead.

As our transformer car approached the big overhead door, it started to open, but I gave the engineer a stop sign and waited until the door was completely open. A Bonneville employee walked up and told me to shove the car to the rail bumpers at the end of the track, which I did very carefully. I set the hand brake on my end of the car and the head brakeman set the hand brake on his end of the car. The engine left the building and headed toward the Pacific Alloy main line. As we did so, the overhead door slowly closed. That was the last time I saw the big transformer that sat on the Bon Spur for so many years. To the best of my knowledge, the BPA never staged another transformer at Bon Spur.

Returning to the Alcoa Local, after switching Alcoa and perhaps Bon Spur, the Alcoa Local ran east to Quincy. The Alcoa Local backed into the West Yard and switched out their train. They set their eastward loads of aluminum onto the Spud Local's east pickup and added their occasional westward loads to the west pickup.

During the spud season, the Alcoa then picked up any iced reefers and any other cars for Ephrata and headed for Ephrata. They switched Ephrata, ate dinner, and returned to Quincy. At Quincy, they set any east loads from Ephrata to the east pickup, held on to any west cars from Ephrata, made the west pickup, and headed to Wenatchee.

In the early 1960s, the Alcoa Local and the West Local handled the switching at Quincy when there was no Spud Local assigned. The West Local's working limits were later shortened up to Quincy. The Quincy Turn and the Alcoa Local continued to share the work at Quincy in the off season.

After the BN merger, the Alcoa Local no longer made the trip to Quincy, but ran west as far as Merritt and back to Wenatchee when they first went to work, and then went east to the Alcoa plant on the second leg of their trip. At the same time, a Quincy Turn was established at Wenatchee to handle all switching between Wenatchee and Quincy except Alcoa. The only potato business that continued to be handled by the railroad was frozen French fries, tater tots, and hash browns from Lamb-Weston shipped in mechanical reefers. The Quincy Turn left the east pickup for the manifest train that came out of Interbay that morning.

➸ The Wreck of the Alcoa Local at Quincy

The Alcoa Local's trip of November 5, 1963 came to a bad end at Quincy at 6:38 AM the following morning, November 6, 1963. The local was supposed to meet Extra 472A West at Quincy that morning. The normal course of events was for the Alcoa Local to back into the West Yard and switch out their train. If they made a meet at Quincy, they cleared the main track by backing into the West Yard. This morning, the Alcoa local did not stop at the West Yard, but continued east on the main track, running head-on into Extra 472A waiting for them just short of the west switch at Quincy siding.

Extra 472A was a drag west, usually called on duty at Hillyard between 6:00 PM and 11:00 PM. When the call time of the drag was closer to eleven, which it often was, the drag often met the Alcoa Local at Quincy.

The local, with RS-2 number 203 and 14 cars, including several loads of aluminum ingot from Alcoa, came over the lip of the Columbia Plateau about three miles west of Quincy, at full power. The local accelerated continuously on the level tangent track until it collided head-on with the extra west standing on the main track. The collision killed engineer Nick Winker and fireman Raymond Barnhart on engine 203. A photo on the front page of the *Wenatchee Daily World* showed the wrecked engine stripped to its frame with a pile of cars atop it.

The only plausible explanation for such a catastrophe was that the crew on the local fell asleep, perhaps lulled by rhythmic throbbing as engine 203 pulled slowly up Trinidad Hill with throttle in the full power 'Run 8' position, doubtless with the cab heaters on during the critical 'fatigue hour' near daybreak.

Many have wondered why the brakeman of the extra west did not open the siding switch so the local could 'head in,' which was the polite thing to do when holding the main when the train to be met had not yet arrived. The operating rules did not require 438A's brakeman to do this; rather, the crew of the opposing train was required by rule to handle the switch in such cases.

The reason nobody made this optional effort on the local's behalf was that the local customarily pulled by the east switch of the West Yard, which was located about 1,600 feet west of the west siding switch, backed into the yard, closed the main track switch, and began switching.

The crew of Extra 472A West, engineer John Bergman, fireman Bob Griffin, and head brakeman Frank Garske, stopped short of the west siding switch at Quincy and made a set out to the industry track. In returning their

Wreck of the Alcoa Local at Quincy early on the day of the accident. This photo shows the original position and condition of engine 203, whose underframe is the white line at the center of the photo. It is upright with everything above the underframe; cab, generator, and diesel engine scrapped off by one or more box cars loaded with aluminum passing through engine 203 above the underframe. GRANT COUNTY JOURNAL.

engine to the train, brakeman John Pruitt of Extra 438A West lined the west siding switch back for the main track, then walked west to the Standard Oil Spur just for something to do. The local blew past the astonished Pruitt and crashed into the extra west at an estimated 65 MPH.

The crew of the extra west was very fortunate to get off their lead unit before the impact. They did not realize that the local was not going to stop until it was almost too late to exit the cab. It is almost impossible for even experienced men to judge the speed of a directly approaching headlight.

Frank Garske, doubtless contemplating the eight-foot jump to the ground, froze in the door of EMD F 3 diesel 472A. Bergman gave Garske a shove so that Bergman himself could get out. Bergman did not get far enough away. Hit in the head by a flying boxcar, he was injured so severely that he never worked for the railroad again. Fireman Griffin was trapped in the 472A for a few minutes. Luke Tevlin of the Alcoa Local crew got him out. Griffin later stated he could hear the 203's diesel engine still running full-tilt when it went over the top of the 472A.

Another oddity, and probable contributing cause, is that the train crew of the local: head brakeman Linn Johnson, rear brakeman Leonard "Bunny" Doran, swing brakeman Luke "L.D." Tevlin, and Spokane extra board conductor John "Jack" Shields, were not aboard the train. They drove by auto from Rock Island to Quincy so they could eat while their train was grinding its way up Trinidad Hill. No doubt they were horrified to see

View to east from main track. The frame of engine 203 in center has been pulled from the nose of engine 472A, and some of the box cars have been moved. The ATSF box lying on the F units was in the Alcoa Local and was thrown forward at least 100 feet to come to rest in this position. GRANT COUNTY JOURNAL.

their train roar past them at the West Yard. Conductor Shields was fired and chose not to return to work, even though he could have been reinstated as a brakeman. The three brakemen were all suspended and returned to work after they served their time.

If the trainmen had been in the Alcoa Local's caboose, someone should have realized that their speed was excessive and pulled the emergency air valve in time to avoid the collision. If the crew had been in the caboose and rode out the actual collision, John Langlot believes they would have been killed or seriously injured. John saw the caboose, which was scrapped soon after, at Quincy. He observed that the stove, normally fastened down by bolts extending through the floor and further secured by steel backing plates under the floor, was torn completely loose, as were all of the interior doors. The car body of this older wood caboose, typical of those assigned to local service at the time, was wracked so badly by the quick stop it suffered that it was no longer square.

Over the years, some gossip has existed to the effect that the train crew of the local all testified at a subsequent formal investigation that they were in the caboose at the time of impact. I believe that this gossip about false testimony is incorrect and, in the absence of an investigation transcript to verify the many facts obscured by passage of time, believe that such false testimony did not occur. The Great Northern at that time was like an extended family. There were not many secrets. None of the local's train crew suffered a bruise or a scratch; it was common knowledge that Tevlin got Bob Griffin out of the 472A. If Tevlin was actually inside the wrecked caboose, he probably would have needed rescuing himself, and been unable to help anyone else.

About six months after Jack Shields was fired, Conductors' Local chairman Gordon Davies informed him that reinstatement, at least as a brakeman, might be possible, but Jack would first have to meet face-to-face with Superintendent R. H. Shober and be interviewed before Shober would assent to restoring Jack to work. Shober's willingness to allow Jack to return to work was customary in those days. Management knew it cost money to train employees, and was aware that when accidents took place, employees lucky enough to survive often learned a hard lesson about rules violations. Men who experienced the consequences of rules violations generally would never again repeat their violation

Engine 472A, lead unit of the drag west at Quincy, showing impact damage from the frame of engine 203. Engine 472A was traded in to EMD on January 20, 1964. GNRHS ARCHIVE (55.05.34).

if given a second chance. The experience often caused a general shift in attitude toward consistent compliance with all the rules.

Gordon and Jack left Spokane on No. 31, the Empire Builder, arriving at King Street Station, Seattle, at about 8:00 AM for their 11:00 AM appointment with Mr. Shober, whose office was across the street in the Great Northern freight house. Jack said that he wanted to "visit a friend" before the meeting and promised to meet Gordon at the station at 10:30 AM. Jack failed to show up, and in fact disappeared. Gordon kept the appointment with Mr. Shober and discussed the matter.

Shober informed the local chairman, regardless of the missed appointment, to tell Jack that he would be allowed to return to work as a brakeman if he would make another appointment and meet with Shober. The Superintendent undoubtedly wanted to give Jack his job back if Jack would show contrition and willingness to comply with the rules. Shober also stated that it must be understood that Jack would never be allowed to be a

Locomotive cranes have arrived at Quincy and are at work at both ends of the accident site. Underframe of engine 203 has been turned upside down and set aside in the clearing process. Engine 203 was officially scraped January 2, 1964. GNRHS ARCHIVE (55.05.40.01).

conductor again. Gordon never saw Jack in person after that day. They spoke by telephone after they returned to Spokane; Jack excused himself by saying that he "just could not face Mr. Shober."

John Langlot believes that there was a pact of silence among the three brakemen. None of them spoke of the accident with fellow employees, even when directly asked about it. John witnessed this several times; someone would ask a question; the only response would be silence. There was not even a "None of your business," or "I do not want to talk about it"—just total, complete silence. John believes that all four of the trainmen involved suffered a hard time living with the memories of this event. Jack Shields certainly experienced trouble living with it.

In addition, there was an issue with the train dispatcher. The railroad fired train dispatcher John C. Shuman, who was approaching retirement age. He never worked another day after the accident.

The Railroad Adjustment Board, in award 13778, exonerated Shuman.[5] In reporting the Board's finding for Shuman, *Train Dispatcher* magazine,[6] the official magazine of the American Train Dispatchers' Association, the union representing him before the Adjustment Board, was scathing in its commentary:

> Not withstanding repeated requests upon the Carrier that it advise the Organization precisely what the indefinitely alleged responsibility was, the Carrier did not see fit to respond, and for obvious reasons. The record did disclose that one of the all too familiar "jawbone" situations was involved. The resort to "jawbone" was known

This photo, a companion to the previous, looks to the west. Underframe of engine 203 is at center of photo. Grade crossing signals at far right protect Third Street crossing. GNRHS ARCHIVE (55.05.37).

> to and sanctioned by local Carrier officers. Indeed, it was they who were responsible for it. However, and for obvious reasons, the practice was never authorized in writing, although it was made clear to the train dispatchers that they were expected to operate on that basis. And, of course, immediately following the collision, the Carrier officers who had originated and sanctioned the practice, and expected the train dispatchers to observe it, moved quickly to put themselves in the clear to ensure that somebody else would tote the hod—in this instance, the train dispatcher.

The exact wording of the questionable train orders is not known. However, several train dispatchers available for comment over fifty years later remember a few pertinent facts about the incident. David Sprau, a NP telegrapher at Auburn at the time, was training to be a dispatcher and knew many of the GN people. He remembers being told by GN dispatcher Jack Frisina that the issue involved Shuman's having the operator at Quincy use his train order signal to hold the extra west at Quincy for the local without issuing any train orders as required under such circumstances. The operator on duty at Quincy at the time, the late P. William Watts, later became a dispatcher and told Sprau that his recollection was that some type of train order existed between the two trains at the time, but it was inadequate.

Dispatcher Harry Parks recollects that the actual offense involved the local moving to Quincy protected against Extra 472A West only by a red train order signal against the extra west at that point. In combination, these recollections suggest that whether or not train orders existed between the two trains, they contained neither sufficient protection nor other instruction to permit the local to move to Quincy successfully.

It is clear from the Railroad Adjustment Board's report that the local left Wenatchee with train orders and clearance as "Work Extra 203," so it held a 'work' order. While it has not been possible to locate the order issued on November 5, 1963, a Great Northern "Dispatchers Train Order Book" for a slightly earlier time frame contains daily work orders issued for the Alcoa Local in format similar to this:

ENGINE ___ WORKS EXTRA 701PM NOVEMBER 5 UNTIL 1101AM NOVEMBER 6 BETWEEN WENATCHEE AND QUINCY NOT PROTECTING AGAINST EXTRA TRAINS

With such an order, the engine could move in either direction between Wenatchee and Quincy for as many trips as desired but would have to observe timetable times of regular trains. In November of 1963, this meant clearing the main track for No. 5, the mail train, at Quincy beginning at 11:50 PM. In like manner, the local was required to clear the main track for No. 31, the Empire Builder, beginning at Quincy at 2:17 AM, and for No 28, the Western Star, leaving Wenatchee 2:40 AM, always respecting these trains' timetable times at intermediate stations. In addition, the work train must either clear the main track for, or provide flag protection against, second class freight schedules No. 492 leaving Wenatchee 4:30 AM and No. 494 at 9:00 AM.

If any extra trains were expected within the limits of the work order, the order would instruct the local to protect against those trains. Protect in this context meaning to station a flagman to afford protection, or to clear the main track. For example, if Extra 472A West was expected at Quincy at 10:30 PM, the order would state:

EXCEPT PROTECT AGAINST EXTRA 472A WEST AFTER 1030 PM

With such a train order in hand leaving Wenatchee in early evening, the local held plenty of time to go to Malaga, Alcoa Spur, or even Rock Island against the extra west and get their station work done at those points. By 10:30 PM, however, if the local had not arrived at Quincy, the extra west was permitted to leave Quincy and enter the work order limits.

With a train order worded as the above, Work Extra 203 was obligated to protect against Extra 472A West as of 10:30 PM. Although it was possible to actually walk a flagman against an overdue train being protected against, as a practical matter, this was seldom done over any significant distance. In practice, such an order pretty much became useless if the work extra was unable to make Quincy before 10:30 PM. The local effectively was 'stuck' wherever it was at 10:30 PM.

Meanwhile, Extra 472A West was delayed far beyond whatever 'protect' time was indicated in the train order. If Work Extra 203 remained at Alcoa, Rock Island, or Columbia River until Extra 472A West appeared, Work Extra 203 would have been badly delayed, and might not have sufficient time to go to Quincy, do their switching, go to Ephrata, and get back to Wenatchee.

Since the crew of Extra 472A West was not short of time to work, the better move was to hold the extra west at Quincy and advance the Work Extra. Doing this properly under the rules required additional orders to both trains. Since there were no night telegraph operators on duty anywhere between Wenatchee and Quincy, the dispatcher would have been forced to either call the agent at Rock Island out in the middle of the night on overtime to copy the train order for the local, or the conductor of the local would have been required to go to a company telephone booth, call the dispatcher, and copy the train order himself.

The dispatcher would have used the Quincy operator to issue the order to the extra west, and either the Rock Island agent or the conductor would simultaneously copy the new orders allowing the Work Extra to advance against Extra 472A West. While there are many different ways such orders can be worded, the most likely form of train order would simply state:

EXTRA 472A WEST WAIT AT QUINCY UNTIL 650 AM

Penalty overtime payments would have been due in any train order case. If the Rock Island agent copied the order, he would have been paid for a minimum of two hours at time and a half. If the conductor copied the order, he would have been paid 100 miles at the rate of pay applicable to the job he was on, quite a bonanza! In addition, the agent would be paid if the conductor copied his own order, because under union rules, the work of copying train orders belonged exclusively to agents and telegraphers. As a professional courtesy, conductors usually made an extra copy for, or would otherwise arrange to inform, the agent/telegrapher who was not called, so that person could file a time claim for the work he was entitled by union agreement to perform.

A 'jawbone,' or verbal procedure, was worked out to avoid what otherwise would have been expensive circumstances occurring frequently with the Alcoa Local. Although it was contrary to operating rules and would have been obvious to any operating official who was paying attention, the procedure was tacitly ignored, if not encouraged, because it was saving the company money.

The dispatcher would 'jawbone,' that is, verbally authorize the operation, by instructing the operator at Quincy to put a red train order board out for westward trains. Then, instead of issuing a train order to accompany the red train order signal, the dispatcher would verbally instruct the operator to hold westward trains until the work extra arrived. When the Alcoa Local conductor called from Alcoa Spur or Rock Island, the dispatcher would simply tell the work extra, "I have a red board on westbounds at Quincy. Get moving and get over there."

John Langlot recalls that the Alcoa Local routinely left Wenatchee with a work order. When they finished switching Alcoa, they would travel from the plant back to the main track. They stopped short of the main track while the conductor went to the phone booth near the switch to call the dispatcher.

The late former Cascade Division Chief Dispatcher Edward Khatain was interviewed about the accident. Khatain was an Assistant Chief Train Dispatcher at the time. He had no direct connection with the accident, but as an employee in the dispatchers' office, was thoroughly familiar with the cause. Khatain was a careful, safe train dispatcher who, like most, followed the rules and did not 'jawbone' any of his train movements. Even 45 years later, he indicated disdain for the whole affair and did not much care to talk about it, but offered the following:

> While it was impossible to "cover-up" that accident, many of the inside details were kept pretty quiet because too many people were involved in it, from the Superintendent down. While most did not have a direct hand in authorizing it, many company officers either knew, should have known, or suspected this kind of thing was going on regularly. They turned a blind eye to it, did nothing, and eventually ***this*** is what happens.

Alan C. Field, another Seattle dispatcher known for working carefully and safely, likewise was not involved, but recalls the event similarly. He believes if a work order existed, its station limits may have not extended as far east as Quincy, the Alcoa Local's move being entirely 'jawboned,' but, in either case:

> When the Alcoa was ready to proceed to Quincy the railroad did not want to pay overtime for the Agent-Operator at Rock Island to come on duty and copy whatever orders were necessary at the time for the local to make his move to Quincy, or to incur similar penalties for the conductor copying train orders. So, the practice was if no trains were coming west, the dispatcher would tell the Quincy operator to put out a red board west, and just tell the local it was okay to "proceed to Quincy." The night of the wreck, as I remember, John Schuman did exactly this, but there was a westbound somewhere east of Ephrata. John figured the local would not delay that westbound much on the red board at Quincy. The westbound got to Quincy before the local and was stopped east of the west switch.
>
> The local came into town with only the engine crew aboard, who were both asleep; they came right down the main and hit the head end of the westbound. The train crew on the local admitted at the investigation that they were not even aboard the train. They had an automobile in Rock Island and they drove to Quincy to get to the beanery. When they recovered the bodies of the men who were killed, a caboose mattress was found in the wreckage of the engine cab. And of course even though most everyone knew what had really taken place, the improper train order handling was never admitted to being somewhat regular practice, by anybody. Nice story.

While content of the train orders, if there were any, on that fateful morning is unknown, the whole issue of whether any orders existed, or how they read, is moot. We know that the train order signal was used to hold Extra 472A West, and that Schuman told the local to go to Quincy on the strength of the train order signal holding opposing movements until the local arrived. As stated, such handling, or mishandling, of train orders was strictly against the rules, but the procedure was common on the division at the time. The circumstances of timing, the process of the meet, the procedure of using the order board to hold the extra west, and the local's train crew driving to Quincy to eat all were typical.

With the crew asleep, the content of the train orders, proper or not, made no difference; the wreck would have happened regardless. The head end crew of the local certainly did not intend to fall asleep but fall asleep they did, and at this point it was "game over." No train order or other paper document could have prevented the accident from happening.

Because of the rules violation and being in the wrong place at the wrong time, the railroad dismissed dispatcher Schuman. Because management either tacitly permitted or verbally instructed him to regularly operate this way, he was eventually recognized as a 'scapegoat' and exonerated by the Railroad Adjustment Board, which ordered his reinstatement. The Board recognized, however, that some of the blame indeed was his, so the reinstatement included only partial payment for lost time.

John Schuman worked as a dispatcher for the Union Pacific and later migrated to the little Pacific Coast Railroad in King County, Washington. During World War II, he moved to the Great Northern. At the time of his reinstatement by the Board, he had reached retirement age and developed an enjoyable part-time occupation growing prize dahlias, for which he was somewhat renowned in the Seattle area. He took the money and retired.

Needless to say, after the events of November 6, 1963, 'jawboning' was not even considered. Whenever existing orders no longer permitted the train to move as required by rules, the conductor of the Alcoa Local would copy whatever train orders were required to authorize further movement.

➻ The Mansfield Turn

Last, and in those days least, was the Mansfield Turn. The Mansfield Turn was called on Sunday morning. Train crews were Spokane men from the chain gang who were not happy to be delayed the extra day it took to get home if they caught the Mansfield. The engineer was off the Wenatchee extra board, so he did not mind catching the job. Power was from one or two of the locals that did not work on Sunday.

Under Washington's Full Crew Law, the Mansfield Turn usually ran with only two brakemen, because it was shorter than 24 cars while it was on the main line. All crews came out of Spokane with a third brakeman on a tonnage train. Our third brakeman stayed in Wenatchee and 'fell back' so that he could return to Spokane with the crew that was called to go east after our crew was called. The third brakeman on that crew fell back when our man was called in his place. This continued until our crew worked back to Spokane with a third brakeman who had fallen back from a previous crew.

The Mansfield Turn was usually made up on one of the river tracks where the cars were accumulated during the week. The operation was elegantly simple. Since all the cars were identical 40-foot boxcars and only grain was handled, any empty car could go anywhere. Since all the station tracks were double ended and rolled toward Columbia River, the elevator operators rolled their loaded cars past their elevators. The trip to Mansfield was simply a matter of spotting the empties.

At Mansfield, there were three or four elevators along the industry track. The engine pulled the entire train beyond the switch and shoved into the industry track putting the caboose against the loads, shoved the loads together, and got them past the elevators. The crew then worked toward end of track, spotting empty cars at the elevators as we went. The crew ran the engine around the wye if they needed to, ran down the main, coupled to the cars, cut in the air, pulled the loads and the caboose from the industry track, shoved the cars up the main to the crossing, left the train to charge the air brakes, and went to lunch. After lunch at the tavern, the only business open in town on Sunday, we made an air test and headed home. At each station, it was just a matter of making a pickup to the head end.

The down grade to Palisades, at the bottom of Moses

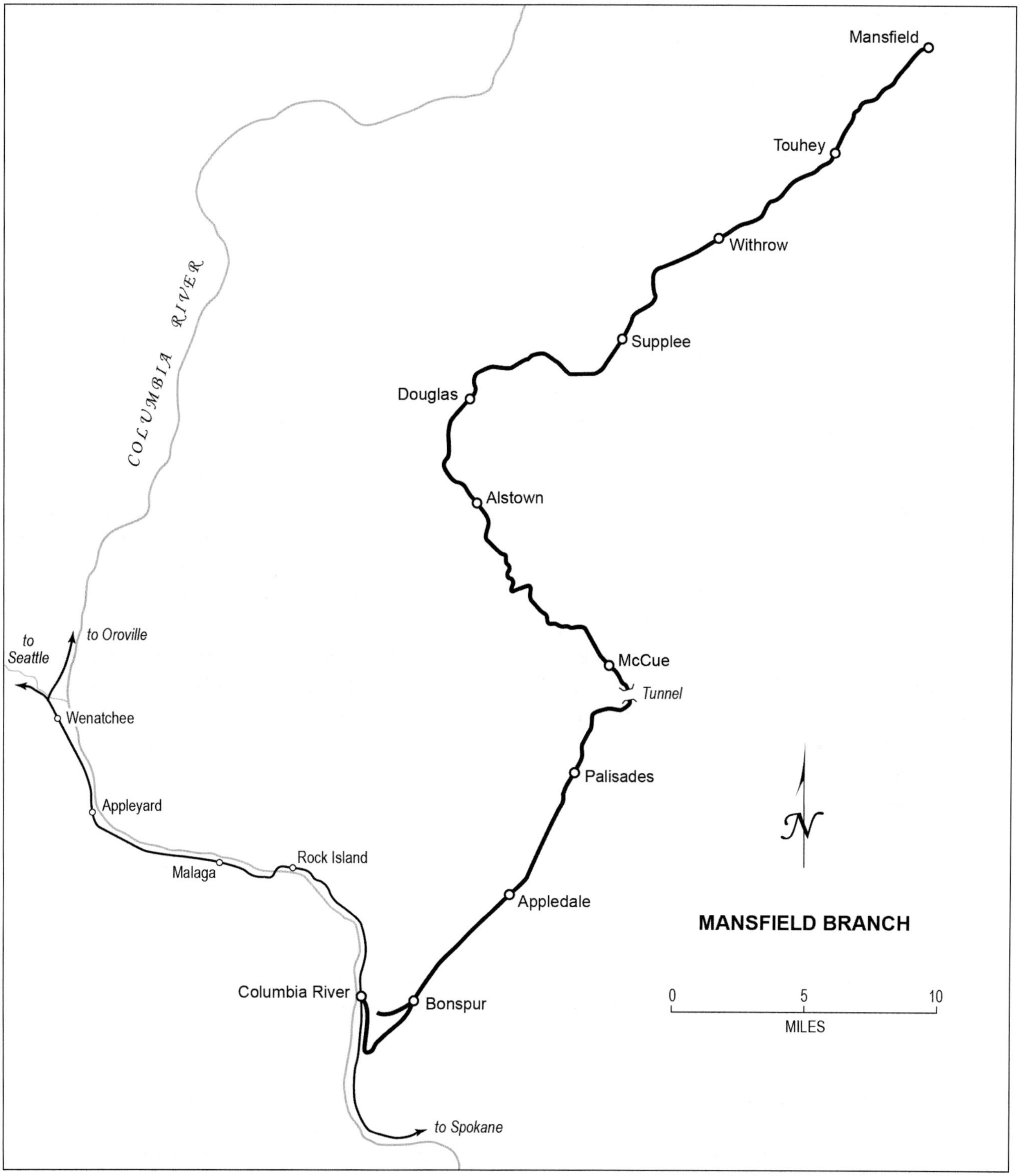
Mansfield
Touhey
Withrow
Supplee
Douglas
Alstown
McCue
Tunnel
Palisades
Appledale
Bonspur
Columbia River
COLUMBIA RIVER
to Oroville
to Seattle
Wenatchee
Appleyard
Malaga
Rock Island
to Spokane
N
MANSFIELD BRANCH
0
5
10
MILES

Harry O. Black, manager of Waterville Union Grain elevators at Mansfield. The Mansfield branch was built to haul grain, predominately wheat, and it did so for its entire existence. Farmers took their grain to the nearest elevator, where it was stored and shipped from. Because Mansfield was at the end of the line and had a tributary area that was larger than usual, it had an extraordinary collection of elevators. Mr. Black came to Mansfield in the 1930s, and several of his grandchildren live in the area to this day. MARY ELLEN WAX COLLECTION.

Coulee, 2.0%, a steep grade. Some engineers directed the brakeman to turn up some retainers, others did not.

I worked the Mansfield eight to ten times and remember one trip in particular. I was the swing brakeman called on duty at 6:00 AM.

Our train was in the West Yard at Wenatchee. I rode the engine west to the train and walked to the rear end. When I got there, I discovered an old heavyweight stockmens' coach at the rear of our train instead of a caboose. Stockmens' coaches were used in days past when the company ran stock trains. The cowboys who accompanied the cattle rode in the stockmens' coach. The inside of our stockmens' coach was a filthy mess due to transients living in the car. The car was a disgrace. The car was equipped with an air gauge, so I was able to make our air test.

I told the conductor, Ed Dewood, about the stockmens' coach when we pulled out on the main. I stopped the rear of the train at the yard office. Ed came out, took a look, went right back into the yard office, and made the yardmaster come out to take a look. I went outside, as there was a lot of screaming and harsh words over the condition of this car.

The carmen were summoned from Appleyard to flush the car out with a hose, washing the garbage and trash out the door. They nailed a piece of plywood across the

The Mansfield Local descends Douglas Creek Canyon during July 1983 with forty-four loads of grain. Air brakes are set and both units are in dynamic braking to hold the train on the 2.0 percent grade. This location is near where Douglas Creek enters Moses Coulee, and is about two miles railroad west of the long-forgotten station of McCue. Palisades is about four miles ahead. The rear of the train is passing through the only tunnel of the branch. PHOTO BY BLAIR KOOISTRA.

armrests of one of the seats for a conductor's desk. The carmen also supplied us with the tools and supplies to re-brass a car. These tools and supplies were routinely carried on cabooses, but not on stockmens' coaches. I asked Ed what this was all about. Ed told me that last night's Extra West set out a tie gang's cars into one of the two storage tracks at Columbia River. We were to pick up the tie gang cars and move them to Mansfield. Ed told me that the Extra West suffered a hot box on the tie gang's water car and we were going to have to re-brass the journal. The message said that the water car would move to Mansfield "without fail" even if we were forced to re-brass the car more than once.

We finally departed Wenatchee with about 20 empty boxcars and the stockmens' coach. At Columbia River, we headed into the siding, pulled up to the water car, and unloaded the re-brassing tools. Then the engine backed the train west to get it out of the way. The head brakeman, Bob Jones, cut the engine off the train, and came against the tie gang cars. I made a cut behind the water car, signaled the engineer to pull ahead a couple of car lengths, stopped him, and signaled the engineer to set the brakes on the cut of cars. The rear car was now the water car. I closed the angle cock and bled the air out of the water car. By having the water car attached to the cut of cars with the brakes set, the water car could not move.

Bob Jones and I set the oak blocks, which are about 4 inches thick, 16 inches wide, and 30 inches long across two ties, the blocks one on top of the other. Then we set the yoke on the oak blocks, placing one end against the wheel. The yoke was a flat steel plate half an inch thick, eight inches wide, and sixteen inches long. One end of the yoke was bent up in an S curve to engage the curved outer lip of the wheel. When a car is jacked up, the yoke holds the wheel on the rail, preventing the wheel from lifting off the rail. If the wheel lifted, it could fall to the rail and kick the jack out. The fall could cause the far wheel to fall to the ground and derail. Having the jack kick out could hurt or kill one of us.

Bob and I placed a hydraulic jack, called a caboose jack, on top of the yoke and under the journal box. The bottom of the journal box was flat the full depth of the journal box. The flat spot was only five or six inches wide, which was just wide enough for the cylinder head of the jack to press on the journal box's flat spot. Each push on the pump handle raised the jack's cylinder only an eighth to a quarter of an inch, depending on the weight of the car. An approximately three-quarter inch machined lip around the outer end of the axle kept the brass from sliding out of the journal. The brass sat on the top of the axle journal behind this lip. To jack the journal box up high enough to pull the old brass out and replace it with a new brass took a lot of jacking. Bob and I raised the journal box four or five inches if my memory serves correctly. Big Ed supervised.

This brass was cracked completely in half. The journal end of the axle was severely scored and galled. The condition of the axle indicated that this water car was not very far from dropping the journal when the other crew had set it out. Dropping the journal means the end of the axle melted off. When the axle melted, the truck side would drop to the top of the rail and the axle, with wheels, would go crosswise, causing a derailment. If this happened at speed, the result could be a 25 to 40 car derailment.

I told Ed that I did not think this car would get to Mansfield without re-brassing it again, and Ed agreed. Bob and I gooped up the new brass with hot box coolant, a thick tar-like substance, slid the new brass into place, and let the jack down. There was no release valve on the jack. To bring the car down, we flipped a lever to the down position and jacked the car down with just as many pumps as it had taken to jack the car up. With the car back down, we put a new oil pad in the bottom of the journal box and soaked the new pad with journal box oil. It took us about an hour to re-brass this car, which was typical time for a train crew on the road.

We put the tie gang cars back together and left them on the industry track. Then we cut off the stockmens' coach, got the empty boxcars off the siding, picked up the tie gang cars, and picked up our stockmens' coach. This put the tie gang cars immediately ahead of the stockmens' coach. We pulled up to the switch for the Mansfield Branch, opened the switch, pulled the train by, closed the siding switch, and headed up the hill.

At Palisades, 15 miles up the line, the journal was on fire. We put out the fire and re-brassed the journal again.

As Bob and I were finishing re-brassing the journal, I looked under the running board and across the bottom of the tank and saw a pipe with a gate valve coming out of it. A pipe, an elbow, and a horizontal pipe with a nipple on the end extended towards the truck side with the re-brassed journal. I took a good look at the pipe nipple and found that it was threaded on the inside. After looking more closely, I decided that it looked like the threads in the pipe were the same size and thread as an air hose. I walked back to the stockmens' coach and returned with two standard replacement air hoses. I screwed one hose into the nipple and hooked the two glad hands together. Fortunately, our bad journal was on an inside axle, so it was possible to reach it with the two hoses. I found a piece of farmer's fence wire and wired the threaded end of the second air hose into the journal box. Then I cracked the water valve and let a small amount of water trickle into the journal box. Off we went, limiting our speed to 10 MPH to keep the journal from overheating.

We set out cars for grain loading all the way to Mansfield while the water car journal steamed for the rest of the trip. The water car made it to Mansfield without having to re-brass the journal again. We set the tie gang cars in the siding, switched the elevators, and started back down the line picking up wheat from station to station. The delays caused by the water car forced us to go dead on our 16 hours of service at Douglas.

Summary

When most people think about working in train or engine service, they think of the old head conductor punching tickets and riding the soft cushions in a nice warm passenger train, and the brave engineer handling a mile-long fast freight, peering into the dark while speeding the mail on No. 28, or protecting his passengers on No. 31. While those visions are accurate, in the sense that they certainly happened, they are incomplete.

In the last decade of the Great Northern's existence, more Spokane Division trainmen and enginemen worked on the locals than in chain gang and passenger service combined. We have discussed 14 year-round locals excluding the two jobs on W–O, the seasonal Pateros Turn, and the Mansfield Turn. With the Beet and Spud locals in the busy season, 19 local crews worked the Spokane Division every weekday.

Yard crews employed both switchmen and enginemen. Wenatchee worked three switch engines on all three shifts on weekdays, for a total of nine jobs. Hillyard, Spokane Yard, and the SC&P Yard between them started 29 switch jobs on a typical weekday.

The fact is that in the 1960s most trainmen and enginemen got a taste of fast running for a small part of their careers. What, where, and how crewmen worked was driven by the single car nature of the business. After the BN merger, management would encourage the growth of unit trains, and shift as much traffic as possible to unit trains and to trains, such as intermodal, that could be operated from terminal to terminal with little or no intermediate switching.

Endnotes

1 HistoryLink, U&I Sugar Company dedicates Moses Lake plant on October 23, 1953, Accessed October 23, 2012, www.historylink.org, 1–3.

2 Northern Pacific Railway, Idaho Division Local Train Brief Train 1234–1235 Wheeler Turnaround Local, Office of General Superintendent Transportation, October 1, 1968, Accessed October 13, 2012, http://sdp45.blogspot.com/search/label/Wheeler.

3 Gary Dinsmore, emails dated October 26 and 28, 2012. Mr. Dinsmore worked as a clerk for the Northern Pacific at Wheeler from September of 1963 through February of 1964.

4 Northwest Council, Columbia Basin Project, Accessed February 22, 2011, www.nwcouncil.org/history/ColumbiaBasinProject.asp.

5 Harold M. Weston, "Award 13778 Docket No. TD-15067" National Railroad Adjustment Board, Third Division, Washington DC, July 29, 1965.

6 C. Harker Rhodes, Editor, RECENT COURT AND BOARD DECISIONS OF INTEREST, "Train Dispatcher Magazine Official Publication of the American Train Dispatchers' Association," September 1965, 254.

9. Working the W–O Branch in the 1960s

➸ Introduction

I started to work the W–O local regularly in 1961. During 1965 and 1966 I could work the brakemen's extra board for a month or two during the summer. In the fall I was back to the W–O, until the spring of 1967, when I was finally able to work elsewhere. Our previous book, *The Rusty Dusty: Great Northern's Wenatchee–Oroville Branch*, includes a tour or the W–O at Chapter 13. This chapter is material not included in that book.

➸ Operating Overview

During the 1960s, train No. 698 operated northward and train No. 697 operated southward between Wenatchee and Oroville. The Keremeos Turn operated as an extra between Oroville and Keremeos, British Columbia.

Trains 698 and 697 were called at 4:00 PM. They were night locals, which meant working with a lantern in your hand all night long. When you went up a ladder on the side of a car to tie the hand brake, as a brakeman on these jobs did as many as 50 times a night, you did it with that lantern in your hand. When you were lining a switch, getting on and off moving cars and engines, in short, everything you did, that lantern was always in your hand. If you were working the lists, you either held onto them and the lantern, or put the lists in your pocket. Woe to the swing brakeman who lost his switch lists!

The schedules published in the Time Table showed the W–O trains running much earlier than they really did and called for the meet to be made at Monse (1953–1967) or Brewster (after July 1, 1967). The solution for this was to issue orders to No. 697 at Oroville and to No. 698 at Wenatchee that established a flat meet at Okanogan. Since the rules provided that train orders supersede the Time Table, the flat meet resolved the problem.

Trains No. 697 and No. 698 met at Okanogan because there was not sufficient room at Omak to meet the two trains, both of them trying to do the industry switching at the same time. With the meet at Okanogan, Omak was switched sequentially. The issue was not siding length; Okanogan was a 55-car siding and Omak was a 66-car siding. The issue was that two crews could not work Omak at the same time.

The southward crew usually arrived at Okanogan soon after the northward crew finished their switching. The crew of train No. 697 picked up the cars for Wenatchee that No. 698 had gathered up for them. They made their pickup, air tested the pickup, pulled down the main to clear the north switch so the northward crew could leave when they finished dinner, and cut the crossing. By making the air test on the pickup before pulling down to clear the north end of the siding, all they needed to do after eating was buckle up the crossing and make a stub air test before leaving.

Both crews walked over the Oak Street Bridge across the Okanogan River into town to The Loop Loop Bar and Grill for the only meal we usually ate until we were off duty at Oroville. The Loop Loop was located in a basement with no structure above the basement. It was the only place to eat in town at this time of night. The food was good but the atmosphere left a little bit to be desired; the place was a dump.

For a short time, both crews were at the Loop Loop for dinner. This gave everyone a chance to talk to someone that he was not spending 16 hours a day, six days a week with at work. When the crews met at Okanogan, the southward crew gave all the switch lists for Oroville,

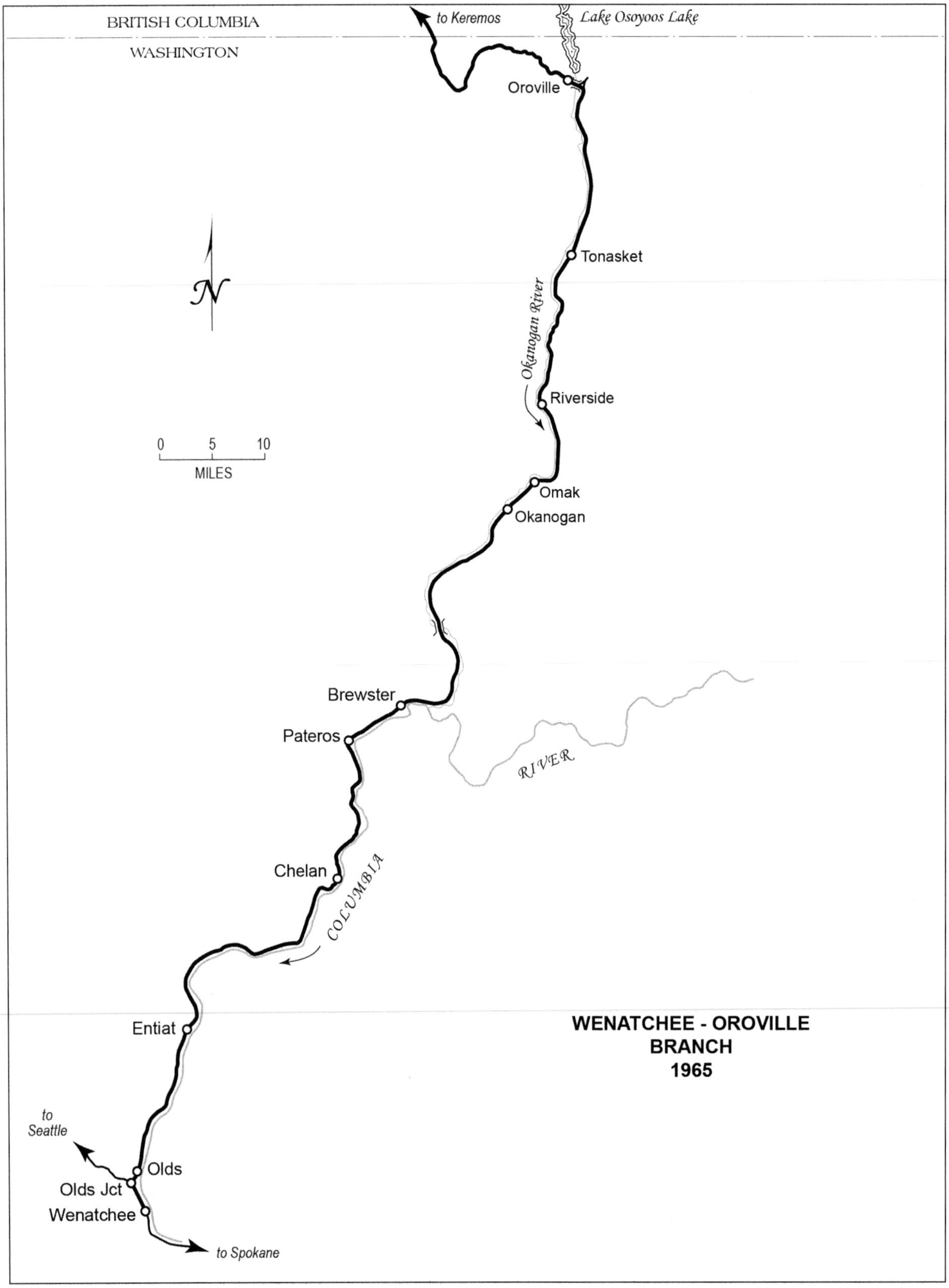
BRITISH COLUMBIA
WASHINGTON
to Keremos
Lake Osoyoos Lake
Oroville
Tonasket
Okanogan River
Riverside
0 5 10
MILES
Omak
Okanogan
Brewster
Pateros
RIVER
Chelan
COLUMBIA
Entiat
WENATCHEE - OROVILLE
BRANCH
1965
to
Seattle
Olds
Olds Jct
Wenatchee
to Spokane

Tonasket, and Omak to the northward crew. This gave the northward crew a sneak peek at what they would do the rest of the night, a little time to study the switch lists, and they could start to figure out how to do the work at each station. We could see which cars in our train spotted at each station, plus where cars that No. 697 left off spot in each track would be spotted back to on that track.

The Great Northern allowed customers on the W–O to load a car at two different stations. These were 'stop cars' to us. On occasion, we got a car of fruit with a red tag on the top of the waybill that said "STOP OVER TO FINISH LOADING." This meant that this car must be spotted at a different station to finish loading.

When No. 697 had a stop car for a station south of Okanogan, the crew of No. 698 gave them the relevant switch lists for the station south of Okanogan so that the crew of No. 697 knew where to spot the car and where all the cars were to be spotted so they could properly re-spot the track. Each conductor kept their lists for a few days in case a question came up. After a few days he threw them away.

After leaving Okanogan, train No. 697 picked up the cars that No. 698 had set up for them at Brewster and Pateros. From Pateros, No. 697 ran straight to Wenatchee unless they got a stopover car to finish loading south of Pateros; in that case they stopped and spotted that car.

Yard Limits were in effect at Wenatchee/Olds, Entiat, Chelan Falls/Chelan, Pateros, Brewster, Okanogan, Omak, and Oroville. Yard Limits allowed trains to move freely on the main track between the yard limit signs to do their work. This was most important at Okanogan, because it let No. 698 work using the main track between the south Yard Limit board and the north Yard Limit board without having to flag against No. 697. The down side of Yard Limits was that within Yard Limits all trains were required to move at restricted speed, not exceeding 20 MPH.

➻ Wenatchee Terminal

During the 1960s, and today, the Wenatchee Terminal extended nearly six miles from Switch One near MP 1647 on the east, to Olds Junction near MP 1652.8 on the west. The yard office is located at MP 1650.1. Locomotives were kept on the 'Roundhouse Tracks' in back of the freight house portion of the yard office. The west end of Appleyard was located at MP 1648.5, and the west end of the Main Yard and the West Yard were located at MP 1650.8 at Wenatchee station. The 'W–O Main' track, adjacent to and on the river side of the main track, extended a bit over four miles from the west end of Appleyard, through Wenatchee, to Olds Junction, and was equipped with block signals. At Olds Junction the W–O main ends at a crossover. The straight side of the switch connects with the W–O branch. The diverging side takes westward trains from the W–O main to the Cascade Division main track for Stevens Pass and Seattle.

When I started on the W–O in 1961, the switch in the W–O main at Olds Junction was a spring switch normally lined for the crossover. Northward train No. 698 was required to stop at Olds Junction, line the spring switch for the W–O, then stop and line the switch back after the train cleared the switch at Olds Junction.

Train 697 would, with the permission of the dispatcher and yardmaster, run through the spring switch from the W–O branch to the W–O main at Olds Junction. That No. 697 was required to get permission from both the dispatcher and the yardmaster was unusual. Normally the only permission required was that of the yardmaster since the switch was within yard limits. Because the W–O main was a main track, and the dispatcher could have been planning to use it for an approaching eastward train, the practice was established of having us call the Wenatchee operator, who contacted the dispatcher for us, and relayed the dispatcher's permission to us. If the yardmaster did not immediately contact us after our discussion with the operator, we called him for authority to move within yard limits.

In April of 1966, Centralized Traffic Control (CTC) was completed from Merritt to Olds Junction and from Switch One at the east end of Appleyard to Columbia River. The main track between Olds Junction and Switch One, and the W–O main between Olds Junction and the west end of Appleyard, remained Automatic

Block Signal (ABS) territory under the jurisdiction of the Wenatchee yardmaster.

After the CTC was in operation, the dispatcher in Seattle controlled the switches at Olds Junction and Switch One. The Wenatchee operator informed the dispatcher that a train needed to be lined a certain direction at Switch One or at Olds Junction. The dispatcher lined the switch for the intended move and gave the train the signal for that movement.

During 1947, the Appleyard ice platform was extended to its final length of 2,805 feet,[1] for a capacity of 120 cars, 60 on track 1 and 60 on track 2. That same year, Columbia Ice & Cold Storage added an ice manufacturing facility at Plant 3,[2] the Ice House at Appleyard, eliminating the need to haul ice from Wenatchee to Appleyard.

As it happened, the peak fruit traffic handled by the Wenatchee Terminal occurred during 1948 and 1949. The ice platform at Plant 2 in Wenatchee was removed during the first half of the 1950s. Loss of the icing platform at Wenatchee meant that all of the reefer cars would be pre-iced and re-iced at Appleyard.

➻ Where at Wenatchee?

Soon after reporting to the yard office at 4:00 PM, the conductor would ask the yardmaster where our train was and if it was OK for his crew to get the engine out of the roundhouse tracks and go get on the train. The yardmaster is the boss of the yard and everyone is governed by his instructions. He can authorize freight trains and engines to occupy the main track within yard limits subject only to the requirement that they not occupy the main track when first class trains are due. Once we received permission from the yardmaster, we got the engine out of the engine house tracks and put it on the train.

In the summer months, our train was usually, meaning something over half the time, made up at Wenatchee west of Orondo Street. During the fall fruit shipping season, when trains were heavy with iced reefers, the W–O and Pateros trains were almost always built at Wenatchee. Since making these trains at Wenatchee required having a switch crew drag the cars up from Appleyard, the only reason I can think of for building the trains at Wenatchee is that Appleyard was too congested to handle everything.

When our train was at Wenatchee, we came out of the roundhouse tracks with the power, ran west on the main track to the Fifth Street, or the Ninth Street crossover if Fifth was blocked, backed through the crossover to the W–O main, went east to our train, coupled on, made our air test, and departed. The W–O Local was usually on the W–O main and the Pateros Turn was usually on Main Yard One, the first track next to the W–O main on the river side of the yard. Sometimes the W–O Local was so long that it fouled the west lead of the Main Yard, blocking access to the main yard tracks. When that happened, the Pateros Turn's crew could not get on their train until after No. 698 departed.

By the late 1960s, Fred Ball was the afternoon yardmaster. Fred made all the locals at Appleyard. This saved his switch engines having to drag the cars for the locals to the Main Yard at Wenatchee. It also simplified the switching since Appleyard possessed more tracks into which cars could be spread to make blocks for stations.

When the train was made up at Appleyard, we took our power east on the main or the W–O main. At Appleyard, the engine coupled onto the train, made our air test, pulled the train up the W–O main to Wenatchee, picked up the train orders from the conductor at the depot, picked up ice for the caboose, got the conductor on and departed, usually between 5:00 and 5:30 PM.

➻ Air Brake Tests

Before our train left the yard track, the engine pumped up the air so we could make our 'initial terminal air brake test' as required at both Wenatchee and Oroville. The term 'pumping up the air' refers to charging the brake pipe and the air reservoirs of each car with compressed air. As the cars are being charged, the air makes a sound as it flows into the reservoirs on each car. Trainmen call this sound 'singing.' When the caboose and the car ahead of the caboose quit singing, the rear brakeman checked the air gauge in the caboose to confirm that there was close to ninety pounds of air pressure in the train line. If so, the rear brakeman signaled the engineer to make the air test. In response, the engineer applied, or set, the brakes on the train.

Both brakemen then 'walked the set.' The head brakeman started at the engine working back, while the rear

Caboose X-494 at Appleyard. This 25-foot wood caboose was typical of GN cabooses built from 1907 through 1930. Car is likely assigned to the Grotto Local, or Alcoa Local. GNRHS ARCHIVE.

brakeman started from the caboose working forward. The brakemen checked each car body for safety appliance defects such as bent or broken ladders, grab irons, and sill steps. They checked the trucks for broken or cracked wheels and missing or worn out brake shoes. They checked the piston travel of the brake cylinder on each car to make sure the air brakes were applied and that piston travel was not excessive. The brakemen met near the middle of the train, gave the engineer a sign to release the brakes, and then each walked back to their starting point, checking to make sure that each car's air brakes released.

The engineer did a leakage test as the trainmen were walking the train, to see that the leakage in the train did not exceed five pounds of pressure per minute. This initial terminal air test was, and is, required by federal law. If the feds caught us not making the air test, each member of the crew was subject to a federal fine amounting to, at that time I believe, around $500.

When I started on the railroad in 1960, the engineer charged the brake pipe with 80 pounds of air pressure. In the early 1960s, as the capacity of rail cars increased from 50, to 70, to 100 tons, the Great Northern decided to increase the brake pipe pressure to 90 PSI to increase the braking capacity of the cars and to partially offset the increased stopping distance caused by heavier cars.

While the brakemen were making the air test, the conductor got the wheel report from the manifest clerk in the yard office. The wheel report is a list of the cars in the train in standing order from the caboose forward, showing whether they were loads or empties, contents, and the destination of each car. He also got a packet of waybills, one waybill for each load in the train. Then the conductor went over to the depot where he registered our train out on the train register book and picked up and checked over our train orders. This done, he waited for us to come up the W–O main from Appleyard. He handed the head brakeman a set of orders for the engineer as the power went by and swung onto the rear platform of the caboose as it went by. If the train was made at Wenatchee, that is west of the depot, he walked down to the caboose where he gave the train orders for

Caboose X212, photographed on the caboose track at Wenatchee, is assigned to the W–O Local. This 30-foot car is one of fifty built from 1941 to 1945. This group had four bunks versus the 25-foot cars' three bunks. Four-bunk cars were required on the W–O local. These 30-foot cars set the standard for length of GN cabooses for many years. COLLECTION OF MIKE BARTENSTEIN.

the head end to the rear brakeman to give to the head brakeman when the brakemen walked the set.

Trainmen made our own outbound inspection at Wenatchee because no carmen were employed to inspect departing trains. Roving carmen were based in Wenatchee to fix bad order cars on line. When a train crew's inspection identified bad order cars at Wenatchee, the roving carmen showed up with their wheel truck and made the necessary repairs.

On the road, each time a crew cut the engine off the train, we made an air test on the cars picked up to make sure the brakes were working. The head brakeman walked the set and walked the release on the cars picked up. The rear brakeman checked to see that the brakes set and released on the caboose and the car ahead of the caboose. This 'stub test' was not done until the caboose air gauge indicated 90 pounds of air pressure in the train line.

Late one summer I was a brakeman on the W–O local crew that started their week on Sunday afternoon. We were having far too many problems with excess piston travel and air leaks in the piping under the cars on the storage reefers. Now and then a crew encountered a stuck control valve. When a stuck control valve happened on line, we cut the air out of such cars, which meant that there were no working air brakes on the car. If we were still at Wenatchee, we called the yardmaster and asked him where he would like us to set out the bad order car(s). A crew could not take a federal bad order car out of a terminal as a matter of law.

Setting out bad order cars irritated the yardmaster and made us late out of Wenatchee. Soon the trainmaster, William Soga, asked the yardmaster why the W–O local was so late departing Wenatchee. The yardmaster told the trainmaster that we were dragging our feet trying to kill time.

Bill Soga was soon following us all night long trying to catch us doing something wrong. After about two weeks of this, we decided to rebel by getting really picky about bad order cars at Wenatchee, especially when it came to the air. Brake cylinder piston travel was required to be not less than 5 inches and not more than 11 inches. We started to actually measure the piston travel rather than eyeball it. Well, we hit the jackpot with 20 to 25 bad orders per night, and our delay increased markedly since we ended up switching out a big chunk of our train each afternoon. Assistant Superintendent Tom Brennan called our conductor into his office to find out what was going on. Our conductor told Mr. Brennan the whole story. Trainmaster Soga found better things to do than bird-dog us all night.

Everyone on the crew learned a lesson about air brakes as a result of being picky about piston travel and leaking brake pipes. I was amazed how much better the air brakes worked with proper piston travel. The air gauge on the caboose showed pressure held in the train line even when the engine was cut off the train for an hour, when before the air pressure leaked down to zero within 20 to 25 minutes after the power cut away from the train.

➻ New Guys

Recall that brakemen and conductors were subject to the bid and bump labor agreements. The railroad could, and would, force the oldest promoted conductor working as a brakeman to the W–O as the conductor if the job went no bid. Our new conductor is not used to doing the thinking part of a conductor's job, and the bookwork. He got away from the W–O years ago and forgot much of what he knew about the W–O line. Put this 'new' conductor on a night local on a line he has not seen for years, and where there have been new industries added or line changes made due to construction of Rocky Reach and Wells dams that created new stations like new Entiat or new Pateros, and he will feel uncomfortable at best.

Since the W–O was low on everyone's list of preferred jobs, any brakeman forced to the W–O would have very little railroad experience. He was often as green as spring grass. A new brakeman on the crew of a local always put added work and responsibility on every other member of the crew, because the crew does not know how the new guy works, how experienced, or how competent he is. When the fruit shipping season was ramping up and the railroad added a green third brakeman to the W–O locals to handle the work, that brakeman again distracted the conductor and the engine crew. The Pateros Turn and the W–O Local sometimes carried two green brakemen. This put a lot of pressure on the conductor and on the engine crew. The fact that these were night locals, and most guys cannot see in the dark, added to the 'new guy' problem.

Give our new conductor a couple of green brakemen, who are so new that they cannot switch an elephant out of a load of hay, and it did not take me long to figure out why some of these new conductors turned prematurely gray and became nervous wrecks.

The quip about a new guy not being able to switch an elephant out of a load of hay included me too when I hired out. I would occasionally see chain gang crews in the Wenatchee yard office when we were going to work or coming off duty. One older brakeman who was working chain gang would always ask, "How is it going, kid?" There was a short pause while the kid tried to think of an appropriate answer. The old head would then say, "You do not learn this stuff overnight, kid, sometimes it takes two weeks," and we would all laugh.

➻ Seasons of the W–O

Apples were the largest volume single product, by car count, handled on the W–O line for decades, including the last days of the Great Northern. Because of the strongly seasonal pattern of apple shipments, volume on the W–O line was also strongly seasonal.

Traffic was lightest in the summer months when no apples moved. 20 to 30 cars out of Wenatchee was a big train. During the summer, a trip from Wenatchee to Oroville took nine to ten hours and both jobs ran with two brakemen. Outbound, or southbound, freight traffic during the summer consisted of lumber, wood chips, and silica rock. This traffic was not strongly seasonal; it continued at about the same rate month to month throughout the year. A few cars of gypsum soil amendments moved in the spring and fall.

Loaded cars to customers on the branch were sporadic and included tank cars of diesel oil or gasoline, knocked down fiberboard fruit boxes, and the paper fruit trays used to separate the layers of fruit within the boxes. When I started, it had only been two or three years since the fruit industry switched from wooden fruit boxes to the fiberboard boxes. I remember stacks of old wooden apple boxes 20 feet high by 100 feet square sitting beside the right of way in the wide-open spaces.

The climate of Central Washington is very arid, and the summers are very hot. High temperatures over 90 degrees are normal in the summer. Temperatures over 100 degrees are common and the nights remain warm until just before sunrise. It was common to see rattlesnakes while we were switching during the warm summer nights.

During the summer, we always hosed down the inside of caboose at Oroville to swell the wood floorboards to hold down the dust. If we did not, the dust would come up through the floor, filling the air in the caboose, and our lungs, with dust. No wonder crews called the W–O line the "Old Rusty–Dusty." No wonder most of the old wooden cabooses were full of dry rot. In the summertime it was dust, in the spring and late fall it was mud, and in the winter it was snowdrifts and ice.

The W–O locals started to get storage reefers during the late summer and early fall, usually in blocks of 20 to 30 at a time. These reefers were cleaned and inspected by Western Fruit Express at Hillyard for apple loading. We were instructed to set these reefers out at 'blind sidings,' that is, stations without agents (and without customers), like Malott, Winesap, and Wakefield, for use during the apple shipping season. The blind sidings were generally used to store reefers for the next agency station to the north. We were also instructed to make a fire break every 15 car lengths. I never did understand this fire break thing; the country was nothing but basalt rock and sand, and most of the cars were steel. It was so dry that even the cheatgrass could barely grow. By the time the apple shipping season started, the company had 300 to 400 clean dry reefers on line.

Pears came off the trees first, around the middle of August, but there were not a lot of pears along the W–O and there was certainly no pear rush. In September, the nights started to grow cooler and the days grew shorter. Apple picking generally began around September 15.

In September, when it was about time to pick apples, they came by the hundreds: the all-American hobo, with everything they owned strapped to their backs. Many nights the W–O local left Wenatchee with well over 100 hobos onboard heading up the W–O line. The boys were there to make money picking apples, and they rode to work in any empty car that they could get into. There were many nights that the W–O Local carried more passengers than the Empire Builder or the Western Star. I remember on those nights the engineer complaining that the tonnage figures for this train were wrong because "the train pulled harder than it should" due to the weight of the hobos. This was imaginary, of course.

Apples began to move in late September and volume grew through October as the new crop moved to market. As business increased, switching increased and the trains got bigger, which slowed everything down. Fruit loading on the north end exploded with apples being loaded on every business track between Oroville and Tonasket.

By around October 1, apple shipments were heavy enough that a third brakeman was put on so that the long locals could get over the road in 16 hours. A long local was any local that worked to a distant terminal for rest and then worked back to its origin terminal the next day. On the W–O line the term was used to distinguish the train 698/697 jobs from the Pateros Turn. For example, "Are you working the long local?"

During October and November, fruit shipments continued to increase due to the demand for apples for the Thanksgiving and Christmas holidays, and the W–O local crews experienced a tough time getting their work done even with the third brakeman. Around November 1, the company would establish an additional local, the Pateros Turn, putting the job up for bid to the crafts involved. The Pateros Turn worked from Wenatchee to Pateros and back Monday through Friday, going to work at 4:30 PM. While the new Pateros Turn jobs were up for bid, they were filled by men called off the Hillyard extra boards for the 10-day life of the bulletin.

The northward Pateros Turn left Wenatchee about half an hour behind train No. 698 and handled all the switching beyond Olds to and including Pateros. Its mission was to gather up all the fruit and get it to Pateros soon enough to not delay No. 697. The Pateros Turn pulled all the fruit loads on its trip north and set out cars for each station at that station. Unlike train No. 698, the Pateros Turn did not leave each station spotted up for the next day's loading on its northward trip. At Pateros, the turn pulled and spotted all the customers. The crew then built a fruit only pickup on the siding for southward No. 697 to pick up, and sloughed the empty and dead freight cars to their caboose in the process. The Pateros Turn crew then went to the restaurant, warmed up, ate, and waited for No. 697 to arrive, pick up the fruit, and head south to Wenatchee.

When the Pateros Turn was operating, train No. 698 did no work until Braker Spur, just south of Brewster. Despite not having to work Pateros and points south, No. 698 took longer getting out of Wenatchee, and, having a much heavier train, their running time was longer from Wenatchee to Okanogan. The high volume of fruit at Brewster and Okanogan, plus switching the petroleum distribution plants at Brewster and Okanogan, lengthened No. 698's night. The petroleum distribution plants were very busy in the fall because of all the activity in and around the orchards during the apple picking season. Even with the Pateros Turn working everything to and including Pateros, the Okanogan meet between No. 697 and No. 698 was still good in terms of time.

Train 697 kept all their fruit on the head end as they worked south. When No. 697 picked up the fruit the Pateros Turn had left for them at Pateros, the reefers were all together in one block on the head end. If No. 697 had a stop-off car of fruit to finish loading at a warehouse south of Pateros, they set it out at Pateros and the turn spotted the car on their return to Wenatchee. After No. 697 picked up the fruit at Pateros, they ran straight to Wenatchee. All of the fruit from the W–O line came to Wenatchee on No. 697.

The Pateros Turn always followed No. 697 south to Wenatchee. Operating rules required that the turn could not leave Pateros until 10 minutes after the departure of No. 697. This rule existed to give No. 697's crew time to flag the turn if they stopped on line for some reason.

The Pateros Turn left Pateros with the occasional stop-off car plus whatever empties and dead freight the crew gathered up on their trip northward. The Pateros Turn spotted all the customers south of Pateros on their way back to Wenatchee using the cars they previously left at each station. Since the Pateros Turn brought only dead freight and empties into Wenatchee, the crew was usually instructed to land in one of the middle yard tracks at Appleyard to keep the dead freight clear of the ice platform.

In November and December, when the apple shipping season was in full swing and temperatures were down, the station agents issued instructions to stop and pick up 10 to 15 of those clean dry storage reefers stashed away months before on 'his' blind sidings to fill out his station's car orders. Dry cars were loaded on line and then iced, or got heaters depending on the season, at the icing platform in Appleyard.

Sometimes the agent would request so many reefers with more than 2000 cubic feet capacity, or reefers with high ceilings, along with 'standard' reefers. If the agent told us to pick up 10 reefers, three of them over 2000 cubic feet and one high ceiling reefer, he would also instruct us to spot the nonstandard reefers to specific locations. Standard reefers were spotted to specified doors at the warehouses, but specific cars did not have to spot to specific doors. The fact that all reefers were not alike meant that we pulled the track of storage reefers out very slowly, checking the small print dimensional data on the side of each car, looking for the high cubic capacity or high ceiling reefers. It was up to us to write down the car number of the high capacity or high ceiling cars so we knew which car to spot at the special spots the agent listed.

Winters were very cold and windy with heavy drifting snow, which made switching and spotting of cars very difficult. Large snowdrifts were everywhere. Drifts five to ten feet high were common, but twenty feet away could be bare frozen ground. I still remember hitting snowdrifts in some of the rock cuts; I could feel the impact and wondered if the train was going to stay on the rail or be all over the ground. Sometimes a crew went blind for better than a half a mile until the wind blew off enough snow so that we could see out the windows.

To give you an idea what it feels like to hit a good size snowdrift, I was called at Yardley one morning for train No. 97 to Wenatchee; my engineer was Richard A. Volavka. Dick and I were the first train west out of Spokane since No. 31, the westward Empire Builder, left Spokane around 1:30 AM. There had been considerable snowfall that night with high winds west of Spokane. Beyond Fairchild we started to run into small snowdrifts. The farther west we went, the deeper the snowdrifts became. By Bluestem the drifts were getting pretty good sized.

At Bluestem Dick and I entered the double track which extends for about 20 miles to Lamona. There are many cuts through the gently rolling terrain between Bluestem and Harrington. As the train popped around a curve on the double track at about 45 MPH, there it was: a drift about 20 feet high across both main tracks. The cut was completely full of compact snow with a slight tint of brown, which is dirt mixed in with the snow. To hit a snowdrift mixed with dirt is like hitting a solid concrete wall. Dick and I both braced ourselves for impact. Our lead unit was a SD 45, just like the 'Hustle Muscle,' GN 400. Well, I almost got knocked off the seat when we hit the drift, and everything went totally white all of sudden. I looked at Dick and he looked at me as we felt the SD 45 start to lift. She felt real light on her feet. It seemed like forever before she finally settled back on the rail. Dick and I looked at each other with a big sigh of relief. Neither Dick nor I could believe that the train was still on the rail.

The whole front of the unit was packed with snow. We traveled about a mile before enough snow blew off so that Dick and I could see out the front windows. When we could see again, he and I knew that we missed one block signal, so Dick immediately reduced our speed to 20 MPH until we could see the next signal.

We were required to wait for an eastbound at the end of double track at Lamona. Since our train was stopped, the rules said I must give the eastbound a roll-by inspection. I tried to go out the front door. That was impossible; too much snow was packed against the door, in fact, it was up to the window in the door. My next option was to go out the back door behind the engineer's seat. Dick followed me out. The front of the engine was packed with snow; the steps, the walkways, everything, even the drawbar, was packed with snow. The only things visible on the front of the engine were the windows, the headlight, and the number boards. When we arrived at Wenatchee there was still a lot of snow on the front of the engine, but I did manage to force the front door open.

One of the first signs of spring on the W–O line was that in the early morning hours the whole valley was filled with oily black smoke from the smudge pots set out in the orchards and lit on frosty nights to protect the fruit tree blossoms from freezing. I could see the fires in the smudge pots through the thick, heavy smoke on the hillsides on both sides of the tracks. The orchard workers used stove oil in the smudge pots and we could see the fire in the pots in the dark. They set the pots between the rows of fruit trees throughout the whole orchard, which made for quite an impressive sight. The sooty black smoke filled the air, made it difficult to breathe, and obscured lantern signals from Omak all the way to Oroville on frosty spring nights in the valley.

Around the middle of March, the fruit business slowed down and the Pateros Turn was pulled off. As traffic dropped further, the third brakeman's job was pulled off, leaving just the two brakemen on each W–O local, completing the seasonal cycle.

➻ The Keremeos Turn

Oroville was the home terminal for the Keremeos Turn, meaning that the crew for this local went to work and tied up at Oroville. The crew went on duty at 8:00 AM Monday through Friday. They worked from Oroville north to Keremeos and return as required, typically, Monday, Wednesday, and Friday. Their power was the engine from No. 698 that had arrived at Oroville that morning.

The Keremeos Turn crew made up their own train which consisted of three or four empty boxcars for lumber loading and three to five empty reefers during the fruit shipping season. Sometimes they got a car of company material for the section crew or bridge timbers and hardware for the Bridge & Building crew to maintain the obsolete timber bridges between Oroville and Keremeos. The Keremeos Turn was back at Oroville no later than 4:00 PM most days.

On arrival at Oroville, the Keremeos crew pulled their train into the north end of yard track 1, cut their caboose off opposite the depot, pulled forward about half a car length, and left the engine and cars there for us. They always lined their train up with fruit on the head end and dead freight behind.

If there were no cars to go north and no loads to pick up at Keremeos, they did not work that day, but got paid for a basic day. On occasion, the Keremeos Turn was called to switch a customer at Oroville on Tuesday or Thursday if one of the warehouses needed reefers spotted to load on short notice. This occurred if the agent messed up a car order or if a customer got a rush order for a load of fruit and there was a suitable car in the yard. They performed work train service both north and south from Oroville as required. Very rarely they would dog catch No. 698 if the crew died on line. During the fruit season, they often made a revenue trip to Keremeos on Tuesday and Thursday.

By the early 1960s the only steady traffic for the Keremeos Turn was lumber from Keremeos. There were two lumber shippers located on the stub of the main track toward Hedley. The fruit shipper was located on the industry track. I made only three trips to Keremeos and was lost the entire time.

On each trip through the Shanker Bend Tunnel, located between Oroville and Nighthawk, small rocks

Oroville depot was the tie-up and on-duty point for both the W–O Local and the Keremeos Turn, so the agent here handled train orders in addition to switch lists and waybills. COLLECTION OF STAN TOWNSEND.

fell on the top of the engine. This rock fall was disconcerting to me as we travelled at 5 MPH through this roughly 1,200-foot long, slightly curved tunnel. Despite being in dry country, the tunnel was wet with occasional dripping from the ceiling. There were springs in the side or bottom of the tunnel, because the ties and ballast were always wet for the entire length of the tunnel.

On what proved to be my last trip to Keremeos, we pulled into the industry track and spotted three iced reefers for loading. I cut the engine off. The engine ran down the main track and headed into the south end of the industry track. We were going to go eat while waiting for the cars to be loaded. About 10 car lengths short of the reefers on spot, the engine spread the old light rail, rolling the rail over. Once the rail tipped over, the rerailing frogs on the engine were useless. To rerail the engine would require the wheel truck from Wenatchee to bring its portable hydraulic jacks to jack the engine up so the section crew could build the track back under it. The conductor went to the fruit shipper's warehouse and used their phone to call the agent at Oroville who contacted the section crew and the dispatcher. We did not leave Keremeos until about 11:00 PM that night.

When I first went to Oroville in 1961, Bill Martin was the conductor on the Keremeos Turn. Bill was a former Marcus Division trainman with Marcus Division seniority. Before I came onto the scene, Bill was working at Kettle Falls when the conductor on the Keremeos Turn retired. This meant that a Marcus Division conductor, who was working as a brakeman, say at Kettle Falls, would be forced to the Keremeos Turn at Oroville as conductor. Bill could see that he would be forced to the Keremeos Turn part of the year and would be bumped back on occasion, and when he was bumped he would have to move back to Kettle Falls. Bill expected that this would continue for a couple of years. Bill proposed a deal to the Marcus men who were ahead

Poling pockets, while dangerous to use, were a standard feature of freight car construction for decades. COLLECTION OF STAN TOWNSEND.

of him in seniority. The deal was that if he bid in the Keremeos Turn, and moved to Oroville to protect the job, they promised not to bump him for the rest of their careers. If they bumped Bill, then he would not go back unless he was forced. The senior men gladly agreed. Bill moved to Oroville and stayed there until he retired.

The Drop at Braker

A basic drop involved both the engine and cars moving in the same direction for the entire move. When we used the engine to get the cars moving, the company called this a 'flying switch.'

Since we switched Braker with the northward train, No. 698, and since the spur opened to the south, we were forced to drop the empty car or cars into the facing point spur. The drop at Braker was accomplished in the following way. After the cars to be dropped were cut away from the train, we closed the angle cock on the engine and bled the cars off to release the air brakes so the cars would roll freely. Then we took the head brakeman to the switch. He lined it for the spur track and waited. The balance of the crew and the engine shoved the car(s) to be dropped back toward the train. We shoved back far enough to get our speed up enough to be sure we could get all the cars up the main track and clear of the switch. One brakeman got on the handbrake on one of the cars to set the hand brake when the car(s) cleared the switch, and one man got on the bottom step of the engine.

The man on the engine step controlled the move toward the switch. When he felt he was moving fast enough, he gave the engineer the sign for a little slack. In response, the engineer made a quick application and release of the independent brake to make the slack run in behind the engine. When the slack came in, the man on the engine pulled the pin to uncouple the car(s). As soon as the cars were uncoupled, he gave the engineer the sign to run away from the car(s). The engine took the curved side of the switch into the spur and stopped in the clear of the switch. As soon as the engine cleared the switch, the head brakeman threw the switch to send the car(s) up the main track. After the car(s) were clear of the switch, the brakeman applied the hand brake on the car(s) to stop them. After the last car cleared the switch, the head brakeman lined the switch for the spur to allow the engineer to bring the engine back out from the spur to the main. The next move of the engine, however was to move ahead to gather up the cars to be pulled from the spur. After the engine pulled the cars and cleared the switch, the brakeman signaled the engineer to stop, lined the switch to the main, and give a come ahead sign so the engine could move to couple to the empty cars sitting on the main track. The cars were then spotted as ordered in the usual manner.

Which way we sent the engine depended on how much room there was in the spur to hold either the engine or the car(s), and what work we planned to do after the drop. If we did not have to switch loads out of the spur, and there was room to stop the cars without running off the end of the track, then we would drop the car(s) into the spur. On occasion, we could ride the car(s) right to spot on the track. If we planned to switch loaded cars out of the spur, then we would drop the cars up the main track and put the engine in the spur so we could pull the spur with the empties out of the way on the main. Everything depended on what was to be done and how much room there was to work with.

There were risks inherent in a drop. The first was that the pin did not get pulled soon enough to give the man at the switch sufficient time to throw it. The second was that the head brakeman made a mistake in handling the switch. The least bad mistake was that he failed to throw the switch, which resulted in the cars following the engine. The man who pulled the pin and the engineer both kept an eye on the head brakeman and the switch, to be sure the cars went where they were supposed to before they stopped the engine to avoid being run into by moving cars if the switch was not thrown. Their ability to run away was severely limited by the fact that there were cars in the stub ended spur, but with luck the man on the cars would get them slowed or stopped. The most serious mistake was that the brakeman threw the switch under the engine or under a car. This was certain to cause a derailment and the odds were that it would be bad enough that the trainmaster would have to get out of his nice warm bed and the wrecker would have to be called to rerail the equipment, a very bad thing. If it happened at Braker, the entire W–O line was shut down.

The final risk was that of getting a car stopped foul. This was usually caused by not getting the car(s) going fast enough before pulling the pin on them. Stopped 'foul' means the car(s) are on the switch and will not roll off the switch by gravity in either direction, so we could not get the engine out of the spur. When this happens, the crew is said to be 'frogged.'

A crew can deal with being frogged in one of two ways. One is to get a chain or cable off the engine and pull the cars far enough to get the engine out of the spur. The other choice was to use a board, pole, or anything long and narrow to push the car(s) off the switch. If you look at each corner of older rail cars, you will see a square stamped steel plate with a dimple in the center. This was used to hold the pole, 2 × 4, or post when someone needed to push the car. The move was called 'poling' a car, and the dimpled plates were 'poling pockets.'

Poling was very unsafe. A man held up each end of the pole as the engine closed on the car, and the pole was always at an angle, so it was apt to pop out of the pocket. Poling was prohibited by the time I started on the railroad, but desperate situations call for desperate measures.

Back at Braker, when the switching was done, the loads were ahead of the engine and the train was behind. Our solution at Braker was to couple to the train and advance to Brewster shoving the car(s) from Braker ahead of the engine at restricted speed. Shoving cars ahead of the power required the head brakeman to ride the lead car as a lookout. The shove from Braker to the south switch at Brewster was about a mile.

The hill over Brewster Flat, a massive sandbar left over from glacial times, began northward about MP 60.5 and was only .2% until the south switch at Brewster, where it stiffened to .4%. When we got close to the south switch at Brewster, we stopped short of the switch, being sure to leave enough room south of the switch for the power and the cars ahead of the power. The head brakeman would stop the move short of the switch. Another brakeman cut the train off, we shoved up to the switch, and dropped the head brakeman, who rode the shove, off at the switch. We then backed up a little and kicked the car or cars up the main track, again with a brakeman on the car(s) at the hand brake. As soon as the car(s) cleared the switch, the brakeman lined the switch and the engine continued into the siding. Since the main is ascending northward here, the car(s) would roll back southward toward the train. The brakeman on the car(s) slowed them down and made an easy joint on the train. Then the brakeman lined the switch for the siding and the power came back to the train after the brakeman relined the switch for the main and got on the power. We finally had the train back together and in proper order. This move at the south end of Brewster was a gravity drop because gravity moved the cars back to the train to complete the drop. The gravity drop works only when the track gradient is favorable.

We were always trying to do more fancy moves to save time. They did save time but the risk also went up as the complexity increased.

Delivering the head brakeman to the south switch at Brewster illustrates the principle "Never walk when you can ride." We got plenty of walking on the W–O despite our best efforts to ride. This brings to mind another old railroad saying, "If you do not use your head you will have to use your feet."

When working the W–O locals it was common to make anywhere from 10 to 15 drops a night. We did them at Pateros, Braker Spur, Okanogan, Omak, Tonasket, and three or four spurs that opened only to the south between Tonasket and Oroville.

➻ Hobos, Cops, and the Wild West Boys

At every station in the fall, we were forced to wait a good five minutes for the hobos to get off the train before we could start our switching. They took any fiberboard dunnage they found in the empty boxcars with them. A big sheet of fiberboard was a nice wraparound blanket if a guy did not have a real one or wanted to keep his real one sort of clean. Some nights, the boys just laid down right where they got off the train with one piece of fiberboard underneath them and one on top; that is where they spent their first night. I do not know how many times we trainmen got off the side of a moving car and stepped on a hobo under a piece of fiberboard, knocking us off our feet. We would go rolling across the ground with the cars rolling by and the hobo screaming at us for tromping though his bedroom and stepping on him. Next morning, they packed up their personal belongings, took the fiberboard with them as building material, and moved off to a safer location than beside the tracks. Most years a W–O crew would accidentally kill one or two who were sleeping on the track or who missed a handhold.

Hobo jungles appeared overnight. Hobos constructed fiberboard shacks with rusty scraps of tin sheeting for roofing. The jungles sprang up like mushrooms in various locations, always close to water and the railroad tracks. I remember switching and spotting industries in an atmosphere filled with heavy smoke from all the hobo campfires. Needless to say, any little scrap of wood was like gold to hobos. Whenever one of the apple warehouses threw out broken pallets, they immediately disappeared and would be nothing more than smoldering campfire ashes come morning.

This influx of hobos, or winos as the townspeople called them, and migrant workers drastically increased the populations of these small communities. Hobos rode the railroad. Migrant workers came by car, often in family groups. Both groups followed the crops. Both groups were required to get the apples picked before they froze. They were essential to the agricultural economy, and the vast majority of them were hard workers.

Human nature being what it is, most of the townspeople considered the hobos to be undesirables. Hobos kept the local police forces extremely busy from sundown to sunup during the apple harvest season. Of course, this is the time when we were switching the industries in these towns, so it was often 'cops and hobos' featuring the local authorities in hot pursuit.

There were no lights at the south end of Brewster. Hobos congregated there because of a water standpipe near the grain elevator and about four stacks of old wooden grain doors they broke up for firewood. The final feature that made the south end a perfect place for the hobo jungle was that it was isolated. The local police did not go there if they could avoid it.

On occasion things got out of hand and the local police would round up some of the boys and ship them south on No. 697. This only relocated the problem to another town and did absolutely no good since all of the lawmen in each of these little towns did it. Running a man out of town on the rail was standard police procedure on the W–O at the time. If the boys ended up in Wenatchee on No. 697 in the morning, they would head north on No. 698 that afternoon. The town/hobo battle was ongoing at Pateros, Brewster, Okanogan, Tonasket and Oroville until the fruit-picking season was over.

Omak was different. The railroad side of Omak belonged to the Indians and they ran the hobos right out of their part of town, and of course the white residents would not tolerate them across the river in their side of town. If the hobos kept coming back or hung around too long, they got severally beaten up. If they did not get the message, then they just disappeared.

Every night was showtime somewhere on the W–O line. Something went on with the hobos, the Indians, or both, every night. Because we were generally in Okanogan and Omak around the time the bars closed, some of the towns' finest residents occasionally got a little crazy which added a special dimension to the mix of confusion and entertainment.

By late October, with the final picking of the Winesap and Macintosh apples coming to an end, the nights consistently dipped below freezing and the sunny weather was deteriorating into the rainy season. With no work and bad weather, the hobos and migrant workers packed up and headed south. Things started to quiet down in these small towns and they returned to their normal pace of life. In short, these communities got their towns back.

It was not until about 1966 that I finally realized what a zoo we were working in. Two brakemen who were furloughed in Great Falls, Montana came out to work the W–O locals until they could hold a job back home. When they arrived, they were full of talk that they were from Great Falls, Montana "the last of the Wild West." Well, two weeks later one of them packed up and headed home, stating as he left, "This place is crazy and too wild for me." Sounds to me like Montana was not as wild as he thought it was. The other brakeman, Bart, stayed for about six months, but would on occasion just shake his head about the unusual nighttime activity on the W–O.

Curly Kills Two Cows

When the railroads imported their first steam engines from England in the 1830s, they soon added a cow catcher to keep the beasts from getting under the wheels and derailing the engine. For ever after, North American steam engines featured a cow catcher on the front of the engine. The tradition continued with diesels as it is still preferable to knock cattle, automobiles, fallen trees, and rocks off the track rather than getting them under the equipment.

One night I was the head brakeman on No. 697 with Walter "Curly" Bradshaw as engineer. We were rolling along peacefully south of Riverside when Curly dumped the air, putting the train into emergency, and yelled that he hit a cow. I did not see the cow before his announcement because she came from Curly's side of the engine, an Alco RS-2. All I saw was the cow going straight up in the headlight beam. The cow was still going up as she disappeared into the darkness above the engine.

After the train stopped, Curly recovered the air. When the brakes released, he whistled three shorts and started to back up. I asked Curly why he was backing up. He said that he needed to know if the cow was dead or just injured. I told Curly that if the cow was not dead on the way up it sure as hell was when it came down. Curly replied that he needed to know because he did not have all the information on his last stock report and he had been chewed out about it. Any time a train hit or ran over livestock, the engineer was required to fill out a 'stock report,' so the claims boys knew about it, when it happened, the location, and how many head were killed or injured.

We backed up about 25 car lengths when the air went into emergency. Curly insisted that I go looking for the cow. It did not take long to find it in the orchard about 100 feet off the track. I was sure glad that the cow had not come down in one of the apple trees, as it was lying about one row deep into the orchard. The stock report did not have a place to report broken fruit trees damaged by flying cattle.

I returned to the engine and informed Curly that the cow was dead. Satisfied, Curly whistled off and started to move forward. The air immediately went into emergency, so I started walking back on the outside of the curve to inspect the train. Once I got about 15 car lengths back, I could see the marker light on the rear of the caboose and three lantern lights alongside the caboose. I flashed my lantern light towards the caboose and got a response in the form of a stop sign. I moved far enough toward the edge of the right of way that I could see the lanterns at the caboose, and Curly could see my lantern.

Pretty soon I started to receive lantern signs: a little backup sign, then stop, then a little go-ahead sign, then stop. I relayed the signs I got to Curly who moved the train as directed. We made several short back and forth moves, with short pauses between the moves, for about 30 minutes. I could hear voices. I could not tell what they were saying, but they sounded very hot. Finally, I received a big highball sign so I ran back to the engine and told Curly to proceed. Curly asked me what was wrong. I told him that I did not know but I was sure we would hear at Omak.

At Omak, I found out that when Curly backed up to check on our flying cow for his stock report, the caboose hit another cow. The caboose, not having a cow catcher, ran over the cow, which ended up in pieces and lodged under the caboose. It is a wonder that the caboose did not derail. All the back and forth was trying to get the dead cow pieces that were wrapped around the brake rigging out from under the caboose. Nobody said anything to Curly at Omak or Okanogan. At Wenatchee, we put the engine to the diesel tracks as usual. When Curly and I came into the yard office, conductor Larry Hayes jumped all over Curly. I can still remember Larry screaming at Curly that when he became a conductor the last report he thought he would ever have to fill out was a stock report. Larry told poor old Curly that he sure took care of that.

Stories, Wrecks, and Near Wrecks

The W–O branch was not the train dispatcher's top priority. Once the dispatcher issued his flat meet orders, slow orders, and clearances for each train, he was done with the W–O.

The way the dispatcher kept track of where his trains were in those days was that the operators at manned stations called the dispatcher with the train departure time after having given the train a 'roll by' inspection. Since all of the W–O station agents worked daylight hours, and all of the trains except the Keremeos were night jobs, the usual 'OS' system did not work. Somebody got nervous, probably after some crew encountered a problem with something, somewhere, and started an unusual 'call home' practice. On Sunday night, the dispatcher's office wanted us to call the Wenatchee operator to let him know that all was well. We figured this was due to the fact that once the W–O Local left Wenatchee, no one except us knew anything until the Oroville agent reported our arrival and tie up the next morning, sometime after 8:00 AM when he came to work

After switching at Omak, we pulled the train up to the depot to unload way freight and put the waybills and company mail in the waybill box. As directed, we called Karl Buschmann, the third trick operator at Wenatchee, on the phone. Karl had been a member of the German military during WWII. He immigrated to the U.S. shortly after the end of the war, went to telegraph school, and hired out on the Great Northern. In the beginning, he was a bit slow with the English language, but by the time I knew him it was no longer an issue.

We told Karl that everything was OK. Karl asked for our location. We told Karl, "Peabody Spur." There was, of course, no Peabody Spur on the W–O. This continued for about six months. One night, Karl came back, in his German accent, with, "The dispatcher said that there is no place called Peabody Spur." We just said, "Goodbye Karl." Our little bit of malicious compliance went on forever with the same comeback, "Goodbye Karl."

I previously mentioned that the normal routine for the meet at Okanogan was that No. 698 took the siding and cut their train so No. 697 could make their pickup and cut their train. Toward the end of my time on the W–O, I found myself working opposite the least cooperative crew on the railroad. This crew always left their train hanging foul of the south switch, which No. 697 needed to make our pickup. Every night this crew was in such a rush to get to the girls at the Loop Loop Cafe that they pulled up to the crossing, stopped short, and ran off. Every night on No. 697, our crew was forced to get on No. 698's train, pull it into the siding, and cut the crossing. No matter how many times we complained, that crew would not pull their train to clear the siding switch on either end. The regular crew was so boneheaded that the third brakeman changed every week or two because no one wanted to work with the other four.

One night for some reason, the dispatcher issued the meet order at Okanogan with No. 697 directed to take the siding. We were on No. 697 and headed in to the siding while No. 698 held the main. As usual, No. 698 left our pickup first out on the south end of the industry track and failed to pull their train clear of the south siding switch. One of us came up with a little dirty trick to get even. To get to our pickup, we were forced to pull their train north to clear the south industry track switch. Of course, our crew needed to cut the crossing after pulling their train north. In the midst of all of our work with their train, we cut their caboose off and wired the caboose markers onto the boxcar ahead of the caboose.

When they came back from the Loop Loop, they buckled up the crossing and the whole crew rode the head end to Omak. They did their Omak work and dropped off at the depot as the engineer pulled the train by. When they saw the markers coming over the crossing, they gave the engineer a big highball and got ready to swing onto the caboose that was not there. One of the brakemen managed to run behind the rear car, open the angle cock, and dump the air on the train to get it stopped. They were forced to back up, cut the crossing at Omak, run south through the yard, and run light engine to Okanogan to get their caboose. When they got back to Omak, they dropped their caboose north on the main, ran north through the yard, coupled up their train, and perhaps coupled to the caboose as well. This cost them at least an hour and a half. That was the last time we were forced to pull their train down and cut the crossing, but from then on we were always on guard, wondering what they were going to do to get even.

On a sunny afternoon in May 1967 engineer Doc Ulrich and head brakeman Gene "Spanky" Sponcler were working No. 698. Train 698 was built on the W–O main in Wenatchee that day and they got right out of town at about 4:30 PM. The Pateros Turn was called out of Wenatchee 30 minutes behind them. Since the Pateros Turn was still on, No. 698 was running for Brewster which was to be their first stop. The train consisted of two 700 series GP 9 units and 35 to 40 cars, mostly empties.

At about 6:00 PM, as they rounded the curve coming into Chelan Falls at about 40 MPH, they saw that the main track switch was open. Doc dumped the air, putting the train into emergency. As they passed over the main track switch, they saw that the inside switch between the storage track and the industry track was lined for the industry track. Cars were spotted on the industry track. Both crewmen braced for impact.

The first of 10 cars spotted on the industry track was an empty reefer. Gene cannot remember if they were knocked off their seats or not when they hit that first reefer. All he remembers is the engine cab being filled with dust and soot from the perforated sheet metal cab ceiling. The dust and soot was so thick that they could barely see out the windows. When they looked at each other they realized that they were both covered in dust and soot. Their clothes, faces, and arms were black with that greasy soot.

The impact derailed the reefer they hit. They shoved this car about 160 feet on the ground before hitting more reefers as they continued into the industry track before coming to a stop. The other nine reefers did not derail but ran out the north end of the industry track and through the main track switch. They stopped in front of the depot at Chelan, about a mile away. The company later found out that one of the warehouse loading crews had just finished pulling their ramp out of the last car that they planned to load that day and just closed the doors and sealed the car when the derailed car hit that car.

When Doc and Gene finally got their bearings, they realized that there was steam coming out of the radiators and coolant was running out on to the ground from the lead unit, so they shut that engine down. As they inspected the unit, they noticed that all the cooling pipes and fittings were broken or cracked and the radiators were torn loose from their mounting brackets. After the trainmaster interviewed them, and the diesel shop foreman inspected both units, Doc and Gene set the lead unit out on the south end of the industry track at Chelan Falls for pick up by the Pateros Turn on their trip south to Wenatchee. Then Doc and Gene took the train to Chelan, put the runaway cars on the siding at Chelan, and continued to Brewster using the second unit.

The FBI was called in, as train wrecking was and is a federal offense. About two days later, the FBI located the 12-year-old boy who took a rock, beat the switch lock open, and lined the switch for the inside. Gene said that the crew never heard what they did with him, if anything. Receiving no information from the justice system was common in those days.

Brakeman Jim Weaver was plowing snow on the W–O during January of 1969 with a Jordan Spreader and two units. They went over the crossing at Chelan Falls at about 25 MPH when, out of the blue, the spreader derailed at the crossing. Everybody in the spreader knew they were on the ground by the way they were thrown around. When they got stopped and everybody got up off the floor, they realized that both the spreader and the lead unit were on the ground. It was not until they got out that they realized that the spreader and the lead unit had jackknifed, putting the spreader a considerable distance from the rail. The spreader had climbed the rail at the crossing, which was full of ice in the flangeways to the top of the rail. No more snow was plowed on the W–O that day.

The most serious derailment on the W–O line during my Great Northern days occurred on January 26, 1970. That Monday the W–O local was called at 4:00 PM with Doc Ulrich engineer, Dick Bethel conductor, Don Moline rear brakeman/flagman, Tom Taylor swing brakeman, and John Kerwin head brakeman. They departed with two GP 9s, GN 728 and GN 719, and about 50 cars.

The Pateros Turn left Wenatchee ahead of No. 698 that night because conductor Bethel, called for No. 698, came from Seattle and was delayed on Stevens Pass. Conductor Bethel arrived about 6:00 PM and No. 698 departed Wenatchee about 6:30 PM. The Pateros Turn was finishing their switching at Entiat and was about ready to leave for Chelan Falls when they heard over the radio that No. 698 was leaving Olds Junction. The Pateros Turn stopped, backed in the clear on the siding at Entiat, waited for No. 698 to pass them, and followed No. 698 out of Entiat.

As No. 698 rolled along on their way north, it started to snow very hard and visibility became very poor between the dark of the night and the snow in the headlight beam. About a mile and a half north of Stayman, Doc and John rounded a curve and all they could see was a deep rock slide across the track. One rock was about the size of a Volkswagen Beetle.

Doc and John braced themselves for impact and the 728 hit the slide with a massive jolt. John was thrown into the front wall of the cab. The impact knocked him unconscious, crushed two vertebrae in his neck, and broke his collarbone. When John regained consciousness, to the screams of Doc hollering for help, John realized that he was up to his neck in ice cold water. Since it was totally dark, neither Doc nor John realized at that moment that the engine was on the rocks and rolled toward the river on its right side at about a 45-degree angle. The right side of the cab was damaged. The right side of the cab floor and the seat that Doc had been sitting on just moments before were destroyed. Unknown to the crew, the second unit, GN 719, had passed the lead unit on the way down to the river, and was fully underwater. It was the 719 going by the 728 that crushed the engineer's side of the cab. The front three quarters of the lead unit was underwater. One rear step of the lead unit was out of the water enough to be visible.

The crew in the caboose knew that there was trouble on the head end because of the quick and violent way the train stopped. The fact that they received no response on the radio when they called the engine crew was their second indication of serious trouble. Don Moline started back to flag the Pateros Turn. Dick Bethel and Tom Taylor ran to the head end of the train. They had not gotten far when they met two hobos running back toward the caboose. The two hobos told Dick and Tom that the train had hit a slide and the two engines were in the river.

With this news, Dick started back toward the caboose to see if he could call for help on the company radio in the caboose. When he got to the caboose, he found that they were too far away from Wenatchee to contact the operator by radio. Dick knew that not too far back there were some houses. There were no phone lines in this remote area. As luck would have it, one of the families in these houses included a 'ham' radio and operator. The ham radio operator was able to raise another ham radio operator in the town of Chelan. The Chelan ham radio operator was able to raise another ham radio operator in Wenatchee, whose call got an ambulance started from Wenatchee.

When Tom reached the derailment site, all he could see was one quarter of one unit sticking out of the dark, cold water. There was no sign of Doc or of John. Tom knew they were dead; he got sick to his stomach. Tom made the logical assumption that the lead unit was totally underwater and that he was looking at the second unit.

When the lead unit hit the big rock on the south end of the slide, it was forced off the track and down the slope toward the river. Tom did not know that the second unit separated from the first and took a parallel course to the right of the lead unit. Propelled by the momentum of the oncoming train behind it, the second unit passed the lead unit as they both slid down the steep bank of sharp and jagged rocks towards the river. Tom was looking at the lead unit; the second unit was completely underwater and out of sight.

Tom stood looking down at the part of the unit sticking out of the dark, cold water feeling sick when, all of a sudden, he thought he heard a cry for help. Tom started down through the rocks covered with ice and snow as fast as he could, shouting as he worked his way down to the unit that was partly out of the icy water. When Tom reached the unit, and was able to talk to Doc, Tom found out that Doc and John were still alive.

Now the question was how to get them out. John tried to open the side cab window, but it was jammed, and with his broken shoulder, he could not get it to budge. With no lights in the cab, neither Doc nor John could see if there was a way out or not, which there was not. Tom climbed onto the steps on the back of the engine that were just enough out of the water, walked along the walkway behind the cab, and looked in the rear cab window on the brakeman's side. The window was intact. Looking around for something to bust the window out with, Tom saw a scoop shovel that the crew used to shovel out switches jammed in the ladder on the rear of the unit. Tom grabbed the shovel and started to beat on the window glass. He hit it several times before the glass finally broke.

Doc climbed out of the cab window. John, with his broken shoulder, could not pull himself out the window. Tom grabbed John's bib overall straps and pulled him up and out of the cab. Tom helped John up the slippery rock slope, working their way over the jagged rocks.

Once the three of them reached the top of the slope, they faced about a half mile walk to the caboose. This walk took a long time. John was in awful pain and Doc was dazed from being beat up in the engine cab on the wild ride into the river. Doc and John were both wet and cold. By the time they finally reached the caboose, John was in shock and suffering severely from hypothermia. Tom and Doc got John onto a bunk in the caboose and covered him up with an old sleeping bag that was there. John told me that he did not get warm until about 3:00 the next morning when he was in the hospital.

While this was going on, Don got the Pateros Turn stopped. They cut their train off, came up, grabbed the W–O local's caboose, and pulled the caboose back to a crossing where the ambulance could pick up John and Doc and take them to Wenatchee. The next day, someone showed up at the hospital with clean clothes for John,

TOP Engine 728, the lead unit in the Stayman wreck, is unidentifiable in this photo at Hillyard in the spring of 1970. The right side, shown in the photo, was damaged by engine 719 passing it on the right. The extensive damage to the front of the unit is obvious. PHOTO BY GENE SPONCLER.

BOTTOM Engine 719, the trailing unit in the Stayman wreck, is at Hillyard in the spring of 1970. This is the left side of the unit, showing damage caused by contact with the 728. Engine 719 has gotten turned around relative to the 728. It was moving with the long hood to the front at the time of the accident. PHOTO BY GENE SPONCLER.

who was released that afternoon. The company sent John home to Spokane on the Empire Builder that night.

The trainmaster picked up the rest of the W–O crew and took them to Wenatchee by auto. This left the Pateros Turn crew to clean up the mess. The Pateros Turn shoved the W–O caboose ahead to the rear of the train, coupled to and air tested the movable portion of W–O local's train, and took it back to Entiat along with their own train. They left both trains on the siding at Entiat, clearing the line so the company could get the wreck train up to the derailment site.

With the arrival of daylight the next morning, things looked worse. Not only were the two units in the river, but the head three cars of the train were also in the river. Three more cars sat on the bank between the track and the river, and the next six cars were derailed, but still on the roadbed.

The first equipment to arrive were two D-8 caterpillar tractors, each with a winch with cables mounted on the back end. They started to clear the rock slide while they waited for the wreck train to arrive with the big hook. The wrecker arrived and started to clear the line and pull the engines out of the river, up the bank, and back onto the track. Of course, the rock slide needed to be cleared off the track and the track damage repaired. The company was forced to have the Chelan County PUD, which operated Rocky Reach Dam, lower the water about eight feet so the railroad could get cables on the units and the cars in the river to pull them back up the bank to the track where they could be rerailed.

Great Northern was one of a very few railroads that set up their GP 9 units to run long hood forward. If they had been set up with the cab toward the short hood, both Doc and John would have ended up submerged in the river and would have drowned.

If the Pateros Turn had run ahead of No. 698 beyond Entiat, they would have been the crew in the river. Two brakemen on the Pateros Turn were on the head end of the train, so three men would have gone in the river. The Pateros Turn ran with three brakemen, so the flagman would have flagged the W–O and the conductor would have been available to attempt to rescue the crew in the engine.

➸ Train 697 at Appleyard

During the fruit season, No. 697 left Oroville with 25 to 30 total cars including 15 to 20 loads of fruit. On the road No. 697 was required to keep the fruit on the head end of the train at every station. We cut the non-fruit cars into the train behind the fruit at every station so that all the fruit was on the head end of the train at Wenatchee.

The Wenatchee yardmaster usually told us to put the train into Appleyard track 1 or track 2, which were located on either side of the icing platform, to be iced and inspected by Western Fruit Express. We spotted our head car to the east end of the icing platform. Having all the fruit on the head end assured that all the loads of fruit would fit alongside the icing platform. It also allowed the Wenatchee switch crew to pull the dead freight off the rear of our train immediately upon our arrival with one move. After the Wenatchee switch crew plucked our caboose and the dead freight off the rear of our train, WFE crews lit the 'blue lights' at the ends of the ice platform, lined and locked the switches for the lead at both ends, and re-iced and inspected our loaded fruit cars.

After WFE was done with our cars, a switch engine pulled the cut from the ice platform and switched it out. Cars for the west and California were set up for a pickup by a westward train to take to Seattle. Loads for the east were blocked by destination and added to train No. 88, which was known as 'The Fruit' to Hillyard crews, and all the way to Minneapolis, where most of the fruit was interchanged for points east.

Our final move was to return the power to the roundhouse tracks, which were the former freight house tracks, located behind the yard office. The yard office was located in the freight house building just west of Chehalis Street.

Our two-day round trip ended between 4:00 AM and 8:00 AM at Wenatchee. We all headed home, or to the hotel, to get our rest, since we would begin our next trip at 4:00 PM.

➸ My W–O Experience

I feel very fortunate to have worked as a brakeman and conductor in the era that I did. It took me six and a half years to build up enough seniority that I was no longer forced to work the W–O locals. What I learned in my early years as a brakeman on those W–O locals was invaluable, and I applied those lessons through the remainder of my railroad career.

In my early years on the W–O locals the only light in the caboose was from the kerosene lamp at the conductor's desk. Marker lights on the rear of the caboose were the kerosene type. The caboose stove was an old potbelly coal stove and the caboose included an icebox to keep your drinking water and lunch cold. We stopped the caboose at the depot in Wenatchee to get a block of ice out of the large storage icebox in the baggage room at the depot.

The head brakeman always confirmed that the engine carried rerailing frogs on both sides. The rear brakeman always checked our caboose to make sure that it was supplied with kerosene, coal, extra air hoses, and an air hose wrench for use in case one of the cars in our train blew an air hose. He always made sure that there was a chain and a couple of extra knuckles in the possum belly of the caboose. The possum belly was the storage compartment located under the caboose used to carry heavy or awkward items such as a cable or chain and extra knuckles. The possum belly was about six feet long, three feet deep, and about 18 inches tall. It was closed by a pair of sliding doors.

The swing man managed the switching at each station under the supervision of the conductor. As they were leaving Wenatchee, the conductor gave a list of the train to the swing man and explained what cars went where and helped the swing man mark up his list of the train for the set outs at each station. Working the list on the W–O Locals was the ultimate 'finishing school' for a Hillyard based brakeman.

Cabooses on branch line locals did not have radios in those days. If we had to head into a siding to meet another train, and our train was too long to let the engineer see lantern or hand signs, he counted telephone poles to determine where the caboose was when heading into or leaving a siding.

Once I got out of Wenatchee, I continued to work locals every chance I got. I liked the challenge of doing the work, both the physical switching and the mental process of lining up the work.

As each man worked different locals, we learned about each station. The most basic things were the names of all the tracks and what industries were served by those tracks. We learned which way the cars would roll on each track, and how many cars each track held. Crewmen memorized all this information so the next time he switched that station he would not have to walk himself to death. Here again, we were using our heads to save our feet. In time, a man memorized the details of all the stations and all the main line trackage that he worked, about 800 miles of track on the Spokane Division.

Young brakemen got pretty good at switching cars as the years rolled by, picking up tricks of the trade from older brakeman. The bid and bump system meant that the younger guys got a chance to work with many other trainmen which helped 'us kids' develop our own style and skills for switching cars. George Kendall on the Coeur d'Alene local was one of the best and smoothest brakemen I ever worked with; there were no wasted moves when George was working the list. I learned a lot from conductor Jack Cartwright when I worked as brakeman with him in the Wenatchee chain gang freight pool. I also learned a lot from conductor Ray Reedy. Ray was just as good and smooth as George. My last extended braking job was with Ray Reedy in the Whitefish chain gang freight pool for about a year until I got set up permanently as a conductor. I learned more from George, Jack, and Ray about switching than from any other trainmen. These three men showed me the importance of looking ahead in my mind when planning the work, and how the order in which the work was done would affect the number of moves required. The way a crew made our pickups could, and would, save extra moves later in the day. The farther ahead a man could look and plan, the fewer moves were required, the less we used our feet, and the quicker we got over the road.

When planning the work on a local, you always needed to be thinking ahead, including the next station, and sometimes about stations ahead all the way to your final terminal. No matter how well you laid things out in your mind, you'd better be prepared to alter your plans. Sometimes what the switch list showed did not match the way the cars were actually lined up on the track. This usually meant that the agent or clerk failed to visually check each track. Sometimes cars were not even listed on the right track. Not physically checking the tracks was called 'steam heating' the yard check and resulted in the switch list being wrong.

Chelan depot was located miles away from the town, which is at the foot of Lake Chelan. Crews received switch lists and waybills from the agent, who left them in a box attached to the depot. PHOTO BY STAN TOWNSEND.

Bad lists made switching more difficult, especially at night. I always said that plan A was good for 30 feet, or 30 seconds, whichever came first. I found that I needed to have at least a plan B in mind, and a plan C and D would not hurt either. There were times that I was altering my plan all night long and other times when what I first laid out held up for most of the shift.

The late Gene "Spanky" Sponcler turned out to be my most steady braking partner. After spending years together on the W–O locals, Gene and I worked the Kettle Falls Turn and the Coeur d'Alene Local together for about seven years before he and I got set up as conductors. These jobs gave Gene and me the opportunity to be home when we were off duty, which was a rare treat after having spent so many years out of town working outside locals and being away from home for days at a time.

After the Burlington Northern merger, I was exposed to trainmen from the other component railroads. That exposure demonstrated that Great Northern trainmen could hold our own with anybody when it came to switching cars.

Crewmen all learned to recognize each of our fellow workers' individual lantern and hand signs. Lantern and hand signs are unique to each man, just like a signature on a check. In addition, engineers can tell immediately by the way a stop sign is given whether to stop in his normal way, or to dump the air in an emergency stop. If you know an engineer from the old school, ask him if he could tell by the lantern or hand signs who was giving the signs, how quickly to stop, and whether to shove cars into a track, or to kick the cars while switching.

One winter the weather at Wenatchee and up the Okanogan Valley had been very cold. For about three weeks it had been well below zero, as low as −20, with constant wind. We went to work one afternoon in Wenatchee and could feel a difference in the temperature; it was noticeably warmer and looked like it could snow. By the time we reached Entiat, it started to snow and the wind was blowing. We switched and spotted the industries. It was snowing hard as we headed for Chelan Falls, where it was coming down about 50% snow and 50% rain. In spotting the industry at Chelan Falls we found that the rain was freezing on the frozen ground, making walking conditions difficult. We headed to Chelan and started to switch as the rain continued, but much heavier, to the point it was like a cloudburst, and the wind was still blowing.

This was the night I discovered that one can even cuss with a lantern. We were spotting reefers on the industry track at Chelan and I was standing on wet ice. Nothing is more slippery than wet ice. It was raining hard and I was soaking wet from the water running off the roofs of the warehouses and the roofs of the reefers and coming down right on top of me. As I was trying to spot the cars, the engineer shoved too far, and when he pulled back, he went too far back. Out of frustration as I swung my lantern, I hollered out loud, "Stop you dirty Son of a ——." After we got the industry spotted and I got up on the engine, the Engineer, Paul Hume, turned on his ceiling light, looked me in the eye, and said, "Do not cuss at me with that lantern, you called me a dirty 'Son of a ——.' " The engine was about 15 car lengths from me when I said it; there is no way that Paul could have heard me.

The company was always after us to look for hazards and danger. Call it a sixth sense if you want to, but on more than one occasion I got a funny feeling and I just knew that I needed to move or get out of where I was—RIGHT NOW! I was usually right; if I failed to move, I would have been knocked down and injured or run over and killed. The potential for getting hurt or killed was always there, and crewmen had to be alert to what was around us at all times. There was no room for daydreaming or looking around at things that did not pertain to what we were doing.

A full moon gives off pretty good light to see by. Streetlights also provide some light, even at a distance. If there are no streetlights and no moon, then the term 'pitch black' does apply and you really are in the dark.

It did not take me long to realize that sounds around the railroad were just as important as the sense of sight. The Spokane Division operated many night locals, and sounds were very important in the dark. For example, railroad cars roll down a track so silently that many times you cannot hear them at all, even if there is nothing else nearby making noise. Sometimes a car will be rolling along as quiet as a mouse and you can hear the rail make a distinctive little 'pop' or a 'snap' as the car moves on the track. That pop or snap is your danger signal. That sound kept me from getting hit by a rolling car more than once. At times other sounds, like the diesel engine and machinery noise from industries, drown out the sounds that are so important.

I always listened to the air flow through the angle cock valve when I cut in the train line air in on the end of a car or engine. You can easily hear the air as it flows through the train line. When the air is turned into a cut of cars, the air flows at a high rate, but as pressure builds in the train line the rate of flow decreases and the pitch and volume of sound decreases. If the air did not sound like it went very far, that is, the pitch and volume decreased too rapidly, then an angle cock was probably closed a few cars away. If the air did not sound like it was starting to slow down by the time I got the angle cock wide open, it usually meant that the angle cock on the far end of the cut of cars was open, or at least one pair of air hoses between the cars was not laced up. The third possibility was a stuck control valve. If we could not reset the valve, then we cut the air out of that car. The number of trainmen who did not pay attention to the railroad sounds that tell so much surprised me.

➸ L'Envoi

Earl J. Currie, a railroad operating official with many years' experience, and a published author on railroad subjects, was kind enough to offer his view of the demands placed on a conductor and brakemen working in local freight service and the skills, job knowledge, responsibilities, and personal attributes necessary to meet those demands.

> My comments are intended to introduce some of the challenges faced by Conductors, and the Brakemen assigned to their crews, on "heavy" local trains. John Langlot has described how he handled the complex moves required to serve customers in the era of single car railroading. Many aspects of the work environment are part of the job of a Foreman of a yard switching crew as well. John's recollections of his career as a brakeman and conductor are one of very few in the literature. Most railroad books are corporate histories, or are about the builders, the financiers, the civil engineers, and the locomotive engineers. John's recollections, as contained in this book, are unique as to time and place.
>
> From the very start of their careers, railroad operating employees learn that the railroad environment is unforgiving. There are mistakes or oversights for which there may not be a second chance. The work can be done safely, and most employees do it without accident or injury for

long careers of 30 or 40 years, or even longer. A strong sense of awareness and concentration is required.

Getting the work done that is entrusted to operating employees who work "on the ground," that is, Conductors and Brakemen, requires teamwork. Each crew member must have or develop the desire, ability and job knowledge to do their part of the work according to the safe work practices that have evolved over the years. They must know how each of those rules or established work practices have to be applied in each job location, and under the conditions they will face each time and each place they begin to move or handle cars.

The employees who work on the ground must have a Locomotive Engineer they can trust to follow their directions (signals) and the work routine they have set up at the outset of each part of the work they undertake. They are also dependent on the dispatcher or yardmaster to protect them from the danger of unknown, overlapping or unplanned interference from a conflicting movement that would jeopardize their safety.

To be able to work safely in this kind of environment requires that each employee understands the work to be done as it progresses, right from the first move to be made, on each trip. Fellow crew members must know that each employee out there with them can be trusted, and that they have the courage, instinct and initiative to act promptly to prevent another employee from being "blindsided" if conditions change, or the work suddenly is not going according "to plan."

Operating employees must be able to get the work done under a variety of conditions. The railroad never shuts down. Local and switching activity has to be done in the rain, cold weather, at night, during and after snowfalls, and even when footing might not be good due to snow, ice, mud, obstructions such as trash, spilled grain or fertilizer, or misplaced track material. To be safe, a crew may have to work more slowly than they would under "good" conditions, but the point is that the work does not stop.

Among the first "commandments" an experienced railroad man will pass on to a new employee is to "never turn your back to a car," until you know it has been secured and cannot roll toward you. When a railroad car begins to move on a track, it makes almost no sound. Never move between cars until you know you are protected, i.e., your team mates know where you are and what you are about to do and will make sure they do not move any cars toward where you have to cross a track, go between the rails to open a knuckle, or for any other purpose. You also must know that any cars on the same track, and not coupled to "your engine," are secure and will not move. You learn that any time you step on a tie, you have placed yourself foul of any moving cars, hence, the old adage, "ties mean trouble."

In getting cars moved to and from customers' facilities, and from track to track as they are switched in a yard or on station tracks, there is much to be learned about how to get the work done "right," and with the least number of switching moves. To become good at this kind of work is similar to the game of chess in some ways. You have to plan your switching moves by studying the lists of cars on hand, as to where they are located in the yard or on station tracks, or where they are positioned in your train, and where they are to be switched to, and what the "end product" should look like. This means getting a somewhat random or scattered number of cars placed in the right order and at the right door or loading/unloading spots at the customer's facility, or in the right order (from the head end to the rear end) in the train that will be departing from that location.

John Langlot describes the thought and effort that was required to serve carload customers very well. This chapter focuses on the W–O Local between Wenatchee and Oroville. Notice how the crews he was part of handled the complex moves, particularly at Omak, while he worked on the W–O Local. The W–O Local handled thousands of carloads of high revenue, high service, and perishable, fruit traffic every year. The skill needed to run a local freight train on this line was such that, no one (not even an experienced Conductor or Brakeman) could walk in "cold" on the W–O job and expect to get the work done without danger of accident, to get it done "right," and within a reasonable amount of time. He would first need to make several trips with an experienced crew to "learn the ropes."

Indeed, the work of a Conductor and Swing Brakeman on a local is an art. The general practice on the Great Northern was that the Conductor allowed the Swing Brakeman to work the list, with more or less coaching. Working as the Swing Man on a heavy local like the W–O was the finishing school for Conductors. Working the list requires the ability to organize the work, to plan ahead for a series of moves, to assess your work environment at that time, to know when and where to apply a large number of the rules and advisories as to how to do the work safely. All crew members must ensure your fellow crew members, who will be several hundred feet from you much of the time, understand what role they have in each of the many parts in the process of moving cars. And, while all of this is going on in your mind, you will have cars and one or more engines or trains in motion all around you to watch out for.

As Linda Niemann, a retired Conductor/Brakeman from the Southern Pacific, wrote in her book, Railroad Noir, about making a "drop" move "... success is dependent upon timing, skill, and judgment. Everyone has to be on their game. If it fails, at the least it can be inconvenient. At the most, it can be a major disaster. When it is successful, it is a thing of beauty."

While not many railroad operating employees would ever think of the work they complete successfully as a thing of beauty, there definitely is pride and satisfaction for a crew from making a good, safe trip over the road, and knowing that all the local work was done right, per instructions from the customers, and as directed by the agents, clerks or others who prepared their paperwork.

John Langlot worked demanding local train assignments such as the "W–O" job as operated by the Great Northern Railway and by the Burlington Northern for many years. Those who are "students" of railroad operations are fortunate to have access to the kinds of writings John Langlot has done. As a real "professional" railroad man, John describes very well the culture, the life, and the skills required to get the job done on what was a very heavy local freight assignment.

Endnotes

1 Great Northern Railway, AFE 74245.

2 Mike Bartenstein, email dated June 3, 2012, based on 1957 Great Northern Station Map.

10. Planning the Merger

Introduction

To this point, we have been describing John's career and experiences as an employee of the Great Northern Railway. This and the following chapter shift to the planning and implementation of the merger of the Great Northern, Northern Pacific, Chicago, Burlington & Quincy, and Spokane Portland & Seattle into the Burlington Northern, which was finally accomplished in March of 1970.

The Burlington Northern merger was the final realization of James. J. Hill's desire to control the Northern Pacific. The bankruptcy of the Northern Pacific Railroad in 1893 opened the door for Hill and other large investors in the Great Northern to gain control of the NP on January 1, 1901.[1] Because it was attained by personal, as opposed to corporate, stock holding, control was of relatively short duration.

This chapter will begin with a description of the railroads serving Spokane as of 1960. That was the year John began his railroad career, and the Great Northern and Northern Pacific were not far into developing their merger plans. This chapter includes an overview the Great Northern, Northern Pacific, and Spokane Portland & Seattle lines across the state of Washington, plus the north/south lines of the GN and NP.

Spokane was a vital point in the merger planning. Decisions about Spokane were driven both by local issues and traffic patterns between Puget Sound and far into Montana and beyond. The descriptions of conditions in 1960 included in this chapter provide the foundations for the extensive changes made in the Spokane area due to the Burlington Northern merger and the Expo '74 World's Fair. A map of the railroads serving Spokane as of 1960 is provided for reference.

The chapter will discuss the line changes and bridges required to link the Great Northern and Northern Pacific main lines at Spokane and Sandpoint, Idaho, and will also discuss merger related branch line changes in Eastern Washington.

The Physical Geography of Spokane

The physical geography of Spokane is dominated by the Spokane River, which drains Lake Coeur d'Alene in northern Idaho and flows westward to Spokane. The river splits to flow around Havermale Island and then drops 150 feet at the downstream end of the island. The first white settlement at Spokane Falls was established on a site adjacent to the falls of the Spokane River in 1871.

Two miles below the falls, the river turns sharply to the north and continues north and west to join the Columbia River. Hangman Creek joins the Spokane River where the river turns to the northwest. The confluence of Hangman Creek and the Spokane River is located roughly in the middle of an unusually straight run of Hangman Creek and the Spokane River, 20 miles long, that marks the eastern edge of the most recent Columbia River Basalt (CRB) flows. There is a roughly 500-foot difference in elevation between Spokane, at about 1,920 feet, and the top of the Columbia Plateau directly west, at about 2,400 feet.

The Northern Pacific near Spokane

The Northern Pacific approached Spokane from the southwest, passed through Cheney, 16 miles from Spokane on top of the plateau, and followed the valley of Marshall Creek down to Hangman Creek. The Hangman Creek Bridge was situated relatively low, about 35 feet, and was followed by a side hill climb into Spokane.

The Northern Pacific built this magnificent elevated and grade-separated right-of-way through downtown Spokane in the 1910s. TIM WHITTIER.

Grades were 1% in both directions between Cheney and Spokane.

Arriving at Spokane Falls on June 25, 1881,[2] the NP continued construction of its transcontinental main line to the east via the broad valley of the Spokane River. The line passed well south of the town, which sat adjacent to the falls of the Spokane River. Spokane Falls was a way station of no particular importance in 1881.

As of 1960, Northern Pacific enjoyed an elevated route through downtown Spokane totally free of grade crossings. The six track wide roadbed extending two miles through downtown Spokane was constructed between 1914 and 1917 at a cost of over $3 million, excluding lawsuits.[3] The NP route through Spokane and east to Sandpoint was superior to that of the Great Northern.

Northern Pacific completed the current passenger depot, located a block and a half west of Division Street, in January 1891.[4,5] A new yard at Erie Street, about a mile east of the depot, opened in 1906.[6] The NP's last and largest freight yard in Spokane was Yardley, located about four miles east of the passenger depot. New shop facilities were erected at Parkwater, which lay north of the yard with the roundhouse at the east end of the yard. Yardley and Parkwater were placed in service on July 1, 1913.[7]

The Great Northern

From railroad east, the Great Northern skirted Sandpoint and entered the Spokane area from the geographic north, climbing a modest ridge to do so. The flat ground at the crest of this ridge became the site of locomotive and car shop facilities in 1893. The town of Hillyard was platted west of the railroad and north of Spokane soon after the Great Northern arrived by people not connected with the railroad.

As of 1960, Hillyard was the most important car and locomotive repair point on the Great Northern west of Havre, Montana. In addition to the shops, a large freight yard served the Great Northern and the Spokane, Portland and Seattle Railway (SP&S). The yard extended to the geographic north, railroad east, from the area occupied by the shops.

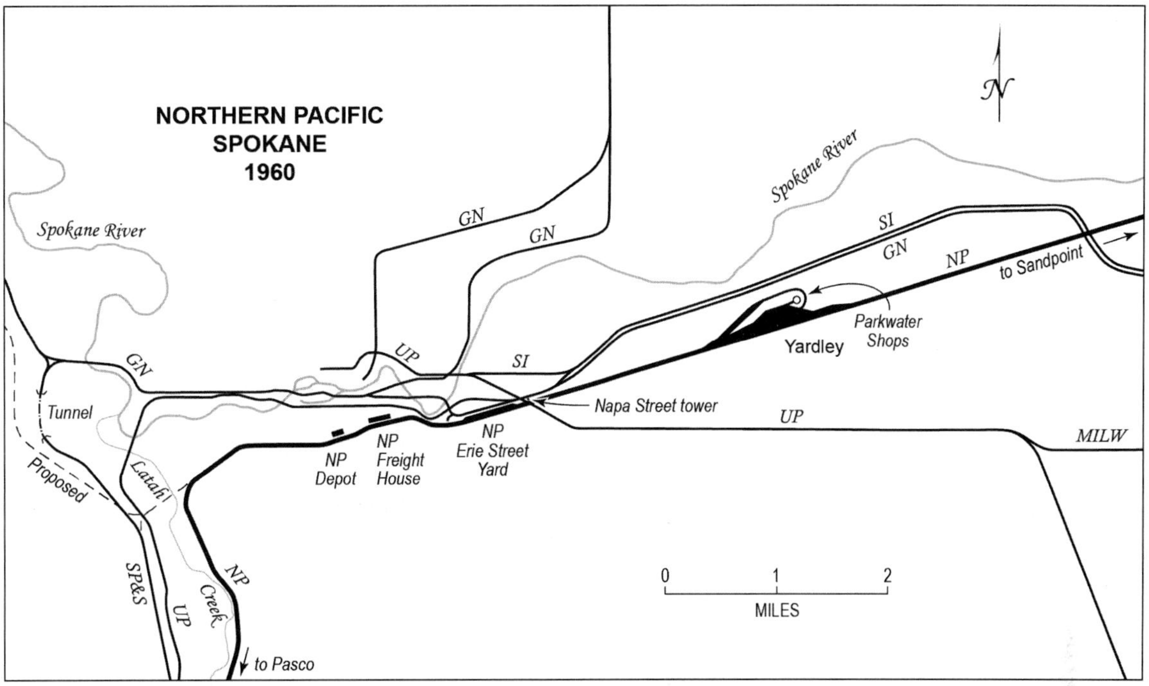

Moving railroad west from Hillyard, the Great Northern main line descended to Spokane. It crossed the Spokane River to the south bank, extended along Spokane Yard, and crossed the Spokane River to Havermale Island, the site of a 48 by 316-foot three story brick[8] passenger depot.[9] A brick freight house sat on the south bank of the river immediately east of Havermale Island. Both structures opened in 1902.[10] The line crossed the river to the north bank to leave the island. The final crossing of the Spokane River was located at the west edge of the city on 1,056-foot long, 140-foot high steel bridge No. 274.

Fort Wright Junction, the connection to the SP&S, was located immediately west of bridge No. 274. Westward from Fort Wright, the Great Northern main line curved to the right and ascended the side hill on a 1% ruling grade to the top of the Columbia Plateau at Fairchild, 15 miles west of Fort Wright. The term 'ruling grade' means the grade that limits the tonnage an engine can haul between any two points, usually over a subdivision.

From Fort Wright Junction, the SP&S turned to the left and ran through a concrete lined tunnel under Greenwood Memorial Terrace Cemetery to Overlook siding, 6.1 miles west, en route to Pasco.

Great Northern's branch line to Kettle Falls, Republic, and Nelson, British Columbia left the main line at Dean, nine miles east of Hillyard. The line to Kettle Falls and Nelson was built by the Spokane Falls and Northern Railway, an independent Spokane Falls company, between 1889 and 1893. The Great Northern attained stock control of the Spokane Falls & Northern system on July 1, 1898. In 1899, to integrate the SF&N into the Great Northern, the Great Northern built 3.57 miles of new line between Dean and the former SF&N at Wayside[11] and constructed a connection with SF&N at East Spokane (Hillyard). The 13 miles of SF&N line between Hillyard and Wayside was soon abandoned. The former SF&N line between Hillyard and its depot site north of the Spokane River remained in service and was known as the 'Spike Yard.'

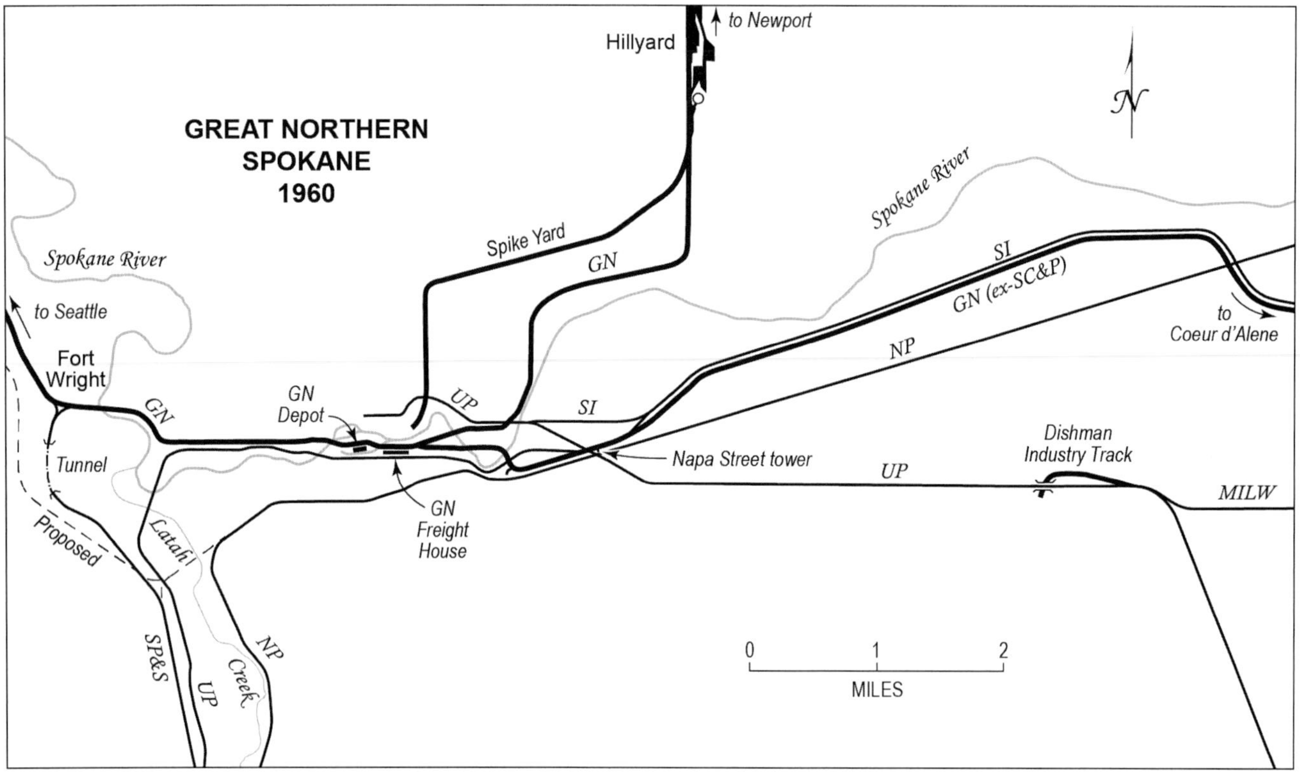

The Spokane, Coeur d'Alene & Palouse

Two electric interurban lines were acquired by a Great Northern subsidiary, the Spokane, Coeur d'Alene & Palouse, in 1927. As of 1960, these lines were the Coeur d'Alene and Moscow branch lines of the Great Northern.

The SC&P main track to Coeur d'Alene extended east from a small stub yard located east of Division Street, south of the Great Northern and north of the Northern Pacific. At the east end of the yard, the SC&P crossed the Spokane River, turned right, and crossed the Spokane River again as it completed its turn to the south on a three span through truss bridge. The bridge was followed immediately by about 110 degrees of left turn which began a long segment parallel with and immediately north of the Northern Pacific. The Coeur d'Alene line crossed the Union Pacific near Napa Street.

As described in detail in Chapter 3, the original route of Moscow line began at the south end of the second bridge over the Spokane River and continued south on a private right-of-way as it headed generally southeast ascending the side slope of Spokane's South Hill on a 2% grade for seven miles to the top of South Hill.

Facing expensive repairs to the Rock Creek Bridge and other wooden trestles between Spokane and Mount Hope, the Great Northern secured 32.2 miles of trackage rights on the Union Pacific between Spokane and Fairfield and built a new connection extending 2.6 miles between Fairfield and West Fairfield, a new junction on the former SC&P main between Mount Hope and Waverly.[12] Service via the new route began on September 17, 1952. The old line between Spokane and Mount Hope was then abandoned, eliminating 22.87 miles of track.

Burlington Northern train No. 82 on Great Northern Bridge 274 over the Spokane River in 1972. The single-track bridge includes two deck truss spans directly over the river with steel viaduct approaches on both ends. Note the semaphore-style home signal for westward trains approaching the end of double track. The lead unit, SD 45 6555, was received in November or December 1971. This line segment and the bridge were abandoned December 6, 1972. DAVID EMERSON COLLECTION, PNRARCHIVE.ORG.

THE SPOKANE, PORTLAND & SEATTLE RAILWAY

The Spokane, Portland & Seattle Railway was a joint venture of the Great Northern and the Northern Pacific which extended from Fort Wright through Pasco and Vancouver, Washington, to Portland, Oregon.[13] From Fort Wright, the SP&S passed Scribner, where an approximately mile long track connected with the NP at Marshall. The main track ascended in the valley of Marshall Creek to leave the Spokane area at Cheney. The westward ruling grade on the connecting track was 1% ascending from the NP.

Long before 1960, the vast majority of SP&S interchange in Spokane was with the GN. SP&S freight trains originated and terminated at Hillyard and picked up or set out NP cars at Scribner.[14] The SP&S operated a daily 'Scribner Turn' from Yardley to set out and pick up cars to and from through trains. SP&S passenger trains used the Great Northern passenger depot on Havermale Island.

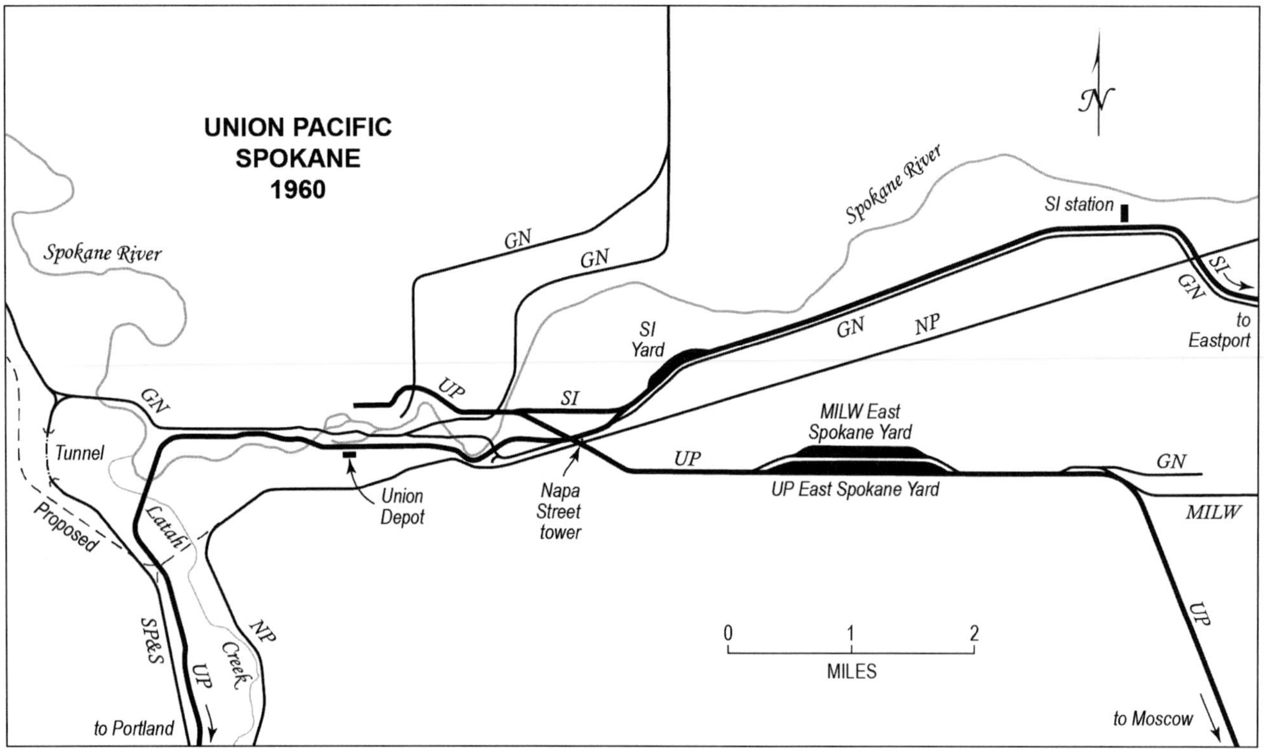

The Union Pacific

As of 1960, the Union Pacific owned a main line through downtown Spokane, a branch line to the southeast, a remnant of its original main track to the north side of the Spokane River, and the former Spokane International line to Eastport, Idaho.

Union Pacific's main line entered the Spokane area from the southwest at Cheney and followed the valley of Marshall Creek to Hangman Creek. It crossed both Hangman Creek and the Spokane River on a high steel viaduct. The line continued east to cross the Spokane River to the new (1914) Union Station in downtown Spokane. Union Station featured elevated track and was located immediately south of Havermale Island, in the heart of downtown Spokane. The 1914 line extended east from Union Station to a connection with the original main line at a point a few hundred feet northwest of the NP main line at Napa Street Tower.[15] Union Pacific's freight yard was located immediately east of Havana Street in East Spokane on the branch line to Tekoa.[16]

Union Pacific predecessor the Oregon Railway & Navigation Company (OR&N) entered the Spokane area from Tekoa to the southeast and crossed the Northern Pacific main track at grade at a point east of Spokane near what would later be Napa Street. From the NP crossing, the OR&N continued to the northwest, then turned to the west, crossed the Spokane River east of town, and continued to the original Union Depot on the north side of the Spokane River.[17] By 1960, the old main line to Tekoa was a branch line, and the old main to the north side of the Spokane River was no more than an industrial switching lead.

The Spokane International

The Spokane International extended from Spokane north and east to Eastport, Idaho where it connected with the Canadian Pacific at Kingsgate, British Columbia. As of 1960 it was a one train a day branch line of Union Pacific.[18] SI owned shops and a small freight yard south of Mission Avenue and east of Greene Street, about 2.7 miles east of Division Street.[19]

Daniel. C. Corbin and others incorporated the Spokane International Railway (SI) at Spokane on January 18, 1905. Canadian Pacific financed the SI in retaliation for Hill's purchase of the VV&E charter and his avowed intention to build between Spokane and Vancouver, British Columbia. It is ironic that Corbin, the first proponent of a line between Spokane and Vancouver, partnered with CP to build the SI in retaliation for Hill's undertaking Corbin's project. Corbin was no friend of Hill or the Great Northern.

Control passed to CPR in 1916. Under CPR control, maintenance was held to a bare minimum and no capital investments were made, so the railroad became progressively more obsolete.[20] The SI entered bankruptcy in June of 1933. It emerged from bankruptcy as the independent Spokane International Railroad in 1941 and began to pay dividends in 1949.[21]

Shortly after the company began to pay dividends, SI management offered their railroad to the Great Northern, which declined to purchase it. SI also offered itself to the Northern Pacific, which was also uninterested. Union Pacific acquired the Spokane International Railroad in a stock swap transaction in 1958. Traffic today is several times what it was in 1960.

➸ Planning Spokane-Area Main Line Changes

One of the economic reasons for the BN merger was 'line rationalization,' that is, to concentrate traffic on the best main lines and to remove redundant branch lines. Planning the changes that would be made at or near Spokane were driven by this concept.

West of Spokane, the merger partners owned three routes to Puget Sound. The Great Northern was the most direct route to Seattle at 329 miles. Ruling grades were 1% in both directions between Spokane and Wenatchee and 2.2% in both directions between Wenatchee and Seattle. The crossing of the Cascade mountains was at an elevation of 2,880 feet at the east portal of the 7.79-mile-long Cascade Tunnel. The tunnels on the Stevens Pass route enjoyed excellent clearances, a legacy of the electrification of the route in the 1920s and its removal in the 1950s. As of 1960, tall boxcars, auto rack cars, and the Boeing airplane parts flatcars with their high and wide

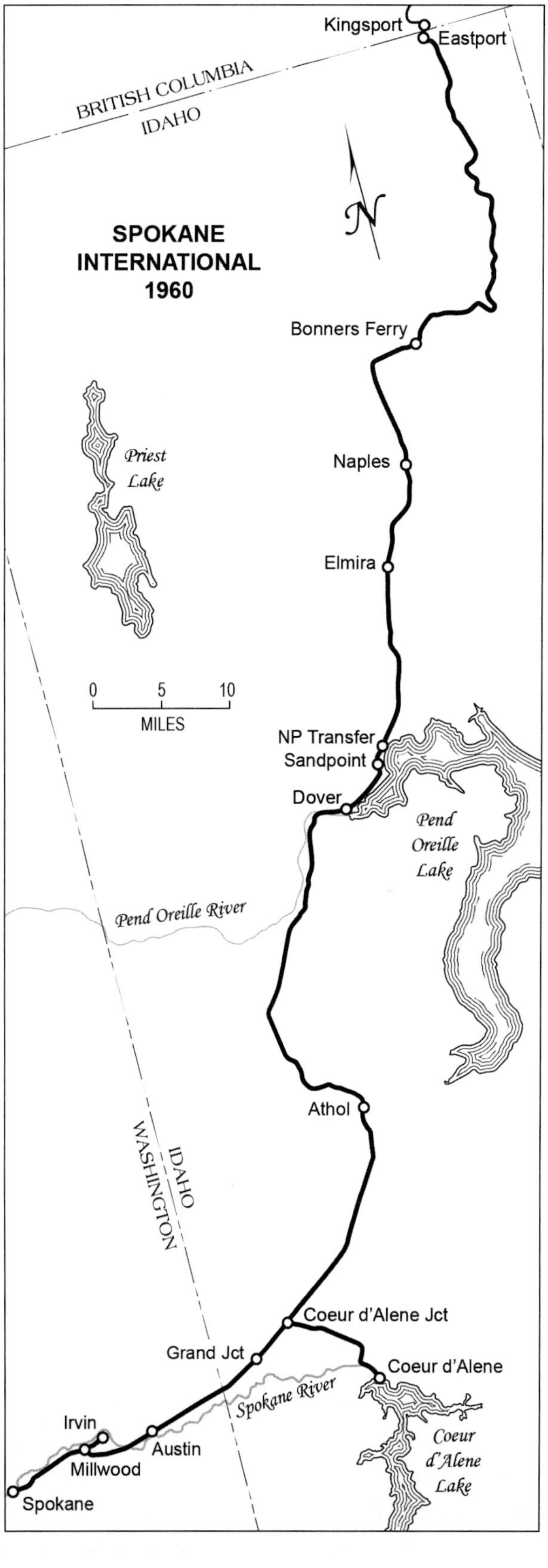

covers all routinely moved over Stevens Pass. The Great Northern required two freight crew districts between Spokane and Seattle.

The Northern Pacific swung south to Pasco and then back north to its yard at Auburn. The NP was 396 miles between Spokane and Seattle, and their passenger train times ran about two hours longer than the Great Northern's. NP ruling grades were 1% in both directions between Spokane and Yakima and 2.2% in both directions between Yakima and Auburn. The crossing of the Cascade mountains at Stampede Pass was at virtually the same elevation as the GN. The NP summit was within the 1.9-mile-long Stampede Tunnel.

The Stampede Pass line could not handle auto rack, or any other high freight cars. Stampede Pass suffered from inadequate clearance ever since the Northern Pacific developed its large, high capacity steam locomotives in the 1920s. The NP operated between Auburn and Easton with World War I era 2-8-8-2 class Z-3 locomotives limited to 30 MPH top speed until the advent of FT model diesel locomotives in 1944. Northern Pacific never improved the original clearances in the Stampede Pass tunnels.

The Stampede line was 67 miles, or 20%, longer than the GN between King Street Station in Seattle and each line's respective passenger stations in Spokane. Northern Pacific required three crew freight districts between Spokane and Auburn. Turnaround locals handled traffic between Auburn and Seattle, Auburn and Tacoma, and Auburn and Everett. The Northern Pacific required effectively three and a half crew districts between Seattle and Spokane. The NP incurred high operating costs due to the high number of freight crew starts, its seven to GN's four, required to make one round trip between Spokane and Seattle. These handicaps were compounded by the problem of inadequate clearances in the Stampede Pass tunnels compared with the Stevens Pass route.

The SP&S owned a line between Spokane and Pasco, and through the Columbia Gorge to Vancouver, Washington and Portland, Oregon. This line featured the lowest eastward ruling grade, .4%, of all of the lines across eastern Washington. Westward, the ruling grade was .8% between Fort Wright and Overlook,[22] 6.2 miles west of Fort Wright.[23] Through the Columbia Gorge between Vancouver and Pasco, the ruling grade was only .3% ascending eastward. The SP&S was a 'super railroad' in terms of both grades and curves. Three freight crew districts covered the 370 miles between Spokane and Vancouver. Traffic to and from Portland, an additional 10 miles, was handled by transfer jobs.

Northern Pacific owned a north/south double track main line between Seattle, Tacoma, Centralia, and Vancouver, Washington, and utilized trackage rights over the double track SP&S between Vancouver and Portland, Oregon. Great Northern enjoyed trackage rights on the entire NP line and on the SP&S between Vancouver and Portland. Trackage rights are a contractual arrangement by which a tenant railroad obtains the right to operate over a segment of trackage owned by another railroad. The NP double track tied the west end together.

The NP and the GN each owned separate lines to Canada, the NP from Black River Junction to Sumas, Washington, and the GN from Everett to Vancouver, British Columbia. The GN interchanged with Canadian National, Canadian Pacific, British Columbia Hydro, and the Pacific Great Eastern at or near New Westminster. The NP interchanged with Canadian Pacific and British Columbia Hydro at Sumas, on the Canadian border about 22 miles east of Blaine, Washington.

Another factor the merger planners considered was the location and capacity of freight yards. Northern Pacific completed a modern hump yard at Pasco in 1955 used by both the NP and the SP&S. To the extent carload traffic could be routed through Pasco after the merger, Pasco could make eastward trains for Northtown, Minnesota, Chicago, Denver, Texas, Kansas City, St. Louis, and other points east. Pasco could also make westward trains for Vancouver, Washington, Tacoma, Seattle, Everett, and Vancouver, British Columbia. By using Pasco in this way, the smaller yards in the Puget Sound region could make their trains with traffic for Pasco and beyond without regard to destination blocking. In like fashion, Pasco could make trains for Everett, Seattle, and Tacoma that would enable Auburn to be shut down and the remaining Puget Sound yards to handle more traffic. Pasco, built on cheap desert land, absorbed much of the work that would otherwise have to have been done at cramped yards on expensive urban ground in Seattle, Tacoma, or Auburn. Pasco Yard is still a crucial asset to BNSF and its carload traffic network.

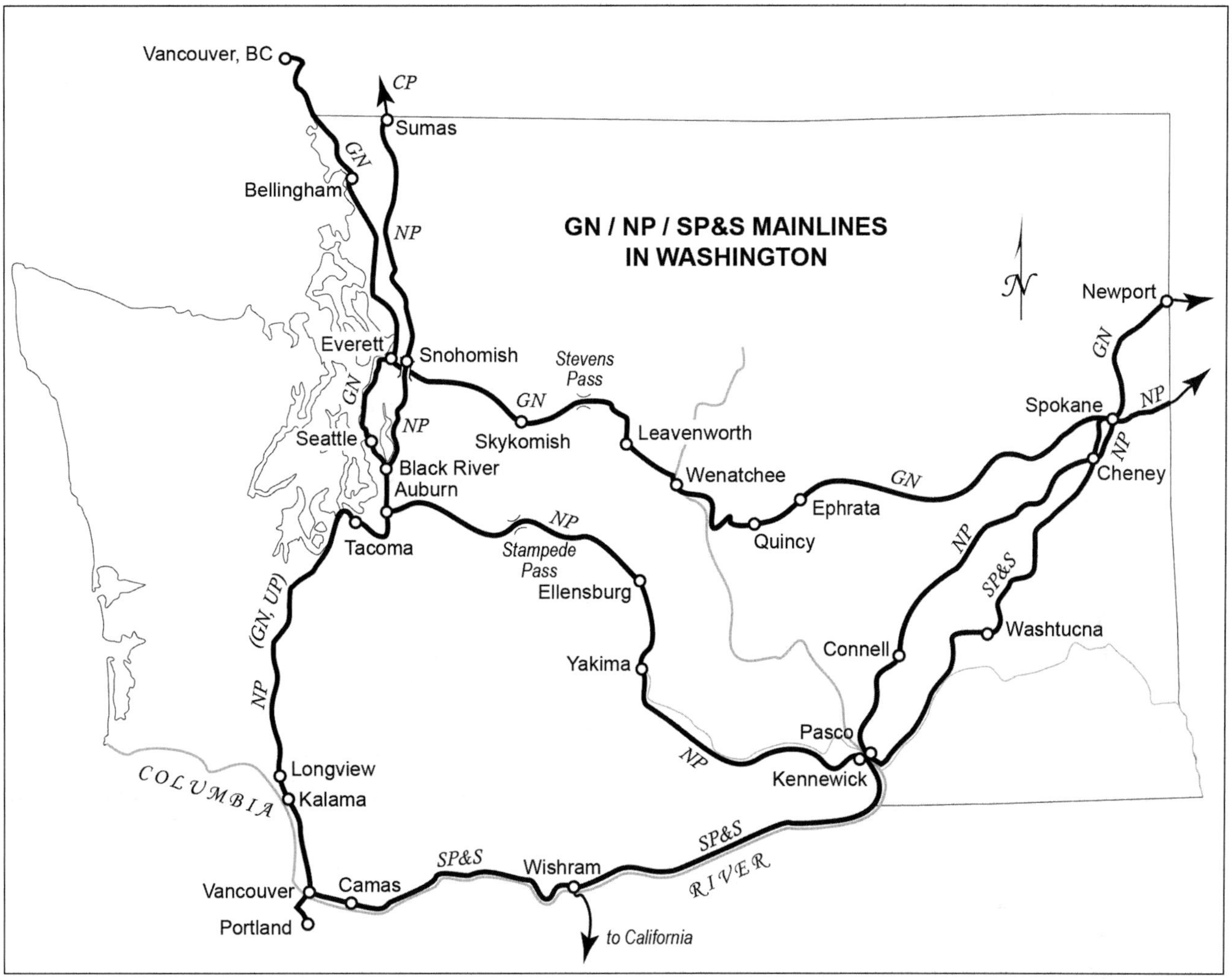

Prior to the merger, export grain in the Pacific Northwest was predominately wheat moving to consuming countries of the Pacific Rim. Export grain moved through the ports of Portland, Oregon, Vancouver, Kalama, and Longview, Washington, on the lower Columbia River, and Tacoma and Seattle on Puget Sound. Over half of the grain moved through the lower Columbia River ports. By long standing agreement, NP origin grain to the lower Columbia River Ports moved via the SP&S through the Columbia Gorge. GN origin grain to the lower Columbia River ports moved over Stevens Pass.

During the 1960s, each route across the state of Washington was handling two pairs of passenger trains and about three pairs of freight trains per day. The obvious merger plan was to route freight traffic away from the more expensive Stampede Pass.

The GN line became the preferred route between Spokane and Puget Sound points. As intermodal traffic to and from Seattle and Tacoma grew after the merger, it moved via the Great Northern route across the state of Washington, which reinforced the importance of the former GN main line. 'Intermodal' is the preferred term for any transportation involving use of two or more modes of transportation for a single trip. In the railroad context, 'intermodal' is transportation of trailers or containers on railroad flatcars.

The SP&S line became the preferred route for everything south of Puget Sound, basically Centralia and

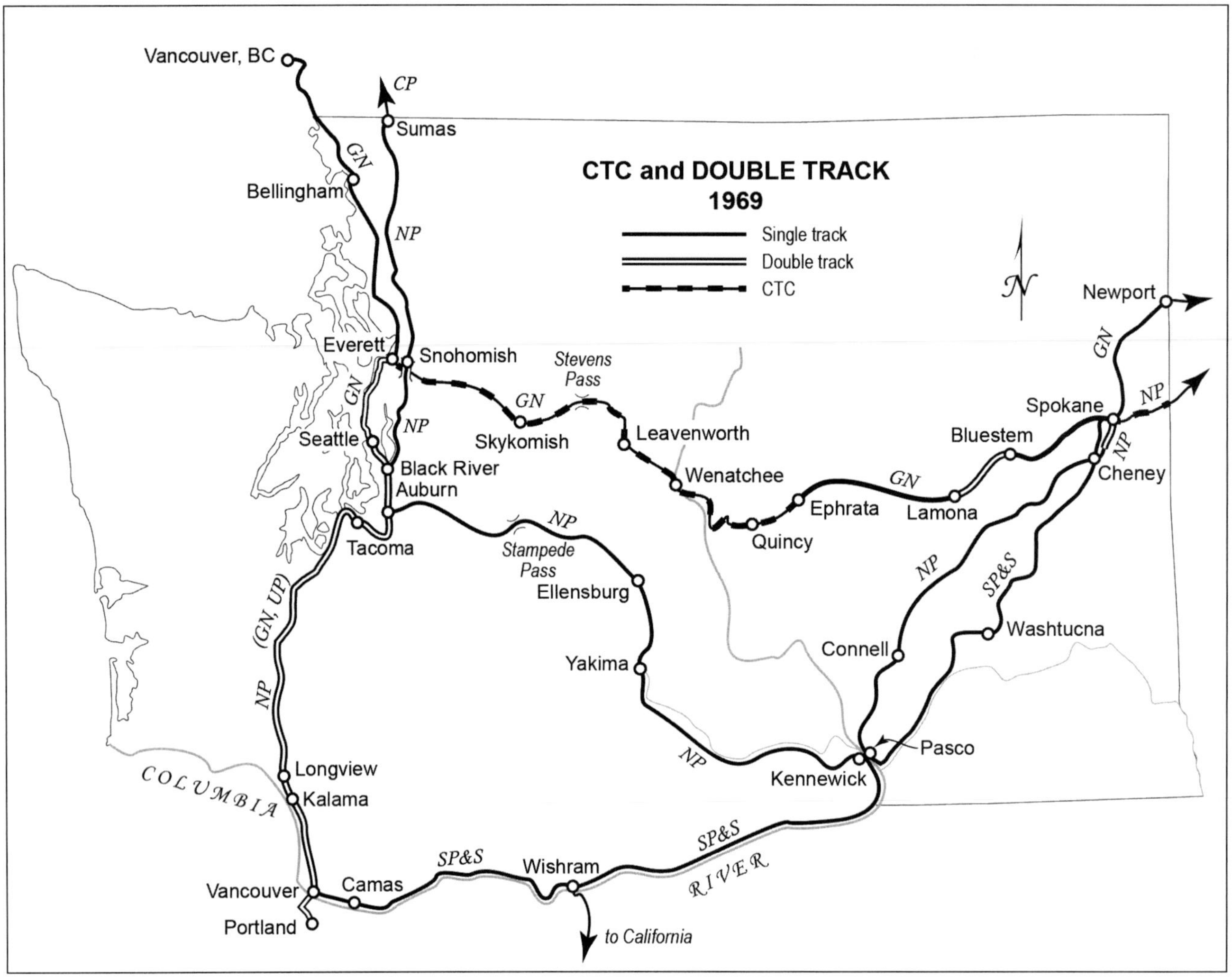

south, including export grain traffic to Lower Columbia River ports. Rerouting GN grain to the lower Columbia River ports via the SP&S would avoid burning the fuel to lift it over the Cascade mountains, require less power, and save time. After the merger, increasing volumes of upper Midwest corn moved in solid grain trains to Washington State export elevators. As the former GN line became ever busier with intermodal traffic, grain trains to Tacoma and Seattle were increasingly routed the longer, but low grade, route through the Columbia Gorge.

Prior to the Burlington Northern merger, the Northern Pacific installed CTC between Yardley and Paradise, Montana. The Northern Pacific also made an extensive line change near Granite, Idaho which eliminated a long tall bridge, one tunnel, two speed restricting curves, and shortened the line by two miles. From the west end of Yardley west to Marshall, the NP was double track, then single track with block signals between Marshall and Pasco.

Great Northern installed CTC between Everett and Ephrata during the 1960s. Great Northern also made three separate line changes near Index on the west slope of the Cascade mountains during the 1960s that reduced curvature, increased speed, and shortened distance.

The Great Northern and the Northern Pacific main tracks both passed through Spokane on an east-west axis. The NP line was double tracked and elevated through town, and the NP route from Spokane to Sandpoint, Idaho was better in terms of grades and curves than was the GN's. The superiority of the NP through the city of Spokane and east to Sandpoint was the reason it became the merger planners' preferred route between Spokane and Sandpoint. East of Sandpoint, the former GN was to be the preferred route to Minneapolis and Chicago, while the former NP as far as Laurel, Montana was to be the preferred route to Denver, Kansas City, St. Louis, Memphis, and Texas.

Unrelated to the merger, the city of Spokane wanted to host Expo '74 on Havermale Island, which the Great Northern occupied with its passenger station, the associated terminal trackage, and its double track main line. The solution to both the railroad's and the city's problems was to connect the GN line from Wenatchee to the NP on the west side of Spokane, and to build a new connection at Sandpoint to move trains between the Northern Pacific and the Great Northern lines. This would allow the Burlington Northern to sever the Great Northern line through Spokane, vacate Havermale Island, and downgrade the GN main line from Hillyard to Sandpoint to a branch. Maintaining service to Hillyard and the Kettle Falls line would require a new connection east of downtown Spokane.

Three bridge projects were required to consolidate the Burlington Northern's traffic on the former Northern Pacific line through downtown Spokane. The largest new bridge was over Latah (Hangman) Creek immediately west of downtown Spokane. A new bridge was required over Sand Creek at Sandpoint, Idaho. These two bridges connected former GN main line segments with the former NP, allowing trains to and from former GN routes to use the former NP between Spokane and Sandpoint. The third bridge, needed to maintain service to the Kettle Falls line, will be discussed in the following chapter.

➻ Endnotes

1 Albro Martin, *James J. Hill and the Opening of the Northwest* (Oxford University Press, 1976), 463.

2 Peter B. Lewty, *To the Columbia Gateway: The Oregon Railway and the Northern Pacific, 1879–1884* (Pullman WA: Washington State University Press, 1987), 63.

3 Verne Alexander, "Rising Above it All in Spokane: The Downtown Grade Separation Project," *The Mainstreeter*, Spring 2010, 4–25.

4 Spokane Falls Review, January 4, 1891.

5 Peter B. Lewty, *Across the Columbia Plain: Railroad Expansion in the Interior Northwest, 1885–1893* (Pullman WA: Washington State University Press, 1995), 181.

6 Northern Pacific Railway, Idaho Division, First Subdivision, condensed Profile and Track Chart, Revised January 1, 1970, nprha.org.

7 John T. Gaertner, *North Bank Road: The Spokane, Portland & Seattle Railway* (Pullman, WA: Washington State University Press, 1990), 36.

8 James Mattson, Great Northern Railway Mileposts, Spokane Division, SP 2–3.

9 *Spokesman-Review*, May 30, 1902.

10 James Mattson, Spokane Division, SP 2-4.

11 Great Northern Railway. Original Track Laying Record, Great Northern Railway, 1862–1932.

12 Clive Carter, *Inland Empire Electric Line* (Coeur d'Alene ID: Museum of North Idaho, 2009), 205–206.

13 Ed Austin and Tom Dill, *S. P. & S. The Spokane Portland & Seattle Railway* (Edmonds WA: Pacific Fast Mail, 1996), 125.

14 Austin and Dill, *S. P. & S. The Spokane Portland & Seattle Railway*, 140.

15 Jeff Asay, *Union Pacific Northwest* (Cheyenne WY: Union Pacific Historical Society), 127–29 and 140.

16 Asay, *Union Pacific Northwest*, 141.

17 Lewty, *Across the Columbia Plain*, 126.

18 Paul Rechnitzer, *Corbin's Road aka Spokane International Railway* (Comanche Press), 149–51.

19 Rechnitzer, *Corbin's Road aka Spokane International Railway*, 19, 88, and 75.

20 John Fahey, *Inland Empire: Unfolding Years, 1879–1929* (Seattle WA: University of Washington Press, 1986), 209–19.

21 Rechnitzer, *Corbin's Road aka Spokane International Railway*, 149–51.

22 Austin and Dill, *S. P. & S. The Spokane Portland & Seattle Railway*, 126.

23 Austin and Dill, *S. P. & S. The Spokane Portland & Seattle Railway*, 134–35.

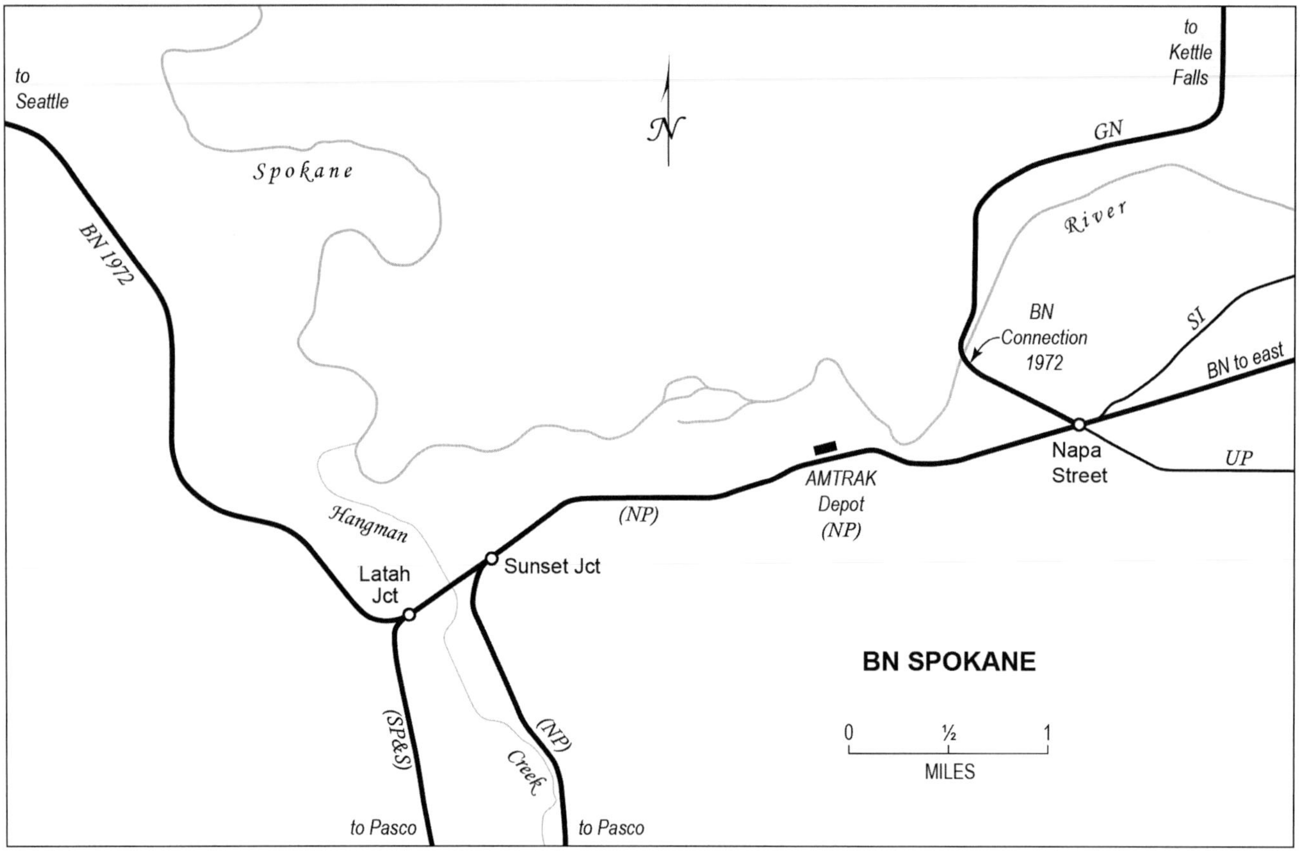
to
Seattle
BN 1972
Spokane
N
to
Kettle
Falls
GN
River
BN
Connection
1972
SI
BN to east
UP
Napa
Street
AMTRAK
Depot
(NP)
(NP)
Hangman
Latah
Jct
Sunset Jct
BN SPOKANE
0
½
1
MILES
(SP&S)
Creek
(NP)
to Pasco
to Pasco

11. Implementing the Merger

LINE CHANGES

This chapter will begin by discussing main line changes in the Spokane area. The next five sections will discuss branch line rationalizations in Eastern Washington related to the BN merger. This chapter will close with a discussion of seniority issues related to the merger and operations on the Kettle Falls line after the merger.

SPOKANE-AREA MAIN LINE CHANGES

Immediately after the BN merger of March 2, 1970, the company started to build the new Latah Creek Bridge and its associated line change. From the new Sunset Junction on the NP main at the west edge of Spokane, the new line crosses the Latah Creek Bridge and passes the new Latah Junction on the bridge. The north leg of Latah Junction continues west, ascending on a 6.3-mile long line change that joins the original GN main line just west of Highland.

The south leg of Latah Junction crosses over Interstate 90 and connects with the original SP&S line about a mile east of Overlook siding, which was not relocated. Overlook is 3.4 miles west of Latah Junction. The Latah Creek Bridge and associated line changes would cost $16.2 million,[1] and was placed in service on December 6, 1972.[2]

The city of Spokane also wanted the Union Pacific track through downtown Spokane, and for Union Depot to be removed so the depot site could be redeveloped in conjunction with Expo '74. To accomplish this, the BN granted the UP trackage rights through Spokane.

The at-grade crossing of the former Northern Pacific main track by the Union Pacific at Napa Street was removed and replaced by a switch in the BN main track, diverging geographic south toward the UP Yard and Tekoa, Washington. Another switch was added to the BN diverging to the geographic north to allow westward trains off the former Spokane International Railroad to enter the BN westward. A third switch was added to the BN diverging to the geographic north to allow continued access to the UP freight line to the north side of Spokane. A pair of crossovers was added between the BN main lines west of these new switches to and from the UP. These connections and crossovers allowed UP trains to come out of their yard or off the SI, get on the BN at Napa Street, and use the elevated main tracks through downtown Spokane. At Sunset Junction, UP trains used the Latah Creek Bridge and the former SP&S line through Overlook.

In Marshal Canyon, about 12 miles west of the former NP Spokane Depot, the SP&S and the Union Pacific were parallel and at the same elevation. The UP line at this point is to the geographic north of the SP&S. As viewed by a westward train on the SP&S, a right hand facing point turnout was placed in the main track at a point where the UP main track was easily tied into the diverging side of the turnout. This new switch was named UP Junction. As the two lines continue westward, up the hill toward Cheney, the UP swings to the north and turns back to the south to pass under the former NP line. Since neither of these UP connections were large projects, the UP was able to abandon its line through downtown Spokane shortly before the GN depot was removed.

When the SP&S line to Pasco was later abandoned, the SP&S segment through Overlook was retained and tied

The Latah Creek Bridge is one of two bridges built immediately after the merger to connect former GN and NP main lines so that traffic to and from GN lines could be handled on the higher-speed NP line between Spokane and Sandpoint. On the morning of December 21, 2018, Chicago–Portland train Z-CHCPTL soars above Latah Creek with high-priority domestic intermodal traffic. PHOTO BY BRUCE KELLY.

into the former NP line at the new Lakeside Junction, located one half mile west of UP Junction. Creation of Lakeside Junction allowed BN trains to use the Latah Creek Bridge, the former SP&S line to Lakeside Junction, and the former NP line to Pasco. Trains could also stay on the former NP line via Marshall between Sunset Junction and Lakeside Junction. The connection at Lakeside Junction created a new segment of two main tracks between Sunset Junction and Lakeside Junction.

Burlington Northern began construction of a new connection at Sandpoint immediately after the merger. Moving eastward, this new main track left the former NP main at MP 2.9, east of the long bridge over the end of Pend Oreille Lake, and immediately east of the NP passenger depot, and joined the former GN main line about one half mile east of the GN depot. Boyer siding was constructed at the GN end of the new connection. Boyer siding extends from Boyer Road for 10,363 feet as the track curves to the east paralleling the original GN main line toward Bonners Ferry and points east.

Within a year after the merger, while the new Sandpoint connection bridge was being built, selected trains were crossing over between the NP and GN main lines using the NP-GN transfer track, also called 'the stem.' The overall pattern was to divert traffic away from Hillyard. The most common moves were westward trains off the GN to the NP, and the reverse, eastward trains off the NP to the GN. There were also some moves west off the NP westward onto the GN, and the reverse.

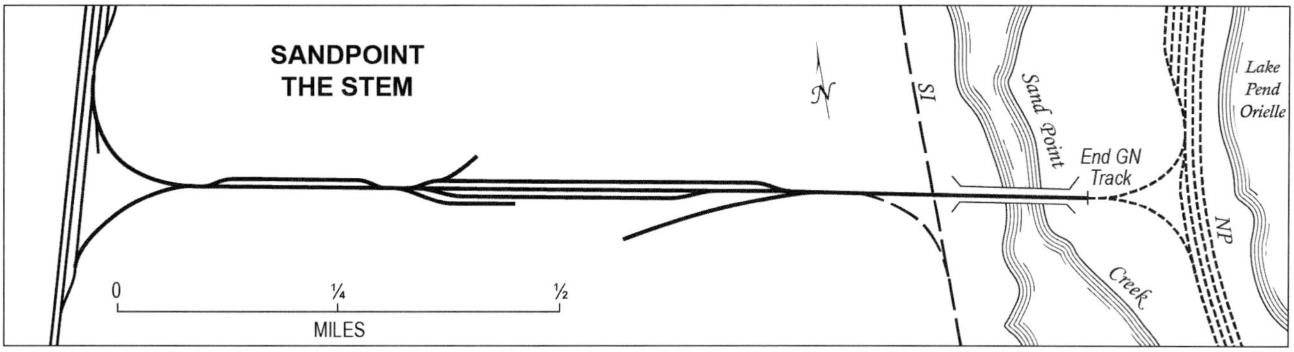

This Great Northern trestle over Sand Creek at Sandpoint, Idaho, was built in 1891 to connect the Great Northern to the Northern Pacific, so rail and other construction necessities could be brought to the GN right-of-way at Sandpoint to allow track to be built both east and west from Sandpoint. COLLECTION OF DAVE SPRAU.

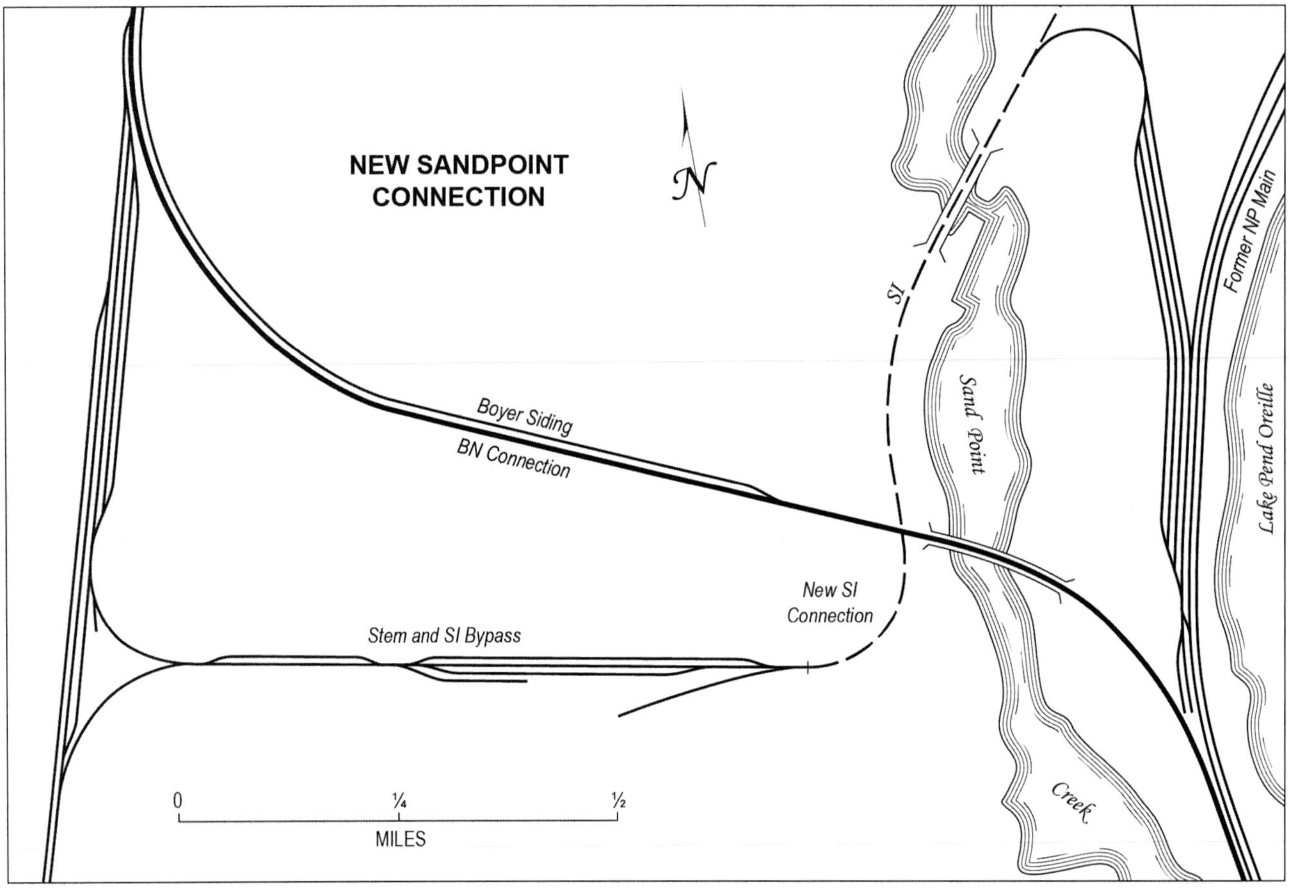

At Sandpoint, the Great Northern siding was located on the north side of the main, with the yard and wye on the south side of the main. A westward train from the GN going to the NP side would come west on the GN main, slow from 50 MPH to a stop and line the switch at the east end of GN Sandpoint Yard. The train would enter yard track 1 at restricted speed and travel about 3,500 feet to the east leg of the wye. The crew would stop here, open the wye switch and, if necessary, line the switch at the top of the wye for their movement. The tail track of the wye was 'the stem.'

The stem crossed the former Spokane International, now Union Pacific, main track. The UP crossing was not signaled but was within yard limits of both lines. BN trains were required to creep up and stop to make sure no one was coming on the UP before they could continue. After crossing the UP, the stem crossed over the highway and Sand Creek on an old wood trestle to the NP side.

On the NP side there was another wye, which meant two more switches to observe or throw. Westward trains took the west leg, which turned to the railroad west and the switch to the NP siding. Entry to the siding was controlled by the NP dispatcher since the siding was part of the CTC system. Permission to enter the siding was obtained from the NP Sandpoint operator who talked to the dispatcher and advised us that we could or could not enter the siding. From the siding, trains entered the NP main line on the authority conveyed by the controlled signal at the west end of Sandpoint.

The stem was about three quarters of a mile long and was constructed of old light rail on old and infirm wood ties. When the crossover traffic started, there was a 5 MPH speed limit on the stem until the section crew could put in a few new ties, dump some ballast, and run the tie tamper up and down the stem a few times. The speed limit was never raised over 10 MPH due to the light and worn out rail and the marginal condition of the wooden trestle over the highway and Sand Creek.

This operation was as colorful as it was unsuitable for use as a main track connection. Each train making this move incurred at least 45 minutes to an hour delay lining all the switches, traveling at 10 MPH, and accelerating back to 50 MPH, assuming no delay in getting onto the NP main at Sandpoint.

When westward trains crossed over from the NP side to the GN side, they were required to pick up train orders at the GN Sandpoint depot before they could leave Sandpoint for Hillyard. Sometimes this would cause a little more delay.

At times, there were trains waiting to cross over from the NP at Algoma and at Kootenai sidings. Algoma was 7.2 miles west of NP Sandpoint. Kootenai was the first siding east of the NP Sandpoint. Kootenai was so close to the east end of the Sandpoint siding that it was and is accessible via a connecting track between the two sidings, which allowed trains to move between the two sidings without using the main track. On the GN side the adjacent sidings were Elmira, 15.2 miles east of Sandpoint, and Laclede, 13.4 miles west of Sandpoint. Trains waiting at any of these points to crossover from one side to the other could incur additional delays of an hour or two waiting to get their turn at Sandpoint. The new Sandpoint connection was finally completed and placed in service in July of 1973.[3] Opening the Sandpoint connection was a great relief to everyone involved in moving main line trains over the stem.

Once the new Latah Creek and Sandpoint connections were in place, the former Great Northern main between Highland and Sandpoint was discontinued as a through route. Track was immediately removed from Highland eastward across Havermale Island along with several steel bridges.

Immediately after the merger, roadbed for a second track was built along the former Northern Pacific main track between Athol and Ramsey. The BN worked for about two months with a bulldozer pulling trees from five to thirty feet tall from the proposed grade, and leveling the roadbed for a second main track, but track was not laid on it until 2017. The BN should have immediately completed this segment of second main track, and others, because as soon as all through trains were routed onto the former NP line between Sandpoint and Yardley, train delay became significant. Adding the former GN traffic to the NP traffic more than doubled the number of trains between Sandpoint and Yardley, creating a bottleneck.

The final main line merger-related change in the Spokane area was construction of a new yard. Consolidation of GN and NP traffic on the former NP line between Spokane and Sandpoint enabled one yard somewhere between those points to perform switching for traffic destined to any point on the BN system. With the merger, Pasco became less than ideally located in that it required a long detour to the south for carload traffic to and from Puget Sound, a condition that would get worse when the company later closed Stampede Pass.

Merger planners intended to rebuild Yardley as a hump yard. Yardley would then assume the role in BN operations that Pasco played in the NP. It would classify cars for 'coastal' destinations and for destinations east of Spokane. Once the reconfigured Yardley was in operation, most of the work that Pasco was performing would be moved to Yardley, and Pasco would be downgraded.

By 1970, Yardley was surrounded by urban land, which would make expansion at Yardley unusually expensive. Shortly after the merger, plans were changed. The company would build a new yard and locomotive facility at Hauser, Idaho, 16 miles east of Yardley. When Hauser was completed, Yardley Yard, Pasco Yard, and the locomotive facilities at both locations would be downgraded.

Burlington Northern found itself unable to complete all of its merger-related projects due to financial constraints, but in 1973 the company did manage to build 10 storage tracks at Hauser.[4] Hauser was initially used as an overflow facility for low priority westward trains and to stage unit grain trains for delivery to export elevators.

BN petitioned the Federal Railroad Administration for a mileage extension waver on the 500-mile inspection rule, since Yardley was just a few miles over the 500-mile limit from Havre. This reasonable request was denied by the FRA. As a result, westward trains from Havre were yarded at Hauser Yard and given their 500-mile inspection by a crew of carmen.

BNSF's new bridge over Sand Creek at Sandpoint, Idaho. Like the Latah Creek Bridge, it was built to connect former GN and NP main lines so that traffic to and from GN points east of Sandpoint could be handled on the NP line between Sandpoint and Spokane. COLLECTION OF JOHN LANGLOT.

Carmen at Hauser made a walking inspection of both sides of the entire train. They ran a support vehicle on each side of the train with brake shoes, air hoses, and knuckle pins so they could make minor repairs on the spot. A torch on the vehicle enabled them to make light welded repairs and to straighten grab irons. Carmen replaced worn out brake shoes and adjusted brake piston travel along with repair of bent or broken grab irons and ladders and repaired any other minor defects that could be fixed quickly. This inspection usually took about an hour in good weather. The road crew sat and waited, spending time but making no miles and no pay since Hauser was then neither a final nor initial terminal. We would set out any car found to have federal defect wheels and the carmen would repair them at Hauser Yard.

All major railroads continued to push the FRA for a 1,000-mile inspection limit, and within a year or two after Hauser was constructed, they were granted the 1,000-mile inspection limit. This eliminated the inspections at Hauser Yard, as trains could now make it to Interbay, Tacoma, and Portland from Havre.

As business increased, secondary trains from Whitefish and Missoula were yarded at Hauser and switched and blocked for 'coast' destinations by the Rathdrum Turn, a switch local. When the building of these trains was completed, the Rathdrum Turn would bring the train into Yardley for the outbound crew. While blocking trains at Hauser, the Rathdrum Turn accumulated traffic for Spokane proper and the locals that worked out of Spokane, and brought this Spokane traffic into Yardley at the end of the shift. This practice continued until Hauser Yard was completed. Transfers between Hauser and Yardley continue to this day.

By 1982, BN had finished the largest part of its investment in upgrading the railroad and expanding its capacity to handle coal from the Powder River Basin. Cash was finally available to build a hump yard at Hauser. Mr. Earl Currie, then Vice President–General Manager of the Seattle Region, was directed to determine whether or not the company should invest approximately $60 million to build a new hump yard at Hauser.

His study began with the obvious; unit grain trains eliminated the need to classify and grade individual grain cars in Eastern Washington. Merchandise traffic, which in the 1960s moved in boxcars, was now moving in intermodal service or lost to motor carriers. In either case it did not need to be classified. That left mainly single car shipments of fertilizer, tank car commodities, and forest products that still needed to be classified.

The Pasco hump yard, while not perfectly located, was classifying traffic to and from Portland-Vancouver, the Oregon Trunk, and the Bieber interchange, and the branch lines in Eastern Washington naturally tributary to Pasco. Between Pasco and the reduction in traffic that required classification in Eastern Washington, the volume was not there to support a hump yard at Hauser. The decision was to add four long tracks and a stub track, expanding Hauser as a flat yard, to partially relieve the congestion at Yardley.[5]

The Kettle Falls Line

Before the Great Northern main track through Spokane could be severed, it was necessary to establish a viable route between Hillyard and Yardley to maintain service to Kettle Falls, Nelson, and Republic.

The new connection left the former GN main line at MP 1475.7, west of Mission Street and about 2.7 miles west of Hillyard. A new 601-foot long bridge over the Spokane River was the key component in the new half mile long connection. In comparison with the Latah Creek and Sand Creek bridges, this was a modest project.

BNSF's new bridge over the Spokane River at Spokane connected the former GN main line to Yardley yard. This bridge was required to maintain service to Dean, Kettle Falls, and Newport when the GN main line through downtown was removed in 1973. COLLECTION OF JOHN LANGLOT.

South of the river, and as part of the general consolidation of facilities in Spokane, the UP granted the BN the trackage rights it needed over a portion of its north side industrial track between the point where the BN's new line from the bridge joined the industry track south to the BN. At the time, UP traffic on this track involved only two switch engine moves per day. BNSF acquired about half a mile of the former UP segment in a 2012 track swap, and now owns it as an integral part of its Kettle Falls line. Today, the UP industry track north of the BNSF has been removed.

The new connection joined the former NP 'Old Main' track at a new switch east of Erie Street Yard. Northern Pacific's Old Main track between Yardley and Napa Street Yard was left in place when the NP completed its elevated main line through Spokane in 1917. In 1970 the Old Main was a yard track connecting Yardley and the Erie Street Yard. Erie Street Yard is located west of Napa Street junction, so moves to or from Kettle Falls do not pass through the Erie Street Yard. The Old Main between Yardley and the switch to the new Kettle Falls line was upgraded to branch line track standards when it became part of the route between Kettle Falls and Yardley. The

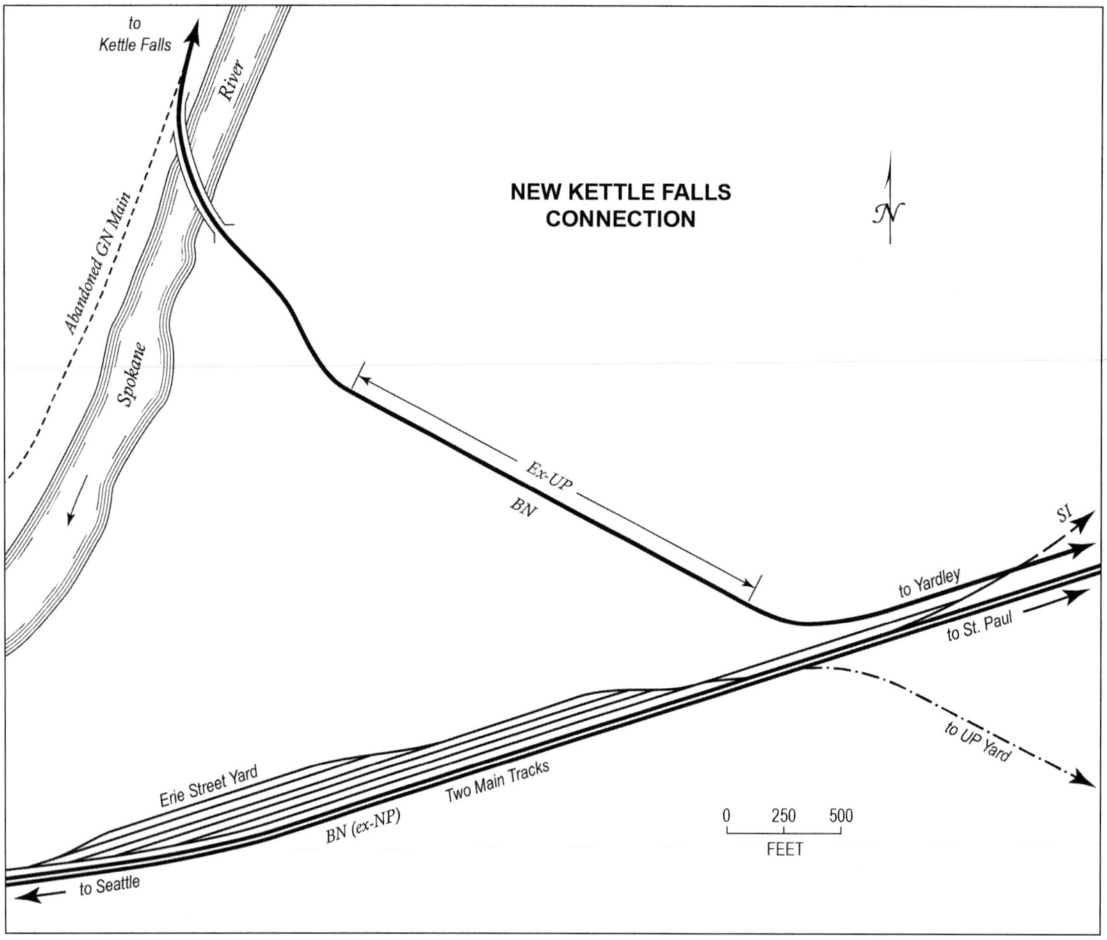

Old Main also continues to be the usual route for transfers between Yardley and the Erie Street yards.

The yard at Hillyard was partially removed after traffic was consolidated at Yardley, but Hillyard continued to build the Kettle Falls Turn. The diesel shop and yard office were removed in 1981, about eleven years after the BN merger and shortly after the SLSF merger. The rest of yard at Hillyard was ripped out and the origin point of the Kettle Falls Turn was moved to Yardley during the early 1980s. Today only the Kettle Falls branch main and a siding remain at Hillyard along with a few customer tracks.

In October of 1984, the former GN main track between Dean and Newport was removed. Two tunnels badly in need of repair between Camden and Scotia speeded up this action, which was the logical result of removing GN through traffic to the NP.

The Moscow Line

Shortly after the merger, the Great Northern's SC&P Moscow Local was eliminated by constructing new connecting tracks between the former Great Northern and the former Northern Pacific Palouse & Lewiston line, the P&L, at Rosalia, Oakesdale, Garfield, and Palouse. There was already an interchange track at Moscow. After the new connection at Rosalia was built, the trackage rights over the UP via Fairfax were relinquished and the GN connection between UPRR Junction and West Fairfield was abandoned and removed. As the connections were installed, the former GN track between stations was removed wherever possible.

Mt. Hope, Waverly, Spring Valley, Seabury, and the entire line to Manning were served from a new connection at Rosalia. Rosalia to Mt. Hope was about 16 miles one way, a three-hour round trip at 10 MPH. Spring Valley to Seabury was 7.5 miles, an hour and a half round trip at 10 MPH. Spring Valley was originally the junction on the SC&P between the line to Moscow and the line to Manning. It was now the junction between the line from Rosalia to the line between Mt. Hope and Seabury. A trip from Rosalia to both Mt. Hope and Seabury required four and a half hours of travel time.

Rosalia to Manning was 25 miles. At 10 MPH, this was a five-hour round trip. These travel times do not include any time for switching. Crabtree and Sokulk were served through the new connection at Oakesdale. Grinnell and Viola were served by the connection at Palouse. For a while, the company established a job at Yardley that made a three-day tour working these fragmented SC&P lines the from the former P&L line twice a week.

Estes, the last station north of Moscow, was served by an eight mile stub out of Moscow. The former SC&P line segments were abandoned piecemeal during the 1970s due to the inability of the elevators it served to ship 26-car unit trains. The elevator operators chose to truck their grain to the river rather than upgrade their elevators. The BN was probably happy to avoid the cost to upgrade the rail and maintain good tie condition to support 100-ton covered hoppers.

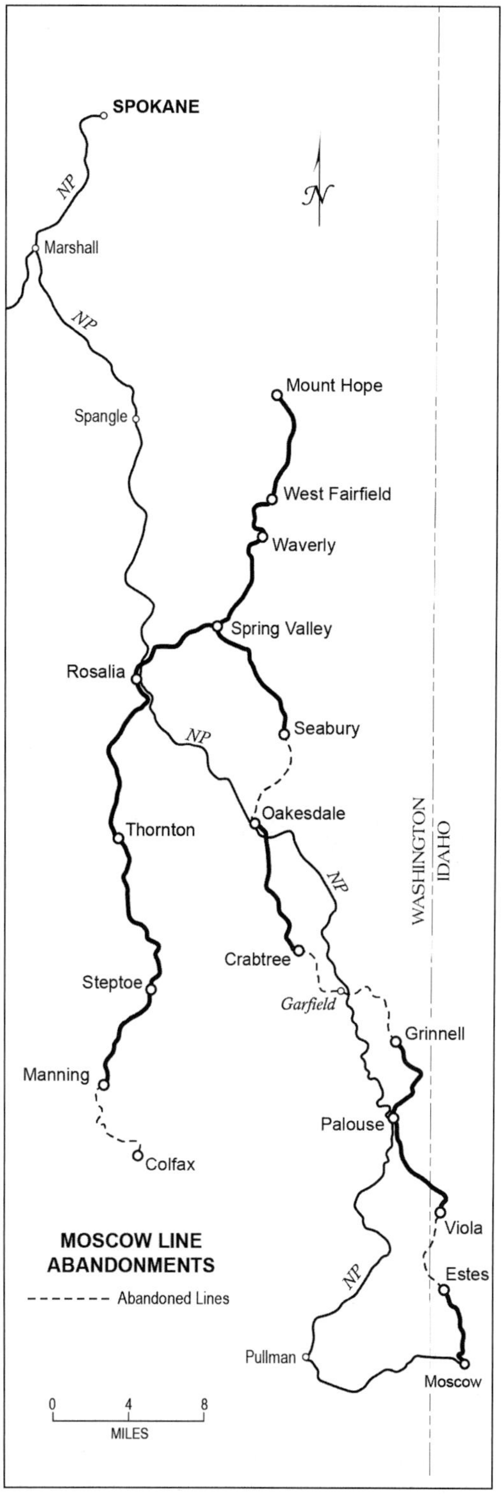

➵ The SC&P Spokane Yard

Immediately after the merger, the on-duty point for the Coeur d'Alene Local continued to be the former SC&P Yard. As the GN main line was removed between Fort Wright and Havermale Island, and then east to Mission Street, the GN Spokane Yard was also removed. Before Spokane Yard was removed, a short new connecting track was built between the east end of the former NP Erie Street Yard and the SC&P main track to Coeur d'Alene.

With the new connecting track in place, the Coeur d'Alene Local was rerouted to leave the SC&P Yard, run via the former NP transfer track to the Erie Street Yard, through the yard, and then over the new connection to the original SC&P line. Cars to and from the Coeur d'Alene Local moved between Erie Street and Yardley on transfer jobs. After a couple of weeks, the on-duty point of the Coeur d'Alene Local was moved to Erie Street

Yard. By this time the Moscow Local no longer existed due to the construction of connections with the former Northern Pacific P&L line, making the SC&P Yard useless.

After the Coeur d'Alene local was moved to Erie Street, the SC&P bridge over the Spokane River, bridge 1.5, was removed in the summer of 1973. The bridge closest to the yard, at MP 1.3, just east of Trent Avenue, stood until August of 1987 when it was removed to allow widening of the Trent Avenue Bridge over the Spokane River.

The Coeur d'Alene Branches

On merger day, the GN and the NP both operated daylight Coeur d'Alene Locals on their separate branch lines. The NP local went to work at 8:00 AM at Yardley and worked to Hauser Junction, where there was a lumber mill to switch. Tri-State asphalt at Hauser Junction received tank cars of asphalt emulsion on their private tracks.

After switching Hauser, the NP job headed to Post Falls where they switched Idaho Veneer a couple of times a week. Then it was on to the Atlas Tie, just past the GN-NP transfer track at Huetter. The NP had their own flat car track at Atlas Tie, which was good for one or two cars a week. The NP local very occasionally came down the NP-GN transfer track and used the GN/MILW branch main to spot a car or pick up a load at Diamond National Lumber Company at Huetter. Diamond National was one tenth of a mile west of the GN-NP transfer track and within Yard Limits on the GN/MILW branch.

The next NP station, about one mile east of Atlas Tie, was Blackwell, site of the track into Northwest Timber. The NP got only two to three cars a week out of Northwest Timber.

The NP local continued east for about a mile and a half to Coeur d'Alene, which had a double ended industry track that served the Coors beer distributor who unloaded beer from insulated fifty foot boxcars into their building. From the Coors distributor it was just over a mile to the NP depot, where Runge Furniture received a boxcar of furniture about once a month. Runge transferred their furniture from the boxcar to their truck and took the furniture to their store; this was called 'teaming' the load. The track Runge used was the 'team track,' which is a railroad owned track available to all customers who want to bring loads to or take loads from the railroad. The name 'team track' goes back to the days when farmers and merchants used horse drawn wagons to meet the railroad.

Even before the merger, there were days that the NP Coeur d'Alene Local did not go to Coeur d'Alene. Soon after the merger, the company put in a crossover connecting track between the NP and the GN/SC&P lines at Post Falls so the SC&P local could switch both sides of Post Falls. The new crossover was located about half a mile west of Post Falls where the former NP line closely approached the former GN line. The new crossover was only about 1,000 feet west of Idaho Veneer on the NP side of Post Falls. The new crossover allowed the NP Coeur d'Alene crew to concentrate on Kaiser at Trentwood, on Tri-State at Hauser, and switch the new Hauser Yard between Hauser and Rathdrum.

After the merger, the SC&P Local served customers on the former NP side of Coeur d'Alene, usually on the trip to Coeur d'Alene. The SC&P Local used the GN-NP transfer track to get on the NP side to serve the Northwest Timber lumber track off Blackwell siding, the Coors beer distributor, and Runge Furniture. The NP never reached PFI, so we were required to go back to the GN-NP transfer track to return to our normal route. If the SC&P job worked the NP side to Coeur d'Alene, the train often waited on the NP transfer track for the Milwaukee to come back from Coeur d'Alene, since the only other place we could clear up for them was in the former GN yard at Coeur d'Alene.

As before, when the SC&P job arrived at Huetter, the conductor called the agent at Coeur d'Alene from the phone in the foreman's office at Diamond National Lumber Company to determine what switching needed to be done on the way into town. The difference was that the scope of work now included the former NP side as described above. Late in 1973, the NP line between Idaho Veneer at Post Falls and the NP transfer track at Huetter, which paralleled the GN line, was abandoned and removed. The former NP line from Hauser Junction to Post Falls remained in place.

In 1977, the Milwaukee went bankrupt, and the west end of the Milwaukee was abandoned in 1980. Other railroads purchased the portions of the MILW they wanted or needed. The Burlington Northern bought the

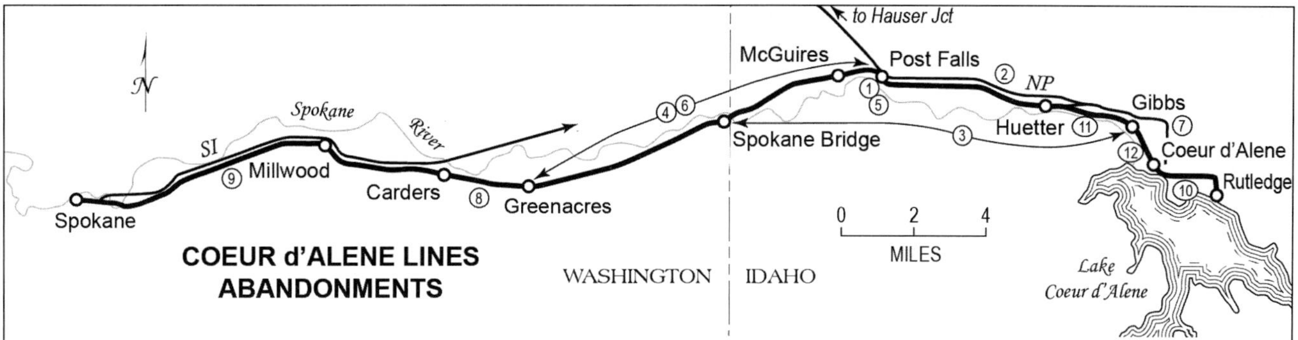

COEUR d'ALENE LINES ABANDONMENTS

① 1970 Install crossover between GN and NP lines at Post Falls

② 1973 Abandon NP between Post Falls and Huetter

③ About 1980 BN buys MILW trackage between Spokane Bridge and Gibbs

④ 1983 BN files for authority to abandon former GN between Greenacres and Post Falls

⑤ 1983 Simplify trackage at Post Falls to connect former NP end to end with former GN and remove former NP trackage across three grade crossings in town

⑥ 1984 Abandon former GN between Greenacres and Post Falls

⑦ About 1984 Abandon former NP between Huetter and Coeur d'Alene

⑧ 1985 Abandon former GN between Carders and Greenacres

⑨ 1987 Abandon former GN between Spokane and Carders, gaining trackage rights on SI between Spokane and Millwood to continue service at Millwood.

⑩ 1987 PFI at Rutledge shuts down, so BN abandons Coeur d'Alene to Rutledge in 1988

⑪ 2001-2008 Lumber mills at Huetter and to the east shut down

⑫ After 2008 BN abandons line between Huetter and Coeur d'Alene

Milwaukee's line from Spokane Bridge to Gibbs to maintain service into Coeur d'Alene via the former SC&P.

In 1983, the BN filed notice of abandonment of 14.4 miles from Greenacres to Post Falls. The abandonment was implemented the following June and the trackage was soon removed. The Coeur d'Alene Local was by then rerouted over the former NP line from Hauser Junction to Post Falls and Coeur d'Alene. To simplify the track arrangement and allow abandonment of a segment of former NP track that crossed three streets in Post Falls, a new crossover was constructed immediately west of Idaho Veneer. Then the crossover switches installed immediately after the merger, about half a mile west of Post Falls, were removed, leaving the former NP and the former GN tracks connected end to end. Now the branch main from Hauser Junction to the west side of Post Falls was former NP, while the track east of the connection was former GN/MILW. When the new job was established it was allocated to the NP prior rights trainmen.

By 1984, the portion of the NP line between Post Falls and the NP transfer at Atlas Tie, one quarter mile east of Huetter, was removed, leaving only the SC&P line from Post Falls to the NP transfer track at Atlas Tie. The former NP line between Atlas Tie and the former NP depot continued in service for several years, but it now ends just beyond Post Falls.

With the closing of the Quickie Box Company, the SC&P line to Greenacres was cut back to Carders in December of 1985. BN abandoned the line from Carders to Spokane in 1987. Union Pacific granted the BN trackage rights over the Spokane International main line from the SI yard to just beyond Millwood. Access to the BN industry tracks at Millwood is provided by a new connection from the SI main line. The Erie Street switch engine serves Millwood today.

Sawmills started to disappear from the Coeur d'Alene branch when Potlatch Forest Inc. at Rutledge closed in 1987. In 1988, the one and half miles of track in the city streets of Coeur d'Alene were removed bit by bit as street repairs occurred. The Georgia Pacific, later Louisiana Pacific, sawmill at Post Falls went out in 1995, followed by Diamond National at Huetter, then owned by Crown Pacific, in 2001, followed by Atlas Tie in 2005. Northwest Timber at Gibbs closed in 2008 as did DeArmond Stud at Coeur d'Alene later that year.

The only shippers left on the Coeur d'Alene branch as of 2018 are Idaho Veneer and the Potlatch particleboard plant, both at Post Falls. The particle board plant is relatively new, having been constructed about 1981. The former SC&P line now (2018) ends about 400 feet east of the crossing of Huetter Road which is west of the former Milwaukee siding and yard at Huetter. This is located about five miles east of Post Falls.

➻ The Palouse & Lewiston

Northern Pacific's Palouse & Lewiston line moved lumber and paper products from Lewiston and grain from the Palouse country at the time of the merger. The grain moved to Portland, Lower Columbia River, and Puget Sound ports for export. This pattern of grain movement existed since the first segment of the P&L line was built in the 1880s. Grain elevators on the P&L were 'single car' elevators designed to load a car or two or five at a spot. About the time of the merger, the railroad offered reduced rates on 26-car blocks of export grain. This was done both to compete with barges on the Snake River and to reduce the cost of switching a few cars here and a few cars there. Since few of the grain elevators possessed the capacity to load 26 cars of grain at once, the BN allowed 26-car trains to be co-loaded at two or more stations.

By the time of the merger, the Army Corps of Engineers was spending hundreds of millions of taxpayer dollars to bring slack water barge navigation to Lewiston, and specifically to divert the Palouse country grain traffic from the railroads to the river. The last lock and dam on the Snake River, Lower Granite, was completed in 1975. Anybody who was paying attention knew what the Army's plan was. The grain elevator operators were paying attention, and knew before the river opened up that it would be cheaper to truck the grain to Lewiston and downriver points, and then barge the grain to Portland or the Lower Columbia River ports, than to ship by rail.

Shortly after the merger, all traffic to and from Lewiston was diverted to a Pasco routing, which put it into or out of through trains at the Pasco hump yard and kept it out of Yardley, both good things. The mountain grade segment from Lewiston up to Moscow, Idaho was taken out of service, and later abandoned once the states of Washington and Idaho decided they were not willing to pay to keep the line.

After the Burlington Northern merger, the Superintendent, Assistant Superintendent, and both Trainmasters at Spokane, all former NP officials, pushed to upgrade the P&L from Marshall to Lewiston, a total of 135 miles, with new ties, ribbon rail, and hard rock main line ballast. They got the money, so much of the track between Marshall and Pullman was upgraded.

This attempt to retain grain traffic in the Palouse country was futile. The grain elevator operators were getting better rates by trucking the grain to Lewiston and shipping the grain by barge to Portland. In fact, several of the elevator operators built their own river terminals.

By 1980, the grain business on the P&L was dead. With most of the grain traffic diverted to the river, upgrading the P&L was a total waste of resources, which the operating wizards would have known if they bothered to talk to the grain marketing guys.

➻ Seniority Issues Following the BN Merger

Immediately after the merger, former Great Northern Spokane Division trainmen could also work the former Northern Pacific main line east to Paradise, Montana, the former NP Palouse and Lewiston branch to Lewiston, Idaho, and the Central Washington branch to Coulee City. In similar fashion, Northern Pacific men working those territories could now work former Great Northern Spokane Division jobs. The NP west to Pasco was covered by crews based in Pasco who were not included on the combined Spokane seniority roster. Later, regional seniority rosters were negotiated that included men from Pasco, Portland, Vancouver (Washington), Seattle, Tacoma, and Klamath Falls.

The seniority issues I experienced with the BN merger were horrible. On merger day I was the senior man on the brakemen's extra board, and had taken my conductor's promotion in 1966. By the time of the merger, I worked as a conductor only a few times when the conductors' extra board was exhausted. As senior brakeman, if a good local came open, I could bid it and get it before any other extra board brakeman.

Shortly after merger day, I was working the former Keremeos Local (which was then called the Oroville to Omak Local), because Ron Bible was off due to an injury. This local worked from Oroville to Omak and back six nights a week. When a man was called off the extra board to protect an outside local, he was committed to that job for a minimum of 10 calendar days whether he liked it or not. If you laid off on call, you would be held off the extra board for the 10 days or until you marked up and protected that outside job.

I came home on Sunday, the job's one day off. I went out to the Hillyard crew office on Sunday with the intention of laying off the job, taking the next three days off, which would have completed my 10 days, and then marking up on the brakeman's extra board. When I arrived at the crew office, I was forced to park two blocks away from the office. It took me over 30 minutes just to get inside the office, which was so crowded it was almost impossible to move inside the room. I watched as men were getting bumped off of jobs as they were bumping someone else off the same job. The crew clerks all looked like they were about to have a nervous breakdown. I took a look at this and said to myself, "I'm going back to Oroville where I know I can work for at least three days." I stayed at Oroville for all of the next week. Ron Bible marked up for work for the following Monday, so I went back home to Spokane. I went to the crew office on Sunday afternoon and found out I had dropped 75 places on the seniority roster. I was in shock.

As unhappy as my experience was, it was far from the worst. I know that some men went five or six days without working because they would bump onto a job and then get bumped just before the job was called to go to work. Then they went through the same thing on some other job. For me it was back to the brakemen's extra board for a long time.

It took almost a year and a half to straighten out the seniority mess. The merger day consolidated roster was created by dovetailing the separate rosters based on hire date with no regard to a man's prior employer. I dropped behind 75 former NP and SP&S trainmen on this roster. Fortunately, business was good, and the company needed pilot conductors and engineers to train everybody on the new territories now available to them. The conductors' and engineers' extra boards were increased dramatically to accomplish the training. As a result, the brakemen's board was able to absorb most of us who lost so many positions because of the dovetailed roster.

I blame the United Transportation Union, the UTU, for the seniority mess. Not long before the BN merger, the ORC&B, Order of Railroad Conductors and Brakemen, and the B of RT, Brotherhood of Railroad Trainmen, merged to create the UTU. As the merger approached, there was still a power struggle going on among the UTU management factions over who would control the new union.

The UTU spent all their energy fighting the merger right up to the time that it was approved. I saw no effort to look ahead to settle the issue of seniority consolation if the merger was to be approved. If only they had accepted the possibility of merger, the union could have written their own ticket in terms of seniority issues. In fact, the union could have worked out the seniority issues even while fighting the merger. Management was confident that the merger would be approved and should have wanted to resolve seniority issues before the merger actually happened. The company was unlikely to object to whatever the men, speaking through the union, wanted to do about seniority.

Six months after the merger, the union came up with the 'ton mile roster' which boiled down to three GN trainmen, two NP trainmen and one SP&S trainman; three GN, two NP and one SP&S and so on until the whole roster was lined up. I moved up about 25 men on this new roster, but gained nothing since by now most, if not all, conductors were qualified on all the 'new' track of the other railroad. The conductors' and engineers' extra boards were cut back a little bit but were still larger than before the merger. The reason for this was an increase in business and mass confusion at Hillyard and Yardley.

Operational blunders included running trains on the wrong routes. I remember trains going to Paradise, Montana and beyond when they should have gone through Troy, Montana and on east. When this happened, the company needed to return them and then send the train the right way. The same thing occurred with Wenatchee and Pasco.

Before the merger 'dog catching,' that is, to call a second crew to relieve the first crew that died on line, was rare on the Great Northern except in a bad winter or in case of a derailment. After the merger, it seemed like we were dog catching all the time, which kept the extra boards turning which supported more men. The major

Train No. 188 near Rock Island on August 23, 1970, shows the mix of paint schemes of merged railroads that made up Burlington Northern that was common shortly after the merger. Today's power is a former Chicago, Burlington and Quincy (CBQ) SD 24; a former GN SD 45; another former CBQ SD 24; a former CBQ U25C; a recently repainted BN GP 9; and a Big Sky Blue former GN GP 9. PHOTO BY MIKE BARTENSTEIN.

factor contributing to the increase in dog catching was that the density of trains on the former NP between Spokane and Sandpoint and on the former GN east of Sandpoint increased as traffic was rerouted. In addition, trains were getting longer which made the short sidings useless, effectively reducing the number of available meeting points.

Trains also experienced much delay getting out of Yardley. Some of the delay was due to congestion at Yardley. Most of the delay was due to bad calls, that is, crews being called long before the outbound trains were ready to go. I was often called to go east from Yardley only to find that the train had not arrived, or that Yardley needed to do some switching before our train could leave, or that failed power had gone to the roundhouse for repair or replacement so many times that I simply came to expect some delay at Yardley every trip. On the rare occasion that our crew got out in good time, I took it as a good omen. Congestion at Yardley also contributed to delays on line as dispatchers would hold us well away from Yardley rather than get us close and plug all of his sidings near Yardley. This was good dispatching, but it was another delay to us.

Coincident with the merger, officials were moved all over the railroad. A former Northern Pacific man, George Heimsjo, became our division superintendent. This wholesale moving of operating officers was done to preclude the development of 'home road' cliques, and to help develop a Burlington Northern identity among the operating officers. It was the correct decision, but it added an element of change and uncertainty among the blue-collar ranks. In the Spokane area, this was particularly true for those of us who were not former NP employees. I knew that morale was not good in the Spokane dispatcher's office, probably due to the combination of former GN and NP dispatchers. When we talked to the Boyer West dispatcher, there was obviously more tension in the dispatcher's office than had previously been the case.

Years later when I was working chain gang to Wenatchee, I was able to talk with crews working out of Interbay about what happened in the Seattle area after the merger. They said that it appeared that the new superintendent tended to favor those employed by the same predecessor company that he had come from. This favoritism applied to all crafts. Subordinate officials were particularly exposed to biased pressure from above. I heard that conditions and morale were not the best in the Seattle dispatcher's office.

Both the Great Northern and the Northern Pacific had postponed hiring trainmen and switchmen for some time before the merger, so Spokane did not have

Train No. 188 moving away from the camera near Rock Island in a companion photo to the previous one. PHOTO BY MIKE BARTENSTEIN.

a surplus of men. I know the Great Northern was very short of brakemen just before the merger. Great Northern trainmen and switchmen did not have joint seniority like Northern Pacific trainmen and switchmen did. NP trainmen and the switchmen were on the same roster and were said to have 'joint rights.' Between the short staffing before the merger, training, dog catching, and good business volumes, I cannot recall a time that any pre-merger trainmen were furloughed at Spokane.

About nine months or a year after the ton mile roster came out, the union went back to the dovetailed roster, but this time everybody retained prior rights on their former railroad. This let me hold a brakeman's job in the Troy, Montana chain gang freight pool, a former GN freight pool.

The seniority issue caused hard feelings and dissension between the GN men and the NP men, with the SP&S men caught in the middle, for many years. In Spokane, the GN and NP trainmen supported separate local union lodges until May 1, 1994. On that date, local lodges 765 and 1076 were voluntarily consolidated into one lodge with a new number, UTU Local 426. The NP lodge, 765, was suffering financial difficulties because it did not have enough members, which contributed to the consolidation. With two lodges, Spokane trainmen got two delegates to the national convention and two legislative representatives to lobby the state. The negative side of the consolidation was that since there was now one lodge in Spokane, we now got only one delegate to the national convention and one legislative representative.

Before the BN merger there were many locations which had two or three UTU lodges, one for each of the predecessor companies. To this day, there are many locations on the BN where the terminals retain their separate local lodges. The animosity has now carried into the next two generations of BN and BNSF trainmen.

What the GN trainmen went through was nothing compared to what the GN engineers went through. The Brotherhood of Locomotive Engineers (BLE) really did a number on the GN enginemen. The BLE used the fireman's hire out date to make up the seniority roster. NP firemen who had never worked as an engineer were put ahead of GN engineers who had worked as engineers for 10 to 13 years. This caused real hatred between the GN and NP enginemen that has lasted to the present time, even among retirees who still carry strong negative feelings about this issue. The BLE would not back down on the way the enginemen's seniority roster was made up using the firemen's hire out dates. The BLE general chairman was a former NP engineer. He determined how the seniority roster was arranged, and he took care

of himself and his former NP enginemen. If he intended to be fair, this roster would have been either a ton mile or prior rights roster.

As the seniority issues related to the merger were being played out, the federal government took over the passenger trains on May 1, 1971 and called it Amtrak. The GN side lost the Western Star and the NP side lost the Mainstreeter and the North Coast Limited; the only passenger train left was the Empire Builder.

When Amtrak took over, former GN trainmen lost 21 trainmen jobs and eight baggagemen jobs at Spokane, while the NP lost 12 trainmen jobs at Spokane. On the GN, baggageman jobs were protected by brakemen, while on the NP, trainmen did not perform baggage jobs. Spokane trainmen lost a total of 41 passenger jobs. Amtrak offered just three trainmen jobs, one conductor and two brakemen, at Spokane, for a net loss of 38 jobs. I went from working the Coeur d'Alene Local as a brakeman back to working the brakemen's extra board for well over a year.

The only source of qualified employees available to Amtrak was current railroad employees. Amtrak operating jobs, conductors, brakemen, engineers, and firemen, were opened to bid. Everybody qualified to work passenger jobs could bid on the Amtrak jobs. Railroad employees could bid back into freight service anytime they desired as long as their seniority allowed them to. The successful bidders were granted a leave of absence from the railroad for six months. The unions negotiated one more year and then added another year. The leaves of absence were never dated, so if Congress decided not to fund Amtrak's continual losses, and some or all passenger trains were terminated, the Amtrak employees could come back to their former railroad with their former seniority.

The reason this was handled this way was that no one really knew how long Amtrak was going to last. After about 10 years, the only way someone could come back to their former road was if they could prove a hardship. Everybody in Spokane who bid on those Amtrak jobs was younger than I was in seniority. One advantage to going with Amtrak was that you could bid on Amtrak jobs in a different part of the country if you enjoyed the seniority to hold it. The use of freight carrier employees to man the passenger trains lasted until April 28, 1987, when Amtrak hired their own operating employees.

My father, John "Jack" Langlot, who was number one on the Great Northern conductor seniority roster in Spokane, could not hold the one Amtrak passenger conductor job to Seattle. The oldest NP conductor at Spokane hired out as a brakeman for the NP in 1936, seven years after my father had hired out as a brakeman for the GN in 1929. The NP promoted their trainmen early, so this NP man was promoted to conductor in 1941 while my father was promoted to conductor in 1943. Just because a man was promoted to a conductor

Train No. 188 is at the center of the horseshoe curve located in Lynch Coulee east of Trinidad. The fill here is about 80 feet high, and the 10-degree curve imposes a 25 MPH speed limit on all trains. PHOTO BY MIKE BARTENSTEIN.

did not mean that he worked as a conductor right away. This was just your promotion date. After Amtrak was created, my father bumped George Rasmussen, a former GN conductor, off the Coeur d'Alene Local.

The NP conductor who previously outbid my father on the Amtrak conductor job retired eight months later. After a few phone calls to find out how the new passenger system was working, my father decided to stay on the Coeur d'Alene Local, working daylight hours five days a week, until he retired in 1973. Amtrak jobs out of Spokane were night jobs.

After the BN merger, the worst thing about the brakemen's and conductors' extra boards was catching helpers on the former NP. The job would help a train from Sunset Junction to Cheney, come back to Sunset Junction, and get in the clear of the main track on the long lead from the westward main to the passenger depot. Sometimes we sat there for six or seven hours and then took the power back to Yardley to tie up. The bad part about this was that if the extra board was turning slowly, you might not go to work for 24 to 40 hours. I suffered one pay period of two weeks wherein all I worked was seven helper turns, and that was not good. That amounted to 700 miles for the pay period when I should have earned 1,900 to 2,500 miles off the conductors' extra board.

Operations on the Kettle Falls Line

Business on the Kettle Falls line increased rapidly during the 1970s. Lumber loading was on the rise, as were shipments of copper smelter slag in C-6 covered hoppers from Grand Forks to United States Navy shipyards in Bremerton and San Diego for sandblasting. The very hard, very black, copper slag was found to last much longer than sand in sandblasting.

About merger time, after the Deer Park sawmill closed and pulpwood was no longer shipped from Denison and Loon Lake, the on-duty point of the Chewelah Turn was moved from Hillyard to Chewelah. By this time, a new magnesium plant was operating at Addy, nine miles north of Chewelah, and the Jump-Off Joe Lumber mill was built south of Lane Mountain Sand at Valley. The relocated Chewelah Turn handled the switching from Chewelah to Arden and from Chewelah to Valley, including Lane Mountain Sand, Jump-Off Joe Lumber, and North American Non Metallics.

The Kettle Falls Turn now set out cars for Valley customers at Valley and set out cars for Chewelah, Addy, and Arden at Chewelah. On the return trip, the Kettle Falls Turn picked up all the south cars from the Chewelah Turn at Chewelah. With this change in the Chewelah Turn, the Kettle Falls Turn handled company material for Deer Park or Loon Lake when necessary, a practice that continues to this day.

This began a long period in which jobs were relocated, renamed, and work limits changed in a constant attempt to serve the local customers with fewer crews and at lower cost. It seemed like every new trainmaster had to tinker with the jobs on the Kettle Falls branch.

Around 1976 or 1977, when I was the conductor of the Kettle Falls Turn, the Kettle Switch began to regularly die short of Colville, which forced us to do their remaining switching and weighing, and then finish building our outbound train. Finally, we had to go back, get our train, yard it, and put our outbound train together. To add insult to injury, we also were forced to take their locomotive, caboose, and cars for Colville back to Colville on our westward trip. This caused the Kettle Falls Turn to die on our hours of service before arriving back at Hillyard. In addition, we were forced to wait for the dog-catch crew to relieve us and take us to Hillyard. The only night the Kettle Falls Turn did not die on line was Sunday, when no other local was working.

After about three weeks of this, I called the trainmaster in charge of the Kettle Falls branch and asked him what he was going to do about our not being able to get back to Hillyard. He told me that as far as he was concerned, the plan was working, not well, but it was working. I told the trainmaster that he could figure on us going to eat Monday through Friday night at Kettle Falls. We were not going to work 12 hours and more without eating. I also told him that he could figure on dog catching us five nights a week until things changed. After another week of dog catching us, the Kettle Switch Local was moved back to Kettle Falls.

Shortly after the Kettle Switch Local was moved back to Kettle Falls, the on-duty point of the Kettle Falls Turn was moved to Yardley with the closing of Hillyard. Train delay increased substantially due to the congestion at Yardley. Congestion at Yardley was so bad that the company was forced to establish a second Kettle Falls Turn crew to dog catch the first Kettle Falls Turn crew, usually at Addy, but really wherever the first crew got to by the end of their 12 hours.

The Kettle Switch Local, the Republic Local, and the Quick Turn were lost to BNSF crews when the lines beyond Kettle Falls were leased to short line operator Kettle Falls International Railroad, a subsidiary of short line holding company OmniTRAX. The current BNSF operation involves a two-man crew, conductor and engineer, operating from Yardley to Chewelah, where interchange is made with the short line. This crew sets out cars for Lane Mountain Sand at Valley. A second crew, this one with three men, is called to run from Chewelah to Yardley pulling and spotting Lane Mountain Sand en route. The current labor agreement provides that a two-man crew (conductor and engineer) can make one set out. If more set outs will be made, or if any industry switching will be performed, then a brakeman is required.

This final view of No. 188, taken as the train is approaching the East Switch at Ephrata, shows the semi-desert vegetation native to Eastern Washington, the firebreak that the railroad graded every spring, and the pole line used to carry railroad message and signal wires, all typical of the Columbia Plateau between Quincy and Fairchild. PHOTO BY MIKE BARTENSTEIN.

When I worked the Kettle Falls Turn as conductor, the track was so bad that we were on the ground with a derailment about once a week. Some of these derailments were just one car. Other times we were not that lucky.

We were headed for Hillyard one night, and had just cleared the Denison Staley road crossing three and a half miles south of Deer Park, when the air went into emergency. I felt the train lurch and jerk as the cars were going on the ground and piling up. The caboose came to a stop and started to shake as I heard the chip car directly ahead of the caboose roll over onto its side and hit the ground with a thud. My brakeman, Bill Fernow, said, "What was that?" I told him that the chip car ahead of the caboose just tipped over on its side. Keep in mind, this is at night and there were no outside lights around. Bill did not believe my answer so I walked to the front of the caboose, turned on the spotlight, and opened the door. Right in front of the caboose, lying on its side, was that carload of wood chips along with three more loads of chips also lying on their sides. Lady luck smiled on us that night; the caboose was still on the rail and standing upright. Call it luck, call it the Lord's protection, or call it fate, but there comes a time when you say enough is enough and it's time to move on.

Sounds are so important. I knew by the sounds I heard that the chip car was rolling over. That is why I grabbed the overhead rod mounted down the center of the ceiling on cabooses. If the caboose was going to roll over with that chip car, I would not be slammed against the wall that would become the floor when the caboose rolled over onto its side. Bill could not figure out what I was doing when I grabbed the overhead rod. Bill thought it was funny until I turned on the spotlight and opened the door. Once Bill saw the chip car laying on its side, it was not funny anymore.

The worst derailment I experienced while I was the conductor on the Kettle Falls Turn happened just north of Clayton when we stacked up 26 cars, and I do mean stacked up. They were all in one egg-shaped pile about 100 feet by 200 feet and 25 feet high. The caboose stopped so hard and fast, it knocked the fire out in the oil stove and sent my rear brakeman, Tom Brass, up against the cupola wall. I was sitting at the back desk watching for

derailment marks in the fresh snow when the caboose went from 23 MPH to zero within about 50 feet.

The jolt knocked me out of the chair onto the floor. Immediately after the train stopped, Tom and I were picking ourselves up when the oil stove exploded, filling the caboose full of thick black sooty smoke. We shut the stove off and opened the doors to get rid of the smoke, picked our personal belongings up off the floor, and put them back in our grips that had been thrown against the front wall of the caboose. We then tied some hand brakes on the rear of the train and started to walk forward.

About 30 cars from the rear of the train, we found an open top hopper with its rear end on the rail and the leading end sitting in the dirt. There was no rail, ties, ballast, or snow for about 200 feet, just plain old dirt. At the end of the 200 feet was a huge pile of 26 cars stacked on top of each other. Tom and I walked up to the derailment and I started to write down car numbers and the condition of each car, whether the car was upright or on its side or top. Tom climbed up on the pile of derailed cars and gave me the car numbers and a description of the damage. As I wrote down the car numbers and the damage to each car, I could not believe what I was hearing. Both Tom and I kind of lost it when Tom told me that a NP skeleton log flat was literally broken in two. The cause of this derailment was determined to be a broken rail.

I was able to bump my way off the Kettle Falls Turn when they pulled the job off due to this derailment and the bosses decided that that line was going to be shut down for five days. I was relieved. I had felt for some time that my luck on the Kettle Falls Turn was going to run out sooner or later.

➻ Endnotes

1 Robert C. Del Grosso, *BNSF Northwest: The BNSF Railway in the Pacific Northwest* (Bonners Ferry ID: Great Northern Publications, 2002), 68.
2 Earl Currie, email, October 5, 2011.
3 Currie, email, October 5, 2011.
4 Del Grosso, *BNSF Northwest*, 71.
5 Currie, email, November 14, 2012.

12. The Burlington Northern

Introduction

This chapter will discuss congestion at Yardley, signal systems, and some stories of working on the railroad in the 1970s through the eyes of John Langlot.

The chapter will also discuss a specific case of railroad competition involving BN and CPR, the Red Dog concentrate. It closes with a discussion of some of the important industry and corporate changes during the decade between the Burlington Northern merger and the Saint Louis–San Francisco, SLSF, or Frisco merger.

Congestion at Yardley

Once the new Sandpoint connection and bridge was completed in 1973, it and the Latah Creek Bridge were used to route all main line traffic through Yardley as planned. The merger planners evidently did not consider the consequences of delay in building their Yardley hump yard. The operating plan did not require that locations such as Pasco, Minot, Whitefish, and Missoula build more trains that could bypass Yardley.[1] It should have.

When all the traffic was diverted to Yardley, operations almost came to a halt. Trains went into Yardley, but they did not come out. The congestion at Yardley was in stark contrast to pre-merger conditions at Hillyard, in which trains got out of Hillyard in a timely manner and the dispatchers knew when to expect them. Dispatchers soon referred to Yardley as "The Black Hole." One dispatcher said that trains seemed to rust to the rail if they were yarded at Yardley.

Dispatchers relied on the operators at origin yards for their information. Wally Morse and Bobbie Campbell at Wenatchee were very good at getting information for dispatchers about when trains would be ready to come out of the yard. June Peterson and Jim Gregson were both very good at obtaining information on when trains would be ready to leave Hillyard.

When the company eliminated their jobs at Hillyard, June and Jim both bumped onto telegrapher's jobs at Yardley. Yardmasters at Yardley would ignore their questions, which meant that they were forced to keep asking the yardmaster and consult other sources. They would talk to the carmen, the conductors if the crew was on duty, the manifest clerk working the train's paperwork, and the roundhouse foreman, if the power was still at the roundhouse, to obtain information. If an operator was dumb, lazy, or just did not give a damn, then the dispatcher would be left blind about what to expect out of Yardley. That put trains leaving Yardley at further disadvantage since they were a surprise to the dispatcher.

Some crews actually went dead on their hours of service without ever leaving Yardley. I was never on a crew that did that, but I did die twice eastward on hours of service at Hauser Yard, 16 miles east of Yardley. I remember being called for a train, and, upon reporting for duty at Yardley, finding that the train was still out on the line somewhere. Sometimes it would be four to eight hours before our train arrived, and then the switchmen would have to switch part of the train. Sometimes the train was there but the power was coming in on another train and it would be four to eight hours arriving at Yardley, and then the power would have to go to the Parkwater Roundhouse for fuel.

Yardmasters at Yardley were generally uncooperative, and at times, even smart mouthed. I believe the reason for this was the increase in their workloads. They were not used to it and could not handle it. We road crewmen referred to Yardley as "The Zoo." Everybody was under the same pressure. Local officials did not want to add any

ABOVE Train No. 88 ascends the west side of Lynch Coulee, closely approaching the horseshoe curve on August 23, 1970. Former GN F 45 has been renumbered to its new number, 6600, but former NP SD 45s have not been renumbered yet. PHOTO BY MIKE BARTENSTEIN.

LEFT Train No. 88 east of the Ephrata depot on August 23, 1970. PHOTO BY MIKE BARTENSTEIN.

help in the Yardley Tower, because to do so would add to their labor budget and they would have to explain why.

The company operated Yardley with the absolute minimum number of clerks. The inbound manifest clerks were regularly overloaded, often having two or three trains waiting for the manifest clerks to work them. Until the clerks worked the inbound trains, the yardmasters did not know what they needed to do. Adding a single manifest clerk at Yardley would have helped the yardmasters by providing timely switch lists so the yardmasters could plan their work and get it done more quickly. If the company would have relieved the pressure on the yardmasters, then they should have been able to plan ahead, done a better job, gotten along better with both train and yard crewmen, and reduced train delays at Yardley. For years, the company lost dollars to save pennies at Yardley.

Working on the BN

Long before the BN merger, the carriers wanted crews to work longer distances to reduce labor costs. This was done by instituting interdivisional runs, by which intermediate terminals were eliminated as crew change points. For example, Hillyard to Troy, Montana was 134 miles; Troy to Whitefish was also 134 miles before the Libby Dam line change. The new line, placed in service in November of 1970, shortened the mileage between

Train No. 97 passing Rock Island Dam on August 23, 1970. The former Burlington GP unit is unusual. Train 97 normally ran with three SD 45 or F 45 six-axle units of 3600 horsepower each. The four-axle GP unit will rob some of the tonnage rating from the trailing six-axle units due to its higher minimum continuous speed. PHOTO BY MIKE BARTENSTEIN.

Troy and Whitefish to 122 miles. In addition to saving on train labor cost due to paying a lower rate per mile for miles over 100, by eliminating crew change points the company could eliminate crew clerks, train order operators, and other support positions and assets associated with changing crews.

Crews began to run through Troy shortly after the Libby Dam line change. The run through freight pool mileage between Yardley and Whitefish was 256.6 miles. Traffic between Spokane and Whitefish was so heavy that crews were regularly going dead on their hours of service. If one train suffered a problem and died on their hours of service, it usually caused enough delay to other trains to make them die on the law also. One dead crew could snowball, causing several trains to go dead.

When a crew died on their hours of service, the company called a second crew to relieve them. The crew that went dead was generally on overtime; if not, they would be on overtime by the time they reached their final terminal. The crew that died was paid the full 256.6 miles for the trip, plus the overtime. The crew that died on line thus earned something more than their base pay of 256.6 miles.

The crew called to dog catch the dead crew was transported under pay from their originating terminal to the location of the dead crew. The dog catch crew was paid 'railroad line miles' for the deadhead move from Yardley to the dead crew. Then they were paid actual miles worked back to Yardley or on to Whitefish. A dog catch usually more than doubled the labor cost of moving a train between Whitefish and Yardley due to the overtime paid to the first crew, the cost of the second crew, and the cost of a van and driver to haul the crews out and back over the highway.

For the longer runs to make sense for the company, crews needed to get over the road. The extra labor cost generated by crews dying on line worked against the company's purpose in creating interdivisional runs. As business continued to increase, more double track should have been installed by connecting adjacent sidings where practicable. No such work was done between Yardley and Whitefish until after the BNSF merger.

After the BN merger, the amount of track that crewmen were required to memorize more than doubled. GN men, for example, needed to learn the entire Northern Pacific and SP&S track in a very short time. With very modest exceptions, I never worked any of this trackage as a brakeman, so I was not familiar with it.

In addition, the men in my seniority bracket were just starting to get used as conductors whenever the conductors' extra board was exhausted in the vacation months of the year. Working the conductors' extra board during this time was not easy. Many times, I caught a job that I had never worked as a brakeman and ran over track that I never saw before. The conductor was in charge of the train and the work to be done, but I often knew little or nothing about the stations that we were to switch. The only source of information was the regular men working the job or the Time Table station information.

I remember getting called for one local when the whole crew was called off the extra board. No one had ever worked the job before, so the whole shift we did everything by braille. The only thing to do was to take the switch list and walk around checking the numbers on the cars on each track just to learn the names of the tracks. These 'three blind mice' days were always very long. Trainmen were forced to guess far too often. We would look at how the cars were sitting on each track. Sometimes we could figure out from the way the cars were sitting how to spot the track, but not always. Sometimes we could only guess how to spot the track and which way the cars would roll. This did nothing for our customers' perception of our competence.

Immediately after the merger, traffic through Spokane grew. After the Latah Creek Bridge was completed, traffic grew even more on the line to Wenatchee due to rerouting traffic away from Stampede Pass. Unit grain trains for Seattle and Tacoma continued to move through Wenatchee. Unit coal trains destined for Roberts Bank, British Columbia moved via Wenatchee and Everett about twice a month.

Ever more intermodal traffic flooded onto the Wenatchee line during the 1970s as merchandise traffic shifted from westward boxcars loaded with American made products to more and more containerized import/export traffic to and from the ports of Seattle and Tacoma. All intermodal traffic to and from Puget Sound points, both international and domestic, moved through Wenatchee. At the same time, carload traffic was preferentially routed via Pasco to make use of the former NP hump yard.

By 1980, intermodal traffic displaced the grain and coal traffic from the Wenatchee line to the long way around through the Columbia River Gorge. The Wenatchee line was down to one carload, or manifest, train a day each way. The eastward manifest train usually arrived at Wenatchee about 4:00 to 8:00 PM.

In the BN days, the manifest train was No.198, which originated at Balmer Yard/Interbay in Seattle. In the BNSF years, the origin point was moved from Balmer Yard to Delta Yard at Everett to avoid the congestion that developed at Balmer, and the train was known as H-EVEGAL. H was the code for a high priority manifest train, while EVE designated the origin terminal of Everett, and GAL designated the final terminal of Galesburg, Illinois. From Everett, it handled Canadian lumber traffic destined for points on its route to Galesburg, and Red Dog concentrate for the Kettle Falls line. Alumina ore for Kaiser at Mead and the aluminum plant at Conkelley, Montana loaded at Everett and moved on the H-EVEGAL until both of these aluminum reduction plants closed.

The H-EVEGAL always set out cars at Appleyard for Wenatchee, the W–O, and the Alcoa locals, and picked up cars for Yardley and east. A new crew took the train from Wenatchee and made the east pickup at Quincy. Trucks had captured the fresh potato traffic so the east pickup was down to some shipments of diatomaceous earth and six or seven loads of frozen potatoes. Once in a while the Quincy elevator shipped a 26-car grain train of wheat for the coast. When they did, it went in the east pickup and was set out at Erie Street Yard near downtown Spokane where it was picked up by a train going through Pasco and on to the coast. Regardless of whether the manifest train included an Erie Street set out, they headed into Yardley where the train was switched, added to, and sent east.

This was also the period when coal traffic from the Powder River Basin in Wyoming was growing rapidly. It was wonderful that BN gained the business, which went east so it had no direct impact at Spokane. All new locomotives went to move coal trains. The rest of the railroad was left with the power that the merger partners had brought into the merger. During the 10 years before the merger, GN, NP, and Burlington combined bought 199 four-axle engines averaging about 2,500 horsepower, and 210 six-axle engines averaging about 3,000 horsepower from EMD and GE. The premier units were 92, 3,600 horsepower, SD 45 models. These 'second generation' units, and the mass of older 'first generation' units, had been run hard since the day they arrived. By the late 1970s, the newer units, which were assigned to the high priority trains, were too often failing on the road. On occasion, delays due to power problems made us go dead on our hours of service, which added to our frustration.

➻ One Day on the Greenacres Turn

I was set up on the conductors' extra board about seven years after the BN merger. Occasionally I would catch a former NP job that I never ever worked before. This happened one afternoon when I was called off the conductors' extra board to work the Greenacres Turn on duty at 4:00 PM. The name Greenacres Turn never made any sense to me. The job started at Yardley and ran via the NP to Post Falls. It never got anywhere near Greenacres, which was a station on the SC&P that by the time of this story, had long since been abandoned.

I reported for duty at Yardley and found out that my crew was brakeman Forest Markham, who was working the Greenacres Turn as his regular job, and extra board brakeman Danny Packard. Danny was there at the yard office, but Forest was not.

I soon found out that Forest showed up at the roundhouse and put the engine on the train. I remembered the name Forest Markham, but I could not remember where or when I had met him before. Dan and I drove down to our train at the east end of the yard. I got up on the engine with the orders, and to see the head brakeman. I asked Forest why he did not show up at Yardley. He told me that he was the head brakeman. I told him that he was the regular man on the job and he should work the list. Forest told me that he was the permanent head brakeman.

Thank the good Lord the engineer knew where the job was supposed to go and what it was supposed to do, or Danny and I would have been totally lost. The engineer told me that this job switched the lumber mill and the asphalt plant at Hauser, and Louisiana Pacific and Idaho Veneer at Post Falls. Then we would wait for the Coeur d'Alene–Post Falls Turn to arrive, pick up their loads, and give them our empties for the Coeur d'Alene branch.

Switching Post Falls was no problem as I had switched both sides of Post Falls hundreds of times. I was concerned about Hauser. I could plainly see that Danny and I were not going to get any help from Forest. It was still in my mind that I knew Forest, but I could not figure out from where or when. We left Yardley, headed in at Hauser, and cleared the main line. Danny and I walked up to the engine, and there was Forest standing by it. I asked him what tracks were what. He told me that he was the head brakeman and he only worked by sign. I felt the hair on the back of my neck stand up and my blood pressure rise. I said, "You mean to tell me you are the regular man on this job and you have no idea what this job is supposed to do?" Forest's answer was "Yup." "You have no idea what the names of the tracks here at Hauser are?" "Nope."

Danny and I walked the tracks at Hauser, checking the car numbers and looking for them on the switch list to figure out the names of the tracks. With the names of the tracks figured out, Danny and I laid out a plan.

I came back and told Forest what I wanted him to do. I gave him the first three moves and his eyes just went to glass. Then I remembered how I knew Forest. He and I were in the same homeroom in high school, over 25 years earlier. That was his look when a teacher asked Forest a question; his eyes immediately turned to glass. I knew right then that Danny and I were on our own for the rest of the night. We switched the lumber mill, pulling four loads off the lumber dock and two loads off the flatcar track, and left the loads on the run around track to pick up on our return from Post Falls.

We headed for Post Falls with our train, which consisted of cars for Post Falls, and for the lumber mills in and around Coeur d'Alene. At Post Falls we switched Louisiana Pacific and Idaho Veneer. Since the Post Falls to Coeur d'Alene Local was not in sight, we settled in to wait.

About an hour and a half later their headlight appeared. The Post Falls Local stopped on the other side of the crossing ahead of our engine. As Danny and I walked toward the engine, I noticed that all they had was an empty flatcar. Their conductor was John Jolgen, a former Great Northern trainman who worked passenger and as a train baggageman every chance he could until Amtrak took over. I had worked chain gang to Troy, Montana with John when he and I were braking for conductor Larry Hayes. John was never much of a car hand. He showed little ability to plan when it came to switching cars.

I asked John where his train was. John replied, "It's been a hell of a day." I then asked where the empty flatcar was supposed to go. John said that it went to the flat track at Atlas Tie. I asked, "What are you doing with it here? You went right by Atlas." Again John said, "It's been a hell of a day."

Then I realized that John's only brakeman was a recent hire named Debbie. I asked John where his other brakeman was. John replied, "I lost him." I said, "You what?!" Again John said, "I lost him." I asked who his lost brakeman was. When John said "Herman Green," some of the jagged pieces of the puzzle started to fall into place. Herman Green was a former GN switchman who hired out in 1952 and had spent time out at the state mental institution at Medical Lake for a tune-up at least twice.

I said, "OK, what happened?" John explained that somebody driving a car hit their train while they were switching in the Coeur d'Alene yard. The motorist then backed up and took off, and Herman started to chase the car. John said the car turned at the corner with Herman in hot pursuit like a rabid dog, and that was the last time he saw Herman. I asked, "When did this happen?" John said, "This morning about eleven o'clock." I said, "You have not seen him since?" John replied, "Nope." John said he called Trainmaster McElroy and told him about Herman's disappearance. McElroy told John to "do the best you can."

I told John that I could not leave Post Falls until I checked with McElroy, since we obviously would not get any loads out of the Coeur d'Alene area. McElroy told me to leave Post Falls with the loads available, finish the trip by picking up at Hauser, and weighing the loads at Velox. He would have the former NP Coeur d'Alene Local come over tomorrow, which was Saturday, and straighten out the mess.

We put the empties for Coeur d'Alene on the run around track and departed for Hauser with our four loads from Post Falls. At Hauser, we picked up the loads we left there earlier in the trip and contacted the dispatcher. I informed him that we were ready to leave Hauser for Velox and we would get in the clear at Velox by backing in.

We were stuck for about 30 minutes waiting for one eastward train before the dispatcher gave us permission to line out and head for Velox. At Velox, we pulled past the switch, lined the switch for the Velox lead, and backed in. Danny had worked the Velox Local once so he kind of knew where the scale track was. Danny and I put the first car on the scale when the clerk from Yardley showed up to weigh the loads. It did not take long to weigh the loads, reline the air, and make an air test. The dispatcher gave us permission to line out and head for Yardley. At Yardley, we went around the horn and into the 'hell hole,' which was once the part of the yard used by trains going to and from the SP&S. While Forest took the power to the house, Danny and I walked to the yard office where I tied up at 1:30 AM.

I heard later that on Monday, the trainmaster and the road foreman showed up at Post Falls and informed Herman that he was out of service. The previous Friday became Herman's last day on the railroad. He was retired on a medical disability. Working the conductors' extra board during this time was not easy.

Signal Systems

In addition to all of the stations, tracks, and industries, crewmen came to know where all the block signals were. When I started on the railroad in 1960, main line trains were protected by automatic block signals (ABS). Block signals did not and do not convey authority to occupy the main track. Authority to occupy the main track was given by schedule and clearance for scheduled trains, or by train order for extra trains.

Blocks are a segment of track with a signal protecting entry to the segment. Block length varied, based in part on traffic density. Blocks were required to be long enough to allow the heaviest and fastest trains operated on the line to stop from the maximum authorized speed in effect at that location using less than a full service brake application. As a matter of practice, blocks on the Great Northern between Wenatchee and Troy were seldom less than 5,000 or more than 6,500 feet long.

The basic block signal aspects and indications were: red—stop; yellow—approach next signal prepared to stop; and green—clear.

Block signal systems function based on occupancy. If a train or cars are on the track between block signals, the equipment is said to occupy the block. The adjoining rails in each block are bonded to each other. Bonding means that short multi-strand copper wires have been welded to the outside of the rail head to carry electrical current from rail to rail to make the rails a continuous electrical path. The rails are then electrified at low voltage to create an electrical circuit using the two running rails. Equipment in the block 'shunts' the electrical circuit established in the two running rails. The shunt is detected by a relay in the signals at each end of the block, and each relay sets its signal to the red aspect and the stop indication. Assuming the engineer complies with the stop indication, he stops short of the signal at the end of the block and does not collide with the equipment in the block ahead.

Approach signals are wired so that if a block signal displays a stop indication, the next signal that a train approaching the red signal would see displays a yellow aspect. The practice of tying adjacent signals together dates to the very creation of the block signal system. The yellow aspect indicates to the engineer that he needs to slow down enough that he can stop short of the next signal, which is very likely to display the stop indication. A signal displaying an approach indication is referred to as an approach signal. The approach signal concept and language were established with the block signal system. Since any signal may be a stop signal, any signal may also be an approach signal.

The third aspect, green, indication clear, is displayed if there is no occupancy in the immediate block and in the next block. If a clear signal is displayed, the next signal may be approach. The practical effect of this three-aspect signal system is that trains can follow each other at track speed with as few as two unoccupied blocks between them. Since there is only one approach signal between a clear signal and a stop signal, it is vital to see every signal, and vital that approach signals are respected as if the next signal is a stop signal.

The block signal system also provides protection against broken rails because a broken rail shunts the track circuit and sets the signals at each end of the block to the stop indication. In a similar fashion, slide fences are tied into the signal system so that if a rock or a slide breaks the fence, the block signals at each end of the block that the fence is in will display the stop indication.

Most railroads, Great Northern included, designed their block signal system so that when a train passed the leaving signal of a station where trains could meet or pass, it set all of the signals that an opposing train would see as far as the next station to 'stop.' This feature, known as APB or 'Absolute-Permissive Block,' gave additional protection for trains moving in opposite directions. The leaving signals at each station were 'absolute,' meaning that a train could not pass an absolute signal displaying stop without permission from the dispatcher. These absolute signals did not have a number plate mounted on the signal mast.

To allow trains to follow each other reasonably closely yet not unnecessarily limit line capacity, signals behind a train cleared up as the train moved out of the block. This is the permissive part of ABP. Intermediate block signals did and do have a number plate mounted on the signal mast.[2] The number is the mile post location down to the tenths of a mile, such as 1970.4. Eastward block signals have an even last digit, while westward signals have an odd last digit. The number plate indicates that the signal was not absolute. It could be passed after stopping for it. Speed of movement to the next signal was limited to restricted speed.

Knowing where all the block signals are located was very important with the three-aspect system, because on a foggy or snowy night if you do not know the location of the block signals, you could miss an approach signal. This could be disastrous since your train would come to the stop signal at track speed, be unable to stop short of it, and be likely to collide with the equipment in the block.

The practice of 'running on blocks' always made me very uneasy. 'Running on blocks' meant that a train was following another train so closely that the crew of the following train would see a yellow block signal go green before they went by the signal. Running on the blocks of a train ahead could be a trap because crews would get used to the block going green, or 'clearing up,' just before they went by it. If the block did not clear, and the crew assumed that it would have if they had been just a bit later, the next thing they knew they could be looking at a red block, and the crew would not be able to get their train stopped before they passed that red block. If a crew was unlucky in addition to being careless, they would find the caboose of the train ahead stopped just past the red block. In this case, a collision was likely. The crew that failed to approach a red block prepared to stop was in trouble regardless of the extent of death, injuries, and wrecked equipment.

Running on blocks always made me feel that my engineer was like a hound chasing a wounded fox, but we would suffer if we caught the train we were chasing. Some engineers simply backed off, while others would crowd the blocks to the point that I had to encourage them to back off. Most took the hint.

On a line equipped with ABS, four block signals are associated with a siding. The signals are arranged in two pairs, each pair located outside the points of the siding switches. One pair of block signals is located at the west end of the siding, west of the siding switch, and the other pair is located at the east end, east of the siding switch. One signal of each pair faces east; the other faces west. Trains leaving the station from either the siding or the main track are required to respect the main track signal that they can see. If the signal is anything other than clear, the crew is to comply with the main track signal until they encounter the next signal.

The Spokane Division included three significant segments of double track: between Lamona and Bluestem, between the east end of the Spokane River Bridge (bridge 274) near Fort Wright, and the west end of Hillyard, and between the east end of Hillyard and Dean. By definition, there is a current of traffic on double track, eastward on one track and westward on the other. The usual convention in North America is to run to the right, and our segments of double track were set up that way.

Since there is a current of traffic, each track in double track territory is signaled in only one direction, for the current of traffic. The converse is also true; double track is not signaled for movements in the 'wrong' direction, except for an approach block signal located about a mile before the 'home' signal which was located immediately short of the switch to enter single track. That lack of intermediate signals means that speed of a movement against the current of traffic is limited to 49 MPH for freight trains and 59 MPH for passenger trains by federal rule. Between Fort Wright and Hillyard, the double track was within yard limits, and speed limits were lower than 49 MPH.

The switch and signals at east end of the Spokane River Bridge were controlled by the manual interlocker at Fort Wright, those at the west and the east end of Hillyard were controlled by the operator at Hillyard, and Dean was controlled by the operator at Dean. The operators routinely lined trains for movement with the current of traffic. If a move was to be made against the current of traffic, the dispatcher would instruct one operator to route the train on the 'wrong' main after he had instructed the other operator to place a block on his apparatus to prevent him from lining an opposing train into the same track. I have run around an eastward train sitting at the signal on the eastward main to get into Hillyard Yard by running against the current of traffic from Spokane Yard to Hillyard. Trains left the interlocking limits by the authority of a controlled signal.

The switches at both Bluestem and Lamona were controlled by automatic interlockers which automatically lined the switch at the end of double track for movement from single to double track with the current of traffic, and lined movements off either double track onto single track. The automatic interlocker also set the signals associated with each switch to display the appropriate aspects.

If use of the wrong main was planned between Bluestem and Lamona, for example, if track work was being done on one of the main tracks, an extra board brakeman or conductor would be called to work as switch tender. They would line the switches as directed by the dispatcher, and advise him when a train passed them.

At Bluestem and Lamona only, if no switch tender had been called and a train was directed to enter the double track for a movement against the current of traffic, the crew had to stop short of the switch to enter double track, take the switch out of power, hand line the main track switch for the 'wrong' main, occupy the track circuit at the switch, and then return the switch to power, which restored control of the switch to the automatic interlocker.

Between Bluestem and Lamona, in the early days, shortly after I hired out as I recall, crewmen were instructed to run against the current of traffic, and that was it. Later, a train order was required to run against the current of traffic, and later still, trainmen were required to copy a Track Permit form.

Double track is NOT the same as two main tracks. Two main tracks, by definition, are each fully signaled for movement in both directions. As a matter of practice, two main track territory is generally also Centralized Traffic

ABS signals at the west end of Stryker, Montana. Note that both block signals are beyond the switch points as viewed from the siding. PHOTO BY WILLIAM MCGINLEY.

CTC signals at the west end of Malaga, Washington. Note that the eastward signal is beyond the switch points as in ABS territory, *but* both leaving signals are well inside the switch as viewed from the siding or main track. PHOTO BY MIKE BARTENSTEIN.

Control (CTC) territory. The former NP line between Seattle and Vancouver, Washington is an example of a double track territory that was upgraded to two main tracks by adding signals in the 'reverse' direction on both tracks, and CTC control of switches and crossovers.

Centralized Traffic Control is a particular type of block signal system featuring signals controlled by the dispatcher. Within Centralized Traffic Control (CTC) limits, authority to occupy the main track is given by a controlled signal indication more favorable than stop. By definition, a controlled signal is one controlled by the train dispatcher. The defining feature of Centralized Traffic Control is that authority to occupy the main track or controlled siding is given by an indication more favorable than stop from a controlled signal.

Controlled signals are also absolute signals. An absolute signal is absolute in that a train or engine absolutely may NOT pass it when it displays a stop indication without the permission of the train dispatcher. This is different than block signals. Block signal rules generally provide a way to pass a block signal displaying stop without any involvement of the dispatcher. Within CTC territory, the signals between controlled signals are automatic block signals. Absolute signals are marked differently than block signals so that they can be distinguished on sight. Absolute signals do not have a number plate mounted on the signal mast.

The first CTC I saw was between Switch One at the east end of Appleyard, and Columbia River. This was placed in service in the spring of 1966 and shows in the

Employee Timetable issued April 25, 1966. CTC was extended to Ephrata about 1967.

When CTC is installed on a line that already has ABS, the four block signals associated with the siding are removed, and six absolute signals are installed, three on each end.

At a CTC controlled siding, the first absolute signal an approaching train will encounter is located at the point immediately before the train would pass over the switch that will route it to either the main track or to the siding. Two such signals are located outside of the points of the siding switches, one at the west end and one at the east end. These signals indicate whether the approaching train is to take the siding or hold the main track at the station. The top head applies to the main track; the bottom head is for the siding.

Two other signals are located inside the fouling point of the switch at each end of the siding. One signal is for the main track; the other is for the siding. These are the 'leaving' signals. Each leaving signal has one head. A leaving signal displaying an aspect more favorable than stop conveys authority to occupy the main track to the next absolute signal. A train leaves the siding, or proceeds on the main track, on the authority of the leaving signals. The other end of the siding is a mirror image.

The train that is to hold the main track for a meet will get a yellow on the top head and dark, or red, on the bottom head, at the entering signal. The train that is to head into the siding will get a red top head. The bottom signal head will be a lunar white if the train is to head in to a non-bonded siding, or yellow if the siding is bonded.

When a line segment was converted from ABS to CTC, the intermediate block signals between controlled sidings were generally left alone and continued to function as they did previously. If greater braking distance was required, the approach signals to the absolute signals at each end of the siding were relocated. In some cases, all of the signals between two adjacent sidings were relocated to provide longer blocks between signals.

CTC introduced the lunar aspect to the Great Northern signal system. A lunar aspect was a restricted speed signal. A lunar aspect meant that your movement was leaving CTC and proceeding into non-block signal territory. Great Northern practice was to not bond their CTC sidings, and the lunar aspect was a reminder that the siding was not bonded. The lunar aspect was a lunar light under the red signal light. These lights were in two different signal heads. A lunar aspect was also used when entering a yard from CTC territory. Under the rules applicable in non-block territory, trains proceeding on a lunar signal moved at restricted speed, being prepared to stop short of trains or engines and/or men and equipment on that track. Later versions of the restricted speed rule required that any movement be able to stop in one half the range of our vision. In a hard snow or in fog conditions, any speed was greater than this definition of restricted speed.

The Great Northern 'route signals' was a very easy system to learn. Each signal told the crewmen what route your train was going to take. The Northern Pacific's CTC signal system was a much more complicated speed-based system.

Northern Pacific's CTC signal system featured a different speed associated with each different signal indication. Several speeds were specified in the NP system, each with a different signal aspect, name, and indication. The 'aspect' is the appearance of a signal as viewed by an observer in the cab. Each aspect is given a name, such as "Proceed." The 'indication,' that is, what a train crew is being told to do, is spelled out separately for each aspect and name.

Most NP approach signal masts mounted two or three heads, which made the NP system more costly to install and maintain. For trains entering a siding or crossing from one track to another, NP indications specified the turnout speed over related switches.

The NP signal system included 22 different aspects, names, and indications. In each case, an engineer was expected to react differently. Twelve NP aspects used the word "approach" within a longer name. The GN used the word "approach" only five times. Ten of the NP aspects used the word "clear" in their name, and at least two of those ten aspects were identical as viewed from a locomotive. If that wasn't enough, two of those 22 NP names used both "clear" and "approach" within a single name, whereas GN used no such combination whatever. The GN used the word "clear" two times, and the engineer's response to both indications was the same. The NP signal system included seven different combinations of "flashing" signal colors, whereas GN had only three.

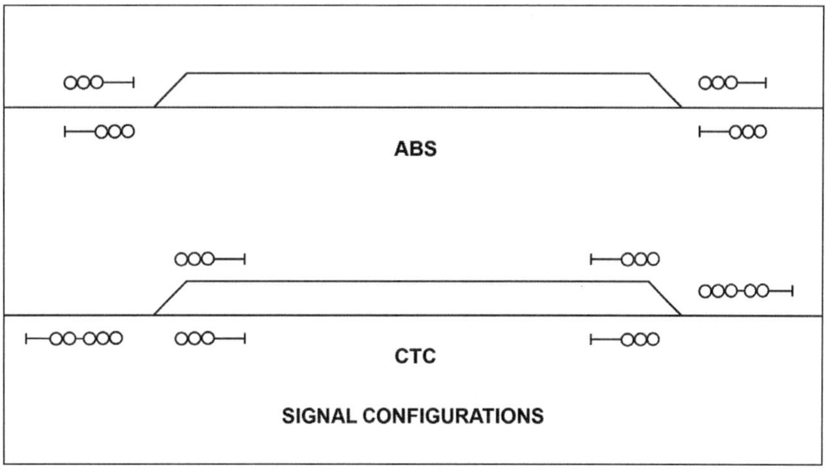

The GN system was much easier to commit to memory than the NP system.

When the merger occurred, everybody was required to learn the CTC signal system of the other railroad. GN and SP&S conductors and engineers were expected to be instantly familiar with a system much more difficult than their own. The SP&S men had no CTC territory. Their block signal rules were identical with the NP but used only three aspects: red, yellow, and green.

Fortunately, management anticipated confusion for employees of each road unfamiliar with the signal system of the other. They provided everyone an Automatic Block/CTC signal 'cheat sheet' with the Great Northern on one side and the Northern Pacific on the other side. Even with the cheat sheet, the NP system was difficult. I was glad to have the cheat sheet.

I remember my first trip to Paradise, Montana on the former Northern Pacific. Well, I'm sitting there looking at my cheat sheet, and I looked over at my engineer, a former NP engineer who I had met just 30 minutes earlier, and he is looking at the same cheat sheet! I said to him, "I thought you were former NP." He said that he was. I asked him why he was studying the cheat sheet on NP signals. He told me he "gets a little confused once in a while" on the signals. I said to myself, "This cannot be good." I did not sleep well that night in Paradise knowing that I would have to work back to Spokane with this engineer. It was a good thing that I brought enough antacid with me to cover the round trip. For quite some time on a trip involving the former Northern Pacific CTC signals I always questioned, "Am I reading that signal right?"

As the cars in manifest trains became heavier, and with the coming of even heavier loaded unit grain and coal trains, the stopping distance of trains lengthened. The three aspect block signal system became inadequate to stop trains safely in the prescribed distance.

The Great Northern, like most railroads, modified their block signal system by adding the approach medium signal indication, which is a flashing yellow aspect. An approach medium block signal meant that a train was required to slow to 35 MPH before any part of the train passed the next block signal. When a train passed an approach medium, the most restricting the next signal can be is a solid yellow, or approach. After passing the yellow approach block, any train was required to be prepared to stop before any part of our train passed the next signal, which was very likely to be red. If your move failed to stop short of the signal, you should expect an invitation to an investigation. Worse, you could have a caboose in your lap.

Adding the approach medium aspect gave the engineer an extra block length of space and the time to safely stop the train at a red block or absolute signal. The extra space was certainly required on heavy grain and coal trains. When the approach medium aspect was added, it was added to all block signals, not just to those near sidings.

I remember one trip to Wenatchee on a grain train with 104 covered hoppers loaded with wheat weighing 13,520 tons. It was winter. According to the talking hotbox and dragging equipment detector west of Odessa, the ambient temperature was about five below zero. The next block signal was flashing yellow, approach medium. I was in the second unit, which was facing west. My engineer, Denny Douville, immediately set some air to start to burn the ice off the brake shoes and heat up the composition brake shoes. Composition brake shoes work better when they are warm than when they are cold. At the same time, Denny was still using the throttle on the engines pulling the train to keep the train stretched tight against the air brakes applied on the train, a technique called power braking. Power braking is used to keep the slack stretched during a brake application or to control both speed and slack while traversing undulating territory. Power braking resulted in fewer slack run-ins and run-outs within the train, and gave the crew in the caboose as stable a ride as possible. Power braking was eventually forbidden by the company as it wears out brake shoes and uses more fuel than dynamic braking. The change in braking practices occurred while there were still men in the caboose.

By the time Denny went by the yellow approach block, our speed was down to 25 MPH, 10 MPH below the maximum allowed speed of 35 MPH. Approaching the east switch at Gibson, Denny dropped the train down to about 10 MPH. He and I could see that the signal at the east end of Gibson was double red: absolute stop. With about 20 car lengths to go to the double red signal, Denny set more air and the train slowed to about 5 MPH. Denny set some more air, and the train slowed down to the point that the speedometer read zero, but the train was still moving. Denny dumped the air, which put the train into emergency, but it still kept moving.

At this point I was getting really nervous. I could see Denny in the lead engine in the light of the double red signal, and he was getting a little jumpy. I was watching the ground slide by in the glow of the step light, as we slowly moved toward the double red signal. I suddenly realized that I was unconsciously shoving my feet against the cab heater mounted against the wall under the front window so hard that my legs began to shake, as if my efforts were going to help us get stopped. I saw by the air gauges that Denny was applying the engine brakes to their maximum. He was sanding the rail, but the train still kept moving with the speedometer reading zero. The whole crew was wondering if it was ever going to stop. It seemed like we went forever in slow motion before the train finally stopped just short of the insulated joint at the double red block. When my hand quit shaking, I picked up the hand set on the radio and said "Whew." After a long pause, Denny replied, "Amen."

About this time, the absolute signal changed to lunar under red, so Denny released the air and started to recharge the train. It took about 20 minutes before he had restored enough air on the rear end of the train that he could be sure the brakes released, and begin to pull very slowly into the siding at Gibson. We spent all that time thinking about what just happened and wondering if the same thing would happen at the west end of Gibson.

About this time the eastward train called us to determine our location. Denny told them that he was just starting to pull into the siding at Gibson, and he would be a while getting in the clear because this grain train did not like to stop. The eastbound crew said, "We understand, take all the time you want. We will start to slow down right now." As our train finally cleared the east end of Gibson, the east bound was just coming up to the west switch when they said that they got a clear signal. They rambled by us as Denny moved us slowly down the siding. The signal to leave the siding at the west end of Gibson was green. All of the crewmen agreed later that they were sure glad that Denny did not have to stop that bad boy at the west end of Gibson.

Some approach signals are less than a mile to the next signal. These short approaches do not leave engineers much time to slow the train down enough to be prepared to stop at the next signal. One particularly nasty example is the westward approach to the approach signal at Lamona after CTC was installed. The end of double track at Lamona is located at the bottom of a descending grade westward.

The original track design involved eastward trains taking the diverging route onto the double track. The turnout speed restriction limited train speed for ascending eastward trains, which slowed every train at a location where it was difficult to impossible for a freight train to recover lost speed.

When CTC was installed, the switch was moved eastward a bit and the switch reversed so that eastward trains took the straight side of the turnout. Westward trains now faced a turnout speed restriction, but it did not hurt them much since they were on a down grade where they could resume speed with no difficulty. This was a wise change.

Problems could occur if a westward train was moving toward the end of double track and the westward controlled signal at Lamona displayed red or stop. The approach signal would be yellow, or approach, as it should be, and the signal west of the approach signal would display a flashing yellow, or approach medium. This signal was only 3,500 feet from the approach signal, so if a train came to the approach medium signal at track speed on the descending grade, it was necessary to quickly make a hard brake application to be able to stop at the controlled signal. Compounding the situation, moving the switch about 600 feet to the east limited view of the absolute signal to about 300 feet, which left no margin for error. The situation westward at Lamona is not good.

After the merger, all new CTC installations were of the GN design, except that sidings continued to be bonded on the former NP lines. Where the siding is bonded, the bottom head of the absolute signal displays yellow if the train is to head in and the siding is clear. If the siding is not clear, the bottom head displays red. In addition, the Burlington Northern replaced the NP system with the GN system over the course of several years as funds were made available.

The Great Northern was very good about informing the work force about changes in track arrangements, track additions or removals, new car restrictions, and new tools, including switches or any equipment that a crewman might encounter. I remember when the Great Northern was about to install CTC, every trainman, switchman, and engineer was taught how to operate a dual control switch. The company mounted a dual control switch to the floor of an old heavyweight baggage car and all employees were required to attend a short class on how to throw the switch and actually take the switch off of power and hand throw the switch. After the BN merger, there were times that I came into Yardley to find some kind of new switch. I would say to myself, "OK, what is the magic trick for this new switch?" Under the Great Northern, a bulletin would have been posted on this new switch, its location, and instructions about how to work it before the switch was installed.

Signal Problems

I was working west end chain gang between Yardley and Wenatchee. Engineer Ron Blank and I were called for the manifest train out of Wenatchee at about 1:00 AM. By the time we were ready to leave, the westward Empire Builder arrived, avoiding that meet. We were a heavy train and worked our way toward Spokane as fast as the power allowed. This was one of the few trips that we did not meet a train between Wenatchee and Spokane. About 6:00 AM, as we proceeded down the hill east of Lyons and rounded the curve while passing through the freezing heavy fog, the approach block to Latah Jct. showed lunar (white) over red, which was an improper signal aspect. The signal was a two-headed searchlight style. The top head could display red, yellow, or green, while the bottom head always showed red.

I told Ron to stop, but he kept going. Ron, who had been a road foreman for the BN, said, "They will just call us liars." I told Ron, "Either you stop or I will stop the train by putting the train into emergency." Ron did stop, but by this time we were about one mile past the signal. I called the dispatcher and informed him of the condition, and was told to sit still and don't move until further advised.

We waited about two hours before the road foreman showed up and interrogated us. The first two questions out of his mouth were, "Do I need to drug test you two?" and "Are you sure that is the aspect you saw?" I stood my ground, as he was implying that we were lying. While this was going on, the signal maintainers were checking out the problem. At 12 noon, they decided to have us proceed to Yardley as we were going to be dead on our hours of service at 1:00 PM.

For about a month I questioned this road foreman about this incident. He got to the point where he would duck out to avoid me if he saw me coming. I never did get an answer and heard later they thought we made the event up. Later I heard that the excuse was that a mouse chewed a signal wire.

Searchlight signals have one bulb, and they display

different aspects by rotating each color lens ahead of the fixed bulb. That morning, the entire signal was covered with heavy frost. My personal opinion is that the freezing fog froze the rotating disc that holds the lenses in a position where none of the colored lenses were between the bulb and our eyes.

Another morning I was called for a train to Wenatchee around 6:00 AM. Engineer Dick McCarter and conductor Dick Perkins were called behind us for Wenatchee with the Z train, which was a hot train. The line was still ABS from Latah Jct. to the end of the double track at Lamona. It was not long before the Z train was getting close to us. The CTC dispatcher lined us into Odessa to let the Z train by, and we soon followed them out of Odessa on a yellow signal. As we were approaching Ephrata close behind the Z train, we heard on the radio the detector at Winchester start to talk, and then someone asked, "Who are you and where are you?" Then we heard Dick Torbenson respond, "We are 82's train approaching Naylor."

Engineer McCarter put his train into emergency and managed to get stopped short of the absolute signal at the west end of Naylor. Engineer Torbenson soon stopped short of the signal at the west end of Naylor, and three signal maintainers were there trying to figure out what was wrong. After about two hours, they let Torbenson pull into the siding at Naylor and let the Z train crew hand line themselves by the west switch at Naylor. When the Z train cleared the west end of Naylor, we got a yellow approach signal at the east end and could move down the main line to the west end of Naylor. We stopped at a red block at the east end of Naylor and also had to hand line ourselves main line to main line at the west end of Naylor.

I found out later that when Perkins and McCarter approached the east end of Naylor they had a yellow approach signal, and began to slow down. As they rounded the curve at the west end of Naylor, they could see the signal was green, so the engineer released brakes, and as soon as he did, the signal turned red in their faces. Within seconds of the signal going red, Perkins and McCarter heard the detector at Winchester go off; they knew it was not because of them, and they knew that we were behind them. That is when they asked, "Who are you and where are you?"

None of us ever did hear what the problem was. I suppose a mouse chewed a wire.

One day a few years after the BNSF merger we went to work at Bonners Ferry with the Georgetown slot train which was full of dirt, rocks and vegetation from the day before. After I received my clearance and track orders, I told Dennis Giles, the Boyer East dispatcher, who participated in the Maintenance of Way conference call, that our first move of the day would be to unload our train from Main 1 at Bonners Ferry between the wye switches.

We moved west on Main 1 to a point between wye switches, and the track hoe operator started unloading the material from the trough. About 15 minutes later, Dennis called me on the radio and said, "Jack, where exactly are you?" This question from a dispatcher who should see your train on his control screen always increased my heart rate. Several times when I was working west end chain gang between Yardley and Wenatchee, the dispatcher called to ask me where I was. This question is especially troubling when you are running at 60 MPH. I told Dennis that the train was about five car lengths west of the east wye switch at Bonners Ferry on Main 1.

Dennis replied, "You were there on my screen earlier but now you have completely disappeared off my screen." Dennis instructed us to "Sit right there and do not move." I responded that I would "sit still until you tell us we can move."

Dennis called the signal maintainers and told them to contact him on the channel that he used to talk with Maintenance of Way and signal maintenance personnel. When I was on a work train, I monitored this channel on my portable radio. Dennis told the signal maintainers that my train had disappeared off his screen. The train sat there for four hours while the signal maintainers ran test after test. Dennis also called the computer programmers, who were located upstairs from him. Later I was told that there was a glitch in the in the computer program. Computer program errors in the safety critical CTC system do not inspire confidence.

➻ Red Dog Concentrate

During the 1980s, Teck Corporation, a Canadian mining company, discovered a huge deposit of high-grade lead, silver, and rare earth metals ore in northern Alaska, about 225 miles North-Northeast of Nome and about 55 miles from the Chukchi Sea. Teck planned to build a concentrator in Alaska, but they needed a place to smelt the concentrate since there was no smelter in Alaska. The ASARCO smelter on the Tacoma waterfront shut down in 1985 due to environmental concerns. In 1986, Teck and others bought all the stock of Cominco, which owned and operated the Trail, British Columbia, smelter, from CP Limited, the holding company that also owned CP Rail. Teck planned to move the concentrate from Alaska to Vancouver, British Columbia by barge and to ship it by rail to their smelter at Trail. Projected volume was 6,000 tons per week.

The only route available to CP Rail was very circuitous, utilizing its main line for the 473 miles between Vancouver and Golden, then 142 miles to Fort Steele, the junction with the Crowsnest Pass line. From Fort Steele west to Castlegar is 178 miles; Castlegar to Trail is 18 miles, for a total of 809 miles one way.

By 1986, the CPR had been handling unit trains of coal from the Crowsnest coal fields centered on Sparwood, about 75 miles east of Fort Steele, to the export terminal at Roberts Bank, for twenty years. From Sparwood to Fort Steele the coal route is gently descending. From Fort Steele to Golden, the line has ascending and descending grades of not more than .6%. Between Golden and Revelstoke, the CPR crosses the Selkirk range at Rogers Pass. The ascending grade against the loads was 2.2% and the descending grade was 2.0%. There were short but steep ascending grades of not more than 1.9% over Notch Hill and the Gold Range, both between Revelstoke and Chase.

In the mid-1980s the CPR used radio-controlled units over every mile of line traversed by its 11,500-ton coal trains. CPR used two SD 40 units on the point plus two cut in behind the 36th car, or behind 40% of the tonnage, over the less than 1% grade territory on both sides of the Selkirk Mountains. In steady state ascending conditions, this arrangement resulted in slack stretched throughout the train. At Golden, the junction with the main line, two units were added to the head end of loaded trains, making six units deployed as four plus two. At Beavermouth, four manually controlled helper units were added for the short but steep climb over Rogers Pass. The helpers cut out at the summit and returned to Beavermouth. Two head end units were cut off at Chase, the western foot of Notch Hill. These units were accumulated and returned to Golden as light engine moves.[3]

Based on CPR practice with the coal trains, we can accurately project how they would have handled 6,000 net tons of concentrate per week. We assume CPR would have assigned dedicated cars to concentrate service to avoid cross contamination rather than utilizing empty coal cars in backhaul service. A unit train of 60 100-ton capacity concentrate cars, with caboose, would total 7,890 trailing tons; say 8,000 tons, well within the CPR's capacity.

The concentrate route was the reverse of the coal route from Vancouver to Fort Steele. At Fort Steele, concentrate trains turned west and faced a 1% ascending grade to Cranbrook. From Cranbrook to Castlegar, the CPR faced a short climb of 1.25% against the loads and a longer descent, also of 1.25%. The branch line to Trail begins at Castlegar. From Castlegar to the Trail smelter, the CPR faced a short climb against the loads, about one mile of 3.6% descending grade, and curves of up to 20 degrees.

Our 8,000 ton concentrate train would require four SD 40 type locomotives on ruling grades of 1% or less; that is from Vancouver to Chase. From Chase to Golden seven SD 40 type units would have been required on an 8,000-ton train to climb the 2% ascending grade over Rogers Pass and for the 2.2% descent to Beavermouth. From Golden to Cranbrook, four units would have been sufficient, but beyond Cranbrook the 1.25% grade required five units. The segment beyond Fort Steele differs from the coal train route, and beyond Cranbrook requires more power than the coal trains.

Based on coal train practice, CPR would have used an in-train slave with power deployed as two units on the point plus three cut in behind 50% of the tonnage between Vancouver and Trail. Between Chase and Golden, the seven unit total would be attained by adding two units to the point, exactly like the coal trains, and utilizing power that would have otherwise been run light back to Golden.

Cycle time for unit coal trains over the 1,406-mile round trip to Sparwood was typically 82 hours, an average speed of 18.25 MPH based on 77 hours of travel and five hours for loading and unloading combined. During the summer track work season, coal train cycle times of 92 hours or more were common.[4]

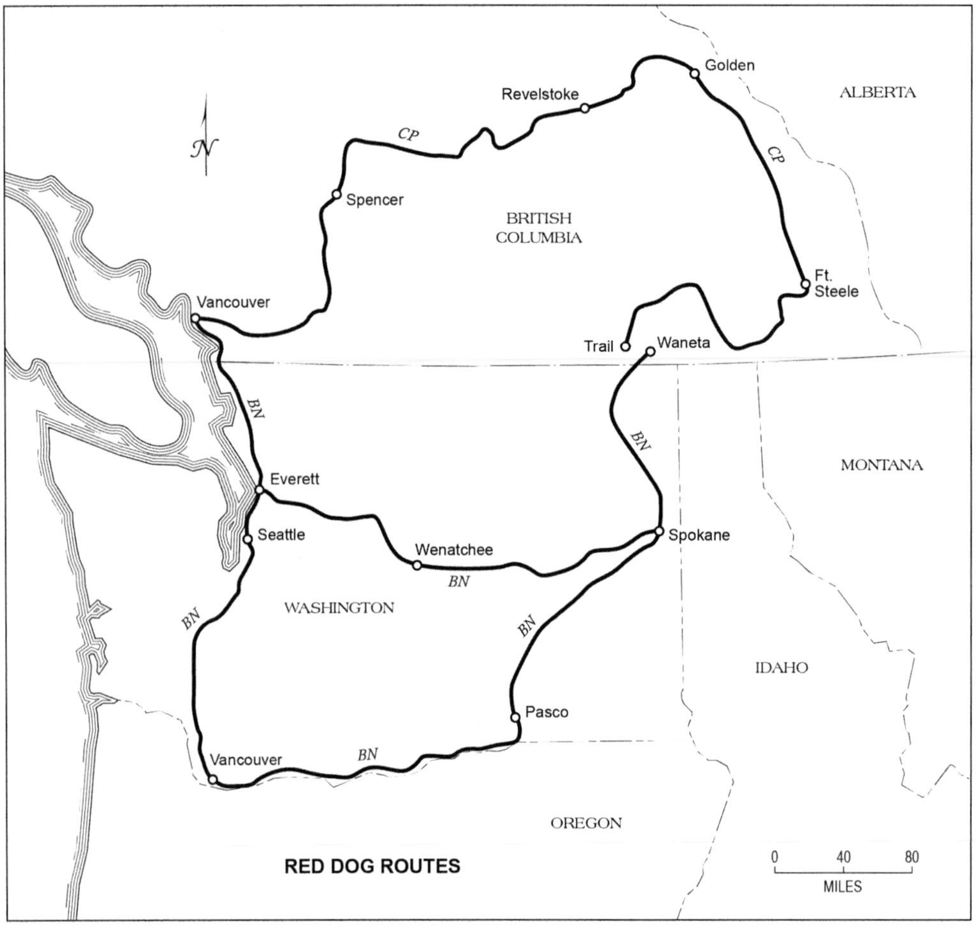

Travel time of the concentrate trains over their 1,618-mile round trip would have been 88 hours at 18.25 MPH. Since the line between Cranbrook and Trail was a bit slower than the rest of the route, assume six hours additional travel time on this slower segment. Loading and unloading of concentrate would have been slower than for coal, so estimate 12 hours for loading and unloading combined. This gives a total projected cycle time of 106 hours, or just short of five days. One set of equipment would have been sufficient for one train per week. CP Rail faced very few track quality issues on this route.

Burlington Northern bid on the contract to move the concentrate, but, since Canadian Pacific had owned the smelter at Trail for decades, BN management did not think they would get the bid. BN train and engine crews at Spokane heard that CP Rail decided not to bid on moving the concentrate because of the excessive mileage of its route, the steep grades between Vancouver and Trail, and the several helpers they would need to move the concentrate.

Burlington Northern faced no grades exceeding 1% using the long mile route via Vancouver, Washington, which would have been the route selected for unit train operations. It avoided the intermodal trains that filled Stevens Pass to capacity and avoided using helpers on a once a week unit train, a poor use of helper power.

Mileage from Vancouver, British Columbia to Waneta via Vancouver, Washington is: Vancouver, British Columbia, to Seattle, 156 miles, then 546 miles from Seattle to Yardley via Vancouver, Washington, plus 140 miles from Yardley to Waneta, for a grand total of 842 miles, compared to 809 miles on the Canadian Pacific via Golden. Due to its lesser grades, not over 1% against the loads, BN would have been able to handle an

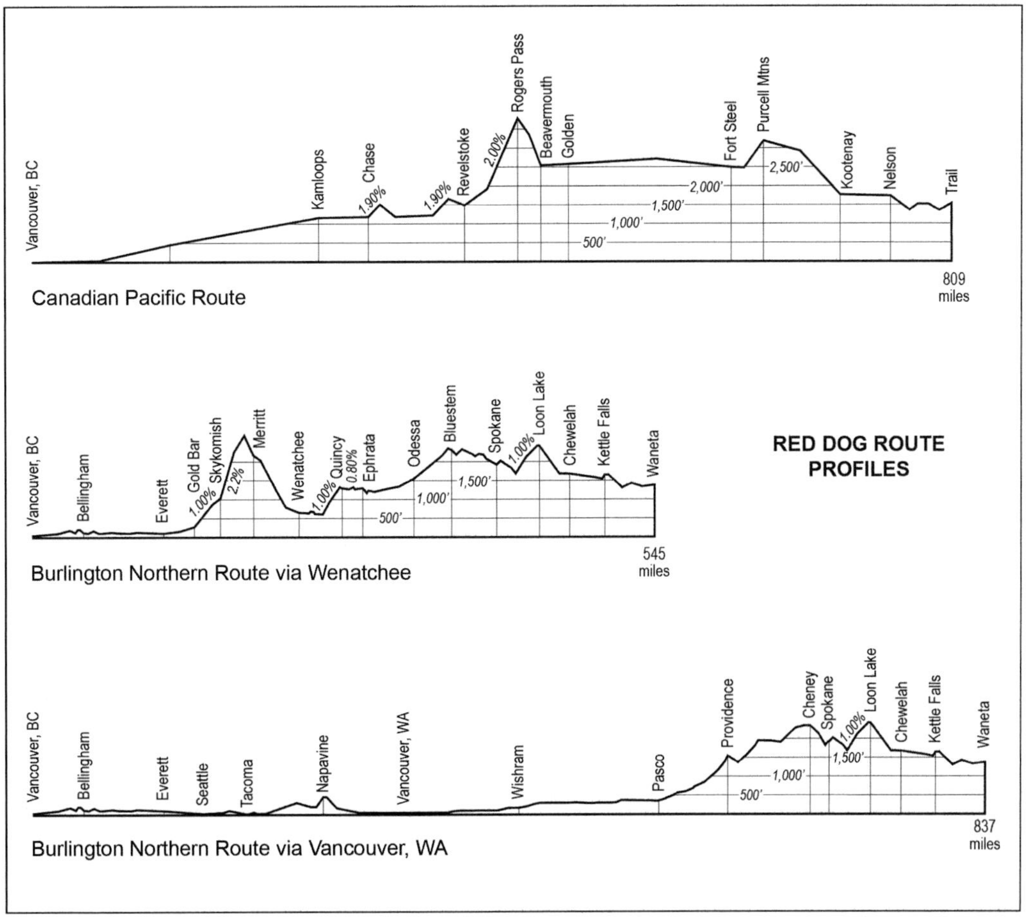

8,000-ton unit train with three SD 40 units, compared to five and seven for CP. CP Rail's mileage was a bit less than ours was, and their eastward helpers would have been free, even if the fuel was not.

BN proposed to transload the concentrate to trucks at Waneta. This avoided both the bad track and the mountain grades between Waneta and Troup Junction, and avoided having to deal with CP Rail between Nelson and Trail. It took advantage of the short, 10 miles long, mostly river grade public highway between Waneta and Trail. Teck agreed that transloading the concentrate at Waneta was a good plan. The competitive spirit of James J. Hill was alive and well at the Burlington Northern in the case of Red Dog concentrates.

Burlington Northern got the traffic and a big investment problem: virtually every foot of track between Dean and Waneta, 126 miles, needed to be upgraded. The track was in very poor shape. The ties were old and rotten; the ballast was round river rock and sand. The rail was lightweight and it was all jointed. Between Dean and Valley, 42 miles, the rail was 110 pounds per yard in 39-foot lengths and at least 50 years old. The rest of the line was 85 and 90-pound rail rolled in the 1900s and early 1910s, except for 19 miles of 80-pound rail in 30-foot lengths that dated to the 1890s. None of this rail was capable of safely supporting an additional 8,000 tons per week in 131 gross ton cars for any length of time.

The company invested tens of millions of dollars in track improvements to handle this traffic safely and reliably. Work to upgrade the route began in 1989 and continued until the first shipment of Red Dog concentrate was made in August of 1990. Teck paid to build new highway bridges from the Quirk reload center 1.6 miles beyond Waneta to the Trail smelter since the existing

A block of Red Dog ore at Yardley. Cars are equipped with white fiberglass covers to prevent concentrates from blowing out of the cars. The two dark vertical items on each side are lifting lugs that allow covers to be lifted on to and off of the cars. Each cover has four lugs. PHOTO BY JOHN LANGLOT.

bridges did not have a high enough tonnage rating to support the heavy loaded concentrate trucks that Teck wanted to operate to the smelter.

BN supplied 50-foot-long flat bottom gondolas with bolt on fiberglass covers to move the Red Dog concentrate in cuts of 15 to 20 cars three or four days per week in manifest train service, rather than in unit trains. Red Dog concentrate now arrives at Yardley on the H-EVEGAL manifest train via Stevens Pass, the shortest available route. The route is Vancouver, British Columbia to Everett 123 miles, 296 miles from Everett to Yardley via Wenatchee, plus 142 miles from Yardley to Quirk, a total of 561 miles. Shipments of Red Dog concentrate continue to this day.

The Appleyard Explosion

At 12:32 PM on August 6, 1974, tank car DUPX 16009 carrying 99,600 pounds of monomethylamine nitrate, standing five cars west of the east end of a cut of 15 cars, sitting in track 12 at Appleyard, near Wenatchee, Washington, detonated. The explosion created a cone-shaped crater 25 feet deep and 75 feet across stripping the rail from the ties, which remained embedded in the ground of the cratered surface. The explosion killed one railroad employee and is known to have killed one transient. There were 67 injured, the vast majority of whom were members of the general public. The blast destroyed 66 freight cars and damaged 101 more. Damage to railroad and non-railroad property was estimated at about $6,000,000.

Author Mac McCulloch was then employed as a District Inspector by the Bureau of Explosives, which was part the Association of American Railroads headquartered in Washington, D.C. Mac was performing an inspection at the Union Pacific agency in Tekoa, Washington at the time of the event. His fiancée, who had been waiting in the car with the radio on, told him when he came out of the depot at 2:15 PM that there had been a big explosion in the rail yard at Wenatchee and he had to get there quickly. She drove the 196 miles to Wenatchee in less than three hours, arriving at the yard office at 5:30 PM, after one stop at Oakesdale to call the BN Chief Dispatcher in Spokane on the company wire, and one stop to accept a speeding ticket on South Wenatchee Avenue, which was posted at a very low 25 MPH.

The scene at Appleyard was astounding. Rail cars on adjacent tracks had been thrown into a twisted pile of steel about 20 feet high beginning about 75 feet from the center of the crater. Parts of the tank car had been thrown up to one and a half miles away, but most were within 4,000 feet. Tank pieces landing on the hill above the yard and across the Columbia River in East Wenatchee, at least half a mile away, were hot enough to ignite grass fires on contact. The explosion ignited a large fire in the body of the yard. August is wildfire season in the Wenatchee area, and airplanes equipped to drop borate and water fire retardant solution were on standby at Pangborn Memorial Airport in East Wenatchee. The borate bombers were called in and they dropped fire retardant on the fires on the hill above Appleyard, across the Columbia River in East Wenatchee, and in Appleyard.

The blast badly damaged Columbia Ice & Cold Storage Plant 3, which was the ice house, and the separate heater house. The blast also destroyed the east end of the icing platform. These ice facilities were all soon removed. The former railroad crew hotel across the Malaga Highway was destroyed. The steel frame brick Electric Shop was still standing, but so shattered that it had to be removed.

At Appleyard, Mac encountered Senior Inspector Ev Coughlan, who had been dispatched to Wenatchee by his boss, Robert M. Graziano, Director of the Bureau of Explosives, since Graziano could not immediately contact Mac. That evening they sought out and introduced themselves to the railroad officials on hand, who were under the leadership of Mr. R. A. Beulke, Vice President–Seattle Region, of BN Inc., who welcomed them to the investigation. Mac and Ev reported developments to Bureau headquarters. The next morning, Mr. Graziano instructed Mac, who had been with the Bureau of Explosives for less than a year, to work with Ev to investigate the incident.

August 7 was spent meeting with the railroad, inspecting the few other cars containing hazardous materials on hand at Appleyard, looking for tank car fragments, obtaining waybill and train consist information, meeting Mr. C. W. Schultz the Bureau's Chief Chemist, and participating in a late meeting with the National Transportation Safety Board (NTSB), who declared that there would be only one investigation, theirs. The BN began to take employee statements, and those of non-employees who they could locate and who had something interesting to say.

Because his crew's actions appeared to have triggered the explosion, the most relevant statements about railroad operations in Appleyard that day were those of Victor Lyon, foreman of Job No. 1. His crew consisted of locomotive engineer Darrel Dearing and helpers Ron Jacobs and Dave Jones. Vic stated that after lunch they left Wenatchee about 12:01 PM, and traveled to the east end of Appleyard, via yard track 5. They switched four cars from track 8 into tracks 2, 7, 8, and 5, in that order. While Ron lined those switches back to the lead, Vic took their engine east through the crossover to the main track, and then came west and coupled to the caboose of train No. 97, which was sitting on the main track and had arrived while they were switching the four cars. Switchman Dave Jones made their cut 14 cars ahead of the caboose and bled the air from the brake cylinders of the five cars they were going to reduce from train No. 97. Vic and Ron Jacobs were on the ground near their engine and the caboose while Dave was bleeding the cars.

When Dave gave a back-up sign, the engineer pulled east past the main track switch. After riding eastward for about 300 feet, Vic dropped off and began walking eastward to line the lead switch at track 9 for the lead. He then continued eastward to protect the road crossing at the east end of the lead.

After clearing the crossover to the east and lining the main track switch for the yard, Ron kicked the five cars loaded with aluminum west on the yard lead allowing them to roll free at 3 or 4 MPH toward track 12. Ron then relined the main track switch and started the engine and the rear of No. 97 west toward Dave, who would control the speed of the closing movement and the coupling by hand signals, and reconnect the air line after the coupling was completed. Dave had remained at the cut point and on the yard side of the train, standing in the shade. Dave was about 500 feet from DUPX 16009.

Vic waited at the road crossing while the rest of his crew was putting No. 97 back together. When the cars went by him, Vic was not sure they were moving fast enough to clear the lead. If they did not clear, then his crew would have to go shove them into the track before they did anything else. Concerned about the rolling cars clearing the switch at the west end of 11 track, and generally keeping an eye on their progress, the next thing Vic remembered was the flash of the explosion. He estimated that he was 400 to 500 feet away from the explosion. In fact, he was about 1,000 feet away. There were cars between him and the explosion. Vic was not physically injured, but he was traumatized in part because Dave Jones, a member of this crew, was killed.

Engineer Tom Ryan and switchman Rick Hanson were working the west end switch engine in Appleyard when the tank car exploded. They had coupled one car onto a cut of cars in track 10 that were to be a fill on a westward train. Rick walked east on the river side of the cut in track 10 to line the air on this cut of cars. When he was done, he signaled engineer Ryan to pull about 15 cars to the west end of the yard. Rick got on the last car and rode the cut out of the track. The explosion occurred as Tom was stopping the engine about 2,200 feet away from the blast site. Had they not pulled east when they did, they would have been so close to the blast that Rick would have been severely injured or killed and Tom could have been injured or killed inside of the engine. Had Rick been on the other side of the car, he would not have been shielded by the car he was riding.

Appleyard is on fire shortly after the explosion of August 6. Borate bomber is dropping fire retardant on the fire. COLLECTION OF *WENATCHEE DAILY WORLD*.

Tom stated that the engine rocked up on its side toward the river and then settled back on the track with a clunk. At the same time Tom saw a mushroom cloud appear over the east end of the yard. Tom got off the engine and ran east toward the end of the cars where Rick was.

The force of the blast slammed Rick against the side of the car he was riding. Rick got off the car at a point about 1,500 feet from the blast site and started to run toward the engine when he immediately got knocked down. Rick got up and felt pain in his right shoulder. The first thing that came to his mind was, "Who is bombing Wenatchee?" as every direction he looked but west was on fire. He started to run toward the engine again as Tom met him. About that time, they heard a strange sound and the side, end, and part of the roof of a boxcar came down out of the sky and hit the ground about 50 feet from where they were standing while smaller explosion debris continued to fall all around them. When they got back to the engine and its radio, the yardmaster instructed them to couple into tracks and pull cars away from the fire area.

Rick stated that walking with the borate fire retardant solution covering the ground was very difficult as it made everything very slippery. Tom stated that he had to have the sanders on the engine running all the time to get enough traction to get the engine to move while pulling the cars to the west, away from the blast area.

The last thing Tom and Rick did was grab five tank cars of jet airplane fuel for Fairchild Air Force Base and take them uptown. They stopped in front of the yard office, went in, and tied up. Rick was taken to the hospital because he had four puncture wounds in his right shoulder. When Rick arrived at the hospital, he noticed a trail of blood from the sidewalk into the emergency room entrance and on the floor inside from people coming in with cuts in their arms and legs from all the flying glass around town. The nurse asked Rick where he was injured and Rick said he had some punctures in his right shoulder, but that he could wait if they were busy with more serious injuries. They were about three hours getting to him.

Conductor Frank Juliano and brakeman Marvin Schultz had just arrived on No. 97, and were waiting for the company van bringing the outbound crew to Appleyard and then take them to the Yard Office to tie up. Frank said that all of a sudden, his ears started to ring and Schultz was spinning around in the air like a pinwheel. Then Schultz got hit by something, was knocked to the ground, and did not move; Frank figured that Marvin was dead. Frank immediately hit the ground and covered his head when he saw Schultz get knocked to the ground. Everything went black with dust, dirt, and smoke filling the air. Debris finally stopped falling and Schultz started to move. Frank told him to stay down and not move. They were picked up by an ambulance and taken to the hospital about 15 minutes later.

LEFT The day before, this pile of scrap iron was railroad cars, taken from about area of track 10. Before the explosion, this area was filled with track, but now the rail has been blown off the ties, which have been covered by fallen debris and make them impossible to see. PHOTOGRAPHER UNKNOWN.

RIGHT The debris field at Appleyard, probably taken from about track 8. The explosion site was to the right and behind the photographer's location. This photo was taken about 6 or 7 PM on the day after the event. Burlington Northern employees surveying the damage are probably wondering what to do next. PHOTOGRAPHER UNKNOWN.

Marvin's grip took the full force of the blast, which charred the side of the leather grip. Both of Marvin's eardrums were broken and he never regained his balance. Marvin retired on a disability pension.

Conductor Dick Perkins was called for an eastward train and was in the yard office when the blast occurred. He said that the yard office, windows shook severely, as did the brick building. They all ran outside and saw the mushroom cloud over Appleyard. Dick and his crew were going to drive to Appleyard to take a look, but the trainmaster told them to stay. They were not wanted there, and there was so much debris on the streets and traffic congestion they might not get there or back.

Dick and his crew were held at Wenatchee for about three hours. The track inspector inspected the track and the larger fires were put out before they were allowed to leave. Dick stated that it looked like a war zone as they pulled by at 10 MPH.

It was fortunate that the explosion occurred during the lunch hour. Two WFE employees were at lunch. Edward F. Hestand had eaten his lunch in the office above the third floor of the heater house, which has an elevated view over the entire yard. He was walking down the stairs from the office to the third floor when the blast knocked him over the banister. The heater house was located on the river side of the yard and about 800 feet from the blast site. Lavern Smart was in 'the office building' in the former rip track area which he estimated to be about 300 feet away from the blast site. He stated that a refrigerator was blown over him as he sat in a chair eating lunch, and he had to dig himself out from under the debris. He was taken by ambulance to the hospital. Both men were knocked around and injured, but not seriously. Two other WFE employees, Jack Sites and David E. Short, were on their way to Appleyard by auto.

Jack Sites was passenger in his brother's pickup. They were about to turn off the Malaga Highway into the former rip track area when the explosion occurred. They went to his brother's house, which was nearby. David Short had stopped to get a snack because he had not yet eaten lunch. He was in the Viewdale Grocery about a mile away when the explosion occurred. He continued to Appleyard where he looked for survivors.

Machine operators Vern H. Cox, H. B. Boehm, and Gary Tagil had just finished their lunches after loading a machine onto a flatcar located west of the electric shop and opposite the turntable, a few hundred feet west of the former rip track building occupied by Lavern Smart. They were near the flatcar and their vehicles when the explosion occurred. Vern Cox stayed at the yard and helped sheriff's deputies search the yard. He found the body of a transient who had apparently been blown into the Shower House of the former rip track. Cox later helped the coroner load the bodies of the transient and switchman David Jones into a funeral home hearse.

Track laborer Paul E. Turnbull took his lunch near the electric shop. He then walked west and was near the west switch to track 12, about 2,000 feet from the blast site, when the explosion happened. He moved east to the tool house where he and others were advised to leave the area. He walked to the Malaga highway, where he was picked up about an hour later. Paul was uninjured.

The blast took out windows all over Wenatchee and East Wenatchee, causing several injuries from flying glass. So many windows were destroyed in the area they had to bring glass in from Seattle. Rail car wheels were thrown about half a mile to a mile away across the Columbia River. Rick Hanson lived in East Wenatchee off Grant Way. A friend of Rick's who lived about two blocks east discovered that a two-foot piece of rail had penetrated the roof of his garage and was stuck in the top door of his chest freezer. That location is over two miles from the blast site. A woman who worked for a non-railroad employer in an office with large windows overlooking the yard was at lunch elsewhere, which probably saved her from serious injury by flying glass.

South Wenatchee resident Archie Ashlin, who estimated that he lived one half to three quarters of a mile away from the blast site, could not see the site of the explosion. He was out in his yard at the time and reported hearing a 'soft' explosive noise, and then the loud bang of the main explosion. His is the sole report of a soft explosion before the main explosion.

Four witnesses located in East Wenatchee reported seeing fire in Appleyard immediately before the explosion. Billy R. Beaty was a carpenter engaged in work at the Douglas County Sewer District building about one and a half miles away. He reported that he could see Appleyard under both Columbia River Bridges. He and his brother, Wesley, had just finished lunch and were looking at a wildfire burning on a hill above and beyond the yard. While looking in that direction, "I noticed a small fire which appeared to be in the railroad yard and more or less between the roundhouse [electric shop] and the big white building towards the river [the ice house]. This appeared to be but a small fire at first. I said to my brother something about the small fire and I then turned to some of the other men in the immediate area and told them to look towards the fire. Turning back to the fire, I then noticed what appeared to be two larger fires which appeared to be coming around the sides of perhaps a boxcar or a tank car and this fire went up in the air 20 or 30 feet. Then there was the huge explosion.... I would estimate the time to be about 30 to 60 seconds from the time I first noticed the small fire until the time of the explosion. I could see the railroad cars in the yard and this fire (the first small one) appeared to be on the ground rather than above the cars.... I did not hear but one huge explosion." His brother, Wesley E. Beaty, saw fire 20 to 30 feet in the air for a few seconds before he saw the explosion.

Donald L Gillis, Captain of Douglas County Fire District #2, was in the shop portion at the main fire station, located at 1100 North Main in East Wenatchee, waiting for his wife to bring him lunch. He looked out the south window of the shop for no particular reason and saw a fire he thought was on the deck of the US Highway 2 bridge over the Columbia River, which was between him and Appleyard. He stated that the flames were hundreds of feet high. He called to volunteer fireman Arnie Willms who had his back to the window. They both looked at the fire which was going straight up. They moved to the garage doorway, arriving there as they saw the explosion. Captain Gillis estimated that he observed the fire for 30 to 60 seconds and that he was 8,500 feet from the explosion.

Arnold L. Willms walked to a good vantage point in response to Captain Gillis' call. He too thought the fire was on the deck of the road bridge. He said that the flames were "not too high" and described the flame as "a real brightish orange to reddish orange in color." Willms estimated that 60–90 seconds elapsed from the time he first saw the fire to the moment of the explosion.

There is one significant area of disagreement among the statements. None of the railroad employees working in the yard, a total of 15 people, saw any fire or smoke in the yard before the explosion, while at least four people in East Wenatchee did see fire. Both groups of reports are probably true.

The fact that the railroaders did not see fire is due to the fact that they were engaged in switching cars or other activities which required their immediate attention, while the East Wenatchee observers were relaxed and looking around when they saw the fire. The view of the railroaders was obscured by other rail cars between them and DUPX 16009, while the observers in East Wenatchee were above the tops of the rail cars and thus had a shallow downward view. The East Wenatchee observers were consistent in their estimates of watching the fire for 30–60 seconds or less, excepting only Willms who reported 60–90 seconds. They were also consistent in the description of the fire, except for Captain Gillis who reported much higher flames than the others. Captain Gillis probably exaggerated the flame height.

The next day, August 8, Mac and Ev took the Bureau's chief chemist Schultz on a tour of the Appleyard site. They asked to sit in on the statement taking interviews and were refused by BN's legal counsel Mr. Larry Silvernale of Seattle, as was his right. They encouraged him to ask if witnesses saw any flame prior to the detonation.

Tank car DUPX 16009 originated from an E. I. Dupont de Nemours Company, Incorporated plant in Biwabik, Minnesota served by the Duluth, Missabe and Iron Range Railway, and was billed to Dupont at Dupont, Washington, located south of Tacoma and near Fort Lewis. Dupont contracted for an annual inspection of many of its plants, and Mac had been into the Dupont dynamite plant before.

Mac and Ev went to Dupont, Washington on August 9 and asked to see the unloading operation, which request was granted. During this inspection, they found out that the monomethylamine nitrate was a component in 'slurry gel' explosives which were being used in large quantities on the oil pipeline then being built from the North Slope of Alaska to Valdez. The tank cars were unusual in that they had stainless steel tanks and fittings, as opposed to the far more common carbon steel. They were of about 10,000-gallon capacity, were insulated with 10 inches of fiberglass insulation placed outside the tank and then covered with a 3/16-inch carbon steel outer jacket. All of the DUPX cars were insulated and were of traditional design featuring a horizontal tank strapped to the underframe.

These cars also had a top operated style bottom outlet valve. The operating mechanism was located on the top of the car with a vertical rod that worked a screw mechanism at the bottom of the car which raised the valve to open it and lowered the valve to close it. Below the valve, product flowed into the bottom outlet leg, which was about two feet long on these cars. The outlet leg was closed by the bottom outlet cap, a large pipe cap. This style of outlet valve always leaked at bit, so the Hazardous Materials Regulations of the Department of Transportation required that all tank cars equipped with a bottom outlet be loaded with the outlet cap off, so that leakage past the closed valve could be known to be no more than dripping.

Since no cars were on hand there was nothing to inspect except the unloading site. Discussion developed that even during the summer season the cars arrived with a layer of crystalized product on the bottom of the tank. As the load cooled, the solution became supersaturated, and the crystals formed. The product was heated by running steam through the heater coil pipes built into the car for that purpose. It took 24 to 96 hours to liquefy the entire mass, depending on the season. Most interesting to Mac and Ev was that though the cars were equipped with bottom outlets, they were not used. The liquid was unloaded by pressurizing the car slightly and taking the product out through the car's liquid line.

Monomethylamine nitrate was classed as a flammable solid, and shipments up to 86% concentration were authorized in specification 111A100W6 tank cars by Special Permit 5737. The unloading plant ran an assay on each car and provided those figures for the last five cars. The lowest assay was 87.0% and the highest was 89.0%, all higher than the 86% limit imposed by the Special Permit. The over limit concentration of product in each car was a separate violation of the Special Permit, and thus the Hazardous Materials Regulations.

Special Permits were a regulatory device used to authorize something not authorized by the Hazardous Materials Regulations of the Department of Transportation. They provided flexibility that the regulations themselves did not, and could be used to gain experience before the provisions of the Special Permit were incorporated into the regulations. The vast majority of Special Permits were requested by shippers who set forth the provisions of the Special Permit.

Ev had been in the Canadian military dealing with explosive ordnance during World War II, and recalled that the British had discovered that certain nitrates in contact with certain metals would form a highly shock-sensitive explosive. Since Dupont never used the bottom outlet, the outlet leg would have filled with nitrate crystals the first time it was loaded, and then cooked each time the car was unloaded and reloaded. If the stainless-steel bottom outlet cap had been replaced with a carbon steel cap, perhaps a very sensitive explosive had formed in the threads, got initiated somehow, initiated the old nitrate in the outlet leg, which then initiated the entire mass. This became Ev and Mac's working theory of the event.

Back at Wenatchee that evening, they found the railroad's officials, who advised them that their preliminary investigation, including an interview with switch foreman Victor P. Lyon, developed that the explosion occurred about the time a five-car reduction off the rear portion of train No. 97 coupled into the east car in track 12. The tank car was the fifth car from the east end of the standing cut and was coupled to the cars on each end.

At a late evening meeting with railroad officials, they found out that the Burlington Northern had an empty DUPX sister car to the one that had exploded on hand in Superior, Wisconsin, and asked the BN to hold the car there for the Bureau to inspect. They were assured that a hold had already been placed on the car. All of the railroad men and all of the Bureau men decided that Mac and Ev should inspect this car and the Biwabik plant as soon as possible and independent of the NTSB and its investigation. The next morning, they updated Director Graziano and arranged transportation to Superior.

The entire next day was spent traveling to Duluth, and renting a car. On August 11, they inspected DUPX 16005, a specification 111A100W6 car of 10,000-gallon net capacity built in 1961. Specification 111A100W6 is a non-pressure car with a 100-pound hydrostatic test pressure, having a minimum 7/16th inch thick stainless-steel tank. A bottom outlet was authorized but not required. Like its sister car, this car had a bottom outlet.

They were looking for any carbon steel caps, particularly on the bottom outlet, and were concerned that removing the bottom outlet cap would blow them to kingdom come. That concern was eliminated when the three BN police officers they met at Superior told them that they had removed the bottom outlet cap the previous day. The Bureau inspectors found an unauthorized bottom outlet extension with flange, another violation of the regulations. In addition, the bottom outlet nozzle was found to be made of carbon steel, supporting our working theory. Mr. Dale Propp, Burlington Northern chemist, reported that on August 9, in the presence of a witness, he had been able to unscrew the bottom outlet cap, which the regulations required to be made wrench tight with a 36-inch wrench, by hand. This was another clear violation of the regulations. In addition, inspection of the underside of the car near the bottom outlet revealed that the insulation was wet with a reddish-brown liquid similar in appearance to the material remaining in the bottom of the tank. The railroad advised that DUPX 16004 was on spot in Dupont's plant at Biwabik; they made plans to visit the origin plant the next day.

BN patrolman O. E. Soltau led the Bureau Inspectors to the Biwabik plant, arriving at 7:45 AM on August 12. The plant manager was used to seeing Bureau inspectors and took Coughlan and McCulloch to the loading site. While photographs were not allowed, Plant Manager Leo Fox explained that they made the product by placing nitric acid in a vat and introducing monomethylamine, a flammable gas, into the vat. The two reacted to make monomethylamine nitrate. This reaction was 'exothermic,' which means it generated heat. The heat of reaction was recorded on a dial recorder which created a paper trace of temperature as a function of time. The temperature started at ambient, quickly rose to normal reaction temperature, and stayed there for the several hours required to make a tank car load of product. Plant personnel advised that the temperature shown on the recorder traces on hand indicated a concentration of 88 to 89%. When reminded of the 86% limit imposed by the Special Permit, Mr. Fox contended that the lower concentration of the startup period reduced the final concentration in the car, a mathematical impossibility given the short startup and long production times. Temperature of the product as loaded was over 200 degrees F.

Tank car DUPX 16004 was on spot. To load the car, a hose was placed in the manway, and the manway cover was closed to secure the hose, and to keep pine needles from the surrounding forest out of the car. The Biwabik plant did nothing with the bottom outlet, despite the regulation requiring that the cap be off for the entire time the car was being loaded to make sure that the leakage through the bottom outlet valve was no more than a drip. Mac and Ev had not yet disproved Ev's super sensitive reaction product theory, and they never would.

They found car NATX 21834, a 20,000-gallon Spec 111A100W1 lined carbon steel car which had made four trips to Dupont, Washington, in this service. This car was not authorized for transportation of monomethylamine nitrate, a gross violation of the Hazardous Materials Regulations. In addition, they found that the placards, which were required to show the shipping name, which was "Flammable Solid N.O.S.", actually showed "86% Monomethylamine Nitrate Solution", yet another violation of the Hazardous Materials Regulations by Dupont.

Upon their return to the office, Mac and Ev were confronted by attorney C. R. Kimmel from Dupont headquarters in Wilmington, Delaware who was incensed that they were on Dupont property. He advised them that the NTSB had promised Dupont that there would be only one tour of the plant, and that he would now call Mr. Brennan of the NTSB to determine our authority to be at the plant. When Ev, the Senior Inspector, did not respond, Mac showed Mr. Kimmel section 173.1 of the Hazardous Materials Regulations which authorized inspection of rail shippers of hazardous material by the Bureau of Explosives at any time. A second Dupont lawyer then stated he would call Mr. Brennan if *we* desired. Since we had seen what we came to see, we left with no further discussion.

The NTSB tour of Biwabik took place the next day. There were 21 non-Dupont people in attendance. Had we not been there the day before, we would have discovered little to nothing as part of this mob. What was interesting is that liquid was leaking past the threads of the bottom outlet cap of DUPX 16004 at a rate of eight or nine drops per minute, which it had not been the day before. When we asked the plant manager about it, he claimed, in the presence of attorney Kimmel, that the car had not been touched. Mac and Ev never could figure out what they were trying to accomplish.

While this was going on, the National Transportation Safety Board had people at Wenatchee trying to prove a coupler override had punctured the end of the car. This was their favorite theory at the time because they had been recommending head shields to prevent such occurrences, which had happened in an accident in Decatur, Illinois, and in several road train derailments involving flammable gasses such as propane and butane. We thought this politically driven theory was ridiculous, given how the cars had been handled in Appleyard. The NTSB decided to recover all of the tank car parts they could, so that they could reconstruct the car, as was their habit with airplane crashes, and began to excavate the crater. When we returned to Wenatchee, we found that the NTSB had found two threaded pieces of carbon steel that we believed were part of the bottom outlet, which supported our working theory.

The National Transportation Safety Board held a public hearing in Wenatchee on September 24, 1974. These hearings are used to place relevant facts on the record. While most of the hearing had to do with how DUPX 16009 had been handled by the railroad(s), which was entirely routine, a few interesting facts were introduced, including the statements of the East Wenatchee witnesses.

Robert M. Graziano, Director of the Bureau of Explosives, reminded the Board that specification 111A100W6 tank cars have a relatively short hydrostatic retest interval of 5 years up to 10 years old, and then a retest interval of 3 years for cars up to 22 years old, and a retest interval of 1 year for cars over 22 years old. The DUPX cars were built in 1961. They should have been retested in 1966, 1971, and 1974. In fact, DUPX 16009 was last retested during August of 1972. The most interesting evidence he introduced was that after the 1972 retest, DUPX 16009 was between 20 and 30 cars behind the locomotive of a DM&IR local train that had collided with a standing ore train at about 25 MPH. The loaded car was not derailed, not obviously damaged, went on to Dupont, Washington, and remained in service until August 6.

The National Transportation Safety Board was curious about the classification of monomethylamine nitrate 86% solution as a flammable solid. The then-current regulations provided for two types of explosives, Explosives A and Explosives B. Explosives A were those that could be detonated when contained in a paper cup by a number 8 blasting cap, such as nitroglycerine, dynamite, trinitrotoluene, and several others. Explosives B were those that functioned by deflagration, that is, rapid burning, rather than by detonation. Solid fuel rocket motors are an example. There were also class C explosives which were manufactured articles containing a small quantity of either class A or class B explosives. Small arms ammunition was a class C explosive.

Since the product met none of these tests, it was classed as a flammable solid.

Testing in Canada, which copied the American Hazardous Materials Regulations virtually verbatim, had revealed that monomethylamine nitrate 86% solution could be detonated if enclosed in a pipe two inches or more in diameter. The outlet leg more than qualified, as did the tank itself.

The Burlington Northern and Dupont jointly retained Failure Analysis Associates of Palo Alto, California to perform "mechanical and metallurgical analyses of couplers, bottom outlet valve and boxcar underframes." Their report was released in November of 1975. In 264 pages of analysis of various couplers, they proved that the cars in track 12 had all been coupled together at the time of the explosion. This means that the cut reduced out of No. 97 did couple into the standing cars, and that DUPX 16009 was coupled to the cars on each end, disproving the NTSB's devoutly desired coupler override theory.

The Failure Analysis engineers also examined the bottom outlet valve mechanism excavated from the crater. They concluded, on pages 270 and 271, that a detonation within the bottom outlet was the precursor detonation, which in turn caused the detonation of the main mass in the tank car.

There were three results of this accident. The Federal Railroad Administration cancelled Special Permit 5737, putting an end to the transportation of monomethylamine nitrate in tank cars. The National Transportation Safety Board was unable to establish a probable cause for the accident, something very unusual for them. Finally, BN attorney Silvernale told Mac many months later that Dupont paid the railroad a substantial amount, well over $1,000,000, to avoid having to defend themselves in a lawsuit, which would have been difficult and embarrassing due to the many violations of the Hazardous Materials Regulations of the Department of Transportation discovered by the Bureau of Explosives inspectors.

Author McCulloch believes that Ev Coughlan's theory of a shock sensitive initiating explosive in the treads of the carbon steel outlet cap is a reasonable explanation. Dupont's loading and unloading practices, combined with normal leakage past the bottom outlet valve, created a plug of old, many times cooked, monomethylamine nitrate in the bottom outlet leg. If that material reacted with the carbon steel outlet cap to create a highly shock sensitive explosive in the threads of the outlet cap, it was set off due to the rattling of a loose bottom outlet cap as found on tank car DUPX 16005 on August 9 at Superior. The motion of a loose cap would have been exacerbated due to the long, heavy, and illegal piping Dupont added below the bottom outlet cap. The coupling of the cars, which should not have done more than rattle the car, was sufficient to trigger the explosion. In this case there would be no time for a fire of any duration before the explosion. The explosive chain would have been initiation in the threads, which initiated the material in the outlet leg, which initiated the main mass. All of this would have taken less than a thousandth of a second.

The other theory consistent with the evidence is that the tank of DUPX 16009 suffered a short hairline crack in the rear end collision on the DM&IR. This caused sufficient leakage to saturate the bottom of the insulation on at least one end of the car with monomethylamine nitrate. Between the heat of the load and the warm, dry summer day of Eastern Washington, a significant amount of water was evaporated from the nitrate in the insulation, and certainly crystals formed due to the lower temperature in the outer portion of insulation as compared to in the tank. Testimony at the NTSB hearing in Wenatchee developed that nitrate crystals are more shock sensitive than nitrate solution, and that the 86% solution would detonate when confined, as in the bottom outlet and the tank itself. In this theory, the initiating event was a slight shift of the tank relative to the oak blocks that supported it at each bolster, or a shift of the oak blocks relative to the underframe and bolster of the car. If the East Wenatchee eyewitnesses are to be believed, this started a fire in the insulation between the tank and outer metal jacket. That such a fire would first break out of the jacket low, then extend 20 to 30 feet over the top of the car and burn for 30 to 60 seconds before initiating the explosion of the old material in the bottom outlet leg, which instantly initiated the main explosion, is entirely reasonable. In this case, heating of the old crystals in the bottom outlet leg initiated the explosion. Since four neutral and independent witnesses reported seeing a fire in Appleyard immediately before the explosion, Mac believes this is the more likely explanation.

Regulatory and Corporate Activities, 1970–1980

Merger Day, March 2, 1970, was among the worst of times to be in the railroad business. Federal rate regulation had starved the carriers of capital for over 60 years; as a result, many fixed plants were ragged at best. The industry was carrying the burden of passenger trains that consumed capacity but did not cover out of pocket costs; forget generating enough money to contribute to overhead or replace the equipment. In fact, the burden of money-losing passenger trains was eating up what little freight earnings the industry could generate. Finally, the Interstate Highway network was far enough along to make motor carriers a competitive reality in every freight market. The Penn Central bankruptcy, which removed the emperor's clothes from the entire rail industry, occurred on June 21, 1970.[5]

A project funded by the Army Corps of Engineers, begun during the final years of the Great Northern, was competed on November 7, 1970 when the Libby Dam line change was dedicated and officially placed in service.[6] The 57.4-mile line change included the 7.01-mile long Flathead Tunnel. The new line is 14.66 miles shorter than the old line but has steeper grades. The old line was not over 0.7 percent grade ascending eastward to Stryker with not over 0.25 percent grade descending eastward from Stryker. The new line has 1 percent grades in both directions. The summit of the new line is at the east portal of the Flathead Tunnel, at an elevation of about 3,650 feet.[7]

Amtrak took over the passenger service in 1971 and eliminated over half of the national passenger train mileage overnight. Spokane went from eight passenger trains to the east and twelve to the west to two and two. Congress required that each railroad company give Amtrak two years' worth of passenger losses in the form of equipment or cash,[8] and give Amtrak virtually free use of the railroad forever.

In 1973, the Regional Rail Reorganization Act, or '3R Act,' laid down the process for dealing with the multiple bankruptcies in the northeast, of which the Penn Central was the largest. For the first time since World War I, the unions did not get what they wanted from the federal government. They did get a $250 million program to guarantee the lifetime incomes of all employees of the bankrupt railroads.[9]

The federal government began to loosen its regulatory stranglehold on the railroads in February 1976 with the Railroad Revitalization and Regulatory Reform Act, known as the '4R Act.' Since it decided to rescue Penn Central and the other northeastern bankrupts, Congress could finally see the wisdom of removing a few of the many burdens it previously placed on the carriers' backs.[10]

At last, in 1980, the railroads were mostly, but far from totally, deregulated as to rates and abandonment by the Staggers Rail Act. They could now enter into contracts and did not have to charge every customer the same price regardless of volume, cost, or the scope of the service. In short, they could act like a rational business for the first time since 1906. It would take the carriers years to figure out how to market their services in the new, partially deregulated world.[11] Burlington Northern moved faster than most other railroads in adapting to the relative freedom of the Staggers Act, due largely to hiring Darius Gaskins from the outside as Senior Vice President Marketing and Sales in 1982. That story will be told in the following chapter.

Four important corporate decisions were made after 1970 that affected the railroad. One was the decision to transport Powder River Basin coal, the second was how best to use the Northern Pacific's resource assets, the third was the formation of a non-railroad holding company, and the fourth was finding a partner for a subsequent merger.

Northern Pacific had owned and operated coal mines from the 1880s until the end of steam engine operations in the mid-1950s. One of NP's larger mines was the Rosebud Mine at Colstrip, Montana, about 100 miles east of Billings, and near the northern edge of the huge Powder River Basin coal fields. The mine had 1.3 billion tons of reserves in 1965.[12]

On May 1, 1969, NP began unit coal train service, jointly with GN, from Peabody Coal's Big Sky Mine at Colstrip, to the Minnesota Power & Light generating plant at Cohasset, Minnesota, located five miles west of Grand Rapids on the GN between Crookston and Duluth. These 105-car trains of nominal 100-ton cars were interchanged initially at Moorhead, a haul of 580 miles on the NP and 261 miles on the GN, a total of 841 miles. Cars were supplied by NP; power was changed at Moorhead, as was train direction. This was the first long distance, large volume, unit coal train service provided by any Burlington Northern predecessor.

Great Northern executive vice president Robert Downing said in a 2008 interview, "It was a first as far as GN and NP were concerned. We had no idea what it would ultimately become, but we knew it was a big deal because we knew where the coal was. We knew there were billions of tons of coal there, and if somebody could use it, why, we were more than happy to move it."[13]

Unfortunately, the Cohasset move was underpriced, meaning that the rate was too low.[14] The inadequate rate problem appeared in the form of greatly increased track maintenance costs caused by 100-ton cars. Since shortly after the beginning of the twentieth century, the standard rail car had been the nominal 50-ton car with a designed axle loading of 20 tons. A 10% overage of the load was allowed, bringing the real maximum axle loading to 22.5 tons. Starting around 1960, almost all new cars being built were of 100-ton nominal capacity, a 33-ton axle loading, or 1.5 times the previous prevailing standard. Track designed for lower axle loads was soon found to need much more maintenance to support the higher axle loading.

A 1970 amendment to the Clean Air Act required that sulfur dioxide emissions from coal fired power plants be reduced. Utilities could either burn low sulfur coal or install and maintain expensive combustion gas scrubbers to remove sulfur dioxide from their exhaust.[15] Coal from traditional sources in Appalachia and Southern Illinois was 'high sulfur' coal, which required scrubbers. The largest reserves of low sulfur coal were centered on the Powder River Basin of Wyoming and extending northward into Montana.

In the winter of 1973, the United States experienced the Arab Oil Embargo, or The Oil Crisis. Oil prices rose dramatically and swiftly.[16] People lined up to buy gasoline, and there was a period when you could only buy gas when the last digit of your license plate was odd or even, matching the even or odd day of the month. Prices of natural gas rose. Since natural gas is a close substitute for oil in many applications, the price of natural gas followed the price of oil for decades. Coal prices increased, but not nearly so dramatically as oil and gas prices, which made coal relatively more attractive for electric power generation. After 1970, and especially after 1973, electric utilities became progressively more interested in burning the very cheap, easy to mine, low sulfur coal located in the Powder River Basin, despite the long rail haul required to get the coal to their generating facilities.

The Burlington (CB&Q) owned a line along the eastern edge of the Powder River Basin (PRB) coal fields of Wyoming. When asked for a trainload rate, the new Burlington Northern repeated the NP's mistake and quoted too low a rate based on incremental costs. Soon utilities from far and wide wanted to move coal at that low rate, which was based on the false premise of marginal costs and was far too low to cover the increased track maintenance costs and the investment in new ballast, ties, and welded rail required to support unit trains of 100-ton cars.

Burlington Northern was forced to engage in a series of legal battles with the utilities for the right to price its services high enough to earn a reasonable return on the assets involved in the coal business, while being drawn into a $2 billion investment in totally rebuilt track required to support the unprecedented tonnage, line relocations, a new line over 100 miles long, hundreds of miles of second and even third main track, a new locomotive shop at Alliance, Nebraska, plus hundreds of locomotives and thousands of coal cars.[17] To conserve cash and protect its credit rating, the BN offered shippers a lower freight rate if they provided the cars.

The rate cases were fought through the ICC and the courts for years, and, on balance, the BN prevailed. PRB coal was a traffic boon, a huge financial risk, a regulatory nightmare, but ultimately a success.[18] During the 1970s when the initial large investment was made, the needs of the PRB restricted investments in other parts of the system.

In the Pacific Northwest, these investment restrictions showed in deferment of capacity improvements between Sandpoint and Spokane, deferment of a tie replacement program in Kootenai Canyon for two years, and operation of secondary and local trains with a fleet of early 1950s vintage EMD F, GP 7, and GP 9 engines, which were becoming unreliable and demanding excessive maintenance. BN addressed this about three years later than they would have liked by assigning 40 new GP 39-2 engines to the Seattle Region,[19] where they were assigned to important regional trains between Seattle and Vancouver, British Columbia; Seattle and Portland; Pasco and Bieber, California; and between Portland and Pasco. The older units in local service were replaced by 1960s vintage GP 30 and GP 35 engines bumped from their previous assignments by the new GP 39-2 engines.[20]

Northern Pacific came into the merger with many million dollars' worth of resource assets. These assets were mostly mineral rights under Montana grazing lands which the NP got as part of its land grant but was never able to sell, and forest land that the railroad owned in Montana and Washington, again from the land grant. Northern Pacific entered into oil and natural gas leases on those portions of its land where oil drillers thought there might be oil. Northern Pacific had a lumber company, Plum Creek Lumber, that bought logs from NP and sold cut lumber, but the NP did not aggressively develop its resources. The NP faction on the BN board thought they should have done better in terms of the stock exchange ratio going into the merger, because their resources were undervalued. Former NP board members were very aware of the Burlington Northern's resource assets.[21]

Most other railroads formed holding companies during the 1960s. The holding company owned the railroad stock. The holding company's stock, not the railroad's, traded on the stock exchange. Some of the railroad's cash flow was invested in non-rail assets owned by the holding company in the hope that stockholders could make a better return in these other businesses than they could with the railroad. Due to regulatory constraints, beating railroad earnings in any other business was not difficult after 1910.

None of the BN predecessor companies had created a holding company. The non-railroad assets of the NP were pledged as backing for two issues of bonds that would not mature for many years. The bond covenants prevented the NP from moving its resource assets into a holding company.[22] The Great Northern did not own any significant non-rail assets. Great Northern management concentrated on the merger and never formed a holding company.

Burlington Northern created two corporate divisions in 1974: Transportation and Resources. The Transportation Division included the railroad, a trucking company, BN Transport, an air freight forwarding company, BN Air Freight Inc., and an aircraft servicing company at the Minneapolis–St. Paul Airport, BN Air Motive.[23] The non-railroad transportation subsidiaries involved very small investments and modest incomes in comparison with the railroad.[24]

The Resources Division, under newly appointed president C. Robert Binger, included Plum Creek Lumber, oil and gas, mining, and land holdings, all largely from the NP land grant. The resources would now be managed separately from the railroad, and more intensely than had been the case previously.

Burlington Northern was the largest railroad in North America. In 1975, for example, BN was operating 24,832 miles of line, compared with Union Pacific at 9,463 miles.[25] In 1970, the Union Pacific was seven years into its attempt to purchase the Chicago, Rock Island and Pacific Railroad Company (Rock Island). That fiasco would continue until November of 1974 when the ICC approved the UP purchase of the Rock Island, but with so many conditions that the UP walked away from the deal. After 11 years of minimal track and equipment maintenance, the Rock Island was a physical wreck that soon fell into bankruptcy and liquidation.[26] Other railroads, the Union Pacific in particular, felt threatened by the sheer size of the BN. The fact that the UP and NP were long established rivals simply reinforced the Union Pacific's fears. All the Class I railroads were looking for merger partners, and a multitude of informal discussions occurred among the presidents of the railroads.

Louis Menk, President and Chairman of the Burlington Northern Railroad from 1970 to 1978, then Chairman 1978–81, spent 20 years of his career on the St. Louis–San Francisco Railway (SLSF or Frisco). He knew and thought highly of the SLSF's President, Richard Grayson, who had succeeded Menk on the Frisco. Menk began merger talks with Grayson in 1975. Menk was bound and determined to buy the SLSF, possibly for emotional rather than business reasons. In 1977 the Burlington Northern and the St. Louis–San Francisco announced that they intended to merge. Many observers have opined that Menk picked the wrong partner; the BN should have merged with the Missouri Pacific. On the basis of traffic and economics, your authors agree. The BN-Frisco merger occurred in November of 1980. The Union Pacific moved to acquire both the Missouri Pacific and the Western Pacific in January of 1980.[27]

In the spring of 1978, the board promoted career railroader Norm Lorentzen from President of the Transportation Division to President and CEO of the Burlington Northern, over both the transportation and resource subsidiaries. About a year after Lorentzen became President of BN, he indicated that he planned to retire fairly soon. Menk then established a committee to search for a new president of BNI. Lorentzen would retain his position as Chairman of Executive Committee of the Board until early 1981 when he retired.[28]

While on an inspection trip in the spring of 1980, the board decided to create a holding company, and to bring in a new President of BN to develop the resource assets.[29] With the holding company concept in mind, Menk recommended and the board selected Richard Bressler, a respected executive at Atlantic Richfield Company (ARCO), a large integrated oil company, to be President of BN with the thought that he would become President of the soon-to-be-formed holding company. Bressler arrived in June of 1980.[30]

Richard Grayson, then President of the Frisco, became President of the Transportation Division, reporting to Bressler, in the summer of 1980. The SLFSF merger, despite approval by the ICC, was still tied up in court.[31] As of 1980, Chairman Louis Menk had 43 years of service in the railroad industry, had led the BN for 10 years, was 63 years old, and approaching retirement.[32]

The holding company, Burlington Northern Incorporated (BNI), was established in 1981 with Burlington Northern Railroad Company as its most significant operating subsidiary.[33] Richard Grayson continued as President and CEO of the railroad until his retirement in 1982.[34]

Louis Menk retired as Chairman in 1981.[35] He had created a Resource Division to manage the resources and led the company through a period of rapid management turnover. He created the holding company, Burlington Northern Incorporated (BNI), leaving with both a structure and people in place to carry out the Board of Directors' vision.

➻ Summary

The decade beginning with the Burlington Northern merger of 1970 was first and foremost a time of implementing the merger. The Spokane area was an important focus of merger implementation with the construction of the Latah Creek Bridge and its associated line change and the new connection at Sandpoint. These new connections between former GN and former NP lines enabled all through traffic to move by the former NP line between Sandpoint and Spokane, including through downtown Spokane. Concentrating all the traffic on the former NP main line overloaded the terminal at Yardley and caused serious congestion between Yardley and Sandpoint.

The capital needs of the Powder River Basin coal traffic constrained all other investment in the railroad.[36] Capital constraints showed in the Spokane area as a delayed tie replacement program in Kootenai Canyon, lack of improvement at Yardley, lack of investment to increase line capacity between Yardley and Sandpoint, continuation of time table and train order operation between Bluestem and Fort Wright, and lack of modernization in the non-coal road locomotive fleet, which resulted in less reliable road power than before the merger. In 1981, 40 new GP-39 locomotives were acquired and assigned to the Seattle Region to replace early 1950s F units, and slightly newer GP type units, used on secondary trains and in local service.

The other crucial event, which rail employees did not recognize the importance of at the time, was the increasing focus of the Board of Directors in natural resources, such as oil, gas, and timber and forest products, none of which suffered from the price controls that had afflicted the railroad industry since 1906. The first clear indication of the board's change in vision was creation of the holding company and the board's selection of Richard Bressler as president of the holding company. The consequences of that change lay in the future.

➻ Endnotes

1 Currie, email November 14, 2012.
2 Martin Envoy III et al., Signaling and the Great Northern, Part V Automatic Block Signaling, Great Northern Railway Historical Society Reference Sheet No. 405, September 2017, 4–5.
3 Robert D. Turner, *West of the Great Divide* (Victoria BC: Sono Nis Press, 1987), 278–80.
4 Turner, *West of the Great Divide*, 278.
5 Stephen Salsbury, *No Way to Run a Railroad* (New York: McGraw-Hill Book Company, 1982), 184.
6 Del Grosso, *BNSF Northwest*, 75.
7 BNSF Railway, Montana Division Employee Timetable No. 6, April 26, 2006, 47, 50.
8 Lawrence H. Kaufman, *Leaders Count: The Story of BNSF Railway* (College Station TX: Texas A&M University Press, 2005), 164–65.
9 Kaufman, *Leaders Count*, 166–68.
10 Kaufman, *Leaders Count*, 188–90.
11 Kaufman, *Leaders Count*, 197–203.
12 Northern Pacific Railway, 1965 Annual Report.
13 Steve Glischinski, "The Train that Started It All," *Trains Magazine*, March 2011, 54–55.
14 Currie, email December 31, 2017.
15 Kaufman, *Leaders Count*, 171–75.
16 Kaufman, *Leaders Count*, 161.
17 Kaufman, *Leaders Count*, 175.
18 Kaufman, *Leaders Count*, 175–78.
19 Currie, email February 19, 2018.
20 Currie, email February 19, 2018.
21 Kaufman, *Leaders Count*, 208.
22 Kaufman, *Leaders Count*, 208.
23 Currie, email December 9, 2017.
24 Currie, email March 2, 2018.
25 Frank N. Wilner, *Railroad Mergers: History Analysis Insight* (Omaha: Simmons-Boardman Books, Inc., 1997), 187.
26 Wilner, *Railroad Mergers*, 204–10.
27 Kaufman, *Leaders Count*, 204.
28 Currie, email February 20, 2018.
29 Kaufman, *Leaders Count*, 207.
30 Kaufman, *Leaders Count*, 210.
31 Kaufman, *Leaders Count*, 209–10.
32 Kaufman, *Leaders Count*, 206.
33 Kaufman, *Leaders Count*, 207–08.
34 Currie, email February 20, 2018.
35 Currie, email January 11, 2018.
36 Kaufman, *Leaders Count*, 176.

Engine 3152 leads the Pacific Zip along a basalt wall approaching tunnel No. 11.1 west of Crater in the 1980s. Engine 3152 is a GP 50 purchased in anticipation of offering a short, fast, short-crewed trailer on flatcar trains across the former GN line between St. Paul and Seattle as the BN was then doing in former Burlington territory. PHOTO BY MIKE BARTENSTEIN.

13. The Frisco Years

The SLSF Merger

With the seniority issues related to the Burlington Northern merger finally starting to settle down, the next shock was the merger with the St. Louis–San Francisco Railway Company, SLSF, or "Frisco," in November, 1980.

Earl Currie reports that well before 1980, Burlington Northern had moved away from the mean-spirited, vindictive management style previously common in the railroad industry and developed an affirmative style of leadership.[1] As part of the 1970 merger that created BN, the company had entered into 'lifetime' job protection agreements with its labor unions. Wages and salaries would be maintained for everyone working on 'M-Day,' provided that employees would exercise their seniority on the highest paying job they could hold. Management rightly saw these agreements as part of the political cost of the merger. The applicants agreed that this lifetime job protection would also extend to lower ranking officers and to exempt personnel. That is, the BN provided the same protection to their nonunion employees that they had agreed to provide unionized employees. The practical effect was that on merger day, BN had more management and exempt employees than were needed.

Original merger plans included four operating regions. To provide jobs for the protected officers and exempts, BN created two additional regions, one at Portland, and one at Billings. As excess employees in these ranks retired or quit, jobs were combined and abolished, reducing the head count by attrition. In time, these two regions were eliminated.[2]

The Frisco merger brought much improvement in engineering practices to the former BN territory. The merger also brought a management attitude of total disdain for anyone who was not a former Frisco manager, although former BN managers who bought into the Frisco attitude were accepted by the Frisco crowd. Relations between management and labor became extremely hostile.

Richard Grayson brought a reputation as a cost cutter. "Within months of Grayson's arrival and the closing of the BN-Frisco merger, many of the top railroad executives were former Frisco officers. '[The BN people] were a good bunch of railroad people, focused on maintenance. But they had never lived on hard times like the Frisco people,' Grayson said. 'I had to shake out the management. Bill Thompson, a Frisco executive who was named Executive Vice President of Operations, could get more out of a maintenance dollar than anyone I've ever seen. There were a lot of things we saw that they could do without.'"[3]

Frisco managers, specifically W. F. "Bill" Thompson, rapidly and substantially improved productivity of maintenance-of-way activities by imposing their standards and their methods on the much larger Burlington Northern. BN managers who wanted to see the new methods in action were encouraged to visit former Frisco territory and watch the gangs at work. BN managers accepted the new standards, set their gangs up on the new plan, and resolved to beat the productivity rate of the Frisco gangs. The Portland Division tie gang accomplished that very soon.

The new standard for tie gangs, who replace ties on a production basis, was 4.0 ties per man-hour. The previous BN standard was between 3.0 and 3.5 ties per man-hour. The new standard was almost instantly met by increasing the size of the gangs from 35 to 42 men and operating them with a double set of equipment.

The productivity rate gradually improved to 4.65 ties per man-hour by 1985.

For relay of new rail, the new standard was 1,100 man-hours per mile. The BN was using 1,500 man-hours per mile. The actual number was reduced to 626 man-hours per mile by 1985. The improvement resulted in part from a decision to set up separate small gangs to rebuild road crossings and to relay switches instead of having the big 70-man rail gangs held up for that slow work.

The new standard for surface correction was 1.0 miles per day. The BN averaged .5 to .7 miles per day. By 1985 the actual rate was 1.85 miles per day, roughly triple what the BN had been achieving. In addition, projects were redesigned so that surface correction was consistently done immediately behind tie and rail gangs to reduce the duration of slow orders behind these gangs.

A decision was made that the company would no longer maintain an inventory of replacement rail lighter than 90 pounds per yard, which simplified rail and other track material inventory. It forced the railroad to replace rail lighter than 90 pounds per yard in yards and on branches with heavier rail removed from the main tracks. That strengthened the yard and branch line track and reduced ongoing maintenance. The company acquired rail pick-up trains, to recover worn welded rail removed from main tracks and relay it on branch lines and in yards.

Men on tie gangs and rail gangs traditionally lived in bunk cars, which were old and obsolete freight and passenger cars converted to bunk service. The company replaced the bunk cars with new 'univans,' which were specially built trailers mounted on 50-foot flatcars. The change was a significant improvement in living conditions for the employees affected.

All of these changes carried the benefit of getting the work done at a lower unit cost, which meant that more work could be done for a given amount of money. These changes allowed each project to be completed sooner, which reduced the number of days the track was out of service to perform the work. Operating employees benefited from the improved quality of track that resulted from these changes. Earnings improved as better work practices wrung unnecessary costs out of these fundamental activities.[4]

I was working the west end chain gang to Wenatchee as a conductor during this time. The reorganized tie and steel gangs were completing their tie and rail replacement projects at lightning speed and the surfacing crew was working right behind them, which drastically reduced train delay and slow orders.

One project that really caught my eye was the welding of the jointed rail on the eastward main between Lamona and Bluestem, 22.48 miles, into ribbon rail. When this project started, I thought there would be delays all summer long, as had been the case when the same work had been done on the westward main the summer before.

The process was to cut out the rail joints to eliminate the batter and surface bending at the joints. Three hi-rail trucks did the work. The first cut out the joints with a saw and pulled the rails together. As they moved along, they inserted a new rail when necessary to fill the lengthening gap between rail ends. The second made the electric weld. Electric welds were a major improvement over the thermite welding process that was used exclusively until the early 1980s. The third ground the weld smooth on the top and inside of the rail head. I could not believe that it took only about three weeks to complete this entire job. Work was being completed faster than I had ever seen before.

The new management made some major changes that improved operations and made the movement of freight more efficient. One example was in the clerical department, with the addition of television cameras to take video of every train arriving and departing Yardley. Cars, loaded or empty, were required to move through terminals in less than 48 hours unless they were being held for material to make repairs, in storage, or held by customer request.

Frisco officials took over and immediately treated the operating employees like trash. We were threatened continually. Intimidation and humiliation were their chief tools. This put our local officials in a bad spot; they had to satisfy the SLSF officials and try to keep the tempers of the blue-collar forces down enough to avoid having a total mutiny on their hands. Knowing what the blue-collar force went through, I can only imagine the verbal abuse and threats that BN officials endured from the new SLSF management, since the officials got the same treatment we did, or worse. The difference between the officials and the blue-collar workers was that the blue-collar force had union representation, while the officials enjoyed no protection. They could be, and were, fired on the spot. If an individual had previously worked in a union position, he could exercise his seniority and go back to his craft. If an officer did not have union seniority, he had no former craft and was out on the street.

One Frisco official was the most ruthless and vicious official that I ever encountered in my 45 years in train service. William F. Thompson was the former SLSF Vice President of Operations who became Senior Vice President Operations after the merger. On his first tour of the former BN territory, he made his intentions known to all. Former BN officials who resisted his new forms of intimidation and control were fired or forced to retire.

Bad news travels with the speed of the wind on a railroad. The only trouble with the grapevine is the need to sort out fact from fiction. We in the Spokane area heard several tales of gross incidents involving Thompson elsewhere on the system. The stories were so preposterous and exaggerated that most of us did not think they were true . . . until he gave us one of our own at Parkwater.

Mr. Thompson arrived at Yardley with two other high officials. Our local officials were scurrying around in a total panic, which I knew was not good. Mr. Thompson, his two bodyguards, and a flock of local and regional officials toured the Parkwater diesel shop, located north of the main body of the freight yard near the east end.

Parkwater personnel were aware that they were going to be inspected, so the shop was spotless and the troops were all lined up for the new general to view. While the inspection was underway, and they were looking at the north side inspection pit, Mr. Thompson walked over to the inspection pit, unzipped his fly while announcing, "This is what I think of this place," and relieved himself into the pit in front of the Parkwater roundhouse employees. Employees occasionally used the pit to change out traction motors or to make other repairs when the main pit on the south side of the building was being used. This crude and gross act drew a line in the sand that remained for many years to come. After this incident, every story we heard about what was going on in other locations was much more believable, whether it was fact or fiction.

Years later, I spotted the power car that my crew used for picking up used rail over the north pit for modifications and repair. Someone made the comment that Pisser Bill made his name right here. People have a long memory for gross insults.

The Frisco upper management gave orders to clean out company storehouses and sell the spare parts for scrap. I saw brand new boxcar sliding doors loaded into gondolas to be sold for scrap. They also decided to scrap our wedge plows, snow dozers, and Jordan Spreaders. This did not happen, but only because resourceful, courageous people hid those invaluable machines on the tail ends of wyes or on back tracks where they could not be seen from a hi-rail vehicle or a business car on the main track. I still remember the comments from the local officials, and how some of them fell out of favor with the SLSF management over this issue.

➻ Rubber Rooms

One feature of labor relations that was peculiar to the Burlington Northern after the Frisco merger was 'rubber rooms.' They were the result of the combination of computerization and labor protective agreements that management believed they were forced to agree to as part of the cost of being allowed to merge.

As mainframe computer hardware and software improved and was applied to railroad operating functions during the 1960s through the 1980s, many clerical jobs were eliminated, computerized, and centralized. Fewer clerks were needed to perform the work required to move the traffic. The clerks, represented by the Brotherhood of Railway, Airline, and Steamship Clerks (BRAC), had negotiated income guarantees before the BN merger of March 2, 1970. This was called the "Orange Book Agreement" because the cover was orange. This agreement provided full income protection for the clerks on the payroll of BN predecessor companies as of the date of the BN merger, and became effective upon the consummation of the BN merger.

After the BN merger, country stations were closed and customer service functions were centralized. Now instead of taking the bill of lading to the local agent, the customer faxed it to the central office. Car orders and releases were now done by long distance rather than local phone calls. Paper records were replaced with computer data. These changes reduced the amount of clerical effort required to perform agency functions.

On May 6, 1980, in anticipation of the BN-SLSF merger, BRAC negotiated a new agreement that protected clerks who hired out after the BN merger. By definition, these people were not protected by the Orange Book Agreement. The new agreement was called the Blue Book Agreement, because the cover was blue. It became effective on December 1, 1980, the date of the consummation of the BN-SLSF merger. Appendix A of the Blue Book provided full income protection for the clerks who were hired after March 2, 1970, once they acquired four years of continuous service. As clerical jobs were eliminated and some of the clerks could no longer hold a job, they stayed home and got paid their regular wages.

During 1986, the company decided to require furloughed clerks who were getting full pay under the Blue Book protections to report to a designated location and stay for eight hours with a half hour unpaid lunch break, five days a week. About May of 1986, the company put the furloughed Spokane area clerks in the vacant Erie Street Yard office. They did not have any work to do, but could bring reading material as long as it was not offensive to others. No televisions were allowed. They were allowed to seek other employment using company telephones, and they could be away from the railroad while seeking other work. Unless seeking other work, they could not leave the property except on their lunch break. They could go outside and walk around as long as they stayed in the designated area near the Erie Street Yard office.

The Blue Book Agreement also provided that surplus clerks could qualify themselves for other clerical jobs, or they could relocate elsewhere on the BN, or they could take severance pay. Most of the surplus clerks saw the new 'show up' program as a way for the company to apply pressure to encourage them to quit. Some claimed that the program was intended to drive the clerks crazy, and the places soon became known as 'rubber rooms.' The clerks proved tougher than the company gave them credit for. Very few of the clerks took the buyout rather than sit in the rubber rooms. Most of the clerks resented the company for the rubber rooms as they felt this move was embarrassing and humiliating to a work force that was proud of their craft as part of the railroad family. The clerks' attitude was consistent with the opinion of the rest of the crafts who were having pressure applied to them by the SLSF style of management.

As new jobs replaced some of the older jobs, some of the clerks sitting in the rubber room were not qualified to work the new jobs. Clerks working the new jobs were often forced to work overtime because too few qualified clerks were available to cover the new jobs on all three shifts. While the clerks that could not hold a job were getting full pay for doing nothing, the clerks who were able to work were collecting large amounts of overtime.

Ken Stockton, Yard Office Supervisor at Yardley, was complaining to the Union Griever, Paul Fishburn, about the amount of overtime he was paying the clerks. Paul told Ken that the excess overtime was the fault of management because they refused to train the extra clerks on the jobs that they never worked. Rule 8 of the clerks' agreement provided the solution to the problem. Instead of paying a guaranteed clerk to sit in the rubber room, or stay home, the agreement provided that they could be assigned to train on any job for which they were not qualified. The clerk who performed the training would be paid an additional $1.00 for each hour they provided training. Once the extra clerk became qualified, he or she could be called in at the straight time rate, thereby avoiding the overtime. Due to the complexity of the new jobs, many of which were created by combining two or more jobs which were already complex, and depending upon the extra clerk's previous work experience, training could take several days to several weeks. Even if it would take a month to train a clerk for a job, the savings of overtime would very quickly repay the additional $160 paid to the training clerk.

Stockton, in an attempt to solve the overtime problem, arranged to have clerks who were not working break in on these new jobs. The training was going well when in walked the Terminal Superintendent, J. B. Scharff. He saw all these clerks breaking in, and blew his stack, screaming to get all these extra clerks out of here, sending them all back to the rubber room. As a result, the company continued to pay large amounts of unnecessary overtime.

Mr. Earl Currie confirms that the cost of clerks sitting in the rubber room was not included in the terminal's budget.[5] There is no other rational explanation for Terminal Superintendent Scharff's reaction to his discovery of the training program. By incurring a modest training cost, the company would have eliminated far more ongoing overtime costs. Scharff, a former BN man, was the most 'Friscoized' Terminal Superintendent ever at Yardley. Either he did not believe that adding clerical help at Yardley would reduce train delays, or he was so intimidated that he did not want to explain how and why doing so would be cost effective.

This was just one more reason why morale was so low around Yardley. Clerks were sitting at home or in the rubber room drawing full pay while other clerks were often being forced to work overtime shifts that they did not really want because management was so incompetent that they could not add two and two and get four.

While the union, some of the clerks, and the media complained that the rubber rooms were abusive, the complainers did not address the fact that the surplus employees were receiving a benefit granted nowhere else in the American labor market, that of lifetime wages regardless of the employer's need for workers.

About a year after the training attempt, the rubber rooms disappeared. No one knew why the rubber rooms were eliminated. The rumors were that in some locations there was some sort of trouble, and the company was afraid of lawsuits for cruel and unjust treatment.

➻ Working on the Frisco

By the time of the SLSF merger of 1980, intermodal business exploded to the point that the company was running trailer and container trains like street cars in the Wenatchee chain gang freight pool, and the intermodal business between Portland and Spokane was almost as heavy. The United Parcel Service business was increasing and many trucking companies like J. B. Hunt, Swift, Roadway, and others were shipping their trailers and containers on intermodal trains.

In mid 1980s, I was working the Wenatchee chain gang freight pool as a conductor and was called one day for the 'Pacific Zip' piggyback train to Wenatchee. My engineer was a young fellow recently graduated from the company's engineer training program. Between Espanola and Edwall, as our train approached the gated road crossing at Waukon, a tractor and trailer rig hauling magnesium ingots from the magnesium plant at Addy, Washington on the Kettle Falls line also approached the crossing. He stopped for us, but too close to the track. One crossing gate arm came down between his tractor and his flatbed trailer. The front of the truck was foul of the main line and the truck driver tried the impossible: to push the crossing gate back up far enough so that he could reverse the truck to clear the crossing. Before he could reverse his truck, the gate was back down.

The engine tore the front bumper off the truck. Far worse, the bumper tore the speedometer cable off the lead axle of the locomotive.

I really felt sorry for this truck driver. He was just in the wrong place at the wrong time. The timing was just wrong and he was trapped in an unavoidable accident. Most people hit at a grade crossing are not paying attention. This truck driver was paying attention, but got trapped.

There was no other west facing unit in the power consist. If we swapped the power around to get a speedometer, the lead unit would have no ditch lights and we would have to stop and flag all the crossings all the way to Wenatchee. This was out of the question. My young engineer informed me that with no speedometer he would have to run at restricted speed all the way to Wenatchee. I asked him, "How, if you do not have a speedometer, are you going to tell when you have exceeded twenty miles per hour?" He sat there in silence with a blank look on his face.

I told the rookie that he and I would be in trouble if we ran at restricted speed, and I was not going to get screamed at for hours of train delay on this very time sensitive train. I told him that I would tell him how fast he was going by counting poles and timing our speed with my watch. He did not believe me at first, but in a little while he figured out that I knew what I was talking about. After he got comfortable with the program, he made the comment that the company did not teach them this at engineers' school. I replied that there were a lot of things that they did not teach at engineers' school.

Later, as communications were transferred from phone lines to microwave, and small town stations were closed with the conversion to Centralized Traffic Control (CTC) and centralized customer service

A westward train approaches Harrington on a clear order board. The next eastward train will pick up orders as indicated by the train order signal. Harrington was located within the double-track segment between Lamona and Bluestem and would become the last train order station between Wenatchee and Spokane. COLLECTION OF JOHN E. LANGLOT.

centers, there was no need for land line communication. The telegraph and telephone wires were removed from the pole lines, and over the next several years the poles themselves were removed.

Working in the Wenatchee chain gang pool between Spokane and Wenatchee we had to contend with the time table and train order dispatching between Bluestem and Latah Junction, which caused unnecessary delays. There were no train order operators on duty between the Spokane depot and Harrington, a station on the double track between Lamona and Bluestem. In addition, the radio communication with the dispatcher between Spokane and Bluestem was very poor. By this time, conductors could and would copy train orders, but the radio reception on this piece of track was so unreliable that crews were forced to stop at a line side phone booth to copy an order. This was a ridiculously primitive arrangement to have on a busy main line in modern times, but that is what it was in the Frisco days of the BN.

The company finally installed CTC between Latah Junction and Bluestem during the winter of 1983–84. Time Table No. 4, dated April 29, 1984, is the first to show this segment dispatched by CTC. The double track between Bluestem and Lamona remained ABS, and trains operated with the current of traffic without train orders, a practice that continues to this day.

The pattern of all the new power going to support the rapidly growing coal traffic from the Powder River Basin in Wyoming continued under the Frisco management. The power assigned to the rest of the railroad naturally grew ever older, less reliable, and more worn out. Unreliable power on the northern lines was a continual source of trouble and delay. I made very few trips in this time period without locomotive trouble causing delay. Sometimes delays due to power problems made us go dead on our hours of service. I remember doubling Trinidad Hill and doubling on the new track west of Latah Junction on more than one occasion because a unit had failed.

Local management at Yardley bought into the SLSF way of managing the blue-collar employees. Things were never pleasant at Yardley. I came to work at Yardley on guard and with a very defensive attitude. It was common to be challenged as soon as one came through the door, or lectured about something that most of the time did not even pertain to you or your crew. This was pure

This is about what my stack train looked like when we came apart on the Latah Creek Bridge. South Seattle to Chicago intermodal train Z-SSECHC is crossing the bridge and about to pass through downtown Spokane on the former Northern Pacific elevated trackage. PHOTO BY BRUCE KELLY.

harassment in our book. At Wenatchee or Whitefish, conditions were respectable and the men were treated like human beings, but at Yardley it was right back to the psycho wars. Three incidents at Yardley illustrate this.

I was working the Wenatchee chain gang freight pool as a conductor and was called for a train to Wenatchee. I received the wheel report and waybills for my train. While going through the train list and the waybills I discovered that I did not have a waybill for a loaded tank car marked "Dangerous." I went back to the manifest clerk and told him that I needed a waybill for this tank car, which I was required to have as a matter of federal law.

The clerk was trying to get the waybill when Assistant Terminal Superintendent Gary Portsche came storming into the room, already hot under the collar. Gary asked the clerk what the delay was. The clerk told him he was having trouble getting a waybill for this loaded dangerous tank car. Gary stormed out of the room. About 10 minutes later Gary was back. When he found out that I still did not have a bill for the tank car he turned to me and said, "Well, it came in here without a bill." I responded, "Well, it's not leaving with me without a bill." Gary threatened, "If you will not take the tank car I will get a conductor who will." I told him, "Gary, you do what you have to and then I will do what I have to and I guarantee you will not like it." Gary again stormed out of the room and did not come back.

About 10 minutes elapsed with no more visits from Gary, so I went up in the tower and asked the yardmaster what he was doing with my train. He told me that they were having the east end switch engine take that tank car out of my train.

The point of this situation was that if I had taken the loaded dangerous tank car without a waybill, then I would be held personally responsible in addition to the responsibility of the company. If the train happened to go on the ground, and that tank car was derailed and leaking, and I did not have the required information for the emergency response crews, then I would be fired and subject to civil liability. It irritated me that Gary tried to intimidate me into taking the loaded tank car without a bill. I had already made up my mind that that if push came to shove, Gary would have to pull me out of service over this issue. If he pressed the point and called another conductor, I decided that I would take it to court if necessary.

Conditions at Yardley deteriorated to the point that keeping our jobs became secondary. The only thing that mattered was our self-respect, dignity, personal pride in being good rails, and knowing that we were not a bunch of low life scum, which was what we were being treated like. Working conditions at Yardley were the subject of discussion in several local union meetings. I knew when I took my stand about the dangerous tank car that several other trainmen had decided that they would pick a winning battle to fight all the way to the end.

The second incident illustrates the difficulty of getting any information, let alone good information, out of Yardley. Yardley was in a league of its own in so many ways, all of them unpleasant and most deliberately inflicted by the Frisco management.

The yardmasters had a trainmaster leaning over their shoulder the whole shift. Some of the yardmasters and most of the trainmasters at Yardley were rude and smart mouthed. All of the trainmasters were new hire college grads. They thought they were a cut above us low life blue-collar boys. They thought they knew everything and thought that trainmen did not have the intelligence to switch our asses off a wet toilet seat. Their attitude reinforced the uncooperative attitudes and behaviors that permeated Yardley.

One of the worst yardmasters at Yardley was Al Cook, who worked the graveyard shift. Bob Gay, who worked days, was almost as bad.

I got called at 6:00 AM for the morning drag west to Wenatchee. When I asked what the scoop on my train was, I got an earful. I was told that right now I was assigned one unit headed east. I needed to get this unit on the train on track 4, and then I needed to get a ride to the east end of the yard, blue flag the track, hang the FRED, make the air hose connections between the cars, and release any hand brakes that might be set as I worked my way to the head end. FRED, herein after Fred, is the electronic box that has virtually replaced the caboose on the rear of freight trains. In polite company, the term Fred is said to be an acronym for "Flashing Rear End Device." Fred's routine duty is to measure the air pressure at the rear of the train and to determine whether or not the rear of the train is moving.

I asked where the rest of my power was. Big Al told me that my other two units were at Keystone on a train headed east that was dead on hours of service, and the dog catch crew had just left for Keystone by auto. At this point I made up my mind that I was not going to take this train out of Yardley. I lined the air and knocked off the hand brakes. When I finished this little chore, the new yardmaster, Bob Gay, told me to make the air test on my train.

I asked Bob what the utility men were doing. He said that they were busy doing other jobs. I then said, "Right now they are playing cards in the lunch room." Bob told me they were at lunch. I said they came to work at 7:00 AM, and it is 9:30 AM. He told me to just do what I was told.

Before I got another ride to the east end of the yard to make the air test, I got a tape measure out of my grip. When I got to the rear end, I told my engineer to set the air. I walked the set and measured each and every car for piston travel and also checked closely for any federal defects on both sides of each car. I even checked to make sure that all the knuckles were equipped with a knuckle pin. I found three knuckles without pins that day. At the same time, I checked the train list against the train and marked the wheel report for mistakes in standing order.

I found about 15 bad order cars. I laid the bad news on Bob Gay's desk. He gave me one utility man to help switch out the bad orders. By the time I switched out the bad order cars and put the train back together, it was high noon and my other two units were just pulling into the yard with their train. I handed the manifest clerk the wheel report and showed him the corrections that he needed to make.

I was told to get a ride to Parkwater, bring the other two units out of the house to the west end, and switch the power together. When the engineer and I arrived at the Parkwater, we were informed that the service crew was going to have to service the power, since the units did not have enough fuel to make Interbay. The fueling rack was full of power being serviced, so we waited for our turn. Two hours later, the power was serviced and switched onto the train. Now it was 2:00 PM. The engineer and I had come on duty eight hours ago and worked continuously. We made a stub test on the train and the yardmaster started to push us out of the yard.

I told Mr. Gay we would be a couple of minutes more. He started to get nasty on the radio. I did not answer him but walked into the Terminal Superintendent's office and informed him that we were going to eat before we left Yardley. Now he got huffy. I said we had already been on duty over eight hours and we were not going to leave until we got something to eat. He got mad and said, "Then I'm going to tie you up and call another crew if you insist on eating before you leave." I said, "Do it," and he did.

The second crew made a pickup at Erie Street and went dead on hours of service at Odessa, far, far, short of Wenatchee. Management's incompetence at Yardley resulted in taking three crews to get one train to Wenatchee. While this was not an everyday occurrence, things like this happened too many times.

The third incident also occurred when I was working the Wenatchee chain gang freight pool. I was called for about 3:00 AM. I was getting my paperwork in order when the trainmaster came into the room and informed the three crews going to work that we would be attending a safety meeting prior to our trip. We all filed back to the conference room and sat down at the table. I did not see any safety film set up, and nothing was written on the blackboard. The trainmaster started the meeting with, "If we catch you doing this or that we will fire you, and if we catch you doing this you will be suspended for 30 days." He kept this up for a couple more minutes until I became fed up, got up and started for the door. He instantly asked where I thought I was going. I told him that this was not a safety meeting but was a harassment and intimidation session. I have not done anything wrong, did not deserve to be treated this way, and I was not going to tolerate it. I walked out. As I walked out, the other crews got up and walked out too.

After Terminal Superintendent John Scharff was transferred to Seattle in 1986, the new Terminal Superintendent caught the Assistant Terminal Superintendent home in bed in the middle of the night when he was supposed to be on duty at Yardley. The Assistant Terminal Superintendent was told to find himself a job somewhere else. After the departure of this Assistant Terminal Superintendent, the situation at Yardley started to improve, but by this time the attitude of the men was so bad and our lack of trust in the company was so deep that it was set in concrete.

I respected the new Terminal Superintendent, Mr. Dennis L. Prewett. He called clerks, switchmen, engineers, and trainmen into his office and closed the door for a little one on one talk with the understanding what was said behind the closed door stayed there and nothing would be held against the blue-collar worker for anything he said. All Mr. Prewett wanted to know was what had been going on at Yardley to drive morale so low. Mr. Prewett made a valiant effort to turn things around at Yardley.

Around 1985, I bid in the Wenatchee pool as a conductor. I could have worked east end chain gang to Whitefish, but there were three to four more months of winter each year in Whitefish than in Wenatchee. The climate was a big factor for me. I do not know how many times I was called to go to Wenatchee and would meet a crew called to go to Whitefish in the yard office. The Whitefish crew would all be wearing heavy winter coats, five-buckle rubber boots, and fur lined winter hats. I was wearing a normal jacket, no rubber boots, and no hat. Even better, when I arrived in Wenatchee, people would be out playing golf in 45- to 55-degree weather. To me, Wenatchee was a no brainer. Granted, the Whitefish pool was far more appealing as far as scenery goes in the summer. The bad winters on the east end far outweighed the scenery, so I stayed in the Wenatchee pool.

When I started to work to Wenatchee as a conductor, I fell in love with it. I could take the calendar for the month and pretty much figure when I would be home, and when I would be out of town. Towards the end of the month I might have to adjust my Spokane days and out of town days a little bit, but not much.

After the dispatchers and crew callers were moved from Spokane to Seattle, the quality of line-ups started to slip. My monthly calendar system no longer worked, and as time went by, the information on the recording that the crew office put out got worse. Then, when the dispatchers were moved to Fort Worth and the crew office went to Kansas City, the line-ups deteriorated to the point that they were useless. It got so bad that I never knew when I was going to work. Many times, I found myself going to work at 10:00 PM, having been up all day after being told that I would be going to work at six or seven the next morning. This is the main reason that after a few years I put chain gang at the bottom of my private list of bid-in jobs, just ahead of the conductors' extra board. I finally told the conductors' local chairman, who followed me in seniority, that if the line-ups did not improve, I would be on the work train instead of him. That is exactly what happened.

Shortly after the BNSF merger in 1995, the crew office was moved to Topeka, Kansas, separating the crew clerks from the reality of what they were doing. They did not know the jobs that they were calling crews for. They did not know the crews they were calling. It seemed that many of them did not care that they did not know. Since they did not know the people, they lost that personal touch. Moving the crew callers broke up the last remnant of the family atmosphere that was pretty much destroyed with the SLSF merger. Everyone knew that the reason the crew office went to Topeka was to save labor costs by placing all the crew callers in one location. This way the company employed fewer people who were constantly busy as opposed to more crew callers each with enough spare time to answer questions.

The Burlington Northern's line from the early 1970s that "Our employees are our greatest asset" fell on deaf ears among the employees. Unfortunately, most American companies of the era treated their employees as expendable, and now companies wonder why they have trouble getting devoted and dedicated employees.

I made a trip to Wenatchee in 1988 as a conductor on No. 21, a train off the MRL. Fred's battery was dead, so one of my brakemen got a ride to the rear end of the train and changed the battery to make sure the engineer got air pressure data from the rear of the train. The MRL crew told us that Fred did not show whether the train was moving or stopped before the battery went dead. I told the train master that our Fred would not indicate when the train was moving or stopped, and we needed a new Fred. He told me he did not have a spare Fred and to leave town with the bad order Fred. There were no rules about Freds at this time so I left town with the half working Fred.

This was during the Frisco era, so everyone was in the habit of asking questions even when the answer was obvious. By asking, the responsibility would fall on management's shoulders if something went wrong. If we did not say anything, then it fell on our shoulders because the local management would claim they did not know anything about it. We always made sure to have a witness to the question. Believe me, this was a miserable way to work, but it is what we were forced to do to protect ourselves.

At this time, the only operating document the crew routinely got at Yardley was a clearance. If there were any slow orders or adverse track conditions between Yardley and Latah Junction, the slow orders would be listed on the clearance and the orders supplied by the operator at Yardley. The Boyer West dispatcher issued this clearance and track conditions orders.

The crew of westward trains got another clearance, and any track condition orders at Spokane Depot. The Seattle East dispatcher, who dispatched the territory between Latah Junction and Seattle, issued the orders crews got at Spokane Depot.

Approaching the Spokane Depot, we realized that there were no orders in the hoop for us. About this time, the operator called on the radio to say he was just coming out the door with the orders. By the time the engineer got stopped, the engine was beyond the depot, so one of my brakemen ran back to the depot to get the orders. We were stopped for about five minutes.

After our train cleared Latah Junction and started up the hill toward Lyons, the Boyer West dispatcher called. He said that he still showed occupancy on the westward main between Napa Street Junction and Sunset Junction, and asked if our train was complete. I told him that our Fred that did not show whether it was stopped or moving and Fred showed 90 pounds of air pressure. About this time, Fred dropped one pound in air pressure and we started to lose contact with Fred. Then the trainmaster who told me to leave town with the bad Fred called on the radio and told us that the rear end of our train was sitting just west of Napa Street on the westward main.

Someone turned both angle cocks and pulled the pin between two cars when the train stopped to pick up the orders. Because the bad Fred did not show whether it was moving or stopped, the engineer got no indication that he did not have all of our train. I told the Boyer West dispatcher to tell the Seattle East dispatcher what was going on, and have him line us into the siding at Lyons. The Seattle East dispatcher did so. After we arrived at Lyons and secured our train with hand brakes, the dispatcher lined us out the west end of Lyons and back down the main to Latah Junction. We returned to Spokane, picked up the rear end of our train, returned to Lyons, doubled our train together, and proceeded to Wenatchee, incurring a delay of about two hours.

The next morning, we were called for a double stack train out of Wenatchee.

Double stack is a type of intermodal service in which containers are stacked two high while in transportation. It was a good trip until the Latah Creek Bridge. The air went into emergency and the train shuddered to a stop. My brakeman walked back to find out why the air went into emergency. Soon I got a "You better come back" on the radio, so I walked back and found a drawbar out of the west end of a double stack car. The drawbar went under the first well of the following five unit well car, where it was wedged under the floor of the car. A well car is a flatcar with deep side sills at the outside edges of the car, separated by a rectangular well into which a container may be placed. The bottom of the container rides about eight inches above the top of the rail. A second container may then be loaded on top of the first, hence the term 'double stack.'

I called Yardley Tower and told the yardmaster that a drawbar was wedged under a well car and we needed the carmen to come out with a cutting torch to cut up the drawbar. Soon the yardmaster called me back and informed me that the carmen were on their way.

About 40 minutes later, the carmen showed up with a cutting torch. One carman crawled under the car, cut the drawbar into three pieces, and spread the pieces out on the ties between the rails so that it would clear the wells of the trailing double stack cars. The drawbar punched at least one hole in the bottom of the first container. A switch crew later took the car to the ramp where it was unloaded so that repairs could be made to the framework on the bottom of the car and the load transloaded to another container.

The pin that holds the drawbar in place fell out somewhere between Lyons and Sunset Junction. The train was in dynamic brake west of Lyons and stayed in dynamic brake all the way down the hill to Latah Junction, which kept the train bunched. When the head end was on the flat of Latah Creek Bridge, fireman Tom Marabello, who was running the locomotive, came out of dynamic brake and went to power. Tom came out on the throttle very slowly to take the slack in the train. As he did so, the drawbar that the retaining pin fell out of pulled out, dropped to the ground, and went under the following car.

Dynamic brakes are an optional feature of diesel-electric locomotives by which the traction motors act as generators to retard the train. Dynamic brakes allow trains to move down grade with less wear on the brake shoes and wheels, and in the case of steep grades, trains can safely move at 25 MPH as opposed to about 10 MPH otherwise. Dynamic brakes eliminate the need to stop to cool the wheels when traversing long down grades. Except for a few early GP series units of GN and NP, all GN, NP, SP&S, BN, and BNSF road units were equipped with dynamic brakes.

While we were waiting for the carmen to cut up the drawbar, the trainmaster and Mr. Prewett pulled up in the company car. They both waved at me to come down to the car, which I did. When I arrived at the car, Mr. Prewett gave me a sign to get in the back seat. His first words were, "What happened?" I told them that the train suffered a mechanical failure and I explained why.

Then I said this has not been a good round trip, considering our crew was on No. 21's train last night. Mr. Prewett immediately asked why I left town with a Fred that was not working properly. I told him that I was told to go with that Fred by the trainmaster. It got very quiet in the car. The trainmaster driving the car was the trainmaster who told me to go with the bad order Fred. The trainmaster

LEFT BN 6481 East between Rock Island Dam and Albus in this unusual view taken from the west bank of the Columbia River. BN 6481 is a former NP 3639, an SD 45; and BN 6593 is former GN 327, a rare SDP 45. This train is at the lowest point on the railway between Wenatchee and Spokane. The basalt cliff in the background is the defining rock type of the Columbia Plateau and covers thousands of square miles. August 1982. PHOTO BY MIKE BARTENSTEIN.

RIGHT BN 6543 West between Albus and Rock Island Dam in view from the west bank of the Columbia River, August 1982. PHOTO BY MIKE BARTENSTEIN.

did not move. Mr. Prewett looked at him, but he did not move or say a word. Neither did I. About that time, the carman came crawling out from under the double stack car, so I said, "I have to go." I left the car and walked up the slope to my train. As I was walking away from the car, I could hear Mr. Prewett vigorously questioning the trainmaster. I was glad that I was no longer there.

Another time, I was working the Kettle Falls Turn as a conductor with a young brakeman named Leo Kenny. Leo was a very good brakeman and always did a good job for me. If Leo did not know he would ask questions or just say he did not know. That was better than some of the knot heads who figured they knew it all and could just fake it or bull s—t their way through.

Leo was nervous and worried that sooner or later his nerves would cause him to make a mistake. I told Leo to relax or he would worry himself into doing something stupid. Leo told me he was afraid that he was going to do something so stupid that nobody else had ever done it before. I told Leo that he could not possibly do anything so stupid on this railroad that someone had never done before.

Boy, did I string myself out to dry on that one.

About six months later, on April 29, 1990, an all Northern Pacific crew was working the Whitefish pool since the Missoula pool now belonged to the Montana Rail Link (MRL). As they were getting themselves and their paperwork together at Yardley, one of crew proudly made the statement that they were a 'pure' crew. He was right; they were all former NP men. Scooter Miller was the conductor. Scooter was always in a big hurry, which I learned at a very early age would cause me grief sooner or later.

They headed east and stopped to pick up several boxcar loads of aluminum at Trentwood. When Scooter cut the power off the train he did not wait for the engineer to toot the whistle to let Scooter know that the air pressure equalized in the train line. Scooter just bottled the air and gave the engineer a go-ahead sign.

To bottle the air means to close the angle cocks on a train or cut of cars so that pressure is contained, or 'bottled' in the brake pipe of the cars to be cut away from the engine. This is accomplished by closing the angle cock on the portion of the train to be kept with the engine, if any, and closing the angle cock on the portion of the train to be left.

The purpose of bottling the air was to expedite departure by avoiding having to bring the train line back up to 90 pounds of pressure from zero. This was no particular problem in the days of the older AB control valves. Bottling the air was forbidden long before 1990 because ABD and newer ABDW control valves are much more sensitive to pressure increase and they dump air from the reservoir on the car into the train line to speed propagation of the release through the train. This is a positive design feature that allows faster release of the brakes than the AB valves provided.

The oldest generation of control valves then in service was the AB valve introduced in 1933. Among the advantages of the AB valve were more reliable release of brakes on the rear portion of long trains, faster transmission of brake application signal, and better control of the rate of air flow into the brake cylinder.

The ABD control valve, introduced in 1963 and made standard for new construction in 1976, is an improved variant of the AB design. The ABD, and later ABDW (1976) control valves, require less maintenance and are more sensitive than AB valves. Their greater sensitivity accelerates both application and release. ABD and ABDW valves dump air from the auxiliary reservoir of each car into the train line to speed propagation of the release signal through the entire length of the train.

As a matter of practice, the engineer sets the brakes by releasing air from the brake pipe at the engineer's brake valve on the locomotive. That creates a pressure differential in the brake pipe between the front and the rear of the train. After the head end of the train reaches the pressure called for by the engineer's brake valve, it takes time for the air pressure to equalize through the entire train, which results in a continuing air release in the cab, as air flows from the back to the front until the entire brake pipe has equalized.

ABD and ABDW control valves require only about half a pound increase to release. If the angle cock is closed before the air equalizes, the air pressure at the front of the train will increase as the air pressure from the rear of the train flows forward to equalize pressure throughout the entire brake pipe. If the increase of pressure on the head end exceeds about half a pound or so, the brakes on the head end will release, dump air into the brake pipe, and propagate the release through the entire train.

They had no more stopped past the switch at Trentwood when Scooter saw that the train was moving west. He lined the switch for the main and they began to chase the train. The runaway train was picking up speed and had just cleared the crossing into the Trentwood rolling mill when the driver of a loaded hot metal truck from Kaiser Mead started across the crossing. Scooter's engines hit the truck. Scooter was riding on the bottom step of the now lead unit. It is a wonder that he was not killed. Scooter did receive some third degree burns from the flying hot metal. The truck driver was not seriously hurt. He was heard to make the statement, "Boy, they sure run those trains close together."

The collision with the truck ended Scooter's great train chase, but the train continued to accelerate. Back at Irvin, where the double track from Parkwater ended, an MRL train was innocently waiting for Scooter and his crew to make their pickup and head east. The MRL crew saw the runaway train coming. They took the safe course; they got off and ran away. The runaway train ran into the MRL train, derailing the cars on the rear of the runaway train, which hit the propane tank for the switch heater. The tank was broken open and the propane released and ignited, setting everything close by on fire.

About six months later, I saw Leo in the yard office. I told Leo I needed to apologize to him. He asked why. I told Leo that I was wrong; all the 'first ever' mistakes on the railroad were not used up, but I was sure Scooter Miller got the last two or three.

Many of us wondered why the BN merged with the SLSF and why were they in charge. It did not take long after the merger for the blue-collar forces to realize what a horrible mistake the SLSF merger was. I have often thought to myself what a great railroad the BN could have, should have, would have, been if only the new management treated their employees with the respect and consideration that they deserved. Railroad workers are a different breed. Crewmen do not require direct supervision to do our jobs. We took pride in being trusted to take care of the shippers since most of us realized that the shippers paid the bills and our pay checks.

The Burlington Northern never got the confidence of the men in the Spokane area back after the SLSF merger. This attitude was mostly due to the conditions the Frisco management deliberately created.

End of the Time Table and Train Order Dispatching

The Time Table and Train Order system, discussed in Chapter 2, and in Chapter 6 under the heading "The 490 Series Second Class Trains," required considerable time and 'on-the-job' training and study to really be well understood. By the time a telegraph operator was promoted to train dispatcher, or from a fireman to engineer, or from a brakeman to conductor, that person would be thoroughly familiar with requirements of the system. While its intricacies no longer held any mystery, it still offered an occasional surprise or two, and was enough like a chess game to make life on the railroad interesting.

Dave Sprau, a retired train dispatcher, points out that the time table and train order dispatching began to be replaced in the late 1930s as Centralized Traffic Control (CTC) installations started to appear on busy, usually single track, lines. Under CTC, the train dispatcher controlled the position of selected main track switches and the lineside 'absolute' signals related to the controlled switches. By lining the switches and clearing the signals, he could cause trains to meet or pass other trains as desired. With this positive control in effect, the rigid time table schedules and the elaborate processes of train orders were no longer necessary. CTC was a substantial capital investment, but it lowered operating costs by eliminating the line side operators and increased flexibility by giving the dispatcher moment to moment control. That increased flexibility translated into reduced train delays which further reduced operating costs.

As CTC was installed on ever more miles of busy routes, the train order system was slowly relegated to secondary and branch lines. By the 1980s, train order operation was very rare on busy segments of railroad. An unhappy consequence of this relegation to near obscurity was that newer employees never got much experience with train orders, and hence did not always understand them well.

An example of this was an incident wherein a 'Work' order for a maintenance train was issued, instructing that a particular engine would "Work Extra 630 AM until 430 PM between stations 'D' and 'E.'" The two stations were nine miles apart and running time between them was approximately 11 minutes. The order went on to list other trains expected in the limits, and a 'protect against' time by which the work train would clear the main track and after which the other trains could pass through the limits unhampered.

An inexperienced crew on an eastbound through freight train, with this order in hand, approached 'E' just before six in the morning and, noting that their train was NOT listed as one of the extras the work train would be 'protecting against,' stopped and refused to enter the working limits, stating they "were not sure it was okay." By the time the dispatcher realized what was happening and could explain that it was perfectly all right for the train to pass through the limits before the starting time in the work order, enough time had passed that the comfortable margin which originally existed to cover the through train had evaporated! By the time the dispatcher was able to issue another train order arranging 'protection' after 6:30 AM, for the train to run from 'E' to 'D' through the working territory, considerable time passed, and considerable delay occurred.

A livid superintendent, who was probably criticized by his superiors for the delay—such criticism flowing downhill until the lowliest party involved has been thoroughly chastised, soundly criticized the hapless dispatcher for issuing the standard form of train order routinely issued for years with nary a hitch. This superintendent was from double track territory in the east. He was not a 'single track' operating man and did not fully understand the system himself. He said, "That order is confusing!" The fact that he was one of the parties confused, and his diatribe was completely wrong, did not help morale in the dispatchers' office that day. The superintendent's response was a hint of things to come.

One rules examiner, a former train dispatcher, told the incredible story that during a staff meeting one day, he overheard several newer officials discussing the time table and train order system, giving it a thorough excoriating. None of them were very familiar with its actual workings. What they *were* all too familiar with was the fact that under its precise and exacting requirements, the train dispatchers and train and enginemen who used it daily seemed to have a 'grip' on things that the young officials were unable to fully comprehend, and therefore found threatening; they could not just barge in and demand a meet be changed, or a train they suddenly considered important be instantly given the right-of-way, as was possible with CTC. As a consequence, some of the more paranoid members of officialdom considered the system to be the 'runes' or 'machinations' of a 'secret society' which undermined their authority. Their conclusion was that the devilish system must go. The rules examiner who overheard all of this, and reported it to the author, was incredulous at the time. He "told it like it was" and the incident is recorded here for posterity, 30 years later.

In spite of such ridiculous assumptions and examples, technology was eclipsing the ancient system. In the early 1980s, train orders were still copied by 'operators,' sometimes known as telegraph operators, although telephone usage long ago eliminated the need of the word 'telegraph.' The written train orders and accompanying clearance form could be given to train and enginemen only at open stations along the line. If a train got delayed or was in some trouble where no operator was on duty, delay to that train was likely to affect other trains. Often nothing could be done to salvage the operation until after the delay occurred and its cause corrected while other trains waited. Issuance of train orders by the dispatcher directly to crews was discouraged; not only was it difficult from a communications standpoint, but labor contracts agreed to by management and the unions often made doing so very expensive from a penalty payment perspective.

Train dispatchers usually have good knowledge about trains on main lines no matter what dispatching system is used, but knowledge about trains within yards was a different matter entirely. Within a yard, train departures and train delays are subject to many vagaries, variables, and individuals: switch crews, carmen, yardmasters, manifest clerks, and roundhouse forces. Unlike on the main line, where the dispatcher has control, a problem within the purview of any of these people is beyond dispatchers' control, and greatly affects departure times.

Most terminal yards in train order days were regarded by train dispatchers as 'black holes' into which trains disappeared. Yardley was the blackest of black holes. Two trains would enter Yardley at approximately the same time; one would be ready to leave within a few minutes, but the other would be delayed for hours. The following day, both trains would disappear for hours, but the day after that, the train normally expected to stop only a few minutes would be interminably delayed, while the train normally spending several hours would be ready to go immediately. Yard departures were almost impossible to predict accurately, which created dispatching problems.

The 40.6-mile long territory between the east end of double track at Bluestem and Latah Junction remained Time Table and Train Order operation longer than almost any other piece of main line on the Burlington Northern. The intermediate sidings at Edwall, Espanola, and Lyons were equipped with spring switches on both ends. The crew was required to stop and open the switch to head in and then line the switch back for the main track, but could leave without stopping. This stretch of railroad could drive the dispatchers nuts and can be cited as a classic example of 'Murphy's Law' as applied to train dispatching.

Harrington was a station within the double track between Bluestem and Lamona and was the break point between two dispatchers' territories. The operator at Harrington dealt with both dispatchers, but the bulk of the work related to the territory east of the end of double track at Bluestem. There were no operators between Spokane and Harrington to copy train orders. The only places that train orders could be issued were Spokane and Harrington. Radio communication between trains and the dispatcher was very difficult with several dead spots. This territory was a headache for dispatchers and train crews.

The most effective way to deal with the unpredictable departure time of westward trains from Hillyard or Yardley was to issue train orders at Harrington, making eastward freight trains of known location and expected running time superior to westward freight trains which may, or may not, leave Hillyard or Yardley while the eastward trains were on the road. The dispatcher would also issue 'wait,' actually passing, times to the eastward trains. The westward train could thus advance as far as possible against the wait times for the eastward train at Lyons, Espanola, Edwall, or end of double track Bluestem. If the westward train failed to depart, the eastward trains moved unhindered. This system worked well but there was one drawback: an important westward train such as No. 97, now inferior by train order to a lesser train such as an eastward drag freight, both running as extras, would be delayed a few minutes taking the siding at the meeting point. Most operating officers understood this necessary exception, but a few did not.

If it was necessary to favor a hot westward train, then the dispatcher needed to issue orders making the westward train superior to the eastward trains, and issue wait times to the westward train. In order for eastward trains with such orders to move past the end of double track at Bluestem and continue toward Spokane, the orders should contain wait times on the westward train that reflected when it was realistically expected to be at the wait points. The dispatcher's problem was that the hot westward train might or might not leave Hillyard, or later Yardley, when the dispatcher figured it should. To favor westbound trains, it was imperative that the dispatcher have accurate information about when the more important train was expected to leave Hillyard or Yardley before issuing wait orders to any trains affected by them.

Problems occurred when operators would not, or could not, obtain good information. Considered 'eyes and ears' of the dispatcher, the operators could make a big difference in the quality of dispatching in train order territory, particularly in onerous pieces of track like between Spokane and Harrington. Some provided excellent service and obtained reliable expected departure time information by consulting roundhouse forces, carmen, yardmasters, and train crews, and reporting the consensus information back to the dispatcher, who could issue train orders which contained realistic waiting times that held up pretty well on important westbounds and allowed eastward trains to meet them en route with very little delay.

Unfortunately, some operators in latter days of train order operation, particularly at Yardley, were neither ambitious nor efficient. The normal polite way for a dispatcher to initiate a conversation requesting departure information would be to ring the operator on the dispatching telephone and ask, "When will 97's train get out of there today?" One clueless operator, instead of taking this hint, simply replied, "I have not heard," and hung up. Others made no attempt to do anything but would simply pull a guess out of thin air. Often, as the result of this bad information, the inferior eastbound train would pick up a fistful of nearly worthless train orders at Harrington. In compliance with those orders, they would head into the siding at one of the stations between Bluestem and Latah Junction for a 'hot' symbol train such as No. 97. The important train failed miserably to depart the yard at the time given to the dispatcher and was nowhere near the 'wait' time in the train orders. The eastward train, or multiple trains in many cases, would then sit for long periods of time, the crew(s) cursing the boneheaded dispatcher for poor work.

From time to time, an operating officer with sufficient authority, but insufficient comprehension of the consequences of such directives, would issue a hard-and-fast edict that train superiority must be arranged so that priority trains were not delayed between Spokane and Bluestem by trains of lesser importance. If a dispatcher disregarded such instruction so that he could move his eastward train(s) expediently, and it was later learned that a high priority train was delayed, for example, at Lyons, for fifteen minutes taking the siding for a train of lesser importance, a livid operating officer would scathingly criticize the entire dispatching force. Superintendent R. O. Hammerstrom, in a fit of temper, once issued further instructions that if there was delay again under such conditions, "Heads are going to roll."

Train dispatchers could be a somewhat independent lot in the face of misused authority. With the above instructions in place, they were forced to reverse their normal, time-tested procedure, and issue train orders making westward 'priority' trains superior to eastward trains between Spokane and Harrington. Dispatcher Bob Stewart, frustrated over similar 'Catch-22' directives, once stated the obvious: "It is fun to comply, to the letter, with stupid instructions." His comment was often cynically repeated in dispatching offices long after he gave voice to it.

Sooner or later, the officers who created these situations would rescind, or more often, not wishing to call attention, quietly relax their hard-and-fast instructions about train priority. It was a struggle to move trains on a busy main line in this territory by the time table and train order system with directives demanding dispatchers to favor hot westward trains in effect. As officers came and went over the years, the initially less comprehending among them eventually learned that the dispatchers were using the best possible system of dealing with the situation.

As ever more routes were changed from Time Table and Train Order dispatching to CTC, and as new dispatchers not adequately trained in the finer points of Time Table and Train Order operation were employed, some strange things happened.

Retired train dispatcher Dave Sprau recalls:

> One time most of the units on a westward train failed. The crew left their cars and caboose in the siding at Lyons and returned with their engine to Yardley. The intent was to get the power repaired, go back up the hill, get their cars and caboose, and continue the trip. Whether the crew copied a train order for the short eastward trip back to Spokane, or they merely 'flagged their way back, is lost to posterity. It really does not matter; the crew still held a 'live' order to run extra to the end of double track at Bluestem. With the locomotive at Yardley, the cars in the siding were no longer a train by rule book definition; without a locomotive displaying classification lights they were just a cut of cars.
>
> This was train order days and a CTC dispatcher (a dispatcher who learned the trade after train order dispatching was passé) was working the job; barely familiar with train orders, he thought himself quite capable. When an eastbound train neared Harrington, the dispatcher did not know what to do because his westbound extra, still holding its uncompleted running order to end of double track at Bluestem, was divided between two physical locations, the siding at Lyons where the locomotive was not, and Yardley where the locomotive could not be seen. Instead of having the crew of the light engines either pick up an additional train order at Spokane Depot, or copy an order on the telephone to annul their westbound running order, which was the proper course, and start over after the eastbound train arrived at Spokane, he issued another order that read: 'EXTRA 2 EAST MEET EXTRA 1 WEST AT LYONS.'
>
> Since there was no engine at Lyons, and it was impossible for the crew of the eastward train to properly identify "Extra 1 West" as required by rule, this was bad dispatching on its face. Compounding his error, he then added to the above order: 'EXTRA 1 WEST TRAIN IS ON SIDING AT LYONS AND ENGINES ARE AT YARDLEY.'
>
> The extra east picked those orders up at Harrington and went to Spokane on them without questioning the order! One can only wonder about stuff like this.

The only reason I know about this incident is that one of the dispatchers on the district west of Harrington heard all this going on and could not believe it. He pointed it out to me a day or so later. I looked in the train order book and sure enough, there it was.

Another time I was working second trick on the Latah Junction to Harrington territory. There was going to be a time table change at midnight. Amtrak schedules would go from daily to tri-weekly. Amtrak No. 10 was operating that night. This train, and its schedule, would turn into a pumpkin around Espanola at 12:01 AM because it was no longer scheduled to operate on that day of the week in the new time table. In addition, it was running about an hour late.

I transferred the territory to an extra board dispatcher, a young woman who believed she knew everything. I told her, "No. 10 is about an hour late and you have two westbound extras, symbols 83 and 77, called at Yardley. Because of the new time table, you will have to run No. 10 as an extra with right of track and some wait times for those two westbound trains or give them a meet depending on whether they really get out or not, and who gets out first." She kind of sneered and looked me as if to say "I know that"—made it plain for me to shut up—so off to home I went about 10:45 PM.

The next day about 10 minutes into my shift I received a very angry phone call from Wenatchee: "Are you the dispatcher who was working this job last night?" Stupidly I answered, "Yes" because I did not know what time 'last night' the caller meant.

"Well, I was on 83's train and we almost had a bad one with No. 10 thanks to those stupid orders you issued. We are not going to say anything about it, but you'd better learn how to issue orders a little better if you want to keep from getting fired." 'Click,' he hung up without identifying himself.

I looked back in the order book and saw to my astonishment she gave them a 'meet,' all right; the first westbound met the passenger train at Espanola and the second one stayed at bottom of hill near Sunset Junction, but here is the order she issued: "No. 10 meet extra 1 west at Espanola and has right over extra 3 west from end of double track Bluestem to CTC Latah Jct."

Turns out she did NOT know what to do, so she asked the dispatcher working the district west of Harrington. As fate would have it, this was the same guy who issued the meet with the cut of cars at Lyons. He did not know what to do either. So instead of doing what I tried to tell her, annulling No. 10, whose schedule evaporated around Bluestem or Espanola anyway and running the passenger train as an extra, he tells her to "Give No. 10 a meet with No. 83 at Espanola. Then 83 has a meet with SOMEBODY for sure." So that is what she did.

Here is what happened: No. 83's extra took the siding at Espanola. Clock ticks, tick, tick, tick. About 40 minutes goes by and no passenger train shows up. Now it is past midnight, the new time table has now taken effect and there is no "No. 10" scheduled in it. Tick, tick, tick; the crew on 83 remembers their training days and the engineer says, "I think this is a test or something, there is NO train No. 10 in the time card anymore, and we should just go." They argue for a minute or two. The engineer, who is correct because this is a classic case used in examples about what other trains may do regarding expired schedules in time tables, wins the argument.

The brakeman starts walking toward the west switch. Just as he gets there and is reaching for his key, the block drops from green to red. Five minutes later, a passenger train goes roaring by at 79 MPH. This scares the crew on 83 speechless because they know that if the timing was different, they might have been on the main line at Espanola two seconds after the passenger train was over the east switch Edwall and there is no telling how badly THAT would have turned out. I have no idea why the second extra west, waiting at the bottom of the hill at Sunset Jct., did not try a similar move. The crew on this train either realized something was wrong and they needed to stay put, or realized nothing, believed the orders were okay and waited for the unscheduled "No. 10." Either way, they too were involved, whether they knew it or not.

Several days later, somebody on one of the three trains involved told Superintendent Hammerstrom about the incident. You can imagine his response to this situation, which did not become a disaster only by the grace of God. I was not privy to it, but I understand he called everybody in the world and chewed them out. I do know that he called Ed Khatain, the Chief Dispatcher at Seattle, chewed on him and told him to "Straighten out those dispatchers." ROH further said that there would be no investigation because too many people were going along with and mixed up in it. This was in caboose days, so at least nine trainmen on three crews including the passenger crew, three engineers, two dispatchers, and the operators at Yardley and Harrington would have been involved in an investigation. I would have been dragged in too since questions would have been asked about my turnover.

Although I kept my mouth shut, I did mention it to the dispatcher who gave the young lady the bad information that was the root of the incident. His response was to get mad at me and say, "Well, they had a meet with SOMEBODY." I tried to tell him, "No, they did not. It is a classic example used in school to teach train orders." He was either clueless, not listening, or perhaps did not wish to admit to having badly misled the younger dispatcher.

I guess after Ralph Hammerstrom got through chewing, all the crews knew about the incident, but knowing nothing more would come of it, the crews made it the talk of Yardley for a few days. I think the passenger conductor was old John Jolgen. I am not sure about that, but whoever it was, that passenger train crew had their necks stuck out a mile. They should never have gone by Harrington with a clearance for a train that would not exist in a few more minutes when a new time table took effect. Sometimes things happen so fast that by the time anyone does the "shoulda, coulda, woulda" part, it is too late.

I learned the true details of what the freight crew said and did at Espanola that night about 10 years later when I was making a dispatcher's road trip to Whitefish. One of the brakemen told me about a trip many years before; how they almost had a headlight meet with No. 10's train, and how he called the dispatcher from Wenatchee the next day and "straightened him out." In telling me this, he did not know the story from my end, nor that I was the dispatcher he incorrectly picked years earlier for the butt chewing. I played dumb, and that is how I got "the rest of the story."

John Langlot referred to the railroad between the end of double track at Bluestem and Latah Junction as "no man's land." John relates: Several times I got stuck for trains between Bluestem and Latah Junction. I did not blame the dispatcher because I knew that Yardley was responsible for some of this delay. This stretch of railroad was probably responsible for some dispatchers not bidding on the Seattle 'Train Order' job, and I cannot say that I blame them.

I recall one trip that tells the way it was when the dispatchers dropped the ball. We were called for 3:00 PM at Wenatchee and left about 4:00 PM on a very long and heavy train No. 198. We picked up 26 cars of grain and about 15 cars of french fries and other loads at Quincy. Leaving Quincy, our train was over 7,500 feet long. I remember the length. I do not remember the tonnage, but the train was heavy. At Quincy, we could still hear radio conversation at Wenatchee, and learned that the Empire Builder would be an hour late arriving and leaving Wenatchee. Train No. 198 left Quincy about three hours ahead of the Builder's time and headed east with all possible speed.

Odessa was the last siding in CTC territory that an eastward train passed before entering double track at Lamona. Harrington, where the two dispatching territories abutted and telegraph operators were on duty 24 hours per day, was 15 miles east of Lamona. Another seven and a half miles east, at Bluestem, an eastward train enters single track time table and train order territory where all the sidings were too short to hold us. Odessa, therefore, was the last good place a long eastward freight could get out of the way of a following superior train. I expected the dispatcher handling the Seattle-to-Harrington territory to head us in at Odessa for the Empire Builder, but our Engineer, Pauly Miles, advised me by radio that the approach block to Odessa was clear. Apparently, the dispatcher wanted us to keep going, so I told Pauly just that: "Keep on going."

Leaving Odessa our speed dropped as the train started up the hill. We were down to 10 MPH at times, grinding it out mile by mile as the train entered double track at Lamona. At Harrington, we picked up train orders authorizing our movement from Bluestem to Latah Junction. I knew the Empire Builder was closing on us at 79 MPH and was not pleased to find no train order advice of No. 8 being late, nor any order relieving us from clearing No. 8 as if it were on time.

Finally, 35 miles east of Odessa and almost two hours later thanks to our crawling pace, our engine was within sight of the automatic interlocking signals at Bluestem. Our speed slowly increased as the grade eased. Pauly took the clear interlocking signal and entered single track. At last nearing track speed, as he started down the hill, Pauly asked by radio if I wanted to head in at Edwall to saw No. 8 by. Our train was only about 10 minutes ahead of No. 8's time table time at Bluestem. Since we held no train orders authorizing us to disregard Rule 86, which required us to clear No. 8's time table time, by rule we should have cleared for No. 8 at Edwall, the first available siding.

Having given our situation quite a bit of thought, I told Pauly that No. 8 must still be at least 40 minutes behind us, and to keep going because there was no siding between Bluestem and Latah Junction that would hold our train in the clear between the switches. Despite Pauly's concern, I made the decision to keep going since we would delay No. 8 far less running ahead of them than sawing them by. Despite my hopeful estimate that No. 8 was 40 minutes behind us, I kept listening for No. 8 to call out an approach block which would mean he was right behind us. Finally, we started down the hill at Lyons and I called the Boyer West dispatcher in Spokane to let him know train 198 was past Lyons. I'm sure he was expecting No. 8 rather than us because his reply, in a voice tone leaving no doubt he felt we might cause a problem, was, "Where is No. 8?" I said, "Forty minutes late."

After all that sweat and worry, not to mention bad decisions by two dispatchers, and my winking at the operating rules, everything turned out all right. Our caboose was passing the Spokane depot when No. 8 called the Boyer West dispatcher to say they were leaving Lyons. But the outcome could have been very different, and our crew would have been defenseless except to use the distasteful but true response that the Seattle dispatchers set us up for what happened.

To this day, I do not know what was going on in that Seattle dispatchers' office. Two dispatchers were involved. They were sitting right next to each other in a warm, well-lighted office, able to freely discuss our situation and aware our train was a 'dog.' Surely, they should have figured out that letting us by Odessa could be a mistake. Meanwhile, Pauly and I were crawling along in the dark trying to guess which course was best to follow. Were those dispatchers brave, chicken, or ignorant?

As for the Seattle-to-Harrington dispatcher who let us go by Odessa and put us on double track at Lamona, smack into another dispatcher's territory, I would suggest 'ignorant' if he simply sent us into the other dispatcher's territory with no thought about what would happen next.

I would suggest 'brave' if the Harrington-to-Latah Junction dispatcher issued an order at Harrington allowing us to run ahead of No. 8 from the end of double track at Bluestem to CTC at Latah Junction, or an order stating No. 8 would run a specific number of minutes late from Bluestem to Latah Junction. Either would have protected us in the event of any official inquiry into the matter, but he did not issue anything. I think the Harrington-to-Latah dispatcher was 'chicken' for not being proactive and giving us an order taking the worry out of possibly delaying No. 8.

The inaction of both dispatchers set us up to either delay No. 8 or violate the rules. I could not do right no matter what. The first mistake was letting us pass Odessa. The die was cast when train No. 198 passed Harrington without orders. The dispatchers put the burden of their decisions on me. I had to figure out how to keep previous dispatching decisions from having a very bad outcome.

How far behind us was No. 8 when we went by Bluestem? I thought about 40 minutes, but I did not know. I could be brave, wink at the letter of the rules, and run ahead of No. 8, or I could obey the letter of the rules, and head in at Edwall. If I headed in, and my 40 minutes late figure was correct, and our crew had No. 198 in position before No. 8 showed up, and all went well, the delay to No. 8 due to our saw-by move would be 30 minutes or more. Fortunately, this was in the days when we still used a caboose, so I had men at both ends of the train to handle the switches.

A saw-by is a meet or pass in which one train is too long to fit in the siding or on the main track between switches where the meet is to take place. Superiority of trains controls which train will take the siding unless superseded by train order or CTC, so the inferior train will generally take siding regardless of train length. The long train positions itself so that the other train can enter the main or siding. The short train enters the track it will use. After the short train clears the switch, the long train moves so that the short train can exit the station at the opposite end. If trains were to pass, the first train must back up to clear the other train at the leaving end of the siding. Backing a long freight train is a delicate maneuver best done slowly for safety's sake.

A saw-by would delay us by the 40 minutes that No. 8 was behind us, by the time required to do the saw-by, and then by the time to pull through the siding, line the west switch back for the main, and leave, another 45 minutes more. If I chose to comply with the letter of the rules, and if someone looked into how the whole thing began, the dispatchers would likely be roundly criticized for setting up a situation where rule 86 required us to delay No. 8.

When I chose to run on No. 8's time to avoid stabbing No. 8, I was open to a charge of rules violation and a possible investigation. Rule 86 said, "Unless otherwise provided, an inferior train must be clear at the time a superior train in the same direction is due to leave the next station in the rear where time is shown." Running on No. 8's time was the correct decision, as long as nothing unusual happened to delay us. Run we did. Fortunately, no unusual event occurred. At the time, rule 86 was enforced very loosely when nothing went wrong or nobody chose to take exception, but enforced very rigidly when things went bad and someone wanted to 'Monday morning quarterback.'

The next morning, I was called at Spokane for a Directors Special to Wenatchee that was continuing to Seattle. The crew rode to the depot in the company van. I went to the dispatchers' office to get the orders, where I was greeted by the chief dispatcher who thanked me for not sawing No. 8 by at Edwall the night before. In an unusual situation that prevailed at the time, the Chief was located in Spokane, but the dispatchers that he was responsible for were located in Seattle. He apparently discovered their rather odd move, letting us by Odessa and onto double track after it was too late, and worried about additional delay to an already late passenger train for at least an hour. When he heard me call to say No. 198 was out of Lyons, he said it felt like a hundred pounds had been lifted off his shoulders. I told him that I figured that there would be less delay to No. 8 if we just kept going. I also told him that I did not appreciate the Boyer West dispatcher announcing to the whole world on the radio that we were on No. 8's time. The Chief told me that the dispatcher got his butt chewed out for doing that.

From my point of view, this was the last portion of the railroad where the conductor could make some decisions about the movement of his train running against wait times of following a superior train as I did running ahead of No. 8 on their time table time. Again, it was that adrenaline rush. It was the last of the train order running on the main line in our area, and I loved it.

Finally, in the spring of 1984, CTC was completed between Bluestem and Latah Junction. I was a conductor in the Wenatchee chain gang freight pool when the CTC was completed. I could not believe that it took so long to install this modest bit of CTC. The CTC saved time almost every trip. Given the amount of train delay between Latah Jct. and Bluestem, this should have been corrected long before it was.

The ability to replace the time table train order system on lines without enough traffic to support the investment in CTC arrived in the late 1980s as microwave and radio repeaters came on line. Now it was possible to communicate clearly with trains, no matter where they were. The days of a train being 'lost' between stations and unable to reliably talk to the dispatcher were over. With this change came the realization that direct communication with crews, and the elimination of the time table and train order system, not only was possible, but could be implemented immediately.

The second approach, after CTC, to eliminating the train order system was developed by the Seaboard Coast Line (SCL) and was called "Direct Traffic Control" (DTC). Southern Pacific Transportation Company adapted and modified the SCL rules to fit Southern Pacific's circumstances. Southern Pacific first used DTC on the Tucson Division early in 1985. DTC was extended to other divisions later that year.[6]

In the SP version of DTC, the railroad was divided into blocks. The blocks were named generally after the station with a siding at one end of the block. The limits of each DTC block were indicated by signs beside the track. By definition, the DTC block included only the main track.

For example, a railroad subdivision running from station 'A' to station 'Z' would have many intervening stations. To illustrate, the first four station names are:

Anna
Bess
Cloy
Doris

Two signs were posted at the limits of each block. The top sign said "End NAME Block" and the bottom one said "Begin NAME Block." This method of designating blocks continued down the line until the entire subdivision was divided into blocks. Assume that Anna is the easternmost station on the subdivision. At the west yard limits of Anna, a westward train would see a sign "Begin Bess Block." The Bess block extended to the west fouling point of Bess siding where a westward train would see a sign "End Bess Block," and immediately below it a sign "Begin Cloy Block." The Cloy block extended to the west fouling point of Cloy siding, and the Doris block extended to the west fouling point of Doris siding.

The location of the signs indicating the ends of the blocks was very important in making DTC work. The signs were all inside the siding switches, at the fouling point, and at ONLY one end of each siding. This allowed the dispatcher to tell either train to take the siding for a meet. If there was a junction at a location otherwise in the middle of a block, then an "End/Begin" sign pair could be placed just beyond the main track switch as viewed in the facing point direction to create two blocks between sidings if there was a need to do so.

The train dispatcher, now able to dependably contact each train, could issue instructions to a particular train authorizing it to "Occupy NAME Block." If the dispatcher wanted to make a meet at a station, he would instruct one train to take the siding at the named block.

The dispatcher could give two types of authority: "Proceed," that is, to move in one direction only, or "Work and Time." Work and Time allowed movement in either direction within time limits. This was functionally the same as a 'work order' in train order practice.

The dispatcher could give authority in one or several blocks at a time. Crews were required by rule to release their authority as soon as the entire train cleared each block. If there were no closely following movements, the dispatcher could tell the crew to release authority only after they cleared some specific block. This was useful to reduce radio chatter.[7]

When railroads other than SCL and Southern Pacific wanted to replace Time Table and Train Order operation, they invented the "Track Warrant Control" system. This was the third approach to eliminating the train order system.

The new term 'track warrant' was substituted for 'train order' in a successful effort by management to characterize the system as new technology. This eliminated labor claims and grievances over existing work rules designed specifically for the Time Table and Train Order system. In fact, the track warrant form that train crewmen fill out as dictated by the dispatcher is a highly formatted descendant of the old 'Running Order,' or Form G train order.

Under Track Warrant Control (TWC), each train, identified by engine number, is separately instructed to run from one location to another. This distance may be as short as between two stations, or as long as an entire subdivision. The only requirement is that the ending location in the warrant must not overlap the authority of any other train. So, like checker pieces on a board, trains are moved against each other, as well as ahead and behind each other, over line segments much like the old "Manual Block System" of 100 years ago. Indeed, the logic behind the two systems is similar.

Unlike the train order system, crews have no knowledge of where other trains are or why their movement authority is often to someplace in the middle of nowhere. The reason could be as simple as trackmen working on the track ahead, an opposing movement, a movement ahead in the same direction, or some other situation or emergency.

The main difference between TWC and train orders was that the train order system required written establishment of superiority between the various trains *before* actual authority for movement, the 'running order,' was issued. Track Warrant Control contains no such precaution. At least one prairie accident occurred when opposing train crews, unaware of each other's presence, suffered a head-on collision resulting in death and injury after one crew member misunderstood his instructions and moved his train beyond the end point on his track warrant. One union officer, after surveying the wreckage, wrote a scathing letter calling track warrants "death warrants," and suggesting restoration of a key feature of the older train order system, namely, listing on each warrant the identification of any opposing train that would be encountered during the trip over the subdivision. The suggestion fell on deaf ears. The Division Superintendent angrily ridiculed it during a post-accident hearing by suggesting it was Luddite in

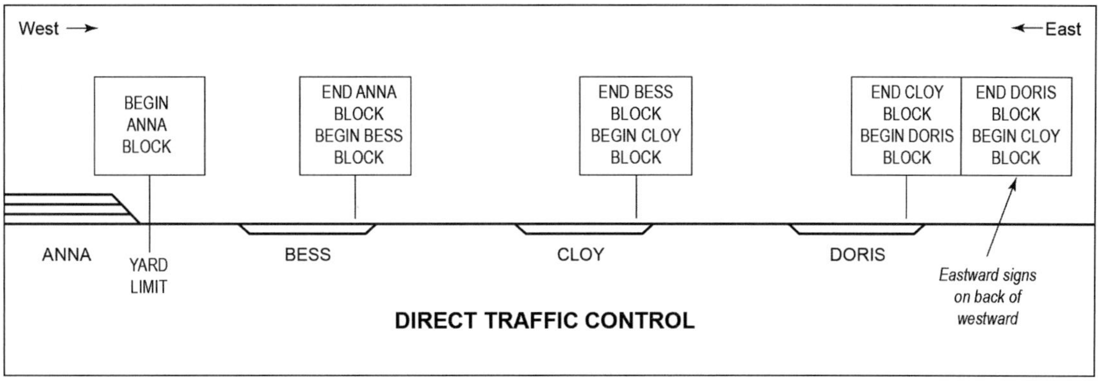

nature, saying, "... and would you also propose to send these instructions by Morse code?"

Burlington Northern began the transition from Time Table and Train Order operation to Track Warrant Control on January 1, 1984, when it was first used on the Fort Worth Division. The Seattle dispatching office issued the last American train order at 2208 hours Saturday January 16, 1988 to UP 3691 at Tacoma, authorizing it to move to the beginning of CTC at Wabash.[8]

The Canadian government was slow to approve track warrants in Canada. The last train order issued by the New Westminster, British Columbia dispatcher's office was dated December 8, 1990.[9] Track warrants have totally displaced the Time Table and Train Order and Direct Train Control systems.

Keeping track of these movement authorities in the dispatcher's office was initially done manually, the train dispatcher relying on his "Warrant Book" and "Train Sheet" to make sure no movement authorities overlapped, same as with the time table and train order system. Issuance of track warrants has, by the time of this writing (2017), evolved into a computer-based system foolproof enough to prevent issuance of any instruction that would permit two trains having no knowledge of each other to occupy the same space.

John Langlot recalls some of his experiences with TWC. TWC was implemented some years before the company abolished his work train and he bumped onto the Kettle Falls dog catch job.

Training Officer Mark McNaghten was giving training classes to new hires at Yardley. John related: trainees made three trips with me on the Kettle Falls dog catch job since it was the only job that worked out of Yardley which regularly copied track warrants. After a few trips, I told Mark that having these guys try to copy a live warrant without ever even having seen the form before was not working. Some of them would try to fake it. About half the warrant would be either wrong or missing. I could see beads of sweat on the foreheads of the students as they tried to copy the warrant. Along with the sweat, their voices would crack, and some of them developed a stutter.

Mark talked to the terminal superintendent. John continues: they offered to pay me a basic day to come in and teach track warrants to the class for three days. I came in on Monday since it was one of my days off. We used two portable radios set to channel 88, a rarely used maintenance-of-way channel. I played the role of the dispatcher and gave them the track warrant over the radio from another room. They copied it, and then repeated it word for word, with Mark looking over their shoulder to make sure they did it right. Each student got about 10 repetitions over the course of three Mondays.

Following this training, the first time a student copied the track warrant for the Kettle Falls dog catch job at Valley, after the student had finished, the dispatcher said, "That went very well." I told him how Mark and I modified the training program. His comment was, "Keep doing it. This is great. I am going to put in a good word in for you with the Chief." This practice is still part of the student training program today where TWC is used.

The only time I experienced a problem with track warrants was at Chewelah when I was conductor of the work train. The dispatcher was giving both my train and the opposing Valley Turn a track warrant to milepost 49. His intent was for the Valley Turn to head in at Chewelah for us. We would then get another warrant and go to Kettle Falls ahead of them before they turned at Chewelah.

I was sitting in my Chevy Suburban that the company installed a company radio in and paid me to use on the work train. My smart mouthed, but good natured, engineer called my Suburban "The Command Module.' I was at Chewelah looking at the physical MP 49.

As the dispatcher started to transmit the warrant, I looked up to confirm the MP 49 location and said "BREAK" to break his transmission. All was quiet for a moment. The dispatcher asked what was wrong. I said, "This is not going to work because the north switch is south of MP 49, not north of MP 49." He fired back that his track profile showed the north switch was north of MP 49. I told him I was in the support vehicle at the north switch looking at MP 49 and the north switch is south of MP 49. I went on to tell him that about five years back the track department shortened up the siding leaving MP 49 north of the relocated north switch.

There was a long moment of silence. Finally, the dispatcher said, "Do not anyone move until I talk to the Chief." About 10 minutes later, the dispatcher came back on the line. I could hear the chief dispatcher in the background as we went through the whole conversation one more time. By the time that conversation was done, someone from the computer track profile department was there and again I was asked about the locations of MP 49 and the north switch.

The dispatcher intended to give us both authority to MP 49 and instruct the Valley Turn to head into the Chewelah siding for us. The problem was that the track plan had not been changed after the siding was shortened. Milepost 49 was located about 300 feet north of the siding switch, so the Valley Turn could not get to the siding holding authority to MP 49.

None of this would have been an issue if the dispatcher had given us both authority to Chewelah, instructed the Valley Turn to take the siding, and instructed us to hold the main. We would have stayed clear of the north switch, and the Valley Turn would have held authority to use it. This was the proper way to issue a track warrant for this routine meet. I have no idea why the dispatcher chose to use MP 49 instead of the station name.

Endnotes

1 Earl Currie, *BN-Frisco, a Tough Merger* (Self-published, 2010), 21.
2 Earl Currie, letter, November 14, 2017.
3 Kaufman, *Leaders Count*, 211.
4 Earl Currie, email, February 15, 2012.
5 Earl Currie, *Transformation of a Railroad Company* (Rails Northwest, 2019), 24.
6 William J. Neil, email, July 24, 2012.
7 Carson S. Lundsten, "Railroad Rules, Signaling, Operations: Direct Traffic Control", last updated July 26, 1998, www.lundsten.dk/us_signaling/dtc/index.html.
8 Burlington Northern Railroad, BN News Update, Volume 2, No 1, February 1988, 1.
9 Dean Ogle, email, July 25, 2012.

14. Difficult Days

➽ THIS CHAPTER WILL DISCUSS CORPORATE activities, labor relations problems, abandonment of the SP&S east of Pasco, the Winona Bridge fight, and the Network Operations Center. Next, we will move to safety, covering two major wrecks and the improvements in BN's safety program during the 1990s.

➽ Corporate Activities, 1980–1995

Several important corporate decisions were made during and after 1980 that affected the railroad. The first was new, non-railroad top management and creation of a holding company; the second was the impact of Frisco and oil company management on the railroad; the third was separation of the resource-based holding company from the railroad; the fourth was finding a partner for another merger.

The Board of Directors brought in the new non-railroad top management for two reasons; one was to help the railroad deal with deregulation. The other, far more important reason was to develop the company's non-rail assets. The first step was the decision in the spring of 1980 to create a holding company.[1]

The board selected Richard Bressler, Executive Vice President and Chief Financial Officer at Atlantic Richfield Company (ARCO), to be Louis Menk's successor; he arrived in June of 1980.[2] Bressler formed the holding company, Burlington Northern Incorporated, in 1981, and established its headquarters in Seattle, about as far away as possible from the St. Paul headquarters of the railroad.[3] The Burlington Northern Railroad Company was now one of several subsidiaries of the holding company. The other companies owned by Burlington Northern Incorporated had previously been subsidiaries of the railroad.[4] Shortly after forming the holding company, BNI purchased El Paso Natural Gas, a gas pipeline and production company, in a hostile takeover.[5]

The Frisco management made profound impacts on the railroad. The Board of Directors saw Richard Grayson as a cost cutter. After the SLSF merger, Grayson put many of his Frisco subordinates in key positions that reported directly to him. Operating, Accounting, and Management Systems, the computers and programs that were by then critical to operation of the railroad, were all soon headed by former Frisco people. The native BN managers felt like they had been invaded.[6]

Among ways that Grayson cut costs was the 'window plan,' what today is known as an employee buyout. Lifetime income protection for all employees was a condition of both the BN merger and the BN-SLSF merger. As a result, the company employed more officers and exempt employees than it needed. In 1981, the company offered officers and exempts age 55 and over a bonus of up to $100,000 paid out over five years to leave the company. When combined with their company pension, the bonus was often enough that if an employee continued to work, his additional income for working was very little. Many of the 1,600 eligible employees took the buyout. The buyout tactic has since become a staple of the railroad business, and American business in general.[7]

At the end of 1982, Richard Grayson retired as President of the railroad. He was replaced by Walter Drexel, formerly Treasurer at ARCO, and Vice President for Planning at its Anaconda Copper subsidiary.[8] Bressler brought Drexel into BNI, the holding company, shortly after he arrived as Senior Vice President–Strategic Planning.[9]

Drexel's goal was to increase railroad operating income, an appropriate goal for anyone in his position. He did a splendid job, telling author Laurence Kaufman that "About 1980 or 1981 the operating income was somewhere in the range of 100 million dollars. In 1985 it was 900 million." Grayson and Drexler slashed the payroll from 60,000 in 1980 to 37,000 in 1984, a period in which revenues were flat.[10] Most of this reduction occurred under Grayson, but Drexel continued the policy with all possible vigor.[11]

In the summer of 1983, Drexel announced that the railroad's headquarters would be moved from St. Paul, the location of headquarters of Great Northern and its predecessors, and of Northern Pacific, since before the turn of the century. He instructed his subordinates to choose a location where many of the headquarters employees would not go. The Operating Department was relocated to Overland Park, Kansas, in 1983.[12] Four hundred employees took early retirement rather than move to Fort Worth, Texas, in 1984.[13] The Operating Department later moved to Fort Worth.[14]

Darius Gaskins joined BN as Senior Vice President, Marketing and Sales, in 1982. Gaskins earned a doctorate in economics and previously worked in several government positions in Washington, D.C. President Carter appointed him Chairman of the Interstate Commerce Commission in 1979, one of the few chairmen who were actually qualified for the position.[15] As Chairman of the ICC, he had been an important advisor about transportation deregulation in President Carter's administration and helped establish the key provisions of the Staggers Act. Having been at the ICC and having worked with Senator Staggers to develop his deregulatory act, Gaskins was in a stronger position and more qualified than anyone else at the time to understand how to apply the new law for the benefit of a railroad company. Grayson wanted Gaskins to come to BN when he left the ICC in 1981, but Gaskins decided to go elsewhere. About a year later, Gaskins put out feelers to the BN and the Santa Fe. Grayson and Bressler offered him the position of Vice President of Marketing and Sales two weeks later. Gaskins became President of the railroad in 1985.[16]

To separate the railroad from its resource assets, the Northern Pacific bonds of 1896 would have to be dealt with. The bonds were a general lien on the resource assets of the Northern Pacific, which came to the NP as part of its land grant. The bonds carried a low rate of interest and were not callable. BNI needed to get the general lien on the resource assets released. After protracted legal wrangling, the railroad and the bondholders reached a settlement in 1987. The railroad paid $35.5 million into a fund that paid $147.50 per $1,000 face value of the bonds that expired in 1996, and $456.25 per $1,000 face value of the bonds that expired in 2046. Face value is the nominal value printed on the face of a bond. The most common face value of railroad bonds of the nineteenth and twentieth centuries was $1,000. Interest is paid on the face value, and at the end of the term of the bond it will be redeemed, or paid off, at face value. In theory, the bond was to be issued, or sold, for its face value. The Burlington Northern Railroad bought back the natural resource lien without otherwise disturbing the bonds.[17]

During 1989, BNI spun off the Burlington Resources Incorporated to its shareholders, leaving BNI with only the railroad. At the same time, Darius Gaskins left the railroad and Gerald Grinstein became President of the Burlington Northern. He correctly concentrated on paying down the debt that the railroad was given in the spin-off of Burlington Resources.[18] Grinstein came from an airline background and was brought in to improve relationships with labor.

The spin-off made no difference to the stockholders on the day it happened. The day before the spin-off, they owned one share of BNI that represented their claim to the earnings and assets of the entire holding company. That share traded at a particular price. The next day the shareholder still owned his BNI share, which now owned only the railroad, plus he owned a share of Burlington Resources. The two shares combined represented the same earnings and assets that the single share of BNI did the day before, and the two together traded at the same value as the combined BNI did the day before. The change from the shareholder's perspective was that now each business would be valued separately by the market. Investors with a taste for resources would tend to bid up the value of the resource shares, while those looking for a pure rail play would bid up BNI.

The question from the stockholder's point of view is, "How did the course that the board and management took with my pile of assets work?" Or, "What are the assets valued at in the market today versus at some time in the past?" The value of a company is its market capitalization, which is the number of shares outstanding times the price per share. The market value of the debt is also part of the market capitalization, but for the sake of simplicity we will ignore that component. A more sophisticated version of the question is, "What would the market value of the company be if a different course had been taken?" This question is much more difficult to answer.

During 1980, the market value of Burlington Northern, that is, the railroad with all the other assets, was less than $1 billion. In 1989, Burlington Resources was spun off to BNI shareholders. The railroad, BNI, and Burlington Resources continued to operate and traded separately on the stock market. Burlington Resources spun off Plum Creek Timber to its shareholders in 1989. Burlington Resources spun off El Paso Natural Gas to its shareholders in 1992, and Bressler went with El Paso. As of April 30, 1993, the aggregate market value of the four publicly traded entities was $13.3 billion.[19] ConocoPhillips, a large, integrated oil company, acquired Burlington Resources on March 31, 2006, for $35.6 billion in ConocoPhillips stock.[20]

Berkshire Hathaway acquired the railroad in February of 2010 in a stock swap and cash transaction. At the price Berkshire paid for the stock it did not already own, the market capitalization of the railroad was $34.193 billion, plus about $10 billion in BNSF debt that Berkshire assumed. Berkshire paid small shareholders, and larger shareholders that did not want Berkshire stock, $16 billion in cash, with the balance paid in Berkshire stock.[21] The Board and management clearly performed their duty for the shareholders.

The fourth major issue in this period was finding a merger partner. With all of the major railroads involved in some stage of merger during this era, the pool of merger partners was shrinking.

The holding companies that controlled the Atchison, Topeka and Santa Fe Railway (Santa Fe) and the Southern Pacific Transportation Company (SP) merged on December 23, 1983. The merged holding company was required to put the Southern Pacific in trust while the holding company spent most of the next three years working to merge the Santa Fe railroad with the Southern Pacific, only to have the railroad merger rejected by the ICC in 1986. After selling the SP, the Santa Fe holding company came under attack. While a hostile takeover was averted, when it was all over the non-rail assets of the holding company were sold off and the Santa Fe was back to being a railroad by 1989.[22]

In 1994, the Burlington Northern and the Santa Fe announced their intention to merge in a stock swap that effectively amounted to the BN buying the Santa Fe. Union Pacific then attempted to purchase the Santa Fe. In the end the UP dropped its bid, but the BN was forced to pay $1.2 billion more than its original offer for the Santa Fe, which most observers believe was the Union Pacific's intention all along.[23]

The BNSF merger was approved and took place in September, 1996. With the merger Robert Krebs, of the Santa Fe, and formerly Southern Pacific, became President of the company.[24] A railroader, probably the best in the country at the time, led BNSF after the merger. Those who believe that a railroad should be run by a railroader were doubtless relieved, since the position of President of the railroad had been held by non-railroaders from the time Richard Grayson retired until the BNSF merger, almost 15 years.

The SP&S Abandonment

A major event in the history of the BN in Eastern Washington was the abandonment of the Spokane Portland and Seattle Railway (SP&S) line east of Pasco. The seeds of this decision were sown when Walter Drexel became President of the railroad at the end of 1982. Drexel made it clear that his job was to manage the assets, not to run trains. A key measure of how well assets are managed is return on investment, which is a ratio obtained by dividing earnings by assets. To increase ROI, one can increase earnings, decrease assets, or both.

The SP&S main line between Spokane and Vancouver, Washington was the best engineered rail line across the state of Washington. Eastward from Vancouver to Cheney, the SP&S faced no grade over .4 percent. Westward trains faced 5.2 miles of .8 percent, beginning immediately west of Fort Wright Junction, and then 11 miles of .4 percent up to Cheney.[25]

In comparison, the NP line between Pasco and Spokane featured 1.0 percent ruling grades westward and 1.1 percent eastward. These grades were concentrated

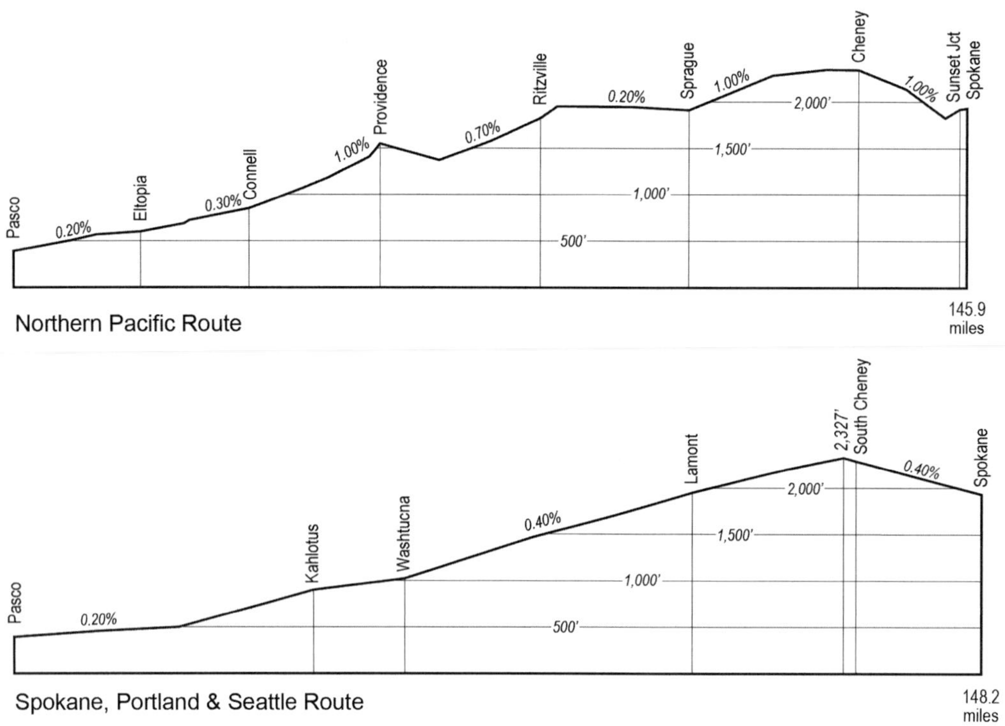

NP and SP&S Profiles
Spokane to Pasco

on Providence Hill between Connell and Lind and between Sprague and Spokane, with 12 of the 16 miles between Cheney and Spokane including a grade of at least 1 percent. The low crossing of Hangman Creek looks like a hole in the NP's profile.

Mr. Earl J. Currie in his excellent book *James J. Hill's Legacy to Railway Operations,* states:

> Of the strategic decisions in which I had a part while serving on the Burlington Northern, the one over which I have considerable regret was the decision to designate the former Northern Pacific line between Spokane and Pasco as the preferred route, and to abandon the parallel SP&S line. In 1982, the question came up as to which of the two lines should be abandoned, as we were in a deep recession and business in the Pacific Northwest was 'in the tank.' It was assumed by the senior level of management that the volume of business handled by railways would continue to decrease. There was little confidence that Burlington Northern would ever get back on a track of growth. As a result, a major driving force was to reduce the asset base by selling and retiring assets, and by limiting capital expenditures to those that would produce high returns in the short term, and hard dollar savings. An operation having duplicating, parallel routes such as we had between Pasco and Spokane became a prime target. Following the merger in 1970, the NP and SP&S were used as double track. The SP&S line had much more favorable grades and was used for westbound traffic because of the heavy movement of westbound unit grain trains.
>
> Besides having surplus assets in place, we needed to relay the rail on much of the SP&S line. It consisted almost entirely of 112 and 115-pound jointed rail. It had a fairly high defect rate, and some of the rail was beaten down at the joints. A rail relay of about 140 miles would be expensive ($300,000 per mile, or $42,000,000 total), and as is the case with any rail relay, it would have a low return on the invested capital. We made a thorough

analysis of all the factors involved, but all of the 'eyes' that focused on the issue had to conclude that the best option we had was to retain the former NP line and abandon the SP&S line. No one in either the Finance or Operating departments debated the numbers we produced. The only argument for retaining both lines was to preserve the capacity that would be needed for long term growth, assuming, of course, that one had faith that our regular business would recover and that international trade would expand.

As for retaining the SP&S line rather than the NP line, the arguments were that the SP&S line had much more favorable grades and less curvature. With trains operating on the SP&S line, the rate of fuel consumption would be more favorable, less motive power would be required and the running time would be lower. However, those advantages were not enough to offset the cost of relaying the rail and future maintenance of a second main track. Finally, there was considerable local business on the NP line, so nearly all of that line would have to be retained, even if the SP&S line were to be used for through trains.

Some Burlington Northern officers cited the exposure of the SP&S line to rock slides in a few locations east of Pasco, in support of a recommendation to retain only the NP line. However, that argument carried little strength as the SP&S had installed an adequate number of slide detection fences and provided enough money each year for a preventative program for scaling rock which could come loose and roll down to a slide fence. The engineering people of the SP&S looked upon the matter of rock slides as just one more item of roadway maintenance they were required to deal with, and not a serious or expensive deficiency. In the end, the only significant disadvantage of the SP&S line was the small amount of locally originated and terminated business it had in comparison with the Northern Pacific's line.

It is interesting to note a list of the projects that have been carried out to improve the NP line since the decision was made to retain it as the main line. Among them are the installation of centralized traffic control over the entire subdivision, construction of a second main track of 14.5 miles over the grades of 1 percent on both sides of Providence, extension of double track four miles east of Pasco, and the lengthening of nine sidings. At the time of the study made in the early 1980s it was determined that all of the through trains operated at that time could be handled adequately on the NP line without making such capital improvements. It is because of the large increase in business since then that the management found it necessary to finance the large capital improvements listed above.

The average number of freight trains operated between Spokane and Pasco has increased from about 15 to today's (2005) level of about 30 per day. This growth in business has been due to the expansion of international business in containers, finished automobiles, and grain. In addition, the revitalization of the "Inside Gateway," the former Oregon Trunk and Great Northern line via Bend, Klamath Falls and Stockton, has produced additional volume as well. Once the SP&S was integrated into the Burlington Northern system, together with the subsequent merger with the Santa Fe, better service was established, and the business grew.

With increases in business beginning in the late 1980s it became apparent to many that the decision to shut down the SP&S mainline between Spokane and Pasco was a major strategic error. Both lines should have been retained. Fortunately, Burlington Northern approved major expenditures to increase the capacity of the NP line and otherwise improve it. However, it still remains a far less efficient line than the SP&S. The SP&S line was placed in a 'bank,' and as part of the agreement that allowed the State of Washington to convert it to a recreational trail, Burlington Northern has the right to reclaim the line and put it back in service.

The way in which this entire matter was evaluated in the early 1980s was in marked contrast with Hill's approach to long term planning. It was reflective of the approach that has become common in much of corporate America in the past 20 years, in which the needs for long term investment are subordinate to the maximization of quarterly earnings. Hill completed major projects such as the SP&S to provide strong capability for the long term. He did not lose faith or become disheartened because some projects may not have produced high returns right from the date of their completion. He withstood the criticism and pressure he received from the financial community, and at times from his peers in the industry. He had the knowledge and the instincts needed to evaluate opportunities, even though he knew some of them might not bear full fruit until years after his passing.[26]

Mr. Currie is too gentle, in our opinion, in his criticism of the Drexel management that carried out the study, and of the Gaskins management that actually abandoned the SP&S in 1987. Drexel's asset management focus 'bit the BN in the ass' almost immediately. Robert W. Downing, who put the merger plan for Spokane together in the late 1960s, was Chief Operating Officer of the BN from 1971 through 1976. By the 1980s he was no longer on the Board of Directors, however, he pleaded with the asset managers not to destroy the SP&S. Mr. Downing called the line a "crown jewel." Downing's pleas were ignored. Drexel was so focused on shedding assets that he never even considered the option of shutting the SP&S down for a while to see how things worked out in practice.

To carry out the abandonment of the SP&S, the Burlington Northern built a crossover at Lakeside Junction between the NP and the SP&S lines. The new crossover took westward trains from the SP&S to the NP. Eastward trains on the NP could either stay on the NP through Marshall to Spokane, or they could move via the SP&S. The crossover created two main tracks between Lakeside Junction and Sunset Junction.

The Pasco freight pool using only the old NP line was a self-inflicted disaster. John Langlot reports: "After removal of the former SP&S between Lakeside Junction and Pasco a good trip on this 144-mile subdivision was one that a crew completed in 12 hours. The Pasco pool traffic just about doubled after the company pulled up the SP&S line. Before removing the SP&S, the company added CTC to the NP line, but even with CTC the NP line between Spokane and Pasco was not able to handle the increase in traffic. Most of the time crews went dead on their hours of service long before they reached Pasco or Spokane."

The decision to destroy the SP&S between Spokane and Pasco was one of the worst decisions that BN management of Bressler, Drexel, and Gaskins ever made. As Robert Downing told John Langlot in 2009, "The railroad should have been expanding with more double track instead of downsizing like they did."

During the summer of 2013, BNSF completed grading for a new siding to be called Lamphier, located between Fishtrap and Sprague, extending the double track eastward over Providence Hill 4.6 miles from Sand almost to Lind, and 3.2 miles westward from Cunningham to Hatton, making a total of 19.2 miles of two main tracks over the ridge between West Lind and Hatton. Babb siding was extended 3.2 miles through Cheney to East Cheney. Cactus siding was extended 3.3 miles to a new control point named West Cactus, only .8 miles from Mesa. Tokio siding, located between Ritzville and Sprague, was extended to create 4.6 miles of second main. Track was laid on these segments in 2014.

Prior to 2014, two and three main tracks were built between West Wye and Glade, including two main tracks around Pasco Center (the hump yard), to expedite moves both eastward and westward into and out of the receiving and departure tracks of the Pasco hump yard.

As of March 2018, the line is all CTC with at least two main tracks from Pasco to Glade, 8.6 miles to MP 137.0, followed by 18.2 miles of single track to West Cactus, with a controlled siding in the middle of the single track at Eltopia. Two main tracks extend 5.6 miles from West Cactus to East Cactus, followed by 12.0 miles of single track to Hatton, with a controlled siding at Connell near the middle of the single track at MP 109.7. From Hatton, 19.2 miles of two main tracks take the line over the ridge between Hatton and West Lind. Single track extends 19.7 miles to West Tokio, with controlled sidings at Paha and Essig, followed by 4.6 miles of two main tracks from West Tokio to East Tokio. From East Tokio, 41.2 miles of single track extend to Babb, with controlled sidings at Keystone, Sprague, Lamphier, and Fishtrap, none farther than 8 miles from another. Two main tracks extend 6.5 miles from Babb to East Cheney, followed by 3.2 miles of single track to Lakeside Junction, from which two main tracks extend to and beyond Spokane.

The BNSF now has nearly the capacity of two main tracks between Yardley and Pasco which they could have had, without the heavy investment since 1987, had the "Oil company" management not destroyed the far superior SP&S line.

➻ Winona Bridge and Montana Rail Link

The Winona Bridge fight and the sale of the lines that became Montana Rail Link were two parts of the

Burlington Northern's attack on rail labor. They are not the only attacks, but were the ones that most affected those of us working at Spokane.

In the early 1980s the Burlington Northern, in an effort to compete with the better service of the trucking industry, introduced its 'Expediter Service.' Expediter trains consisted of a locomotive and trailers on flatcars, known as TOFC. The marketing concept was to provide frequent service with short trains between selected points. This would reduce the wait time at origin terminals and increase the quality of TOFC service. Crew costs were a significant portion of rail operating costs, so for the company to have a chance to make money with the service, they needed to operate with less than a full crew of four men.

The company proposed that expediter trains be limited to 25 cars and be operated with a two-man crew: one engineer and one brakeman, eliminating the position of conductor. Since the Expediter Service was designed to bring new traffic to the railroad, its net impact on employment should have been positive. Most of the local committees of the UTU accepted the change in the crew consist for the Expediter Service in exchange for special allowances and productivity gain sharing. As a result, the Expediter Service was available on two-thirds of Burlington Northern's system.

The company proposed the Expediter Service to the Northern Lines General Chairmen, Mel Winter, for the former Great Northern trainmen, and to John Filter for the former Northern Pacific trainmen. The two general committees were made up of all the local chairmen from the lodges on each former railroad and handled issues that pertained to their former pre-merger territory. The Expediter Service issue affected both the former GN trainmen and the former NP trainmen. Both Mel Winter and John Filter recommended that their general committees reject the Expediter proposal. The Expediter Service issue was one of the few times that these two general committees worked together to oppose the company's proposal.

General Chairmen Winter and Filter passed the proposal down to each of their local chairmen and the local chairmen presented the proposal to the individual members in their lodges. Passing the proposal down to the men was normal practice, and the general chairman would often recommend acceptance or rejection of a proposal. This was a special case. Mr. Winter visited all the GN lodges and explained the adverse effects on the number of jobs that we could, and would, lose if this proposal was accepted. I attended that union meeting and recall that it was a very grim and depressing meeting.

The men voted on the proposal to determine the decision of each lodge. Each local chairman then voted at the general committee level, casting their single vote to reflect the majority opinion of their lodge members. The general chairman informed the carrier of results of the voting of his general committee. The men and the local chairmen of both the Great Northern and Northern Pacific lodges voted the Expediter proposal down; it was rejected on both former GN and former NP lines.

One of the reasons the Northern Lines committees voted the proposal down was that the carrier proposed to eliminate the position of the conductor. The men felt that the crew should be an engineer and conductor. Our other concern was how long it would be before the carrier would violate the 25-car limit or file a Section 6 notice to raise the car limit. The men had been down this road before with the carrier with different issues. In past working contracts, the ink would not even be dry before the carrier would violate the contract by cutting valid claims and force the union grievers to write the grievance up and submit it to the labor relations board for review. I personally have had valid claims paid over six years after the carrier denied the original claim. The reason it took so long for these claims to be reviewed by the labor relations board was the glut of claims that were backlogged waiting to be reviewed by the board. Our union general chairman told anyone who asked that he felt that this was a deliberate tactic by the carrier to overload the review system.

Darius Gaskins became President of the railroad in 1985. The Gaskins management, undaunted by its setback at the bargaining table, devised another means of implementing its Expediter Service on the Northern Lines that avoided the necessity of union negotiations. Burlington Northern granted its wholly owned subsidiary, Winona Bridge Railway Company, trackage rights over the former Great Northern line. A trackage rights agreement grants the new carrier rights to operate trains over the grantor's track.

The Winona Bridge trackage rights agreement called for Burlington Northern to supply all necessary equipment. The agreement limited Winona Bridge's right to pick up and set out only at Burlington Northern's trailer-on-flatcar terminals in St. Paul, Spokane, and Seattle. The agreement thus covered approximately 1,860 miles of track from Winona Junction, Wisconsin, to Seattle. The agreement could be modified, however, to include such other terminals as Burlington Northern might authorize in writing. The only impediment to Winona Bridge's unfettered right to use Burlington Northern's track and terminals was BN's written permission.

Everyone believed that BN would open more routes, and all of its terminals, to Winona Bridge within a very short period of time. Once the company opened all of its terminals to Winona Bridge, it would not take long until all intermodal traffic would be handled by Winona Bridge crews. Winona Bridge was a huge threat to our jobs since intermodal traffic was becoming more important every year.

When the trackage rights agreement was entered into, Winona Bridge Railway Company's assets consisted of one out-of-service bridge and 1.07 miles of track. Winona Bridge Railway employed five people, none of whom ever operated trains. Winona Bridge, as a new carrier, would employ newly hired crews, who would have no collective bargaining agreements with the UTU and BLE. Winona Bridge was not subject to the Expediter Service 25 car limit.[27]

As required by statute, Winona Bridge sought ICC authorization to implement the trackage rights agreement, which fell within the reach of the ICC's expedited procedure for approval of certain rail transactions. An applicant filing a notice of exemption under 49 U.S.C. sections 10505 and 13343 was essentially granted an automatic exemption from the typical ICC filing and hearing procedures; the exemption was routinely granted upon a filing received seven days in advance of the proposed transaction.

In response, the unions filed a petition to reject the specific exemption as well as a petition to revoke the exemption process. The ICC denied the petition to reject the exemption, finding no reason to void on its face the notice of exemption, and declined to consider the underlying motivations behind the proposed transaction. The ICC took no action on the petition for revocation.

After unsuccessfully moving for reconsideration by the ICC, the UTU appealed to the Court of Appeals for the Eighth Circuit, which dismissed the appeal for want of a final order since the petition for revocation was still pending. (See *Winter v. Interstate Commerce Commission*, 1988.)

While the issue was still in court, in December, 1987 the UTU and BLE each served notice on the Burlington Northern as provided by Section 6 of the Railway Labor Act, insisting that the trackage rights agreement with Winona Bridge constituted a unilateral change in the collective bargaining agreements by Burlington Northern. Burlington Northern argued that Winona Bridge's operations would not affect the working conditions of Burlington Northern employees, and that in any event, the ICC authorization relieved Burlington Northern of any responsibilities imposed by the Railway Labor Act. Both disputes were submitted to the National Mediation Board.

On November 18, 1988, the United States Court of Appeals, Seventh Circuit, granted the appellants UTU and BLE a preliminary injunction enjoining the proposed trackage rights agreement between Burlington Northern and its wholly owned subsidiary, Winona Bridge Railway Company, pending resolution of a major dispute under the Railway Labor Act.[28] While the injunction remained in effect, crews on the Northern Lines intermodal trains would remain one engineer, one conductor, and two brakemen. After the unions secured the injunction, the company dropped the Winona Bridge idea.

This entire process started early in 1980 and ended in November of 1988, taking over eight years to play out. Early in 1989, Mel Winter received a standing ovation after he was introduced at our local lodge meeting on the occasion of his last trip to visit the lodges before he retired. After the crowd quieted down, he informed us that we could have lost it all if the Court of Appeals had ruled in favor of the Burlington Northern.

While the Winona Bridge fight was in court, in 1987, the Burlington Northern leased part of the former Northern Pacific main line to Mr. Dennis Washington.

The trackage covered by the lease was between Huntley, Montana, a few miles east of Billings, and Sandpoint Junction, Idaho, with trackage rights from Sandpoint Junction to Yardley. This transaction formed a new railroad called Montana Rail Link, or MRL. This new railroad would handle BN through freight traffic between Huntley, Montana and Yardley. I personally believe that the BN entered into the MRL transaction in retaliation for the men turning down the Expediter Service proposal.

Dennis Washington was a self-made billionaire. He worked construction in Alaska after high school. Two years later he returned to Montana and worked for his uncle's construction company. At age 29, he entered the heavy construction business for himself, and by 1969 was the largest contractor in Montana.

In 1977, Anaconda Copper Company, owner of the copper mines at Butte, Montana, was purchased by Atlantic Richfield Company (ARCO), a large oil company, for $700 million. ARCO knew nothing of hard rock mining and appears to have bought Anaconda for its Wyoming coal holdings. Faced with a sudden drop in copper prices, ARCO suspended mining in Butte in1983.

Washington acquired ARCO's mineral assets in Butte in 1986, leaving the liability for environmental cleanup related to previous mining with ARCO. Washington reopened the mine as a copper and molybdenum mine. Thanks to a presumably low purchase price, higher metals prices, and operating as a non-union mine, the mine is said to have proved very profitable. Since Washington's companies are all private, there is no public data about their profitability.[29]

Because MRL was a new carrier, like Winona Bridge, it did not have a union contract. Before the lease of the MRL was finalized, the BLE negotiated a sweetheart deal with the MRL for crews to consist of an engineer and an assistant engineer. This agreement included no trainman positions. When the MRL was created, BN employees working in that territory could either go to work for the MRL under the new BLE agreement or move elsewhere in their region. Some stayed, most moved.

Both the Winona Bridge and the MRL lease were union-busting moves by the Burlington Northern. This pretty much was the icing on the cake for the long-time employees, especially the former NP men, since it was their line, and their jobs, that were being given away. The MRL transaction caused hard feelings among the trainmen and the enginemen against the Burlington Northern.

In the course of the Burlington Northern merger of 1970, the company and the operating unions agreed to expand the geographic scope of seniority from the division to the region. By the time of the MRL lease, our region included everything west of Whitefish and west of Missoula.

To enable Missoula men to bump into Spokane and Whitefish, the UTU overrode our prior rights to former GN jobs. They did this by allocating a certain number of jobs on former GN territory to former NP men. This made room for the displaced NP trainmen by allocating turns in the Whitefish and Wenatchee chain gang freight pools. I personally went from a conductor in the middle of the Wenatchee pool, in terms of seniority, to the youngest conductor in the Wenatchee pool. I did not get bumped out of the pool, but I spent a long time as the youngest conductor in the pool. This meant that if I was close to not making my miles for the pay period, I was sweating it out wondering if I was going to get bumped out of the pool and hoping that the average mileage would be high enough to keep me from getting bumped out of the pool. Bob Marsh, who followed me as conductor, was bumped out of the Wenatchee pool to a less desirable job several times.

Allowing the former NP men into the Wenatchee pool irritated several of us since the NP trainmen had never worked west of Spokane in chain gang service before the merger. The NP west end chain gang from Yardley to Pasco belonged to the Idaho west trainmen and enginemen, which was a different seniority district than east of Yardley. Most of the GN trainmen felt that the NP trainmen did not belong in the Wenatchee chain gang freight pool because historically they had never worked west of Yardley.

This point of view was raised by former GN conductors and brakemen at our UTU local lodge meetings several times. Our local UTU Conductors' Chairman, Warren Shoop, worked the Whitefish chain gang freight pool as a conductor. Warren felt that the Whitefish pool was more desirable than the Wenatchee pool. Many of us expressed our displeasure with his decision to give away our Wenatchee pool jobs to the NP trainmen on several occasions. Many of us in the Wenatchee pool felt that Warren decided to protect his own position in the Whitefish pool, rather than allocating more men to the Whitefish pool and none to the Wenatchee pool.

At the same time, Warren was also giving away our local freight jobs and keeping the chain gang jobs because he felt that the chain gang jobs were the better jobs, another personal preference on Warren's part. This meant that these locals were now allocated to the NP trainmen. In several cases, former GN trainmen who were working an out of town local by choice were forced back to Spokane because a NP trainman now owned their job.

One example of this was Gene Sponcler, my long-time braking partner, who lived way up north of Spokane. Gene was working the Newport to Sandpoint local. Gene told me that he could drive to Newport in about half the time that it took him to drive to Yardley. The Newport Local was a five day a week job, which meant he had Saturday and Sunday off. Having the weekends off on the railroad was rare, as only a few locals worked daylight with the full weekend off. Gene was very upset with Warren Shoop when Warren informed Gene that he would have to move to a different job because his local was now allocated to NP trainmen.

Since Gene could no longer work his five day a week daylight local, his choice was to work chain gang or a night local for the rest of his railroad career, a bit over 10 years. Gene did not like chain gang, so he bumped onto the night Kettle Falls Turn as conductor. By this time, the Kettle Falls Turn worked out of Yardley, and it took two crews to get a round trip over the road. I did not particularly care for chain gang any longer because the line-ups were so bad that half the time, I found myself going to work without proper rest. So, if I could not hold a work train as conductor, I would bump onto the second Kettle Falls Turn as conductor. On this job, my crew and I were driven up in a company van to dog catch Gene and his crew.

The BLE sweetheart deal with the MRL was the third time that I know of when the BLE tried, or succeeded, in selling another craft's job for financial gain. The first time was back in the late 1960s when the BLE sold the fireman's job for $1.50 per day. This meant that the engineers agreed to work without a fireman and to be compensated $1.50 per day extra for working without a fireman. With no fireman, when someone was required to go back and check a unit because of locomotive trouble, it was the head brakeman who received no compensation for performing the fireman's work.

About three years later, the BLE made an offer to carriers that they would line their own switches when heading into sidings, and open the switch when leaving sidings, for $1.50 per day, which would have eliminated the head brakeman's position on through freight trains. This offer was made on a national basis to all Class I railroads working under a BLE contract. The railroads turned down the BLE's offer, and it was never brought up again.

Years later, in 1988 or 1989, I was watching a movie with several other rails in the crew room at the hotel in Wenatchee. Negotiations were taking place between the UTU and BLE top brass about the unions merging, since the BLE was broke. Matt Wilson, the BLE general chairman, who worked the Wenatchee pool, came in and rudely started an argument about the possible union merger, stating that the BLE would never merge with the UTU. I immediately fired back that the BLE would be forced to merge with the UTU since they did not have anything left to give away. I brought the house down with that one. The BLE general chairman had nothing to say; he did give me his best icy stare. Today, the BLE is part of the Teamsters Union. How the mighty have fallen!

➻ The Network Operations Center

Immediately after the 1970 merger, BN operated dispatchers' offices at Spokane, Seattle, Maple Valley, Tacoma, and Vancouver in the state of Washington alone. Over time the Washington offices were all consolidated at Seattle, a process completed in October, 1988, with the opening of a new office at 2454 Occidental. Positions from the office in Billings were moved to Seattle and to Minneapolis in January of 1989, consolidating BN dispatchers' offices to Seattle, Minneapolis, Springfield, and Galesburg. This arrangement provided regional supervision and left the dispatchers within reasonable physical distance of the territory they dispatched.[30]

By the 1980s, telecommunications technology advanced to the point that it became technically possible to centralize dispatching and many clerical functions, including crew calling and customer service/agency work. All of the large carriers embraced centralization of clerical functions for improved efficiency and the job cuts that centralization enabled.

Around this same time, many of the large carriers centralized dispatching of their entire railroad in one location. CSX opened its centralized dispatching center in Jacksonville, Florida in 1988. Southern Pacific opened a similar facility in Denver shortly after.[31]

Union Pacific officially opened its Harriman Dispatching Center in Omaha, Nebraska in June of 1989. This $50,000,000 facility consolidated all of UP's dispatching in one place for the first time in modern history. UP was the first large railroad to totally centralize its dispatching function. UP claimed that the new facility enabled them to eliminate 600, mostly management, jobs.[32] Subsequent experience showed that they cut too deeply, and some of the previously eliminated positions were restored.[33]

Union Pacific was BN's most important rail competitor, and as a result, BN management watched the UP very closely. Union Pacific officers told glowing tales of the success of the Harriman Dispatching Center at every opportunity.

Gerald Grinstein became President and W. E. Greenwood became Chief Operating Officer of the Burlington Northern in 1989.

Mr. Greenwood states for this book:

> The decision to centralize was driven by the need to adopt the new and improved technology that had become available for a railroad's dispatching function. These benefits in turn could be coupled to the need for a better system for network management. The proposal for centralization originated with the Operating Department. Approval for the project followed and exhaustive review through BN's established budgeting process.[34]

Despite the need to pay down debt, the Board of Directors accepted management's recommendation to construct a single centralized dispatching center. The Network Operations Center opened in March 1995.

Dispatcher Dave Sprau has this to say about the new Network Operations Center:

> I walked out the door of the Seattle dispatchers' office at the end of second trick on the Bainville to Havre district on June 15, 1995 sick and tired of working almost 40 years for what I felt had come to "nothing." We, and our union, had worked very hard, and made many concessions, in order to put together what we considered a state-of-the-art centralized office in Seattle only six years before, complete with quiet, private cubicles for each dispatching district, which included the traditional speaker sets for efficient communication, but now we were going to be moved to Texas, put into an open-concept 'boiler room' where we would have to wear cheap, uncomfortable headsets for eight hours, tethered to our desks like dogs on a leash while multiple phone and radio channels were fed into our heads whether we needed to listen or not.
>
> I never returned to work for the BN. I was pretty bummed out by the whole thing and had nothing good to say about what many of us considered a foolish decision to consolidate all the eggs into one basket. The company gave many reasons for wanting to do this, but all rang hollow as far as actual dispatching efficiency goes. All the pre-construction bragging that was being done to us clearly suggested that one really big reason for doing it was for show, so some latter-day 'Empire Builder' could have a huge, big 'Star Wars' type of room that could be shown off to people and try to dazzle them. They spent an obscene amount of money constructing that facility and paying the cost of moving all the people and equipment from the four regional offices that preceded it, and then paying huge amounts of overtime for many years after because too many people had quit and they did not have adequate help. The decision to put everything together was approved if not made by Senior Vice President–Integrated Network Management, that is, the head of the Operating Department, William W. Francis, who earlier said he did not favor such consolidation, but later excused his decision reversing his earlier views by saying "They wore me down."
>
> I was not the only dispatcher who left the service; several dozens of us with considerable experience and seniority elected to do something other than move to Texas. One guy, who already had endured 'consolidation' moves from Glendive to Billings, and then from Billings to Seattle, asked one of the flunkies who came to Seattle to try to assuage our concerns about moving and to explain the expensive 'moving package' BN was

offering each of us. He bitterly asked, "What happened to your promise, when we were being moved to Seattle, that 'this would be our last move' and that we could 'burn the moving boxes'?" Of course, he received no reply. Besides those who resigned, many returned to clerk status. Families were disrupted and divorces ensued. Many boarded the plane for Texas knowing that aged relatives living within visiting distance were now so far removed that they would seldom be seen again, if ever. One fellow had an ill, aged mother who he and his wife had been caring for in their home. They had to move her to Texas. The trip was too much. She died on the airplane en route to Texas.

Shortly after the move was made, several train and engine men whom I had known for many years made the comment, "We used to gripe and complain, and sometimes we thought you guys made bad decisions, but we were wrong. You guys were rocket scientists compared to the kind of dispatching we get nowadays."

I think the main reason the quality of dispatching went down the tube was the element of bringing local people into local areas and familiar railroad territory had been lost, and the company soon found itself hiring dispatchers for all four corners of their railroad off the street in Texas. Of course, the official company line about the consolidation admits no such failure, but all one needs to do is interview any conductor, engineer, or trackman who worked both before and after the event and get their opinion of the so-called 'improvements.'

To add insult to injury, it wasn't long afterward, and particularly after September 11, 2001, that strong rumors emerged to the effect that both UP and BNSF were disillusioned with their consolidated offices and would be 'decentralizing.' BNSF then opened offices in Spring, Texas, Kansas City, Kansas, and San Bernardino.[35]

John Langlot confirms that when the dispatchers were moved to Fort Worth, the quality of dispatching deteriorated rapidly. Of course, bad dispatching is as old as railroading. Dispatching was, and is, an art that takes time to learn. The problem was that with so many experienced dispatchers choosing not to move to Fort Worth, the NOC opened with an unusually high proportion of new dispatchers.

Many of the new dispatchers struggled with basic dispatching concepts like holding a low priority train back one or two stations for the top priority trains. Being new, they could not do as good a job as the average experienced dispatcher they replaced, and there were not enough experienced dispatchers to sufficiently train the new people.

In addition, most of the dispatchers had never seen the territory that they were dispatching, so they did not have any knowledge of some of the basic problems in their territory. Most of the new, and some of the old, dispatchers had no idea what the problems that came with running trains in winter weather were, such as switches clogged with ice, and air brake problems due to extremely cold temperatures.

I was working as a conductor in the Wenatchee chain gang pool in 1995 and 1996. By this time, through freight crews were just me and the engineer. The following are just a few of many examples of bad dispatching during the transition period as the new employees learned their jobs. The bad dispatching made our days longer than they needed to be and cost the company an incalculable amount of money due to the excess costs of labor and equipment due to unnecessary train delay.

One night as we approached Edwall with an eastward freight train, the dispatcher informed us that we were going to have to saw-by a very late No. 8, the eastward passenger train. I asked the dispatcher why he had not run us up the double track against the current of traffic and let No. 8 around us on double track. I did not get an answer. I told the dispatcher that we would have to stop short of the crossing at Edwall and wait until No. 8 was getting close, as I couldn't block the crossing at Edwall that long. The practice of stopping short of this crossing, which was located about 1,000 feet east of west switch, until the other train was closely approaching had been in place for longer than I can remember. The elevators at Edwall were located on the south side of track, the town was split between the north and south sides of the track, and the main crossing was State Highway 231. It was wheat harvest season, so the farmers were busy hauling grain to the elevator. Lincoln County deputies did not tolerate extended blockage of this crossing, and if they wrote a ticket, they wrote it to me. The dispatcher told me he didn't care about blocking the crossing at Edwall because he wanted to cut down the delay on No. 8. I told him that it was a little late for that now.

I also told the dispatcher that when we finished sawing No. 8 by, I would have to ride the rear end of train to the next crossing west of town as we could not shove over this crossing blind, and when we were completely backed out of the siding, I would have to walk about 30 car lengths to the head end of the train. His response was that he had a hot westward train waiting at Sunset Junction for No. 8 and for us since the westward train was too long to fit in any of the sidings between Latah Jct. and Bluestem. By this time, both the dispatcher and I were getting a little hot under the collar, so I just said that I would do the best that I could. The whole process took us about an hour and a half and delayed No. 8 by 30 to 40 minutes.

A dispatcher with more experience would have held us at the end of double track at Bluestem. Failing that, he should have let us run ahead of No. 8, which would have delayed them far less than the saw-by did. We, No. 8, and the hot westward train all would have been better off if he had made either of these decisions.

On another trip, we had departed the end of double track at Bluestem and were approaching Espanola on a yellow block, figuring we were going to meet a westward train. We were approaching the west switch when the dispatcher came on the radio to ask me how long our train was. Dispatchers have needed to know how long the trains they dispatch are since God made dirt, so this question was not a good sign. I told him that our train, with engines, was about 6,800 feet. The dispatcher responded, "That is just great, you are both too long for the Espanola siding."

After thinking about it for a minute or two, and trying to minimize our delay and help the dispatcher out of his mess, I told the dispatcher that when we went west the day before, the industry track at Espanola was clear, and if it was still clear, he should have the westward stop well short of the east switch. With that done, he could give me permission to occupy the main track east of Espanola to double the head end of our train into the industry track, and we should then be clear of the main track. The dispatcher told the westward train to stop and let him know when they were stopped. We started to enter the siding when the westbound reported that they were stopped at the approach signal to Espanola. The dispatcher then gave us permission, after stopping, to proceed past the absolute signal displaying stop so that we could move east on the main.

We stopped short of the signal and pulled east to the main track. I told the dispatcher to let us know as soon as our rear end showed in the clear at the west end of the siding. We stopped as soon as he told us we were in the clear. I made a cut to clear the industry track switch and set the head end of our train into industry track which did clear the main track. The dispatcher cleared the approach signal for the westward train. He came west cautiously until he could see the clear absolute signal at the east switch, then left Espanola with all possible speed. The dispatcher lined us out of the siding and we doubled our train back together and proceeded east.

One evening we were westward approaching Quincy and could see that the dispatcher had us lined into the siding at Quincy. Around that time, we heard Amtrak No. 8 call Wenatchee to let them know that they were coming through Monitor, which is about seven miles west of Wenatchee, where No. 8 would make a station stop. I rang up the dispatcher as I knew there were no east trains out of Wenatchee. I asked who we were heading into Quincy for. A female voice that I had never heard before told me, "You will be there for No. 8." I said, "No. 8 is not even to Wenatchee yet." Her response was, "Oh yes they are." The crew of No. 8 heard all this and confirmed that they were still west of Wenatchee. Her response was, "You will be at Quincy for No. 8," and we were, incurring about a 50-minute delay. She should have advanced us down the grade to Columbia River, where we would have met No. 8 with very little delay to us and none to No. 8. This is an example of a young dispatcher still learning the territory.

One night we were eastward approaching Gibson on a yellow approach. The absolute signal at West Gibson was double red for no obvious reason. We stopped and waited for a minute or two. I rang up the dispatcher but got no response. After about five minutes, the dispatcher came on the radio, calling the eastward train at Adrian. No one answered, because there was no train at Adrian. I responded, "There is the extra east stopped at the double red block at West Gibson." No answer. The dispatcher again called the east train at Adrian, and again I responded that we were the eastward train stopped at the double red signal at West Gibson. No answer. My engineer asked me what to do. I replied that "We will just have to sit here until the dumb son of a bitch wakes up." We sat there for about 15 minutes and finally the signal went green for the main line. We proceeded east, but since the dispatcher had obviously lost track of us, we were on high alert the rest of the night.

I was not involved in this last incident, but it was the talk of the train and engine crews at Yardley and Wenatchee for weeks. It occurred at Espanola, and again, both trains were much too long for the siding. This meet required a double saw-by to accomplish and the dispatcher had to send a company van and driver from Yardley to assist in the complex process which took close to four hours.

We knew that relatively few of the experienced dispatchers had moved to Fort Worth. The only source for dispatchers was to hire off the street. Most of these new dispatchers had never worked as a train order operator copying train orders, and, quite frankly, had no idea how the railroad worked. You could tell this by some of their comments and their actions. The new dispatchers did not talk like a dispatcher or act like a dispatcher, they acted like the rookies they were. Despite the fail-safe design of CTC, the inexperience and incompetence of the new dispatchers gave everyone a very insecure feeling and no one trusted them.

Lawrence Kaufman, in his authorized history of BNSF Railway, *Leaders Count*, describes Robert Krebs' first reaction to the Network Operations Center.

> Krebs recalled one of his first visits to the NOC, a huge multistoried dispatch center that looked like it could be used to manage the NASA space program:
>
> Grinstein had me come down and look at it. I remember my comment. I walked into this place and I looked at it. I was stunned. I think my comment was 'Oh, s—t!' But it was built, and there was nothing you could do about it.[36]

By contrast, two major railroads, Conrail and Norfolk Southern (NS), never adopted the totally centralized dispatching model. Conrail was later split between NS and CSX. NS, thought by many to be the best managed railroad in North America, dispatches its railroad from regional offices to this day.

The Lamona Rail Grinder Collision

In June of 1990, I was working the Wenatchee chain gang pool as a conductor, when an out of control westward rail grinder ran by the absolute signal at Lamona and hit the eastward Quincy Local. The crew on the Quincy Local was conductor Tom Taylor and brakemen Vic Lyon and Joe Engley, all former GN men. The engineer was Rick Avery, a former NP Idaho west man. The pilot conductor on the rail grinder was a BN man who is still working for the BNSF and prefers to remain anonymous.

The rail grinder belonged to Loram, a specialty contractor to the railroads. Railroad management considered the rail grinder "just a piece of maintenance equipment" and allowed the contractor's employees to run it. Most of the operators for these contractors came from the southeast part of the country. Working on this contract equipment is the only way they could come close to making a decent living, but their income was well below our standards.

The rail grinder consisted of about five rail grinding cars with a control unit on both ends which enabled the equipment to be controlled from ether end. There were two tank cars for water to put out any fires started by grinding the rail, which produces a torrent of red-hot sparks.

The locomotive of the rail grinder was a reconditioned freight locomotive. The front drawbar and knuckle were removed, the draft gear pocket welded over, and other cosmetic changes made so it would not be considered a train worthy of putting an engineer or pilot conductor on. It was as big as a train, and shunted track circuits like a train, but the Frisco management insisted it was not a train.

On June 8, 1990, this rail grinder needed to be moved from Spokane to Wenatchee. The railroad happened to call a conductor who had recently been promoted and had made very few trips as conductor to pilot the rail grinder operator to Wenatchee. He told the crew clerk that he did not feel he was qualified to be a pilot conductor, as he had made only a few trips to Wenatchee and did not know the line that well. This young conductor was told that he was going to be the pilot, period, and was thus intimidated into taking the call.

As the rail grinder left Spokane, the pilot conductor

and the operator noticed that the rail grinder brakes seemed very weak, slow to respond to a brake application, and took a long time to slow down and stop the equipment. The pilot conductor insisted that they stop at a level spot at Harrington on the double track between Bluestem and Lamona and inspect the braking system. The operator tried cutting in the brakes from the other controls on the back end of the rail grinder, and then cutting them out and back in on the west end of the consist. This seemed to help a little bit.

Everything on this rail grinder was in poor condition, the pilot conductor later said. A more experienced and confident pilot conductor would have insisted that the braking system be made safe, even if BN mechanical forces were required to come from Yardley to make repairs. He did not, and they proceeded west toward the end of the double track at Lamona.

The pilot conductor later told Rick Avery that as they were going through Downs, 4.67 miles east of Lamona, he told the operator that he'd better slow down. Well, the piece of junk rail grinder did not slow down. About three miles west of Downs, and one and a half miles east of Lamona, the down grade increases significantly. When they went by the approach block to Lamona, the conductor told Rick that he knew then and there that they would never get stopped at Lamona. He jumped shortly before they entered the rock cut immediately east of the absolute signal at Lamona. The machine operator also jumped. If they had not jumped, they would have been killed.

At the same time, the Quincy Local was moving at about 50 MPH on a clear signal to enter the double track at Lamona. Engineer Rick Avery and conductor Tom Taylor were in the lead unit. Vic Lyon and Joe Engley were in the second unit. As the local approached the switch to enter the double track, the crew was shocked to see the rail grinder coming around the curve approaching the rock cut and the end of double track at a speed that was obviously too high to get stopped short of the switch. This curve ended about 500 feet east of the switch and the rock cut extended for about 200 feet along the straight track. Rick and Tom saw the pilot and the operator jump off the rail grinder after the end of the curve and before the beginning of the rock cut.

Without forming the complete thought, Rick knew that the rail grinder was out of control. Operating on instinct and experience, Rick instantly dumped the air, putting his train into emergency. Both men's first thought was to jump. By this time, the rail grinder was approaching the fouling point of the switch at 20 MPH. Tom moved across the cab and started out the back door located directly behind Rick. Rick was going to follow Tom, but Tom was in his way. Rick dropped to the floor behind the control stand and braced for impact. Rick said that he knew was going to die.

The rail grinder sideswiped the fireman's side of the lead unit. The sound of the impact was deafening. Rick felt the unit rise up and derail. He thought it was going to tip over. The noise and motion finally came to a stop. Rick's entire body felt numb. He could feel the left side of his face and right forearm burning due to battery acid sprayed from the ruptured lead-acid batteries under the fireman's side of the cab. As Rick raised his head, he bumped it on a two-inch diameter piece of pipe about an inch and half above his head that was driven into the electrical panel at the back of the engine cab. Rick still does not know where this piece of pipe came from.

Tom never got the chance to jump. The impact threw him back against the cab door. Tom rode out the derailment of the lead unit hanging on the hand rail on the edge of the locomotive walkway. He was pinned against the outside of the cab door by the rapid deceleration of the derailed unit.

The collision with the rail grinder sheared off the left side front steps, the fireman's side of the cab, and removed the walkway behind the cab for about 20 feet. The lead-acid batteries under the fireman's side of the cab were destroyed, throwing acid all over the cab. The lead unit of rail grinder was knocked into the ditch, missing the second unit, but the rear of the lead unit of the rail grinder ran into the third unit of the local, stripping the entire side off it, rupturing the fuel tank, and damaging the head car, a loaded covered hopper car of diatomaceous earth from Quincy.

The locomotive portion of the rail grinder tipped over on its side and caught fire along with the third unit of the local, generating intense heat and large billows of black smoke. Rick told me that he pushed 911 on the radio to ring up the dispatcher, but he does not remember which locomotive unit he did this from. Rick thinks he radioed from the second unit, since it was the only unit in this three unit consist that was not severely damaged. The batteries on the lead unit were destroyed, so it did not have electrical power. The third unit was burning, so it was not available.

About this time, conductor Tom Taylor started to have chest pains. Rick knew that Tom had a history of heart problems, so Rick told the dispatcher that they thought Tom was having a heart attack. The dispatcher told Rick he was going to call for a helicopter to transport Tom to Spokane. The rest of the crew got Tom to lie down on the ground and Tom took a nitroglycerin tablet from the bottle that he always kept in his pocket. The five of them, Rick, Tom, Joe, Vic, and the pilot conductor all waited for the helicopter to pick Tom up.

The rail grinder crew was gone. Apparently the Loram support vehicle picked up the operator and left. Rumor has it that they went to the Moses Lake airport where the Loram company jet picked them up and flew them home.

When the helicopter arrived to pick Tom up, they were going to take Rick too, but there was not enough room, so Rick was forced to wait for the Odessa ambulance to arrive. Both brakemen, having been in the second unit at the time of impact, came through with just bumps and bruises. Not long after the helicopter left, the ambulance arrived, picked up the four remaining men, and took them to Odessa.

At the Odessa Hospital, Rick's clothes were literally falling off his body due to being soaked with battery acid from the accident. Hospital personnel stripped Rick of all clothing. By this time, Both Rick's and Tom's grips were starting to fall apart from the acid. Luckily Rick had brought a complete change of clothes in a plastic bag in his grip, so when the hospital got Rick cleaned up, he had fresh clothes to put on.

Rick was off work for about six months. As he began to recover from the shock of the accident, he developed back pains. The acid burns healed without scars, but he still has some discomfort if he over works himself from the three discs in his back that were damaged in the accident. Tom Taylor came back to work within a short period of time, as did both brakemen.

One grinding unit and the motive power unit of the rail grinder were cut up for scrap right there and trucked out about three months after the wreck.

The BNSF did not hold a formal investigation of the incident. Rick said that there was what the company called an 'inquiry' and that the Federal Railroad Administration and Loram were invited and attended as observers. Other than this, the event was hushed up, covered up, and swept under the rug. I could not believe there was no formal investigation. Why there was no investigation is still a mystery to me. I experienced some dealings with the FRA about this time and found the FRA was a Paper Tiger.

This piece of junk rail grinder should not have been on the railroad. Before the Frisco took over the railroad, it would NOT have been allowed on the property. According to the grapevine, many in the dispatchers' office were amused by the incident, seeing it as "another lesson for those Frisco management dinks who think they know everything."

Fred and Mary

The technology that killed the caboose was the pair of telemetric communication devices known as Fred and Mary. Fred is the rear end device. The R.E.D. in FRED stands for rear-end-device, which was the original official name of the device. In service, the Fred is hung on the rear coupler and connected to the train line. Fred's basic functions are to monitor the brake pipe pressure at the rear of the train, and to detect whether the rear of the train was stopped or moving. Fred also has a flashing red light that functions as the rear end marker under low light conditions. The Flashing Rear End Device became quickly and universally known as 'Fred.'

Mary is the electronic box attached to the top of the engineer's control panel that displays the air pressure at the Fred. Mary is so called because Fred needed a female counterpart to talk to. Who first used the term, and where, is lost in the fog of history. Mary has a distance counter electrically driven by the lead axle. Mary can count the distance in feet that the train has traveled at any speed. The engineer can reset the counter at any time. The engineer uses the counter to know when the rear of the train has passed a slow order or when the rear of the train has left a siding so that he can resume track speed.

A toggle switch on the front of Mary, under a

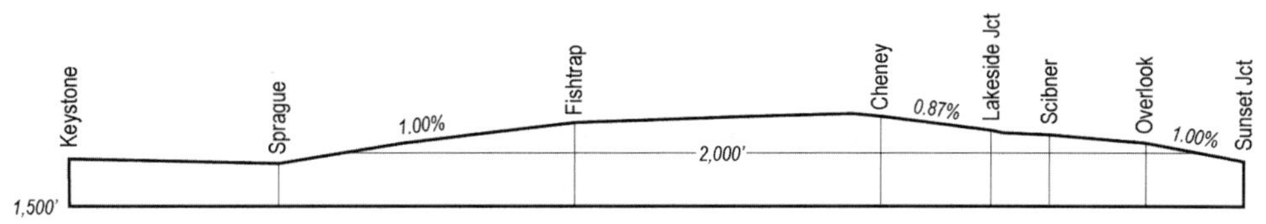

SPOKANE to KEYSTONE PROFILE

spring-loaded protector, allows the engineer to signal a smart Fred to put the train into emergency by dumping the air from the rear of the train. To initiate the emergency application, the engineer has only to flip the toggle switch to the up position. Freds with the ability to dump the air, that is, to cause an emergency application of the brakes, are 'smart Freds.' The Federal Railroad Administration now requires that a smart Fred be used on main line trains. All Freds now in service on BNSF are smart Freds.

The first Freds did not have the ability to put the train into emergency. The BN was in such a hurry to get rid of the cabooses that sometimes trains were run with just a red flag in the knuckle. Trains coming off the MRL were notorious for having no Fred or a non-working Fred. Most of the time, if a MRL train carried a Fred, its battery was dead, and replacing it caused train delay.

The Sprague Wreck

When things go wrong on the railroad, they usually happen so fast that one has no time to reason things out; you just react, usually on a combination of instinct, experience, and training. Even though the time elapsed in this event was only the 10 minutes or so required to travel from half a mile west of Fishtrap to the east switch at Sprague, 12 miles, it would have seemed like an eternity. With time to think of one's fate and to realize that this could be the end of one's life, the event that follows was one of the most agonizing experiences of these four men's lives. They ran out of options and came to the realization that any railroader's worst fears had become reality. This is engineer Michael S. Olin's story.

On a hot Sunday August 18, 1991, engineer Michael S. Olin, conductor Dennis Wright, rear brakeman Richard Skirvin, and head brakeman Darrell Parsley were called at Yardley for train No. 121 to Pasco. A Montana Rail Link crew brought the train from Missoula, Montana and left it on the westward main track. Attached to the train manifest was a document prepared by the Burlington Northern which indicated that our train was supposed to have front and rear telemetry devices commonly called "Mary and Fred." When I got on the train, I notified conductor Wright that there was no Mary on the lead unit as the message indicated there should be. Conductor Wright called trainmaster Curt Bettis, who brought a Mary to the lead unit. When I hooked up the Mary to the control panel and dialed in the number we had for Fred so they could communicate with each other, the Mary received no data from Fred.

Conductor Wright asked brakeman Skirvin to check the train brakes by doing a "roll-by inspection." Trainmaster Bettis said no, we were ordered to leave. As we began to leave the yard, another crew informed us that we did not have a Fred on the rear of our train, only a red flag jammed in the knuckle of the last car. Now the yardmaster in the Yardley tower instructed us to stop at Napa Street and wait for a driver to come down and pick up the Mary, since Yardley did not have a Fred for our train. As the train approached Napa Street Junction, I used the dynamic brakes on the engines. Then I set the air brakes on the train and slowed to a normal stop at Napa Street. When the clerk/driver showed up we gave him the Mary. I released the train brakes and felt the train start to roll westward as the air brakes released.

A railroad special agent stopped the previous westward

train, which happened to be headed to Wenatchee, and removed three Hispanic transients from the train. We did not know this at the time and would not have thought much of it if we had known. We headed across the Latah Creek Bridge and were lined toward Overlook on the former SP&S at the west end of the bridge. We proceeded through Cheney and Babb. I had not used the air brakes since Napa Street Junction. The train was handling fine up the hill.

We left Fishtrap at 57 MPH on a clear signal and started downhill. I put the locomotives into dynamic brake mode immediately past Fishtrap and was soon in full dynamic. Less than a mile beyond Fishtrap the grade steepened to 1 percent. The dynamic would not hold the train's speed on the 1 percent grade so I made a minimum service reduction about half a mile west of Fishtrap. (Note: a minimum service reduction is the least reduction of air pressure from the brake pipe that can be made with modern 26-L locomotive brake equipment. For a train carrying 90-pound brake pipe pressure a minimum service reduction is about 7 pounds, which will yield about 10 pounds of pressure in each car's brake cylinder.)

The combined dynamic and air brake application should have held our train speed steady, but the train started to pick up speed at a rapid rate. When I set the air, it did not sound right. Instead of getting the normal long and loud exhaust from the brake valve I got just a small puff of exhaust. This was my first indication of a brake problem. I immediately set 10 more pounds of air and got the same puff of exhaust from the brake valve. I then went to a full service application, the highest amount of air brake available short of emergency application of the brakes.

The train continued to pick up speed. Our entire train was now on the 1 percent down grade. I dumped the air, putting the train brakes into emergency to no avail. The train continued to pick up speed. I called conductor Wright on the radio and told him to dump the air from the third unit where he and brakeman Skirvin were riding. He did, but nothing happened. The head brakeman, Darrell Parsley, riding in the lead unit with me, asked, "What do you want me to do?" I said, "Pray."

I tried to call the dispatcher on the train radio but she did not answer. I do not know if there was something defective about the radio system or not. Radio communication was sometimes a real problem in this area. I could not talk directly to the dispatcher in this horrible emergency situation.

When I saw that the approach block to Sprague was flashing yellow, I knew that our train was lined into the east end of Sprague siding, a bit over a mile ahead. If we got around the gentle two degree curves above Sprague, the diverging side of the turnout into Sprague siding had a 35 MPH speed limit. We were all dead when we hit that switch.

I had hoped the dispatcher could help us out by lining the switch at Sprague for the main and by stopping the eastward train that we were going to meet at Sprague far enough back from Sprague that we would stop on the upgrade west of Sprague if the train did not derail in the four, five and six degree curves west of Sprague. If we could get past Sprague, sooner or later we could get the train stopped in the bottom of the sag at Sprague.

The eastward train we were going to meet was somewhere west of Keystone, 9.8 miles west of Sprague. Westward train No. 171 was switching at Keystone. The grain elevator is at the east end of the siding, so No.171's crew cut their train off east of the east switch and were switching the grain elevator from the east end when they heard me say on the radio that we had a runaway train and were out of control. Conductor Bob Riggs of No. 171 told his crew to get the power back on their train and leave Keystone. Bob was thinking that if we were lucky enough to get through Sprague and get around the tight curves at the west end of Sprague without derailing, we could run into the rear of his train which only 8.8 miles beyond Sprague. They left Keystone as fast as they could, hoping that they had avoided the possibility of us rear ending them which surely would have killed me and Darrell Parsley.

My train was roaring out of control down a 1 percent grade, with three big units and 87 cars weighing over 8,200 tons, at about 80 MPH approaching a 35 MPH turnout with tank cars of hazardous material not far back in the train. I knew none of us had a chance of surviving the coming derailment. There were so many things racing through my mind in the terror of the moment. I thought we were all going to die. I knew the train would not make it through the turnout at the east end of Sprague siding at the speed it was going without turning the units over on their sides and all the cars in our train stacking up on top of us. If we survived that, the toxic exposure from the

LEFT Lead unit of the Sprague wreck came to rest on its side, making escape from the unit more of a challenge than if the unit had been upright. COURTESY OF TIM WHITTIER.

BELOW Cars smashed up and stacked up like cordwood in the Sprague wreck. The extent of the damage shows the unusual forces generated in this high-speed derailment. COURTESY OF TIM WHITTIER.

hazardous material loads in our train was sure to kill us.

Suddenly I had the strange feeling that my grandmother, who passed away about fourteen years previously, was in the cab with me and that she said, "Mike, it's going to be OK." After that I felt a little bit at ease with our situation, and that it would be OK to die. I cannot explain this. If I could, I do not know that I would want to.

I unconsciously kept blowing the whistle through all the road crossings without even thinking about it. I did hope that no one was going over the track at the crossings. The train was way over the speed limit through the town of Sprague. The train went over the three crossings at Sprague so fast that the crossing gates were not all the way down as the engine went over them.

I remember looking at the speedometer just before the switch at Sprague; it read 78 MPH. When we hit the east switch at Sprague, which diverged to the right, our locomotive rose up on my side, the right side, and stayed up on the wheels on the fireman's side. The unit must have rolled over immediately beyond the switch because it landed on the fireman's side and slid for about 1,500 feet on top of the rails of the main track before coming to a stop. In my mind it seemed like this took forever. In fact, it took about 20 seconds to stop from our high speed at the point of the east switch.

As the locomotive started to roll over, I remember bracing myself, not knowing what to expect or from which direction the biggest threat would come. I was worried about all the cars from our train piling up on top of us. I also knew that we could not help but have a serious hazardous chemical spill, so if we were lucky enough to survive the derailment, we would die from chemical exposure.

I was told later that the noise of the wreck was deafening, but I do not remember hearing anything. I remember standing in the cab looking up and out my side window, which now was facing straight up toward the sky. I stepped up on the control stand and out onto the side of the unit and looked around in shock. About the same time there stood Dennis Wright and Richard Skirvin who had worked their way up to the lead unit to check on Darrell Parsley and me. All three of us were glad to see each other alive.

Then we realized that Darrell was not with us. I looked down into the cab of the unit that I had just crawled out of. Darrell was in the cab standing on the fireman's side window that was now parallel with the ground. I hollered at Darrell, but he did not move. We all climbed back into the cab. Darrell stood there motionless. Darrell did not answer or acknowledge our calls to him. I figured that Darrell was totally shell-shocked standing there on his feet. We helped Darrell out of the cab of the unit and walked him a short distance away.

All we could think about was getting far away from the derailed, leaking, and burning chemical cars. It seemed like everything was on fire. By this time, people from the town of Sprague had started to congregate. About 30 minutes later an ambulance showed up and transported us all to Sacred Heart Hospital in Spokane. The first thing they did at the hospital was take a blood samples and test them for drugs and alcohol. These tests came back negative for the whole crew. I was off work for over a year healing both physically and mentally from this ordeal.

Later I found out that there was a big pile of cars at the east switch and another pile behind our engines, which ended up about 1,800 feet west of the east switch. Sometime during the derailment, the train separated. The air hoses came apart and dumped the air putting the train into emergency. This was proven by the fact that those brakes that could be found were found with their pistons out, which indicated that the brakes had applied.

The company investigates any accident or apparent violation of the rules. Many times, these investigations are on the order of a 'kangaroo court' since the company is prosecutor, judge, jury, and hangman. This investigation was a real investigation because it involved something that is simply not supposed to happen and had never happened in the collective experience of anyone on the railroad.

The accident was also investigated independently by the Federal Railroad Administration (FRA) and the National Transportation Safety Board (NTSB). Both of these federal agencies are generally unbiased as between management and labor, but they always have political agendas. The NTSB in particular tends to use a specific accident to build a case for change. If there are a series of similar accidents, they repeat the same recommendations in drumbeat fashion.

Everybody soon focused on the air brakes. Air brakes

apply when air is removed from the brake pipe, which provides positive protection if a train breaks in two. This fail-safe principle dates to the early days of the Westinghouse air brake design when break in twos were much more common than they are today.

The failure of the dynamic brakes to hold the train was no surprise to anybody. Dynamic brakes are at their most effective at 25 MPH; their retarding power falls off as speed increases. Mike did not start to use the dynamics until the train was doing about 57 MPH, and it was approaching 60 MPH when he went for the air.

Each car has a brake pipe, which runs the full length of the car, angle cocks, which are shut off valves at each end of the brake pipe, and air brake hose on each end of the car. Each air hose has a quick connect fitting called a glad hand at the end. These components are collectively called the train line.

On each car, a pipe branches off the brake pipe and goes to the control valve. The control valve routes pressurized air from the train line to the car's auxiliary air reservoir to charge the brake system, from the reservoir to the brake cylinder to apply the brakes, and from the brake cylinder to the atmosphere to release the brakes. Control valves function by detecting pressure differentials between the train line and the auxiliary reservoir.

During the charging or release process the control valve feeds air into a two-compartment auxiliary reservoir on each car. One part is the service portion; the other is the emergency portion. With the reservoirs charged, a reduction in the brake pipe pressure causes the air brakes to apply. When the control valve senses a reduction of pressure in the brake pipe, it exhausts a bit of air from its own train line to assure the propagation of the brake pipe reduction to the next car. Simultaneously, the control valve closes the charging port between the brake pipe and the reservoir and sends air from the service portion of the reservoir into the brake cylinder. The air pressure in the brake cylinder causes the brake shoes to press against the wheel tread, which slows the train down. As more air is withdrawn from the brake pipe, the control valve will send more air into the brake cylinder, increasing the retarding force.

The question in the investigation was, "Why did the air brakes not work?" The very weak air flow that Mike got from the engineer's brake valve indicated that very little air was exhausted from the brake pipe. That implied that the reduction was not travelling through all of the cars as it should. In fact, it implied that only the first few cars saw the reduction. The most likely cause for that was that an angle cock had been turned to the closed position on a car near the head end of the train. During the cleanup of the wreck, human remains were found near the front of the train, as was a closed angle cock between the second and third cars.

No one knows for certain what happened. The most reasonable explanation for the known facts, and the general consensus for the cause of Mike's air problem, was that one of the transients removed from the train to Wenatchee ahead of Mike got on his train when they stopped at Napa Street to give the Mary to the driver. Presumably he figured closing the angle cock between the second and third car would stop the train when he discovered that he was not headed to Wenatchee. When, and where, he closed the angle cock is anybody's guess. Closing the angle cock did not stop Mike; it isolated the portion of the train behind the closed angle cock from the brake valve. The closed angle cock prevented the brakes from applying on the portion of the train behind the closed angle cock. The rate of leakage in the isolated portion of the train was not sufficient to cause any of the control valves on the rear portion of the train to function.

About the same time down in California on the Santa Fe, pretty much the same thing happened, but on a 2 percent grade. The National Transportation Safety Board and the Federal Railroad Administration investigated both the Sprague and the California accidents. One of the recommendations that the NTSB, which has no regulatory authority, made to the FRA, which does have regulatory authority, was to require main line trains to be equipped with a rear end device that can make emergency application when given a manual command from its Mary by the engineer. The FRA accepted this recommendation and undertook rulemaking to create that requirement in a form that they could enforce as a matter of law. Most of the railroad companies recognized that this was a good idea, since it simply restored a safety feature that had disappeared with the cabooses, and did not fight the rulemaking. Such devices came to be known as "smart Freds." They are the current industry standard. No main line train leaves a terminal on BNSF today without a smart Fred.

Safety

During the later years of the BN, the younger employees who were dissatisfied with working conditions on the railroad started to falsely claim 'on the job' injuries. They sued the railroad using lawyers referred by the union, got big settlements and quit the railroad. After the SLSF merger, this racket really got out of hand. This made life miserable for the honest employees who were devoted to their jobs, since management rightly concluded that the ranks were full of thieves and lowlifes.

Under the Federal Employees Liability Act, the company is obligated to create a safe working environment for their employees. The unique requirements of FELA are the reason that the fake injury scam worked so well; the company had no defense.

In 1991, a decade after the SLSF merger, personal injury claims were totally out of control. That year BN reported 2,887 injuries to employees that resulted in at least one day lost from work. Employee injuries were costing the company millions of dollars per year.[37] The company needed to cut the injury numbers down.

I remember mainline ballast being thinly spread in Yardley Yard. This 2- to 2½-inch size rock ballast rolled under your feet. No matter how many times this was brought up at the company's safety meetings, the response from the trainmaster holding the meeting would be, "I'm sure everyone is aware of this condition." I remember hearing this same response when safety issues were brought up at safety meetings during the BN and SLSF era. The Frisco management finally brought in a tie gang to replace ties in the yard tracks. In the course of this project they swept the large ballast into track and then brought in a train load of smaller sized rock to use as surface material in the toe paths. Making a decent walking surface between and alongside the tracks was something that could, and should, have been done decades before, but was not.

In 1991, Gerald Grinstein hired General John Chain, a recently retired four-star Air Force General whose previous job was running the Strategic Air Command, to be Executive Vice President of Operations. During the spring of 1993, Chain was replaced as VPO and moved to Executive Vice President of Safety and Support. By 1995, Chain flooded the railroad with safety equipment, including safety boots and eye protection for trainmen and enginemen, and prohibited getting on and off moving equipment.[38] This last change was revolutionary as it abolished a practice dating back to the beginning of railroading.

Employee members of local safety committees had long been sensitive to what I call 'condition issues,' like the ballast at Yardley. When management decided to get serious about safety, they needed to deal with the condition issues if they expected to have any credibility with the men. During 1997 and 1998, the BN got serious about cleaning up the working conditions for switchmen and trainmen. The result was extra work for the Maintenance-of-Way Department, cleaning up around switches and in yards, and along the right of way. The Maintenance-of-Way Department removed all tripping hazards and groomed the ground around switches to provide level work areas. This created more work for work trains hauling train loads of fines and rock chips to be spread around switches and in yards.

By the end of the 1990s, the company was strictly enforcing the prohibition against getting on and off moving equipment, crewmen were routinely wearing steel toed work boots and safety eye protection all the time we were on duty, and the condition issues had been dealt with. The continual flow of improvements over the four or five years beginning in 1993 when Chain moved to emphasize safety was effective. As Director Dan Evans said, "Jack did a whale of a job in that respect. Our accident rate was cut in half, cut in half again, and then cut in half again. That was Jack's leadership."[39]

Endnotes

1 Lawrence Kaufman, *Leaders Count*: The Story of BNSF Railway (Austin: Monthly Custom Publishing/Texas A&M University Press, 2005), 207.
2 Kaufman, *Leaders Count*, 209.
3 Kaufman, *Leaders Count*, 220.
4 Kaufman, *Leaders Count*, 236.
5 Kaufman, *Leaders Count*, 239.
6 Kaufman, *Leaders Count*, 210–11.
7 Kaufman, *Leaders Count*, 213.
8 Kaufman, *Leaders Count*, 227.
9 Earl Currie, email, December 11, 2017.
10 Kaufman, *Leaders Count*, 227.
11 Earl Currie, email, January 31, 2012.
12 Earl Currie, email, September 29, 2013
13 Kaufman, *Leaders Count*, 229–30.
14 Earl Currie, email, September 29, 2013
15 Kaufman, *Leaders Count*, 241.
16 Kaufman, *Leaders Count*, 240–43.
17 Kaufman, *Leaders Count*, 237–39.
18 Kaufman, *Leaders Count*, 272.
19 Gordon Donaldson, *Corporate Restructuring: Managing the Change Process from Within* (Boston: Harvard Business School Press, 1994), 134–135.
20 ConocoPhillips, "Burlington Resources Company History." accessed August 29, 2012, http://conocophillips.com/EN/about/who_we_are/history/burlington/Pages/index.aspx.
21 Bloomberg.com, "Railroads Couple More Cars as Housing Boost Shipments." Accessed August 8, 2012. http://bloomberg.com/news/2012-08-08/railroads-couple-more-cars-as-housing-boost-shipments.
22 Kaufman, *Leaders Count*, 253–262.
23 Kaufman, *Leaders Count*, 298, 302–307.
24 Kaufman, *Leaders Count*, 309–313.
25 Earl J. Currie, *James J. Hill's Legacy to Railway Operations* (Earl J. Currie, 2007), 300.
26 Currie, *James J. Hill's Legacy to Railway Operations*, 303–305.
27 Clinton J. Miller, General Counsel, United Transportation Union, email December 6, 2011.
28 BN vs. UTU, 862 F.2d 1266 (7th Cir. 1988).
29 Washington Companies, "Dennis R. Washington Biography." Accessed February 12, 2012, http://washcorp.com/dennisrwashingtonbiography.php.
30 Dave Sprau, emails, September 30 and October 29, 2013.
31 Currie, email, September 29, 2013.
32 Maury Klein, *Union Pacific: The Reconfiguration America's Greatest Railroad from 1969 to the Present* (New York: Oxford University Press, 2011), 260–61.
33 Klein, *Union Pacific: The Reconfiguration*, 264.
34 W. E. Greenwood, email, October 15, 2013.
35 Sprau, emails, September 10 and 19, 2013.
36 Kaufman, *Leaders Count*, 317.
37 Kaufman, *Leaders Count*, 279.
38 Kaufman, *Leaders Count*, 278–82.
39 Kaufman, *Leaders Count*, 284.

A loaded export grain train rolls west on Main 1 in a granite rock cut near Granite, Idaho, on June 1, 2014. This is the Northern Pacific's third alignment in the area, built as single track in 1965, and made two main tracks by BNSF in 1997. PHOTO BY BRUCE KELLY.

15. Burlington Northern Santa Fe

The BNSF Merger

The merger of the Burlington Northern and the Atchison, Topeka & Santa Fe to create the Burlington Northern Santa Fe (BNSF) in September, 1996 brought Rob Krebs to head the combined company. Finally, a railroad man was running the railroad. Morale was still low, but some of the management pressure lightened up, which eased tension between management and the blue-collar work force.

Within six months after the merger, Mr. Krebs and Vice President Matt Rose travelled around the entire system holding town hall meetings with employees. They explained their plans and the projects that were going to happen in the near future. Mr. Krebs informed us that we were now a family and his goal was to make BNSF the best railroad in the country. We employees listened to what Krebs said, but by now there was not much trust since the oil men told us the same story for years. Employees took what Krebs said with the attitude of "Show me and maybe I will believe you."

Our engines were worn out and needed to be replaced or were long overdue for major overhauls. Our engines were so bad that power problems were constantly causing delays to our hotshots. Mr. Krebs soon approached the Electro-Motive Division of General Motors (EMD) about purchasing new units. EMD informed him that they could not commit to a delivery date because EMD was going through a reorganization and their first delivery date guess was in about two years.

Mr. Krebs approached General Electric about purchasing new units. Their answer was, how many and how soon would you like them? Mr. Krebs' answer was, a bunch, and soon as I can get them. Soon new GE Dash 9 units were rumbling through Yardley. The northern lines enjoyed a continual flow of new units for the next three years. Mr. Krebs bought hundreds, and then thousands, of big GE units.

The Dash 9 units were GE model Dash 9-44CW, which the railroad called C44 9W. Santa Fe brought 100 of them into the merger, and BNSF bought almost 1,700 more. In addition, BNSF acquired over 1,500 subsequent and derivative six axle GE models.[1]

Intermodal traffic grew substantially through the 1980s. Most of that intermodal traffic growth moved on the former Great Northern route. By the early 1990s, the line over Stevens Pass was approaching capacity. The ports of Seattle and Tacoma, and the state of Washington, became concerned about BN's ability to handle the ever-increasing international intermodal traffic they projected. When the BNSF merger was proposed, the ports and the state became very concerned that, since the Santa Fe owned a mostly double track route between Los Angeles and Chicago, the merged company would preferentially market international intermodal over Los Angeles versus Puget Sound.

The ports, the state, and BN began a joint study regarding future import/export traffic through Puget Sound and how the railroad could most cost effectively meet their demand. The result of this study was that BN would, among other things, reopen Stampede Pass and rebuild the former Milwaukee line between Ellensburg and Lind, abandoned since February of 1980.

As part of the BNSF merger proceedings, Washington State demanded, BN did not resist, and the Surface Transportation Board imposed a 5-year, $541,000,000 program to increase east–west capacity by reconstructing the line between Ellensburg and Lind and placing a second main track along much of BN's line between Spokane and East Glacier, Montana.[2]

The former MILW right of way between Ellensburg and Lind was owned by Washington State. It was 109 miles long, versus 189.7 miles via Pasco, but the MILW was not as attractive as indicated by this mileage comparison. Since Pasco was by this time BN's most important carload freight yard in Washington, little, if any, carload traffic would utilize this route. In addition, it featured a 17-mile long, 2.2% grade climb westward from the Columbia River at Beverly to Boylston, and a 9.5-mile long, 1.6% grade climb eastward from Kittitas to Boylston. These grades were much steeper than on the former NP route between Ellensburg and Lind. Only intermodal trains were routinely given sufficient power to get over these grades, but the ports and the state were concerned only about intermodal traffic.

The Washington legislature passed legislation allowing the governor to lease the right of way between Ellensburg and Lind to BNSF for railroad purposes. Adjacent landowners then asserted revisionary rights to portions of the right of way, beginning a court battle that went to the Washington Supreme Court. BNSF may have been relieved to see this expensive project flounder under the state's management.

Reopening Stampede Pass was complicated by the fact that BN previously sold the line between Kennewick and Cle Elum to the Washington Central Railroad Company (WCRC). To solve this problem BN purchased WCRC for $40,000,000 in 1996. BNSF then spent $125,000,000 to rehabilitate the line over Stampede Pass, to install many miles of concrete ties and new rail, and to install remote controlled switches at both ends of several sidings between Auburn and Kennewick. Stampede Pass returned to service on December 7, 1996, but with no improvement in tunnel clearances, which meant that double stack intermodal equipment could not use the line.[3]

It is odd that BNSF did not lower the floor or raise the roof in the Stampede Pass tunnels, a job estimated to cost $25,000,000 and take about one year with the line shut down, or two years under traffic with a 12-hour work window. Perhaps BNSF did not believe that the line between Ellensburg and Lind would be restored. To restore the MILW route for intermodal and not clear Stampede Pass tunnels made no sense. It is also possible that BNSF decided that they preferred to raise the roof, and they could do that while they were rebuilding the line between Ellensburg and Lind.

The second important part of the agreement between BNSF and the state of Washington was to increase capacity between Spokane and East Glacier, Montana. Spokane operating employees were living with a series of bottlenecks starting at Yardley and extending to Whitefish.

➻ Easing the Bottleneck

As mentioned in Chapter 10, before the BN merger 'dog catching,' or calling a second crew to relieve a crew that died on line, was rare. After the merger, dog catching became far too common. Train density on the former NP line between Spokane and Sandpoint increased as total traffic volume increased, and as ever more, and finally all, trains were rerouted to the NP line. This portion of the network became a bottleneck with two high capacity lines from the east and three from the west feeding trains into it.

As of 1970, there was only one segment of two main tracks between Yardley and Sandpoint. It extended from the east end of Yardley at MP 66.6 to Irvin at MP 63 and was not much more than a long yard lead. Eastward from Irvin was single track with sidings about two miles long at: Otis Orchards, MP 57.4; Rathdrum, MP 44.5; Athol, MP 31.4; Cocolalla, MP 16.9; and Algoma, MP 10.2. Hauser, the junction with the Coeur d'Alene branch, was at MP 51.5. Sandpoint depot was at MP 3.0. After the merger, Sandpoint Junction was created at MP 2.9. BNSF mileposts between Sandpoint and Spokane start from zero 3.0 miles east of Sandpoint depot, are unchanged from their former Northern Pacific locations, and increase westward.

Northern Pacific equipped the entire line between Yardley and Paradise, Montana with CTC during 1963. Northern Pacific also built a 3.34-mile line change, opened in 1965, to bypass Granite. The Granite relocation eliminated a long and high bridge, one tunnel, two speed restricting curves, and shortened the line by two miles making MP 28.84 and MP 30.84 the same points.

The line change eliminated the sharp curve and bridge over Granite Lake where train No. 25, the North Coast Limited, derailed at high speed on March 2, 1962, killing the engine crew. After the Granite line change, there were no sharp curves and the speed limit for freight trains was generally 60 MPH, except for one 40 MPH curve beside Cocolalla Lake between MP 15 and MP 14, 45 MPH through a series of curves between MP 6 and MP 5, and 35 MPH from MP 5 over the Lake Pend Oreille bridge to Sandpoint Junction.[4]

The Frisco management built a second segment of two main tracks in 1982 extending the siding at Algoma, MP 9.5–11.7, by 2.0 miles on the east and less than one mile on the west to create a short segment of two main tracks between MP 7.5 and MP 12.6 incorporating the former Algoma siding.

The Krebs management quickly recognized they needed to upgrade the northern tier with second main track and more sidings. The most important improvement was to eliminate the bottleneck between Sandpoint and Yardley which was handling all traffic to and from Washington State. It was very congested, handling up to 50 trains per day.[5] Your authors believe that Krebs would have increased capacity east of Spokane regardless of the agreement with Washington State.

Capacity expansion projects east of Spokane began in 1997. Grading was done at the site that would become Hauser Yard that year, but the more spectacular projects were grading for and construction of second main tracks.

To avoid confusion, we will digress for a moment to discuss the difference between 'double track' and 'two main tracks.' These terms refer to different signal arrangements and methods of operation, but are often confused by casual observers.

Under double track operation, each track is signaled for movement in only one direction, defined as the 'current of traffic,' typically either eastward or westward. Tracks are called the eastward or westward main, based on their current of traffic. BNSF's projects between Spokane and Sandpoint involved two main tracks, each signaled for movement in both directions. Current of traffic does not apply in two main track territories. Tracks are called simply Main 1 and Main 2. BNSF practice between Sunset Junction and Algoma is that the track to the railroad north is Main 1, while the track to the railroad south is Main 2.

Contractors moved massive amounts of earth to widen the roadbed for new second main track between the east end of Athol at MP 30.8, through the Granite line change to the west end of Cocolalla siding at MP 18.3. The heaviest work was widening a cut about a mile long in unconsolidated material near MP 28 and using that material to widen fills to the east. A second cut, east of the first, was through rock. That material was also moved east to widen fills to the east.

Second main track between Athol and Cocolalla was placed in service on January 3, 1998. The former west switch at Athol at MP 33.5 became Control Point (CP) Athol, and the former east switch at Cocolalla became CP Cocolalla at MP 16.4, a total of 15.1 miles.

BNSF wanted to extend both ends of the short two main track segment at Algoma to create a long segment of two main tracks from just west of the Sandpoint Bridge to Cocolalla. They were not able to lay a second main track to Cocolalla, because where the track ran between the highway and Cocolalla Lake there was no room for a second track. The state of Idaho refused to move the highway, and the EPA would not let BNSF fill a 100-foot by 400-foot strip along the southeast corner of the lake.

The company settled for extending the west end of the two main tracks at Algoma about a mile and a half west during 1997. Early in 1998, BNSF excavated two miles of rock eastward from Algoma to extend Algoma two and a half miles east to a point about one quarter mile west of the bridge over Lake Pend Oreille. On August 14, this 2.5-mile segment of second main track from MP 7.5 to MP 5 opened. These projects created a 9.1-mile long segment of second main track between CP East Algoma and CP West Algoma. When all was said and done, there was a 2.1-mile long single track segment through Sandpoint and over Pend Oreille Lake, a nine mile stretch of two main tracks and about two and a half miles of single track to Cocolalla.

The two main track project was completed when 14.4 miles of second main track opened between Otis Orchards, Washington and Rathdrum, Idaho on September 29, 1998.[6] This project, in the wide Spokane Valley, did not involve the massive earth moving of previous

On the afternoon of June 6, 2013, Chicago to Portland high-priority domestic intermodal train Z-CHCPTL climbs the 0.8 percent grade through the mile-long cut between Cocolalla and Athol, Idaho. Northern Pacific built this line segment as single track in 1965, and BNSF in made it two main tracks in 1997. PHOTO BY BRUCE KELLY.

projects. This new second main track extended through Hauser Jct. and the future site of Hauser Yard.

BNSF gave up the idea of straightening the slow curve at Lake Cocolalla and constructed a new roadbed between West Algoma and Cocolalla in 2018, and built a second main track that was placed in service August 2019.

Irvin remains the end of two main tracks. Single track now extends 4.1 miles from Irvin to the beginning of two main tracks at Otis Orchards and includes the long Spokane River Bridge. From Otis Orchards, two main tracks extend 25.4 miles to Athol and incorporates the former 2.1-mile long siding at Ramsey. From Athol, two main tracks extend 26.5 miles to East Algoma, and are followed by 2.1 miles of single track to Sandpoint Junction. This last segment includes the 4,770-foot long bridge over Lake Pend Oreille.[7] In 2019 BNSF filed for the environmental permits to build a second bridge at Sandpoint.

BNSF also made capacity improvements east of Sandpoint on its former Great Northern line. During 1997, the company created two main tracks between Bonners Ferry and Crossport, about seven miles, by connecting those two sidings. The Bonners Ferry depot was removed to allow a second main track to be built over the site it previously occupied. Bonners Ferry siding was also extended about half a mile to the west. A set of double crossovers was added at Control Point 1366.3, near the middle of this new second main track, to give dispatchers more flexibility in meeting trains.

Another improvement was the addition of a new

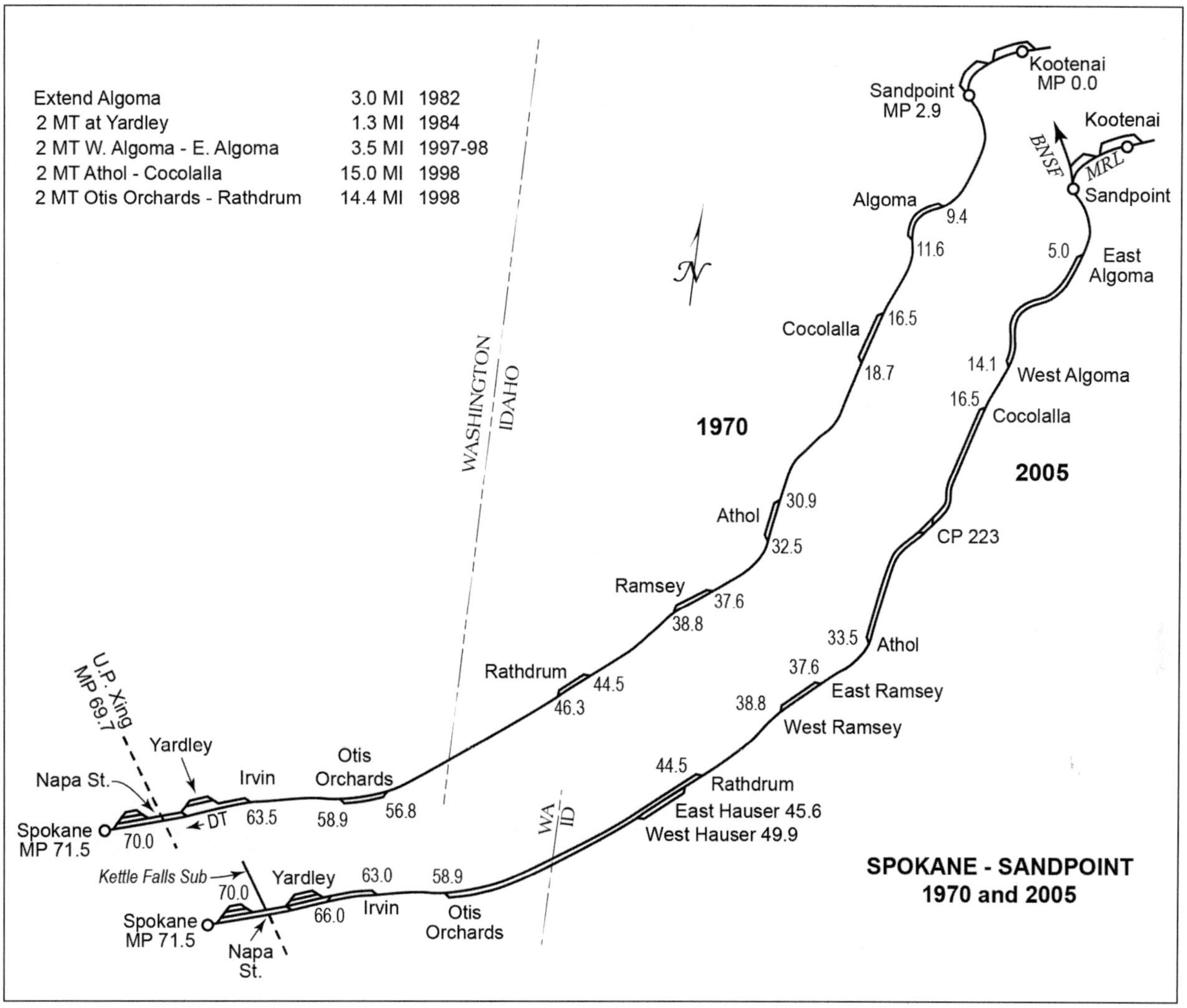

siding in the Kootenai Canyon of Idaho, called Katka. Crossport and Leona were 13.5 miles apart with a 30 MPH speed limit. Travel at 30 MPH equals two minutes to go one mile. Travel time between Crossport to Leona at track speed was 27 minutes. Before I hired out there had been a siding at Katka, but it had been shortened up to a spur track by 1960.

BNSF constructed roadbed in 1997 for a new siding located east of Old Katka Spur and named it Katka. The new Katka siding was 10,440 feet long. The west switch at new Katka was about 200 feet east of the switch for Old Katka Spur, which was the former east switch of old Katka siding. Old Katka Spur switch and track was removed after new Katka was constructed. I do not know why they did not include the roadbed from old Katka siding in the new siding. This would have given BNSF another 3,000 feet of siding without moving any dirt. A longer siding would have allowed dispatchers to put two trains into new Katka siding at one time. There are times when putting two trains into new Katka would have cut down on delays for both east and west trains. Track at new Katka was not laid until 1998. New Katka was six and a half miles east of Crossport and about six miles west of Leona. The new siding at Katka and the second main track between Bonners Ferry and Crossport cut train delay considerably.

For the first time in long time, the company was straightening out its operations, adding capacity, and

Train Q-CHCPTL, carrying domestic intermodal traffic from Chicago to Portland, crosses the former Northern Pacific 4,769-foot-long single-track bridge at Sandpoint, Idaho, on September 13, 2014. PHOTO BY BRUCE KELLY.

reducing train delay. We men were pleased to see progress.

As described in Chapter 11, the plan to build what became Hauser Yard near the Washington-Idaho border dated back to planning for the BN merger, but other things took precedence for years. By 1984 the yard itself attained its current configuration.

The final major project at Hauser Yard was addition of a 'run through' fuel facility on the south side of the yard. Traditional practice was to fuel engines at the origin terminal of each train, and then at selected intermediate points when fuel ran low. Growth of intermodal traffic at the Puget Sound ports of Tacoma and Seattle, and domestic intermodal at South Seattle resulted in engines available for refueling, and needing fuel, at locations where there was no fueling facility. Many wasted engine hours were spent running to fueling points at Interbay and Tacoma and then back to the origin point of the outbound trains.

Somebody figured out that if westward trains were fueled at Hauser, they could run to any turn back point on the west end of the railroad, turn back without being fueled, and be refueled eastward at Hauser. This would improve power utilization by more than enough to pay for the facility. When BNSF applied for the permits to undertake this project, it ignited a firestorm of protest since Hauser is located on top of a major aquifer. The ins and outs of this permit struggle could be a book in itself. It went on for years and the railroad finally got the permits it needed.

Track work for the fuel facility was done in 2003–2004. Three long lead tracks, officially designated as

RIGHT A westward domestic intermodal stack train passes Lake Cocolalla on October 27, 2019, just days after BNSF placed about 2.5 miles of second main track in service here, eliminating a short section of single track. PHOTO BY BRUCE KELLY.

BELOW Snow still lingers on the peaks of northern Idaho's Selkirk Range April 19, 2015, as an eastward empty grain train approaches the end of two main tracks at Crossport, Idaho, on former Great Northern trackage. PHOTO BY BRUCE KELLY.

Main 4, Main 5, and Main 6, with controlled switches and signals on both ends, were built to get trains off the main tracks as quickly as possible and to bypass the yard. These main tracks are about four miles long. The grade crossing of Greens Ferry Road, originally located where the east switch of Hauser is now, was relocated to a point about half a mile east, and the crossing was eliminated by constructing a new underpass for the road.

The new fuel facility has four run-through tracks, one from the yard plus Main 4, Main 5, and Main 6. These tracks are long enough to hold an entire train, in either direction, in the clear of any other moves into or out of the fuel facility and Hauser Yard. Fuel is dispensed to engines on any of three main tracks. The fuel facility is located in the center of the fueling tracks and there are controlled crossovers between tracks 4, 5, and 6. The west crossovers are at West Downing, while the east crossovers are at East Downing. Both are named after Robert W. Downing, who retired from the position of Vice Chairman–Chief Operating Officer in 1976 and from the Board of Directors in 1979.[8]

The crew change point for through trains was moved from Yardley to Hauser in 2004, since virtually all trains would now stop at Hauser for fuel.

The new fuel facility entered service in 2006, only to be shut down due to a leak caused by a cracked line. This resulted in immediate excavation of thousands of yards of contaminated material and cries of "I told you so" from opponents. The leak was fixed and Hauser fueling station continues in service to this day.

My Last Years on the Railroad

The last seven years of my career, I was either on a work train or the Kettle Falls dog catch crew. On work trains, I set our call time and told the crew office what time we would be on duty. My last three years on the railroad I worked the Kettle Falls Turn dog catch. The first Kettle Falls crew was called for 9:00 PM at Yardley. Our usual call was for about 4:00 AM Tuesday through Saturday.

The Kettle Falls dog catch was a regular job bulletined from Yardley to Addy and return. It paid 73.5 miles from Yardley to Addy and the same back, for a total of 147 miles. If our crew relieved the first crew on their return trip anywhere within our bulletined limits, we got paid our bulletined miles. If our crew relieved them beyond our bulletined limits, then we got our bulletined miles, plus another basic day. Since Yardley was always congested, they usually held us out between Euclid Street and Old North Center, a pedestrian crossing. Once our train was held out, we went on Final Terminal Delay at 16.25 miles per hour. We were not paid for the first hour of FTD, but were paid for everything thereafter until we went off duty. It was not unusual to sit at Old North Center for longer than it took to sign in, get our paperwork, ride a van out to our train and get the train to Old North Center.

During the last six months I worked, crews were called by a computer voice system and we responded by pushing buttons on our phone keypad. Now, this was not too bad during daylight hours. However, being woken up by a ringing phone and responding by pushing keypad buttons on your phone was not the easiest thing to do coming out of a deep sleep. I did not have much trouble with it, but I have always been able to jump out of bed on a dead run. No one liked this new way of calling crews, but we did not have anything to say about it.

Computerized crew calling was yet another way of cutting down on human crew callers. One crew caller could call two to three times as many crews with this computerized system. I remember being told about this new system before it went in, and I thought, "This could be a big mess." I later heard comments from those who were still working chain gang that line-ups were a little bit better, but there was still room for improvement. The people who come up with these ideas, and who buy into them, do not have to live and work with them. All that management can think about is cutting cost and employees.

After the BNSF merger, the company put in a new system for reporting the location of cars set out or picked up at each station. This system was used on the ATSF and was extended to former Burlington Northern routes. This system gave each track, including all industries, a unique number, so that each number was different from all other numbers at all other stations. Station numbers were changed from a number to the name of each station. This was OK, but all the tracks at every station were changed from a name such as house, elevator, dock, and chip track to a number. Spot numbers remained unchanged since the shipper usually numbered his spots.

This change to track numbers caused much confusion. I, and every other BN trainman, knew the tracks by name and field support knew them only by number. I will admit this was a good system except for one thing: they did not give this new numbering system to the conductors. This meant that when a conductor called field support to let them know where he left his cars, or where he picked up cars, all you could tell field support was the name of the track that you knew it by.

After about six months of this I decided to make my

own list of new station, track and industry numbers for my entire seniority district. I called field support on the company phone and asked them to fax me the new numbers for three or four stations at a time. When I received these faxes, I cut the information out of the sheet of paper, glued the information on a fresh sheet of paper, and ran it through a copy machine. Once I got all the pages, it took me about two days off and on to put an entire book together for the territory that I worked. When I was finished, I owned a complete book of new track and industry numbers all lined up in station order. About a year later, the company came out with this information for everybody.

About three years later, when the company started to hire new employees, they came out with a book of track diagrams for all stations. This book listed all the tracks and track numbers, plus the names of the industries at each station. The direction each track would roll and how to spot each industry was also listed. Finally, all the information about each station which everyone had spent so much time memorizing and remembering in earlier years was now available in print. This should have been done the first day of the BN merger of 1970. Words cannot express how handy those station diagrams would have been on merger day! I hate to think of the times that I walked a track in a town that I had never seen before, trying to figure out the names of the tracks.

Hauser and Yardley in 2020

Hauser continues to be the 1,000-mile inspection point for westward trains, and a grain holding point. Several trains set out and/or pick up blocks, a practice known as "block swapping." All through power is fueled and fully serviced at the Hauser fueling facility.

Yardley handles switching of carload traffic and builds locals and manifest trains. Manifest trains that terminate at Yardley originate at Pasco, Northtown, Great Falls, Everett, and Longview. Yardley builds westward manifest trains to Pasco, Everett, and Longview. The train to Everett runs via Wenatchee and is the only carload train through Wenatchee. The train to Longview has a set out for Pasco and picks up there as well. Yardley makes only one eastward manifest train, to Northtown via the former Great Northern main line.

Yardley also adds cars to, removes cars from, and switches several though manifest trains. The Pasco to Laurel and Pasco to Lincoln trains are filled with traffic for Missoula, Laurel, and beyond. The Kansas City to Pasco train sets out and is filled at Yardley. These trains run via Montana Rail Link. Yardley adds a fill of shorts for Whitefish, Shelby, and Great Falls Montana to the Pasco to Minot train.

Most intermodal trains bypass Yardley, but two westward and two eastward trains set out and pick up traffic daily to and from the intermodal terminal at Yardley. On low traffic days, some of the through intermodal trains come into Yardley and are split, with one part going to Seattle, Washington and the remainder going to Portland, Oregon. In similar fashion, trains from Seattle and Portland are consolidated at Yardley on light traffic days before they continue eastward.

Yardley still has two switch engines in the yard each shift, plus three 'outside jobs,' the Tramp Job, the South 40, and the Erie Street switch engines. These jobs go to work at Yardley and switch customers in their assigned territories. After they return to Yardley, these jobs switch out the cars they brought in as directed by the yardmaster.

The Tramp Job works anywhere it is needed, typically making a trip eastward to Velox. This job can go east as far as Rathdrum since switching limits were extended to include Rathdrum in 2004. The South 40 job works the industry track that lies south of the main track. The Erie Street job switches Erie Street Yard and works the jointly used Union Pacific industry track as far as Millwood, serving customers formerly located on the SC&P line, but from the Union Pacific side. These are all daylight jobs working Monday through Friday. Yardley also originates and terminates three locals, the Lind Turn, the Chewelah Turn, and the Sandpoint/Coeur d'Alene Local. The Chewelah Turn is a shortened version of the Kettle Falls Turn instituted when the BNSF leased the north end of the Kettle Falls line to a short line operator after I retired.

The Iron Triangle

Early in 2012, BNSF made an important operating change in the state of Washington. BNSF invested another $26,000,000 in the Stampede Pass Line and, with union agreement, established a new three-legged crew pool at Pasco to enable semi-directional running westward on the former SP&S line through the Columbia River Gorge and eastward over Stampede Pass.

Before this agreement, BNSF operated heavy export grain trains, export coal trains, and unit crude oil trains westward down the SP&S to Vancouver, Washington and returned empty equipment eastward via the same route. The new operating plan continues to move loaded bulk trains westward down the SP&S to Vancouver. The new thing is that crews then work north to Auburn. From Auburn, crews work empty grain, coal, and oil trains, plus previously established eastward merchandise trains to Pasco. A new agreement with the operating unions was required to operate in this circular pattern, as opposed to the traditional out and back home pattern.

This 'Iron Triangle' plan leaves heavy loaded bulk trains on two lines that have no more than 1% grades and uses the same power to return empty bulk trains over the 2.2% grades of Stampede Pass. This improves capacity by using the previously under-utilized, but shorter, Stampede Pass line to return trains to Pasco. The big gain is that removing returning eastward bulk trains from the Columbia Gorge line between Pasco and Vancouver allows all westward trains to operate with fewer meets and associated train delays, improving capacity and velocity on that line. In a similar fashion, with Stampede Pass handling predominately eastward trains, few meets are required. This paired track arrangement substantially reduces the total number of meets.[9]

➛ I Left My Train at Espanola

One afternoon I was called for a dead freight to Wenatchee at 3:00 PM with a main line crew change. We left Yardley, picked up our orders at Spokane depot, and started up the hill toward Lyons at about 15 MPH. About two miles from Lyons, the Seattle East dispatcher called and told us that he was going to head us in at Espanola for us to cut all the crossings, tie our train down, and take the power and Fred to Wenatchee.

I told the dispatcher to line us out the west end of Espanola and as soon as our engine showed west of the main line signal, to line us east on the main so I could cut the east crossing from the rear and pick up Fred. I asked my engineer if he would cut our power off at the west end of the siding after I made my cut on the west crossing. He agreed to do so. I told him to stop about 10 car lengths back from the signal to leave room to cut the west crossing wide enough so the crossing signal lights would go out. As our train pulled into the siding, I dropped off at the west crossing. When my engineer stopped, I made a cut and gave him a go-ahead sign. He pulled west so that our head car was just clear of the track circuit bond beside the departing signal on the siding, and stopped. I tied hand brakes on both cuts of cars and soon my engineer was coming east on the main. He stopped, picked me up at the crossing, and we were off.

The east end signal was clear, so my engineer stopped east of the signals to enter the siding. Before I could call the dispatcher, the signal changed to lunar under red and my engineer started into the siding. The dispatcher called me on the radio and asked me what I needed next. I told him that as soon as our power passed the signal to clear us east out to the main on the east end, then after we were east of the main line signal, to line us west on the main. My engineer would pick me up at the crossing and we would be ready to proceed to Wenatchee.

We stopped short of the end of our train. I pulled the Fred off, strapped it to the hand rail on the nose of our engine, and then coupled into our train. I cut the air into the rear of our train and walked 10 car lengths to the gated crossing into the grain elevator. This gated protection on this crossing was supposed to have been put at a public road crossing just east of the east switch at Espanola, but was mistakenly put at the grain elevator access road crossing, which ended at the elevator.

When I arrived at the crossing, I turned the angle cock and gave my engineer a backup sign. He took the slack and started east. As soon as the crossing gates started up, I gave him a stop sign. He got out of his cab, turned both angle cocks, pulled the pin, backed out of the siding, and waited for the dispatcher to give him a signal to come west on the main. I tied hand brakes on both cuts of cars and waited for the engine to come pick me up.

As I was waiting, a car approached from the south. I gave the car a sign to come across the crossing, but it stopped just south of it. Both doors opened, and two police officers stepped out. The officer on the driver's side of this unmarked car was wearing a tan shirt and forest green pants that looked like a Spokane County Sheriff's Department uniform. The officer stepping out of the passenger's side was wearing a uniform that was two different shades of blue and that I did not recognize.

I thought this was very odd; I never saw officers from two different police departments travel together in one car, let alone an unmarked car. Both officers then opened their back doors, reached into the back seat, and came out with shotguns. I thought, "This can't be good." Both officers left their front doors open and walked toward an old, isolated, low budget motel.

There were three structures at Espanola: the grain elevator, an old house, and a motel. This motel was said to be a stopover for Hells Angels and other bad bikers wanted by the law.

While these two officers were walking toward the motel, my eye caught another movement. I saw about 15 men walking around the old house about 200 feet east of the motel. They too were headed toward the motel. Most, if not all, were wearing blue windbreakers with big yellow letters "ATF" on their backs. All these men carried either AR 15 rifles or shotguns.

As I watched this small army approach the motel, I decided that I needed to get out of Espanola NOW! About this time my engineer pulled up and stopped as I got on our engine. I came through the nose and up into the cab as fast as I could. My engineer gestured toward the motel and asked, "What is going on over there?" I said, "Just get the hell out of here; we are the only ones without a gun!" He pulled back on his throttle; we were gone and on our way to Wenatchee with all possible speed.

I never did hear what went on at Espanola that afternoon.

➻ Work Trains

My first choice in jobs was a work train, both as a brakeman and as a conductor. Work trains were almost always daylight jobs, which was a plus. I liked work trains because every day was different, always something new or unexpected. I liked the challenge, and as a conductor I was my own boss. I was in charge of the train and decided how to line up our work to be done. By the time I could hold a work train conductor job, crew size on work trains and local trains was one engineer, one conductor, and one brakeman. The conductor and brakeman each carried a portable radio and the engineer used a radio in the engine.

In work train service, we worked for the Maintenance-of-Way Department unloading new rail, picking up old rail, spreading ballast, or cleaning up after derailments. Many times, I did not know where our job was going to tie up that night until late afternoon, so I made motel reservations in two or three different towns. When the afternoon got late, I would tell the person in charge of us that day that he must to decide where to tie up that night because I needed to cancel some of my reservations "right now." I delighted in staying one or two steps ahead of the Maintenance-of-Way Department.

One of my early experiences with a work train occurred when I was called off the conductors' extra board for a work train one day in 1984. BN was building a second main track from Havana Street to Park Street in Spokane to improve the flow of main line traffic through Yardley. The Maintenance-of-Way Department worked twenty-four hours a day, seven days a week to complete this project. Our job was to work between Yardley and Highland from 6:00 PM to 6:00 AM loading ballast at Highland pit and spreading it on the new main track at Yardley.

At the beginning of the day, the roadmaster and the trainmaster approached me with an offer that if my crew did not stop to eat for the full 12 hours, they would give us two more hours of overtime. Everyone in the crew agreed. Our train was 10 ballast hoppers. Our first move was to take them to Highland. As soon as the front-end loader operator loaded our 10 cars, we backed out of Highland and proceeded to Latah Jct. and Yardley. At Yardley we waited for the tie tampers to move away so we could spread ballast on the new track. The Maintenance-of-Way Department set up floodlights mounted on pickup trucks with portable generators so that they could move along with the tampers lighting the track, and the tamper-liner operators could see to tamp the ties. When our ballast was spread, we departed for Highland pit for another load. We made four complete round trips.

Project work in the Spokane area was and is seasonal;

While this Great Northern ballast train at Fort Wright predates John's story about hauling ballast from Highland Pit, east of Fort Wright, to Yardley, it shows the general look of his train that day. COLLECTION OF JOHN E. LANGLOT.

work is done when the ground is not frozen and there is no snow on the ground. Tie gangs and steel gangs are put up for bid in early spring and men are hired to fill out these gangs for the season. The gangs worked until their projects were done, usually sometime in late fall. Local section crews do not perform project work, but they usually help with the final cleanup associated with the projects.

In the spring of 1997, new seasonal work trains were put up for bid. I bid in a work train that worked between Yardley and Sandpoint. Our first job was to spread new wood ties beside the sidings at Athol and Cocolalla, Idaho. This was done to bring tie condition in these sidings up to main line standards in anticipation of sidings becoming incorporated into the two main track project. Soon, a mechanized tie gang showed up and replaced the bad ties in these sidings.

A massive amount of earth moving was taking place between Athol and Algoma widening the road bed for new second main track. After the earth moving was done and the roadbed widened, sub ballast was placed by off track equipment. Another work train crew had previously laid new rail on bare ground beside the existing main track where new main track was to be laid.

My work train was assigned to keep the Track Laying Machine (TLM) supplied with new concrete ties from the concrete tie plant at Velox. We returned the empty tie flatcars for loading and come back with more concrete ties. Our first bit with the TLM was west from Algoma to the new west end of the two main tracks at MP 14.1 where a new west switch had been installed.

Then the TLM laid new concrete ties and new ribbon rail from a new double crossover at Mile Post 22.3, westward to the east end of Athol siding. We turned the TLM around on the wye at Sandpoint and it laid ties and rail from the new double crossover, which became Control Point 223, eastward to the west switch at Cocolalla.

We came back in with the work train to spread ballast over the track. A surfacing gang used tamper/liners to raise the track by tamping ballast under the ties. When the surfacing gang was done, the track was placed in service, initially with a speed restriction. Once trains settled the track, the surfacing gang gave it a final lift and alignment, and the project was done. We now enjoyed two main tracks between Athol and Cocolalla. The second main track for that year between Yardley and Sandpoint was thus completed.

Then we moved the TLM to Bonners Ferry and laid new rail and concrete ties from the east end of Bonners Ferry to the west end of Crossport. This now all needed to be ballasted. Another work train arrived with a ballast train, and the next morning our job spread ballast on the newly laid ties and rail. This ended our season as it was now November and winter was about to close in.

The most dangerous job I did in work train service was to pick up used rail with a rail pickup train. In January of 1998, my crew began to pick up rail in Kootenai Canyon. There was lots of rail to pick up since three curve relay programs had been done with no rail picked up. We would fill the rail train completely before our job was done.

The head end of this train was special; first was a boxcar used as a tool car. Next was a power car, which had a diesel engine that ran the machinery that could pull the old rail up off the ground, and move it through powered feeder rollers that pinched the rail from both sides to feed the rail onto the ribbon rail train. The tunnel car was located immediately behind the power car. It featured a platform that could be raised or lowered to get rail being loaded to the correct elevation, of five possible levels, to be fed onto the rail train itself. The rest of the train was specially modified flatcars used to transport the rail with an empty gondola or boxcar as a buffer car on the rear to protect the caboose. When the rail train moved to or from a welding plant, it carried a buffer car on both ends.

Pulling old rail off the ground and feeding it onto the train sounds simple enough but several things could and did go wrong. This old rail had been in place for years, being heated and cooled by the weather several thousand times and it had developed a 'set.' Set means that it is 'set' in its condition, straight, curved left, or curved right. Simply picking this rail up is likely to make it bend in a direction that it is not used to. Believe me, the rail acts just like a snake. You would swear that rail was alive when the rail crew fed it through the starting box which was low on the side on the power car. Rail with a set in it will bob and weave from side to side and up and down simultaneously as it fed into the starter boxes and as the operator would lift or lower it with his hydraulic hoist. Sometimes, if the operator just lifted the end of the rail as high as his hoist would allow, and lowered it back down to the ground, the rail would relax and feed smoothly through the starter boxes.

To load rail, the starter box is first lowered and the train moved forward to get the rail into the first box. The motion of the train moves the rail toward the next box, while the rail men guide the rail through the second box and toward the box entering the power car. From the starter boxes, the rail goes through a set of steel rollers as the engine pulls the train under the rail. Once the rail has entered all of the feeder boxes, the power car can pull the rail on its own.

A rail train is loaded from the bottom up. The rail men attach a pointed steel 'shoe' to the leading end of the rail to help guide it through the pockets on each car. Now they are ready to feed rail onto the train and push it toward the rear of the rail train. Once rail is started onto the train, and onto the ribbon rail cars, rail crewmen walked the rail onto the cars keeping the shoe on the rail end feeding through the correct pocket on each car of the rail train. To help this procedure, the train crew kept the rail cars on straight track while loading the train.

Since these were random lengths of welded rail, and

Quarter-mile-long strings of welded rail, also referred to as "Ribbon Rail," are moved on special trains like this one at Wenatchee from centralized welding plants to where the rail is to be placed. GNRHS ARCHIVE.

the rail train length was fixed at 1,440 feet, any particular piece of rail was likely to be either too short or too long. If a rail was too short, the power car operator left the rail end sticking out of the starter box just enough so that the rail men could torch cut bolt holes in the first piece, torch cut bolt holes in the next piece, apply flat connectors called 'fishplates' to attach the next piece of rail, and continue loading. When a pocket would not hold any more rail, then the rail men would torch cut the rail at the tunnel car and start this new rail end down an empty pocket. When a pocket is filled with rail, the rail men clamp it down at the tie down car in the middle of the train. The reason the tie down car is in the middle of the train is that a central tie down gives the rail a chance to move on both ends as the train goes around curves, while the central tie down prevents the rail from shifting either way on the cars.

I have seen rail jump the pocket and dive clear off the side of a rail car before the power car operator can get the rail stopped. Sometimes the rail jammed against a stanchion, which caused it to kink. When a rail kinked, section men would set their cylinders and cutting torch, which were mounted on a frame, on the ground using a hydraulic lift on the tool car. We pulled the train ahead so they could make the cuts. The rail men cut the kinked rail out and applied fishplates at the two ends to get the rail back together before they could finish loading that piece of rail. Then we backed up and reloaded the torch and tanks.

In the winter, when the old rail is frozen to the ground, our engineer helped the power car by running our train under the rail for hundreds of feet. After the rail was fed through the feeder box and the power car, our engineer would pull the rail pickup train toward the rail lying on the ground. This broke the rail loose from the frozen ground and fed the rail onto our train, which made the job easier for the power car. After he got quite a bit of rail fed onto the car, the power car operator would call our engineer and tell him to come to an easy stop because he could now pull the rail onto the train without our help.

While running the train under a rail, everybody was ready to put our train into emergency at any sign that something was going wrong. The power car operator had a brake valve and the best view of the train. In addition, there were air dump valves by the feeder boxes on the power car and our engineer could dump the air. As we fed the rail onto the rail train, rail men walked the point of the rail through each pocket and they all carried a portable radio and would holler "stop" if a rail jammed or jumped the pocket and started to dive off the train.

Having everybody ready to dump the air prevented us from tearing up our equipment, which I have seen happen. If equipment got torn up and needed repairs, we were through loading rail until repairs could be made. If equipment was torn up badly enough, we would take our train to our tie up location and tie up. The rail gang would work all night to fix the equipment if need be so that everyone could start to pick up rail the next morning.

In the spring of 1998, I again bid in a seasonal work train. That spring my crew was assigned to the Georgetown Slot Train, which is 13 articulated gondola sections that are continuously open between all the sections except on the ends of the first and last section. Each section shares a truck with the section next to it, except the first and 13th gondola have a truck under the outside end of their sections.

TOP Rail is recovered onto rail trains for relocation, reclamation, or scrap depending on the amount of wear. Feeding rail into the roller box is the first step in getting rail onto the train. PHOTO BY JOHN OVERDORF.

BOTTOM This view shows the key parts of a rail recovery train, with power car on the left and transport cars on the right. PHOTO BY JOHN OVERDORF.

Our train consisted of this one articulated gondola with a mobile excavator, a GP 30 or GP 35 engine, and a caboose. We went out and removed material accumulated in track side ditches and cleaned up around tunnel portals. When the trough was full, we moved to a nearby location, selected by section foreman Mark May, where the roadbed on the river side was getting narrow and unloaded our spoils. Our excavator operator would flatten the top of his fill with his bucket to restore a toe path so that trainmen could safely walk along a stopped train.

We spent three months between Elmira, Idaho and Troy, Montana, ditching the up-slope side of the track. Most of this work was in Kootenai Canyon along the Kootenai River between Crossport, Idaho and Troy, and most of the time we went to work and tied up at Bonners Ferry, Idaho. We spent another month working between Chewelah, Kettle Falls, Northport, and into Canada above Waneta, British Columbia, cleaning out drainage ditches and culverts that were plugged with mud. We spent about one week on the Republic branch between Barstow and Orient. Then we went back to Bonners Ferry for one more month of ditching in Kootenai Canyon. This was one of the best work trains I ever worked; every day was fun. The railroad was our sandbox and every day we went out and played in mud and rocks for twelve hours.

Around July 1998, we began to participate in a project to extend the east end of Algoma. Our first job was to build a new east switch at Algoma at MP 5.0. While we were doing this, a lightning storm blew in and caught all of us out in the open. A lightning bolt struck a rail lying unattached beside the roadbed with a terrific BOOM. With the smell of ozone in the air, we counted noses and determined that no one had been hit. We were all a little shaky for the half an hour it took for the surprise of that near miss to wear off.

In August of 1998, I was again working with the TLM, adding 2.5 miles of new concrete ties and new rail from the new east switch to the old east switch of Algoma. A roving roadmaster, a new roadmaster who does not yet have a designated territory, was in charge of the crew working the TLM. They handled assignments like the TLM or a tie gang replacing old wood ties with new concrete ties. Indy Sandoval was the roving roadmaster in charge of us and the TLM.

Our crew came out of Boyer Yard, the former Great Northern yard on the north side of Sandpoint, with the TLM, and proceeded west, shoving it across the Sandpoint Bridge to the new switch that we lined, and shoved in to a D-8 Caterpillar sitting just beyond the end of track. It takes about an hour to hook up everything between the transition unit that connects the Cat to the rest of the TLM. When laying track, the Caterpillar pulls the entire train, including the flatcars full of concrete ties and our engine.

Once engineering forces hooked up the TLM, they started to lay track. The TLM lays concrete ties, and then pulls rail previously placed on the roadbed outside of the space the ties will occupy onto the ties, positioning the rail correctly on the ties. Well, it did not take me long to realize that there were no section men clipping this new rail to the new concrete ties behind us. I walked forward and asked Indy when he was going to start some men clipping new rail to the ties. Indy said that it would be OK. I told Indy that if the rail tipped over, I would not be held responsible when our engine or part of our train went on the ground.

For two days, our work train crept out with empty tie flats and crept in shoving loads of concrete ties to the TLM, all on unclipped rail. We were about two miles in from the east switch on unclipped rail. It was about 4:00 PM and extremely hot. The time and temperature sign at the Quick Stop gas station/convenience store across the highway read 103 degrees as a very large black cloud approached from the southwest. Wind started to blow as that cloud came closer. Soon it started to rain. The wind picked up and was now blowing about 40 to 50 MPH, and the rain became a cloud burst. Rain came down in waves. Tree limbs landed on the main track, on our freshly laid track, and all the way out onto the highway. This storm was so violent that highway traffic slowed to a stop. At times, I could barely see the Quick Stop. When I could finally see their temperature sign through the rain again, it read 54 degrees.

I happened to look ahead and could not believe my eyes; the unclipped rail was literally dancing up and down and wiggling like a snake as it began to shrink from the rapid temperature drop. Needless to say, we could not move our engine until Indy's section men clipped the new rail to the ties. My crew left our engine and empty tie flats right there until morning. Indy's section men worked overtime that night clipping new rail all the way back to the switch.

After completing Algoma, our work train moved to the new siding at Katka, between Crossport and Leonia, to lay concrete ties and new rail. Leonia is on the Idaho-Montana border, 13.5 miles west of Troy, Montana.

Katka is in Kootenai Canyon. Roadbed for Katka siding was built the year before, but not soon enough to get track laid. We set up Indy's TLM at Katka just like we had at Algoma and started to lay new concrete ties and rail. New Katka siding was going to be 10,440 feet long. About a mile and a half into the siding, the TLM ran out of concrete ties, and again Indy did not have anybody clipping rail to the new concrete ties. Ties for our job were coming from a tie plant near Denver. I could not understand this, since there is a concrete tie plant at Velox, east of Spokane.

The next morning, I was told to run light engine to Trentwood, Washington and pick up 12 cars of concrete ties. These ties were originally supposed to go to another work train which was replacing wood ties between Cheney and Babb. Trentwood was the name of the two-track yard that provided access to Kaiser Aluminum at

Trentwood. Velox was west of Trentwood and was connected with Trentwood by a running track. Our train would leave and reenter the main track at Trentwood.

We left Bonners Ferry about 6:45 AM headed west to Trentwood light engine. Every time we met an eastward train, we took the siding, which was good dispatching, but our running time to Trentwood was a little long. We arrived at Trentwood about 9:30 AM, picked up our ties, hung Fred on the rear car, made our brake test, and shoved back out of Trentwood Yard to the main track. Before fouling the main, I contacted the dispatcher and told him that I was ready to head to Crossport where we would have to run around our cars of ties and shove to Katka.

We left Trentwood at about 10:30 AM after waiting for a couple westward trains to go by. About this time, it dawned on me that I had not received a cell phone call from Indy. This was not normal for Indy; he was usually calling me every 30 minutes. I told my engineer, Bob Huguenin, and my brakeman, Jeff West, that something was wrong at Katka. I never got a call from Indy. We arrived at Crossport, ran around our cars at the short material and storage track off main 1, and I called the dispatcher to let him know we were ready to shove to Katka; still no call from Indy.

As I mentioned before, Indy did not have anyone clipping rail. That night, the temperature in the Kootenai River Canyon dropped to 36 degrees. Indy's unclipped rail all rolled over, except for the one section that the TLM was sitting on. Indy's whole crew spent that morning standing up quarter mile long sections of rail and clipping them to the ties. Sometimes I could only wonder!

Our last major track project was construction of the second main track between Otis Orchards, Washington and Rathdrum, Idaho, again using concrete ties and the TLM. In addition to the usual hauling of concrete ties and spreading ballast, we delivered four switches for main track crossovers between MP 49 and MP 50, just west of the west end of Hauser Yard, and several more for Hauser Yard itself. This project was completed in September of 1998.

➻ Plowing Snow

One of my duties on a work train was to plow snow. In my Great Northern days, I was occasionally called for a snow plow off the brakemen's or conductors' extra board. The Great Northern assigned a Jordan Spreader, a dozer, and a rotary to Hillyard. A dozer was assigned to Kettle Falls and a dozer was assigned to Bonners Ferry. I have plowed snow with both Jordan Spreaders and dozers.

Jordan Spreaders are designed for heavy work at low speed. A Jordan can big wing snow or repair trackside ditches. Ditch restoration involves moving rocks, mud, and dirt washed or sloughed down into ditches. In extreme cases, the debris has left no room for water to run off. A Jordan has more control over its big wing than does a dozer. The profile and position of snow removed can be adjusted on a Jordan while moving at low speed. On both pieces of equipment, 'big wings' refers to wings that can extend many feet from the side, while 'bat wings' are smaller wings on the front of the machine.

Jordan Spreaders have two-piece wings on each side of its car body attached about ⅓ back from the front. Wings are attached to 'the post' by large hinges. Wings can be adjusted up or down on the post to set the depth of the bottom of the wing. The trailing end of each wing is attached to a big hydraulic arm that pushes each wing out and away from the side of a Jordan or dozer. When a wing is out as far as the operator wants, someone will put a pin in the appropriate hole in the arm to secure the wing. While big winging, the operator can move both the large wing and the short outer segment of the wing up and down separately to taper the cut through snow so that it is not a vertical wall. When used for ditching, the shape of the bottom of the main wing is designed to clear ditches and establish the correct profile of the ditch. The versatility of the adjustments provided by the outer wings makes it possible to produce an infinitely variable angle on the slope of the ditch away from the track.

Great Northern snow dozers were all products of GN's shops. BN and BNSF assigned one dozer to Yardley, one to Kettle Falls, and one to Bonners Ferry. The design of the ones I worked with dates back to 1926, and the first 16 cars were built on steel underframes of Hart ballast cars.[10] All GN dozers have bat wings that attach to the bottom front of the cage at the front of the dozer. The cage is a framework to which is attached a low V-shaped, viewed from above, plow, mounted under the front drawbar, and a snow shield extending about five feet above the top of the drawbar. Bat wings are mounted to the front of the cage near the bottom. Each bat wing has a pivot at the bottom of the wing. The cage and attached bat wings are raised by air pressure and lowered by gravity. Bat wings are kept up when travelling or put down to plow. The cage on a dozer can be raised or lowered to clear crossing planks, switches, or anything that is a bit higher than the rail. Each bat wing has separate controls located in the front of the cage for raising each bat wing. When in the down 'plow' position, the bottom edge of the bat wing is even with the bottom edge of the plow located under the cage.

LEFT A snow plow extra at Apex on the Nelson line. The plow, BN 972507, is one of many "snow dozers" the Great Northern built or modified to that service in its own shops. It was built as second X1671 in May 1942 at St. Cloud as an all-steel car to the classic lines of a GN design, featuring a wooden car body on steel underframes reused from Hart Convertible gondolas. Snow dozers were necessary to keep the railroad operating during the winter. PHOTO BY LOREN GUENTHER.

BELOW Jordan Spreaders may be used to plow snow, and they can move snow off an adjacent track using its big wing. They were originally intended for making and clearing ditches, so they have very heavy side blades that can be adjusted in motion using compressed air from an adjacent engine. GNRHS ARCHIVE.

Snow dozers have a single piece wing on each side of the car body, attached about ⅓ of the length back from the front. Like the Jordan, dozer wings are attached to 'the post' by large hinges and can be adjusted up or down to set the depth of the bottom of the wing. The back of the hinge is a long flat plate that rides in a vertical trough. This hinge allows the big wing to be held in against the car body for travel or extended to move snow away from the track. Each big wing can be pulled up with cables on both ends to clear obstacles such as switch stands, rocks, or anything that is so close that the wings would hit it if they were in the down position. Wings are lowered by gravity. Adjustments to a dozer require that it be stopped and each big wing adjusted manually, so it is not as flexible as a Jordan. A dozer can be used for ditching, but is not as versatile as a Jordan when used for this job.

Dozers also have a flanger mounted below the underframe just ahead of the rear truck. The flanger is a V-shaped plow similar to what people around Spokane see mounted on the front of pickup trucks. The flanger is notched so that when it is down in position to plow, the bottom of the flanger is lower than the rail head. This flanger plows snow out from between and outside of the rails to a maximum depth of four inches below the top of the rails. It clears a swath of about a foot outside of the rails. Depth of the flanger is adjustable. Shallower cuts are taken on light, short, branch line rail than are taken on the main line.

For plowing at track speed, a dozer is, in my opinion, better than a Jordan Spreader. Bat wings on a dozer extend about three feet beyond the side of the dozer, while a Jordan has only the big wings, which must be in against the side of the machine when running at speed. The result is that at speed a Jordan can plow a narrow trench only its own width, about 10 feet wide, while a dozer removes a roughly 15-foot wide swath of snow.

Big winging refers to plowing with a dozer or a Jordan Spreader with the large side wings extended. When big winging, snow can be moved 8 to 10 feet away from the edge of the machine. This is enough to put snow onto an adjacent yard track, so that on the next pass the operator can move it to the next track, and so on, until there are no more yard tracks to clear. Big wings in their extended position will not clear obstructions. At every switch, block signal, or slide fence, we had to stop, bring in the big wing, move past the obstruction, and reset the big wing. Big winging with either machine is a low speed process, not over 5 MPH and often less.

Bat winging refers to plowing with a dozer with the small bat wings in front in the down position. In this position, bat wings stick out about three feet on both sides of a dozer. With the bat wings down, you can run along the main track at 60 MPH throwing snow 50 to 100 feet out into the brush. Two men operate a dozer when bat winging. One man controls one bat wing and the cage. The cage is down when plowing, but must be raised to clear roadway crossings and switches. A second man controls the other bat wing and the flanger. The flanger is normally down when plowing, but it also must be raised to clear roadway crossings and switches. Bat wings in the down position will not clear obstructions such as switch stands and slide fences. Most bat winging is actually done at track speed. The two operators must

This Diesel Electric crane at Bonners Ferry is typical of the breed, and may be the one that worked with the snow plow trains I worked out of Bonners Ferry through Kootenai Canyon. PHOTO BY "BOXCAR BOB" FOSTER.

raise the bat wings and the cage to clear switch stands, slide fences, and grade crossings to avoid damage.

My first snow plow job was during the winter of 1968–69. We were all called off the extra boards to deadhead to Bonners Ferry on No. 28, the Western Star, to work this plow job. When we got off the Star at Bonners Ferry, an engine was sitting on the house track, but no snow plow. A snow dozer was always kept at Bonners Ferry to deal with snow in Kootenai Canyon. Soon, a westward freight train stopped at Bonners Ferry. They set out a snow dozer, picked up our engine, and left for Hillyard. Now we did not have engine. This dozer was useless; one bat wing had been torn off in Kootenai Canyon at Old Katka.

About seven hours later, an eastward train stopped and set out a GP 7 and a caboose for us. Our first move was to grab the Diesel Electric Crane and its boom car, run out to Katka, dig the missing bat wing out of a snowdrift, and return to Bonners Ferry. We spotted the crane on the house track next to the front end of the snow dozer and headed for the hotel on our 16 hours. The crane operator positioned the bat wing on the house track rail and was dropping his bucket on the bat wing in an attempt to put the curve back into the bat wing. A welder was there to weld up the cracks and tears in the bat wing as they put the curve back in it. This repair crew worked most of that night repairing and reinstalling the bat wing.

We were back on duty at 6:00 AM. Our first chore was to hook up and test the snow dozer, put the Diesel Electric Crane and its boom flat behind our caboose, and head east toward Troy, plowing snow. The line between Newport, Washington and Troy, Montana had received about four feet of heavy, wet snow. Kootenai Canyon was a mess. Snow slides filled the slide fences with snow and trees and brush, breaking the electrical continuity of the slide fences and setting many block signals in the canyon to red. The red signals limited trains to restricted speed; that is, being prepared to stop short of a train or obstruction on or foul of the track, or a switch not properly lined, and being on the lookout for broken rail, not exceeding 15 MPH.

Our crew stopped and cut the crane off at the first slide fence east of Crossport, then proceeded east to Troy plowing snow. The crane started to clean out behind the slide fences, and signal crews restrung and rewired the slide fences, restoring them to service and clearing up the red signals. It was common for slide fences and phone lines to be severed in several locations. When snow slides took out slide fences, they also took out the company telephone lines, so communication with the dispatcher became impossible. The main line between Bonners Ferry and Troy had become a black hole. Trains went in, and everyone involved could only hope they came out on the other side. This situation was particularly aggravating for the dispatcher, who was used to being in control of his territory.

This was in the Great Northern days of ABS signals and train orders. Operators were always on duty at both Troy and Bonners Ferry. When a crew was working in snowplow service, our running order designated us as a Work Extra, which allowed us to move in either direction within the limits given in our work order. Normally our limits were between the west siding switch at Bonners Ferry and the west siding switch at Troy, a distance of 32 miles.

The dispatcher could get fresh orders to us in three ways. First, we could go to Bonners Ferry or Troy. Second, a passing train could deliver train orders previously copied by an operator at Bonners Ferry or Troy. Finally, if we were stopped in Kootenai Canyon to wait for a train to meet and the train did not show up after an extended period of time, then our conductor would go to the phone, talk to the dispatcher, and perhaps copy a train order. The problem with us going to the phone to copy train orders was that the phone lines had probably been taken out by snow slides.

Radio communication was limited to Bonners Ferry and Troy and the radios on the engines and cabooses. The dispatcher did not have a radio, and there were no radio repeaters. Radio range was short in Kootenai Canyon. On the Bonners Ferry end, once a train was east of tunnel 10, about six miles east of Bonners Ferry, it was impossible to talk to the operator at Bonners Ferry. Once a train was about eight and a half miles west of Troy, it was impossible to talk to the operator at Troy. This left about 18.5 miles in the canyon with no communication with the dispatcher. Many times, a train would chase us into the clear after I had flagged them to a stop. They often brought train orders for us.

Late one day, our plow train was sitting in Old Katka Spur waiting for an eastward freight train to arrive so that we could go west to Bonners Ferry to tie up. It looked like we were not going to make it on our hours of service, so my conductor, Ed Otto, told me that I was going to have to walk 4.7 miles to Crossport Pit Spur and set up a flag so our train could get back to Bonners Ferry after the eastward train was by Crossport Pit Spur.

To flag another train with only fusees, torpedoes, and a red flag by day, plus a white light at night, is a lot of responsibility. The first time I flagged a following train, my heart was up in my throat. I learned to flag following trains on the W–O line which made me much more confident as a flagman when I got on the main line. It's one thing to read how to do something in the rule book, but until I physically did it, I did not feel comfortable with it. I was particularly glad for my flagging experience when I set out on this trek.

I reached Crossport Pit Spur wringing wet with sweat even though the temperature was about zero. When the eastbound arrived at Crossport Pit and I got them stopped, they called my Plow Extra and told them they were waiting at Crossport Pit until my Plow Extra arrived. I was happy that I could get in their engine cab to start to dry out. Once my Plow Extra knew the eastbound was stopped in the clear, they backed out of Old Katka Spur and headed west to Crossport Pit.

Every day, all day and all night, it continued to snow. Some mornings there was to six to eight inches of new snow to plow. We went back and forth between Sandpoint and Troy on our snow plow, often having to flag trains in Kootenai Canyon since the slide fences were out and the block signals were all red.

My first plowing campaign lasted for three weeks before all slide fences and telephone lines were back in service. It seemed like a signal crew would get a slide fence back in service and another slide would come down and take a slide fence out again, sometimes with telephone lines at the same time. Our train left Bonners Ferry every morning with the Diesel Electric Crane behind our caboose. We stopped and cut him off at the first slide fence that need cleaning out before moving on plowing last night's snowfall. I was out flagging trains every day so the rest of my crew could get some big winging done in the canyon.

The second time I got called for a plow train, I figured out that when the company called for a snow plow, conditions were already so bad that the railroad was close to being shut down. The company always hoped that the snow would stop, the temperature would warm up, the snow would melt, and the problem would be solved by nature at no cost. When a crew started to plow snow, the first priority was to keep the main line clear, and then clear out the sidings. Keeping the main line clear was done with the bat wings only, travelling fast to throw the snow as far away from the track as possible. Once we got the main line and sidings open, we cleaned up yards, industry tracks, and drift and slide areas with the big wings.

The only snow plow I ever worked on which everybody was not in a total panic mode was the Nelson Local out of Kettle Falls to Nelson, British Columbia. The only reason snow plowing was calm on the Nelson branch is because in the winter time the local took a dozer almost every trip, and never let the snow get out of control.

I remember one trip on the main line between Colburn and Elmira. Our train was going east plowing snow at 60 MPH, throwing snow onto the highway that was about 100 feet from the main line. The men running the snow plow did not get the cage up in time, and the cage hooked the crossing planks, dislodging them from a crossing. I was in the caboose cupola watching the stream of snow landing on the highway when I felt a jolt when the plow hit the crossing planks. All I could see was four crossing planks sailing over the top of the dozer and the engine and starting down toward me. Instant visions of crossing planks coming right through the cupola windows flashed through my mind. I immediately decided that this was not a good place to ride, so I got down and sat at the back desk and watched out the back window. The crossing planks sailed right over my caboose; all was well.

When this crew started plowing, the roadmaster told us that as soon as it quit snowing and everything was cleaned up, he would pull the job off and we could go home. The snow quit 26 days later, so after 26 days of 16 hours a day plowing snow, we got to go home.

In the early 1970s, I was called off the brakemen's extra board for another snowplow. This time we went to work at Hillyard with a GP 7 and a Jordan Spreader. We were told to run to Bonners Ferry where the roadmaster would further instruct us. This was the first time I met spreader operator Garfield Stone. I rode with Garfield to Bonners Ferry and got a crash course on how to run a Jordan while it was being towed behind our engine and was not in service. By the time we got to Bonners Ferry, I knew what all the controls did and I could tell that Garfield was proud of his ability to run that Jordan Spreader.

I found out just how good Garfield was during the next three weeks. I could not believe how smoothly Garfield ran that Jordan despite the fact that he suffered from cataracts in both eyes. Every once in a while, he would ask one of us how far something was away from the Jordan or the wing. My conductor always made sure that someone was up in the Jordan with Garfield to help him with his vision problem.

Garfield was restricted from operating machinery because his eyesight was so poor that he lost his driver's license and his wife drove him to work. His glasses were as thick as coke bottle bottoms. He worked with various track machinery for his entire career, but he had a soft spot for the Jordan spreader, which he referred to as "his baby." In the spring and summer, the Jordan was used to clean out right of way ditches for good drainage. This kept Garfield busy, making sure his Jordan was in good repair. Ditching is hard on equipment. The big wing was always hooking large rocks hidden under the dirt, which could shear the bolts on the big wing in a split second. Garfield kept a large bucket full of bolts, nuts, and lock washers in the Jordan just for those inevitable breakdowns.

Garfield told us that he had been telling the roadmaster for about a year that he needed to have someone break in with him on the Jordan so someone at Hillyard would know how to run it, but the roadmaster failed to respond. Winter came, and the roadmaster did not have anybody who knew how to run the Jordan except Garfield, so he looked the other way and called Garfield. That he could barely see was not obvious when he was on the Jordan. Only when he asked something pertaining to distance did I remember that he was legally blind. Garfield ran that Jordan Spreader like their blood ran through each other's veins and they became as one.

At Bonners Ferry the roadmaster instructed us to get our snow dozer out of the yard at Bonners. We put the dozer on one end of our engine and the Jordan Spreader on the other end so we could plow snow in either direction. This year conditions in Kootenai Canyon were not as bad as in my previous experience, but with the continuing snowfall the roadmaster was getting nervous remembering what happened a couple of years before. That winter, the blizzards that hit between Sandpoint and Troy were accompanied by high winds, so there were several areas with very large and deep snowdrifts. Our crew was always putting out the big wing on our Jordan Spreader and cutting through and widening those large snowdrifts. Some of these drifts were 10 to 15 feet high and 50 to 100 feet long. It was unusual to have snowdrifts that large and high in this part of the country, but there they were.

Every day we woke up to about two feet of fresh snow that had fallen during the night so there was plenty of snow to plow. One morning, still in the days of ABS block signals and train orders, we came to work and found that the phone lines were out and we were starting to have slide fence problems. In addition, there were some slides between Katka Spur and Leonia that needed to be cleaned up. A westward freight would be waiting for No. 28, the Western Star, at Leonia before they could come west to Bonners Ferry. My conductor put me on No. 28. They dropped me off about one mile east of Katka Spur where I set my torpedoes on the rail 150 feet apart and walked back to Katka Spur. When I was riding the lead unit of No. 28, I called the westbound at Leonia and told them I would be flagging them at Katka Spur so that our snow plow train could clear the main at Katka for them.

While I was waiting for the westbound and our snowplow to show up, all I could do was stand by the phone booth at Katka Spur and wait. I tried to use the company phone, but it was dead, so I just stood there listening for either train. The whole time I could hear the heavy, wet snow breaking tree limbs on the steep hillside above me. This made me extremely nervous since the distance between the hillside and the Kootenai River was only about 50 feet. All along that hillside I could hear limbs breaking and snow sliding for at least 200 feet on either side of where I was. All I could think about was which way I was going to run if a snow slide came down. Every time I heard something snap or pop, I felt my heart race. I sure was glad when my train arrived at Katka Spur, and we backed into the spur and waited for the westbound train. The westbound arrived shortly after our train cleared the main line. After they departed, we left Katka Spur and headed east, clearing snow slides as we worked toward Leonia. Fortunately, it did not occur to me at the time that a big slide could have shoved the Jordan, engine, dozer and all of us into the Kootenai River.

We plowed snow all day long, moving from one slide to the next, trying to keep the track clear. We got word that some slide fences were out, and some were full of snow and debris and could not take much more before they would become unplugged and set their signals to red. Our conductor asked where the Diesel Electric Crane was and found out it was at Port Hill.

That night, when we arrived back at Bonners Ferry, our conductor was told that the next morning we were to plow out the Kootenai Valley branch to Port Hill, located just south of the Canadian border. Our objective was to get the Diesel Electric Crane that was snowed in at Port Hill, and get a Caterpillar that had been clearing mudslides on the KV line and was now at Camp 8 siding. I never did understand why this equipment was left up the KV line this late in the year, but it was.

The Kootenai Valley (KV) branch ran northward out of Bonners Ferry 27 miles to Port Hill. It was the remnant of the Kootenai Valley Railway which, combined with the Bedlington and Nelson in Canada, extended 50 miles from Bonners Ferry, Idaho to Kushanook, British Columbia on the south arm of Kootenay Lake. This branch was built to provide an outlet for ore that originated on the narrow gauge Kaslo & Slocan and was brought to Kushanook by steamboat. The entire Canadian portion was abandoned and scrapped in 1916. By the 1960s, the only traffic the KV branch handled was outbound grain in the fall.

As ordered, the next morning we left for Port Hill. The KV line lay unplowed since it had started to snow. As soon as our train started down the east leg of the wye and crossed the Kootenai River Bridge, we were in five to six feet of snow. Pushing that Jordan Spreader through five feet of compact snow was all that our GP 7 could do while dragging a snow dozer behind us. Sometimes our engine could not push through the snow. When this happened, the engineer backed up to clear all the snow out from under our engine and then hit it again. Our conductor had been instructed to clean out the siding at Ritz, 7.6 miles east of Bonners Ferry, or north by compass direction. Our crew plowed the KV main to Camp 5, 14.1 miles east of Bonners Ferry, where we plowed the main and the siding. By this time, I lost track of how many times our engineer had to back up and hit the snow again. We did not leave Camp 5 until shortly past noon, so I figured this was going to be a two-day job, more if things did not go well.

At Camp 8, 21.8 miles from Bonners Ferry, everything was going pretty well for a change. The Caterpillar was at Camp 8 and the operator was plowing snow. He plowed the main line and the siding and was pushing snow out of a cut at the east end of Camp 8. I was riding in the Jordan Spreader with Garfield Stone. We were easing up the main track and began to slow to a stop when I felt the Jordan Spreader derail. Garfield immediately dumped the air and we came to a quick stop. He and I got down on the ground and looked behind the side of the operator's cage to see how bad the Jordan was derailed.

Next thing I knew, Garfield was there with a couple of big wenches; he started to unbolt the back of the cage side skirt so we could swing the metal skirt open. Three hinges hold the front of the cage side skirt. With the side skirt open and swung out of the way, all could see that there was no rail under the front truck of the Jordan. A piece of rail four feet long was broken out and lying close to the rail on the other side. The section men figured that when the Cat turned on its tracks, one of its treads broke the rail and snapped that piece of rail right off the ties. There were some oak blocks on the flatcar for the Cat, so we brakemen grabbed a re-railing frog off the side of our engine and set blocking and the frog. In about an hour and a half, the Jordan Spreader was re-railed with the cage bolted back together. Now the section men needed to go get a rail to replace the broken one and it was about 8:00 PM. Everyone got in the section trucks and headed for Bonners Ferry and tied up on our 16 hours.

The next morning everyone rode back to Camp 8. The section men replaced the broken rail and we started to plow the final 5.3 miles to Port Hill while the Cat stayed at Camp 8. The operator was told to clean up around Camp 8, then get loaded on his flatcar and get tied down since our train would pick him up on our way back to Bonners Ferry. Now our engineer hit the snow again and again to break through the deep drifts near Port Hill. Our plow train arrived at Port Hill at noon. The section men dug the crane out by hand so that we could couple to the crane, which was sitting on the tail of the wye. It took a lot of big winging at Port Hill just to get out of there.

Our train left Port Hill at 5:00 PM with the Diesel Electric Crane in tow. At Camp 8 we picked up the Cat on its flatcar and arrived at Bonners Ferry about 8:30 PM. We spotted the flat with the Cat so the operator could unload it and start to clean up around the house track the next morning. By the time the Jordan Spreader, our engine, and the dozer were spotted so that the local fuel company could fuel our engine and add stove oil to the Jordan and the dozer in the morning, our 16 hours expired again.

It was rare to big wing between stations, but this year the snow depth was 8 to 15 feet, so the whole railroad was like an open top tunnel. Our crew was big winging in Kootenai Canyon before our trip to Port Hill, so the canyon was in good shape. Our conductor was told to big wing between Bonners Ferry and Elmira, a piece of main track that included several snowdrifts and slides. This turned out to be complicated because signalmen had started to replace old semaphore signals with new searchlight signals and installing them in new locations for the changeover to CTC. This meant that as our train was big winging between Bonners and Elmira, we were required to stop at each block signal mast, pull in the big wing, shove ahead past the signal mast, put the wing back out, and then back up so the big wing was right next to the signal mast. Then we set and locked the big wing and started to plow snow again. This may not sound like it was much work, but when you figure that there were twice the usual number of signal masts between Bonners Ferry and Elmira, stopping and adjusting the wings consumed a lot of time. Our conductor asked if we could push the old masts over since the semaphore signal heads had been removed and the wires cut. The signal supervisor said no because come spring, tipped over masts would make unbolting and removing the old masts more difficult for the crew of the Diesel Electric Crane.

Our plow train was big winging about three miles east of Elmira on a long sweeping curve to the right at about 5 MPH when the big wing hit a rock buried under a snowdrift. The Jordan started to lift up on her left side.

Garfield dumped the air, but not soon enough. When our engineer got stopped, we discovered that all four one-inch bolts sheared off the large support arm bracket that attaches the support arm to the wing. As the bolts sheared off, the Jordan fell back onto the rail during the stop. After thanking God that the Jordan was still on the rail, everyone stood there in silence looking at the broken wing on our Jordan. Garfield broke the silence; he said, "Well, we have two choices; we can send the Jordan in for repair or fix it ourselves." There was no question; everyone knew that we were going to fix the arm ourselves.

The support arm probably weighed three or four hundred pounds. Four of us were elected to hold up the arm while Garfield got his first bolt started through the bolt hole in the wing. Then he lined up the bracket on the end of the arm to get the first hole in the bracket over the bolt. He finally got the first bolt through the hole and got the nut started on the threads on the bolt. We wing holders took a short break to catch our breath; everyone but Garfield needed it after holding that arm up for so long. We then used a pinch bar to turn the arm to line up the bracket with the next hole and get the second bolt through the wing and bracket. After that, there was no problem getting the other two bolts in and tightened up. We picked up our tools and blocking and were off plowing snow with the big wing again with smiles on our faces.

The snow seemed to be letting up. Our next trip was to Troy, spending about half a day there cleaning up the yard with the big wing and working our way back to Bonners Ferry to tie up. The next day our conductor was told to work our way to Sandpoint, big wing the yard, and head to Hillyard to tie up. That was the end of this snow plow job.

About three years later I got called as a conductor for a snow plow to Coeur d'Alene and back. My crew went on duty at the SC&P Yard. I picked up our train orders at Hillyard and drove to the SC&P Yard. I could not believe my eyes; there right behind our engine was a Jordan Spreader and a caboose. Some section men were there, but not Garfield Stone. I asked who was going to run the Jordan at Coeur d'Alene since the reason for this trip was to big wing the yard at Coeur d'Alene. I got a funny look when I asked this question, but I did not get an answer. Our train arrived at Coeur d'Alene about two hours later and switched the Jordan Spreader so that it was ahead of the engine. The section men hooked up the air to the Jordan but every time they tried to move a wing, the air brakes set up on the engine, the Jordan, and the caboose.

I walked up to find out what was going on. The section men hooked the Jordan's main reservoir line to the engine's train line. Every time the Jordan needed air pressure to move a wing it would set the brakes on our train. I showed them how to hook up the main reservoir hose on the Jordan to the main reservoir hose on the engine. Then I showed them how to run the wings on the Jordan. Between what I could remember about running a Jordan, and one of the section men who worked with Garfield just before he retired, we got the yard big winged and plowed out the wye for the Coeur d'Alene local. We also big winged the main track back to Gibbs and Huetter before we secured everything on the Jordan, switched it between our engine and caboose, and headed to Spokane.

My final time on a Jordan Spreader was in 2001 when I bid in the work train. We big winged Hauser Yard, Boyer Yard, Bonners Ferry station tracks, and the main track from Hauser Yard to Bonners Ferry. I was astounded at the difference in snow depth between the east end and west ends of Hauser Yard. On the west end, snow was about two and a half or three feet deep, while on the east end snow was four to five feet deep. At Boyer Yard, snow was five and a half feet deep which made switching nearly impossible.

➻ A Look Back at the Changes I Saw

As I reflect on the changes I saw in railroading, the most obvious operating change is the greatly reduced volume of switching and the deterioration of switching skills. The economy of the region has changed due to marked declines in the production of wood products and aluminum, both of which were important parts of the Great Northern's traffic base in the 1960s.

The railroad is far more efficient today due to bigger cars, less switching, and the proliferation of unit trains. Railroads were partially deregulated as to rates and service in 1980. As a result, the carriers concentrated their marketing efforts on profitable traffic, real rates fell, and thousands of miles of light density branch lines were either abandoned or spun off to short line operators. All railroads reduced employee counts under the pressure of falling rates and sharper competition from both trucking and other railroads.

When I started railroading in 1960, the business was 130 years old. The carriers and the men had a system, and the work was pretty well figured out. The system was single car railroading, which some would later call 'loose car railroading,' as compared to unit trains, which came along later.

Larger cars introduced in the early 1960s cut the number of cars required to move a given tonnage of lumber, coke, alumina, and aluminum in half. When I started the nominal 50-ton, net, car was standard. Now 100-ton cars are being replaced by 110-ton cars. Tare weight has gone from 22–25 tons to only about 30 tons. Payload has doubled with a very modest increase in tare weight. This doubling of car capacity alone accounts for a 50% reduction in car count and switching, holding traffic volume constant.

In the early 1960s, railroads started buying 100-ton covered hopper cars for grain and alumna ore service. Covered hoppers are much better suited for handling grain and alumna than boxcars. Shippers had to 'cooper' boxcars with railroad supplied grain doors. Coopering referred to installing grain doors, which were about four feet tall, across the inside of the car door to prevent significant leakage from the doorway. Boxcar loading was slow, and required a man be in the car to direct grain more or less uniformly on the floor. At the unloading elevator, tilt tables which tilted the car enough to make the grain run out the car door were required, which made unloading slow and expensive.

Covered hoppers increased the net load per car in bulk service from about 60 tons to 100 tons. Loading covered hoppers was much quicker and easier than loading boxcars, and coopering was eliminated. Unloading was also much quicker and easier. Grain and alumina ore could simply be dumped between fixed rails into a conveyor system to be unloaded. With the reduction of handling costs provided to both the shipper and consignee, railroads did not have to offer a lower rate to encourage conversion of existing traffic to this new technology.

Lumber was a staple traffic for the Great Northern in Washington. Pacific Northwest lumber suffered from two specific problems. First, the federal government locked up federal forests to "save" the spotted owl. Independent mills on both sides of the Cascades relied on logs from the national forests. When the federal government locked the loggers out of the west side fir, spruce, and cedar forests, independent mills were cut off at the knees. Large corporate owners of timber, like Weyerhaeuser, were relatively unaffected and were able to remain in business.

East of the mountains, the problem was a classic case of source competition. Eastern Washington forests are predominately pine and extend north far into Canada. Canadian governments, both federal and provincial, consistently did all they could to help their lumber industry. Canadians ignored the spotted owl, for example. Canadian mills are even more dependent on logs from government land than are American mills. Canadian governments consistently encouraged their mills by charging such low fees to Canadian loggers that American lumber men accused the Canadians of "dumping" their lumber. The American government took up the cause of American loggers and mill operators and threatened to impose import duties on the flood of Canadian lumber coming into the United States. Of course, the Americans were bluffing. Canadian lumber continues to move in huge volume to the U.S.

Railroads in Eastern Washington, especially the Northern Pacific and the Union Pacific, which served the Palouse country of southeastern Washington, transported wheat to the ports of Portland, Vancouver, Kalama, Longview, Tacoma, and Seattle for export since the 1880s. During the 1960s and 1970s, Congress spent hundreds of millions of dollars to build dams and locks on the Columbia and Snake Rivers. The dams were built to generate electric power, but the locks were for the sole purpose of diverting Eastern Washington export wheat from rail to truck-barge transport. The last dam on the Snake River, Lower Granite, was completed in 1975, which brought barges as far upriver as Lewiston, Idaho. Virtually all wheat grown in the Palouse country immediately went to the river as Congress intended.

Once deregulated by the Staggers Act in 1980, Eastern Washington railroads could either cut their rates to compete for what was relatively low rate/high cost short haul traffic, or hold their rates up and see the grain continue to go to the river, and see traffic on hundreds of miles of branch line disappear. BN maintained rates that ceded almost all grain traffic south of the former Great Northern main line to the truck-barge combination. Rates from the former GN main and the former NP Central Washington line for 26 car units were and are competitive with truck-barge. The railroad and the truck-barge combination split the traffic from this area. Eastern Washington grain traffic is only marginally profitable to the BN since the monthly earnings of the equipment are much better in the longer hauls from Montana, Minnesota, Iowa, and Nebraska.

Great Northern's Mansfield branch, while not in the Palouse, was by the 1960s strictly a grain line. It still used 68-pound rail rolled in 1892 and 1893 and re-laid on the Mansfield branch when it was built in 1909. Because of this light rail, BN stayed with 40-foot single door boxcars on the Mansfield long after every other grain line in Washington State converted to covered hopper cars. The shipper, a single elevator operator, owned all the elevators along the line, and could truck to the CW line at Coulee City, to a former Centennial Mills elevator it owned in Wenatchee, and to the river at Pasco. As the customer exercised these options, traffic on the Mansfield branch declined; the BN abandoned it in 1985 and sent the last of its 40-foot boxcars to scrap.

BN and BNSF owned two former Northern Pacific lines in eastern Washington on which grain was the predominant traffic; the P&L line in the Palouse, and the Central Washington line in the 'Big Bend' region. Most of the grain traffic on both lines went to the river almost immediately after navigation was opened to Lewiston in 1975. BN and BNSF continued to operate the lines, almost certainly at a loss, until 1996 when BNSF sold both lines to short line operator Watco in a single transaction. Watco, not able to earn sufficient revenue to maintain the lines, let them deteriorate to the point that train speeds of 10 MPH were an adventure.

Washington State Department of Transportation (WSDOT) purchased both former NP lines, plus a former UP line to Colfax, from Watco in 2007. In fall of 2011, WSDOT began an $8.6 million capital investment program to bring bridges and ditches into a state of good repair. The current operator is struggling to stay in business, even with financial help from the state.

Today, BNSF serves two export grain markets terminating at Pacific Northwest (PNW) ports. The first is the long established export wheat from Eastern Washington, Eastern Montana, and North Dakota.

The second is export corn from Minnesota, Nebraska, and Iowa. Before deregulation, export corn generally moved by rail or truck to the Mississippi River and by barge to New Orleans. Corn destined to Pacific Rim countries went by ship through the Panama Canal. The grain marketers at BNSF figured out that they could offer price competitive service through the PNW ports on corn to the Pacific Rim, in part due to lower ocean freight costs from the PNW as compared to the Gulf. They offered 26-car unit rates on export corn, and soon expanded their offerings to 52-car and 104-car units. Each increment increase in size offers a roughly 10% rate reduction.

When elevators ship 26- and 52-car units, BNSF still has to aggregate them to make a full train of 104 cars over Marias Pass or 130 cars west of Spokane via Pasco. Aggregation is generally done at consolidation points near origin, or the units may move as a block in manifest trains. Either way, the increase in efficiency was phenomenal. First and most obviously, it greatly reduced origin switching required by eliminating the need to gather up a few cars here and a few cars there. The practice of stopping cars for grain sampling and staging for export elevators as described in detail in Chapter 3 was discontinued. This saved the cost of switching and hundreds of thousands of car days spent each year by cars functioning as grain bins. The cost of switching and wasted car days was absorbed by the railroad and reflected in the rate. Revenue trips per month nearly doubled in the conversion from single cars to unit trains, even as the average length of haul increased.

Burlington Northern's final grain marketing innovation was the "Certificate of Transportation," or COT program. This is an auction program for guaranteed availability of cars. Under the traditional car ordering program, shippers order cars for the date they want them and the railroad does its best to fill the orders. If cars are surplus or in balance, the system works fine, and cars are supplied on or near enough the date ordered. When cars are short, which means that the traffic wants to move in higher than normal volume, the railroad is not able to fill car orders on time. In response, shippers over order, figuring that they will get at least some of what they order, but also making the car shortage appear worse than it really is.

The COT program allocates cars to those shippers who need them the most, since they will pay the highest premium over the published rates to secure the cars. This is a classic free market response to excess demand: raise the price. Truckers and barge lines float their rates constantly and no one gives it a second thought, but the COT program was a revolutionary and much excoriated change when it was introduced.

The practical effect of the COT program is to demarket Eastern Washington grain when cars get tight. BNSF defines Eastern Washington part of their Northern Corridor. The other important parts of the Northern Corridor for wheat are Montana and North Dakota. COT bids are in terms of dollars over, or under, the published rates from stations in the corridor. Since the absolute rates per car are higher from Montana than from Eastern Washington, any specific dollar amount over tariff is a lesser percentage amount to a Montana shipper than to a Washington shipper. In addition, Washington shippers have the alternative of going to the river that Montana shippers do not. Washington shippers tend to bid lower than Montana shippers.

Another factor that contributes to the reduction of switching is that aluminum, alumina, coke, and pitch traffic the railroad carried in the past no longer exists. The number of aluminum reduction plants in the Pacific Northwest fell from seven to two due to global competition and increasing electricity costs in the PNW.

The fruit and most of the fresh potato traffic went to trucks. Virtually none of the perishable traffic the Wenatchee, Wenatchee Valley, and W–O line apples and pears, and the Quincy potatoes, is left on the rails. The federal government, through its highway financing policies and the regulatory straitjacket it placed on the railroads, caused the diversion of perishable traffic to the truckers. Since the railroads have been deregulated, they want only profitable traffic, which in the recent past has been the long-haul nonperishable freight business. In addition, perishable traffic has been gone for so long that BNSF has no institutional memory in its Marketing Department of what the perishable business was and what it could and should be.

For all these reasons, switching has come to an all-time low on the former Spokane Division. When I think of all the switching in the early years of my career, I am struck by how much the world has changed. Today's new employees do not have much to memorize and they have their little booklets to fall back on.

I wonder how long it will be until BNSF wakes up to the fact that it is running past hundreds of millions of dollars in annual perishable revenues in the state of Washington alone. At some point the costs of trucking will become so high that producers and shippers may begin to think that lower rail rates would be a good thing to have. I believe that in the future the railroads will re-enter the perishable business due to rising fuel costs and the high cost of labor. Trucking is far more sensitive to fuel and labor cost increases than are the railroads. Unfortunately, the railroads have lost the intellectual capital, or institutional memory, of what the business was and is. The way the railroads will recapture the perishable traffic will be with refrigerated containers, perhaps as a joint venture with motor carrier operators who know the traffic and what its service needs are.

How I Feel about It All Now

In the blue collar world, only a select few were trusted to perform their daily duties without constant supervision. Railroad crewmen were proud of the fact that the company trusted us enough to perform our work without oppressive oversight. As long as the shippers were happy, crews went weeks without seeing the trainmaster in charge of their territory. Even under the BN, and especially after the SLSF merger, with all the officials watching everybody all the time, my crew and I seemed to be left alone. When I started to bid on work trains, I asked the trainmaster in charge why I never saw him. He told me that he knew I would take care of the store and it would be a waste of his time for him to be checking up on me and my crew.

Later in my career, I was glad that I got a chance to railroad on the W–O in the traditional manner as we did in my earlier years. It made me appreciate the modern conveniences like electric lights and radios in cabooses. The art of using lantern and hand signs to communicate

Two Spokane Division crews brought No. 97 from Whitefish, Montana, to Wenatchee. A Seattle Division crew is leaving Spokane Division trackage at Olds Junction one afternoon in June 1978. In just a moment, they will turn into the valley of the Wenatchee River and begin their climb over the Cascade Mountains. PHOTO BY MIKE BARTENSTEIN.

with the rest of the crew for movement of the engine while doing your work vanished with the coming of portable radios. This is fine . . . until the battery goes dead or the radio quits, which happens on occasion. When a radio failed, the old heads went back to their hand and lantern signs to complete the work. New employees do not have that ability, for they were never taught all the hand and lantern signs.

I feel that having to learn how to do the job the traditional way made me a better rail, especially in making me think about how to accomplish the task at hand before doing it. I could actually visualize every move in my mind from start to finish. While writing this book I found myself mentally transported to those days and nights visualizing the moves, just as I did them 50, 40, 30, or 10 years ago.

The seniority mess of the Burlington Northern merger caused everyone some degree of anxiety. The hostility of management toward the men after the SLSF merger set everyone on edge. The toxic atmosphere of those days was unlike anything on the Great Northern, and was worse by far than anything on the BN before 1980.

The oil company management did not understand the railroad, and did not seem to care. They were focused on separating the former Northern Pacific's natural resources from the railroad. That separation was driven by former NP directors on the early BN Board of Directors, and by other directors of similar inclination who came to the board later. Separating the resources was the correct thing to do for the stockholders, but the railroad drifted due to lack of management attention, and what little attention there was focused on cutting costs and shrinking the asset base. Cutting costs was necessary and forced by deregulation, but shrinking the asset base went too far in the destruction of the SP&S line between Spokane and Pasco.

The BNSF merger of 1996 brought a railroader back to the presidency of the company for the first time in 15 years. Robert Krebs and his management team found a property that needed more engines and more track capacity due to a growing business. It was a pleasure to work with reliable power again and to participate in the capacity expansion projects that characterized my time as conductor on the work train.

After the BNSF merger, the relations between labor and management mellowed out a little bit. Labor no longer felt like hunted animals. The Frisco/oil man management's attitude was mostly gone, and conditions started to improve little by little. For the first time in a long time, the men felt like we belonged and were wanted. But after all the men went through, the total trust of trainmen and enginemen will never return until the employees who lived through all the turmoil have retired. Then, and only then, can the company cement relations with their employees. BNSF will have to wait for almost a full generation to pass until the wounds will heal and employees' trust in the reasonableness of management can be restored.

I am proud of the job I did over the years taking care of the shippers, who were the people who paid my paycheck. I prided myself on the professional way I performed my job. When I was the conductor, I felt it was my personal responsibility to take care of the whole crew. Taking care of the crew meant making sure that everyone worked in a safe manner with no one getting injured or killed while getting all the work done.

Endnotes

1 Wikipedia, List of GE Locomotives, Accessed November 3, 2012, http://en.wikipedia.org/wiki/List_of_GE_Locomotives.

2 Robert C. Del Grosso, *BNSF Northwest: The BNSF Railway in the Pacific Northwest* (Bonners Ferry ID: Great Northern Publications, 2002), 35.

3 Del Grosso, *BNSF Northwest*, 33–36.

4 Northern Pacific Railway, Condensed Profile and Track Chart, Idaho Division First Subdivision, Paradise, Mont. To Spokane, Wash, Office of Chief Engineer, Revised January 1, 1970.

5 Del Grosso, *BNSF Northwest*, 37.

6 Del Grosso, *BNSF Northwest*, 37.

7 BNSF Railway. Track Chart Spokane Subdivision, Sandpoint Jct., ID to Lakeside Jct., WA, October 15, 2012.

8 Earl J. Currie, *Robert W. Downing: One of the Best and Brightest* (Earl J. Currie, 2011), 20.

9 Bruce Kelly, "Three-sided Traffic Solution," *Railway Age*, November 2012, 43–45.

10 Kenneth R. Middleton, "Great Northern Dozers, Drags, Flangers and Spreaders," Great Northern Railway Historical Society Reference Sheet No. 393, March 2015, 8–15.

Bibliography

Air Brake Association, The. *Management of Train Operation and Train Handling.* Chicago: The Air Brake Association, 1972.

Alexander, Vern. "Rising Above it All in Spokane—The Downtown Grade Separation Project," *The Mainstreeter,* Spring 2010.

Alt, David D., and Donald W. Hyndman. *Roadside Geology of Washington.* Missoula, MT: Mountain Publishing Company, 1984.

Austin, Ed and Dill, Tom. *S. P. & S. The Spokane Portland & Seattle Railway.* Edmonds, WA: Pacific Fast Mail, 1996.

Asay, Jeff S. *Union Pacific Northwest: The Oregon-Washington Railroad & Navigation Company.* Edmonds, WA: Pacific Fast Mail, 1991.

Bartenstein, Mike. *emails of various dates.* Mr. Bartenstein is a descendant of the Cedergreen Family, owners of Columbia Ice & Cold Storage at Wenatchee, WA.

Becker, Duane. *The Great Northern Railway, Priest River, Idaho to Hillyard, Washington 1890 to 1920.* Great Northern Railway Historical Society Reference Sheet No. 376, June 2012.

Becker, Duane. Email dated September 3, 2016.

Bloomberg.com, "Railroads Couple More Cars as Housing Boost Shipments." accessed August 8, 2012. http://bloomberg.com/news/2012-08-08/railroads-couple-more-cars-as-housing-boost-shipments.

Burlington Northern Railroad. *BN News Update,* Volume 2, Number 1, February 1988.

Burlington Northern Railroad, Train Briefs: No. 97 Revised 12/1/70, No. 83 Revised 10/13/70, No. 82 Revised 1/20/71, and No. 88 Revised 1/28/71.

BN vs. UTU, 862 F.2d 1266 (7th Cir. 1988).

BNSF Railway. *Montana Division Employee Timetable No. 6,* April 26, 2006.

BNSF Railway. *Track Chart Spokane Subdivision, Sandpoint Jct., ID to Lakeside Jct., WA,* October 15, 2012.

Burrows, Roger G. *Railway Mileposts: British Columbia Volume II: The Southern Routes from the Crowsnest to the Coquihalla.* North Vancouver, BC: Railway Milepost Books, 1984.

Carter, Clive. *Inland Empire Electric Line.* Coeur d'Alene, ID: Museum of North Idaho, 2009.

ConocoPhillips. "Burlington Resources Company History." Accessed August 29, 2012. http://conocophillips.com/EN/about/who_we_are/history/burlington/Pages/index.aspx.

Currie, Earl J. *BN–Frisco: A Tough Merger.* Earl J. Currie, 2010.

Currie, Earl J. *James J Hill's Legacy to Railway Operations.* Earl J. Currie, 2007.

Currie, Earl J. *Robert W. Downing: One of the Best and Brightest.* Earl J. Currie, 2011.

Currie, Earl J. *Transformation of a Railroad Company: Burlington Northern, 1980–1995.* Rails Northwest, 2019.

Currie, Earl J. Emails of various dates.

Del Grosso, Robert C. *BNSF Northwest: The BNSF Railway in the Pacific Northwest.* Bonners Ferry, ID: Great Northern Publications, 2002.

Dinsmore, Gary. *emails dated October 26 and 28, 2012.* Mr. Dinsmore worked as a clerk for the Northern Pacific at Wheeler from September of 1963 through February of 1964.

Donaldson, Gordon, *Corporate Restructuring: Managing the Change Process from Within.* Boston: Harvard Business School Press, 1994.

Ehnbom, Staffan. Email December 14, 2011.

Envoy, Martin III, et al., *Signaling and the Great Northern, Part V Automatic Block Signaling,* Great Northern Railway Historical Society Reference Sheet No. 405, September 2017.

Fahey, John, *Inland Empire: D. C. Corbin and Spokane.* Seattle: University of Washington Press, 1965.

Gaertner, John T., *North Bank Road: The Spokane, Portland & Seattle Railway.* Pullman, WA: Washington State University Press, 1990.

Glischinski, Steve, "The Train that Started it All," *Trains Magazine,* March 2011, 54–55.

Great Northern Railway. *Authority for Expenditures,* Great Northern Railway Historical Society, 1893–1970, http://www.gn-npjointarchive.org/default.aspx

Great Northern Railway. *Consolidated Code of Operating Rules,* Great Northern Railway, 1959 Edition, Effective December 1, 1959.

Great Northern Railway. *Original Track Laying Record.* Great Northern Railway, 1862–1932.

Great Northern Railway. Pamphlet entitled *Hillyard and the Great Northern Railway 1892–1954,* Great Northern Railway, November 1954.

Greenwood, W. E. Email October 15, 2013.

Hatler, Chuck, *The Western Star: Train of Many Routes,* Great

Northern Railway Historical Society Reference Sheet 368, June 2011, GNRHS.

Hidy, Ralph W., Muriel E. Hidy, Roy V. Scott, and Don L. Hofsommer. *The Great Northern Railway A History.* Boston: Harvard Business School Press, 1998.

HistoryLink, *U&I Sugar Company dedicates Moses Lake plant on October 23, 1953.* Accessed October 23, 2012, www.historylink.org.

Kaufman, Lawrence H. *Leaders Count: The Story of BNSF Railway.* College Station, TX: Texas A&M University Press, 2005.

Kelly, Bruce, "Three-sided Traffic Solution." *Railway Age,* November 2012.

Klein, Maury. *Union Pacific: The Reconfiguration America's Greatest Railroad from 1969 to the Present.* New York: Oxford University Press, 2011.

Lewty, Peter B. *Across the Columbia Plain: Railroad Expansion in the Interior Northwest, 1885–1893.* Pullman, WA: Washington State University Press, 1995.

Lewty, Peter B. *To the Columbia Gateway: The Oregon Railway and the Northern Pacific, 1879–1884.* Pullman, WA: Washington State University Press, 1987.

Lundsten, Carson S. "Railroad Rules, Signaling, Operations: Direct Traffic Control." Last updated July 26, 1998, www.lundsten.dk/us_signaling/dtc/index.html.

Martin, Albro. *James J. Hill and the Opening of the Northwest.* New York: Oxford University Press, 1976.

Mattson, James C. *Great Northern Railway Mileposts, Spokane Division.* Unpublished manuscript, 2011.

Miller, Clinton J. III, General Counsel, United Transportation Union, North Olmsted, OH.

Middleton, Kenneth R. *Great Northern Dozers, Drags, Flangers and Spreaders.* Great Northern Railway Historical Society Reference Sheet No. 393, March 2015, 8–15.

Neill, William J., former SP Train Dispatcher. Email to D. T. Sprau, July 24, 2012.

Northern Pacific Railway. *Idaho Division, First Subdivision, condensed Profile and Track Chart, Revised January 1, 1970,* nprha.org.

Northern Pacific Railway, 1965 Annual Report.

Northern Pacific Railway. *Idaho Division Local Train Brief Train 1234–1235 Wheeler Turnaround Local,* Office of General Superintendent Transportation, October 1, 1968. Accessed October 13, 2012, http://sdp45.blogspot.com/search/label/Wheeler.

Northwest Council. *Columbia Basin Project,* Accessed February 22, 2011. www.nwcouncil.org/history/ColumbiaBasinProject.asp.

Ogle, Dean. retired BN Train Dispatcher at New Westminster British Columbia, emails various dates.

The Official Guide of the Railways. New York: National Railway Publication Company. December 1968.

Rechnitzer, Paul. *Corbin's Road aka Spokane International Railway.* Sagle, ID: Comanche Press, 2007.

Rhodes, C. Harker, Editor, RECENT COURT AND BOARD DECISIONS OF INTEREST, *"Train Dispatcher Magazine Official Publication of the American Train Dispatchers' Association,"* September 1965.

Salsbury, Stephen. *No Way to Run a Railroad.* New York: McGraw-Hill Book Company, 1982.

Southern Pacific Transportation Company. *Direct Traffic Control.* A Southern Pacific Instruction Booklet.

Spokane Falls Review, January 4, 1891.

Spokesman-Review, May 30, 1902.

Sprau, David, *emails and telephone conversations of various dates.* Mr. Sprau is a retired NP/GN/BN/BNSF Train Dispatcher and short line Superintendent.

Strauss, John. Emails dated November 2, 2016, and December 4, 2016.

Turner, Robert D. *West of the Great Divide* (Victoria, BC: Sono Nis Press, 1987).

Washington Companies. "Dennis R. Washington Biography." Accessed February 12, 2012, http:www.washcorp.com/dennisrwashingtonbiography.php.

Weston, Harold M., "Award 13778 Docket No. TD-15067" *National Railroad Adjustment Board, Third Division,* Washington, DC, July 29, 1965.

Wikipedia. *List of GE locomotives,* Accessed November 3, 2012, http://en.wikipedia.org/wiki/List_of_GE_Locomotives.

Wilner, Frank N. *Railroad Mergers: History Analysis Insight.* Omaha: Simmons-Boardman Books, Inc., 1997.